Oracle Programming with Visual Basic

Oracle® Programming with Visual Basic®

Nick Snowdon

SYBEX®

San Francisco • Paris • Düsseldorf • Soest

Associate Publisher: Richard Mills
Contracts and Licensing Manager: Kristine Plachy
Acquisitions & Developmental Editor: Maureen Adams
Editor: Diane Lowery
Technical Editors: Allen Dong, Russ Jacobs
Book Designer: Bill Gibson
Graphic Illustrator: Tony Jonick
Electronic Publishing Specialists: Bill Gibson, Nila Nichols
Production Coordinators: Rebecca Rider, Julie Sakaue
Indexer: Nancy Guenther
Cover Designer: Design Site
Cover Illustrator: Gregory MacNicol

Screen reproductions produced with Collage Complete.

Collage Complete is a trademark of Inner Media Inc.

SYBEX is a registered trademark of SYBEX Inc.

TRADEMARKS: SYBEX has attempted throughout this book to distinguish proprietary trademarks from descriptive terms by following the capitalization style used by the manufacturer.

The author and publisher have made their best efforts to prepare this book, and the content is based upon final release software whenever possible. Portions of the manuscript may be based upon prerelease versions supplied by software manufacturer(s). The author and the publisher make no representation or warranties of any kind with regard to the completeness or accuracy of the contents herein and accept no liability of any kind including but not limited to performance, merchantability, fitness for any particular purpose, or any losses or damages of any kind caused or alleged to be caused directly or indirectly from this book.

Library of Congress Card Number: 98-86743
ISBN: 0-7821-2322-8

Manufactured in the United States of America

10 9 8 7 6 5 4 3 2

To Jenny and Kelsey

FOREWORD

When asked to write a foreword for Nick's book on Oracle, I was flattered but also a little confused. I never tout myself as an Oracle "expert" because most of my work involves Microsoft SQL Server (I'm sure you've heard of it) and DBMS architectures. I also know that while the number of books on Oracle could fill a small canyon in Arizona, the number of *good* books on Oracle and my other love, Visual Basic, were in short supply. For years, I have seen developers all over the world struggling with Visual Basic and Oracle, trying to get these two world-class tools to work together. After having read Nick's book, I can safely say that this work is worth reading and certainly fills this void.

Now, don't get me wrong. I don't fully concur with everything Nick says, but his characterizations of DAO, RDO, ODBCDirect, ADO, and OO4O are generally fair and well balanced. The technical depth is within the grasp of any developer, and he provides plenty of examples and helpful tips. In addition, his earlier chapters on architecture and design should help most developers get a good running start at their database projects.

And that's the key. We in the computer industry spend most of our time writing applications to store and retrieve data. We also seem to be inordinately focused on performance. If I had a nickel for every time I was asked "Why does it seem that XDO is faster than YDO?" I would have enough money to buy a small country. Most developers just getting started with a DBMS don't realize that all of the interfaces, languages, and CPUs *wait* at the same speed. No matter how fast your system, no matter how fast the interface, if you ask a question that takes the server five minutes to process, your application still has to wait for five minutes before continuing. Smarter, "faster" applications ask smarter questions that take the server less time to process. Nick seems to be aware of these issues and keeps those DBAs needing an introduction to successful Oracle-based applications from making some basic mistakes.

Another issue you need to focus on when choosing your tools is productivity. Although application or system performance does not easily translate to a lower total cost of ownership, developer productivity clearly affects the company's bottom line. If a developer can write five serious programs in a year, his or her customers are five times happier than the ones who see only one new application, or upgrade, or bug fix in a year. Today, the tools developers are being asked to use vary widely in their integration with the operating system, their integration with each other, and their integration with the developer and the way he or she creates solutions. Frankly, it would be hard to recommend a tool that created 20 percent faster code over a tool that takes 50 percent less time to create a workable solution.

As you read this book and others, I suggest that you keep your options open. Many of us hate to reengineer existing applications to make them work in other situations not considered in the original design. This strategy is expensive to implement and rarely satisfies the customer or management. Consider that ADO is Microsoft's strategy for "universal" data access; in the future, we'll see a lot of effort put into ADO to make it the best possible portal to OLE-DB. Because OLE-DB is not restricted to *just* relational data sources, you can use its flexibility to access a myriad of other data sources, as well—and not just those from Microsoft. Since you can write your own OLE-DB providers (right in Visual Basic if you want to), you can use ADO to integrate your own proprietary data sources into your most sophisticated designs. Visual Studio 6.0 now includes a new OLE-DB native provider for Oracle along with new ODBC drivers.

No matter what interface you (as a developer) choose, no matter what language or tools you choose, and (for the most part) no matter what DBMS you choose, if your initial design is flawed, your application will ultimately disappoint your customer and your boss. Invest in success by spending more time and effort on planning, learning, and evaluating your options—long before you write your first line of code.

William R. Vaughn

Visual Studio Enterprise Product Manager

Author of *Hitchhiker's Guide to Visual Basic and SQL Server* (Microsoft Press, 1998)

ACKNOWLEDGMENTS

An incredible number of people are involved in moving a book from the conceptual stage to the point where you can hold it in your hands. Lee The, the editor of *Visual Basic Programmer's Journal,* supported an article on this topic, which Associate Publisher Fred Slone at Sybex picked up and then convinced me to devote some time to for this book. Acquisitions and Development Editor Maureen Adams brought my first few chapters into shape, and Editor Diane Lowery continued this daunting task. Rebecca Rider and Julie Sakaue, the production coordinators, and Bill Gibson and Nila Nichols, the electronic publishing specialists, did more work than I know about. Allen Dong did the Oracle technical editing and contributed greatly to the validity and usefulness of the text. Russ Jacobs did a subsequent technical review after Allen and Diane finished with it.

Although some of what the book contains was found out the hard way, I cannot stress too much how many sources of information go into a book like this. It is not just the white papers, newsgroups, and knowledge bases that are necessary but also the conversations with colleagues who provide answers and solutions. (I must mention Karen Lo and Steve Welch.) Vital to my understanding and the accuracy of these pages has been the extremely helpful support of Sam Carpenter and Gopal Kirsur as well as many other technical support engineers.

To all of these people and the many others who have helped that I did not remember to name, I give you a big thank you. My final thanks go to my family who have had to do without me for somewhat longer than we first imagined.

CONTENTS AT A GLANCE

Part IV: **Advanced Oracle Techniques**

TABLE OF CONTENTS

INTRODUCTION

Why a Book on Oracle and Visual Basic?

This is an unusual book as far as computer literature goes in that it covers two quite separate areas of information technology. Many good books are available on Oracle, although nearly every one is designed as a source of information for database administrators. There are probably more books on Visual Basic than any other topic except perhaps the Web, but you will rarely see the word "Oracle" in the indexes. The lack of information is what I found myself dealing with a few years ago. Even with my strong background in Visual Basic (version 3 at the time), I found getting myself connected to an Oracle database and making it perform efficiently and effectively posed a problem that needed an answer.

This book is a personal one because it provides the resource I would have liked to have had a few years ago. It combines an understanding of the basic concepts about Oracle without which you will have a hard time communicating with database administrators or carrying out the administration role yourself if you are caught in that situation. (Oracle is not the simplest of databases to administer, which is something that is not always appreciated by project managers.)

Most Oracle texts are generally too complicated for the novice who has a hard time trying to decide which things are important enough to learn and which can be safely discarded until more time is available for training. Visual Basic books, on the other hand, are either introductory or deal exclusively with Microsoft SQL Server. So many questions are left unanswered for Oracle developers, even if it is just seeing an example of how something works.

The paucity of books for Oracle developers and the absence of any coverage of Oracle in the Visual Basic literature has led to the need for such coverage; this book will provide you with the information to proceed with your VB front ends to Oracle.

Who Should Read This Book?

The aim of this book is to provide a journey into the world of Oracle for experienced Visual Basic developers. You will not find any details about Visual Basic programming apart from those aspects that apply to data access, and there is little of use to those working with Microsoft Access or SQL. The "Resources" section, later in this introduction, points out several places to find information for novices and more advanced developers. You should keep the following pointers in mind when deciding if this book is for you:

- You need a developer's view of Oracle.

- You have to provide assistance to database administrators, or you need a concise text to help fulfill that role.

- You are a Visual Basic developer new to the world of interfacing with Oracle.

- You are an experienced Visual Basic developer who needs the latest information about how to get the most from an Oracle database.

- You want one book that can be used as a reference to Visual Basic and Oracle without having to search through huge numbers of manuals, help files, and online knowledge bases.

The Structure of the Book

This book is divided into four sections, two sections on Oracle from a Visual Basic viewpoint and two sections on Visual Basic from the Oracle viewpoint. The book is set up so that it can be read from one end to the other, progressing from concepts to database creation in the first half and from concepts to the more advanced techniques in the second half. However, each chapter is relatively self-contained so you can dip and dive into it as you see fit.

The book is organized into the following sections:

Introducing Oracle describes the features that make Oracle the enterprise-quality database that it is as well as the architecture that distinguishes it from a file-based system such as Microsoft Access. We describe the internal architecture of an Oracle database from the system processes and memory utilization to the data files that form the permanent storage for the database, and then we see how to create and maintain an Oracle database. You will also see the fundamentals of database design from the conceptual model to the physical implementation.

Queries and Stored Procedures first describe how to access and update data in the database using standard SQL commands. There is coverage of these commands at the introductory level but also information on how to use the more sophisticated features available in Oracle. The section includes the SQL commands as well as an introduction to the procedural programming language PL/SQL, including how to write stored procedures that can communicate with Visual Basic.

Data-Access Technology gives an overview of the various components necessary for communicating between Visual Basic on the client and an Oracle database server. We will see Oracle's networking solutions as well as the ways Visual Basic can communicate with this networking layer. The section introduces the most common data-access technologies used from VB and covers some design issues you need to be aware of before starting your application development.

Advanced Oracle Techniques goes into depth covering the five most common data-access technologies. We will see the object models of each, how to set up a connection with the database, and how to retrieve result sets from the database. We will see how to use read-only and updatable result sets and then move on to accessing stored procedures and other advanced capabilities. We also look at how to use each of the methods to look at the structure of the database.

Resources

There is a variety of resources that you will find you need as technology changes and you run into problems that are not covered in this book. The following is a personal list, and no doubt you will find your own resources to add to it.

Courses

Oracle offers a large number of courses in many aspects of the Oracle database, from an introduction to SQL and PL/SQL to Advanced and Oracle Parallel

Server. These courses are important to a thorough understanding of the product. Contact your local Oracle support team for your nearest education site.

There are now many courses in Microsoft technologies leading up to certified developer status. You may also find courses at your local educational centers at a more affordable rate.

Books

At any good bookstore, you will find more advanced texts on Oracle, for those of you working toward being a database administrator, as well as more introductory books on Visual Basic. Some of the books you may wish to investigate are listed below. You should note that none of the Visual Basic books you will encounter other than this one cover Oracle except in passing; similarly, Oracle books will not mention Visual Basic.

- *Mastering Visual Basic 6* by Evangelos Petroutsos (Sybex, 1998)
- *Database Access with Visual Basic* by Jeffrey P. Mcmanus (SAMS, 1998)
- *Database Developers Guide with Visual Basic 4* by Roger Jennings (SAMS, 1997)
- *The Hitchhiker's Guide to Visual Basic and SQL Server* by William Vaughn (Microsoft Press, 1996)
- *Mastering Oracle 8.1* by Jatinder Prem, (Sybex, 1999)
- *Oracle PL/SQL Programming* by Steven Feuerstein, (O'Reilly, 1997)
- *Oracle Performance Tuning* by Mark Gurry and Peter Corrigan (O'Reilly, 1996)

Periodicals

Over the years, I have found several periodicals useful. Although books are an excellent reference resource, periodicals capture the latest technology changes as well as give you a variety of views. Those periodicals you should investigate are

- *Visual Basic Programmers Journal* (www.devx.com).
- *Microsoft Systems Journal* (www.microsoft.com./msj/).
- *Oracle* magazine (www.oramag.com). You may be able to get a free subscription.
- *Database Programming and Design* (www.dbpd.com). This periodical is due to be replaced by *Intelligent Enterprise*.

Web Sites

The Internet is vital for keeping in touch with the latest technology as well as allowing you to download sample code. There are any number of sites devoted to Visual Basic and several to Oracle.

- One of the most important Web sites is Carl and Gary's Visual Basic Home Page. It has links to other VB sites; you can even add your own link. Visit Carl and Gary's at `http://www.cgvb.com`.

- Microsoft's Web site is `http://www.microsoft.com`.

- Oracle's Web site is `http://www.oracle.com`.

Newsgroups

Newsgroups are useful for posing technical questions to the computer community as a whole. There is no guarantee you will get an answer or, if you do, that it will be correct, but you will usually get enough information to get you started. Typical news groups are listed below. Note that you must have access to a news server through your Internet provider.

- `comp.database.oracle.misc`

- `comp.database.oracle.serve`

- `comp.lang.basic.visual.database`

- `comp.lang.basic.visual.misc`

- `microsoft.public.vb.database.rdo`

NOTE   Carl and Gary's Web site has an archive of many of the VB-related sites at `http://www.cgvb/gcgi/news_form`.

Technical Assistance

Oracle technical support has a knowledgeable staff in most of the Microsoft technologies, and Microsoft has equally excellent staff experienced with Oracle. There is usually a charge associated with this support, but it is worthwhile considering the amount of time you can spend, unsure why something is not working or wondering if it ever works. This book could not have been produced without the help of these companies' technical support staff.

- `http://support.oracle.com/MetaLink` covers questions and answers on many Oracle related topics

- Technical Forums for ODBC and OracleObjects for OLE at `http://support.oracle.com`

- `http://support.microsoft.com/support`

- Oracle's new Technology Network for Developers at `http://technet.oracle.com`

Other Resources

Over the years, I have found that the Microsoft services, Technet, and the Microsoft Developers Network (MSDN) are invaluable sources of information. There is a charge for both of these services on CD, though you can get access to the online knowledge bases on the Microsoft Web site.

A Final Note

Putting this book together has been a demanding task especially because some of the information has been hard to come by. We have made every effort to present as complete and accurate information as we can. Any feedback is useful, whether it is positive or negative, so long as we can improve the source of information for VB developers in an Oracle environment. You can send your suggestions by using the Contact area of the Sybex Web site (`www.sybex.com`). Once on the Contact page, you can choose the "Book Content Issues Form."

PART I

Introducing Oracle

CHAPTER
ONE

1

Oracle and Visual Basic

- A Brief History of Oracle

- The Architecture of a Relational Database

- The Oracle Server

- Oracle Server Advanced Features

- Visual Basic in an Oracle World

- Moving Up to Oracle

Oracle and Visual Basic are two completely different products from two completely different corporations and are designed to tackle two completely different types of problems. Yet as a Visual Basic developer, you are expected to write applications that work seamlessly with an Oracle database. This book is designed to give you the concepts, operational details, and coding examples to be able not only to understand the dual environment but also to write the most efficient and powerful applications.

This first chapter will set the scene with an introduction to Oracle and the use of Visual Basic against an Oracle database. The topics we will cover are

- A brief history of Oracle

- The architecture of a relational database

- The Oracle server

- Oracle server advanced features

- Visual Basic in an Oracle world

- Moving up to Oracle

A Brief History of Oracle

What we now know as Oracle Corporation, one of the largest software companies in the world, started out in 1977 as a small start-up company called Relational Software Incorporated (RSI). Larry Ellison and the other cofounders of this company drew inspiration from work done at IBM's research labs to develop the world's first relational database, portentously called Oracle. Part of the plan was to make the database compatible with the newly created SQL language for communication between the database and external applications. Another equally important decision was to write the database software in the C language, with the aim of making it portable across platforms. The foresight of this decision has prevailed through 20 years of development and has contributed greatly to the success of the Oracle database.

Version 2 of Oracle was the first released, with version 1 being merely a prototype. Version 3 saw the change of the company's name from RSI to Oracle Corporation. Although stability and reliability of the database improved steadily, it was not until version 5 that Oracle supported the type of architecture that we now take for granted: the client/server architecture. This version also saw the development of the Parallel Server option. Versions 6 and 7 continued the trend toward high performance, high reliability, and greater scalability.

With the release of Oracle8, there has been another shift in the architectural design of the database. The shift was toward the concept of the Network Computer Architecture, with the Oracle database as a fundamental part. Although several of the Oracle8 features had started to appear in Oracle7, this new version moved close to the ideal of the universal database, a database implementation that could store and process data of any type, not simply relational tables. This concept is demonstrated in the ability of Oracle8 to store a variety of large objects (LOB), structured objects with the Object option, and the provision of an assortment of plug-in cartridges that allow the user to process such diverse data types as graphical information and videos. Meanwhile, the trend toward more users, more data, and better performance has continued.

The Architecture of a Relational Database

When we think of Oracle, we think of a powerful, enterprise-capable relational database management system (RDBMS). In Chapter 2, *Oracle Database Architecture*, we shall see the structure of the RDBMS, the tables, the columns, and the relationships between tables that give rise to the term *RDBMS*. However, there is a more basic and fundamental architecture issue for an RDBMS, which separates the advanced from the more simplistic models. In this section, we will examine three fundamental architectural types: file-based systems, client/server systems, and multitier architectures. We will also look at the Oracle implementation of the multitier architecture, the Network Computing Architecture (NCA). It is important to understand the differences between the architectures so you can see the need to switch from one type to another as your applications and databases grow in size and complexity.

File-Based Systems

The simplest form of relational database is exemplified by products like Microsoft Access. Access consists of one file with the extension .mdb. This file contains all the database tables, queries, and forms that apply to the database as well as any locking information. This file can reside on a user's own machine or anywhere on the network.

Although you would normally use display forms and queries of the Access product against the database file, you can also use other software, such as Visual Basic. Each user application must understand exactly how to read and write to the tables in the database as well as how to use any lock management scheme so that the database can be used by more than one person concurrently. Understanding the interface must be complemented by strict adherence to the access rules. For Microsoft Access, the interface is provided by the JET engine. If you use any other method to reach the data, you may corrupt the database.

Figure 1.1 shows an Access database connected to several potential database users on the network. In this diagram, the database is placed on a File Server; there is no active database software on this server, so it is up to the applications to know how to use it.

FIGURE 1.1:

The architecture of a file-based database

The problem with a file-based database is basically in its scalability. A file-based database is more suitable for a small workgroup. Although a file-based database can successfully deal with 100MB of data, it falls down when it comes to handling more than a dozen users and when the number of records in the tables starts to increase. For example, if you want to search for the maximum value of a column in one million records, a file-based system will have to retrieve all of those records over the network, process them locally, and find the required values. With one million records to retrieve, you are going to be waiting a long time for the results.

Client/Server Architecture

As you scale up your requirements with more data and more users, a file-based approach simply reaches the point of being too slow to be useable. Depending on the volume of records and users and the speed of the network, this point may come earlier than you expect. What we need is a way to process the data on a very fast machine; we need to transfer over the network the smallest amount of information that will still do the job. In the case of the million-record search, we have to retrieve just the one value we need. The solution is what we now call a client/server architecture, and this is where products such as Oracle become important.

You can see in Figure 1.2 that the client/server architecture consists of, as its name suggests, both clients and servers. The clients in this case, are the individual users, running applications like Visual Basic; the servers are powerful, often enterprise-level, pieces of equipment running an active Database Server.

FIGURE 1.2:

The client/server architecture

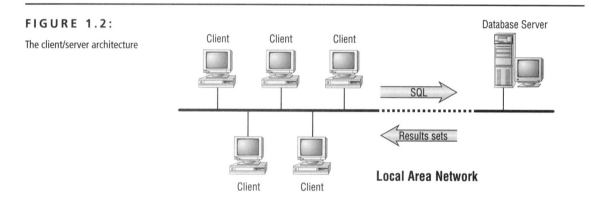

For the purposes of this book we shall consider client applications that are written in Visual Basic and run on either Microsoft Windows 95 or NT Workstation. However, in reality, these client applications can be created in many different languages and on many different hardware platforms and operating systems. As for the server software, we will be looking exclusively at Oracle, which can reside on nearly any hardware and operating system.

What are the advantages of a client/server architecture? Most of the advantages reside with the server and the capabilities it brings to the processing of data. With the presence of an existing networked desktop computer, it makes sense to do away with dumb terminals anyway. The modern PC has tremendous power to process data and display it in a variety of graphical ways that we have come to expect from desktop applications. The server no longer has to devote precious processor cycles for data formatting and report generation; instead, it merely ships the data to the client. The network potentially has to transmit less data, though this is not always the case.

What Is a Client?

From an Oracle perspective, we are dealing only with a server part of the architecture. But what about the client? With the early database architectures, the database and all the database applications were hosted on a mainframe computer. Users had access to the applications via networked terminals. These terminals were often called "dumb" due to the fact that they were display devices with no capability for processing the data.

With the advances and availability of personal computers, it became practical to have desktop machines, which could process the data locally and thereby offload the servers. The active replacement for the dumb terminal is today's *client*. The role of client software is performed by applications written in Visual Basic, among many others. Along with the flexibility and graphical impressiveness of our Visual Basic applications, we now have to accept the responsibility of managing the initiations of connections, the request and retrieval of data from a networked database, and the interpretation and display of that data in a controlled and reliable manner.

Multitier Architecture

The standard client/server architecture that we saw in the previous section has certain problems with scalability, and there have been various solutions to the situation. The very term *multitier* implies that there are various software tiers, each with its own responsibility for a certain task. As you can see in Figure 1.3, the tiers are generally divided into three parts: the client or GUI tier, the middle or business tier, and the data tier. Although the term *three-tier* is often used for this architecture, the term hides the fact that the software can be spread over many computers, with each computer performing a small part of the whole.

FIGURE 1.3:

The multitier architecture

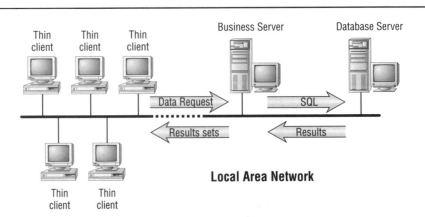

In this multitiered approach, Visual Basic applications can play a role on the client as they do in a traditional client/server architecture, although typically they will contain much less data processing and focus more on the display aspect. But Visual Basic can play a growing role in the middle tier where most of the processing and business rules are captured. This role is made possible because Visual Basic can now create ActiveX software *components* that can be run on a server under a transaction-processing environment, such as Microsoft Transaction Server (MTS).

The multitiered approach was designed to solve as many of the client/server failings as possible. The kinds of features you will find are as follows:

- Applications are easier to deploy and keep current with a multitier architecture. This is especially important when you have to scale your application for use on the Web.

- Business rules in a "thick" client means that each client application has to be altered whenever the business rules change.

- By encapsulating all the business rules in the middle tier, any application that needs to access these rules can make use of shared components rather than coding the same rules into every application on the client.

- The business layer can ensure the security of data in a standard manner and assure that the applications are as stable as possible.

- Scalability issues are covered. Although the multitier architecture has some overhead for small applications, the benefits pay off when scaling up because you can easily include more middle-tier hardware.

NOTE   The techniques we discuss in this book work equally well in either a traditional client/server approach or when built into components that run on the middle tier.

Network Computing Architecture

Oracle's implementation of the multitier design is called the Network Computing Architecture (NCA) and follows the same basic features as we saw in Figure 1.3. However, the emphasis of NCA is more on the middle and back-end tiers with the client side relegated to a minor role in the processing of data. Just as with multitier architecture, NCA consists of three or more layers as you can see in Figure 1.4.

FIGURE 1.4:

The Network Computing
Architecture

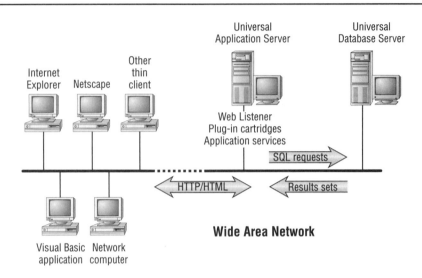

Each of the three tiers falls into one of the categories described below. You will notice that products like VB (whose real strength is as a visual interface) do not have much of a role at the current time. This should change in the future as Oracle expands the types of components (or *objects*) that can fit into the middle application server tier.

Client

The client is a "universal" thin client that can be any of the following:

- A traditional Web browser

- A Java-based client

- A Network Computer (a low-end, low-maintenance variation on the PC)

The aim of using a thin client is to make applications available to any user with an operating system and access software of choice. The client is only used as the GUI front end with limited processing power. Notice that the generic multitier design does not dictate a thin client. You can put front-end and middle-tier software on a client; it is a design issue. Microsoft's architecture is more of a services role, and services can be combined on one machine if necessary. Oracle's NCA, on the other hand, is more strict about keeping business logic off the client. However, there is no technical reason to stop using a Visual Basic application as a client.

Application Server

The *Application Server* is a term not everyone has become familiar with; it is the implementation of a specialized piece of software and the associated hardware that provides an efficient and scalable base for the middle tier. One of the aims of any middle-tier software is to ensure that any piece of code, object, or component can be used by any request coming into the server. In the old days of CGI scripts for Web servers, the server would start up a new process for each request. With all the overhead of starting the process, CGI scripts did not prove scalable. With an Application Server, any type of compliant software can be used in the same process space, and they can be pooled among all the user requests. For Oracle's Application Server, the objects are based on CORBA (Common Object Request Broker Architecture). The equivalent on the Microsoft front is to use Microsoft Transaction Server, which is COM, or Component Object Model, based. At the current time these two architectures, CORBA and COM, are not interchangeable, although there is work proceeding to tie them more closely together. As a result, you can write ActiveX components for MTS but not for Oracle's Application Server (at least not yet).

The Application Server is a flexible design because of what Oracle calls *cartridges*. Cartridges are products that can be run on top of the server software in the same manner as plug-ins in your favorite Web browser. By using a cartridge, you are basically extending the base application software with your own code. One strong point about the cartridges is that a failure in your code does not bring the Application Server down, so reliability is not compromised. There are currently plug-ins cartridges for Java, PL/SQL, PERL, and C.

Universal Data Server

The Data Server layer is often referred to as the Universal Data Server because of the design philosophy that database servers should be capable of handling any type of data. Oracle8 has been designed to fill this role in two ways: features and expandability. The feature set of Oracle8 is the richest yet released. One of the most important things to note is its ability to handle data items up to 4GB. This capability is especially useful for graphics and video information. However, despite whatever built-in capabilities a Universal Data Server has, the expandability is critical to its success. This expandability is made possible by the same cartridge concept that we saw in the section on the Application Server layer.

The types of cartridges you can use currently are

- A PL/SQL cartridge for creating stored procedures
- A ConText cartridge for sophisticated text search and profiling capabilities
- Image/VIR cartridges for native-image management to support multimedia applications
- A Spatial cartridge for specialized geographical information management and manipulation
- A Time Series cartridge for maintaining and querying time-based data

The COM Cartridge

As this book was being prepared, the new beta version of the COM cartridge was announced. This cartridge, which is available as a DLL for Windows NT, will allow you to use remote automation to control COM objects from within Oracle8. For example, you can control the methods and properties of Microsoft Excel and Word from stored procedures. It is expected that you will be able to create your own COM objects (hopefully, with Visual Basic) to extend the capabilities of the database.

The Oracle Server

When we look more closely at the Data Server layer of the NCA, we find that Oracle has developed a very powerful, scalable, and extensible series of products. Oracle was designed as a high-level database server and has matured over the last 20 years, gaining the performance, reliability, and availability features that you expect and need from an enterprise-level tool.

Although the names of the product line have changed more than once over the last few years, the current lineup is as follows:

Oracle8 Server   This is a low-cost, work group–level database that includes the basic features but lacks the expandability of the Enterprise Edition.

Oracle8 Enterprise Edition   This is a full, enterprise-ready database that allows you to use advanced features, such as the ability to make use of multiple CPUs with parallel operations, and to use the specialized data cartridges. This edition includes Advanced Replication, and you can, at extra cost, move up to Oracle Parallel Server.

Oracle Lite   This is a small footprint, personal database suitable for mobile computing.

Standard Features

We would expect to see several standard features from an enterprise-level database, and these are all found in Oracle. These features are itemized below and are fully described in the rest of the chapters in Parts I and II of this book.

- Relational architecture

- Administration tools

- Security management

- Backup and recovery facilities

- SQL interface for queries and updates

- Connection management for external applications

- Stored procedures and triggers

Although the advanced features that we will see in the next section put Oracle in a league of its own, even the standard version stands out in terms of two areas that we will next investigate: scalability and multiplatform personality.

Scalability

Scalability is a word used often these days, especially when applied to the need to create systems that can deal with Web-based clientele who demand high availability and any number of users. In fact, scalability can be many things to many people. Some of the more important issues are

- You can start off with the cheapest of hardware and scale up to more powerful hardware as your needs increase.

- You can have a range of different hardware platforms within one company, choosing each with respect to the requirements for the individual work groups. The Research and Development department may only need a small database while the Accounting and Billing database may need to be of mainframe size.

- You are not tied to a single hardware manufacturer or operating system. In the worst case scenario, you can port your database from any platform to any other platform quite easily.

- You do not have to buy new hardware if you already have a suitably powered server. You can retain your investment in equipment and staff experience.

The multiplatform support has some issues you should be aware of. It is impossible for the database development teams to work on all the different platforms concurrently. Oracle has *reference* platforms on which the database is first developed before being ported to the other platforms. The reference platforms are currently UNIX and Windows NT. If you are using another operating system, you may have to wait for several months before the latest version appears on your chosen operating system.

NOTE   Although the Database Server runs on a wide variety of platforms, not all the support tools do the same. NT is where most of the administration tools, such as Enterprise Manager, make their earliest, and maybe only, appearance.

The Oracle Server Advanced Features

This book is an introductory text to Oracle, so implementing any of the advanced features of Oracle is beyond our scope. However, the following sections conceptually examine a few of the advanced features that an Enterprise installation would have. It is important to be aware of these advanced features because, even though you may not be supporting them, you may have to interface with them as a Visual Basic developer.

The main benefits of these advanced features are to improve the performance, scalability, and availability of the database, features of Oracle that are rarely equaled. However, these options do require a significant amount of planning and training. In the case of Oracle Parallel Server, there is also a significant increase in cost compared to the standard Enterprise Edition.

Distributed Databases

Oracle includes the Distributed option in all the Enterprise-level servers it sells. This option allows you to set up database *links* from one database to any other on the same network. For example, the Accounting department may need to access data in other parts of the company, departments that each have their own databases. We can easily set up a one-way link from the Accounting database to the Engineering, Manufacturing, and Research and Development departments as shown in Figure 1.5.

FIGURE 1.5:

Database links in a distributed database

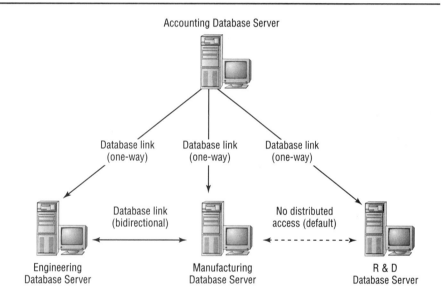

In this distributed situation, the users in the Accounting department can easily request data from any of the databases for which links have been set up. The technique is as simple as adding a table's location when doing your queries. You can even make the data link transparent with the use of synonyms. There are a variety of security measures you can take to ensure that only those users who have the correct passwords can use the links.

The advantage of the distributed database is that a certain amount of separation (both physical and political) can be achieved for the data. You can rest assured in the knowledge that if one database crashes, none of the others will be affected (though in this case, you can no longer run distributed queries). You can also access Oracle databases that are on different operating systems as long as they are on the same network. The versions of Oracle do not even have to be the same.

Parallel Server

The traditional RDBMS is one or more application processes with associated memory against a set of database files. Oracle has proceeded to the next level with what it calls the Parallel Server option. This option enables more than one server to access the same database files (see Figure 1.6). Complicated techniques (such as the Distributed Lock Manager) are required to enable this option to work properly so users on each server can make changes to the same data in just the same way they would when there is only a single server. The servers have to be clustered, so UNIX and OpenVMS have been the traditional operating systems of choice; however, the Parallel Server option is slowly being brought into the world of NT. The most common situation is for two servers in parallel, but there may be tens or even hundreds of servers.

FIGURE 1.6:

Oracle Parallel Server functionality

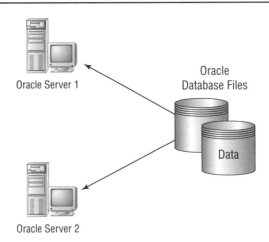

Oracle Server 1

Oracle Database Files

Data

Oracle Server 2

The advantages of Oracle Parallel Server include:

- **Performance**   You now have much more processing power and through-put capability for a small sacrifice in overhead.

- **Reliability**   If any one of the servers fails for any reason, the user applications can be failed over to one of the remaining servers.

Oracle Parallel Server is not free; there is a substantial additional charge, and it requires careful planning and implementation. You will also need additional training because if Parallel Server is not configured properly the performance will not be good. However, where high reliability and throughput is required, the Parallel Server option is definitely worth investigating.

NOTE   Parallel Server does not protect against hard-disk failure. For this, you should use a RAID disk array and preferably a hot-standby database or replication to ensure that you can move to another database if the first one fails.

Replication

There are times when your data availability is so critical to your business that you cannot afford to be without it for more than a short period of time, perhaps minutes or even seconds at the most. With a single database server, there are going to be times when your database fails you. You can, to a certain extent, protect against disk failure by using RAID (Redundant Array of Inexpensive Disks), but many other things can go wrong, from someone accidentally shutting the power supply down to hardware or network failure. Identifying the problem is going to take time, as is pulling in the right support personnel to fix the problem.

In critical situations, the only real solution is to have more than one database. A second server may be clustered with the first one, which is useful when a server crashes, but to be completely secure, you have to be prepared for what is called a "site failure" in which your whole site is unavailable. This second (or third) alternative database is another one of Oracle's strong selling points. There are two ways to provide alternative databases, and the first is called *replication*, the second is called *hot-standby*.

The term *replication* can refer to many things in the database business, but with Oracle, it means, in simple terms, taking the data from one database and transferring it to another. You can do this with simple snapshots in a master/slave relationship where the transfer of data is always one way; the alternative is a master/master relationship where data can be entered into any database and will be transferred to the others. The possible configurations are shown in Figure 1.7.

FIGURE 1.7:

The possible configuration for replication

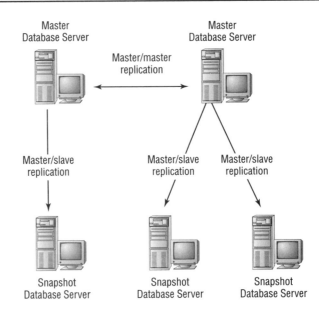

The following are the types of replication you should be aware of in an Oracle replication situation.

Snapshot replication—A periodic copy is taken of the master database and either incrementally or fully updates the slave databases.

Synchronous replication—Data is entered into the two master databases at the same time. If the databases cannot communicate, then no data can be entered; however, the databases are always synchronized.

Asynchronous replication—Changes in a master database are entered into a queue and transferred to other databases on a periodic basis. If the communication or a server is down, then this system will simply delay the transfer of data. Because of this situation, the databases can become out of synchronization.

Although many database vendors offer these features, one of Oracle's strong points is in its conflict management. When you have asynchronous replication, conflicts can occur when updates are transferred to other databases. For example, what if an update is done against a row that is deleted on another database? Oracle not only allows you to detect these conflicts but also provides several standard ways of dealing with it. You can even create your own rules to handle the conflict.

Although it is not generally considered replication, there is another alternative solution to the availability dilemma and that is to transfer logs of the data changes to another machine. This second database is called a *hot-standby machine* and runs in what is called *Constant Recovery mode*. This machine is a much simpler database setup to create and manage; the penalty is that your second machine cannot be used until you make it the master machine (at which point your first machine cannot be used).

Visual Basic in an Oracle World

Visual Basic is the most popular programming language in the world, but does that make it suitable to use as a front end for Oracle? Oracle has its own set of high-productivity tools in the Oracle Developer 2000 series, apart from the other tools that can duplicate what VB can do, such as C++, Java, and Delphi. There is no easy answer to this question, and it may come down to individual preferences. However, there are some important reasons to use Visual Basic rather than any of the others.

Capability   VB is capable of producing software as sophisticated as any of the other data-access techniques available. There is little you can do in say, Developer 2000 that cannot be implemented equally well with ADO or OO4O.

Flexibility   You do not have to use VB for database access. You can use it to write a text processor, an e-mail listener, or 10,001 other tasks.

Familiarity   Being the most popular programming language in the world means there is a steady supply of talented staff for you to add to your development teams. When the general supply is short, you will still be more likely to find development staff than for other languages.

Popularity   The popularity of a product is important for you to become familiar with because you will see more magazine articles and books as well as have a better supply of third-party products from companies who will devote their resources in which there is a payback.

The Past

For the last few years, Visual Basic support for Oracle has not been as good as we would have liked. Until Visual Basic 3, there was no support for remote databases. (Table 1.1 gives an approximate summary of support for Visual Basic methods.) Oracle Objects for OLE (OO4O) is a product from Oracle Corporation that has always supported a large number of features for Oracle-specific syntax. We will cover it in detail in Chapter 18, *Oracle Objects for OLE*. However, the support from ODBC products has been less than stellar.

TABLE 1.1: Historical View of Visual Basic Support for Oracle

Versions	JET	RDO	ADO	OO4O
VB3	JET 1.1	N/A	N/A	OO4O 1.0
VB4	JET 2.5	RDO 1.0	N/A	OO4O 2.0
VB5	JET 3.5	RDO 2.0	ADO 1.5	OO4O 2.1
VB6	JET 3.51	RDO 2.0	ADO 2.0	OO4O 2.3

Accessing Oracle from Data Access Objects (DAO) and Visual Basic 3 was the first time ODBC became viable, but DAO did not support many Oracle-specific features; even accessing schemas and packages was difficult, if not impossible. To a certain extent, DAO still doesn't support as much as we would like, so there has been a move to products that better support remote databases. Remote Data Objects (RDO), which we cover in Chapter 16, was the first ODBC method to provide some of the features that we need, but things were still not perfect. With the introduction of Visual Basic 6 and ADO and the continuing improvements in OO4O, we have a much better position as Visual Basic developers in an Oracle environment than we did a year or so ago.

The Present

Now that Visual Basic 6 has been released, we have access to a more universal ActiveX Data Objects (ADO) data-access model than we have had before. We will see the details in Chapter 17, *ActiveX Data Objects*, but the product provides more support for Oracle-specific syntax and features than any other product apart from OO4O. In addition to supporting Oracle, ADO will support a vast variety of potential data sources. Initially, this will be restricted to current ODBC data sources, although it is noticeable that Visual Basic 6 has been released with what is called a *native OLE-DB provider* for Oracle along with one for Microsoft SQL Server. OLE-DB is an alternative to ODBC, something we will cover in Chapter 11, *Client-Side Technology*.

Along with ADO, which comes with the Professional Edition of Visual Basic, the Enterprise Edition also provides us with database design tools that work well against an Oracle database. Although they do not provide complete support, they are the equivalent of products that cost as much or more than Visual Basic itself. For example, these tools can make creating tables almost as easy as working with Microsoft Access. As with any GUI tool, however, you need to understand what is going on beneath the surface, or your designs will not be efficient.

The improved support for Oracle has become noticeable throughout Visual Basic. Although previous releases of Visual Basic left much to be desired by the Oracle developer, the improvements version 6 provides are summarized below:

- OLE-DB native support for Oracle

- Support for schemas, synonyms, and packages

- Partial support for packages

- Support for PL/SQL tables through ADO

- More knowledge-base articles on Oracle

- Database design tools

There are still a few weak areas. The database designer tools cannot create or test PL/SQL packages. This is not a critical problem, but packages (which are covered in Chapter 9, *Introduction To PL/SQL*) are a sign of a more professional design approach. In a similar way, the ADO GetSchema method cannot retrieve package information, and even ADO has no support for PL/SQL cursor variables.

One final point on the current situation. Oracle8 has introduced such things as new data types and the object-relational features. These are not supported from Visual Basic yet, even with OO4O.

The Future

It is a brave soul who predicts anything in the world of information technology, but sometimes this is the most exciting part of working with new technology. In the realm of performance, it is not likely we will see much of an improvement from the data-access technology in which OLE-DB runs as a forward-only, read-only cursor. The advances we see in performance will be from faster clients, servers, and networks. We may, however, find that techniques for improving the performance of slower data-access techniques (such as updatable cursors) do become more efficient.

In the area of features, we can look to several interesting developments. There is no doubt that OO4O will lead the way and has the following enhancements in store for us:

- Support for Oracle8 data types, such as LOBs

- Support for Oracle8 object-relational features

- Capability of registering for database events as an alternative to polling

- Asynchronous operation (similar to that available in RDO and ADO)

- Support for OLE-DB and ADO

Moving Up to Oracle

Many applications are prototyped in a desktop application such as Microsoft Access. This is a cost-effective solution if it is done carefully. However, you must keep in mind that Access is not an enterprise application; it does not have the features you would expect (such as stored procedures), and it certainly does not have the performance that you need. You can easily get the wrong impression about how an application will perform, and you may end up developing forms and queries that will have to be completely be rewritten. If you do decide to prototype in Access or you have an existing application in Access or SQL Server, then the next two sections will give you some idea of the differences to expect.

Moving from Microsoft Access

If you have been working with Microsoft Access, you have been using a file-based system. The database is stored in a file with a .mdb extension, such as `biblio.mdb`.

Any application has driver .dlls installed on their machine and can access the files locally or over a network. Technically, this can be called client/server; however, the server we are dealing with is a File Server, not a Database Server.

Assuming that you have decided that Oracle is where you are headed, you now have to review how easy it is going to be to migrate. In general, it should be a relatively easy move, but the following points need to be kept in mind.

- Microsoft Access includes more than just database tables; it includes reports, code modules, queries, and screens. None of these features are included in Oracle (or generally in any other RDBMS), so you will have to move these to Visual Basic equivalents.

- In the short term, if you do not have the resources to rewrite all your applications, you have the option of attaching the new Oracle database tables to your Access database and running that way for a while. This is covered in Chapter 12, *Accessing Oracle From Visual Basic.*

- Access includes a *counter* column to make an auto-incrementing indexed field. Oracle uses independent number generators called *sequences.*

- Oracle likes table names that are uppercase with no spaces, whereas Access is much freer.

- Access does not include stored procedures, so there is nothing to be converted.

- Access SQL syntax is not entirely compatible with Oracle, for example, the text-string delimiter is " in Access and ' in Oracle, and the delimiter for a date in a SQL statement is # in Access, while it is ' in Oracle.

If you need to migrate from Access to Oracle, use one of the two methods described in Chapter 12: Access Export and the Oracle Migration Wizard. The latter is far preferable.

Moving from Microsoft SQL Server

Microsoft SQL Server is quite a different product from Access; although it is fairly compatible with Access (for example, the data types), it is an active server like Oracle and contains many extra features, such as stored procedures, many built-in functions, and a more complicated architecture. The learning curve for Oracle is longer than for SQL Server partially due to Oracle having many more high-end features.

Oracle is quite different from SQL Server and, as a result, this can be confusing for those moving between the different databases. This section will cover a few of the main areas of concern.

- Oracle is a multiplatform RDBMS whereas SQL Server is restricted to NT Server workstations. Most high-end Oracle systems currently use UNIX.

- Oracle does not include the concept of a master database. All databases run independently, with their own data files, memory management, and control.

- The architecture of Oracle is quite different from SQL Server, and you should read Chapter 2, *Oracle Database Concepts,* to get a good understanding of this difference.

- Oracle is not as integrated into the Windows world as SQL Server.

- Both products support SQL and include stored procedures. Whereas SQL Server uses Transact-SQL extensions to SQL, Oracle uses PL/SQL. The functionality of these languages is similar, but they look very different in syntax.

- SQL Server stored procedures return a Recordset if you do a SELECT command in the procedure. Oracle only supports this through *cursor variables,* which can be a difficult concept for some developers to accept.

- In stored procedures, Oracle automatically uses transactions; in SQL Server data changes are automatically committed by default.

- SQL Server shares the auto-incrementing column concept with Access, and this time it's represented by the identity property of a column. In Oracle, you will need to work with sequences.

- SQL Server supports temporary tables, whereas Oracle does not.

- In Oracle, you do not have seamless debugging between client and server as you do in SQL Server.

- Functions may differ between the two systems, and some functions may not have an equivalent.

- There is a much larger set of fundamental data types in SQL Server than in Oracle.

- The Oracle server does not support server-side cursors. (These are generally to be avoided anyway.)

- Oracle uses row-level locking, while prior to version 7, SQL Server used page-level locking.

In general Oracle is a more mature product, better suited to more enterprise environments where there is a need for high throughput and availability and reliable backup and recovery.

NOTE   Oracle has recently announced a series of migration tools that will make it much easier to move from SQL Server to Oracle. There are conversion kits available for migrating the database itself as well as your SQL Server stored procedures.

Summary

In this chapter, we took a brief run through the capabilities of the Oracle server and took an introductory look at how Visual Basic and other Microsoft products relate to it. In the rest of the book, we will take a much closer look at the architecture and operation of the database, building up well-designed applications. Then we will move on to viewing how Visual Basic fits into this world, covering the five basic ways to interface with the database, produce the most efficient applications, and use the most Oracle features.

CHAPTER
TWO

2

Oracle Database Architecture

- The Difference between an Instance and a Database

- The Memory Structures Needed on the Server

- The Processes Involved in Running an Instance

- The Database Files

- Concurrency and Consistency Issues

- Schemas, from the Developer's Viewpoint

- An Overview of How Oracle Works

If you have never used Oracle before, then you will be encountering some very strange concepts. As a Visual Basic developer coming to Oracle for the first time and working with a self-assured database analyst, I distinctly remember my confusion surrounding the whole idea of what an Oracle database really is.

If you are used to the file-based architecture of Microsoft Access, then there is much to learn. Even those of you who are used to relational databases, such as Microsoft SQL Server and Sybase, will find the concepts and terminology confusing.

Although there is much more to being a database analyst than what this book could possibly cover, a thorough understanding of the underlying architecture will be valuable to you as you deal with Oracle from the application side: this chapter will provide that basic understanding. In fact, you may never know when your duties will overlap with that of a database analyst (DBA), even if it's something as simple as knowing that it is not your code causing the problems.

In this chapter, we will be looking at the structures that exist in each Oracle database. We will cover

- The difference between an instance and a database
- The memory structures needed on the server
- The processes involved in running an instance
- The database files
- Concurrency and consistency issues
- Schemas, from the developer's viewpoint
- An overview of how Oracle works

Each of the components, memory, processes, and data files are completely intertwined, and it can be difficult to understand one without understanding them all. You may find that you have to go through the details several times, but it is a worthwhile feeling when everything comes together.

Instances and Databases

An Oracle database can be thought of in two ways: as a *database* or as an *instance*. Technically, an Oracle *database* is the physical collection of files that store the data that exists in the database. But on its own the database cannot do anything because there isn't a way for a user to interact with it. The term *instance* applies to the running Oracle database and consists of the memory structures and the associated processes that interact with and manipulate these structures. People who work with the Oracle Relational Database Management Systems (RDBMS) often interchange the terms *instance* and *database*. The difference between the two becomes clearer when you realize that it is possible to have multiple instances connecting to a single set of physical database files. This is the Oracle Parallel Server option.

When a script is run to start up the Oracle instance, it allocates the memory required and starts up the processes. It then *mounts* the data files that constitute the database. In this way you can have more than one database instance on the same server that will run independently of each other. With Oracle Parallel Server, more than one instance mounts the same single set of data files. The memory, Server processes, and data files constitute the three basic organizational structures vital to understanding Oracle.

Memory Structures

The first structure of Oracle that we will look at is the use of memory. The *System Global Area (SGA)*, sometimes called the *Shared Global Area,* is the main memory component in Oracle. Oracle is a memory-based database, which means that data, locks, and so on are all held in memory. The size of the SGA should never exceed the amount of physical memory available on the server machine, otherwise virtual memory paging may occur on the SGA; this paging activity will degrade the performance of the database.

NOTE   In an operating system that uses a virtual memory model, sometimes not enough physical memory is available for all applications. The system solves this problem by moving out the contents of sections of memory, called *pages,* to disk. This process is called *paging,* and the size of the pages is typically 4KB or 8KB. Before operating systems were so sophisticated, whole applications were moved out to disk; this process was called *swapping.* The disk file that is used is still called a *swap file.*

The SGA consists of the following components:

- Database Buffer Cache

- Redo Log Buffer

- Shared Pool Area, which is made up of the following components:

  - Library Cache (which includes a Shared SQL Area)

  - Data Dictionary Cache (also known as the Row Cache)

Oracle allocates the memory for the SGA when the instance starts up. It will grab additional shared memory pages as needed until the size of the SGA reaches that specified in the Initialization file. Oracle controls the use of the memory itself and never releases any until the instance shuts down. Equally, the memory cannot be increased dynamically. To change the memory allocation, you must shut down the instance, make a change to the initialization parameters, and restart.

WARNING   Shutting down the instance on a production database is not an action you should take lightly. It requires that you understand the effects of many of the initialization parameters. If you have not taken courses in Oracle database administration and tuning, you should try to get an experienced DBA to assist.

The overall structure of Oracle, its memory organization, and the commonly used processes and files are shown in Figure 2.1. We will examine each part in detail in this chapter, but you may want to refer back to this diagram to remind yourself where each part fits into the whole. In the diagram, you will notice the SGA, which is made up of several parts that are described in the following sections.

The Database Buffer Cache

The Database Buffer Cache is the component of the SGA that stores in-memory copies of the data read from the database data files, ready to be accessed by your Visual Basic application. The cache is composed of buffers whose individual size is equal to that of a database block in the physical database files. This cache is filled on demand by a request from an application if the data is not already present in memory (see Figure 2.2). When you connect to the database, Oracle creates a *Server process* (also known as a *Shadow process*) that handles application requests on your behalf (or you might share an existing process). We will cover these processes in the "Server Processes" section, later in the chapter.

FIGURE 2.1:

The major components of the
System Global Area (SGA)

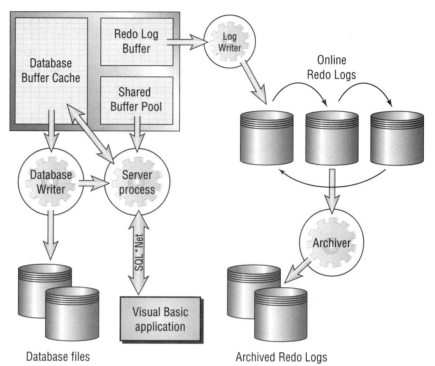

Database files

Archived Redo Logs

FIGURE 2.2:

The operation of the
Database Buffer Cache

Database Buffer Cache

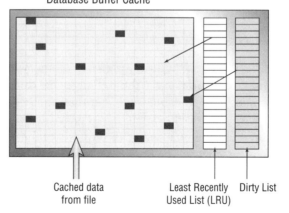

Cached data
from file

Least Recently
Used List (LRU)

Dirty List

There are two lists that manage the buffers in cache: the *Least Recently Used (LRU) List* and the *Dirty List*. The most important is the Least Recently Used List. Every time a data buffer is accessed, such as by a SELECT statement, it is moved toward the top of the list (the *Most Recently Used* end). Buffers that are not accessed head toward the bottom of the list. This LRU scheme ensures that the more often and more recently a buffer is accessed, the less likely it will be removed from memory. The aim of this LRU algorithm is to minimize the number of physical disk reads that have to be done.

Oracle also has a Dirty List that keeps track of any data buffers that have been changed (that is, "marked dirty"). When a request has been made for data that is not in the Database Buffer Cache, Oracle (specifically a Server process) will search the LRU List for a free buffer. If dirty buffers are encountered on the LRU List during this search, the Server process will move them to the Dirty List. After a certain number of buffers have been scanned and no free buffer has been found, the Database Writer process (DBWR) will write some dirty buffers out to disk, which frees them up. Buffers that are not dirty can, of course, be moved out at any time, and the ones at the bottom of the LRU List are the first to go.

If you could look at the Database Buffer Cache, you would see data being brought in, perhaps modified, and written out to the appropriate data file. In Figure 2.2, you will notice several buffer areas are blacked in to indicate that they are dirty. If you used this visual to view the database in action, you would see buffers changing from clean to dirty and back again. This is often viewed as a *twinkling* effect, one of the many colloquial terms you may comes across in connection with Oracle.

Redo Log Buffer

The Redo Log Buffer is the area of memory that holds a journal of all the changes made to the database; these changes are called *Redo Log Entries*. They are not copies of the datablocks; rather they are the information required to reconstruct the changes to the datablocks. The entries are tokenized to make them as small as possible while capturing the entirety of the change. They are used in database crash recovery. The buffer is treated as a circular area of memory, so when it reaches the physical end of memory, it starts again at the beginning. Of course, the Redo Log Entries have to be written to permanent storage, or the log of changes will be overwritten (see Figure 2.3). The Log Writer process (LGWR) monitors this buffer and flushes its contents to a set of files called the Redo Log files when necessary. The Server processes control the writing to the Redo Log Buffer, and LGWR writes the changes to the buffer as Redo Log Entries.

FIGURE 2.3:

The operation of the Redo Log Buffer

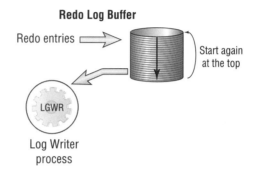

Redo Log Buffer

Redo entries

Start again at the top

LGWR

Log Writer process

Shared Pool

The Shared Pool is an area of the SGA memory that contains the parts of memory that can be shared among users. As shown in Figure 2.4, it consists of several smaller areas, all of which are described in the following sections.

Library Cache

The Library Cache consists of several components that are shared among database users. The most important component is the Shared SQL Area. The Shared SQL Area contains the details of each SQL statement as well as an execution plan (also known as a *parse tree*) when the statement is actually executed. Being a shared area, it can hold SQL statements that can be used by more than one user, as long as they are identical. The SQL statements must be lexically identical, right down to case and spacing. In addition, the statements must refer to the same objects. Because of this restrictive criteria, *bind variables* are often used to make statements lexically identical. This component has the obvious benefit of improving performance if a user is executing the same statement as another user because the code is already parsed and optimized.

NOTE   Bind variables are parameters passed through a SQL statement, allowing statements to be identical except for the values of the variables passed to them. We
will discuss the use of bind variables in Chapter 18, *Oracle Objects For OLE*.

Data Dictionary Cache

The Data Dictionary Cache in the SGA stores information about the tables that are
being used. It will store table names, column names, and data types. In this way,
the information is already at hand when required to parse SQL. It is available to
all memory areas and processes, and it contributes to overall performance. Parts
of the Data Dictionary Cache can be flushed in just the same way as the Database
Buffer Cache (that is, on an LRU basis).

FIGURE 2.4:

The layout of the Shared Pool

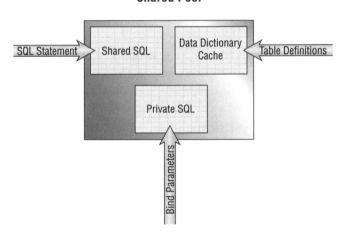

Additional Memory Areas

Two other memory areas worth mentioning. These are

- *Program Global Area* or *PGA*, which is used to contain control information for
  the server processes.

- *Sort Areas*, which are used for memory-based sorts.

Processes

Now that we have seen the memory structures that Oracle needs, we can look at the processes needed for managing that memory. These processes, along with the memory structures, form the heart of Oracle—the instance—and the two work hand in hand.

An Oracle instance is comprised of several background processes, each of which contributes to the database in a different way. These processes are briefly described in Table 2.1. Four of the processes shown are mandatory: the Database Writer (DBWR), the Log Writer (LGWR), the Process Monitor (PMON), and the System Monitor (SMON), and these will be covered in more detail in the next section. We will also cover the Archiver process (ARCH) because without this, you will not be able to completely recover your database after a disk failure. (You can always recover to the time of the last backup, but then you could lose a substantial amount of data.) Finally, we will cover the Listener processes, which enable a network user (such as a Visual Basic program) to connect to the database.

TABLE 2.1: The Various Processes Involved in an Oracle Instance

Process Name	Description
ARCH	The Archiver process copies the *Redo Logs* to disk or tape to archive them.
CKPT	The purpose of CKPT is to update data file headers with synchronization numbers during a checkpoint event. The process is optional; if you do not use it, the LGWR process will take this job.
Dnnn	The Dispatcher processes control shared access to the database for one or more User processes. The Dispatcher processes are enabled when the Multithreaded Server option is used. They replace the Server processes, which handle SQL requests on behalf of User processes.
DBWR	The Database Writer writes data that has changed in the Database Buffer Cache out to file, normally to make room for newly requested data to be pulled into the SGA. It is not used to commit a transaction.
LCKn	The Lock processes are enabled only for the Parallel Server option. They are used to resolve interinstance contention for datablocks.
LGWR	The Log Writer moves data from the SGA to the Online Redo Logs. It also coordinates the checkpoint event as well as switches from one log file group to another.
Pnnn	The Parallel Query processes are used to distribute the work of satisfying a database query.

Continued on next page

TABLE 2.1 CONTINUED: The Various Processes Involved in an Oracle Instance

Process Name	Description
PMON	The Process Monitor performs transaction rollback in the event of a Server process failure. PMON ensures that database resources locked by the failed process are released.
RECO	The Recover process cleans up distributed transactions after a networking failure.
Snnn	Shared Server processes are used only in the Multithreaded Server option; they process SQL requests submitted by the Dispatcher processes.
SMON	In a crash recovery situation SMON will replay database changes since the last checkpoint event. The changes are stored in the Online Redo Log files.
SNPn	The Automatic Snapshot Refresh processes are used in a distributed database configuration to propagate changes in a master database to other databases. You can also use them for your own tasks, such as repetitive administration jobs.

The most important processes are DBWR, LGWR, PMON, and SMON. If any of these fails, then the Oracle instance will fail. One process that is optional but highly recommended is ARCH; without this process, data can't be archived, and there is much less chance of a complete recovery after a failure. You would probably have to resort to your last full backup and lose any changes since that point in time.

NOTE   There is a single-user version of Oracle that has only one Server process, but this version is seldom used; one of the main benefits of a RDBMS is its multiuser features, and most instances are multiprocess as described previously.

Oracle Processes Running under Windows NT

Oracle on Windows NT is not implemented in exactly the same way as on other platforms, such as UNIX and Open-VMS. Instead of processes, Oracle uses a single *service* to run all of the processes listed in Table 2.1 as background threads of the service. A service is an executable process that is installed on the NT machine and can run even when no one is logged on. The Oracle service that runs these threads on NT is called OracleService*sid*, in which *sid* is the name of the instance.

Continued on next page

You will also see several other services running. The first is OracleStart*sid*, which automatically starts up Oracle if NT ever restarts, and OracleTNSListener, which is a service that starts the Listener process, which connects users coming in over the network to the database. Native connections, such as when you run a SQL*Plus session on the server itself, do not require the Listener process to complete the connection.

Database Writer (DBWR)

Any changes you make to data in the database are initially made in memory. It is only later, at an opportune moment, that Oracle updates the data files: this is handled by the Database Writer process. This is the only process that writes data from the System Global Area to the data files. This process is shown in Figure 2.5. Data requested by a user is read from the database files into the Database Buffer Cache if this data is not already in the cache.

FIGURE 2.5:

The Database Writer process writes dirty blocks from the Database Buffer Cache to the database files.

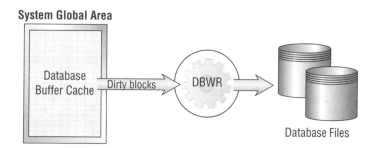

Whenever these buffers are changed, such as with an INSERT, UPDATE, or DELETE SQL statement, they are marked as "dirty." When the number of buffers in the Dirty List has reached a threshold value, the Database Writer uses the Least Recently Used List to find the buffers that are most suitable to write out to file to free the buffers up. Because Oracle uses it own file structure, the Database Writer can write out many blocks at the same time to file efficiently (a "multiblock write"). However, because it does not write out data continuously, a crash could leave changes in memory and not save them to a data file. This problem is solved by the Log Writer.

Log Writer (LGWR)

Any changes you make to the data in your database appear not only in the Database Buffer Cache but also as entries into the Redo Log Buffer. If your Oracle instance were to crash, the entries in the buffer would be lost. To enable recovery after a crash, the entries must be stored in external-disk files. The Log Writer process writes these entries from the Redo Log Buffer to one or more Online Redo Log files. Figure 2.6 should make this a little easier to understand. Remember that the Redo Log Buffer stores any changes to data as Redo Log Entries so that Oracle can replay your changes in the event of a database crash. If you do not enable the Checkpoint process (CKPT), then the Log Writer will perform data file header updates during the checkpoint event.

The Log Writer process writes out the contents of the Redo Log Buffer when

- A database transaction is committed

- The Redo Log Buffer becomes over one-third full

- The Database Writer completes writing buffers to disk during a checkpoint event

If none of these events occurs (the database is relatively quiet), then the Log Writer will write data out periodically anyway (every three seconds).

FIGURE 2.6:

The Log Writer process writes Redo Log Entries from the Redo Log Buffer to file.

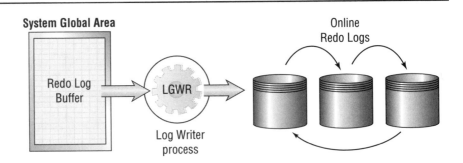

System Monitor (SMON)

The duties of SMON are as follows:

- Perform instance recovery if the previous database shutdown did not include a system-wide checkpoint. This is the primary duty of SMON during startup.

- Coalesce adjacent extents of free space in the data files. This action can be turned off at the tablespace level by setting PCTINCREASE = 0 in the default storage parameters for the tablespace.

- Reclaim temporary segments residing in a "permanent" tablespace after they have been released by a Server process performing a sort operation.

Process Monitor (PMON)

The Process Monitor process cleans up to the SGA when a Server process fails. Specifically, PMON will roll back the transaction of the failed session and release any resource locks associated with that transaction.

Archiver (ARCH)

The Archiver process is not mandatory but is highly recommended because without it, you may not be able to fully recover a database after a media failure, such as a disk crash (see Figure 2.7). Although the LGWR process writes data from the Redo Log Buffer to disk, these disk files are naturally limited in size and number. They are treated as a circular resource so when the last has been filled up, the LGWR starts back at the first again. When this happens, the first one gets overwritten and the data is lost. This setup, known as NOARCHIVELOG mode, is the default for Oracle.

To avoid overwriting the Online Redo Log files, you must start the Archiver process that copies each file to an archive area whenever the file fills up. You must also ensure that the database is in ARCHIVELOG mode. This means that there are two distinct steps to enabling archiving: the latter is often forgotten. Because Online Redo Log files are used to recover the database, you can see the importance of this process. (We will see how to do this in Chapter 4, *Database Administration*.)

The Archiver is partially responsible for keeping the Control files up-to-date, although this task is shared by other processes, such as the LGWR, which updates the Control files with checkpoint and log sequence information at a log switch, and the Server processes, which will update the Control file when a tablespace is added or an ALTER DATABASE command is issued.

WARNING   If the archive destination fills up and archiving is enabled, Oracle will not overwrite the Online Redo Logs; it will eventually just hang.

The Archiver process writes data from the Online Redo Logs to files in the archive destination directory.

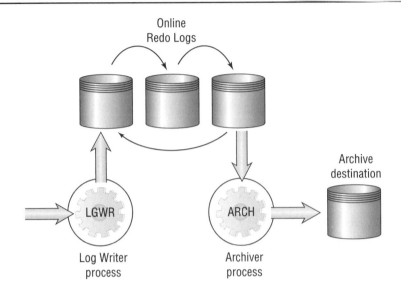

Server Processes

The Server processes are named this way because they are the only processes on the server designed to deal with user requests; however, they are often incorrectly thought of as user processes, which are the actual applications (like Visual Basic). For every user application, such as creating a session from your Visual Basic program, a Server process is created to handle your requests. This setup is the most basic one for users: to enable Oracle to scale to more users, you can use the Multi-threaded Server option, which uses Dispatcher processes as well as Shared Server processes to handle user requests. The creation of these Server processes is dealt with in the next chapter; however, Figure 2.8 gives an overview of how they work.

These are the main tasks of the Server processes:

- Parse SQL statements and execute them

- Return the result sets to the user (e.g., your Visual Basic program)

- Read data blocks into the Data Buffer Cache when they are needed and not present in the Cache

- Write changes to data to the Redo Log Buffer as Redo Log Entries

FIGURE 2.8:

Connecting to Oracle through
a server process

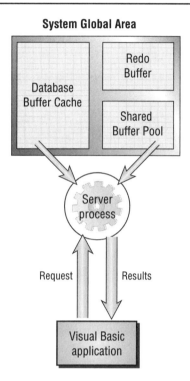

System Global Area

Listener Process

The Listener process is not one of the required background processes but is necessary if anyone wants to access the database from the network (as opposed to running on the server itself). You start this process to "listen" for connection requests
coming in from the network. (It is much like an HTTP listener in a Web server.) It
then creates the Server process to handle the communication between the user
and Oracle. We will cover this process more in Chapter 3, *Creating a Database.*

Database Files

Although an Oracle instance consists of the memory structures and the processes
which manage that memory, the physical database files are what make the system

useable. They hold all the data associated with the database for the following reasons:

- To allow the database to deal with more data than it can hold in physical memory (remember that OS swapping and paging is to be avoided at all costs).

- To allow recovery of database transactions either to the point of failure or to a previous point in time.

In a real-life database, these database files are, of course, of vital importance to the operation of a useable system. There are four types of database files:

- Control files
- Initialization (or Parameter) files
- Online Redo Log files
- Data files

All of these files are important to running Oracle, and we shall review each of them in turn.

Control Files

The Control file is a small file that describes the current database structure. You might think of it as an online database header file. It is a binary file, so you should not edit it; you shouldn't even consider editing it. It is read by the Oracle instance at start up and is kept open and up-to-date until the instance shuts down. Its purpose includes

- Keeping the database name
- Identifying the database files and Log files
- Synchronizing the information needed for recovery, including checkpoints, without which you could never recover the database

Each time the database structure is changed—for instance, when creating or dropping a table or perhaps adding a Log file—the Control file is updated with this physical change.

The Oracle default is to have just one Control file. If you value your database, you should ensure that at least two Control files are configured. We will set this up in Chapter 3, *Creating a Database*.

Parameter File

The Parameter file contains information about all sorts of start-up options for the Oracle instance. It is read when the database is started and as such is similar in concept to an *.ini Initialization file in Microsoft Windows: you can edit it with your favorite editor and manually set the parameters you want. If you change any settings, they will not take effect until the Oracle instance is restarted.

A typical Parameter file is shown in Listing 2.1. By default, it is named `initSID.ora` (where SID is the instance name), but this name will be set for you if you generate it with the provided utilities. You can also change the name to whatever you want. We will see how it is used in the next chapter.

Listing 2.1

```
##########################################################################
# Example INITtest.ORA file
#
# This file includes the settings you want for a particular Oracle
# instance.
##########################################################################

db_name = test
db_files = 20
control_files = (C:\ORANT\DATABASE\ctl1test.ora,
                 D:\ORANT\DATABASE\ctl2test.ora)

compatible = 7.3.3.0.1

db_file_multiblock_read_count =  8
db_block_buffers =  200
shared_pool_size =  6500000

log_checkpoint_interval = 10000
processes =  50
```

```
dml_locks =  100
log_buffer =  8192

sequence_cache_entries =  10
sequence_cache_hash_buckets =  10
max_dump_file_size = 10240       # limit trace file size to 5 Meg each
log_archive_start = true         # sets automatic archiving
oracle_trace_enable = false

# define directories to store trace and alert files
background_dump_dest=%RDBMS73%\trace
user_dump_dest=%RDBMS73%\trace
db_block_size = 2048
remote_login_passwordfile = shared
text_enable = true
```

Online Redo Log Files

Although data changes are made in memory (in the Redo Log Buffer), there has to be a backup in case the instance fails. This is accomplished through the Log Writer process, which, as we saw in previous sections, writes data from the Redo Log Buffer in the SGA to the Online Redo Log files. These Redo Log files are again treated as circular storage areas (when the last one fills, LGWR starts again at the first), and if the database is not in the ARCHIVELOG mode, they will be continuously overwritten.

The terminology for the Redo Log files can get a little confusing. The Oracle default is for two Log files; let's call them redo_1a and redo_2a. They are considered *members* of separate *groups*, though in this case only one file (or member) exists in each group. In fact, it is far better to have at least one more group for performance purposes, so let's add a third group with one member file in it, redo_3a. The Log Writer writes to redo_1a, redo_2a, and redo_3a. After that, it starts writing to redo_1a again, by which time it has been copied to the archive destination. The group that is being written to is called the *current* group.

NOTE   So to remember the terminology: the Log Writer writes to one log group, then the next, and the next. Each log group can consist of one or more members, and members of one group should all be on different disks. Figure 2.9 illustrates this concept well, and you may occasionally need to refer back to this diagram for a refresher.

Redo Log files should be mirrored to secure data.

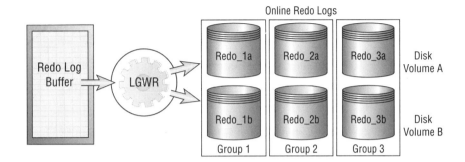

To reduce the risk of losing these important Redo Log files, which are vital for database recovery after a disk crash, follow these guidelines:

- Add more than one file to each group to mirror the data. You could add redo_1b, redo_2b, and redo_2c as new members for the three groups.

- Make sure that the mirrored files are on separate disks so that you have a backup when one fails.

- Ensure that Archiving is enabled.

- Make sure that the Redo Logs are on different disks from any of the database data files as performance will suffer otherwise.

We will be setting up our database along these guidelines in Chapter 4, *Database Administration*.

TIP   Although mirroring with software is far better than not mirroring, many DBA's recommend that if you have a RAID (Redundant Array of Inexpensive Disks) box, then this is the best way to go. In fact, if you are paranoid, use two RAID boxes! Specifically, Oracle recommends RAID 0+1 for Redo Log files. RAID 5 is acceptable for data files, but not for Redo Log files.

Data Files

Finally, we reach the database data files. These are the physical files where the data is stored and can be considered as the physical representation of the data. You should back up these files at regular intervals.

Each of the data files, which normally have a .ora or .dbf extension, is made up at the lowest level of a set of data blocks based on the native operating system file structure. Above this base level, Oracle imposes its own logical structure. This is one of the ways Oracle gets its database running on so many different platforms: there is little dependence on the native OS.

The Logical Structure

Oracle builds up its logical database structure out of the disk space that the OS data files provides for it. (Remember that the term *database* actually applies to the file part of an Oracle database as opposed to the memory- and process-based instance.) Oracle maintains the logical structure based on tablespaces and uses files as a resource for each tablespace. The structure is shown in top-down form in Figure 2.10 and described in Table 2.2.

FIGURE 2.10:

The logical structure of an Oracle database

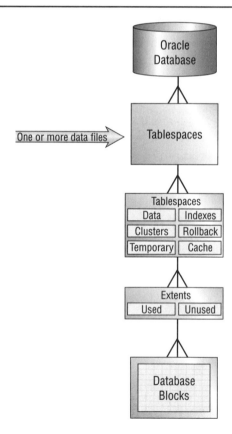

One or more data files

TABLE 2.2: The Logical Structure of an Oracle Database

Structure	Description
Database	A database is the total collection of data that is considered a discrete unit. Physically, it consists of a series of data files. Logically, it consists of a group of tablespaces.
Tablespace	A tablespace is a logical unit of storage that can be set up by the DBA for specific purposes. The SYSTEM tablespace is required and is created automatically and used for dictionary information and system definitions. You should also add a TEMPORARY tablespace as a temporary work area for sorting.
	You should definitely add at least one more tablespace for user data (otherwise users would need access to the SYSTEM tablespace). You will usually want at least one tablespace for each application area and perhaps a separate one for indexes. Another recommended tablespace is the one reserved to hold rollback segments. The reason to create this special tablespace is the fact that a tablespace may not be taken offline if it contains an online rollback segment. Therefore, rollback segments should be isolated from all other segments.
	Each tablespace consists physically of one or more data files that you could keep on the same disk if you do not have plenty of disks to spare.
	Logically, a tablespace consists of a group of segments for organizing the internal structures. Tablespaces can be taken offline or independently backed up without affecting the rest of the database. The SYSTEM tablespace, however, cannot be taken offline.
Segments	Each segment represents one particular type of database structure. Each segment is composed of a group of extents. There are several types of segments:
	Data segments There is one data segment for every nonclustered table in the database.
	Cluster segments There is one cluster segment for every cluster. These hold one or more tables that the database designer has decided to place physically close together to improve the access time with certain queries.
	Rollback segments There is always at least one rollback segment (which is in the SYSTEM tablespace) and normally more. These segments are used to store information about how a transaction can be rolled back if required.
	Index segments These store individual indexes.
	Temporary segments These areas are used as temporary work areas, typically for sorting result sets. These segments normally reside in a temporary type tablespace. You should always define one and specify it in the CREATE USER command. If you don't then Oracle will assign the SYSTEM tablespace.
Extents	Extents are contiguous groups of data blocks in a data file that hold a particular type of information. Extents are grouped together logically to form a segment.
Database blocks	Database blocks are the lowest level of logical storage in a database. You use database blocks to define storage requirements for the schema objects (such as tables) when you create them. Each logical database block is represented by one or more physical operating system blocks.

Data Concurrency and Data Consistency

Now that we have reviewed the major components of an Oracle instance and database, let's address an area of concern for every developer: how Oracle manages to provide a consistent view of the data and achieve concurrency, especially in a multiuser, transaction-oriented environment.

Whenever you allow more than one user to access a database, it is natural to be concerned about what happens when two users want to change the same row of a table at the same time. This is true in Access and Oracle databases as well as anywhere in between. How well a database deals with this multiuser issue is very important to a developer; however, Oracle's solution to these problems is sophisticated, and as a result, you can almost forget the whole issue.

The following Oracle functions deal with multiuser issues are:

Data Concurrency   The ability of the database to manage different users updating the same data at the same time. It relies on a sophisticated locking scheme. If you are updating a table row, Oracle locks that row, and other users have to wait until your transaction is complete.

Data Consistency   The ability to retrieve a consistent result set with a SELECT statement; that is, it is not affected by other updates possibly altering the same set of data at the same time. It should also include any changes made by the user and not yet committed. This function is often called *Statement Level Read Consistency,* which is more descriptive.

NOTE   Most Visual Basic developers will probably be very happy with the default locking scheme. Oracle even automatically detects and corrects a deadlock situation where two users are waiting for each other to complete an operation before they can proceed. However, for the developer with more stringent requirements or who is trying to get the most out of their system, there is a full complement of commands to manually control table locking. These should, of course, be used with great care.

Locking Strategies for Concurrency

When a user wants to change the data, Oracle places an exclusive lock on the affected rows. This stops any other user from changing the same rows (what is called *destructive interference*). Also, Oracle places a *share lock* on the table. This lock prevents any other user from altering the structure of or dropping the table through Data Definition Language (DDL) statements.

NOTE   Oracle's ability to lock at the row level is a great assistance to its concurrency abilities. Many databases use page-level locking, in which several rows are locked even though only one is being updated.

How Is Consistency Achieved?

Consistency is achieved in a clever way. When you submit a SELECT statement to Oracle, it notes down the start time of the request and then retrieves the data. Any rows that are changed after the start of the SELECT statement contain data that would violate the consistency rule. Oracle solves this problem by writing the data as it was before the change into a rollback segment. This rollback segment therefore contains the *before image* of the row. When the SELECT statement reaches the changed rows, Oracle directs it to the rollback segment to retrieve the consistent before image. This behavior applies to the SELECT statement regardless of the commit state of the changed rows.

NOTE   As you can see, Oracle has a very sophisticated consistency and concurrency mechanism. The beauty of this feature is that as a developer you can put it in the back of your mind, confident that Oracle does everything for you.

Schemas

So far we have seen the structure of Oracle from under the hood; it is a database engine that includes processes, memory structures, and the underlying data files. We have also seen how tablespaces include various types of data segments that can hold all the logical structures of the database. We have also seen how Oracle's locking scheme handles many users at the same time. This is the view that the database analyst always sees.

The developer sees a different structure. The database is a system that provides the user with various database objects and whether or not they exist in segments is less relevant. The developer's view is based on *schemas*. Each user in Oracle has a schema, which is a way of grouping database objects (such as tables and indexes) so they are owned by that user and can be protected from other users.

This section is an introduction to the schema objects—users, tables, indexes, clusters, sequence generators, procedures, views, synonyms—that developers can create when given the privileges to create them. In later chapters, we will cover the administrative tasks to create users as well as how we actually design these structures.

To illustrate the ideas behind the schema view of a database, we will consider a simple Human Resources database and identify the sorts of tasks that need to be achieved to produce an acceptable production database. In Chapter 6, *Implementing a Database*, we will use these concepts in a practical example and see how each step is completed.

Users

Without a user name and password, you will simply not be able to log on to an Oracle database. Oracle keeps track of all the users and their encrypted passwords. When you create a new user, an associated schema is created, and the user has access to any objects in that schema. However, the new user has to have certain privileges before being allowed that access, such as the ability to create a session in Oracle and the right to use a certain amount of space in a tablespace (the *quota*).

For our Human Resources database, our first set up is a test and a production database with one or more DBA accounts and also at least one user account for the developer to produce the application. Then, the developer sets up the user accounts for each employee who needs access to this data. (This process would normally be strictly controlled.) The DBAs have to be especially careful as some of the data in the database will be personal or sensitive. To this end, we can set up certain tables to hold the confidential information and restrict access to them through privileges.

Tables

Tables are the fundamental storage unit for data. They consist of rows and columns in much the same way as a spreadsheet grid. This is a good analogy when thinking of tables and is demonstrated in Figure 2.11. Each table in a schema must have a unique name. Each column also has a unique name and has an associated data type such as NUMBER or DATE.

Each table exists in a tablespace that may span one or more data files. The dba_extents and dba_data_files views can be used to locate the extents of a table.

Although Oracle7 restricts tables to a single tablespace, Oracle8 allows for partitioning of tables and indexes. This means that you can spread a single table across multiple tablespaces usually according to a range of values in a key. This is one of those features that allows Oracle8 to handle extremely large databases with potentially huge tables. Chapter 6 covers creating tables and indexes in detail.

In our Human Resources database, the developers need to implement their logical database design with the addition of the required tables. The types of tables they may have here would be employee data, education records, department data, salary information and history, and so on. As mentioned in the previous section, care needs to be taken so that confidential data is only available to those who have approval to see it.

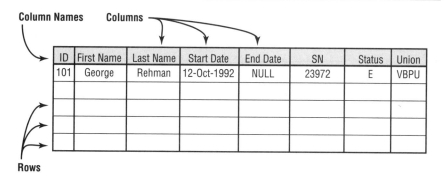

FIGURE 2.11:

The layout of a table is much like a spreadsheet with rows and columns.

Indexes

Indexes are another schema object that is stored in its own segment. The most common technique in creating indexes is to use *B-trees*. Oracle uses a popular variant called a "B*-tree" to store indexes. These are balanced trees, meaning that the branches of the tree are all roughly the same length (see Figure 2.12). In this way, it always takes about the same amount of time to find the pointer to any row of the table. B*-trees are fast for SELECT statements and efficient for INSERT, UPDATE, and DELETE statements.

As with any tree structure, when you are looking for a particular data row, you start at the top (the *root* node) and work your way down through the *branch* nodes to the *leaf* nodes. The leaf nodes contain all the keys as well as the ROWID (a ROWID is a pointer to the actual row) for the row. At each nonleaf node the route to follow is determined by doing a comparison between the key you are looking for and keys stored in the node.

In Figure 2.12, you can see how we can move from the root node through to a leaf node. Let us take our search for the name "Garrett" as an example. We first check the search name against the root node ("Mills"). It is less than the root node (in a string comparison), and so we move to the branch node that contains "Garrett" and "Lo." A second string comparison is now done, and because the search string is not less than "Garrett" or greater than "Lo," it takes the middle pointer, which in this case points to the leaf node that we are looking for. This leaf node also contains the ROWID that points directly to the row we are searching for in the table. We have arrived there in three reads rather than scanning the whole table.

NOTE　　Oracle 7.3.3 introduced the concept of bit-mapped indexes in which each key is represented by setting a bit in the bitmap. This type of index is useful for columns that have few distinct values over the range of rows and can make searches on these columns substantially faster.

FIGURE 2.12:

An example of the B*-tree indexing scheme used by Oracle

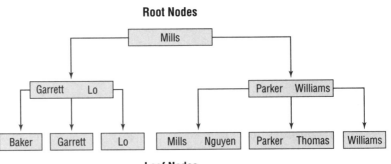

In our Human Resources database, the database designers have come up with an indication of how the data is going to be accessed. Every table should have a primary index, and these will now be created. In many cases, the designers will have realized that performance would not be acceptable if we did not have some additional indexes. For example, the column Last_Name in the Employees table may well need an index if data is going to be regularly accessed by that column.

Clusters

Clusters are an alternative way of storing database tables. The idea is that you can control the way data is physically stored so that you can efficiently retrieve streams of data in the order they are indexed.

When you create a cluster segment, you identify the cluster columns. When you create tables, you indicate into which cluster you want to put them. Any table that you add to a cluster must have the same cluster columns. The table rows are in fact physically stored in cluster index order, though they can also be stored by a hashing algorithm.

You can add several tables to a cluster, but you should only do this if they are always used together. With two tables stored in the cluster, preferably in the way that they are normally joined, the join and retrieval should be faster because the rows that are joined are retrieved in the same data blocks.

In the Human Resources database, the developers may decide that because employee data is nearly always retrieved along with department data, these two tables should be in the same cluster. Clusters need to be monitored to ensure that they do provide some overall performance improvement.

NOTE   Clusters are not commonly used because the performance benefits are realized only when the tables in the cluster are static. Tables subject to frequent DML are not suitable candidates for storage in clusters.

Sequence Generators

A sequence generator is a built-in way of creating unique sequential numbers. Its main use is to provide unique keys for tables. (Oracle does not have a table column type that can automatically do this.) It can be used by many users without any additional overhead and with none of the locking problems seen where the number has to be created in other ways.

Users can have access to the sequence by requesting the next available number, and once they have done that, they can read the current sequence number at any time in the same session. Different users will never have the same sequence number from the same sequence generator (unless the the sequence has the CYCLE option enabled). We will discuss these in greater detail in Chapter 6.

In the Human Resources database, the developers would typically set up one sequence generator for each table to ensure that there is a uniform approach to providing primary keys for the tables.

Procedures

Oracle allows you to write procedural code that can be stored in the database. These procedures are written in PL/SQL, Oracle's procedural extension to SQL. It allows you to write procedures, functions, and database triggers (code that is automatically run when a specific action is taken to a table). These are all schema objects and are the subject of Chapters 9, *Introduction To PL/SQL*, and 10, *Creating Stored Procedures*.

The developers of the Human Resources database have to make a decision up front about how secure the data needs to be. Stored procedures ensure the tightest control of the data by restricting not only who can have access to what data but also *how* they access it. In other words, the stored procedure allows you to encapsulate the business rules in a controlled manner, not one that relies on the client-side developer to remember to integrate the business rules or, even worse, relies on the integrity of the employees.

Views

A view is a predefined way of looking at one or more joined tables, which are called the *base tables* for the view. It is similar in concept to a query in Microsoft Access. Views can be used to hide the information in the base tables, typically to give users access to only some of the available columns. One useful feature is that columns can be added to the base tables, but applications based on the views will still work. They are also useful to hide the complexity of multiple table joins from users.

You can use views in much the same way as you use the base tables with the SELECT, INSERT, UPDATE, and DELETE commands, although there are some restrictions you should check out.

Views are a tool that may well appeal to Oracle developers in a situation like the Human Resources database. They allow the developer to provide access to parts of a table; for example, if salary information existed in the Employee table, we could set up a view that represented all the data except the salary. Developers of client applications would want to ensure that their development tools allowed them to access views before this technique was entrenched. Note that PL/SQL cursors, which we shall see in Chapter 10, *Creating Stored Procedures*, are another way to achieve the effect of a view, but they do need a tool like Oracle Objects for OLE (described in Chapter 18, *Oracle Objects For OLE*) to be able to access them.

Synonyms

A synonym is another name (or *alias*) for an object. In Oracle, a synonym allows you to specify an alias for tables, views, procedures, and sequences. Synonyms can be public or private and can provide the security of hiding the schema name for an object. Synonyms are peculiar to Oracle, and so as a VB developer, you should be especially cautious of using them because there has traditionally been little or no support in Microsoft's Open Database Connectivity (ODBC) technology. (We will look at ODBC in more depth in Chapter 11, *Client-Side Technology.*)

Because synonyms provide an additional level of security, the database developers working on our Human Resources database would probably be inclined to use them. With Visual Basic 6, support for synonyms has improved. Oracle Objects For OLE has always supported synonyms, as we would expect.

Tying It All Together: How Oracle Works

There is no doubt that the internals of Oracle can be difficult to grasp. In practice, you do not need to retain all the details, but you should try to have a general understanding of what is going on. You will be surprised how often this knowledge can be of use to you even if you do not end up performing the duties of a database analyst. So it is worth finishing this chapter by tying it all together with an overview of how a typical session in Oracle actually works.

1. The DBA initiates the database start-up procedure that

   - Reads the Parameter Initialization file
   - Allocates the memory for the SGA
   - Starts up the required processes
   - Opens and reads the Control file
   - Opens the database data files for general access

2. The DBA starts up a Listener process to wait for user-connection requests.

3. A Visual Basic user makes a connection to the database through the network using ODBC or Oracle Objects for OLE.

4. The Listener process dispatches a Server process to handle the user's SQL requests (or it may be able to share a Server process).

5. The Visual Basic application passes a SQL statement to the database.

6. An area of the Shared Pool is allocated for the SQL statement.

7. The required data is pulled into the Database Buffer Cache if it is not already there.

8. Any data changes are made in memory and stored as Redo Log Entries in the Redo Log Buffer.

9. Control returns to the Visual Basic application with a result set if appropriate.

10. The Database Writer process writes data changes back to disk when certain criteria are met.

11. The Log Writer writes changes to the Redo Log files when the changes are committed.

Summary

This chapter has presented an overview of the internal memory structures, processes, and data files of an Oracle database. We also covered the data files needed to hold the total data in the database and allow setup and recovery. We have also seen how the developer views Oracle—from a schema. It should come as no surprise that there is much more to Oracle under the covers, and much of that is beyond the scope of this book. We will cover enough to ensure that you, as a Visual Basic developer, can understand the concepts. These include the memory structures that Oracle is based upon and the processes to manage that memory.

To be a good DBA, you will need to get much more involved in what is going on, and I recommend that, if you want to develop this side of your expertise, then you should take a few courses and read some more detailed texts. One sign of a good DBA is how tattered your copy of *Oracle Server Concepts* is.

In the next couple of chapters, we will move from the theoretical into the practical with the setup and maintenance of an Oracle database.

NOTE   For more in-depth Oracle information, see *Mastering Oracle 8.1* by Jatinder Prem (Sybex, 1999).

CHAPTER
THREE

Creating a Database

- Using the Administration Tools

- Installing Oracle

- Installing Initialization (Also Called Parameter) Files

- Starting Up and Shutting Down the Database

- Creating the Database

- Configuring the Network

3

Now that we have seen the architecture of Oracle, we are ready to create our first database and instance. This step is viewed as an advanced operation in some Oracle manuals, and it can become a complicated task. In this chapter, we will create a database from start to finish. As a Visual Basic developer, you will seldom have to create any databases; however, you would not be the first developer to take on more of the database administrator's role.

When you start creating databases, you will make many mistakes or wish you had done things differently. If you can, get a hold of a test machine for your experimentation, so that you can build and rebuild your database and make all the mistakes you want without interfering with a production environment. If you use a reasonably high-end Windows NT server (the 266MHz Pentium II with 64MB of memory that I use is fine for small databases, but 128MB of memory would be better), you can develop your database and your Visual Basic code on the same machine. However, sharing disk and memory resources on a single machine is not ideal from the performance point of view.

There are several steps to setting up a database. In this chapter, we will cover the following points:

- Using the Administration tools
- Installing Oracle
- Installing Initialization (also called Parameter) files
- Starting up and shutting down the database
- Creating the database
- Configuring the network

A Quick Note on Platforms

One of Oracle's strengths is its ability to run on a vast variety of hardware platforms. Although Windows NT is fast becoming a favorite, especially for entry-level systems, the high-end platform is still the preserve of Unix, OpenVMS, and mainframes. These platforms provide a level of scalability and stability that NT has not yet reached.

Continued on next page

This chapter is the only one in which the platform you are working on makes a difference. Although that difference is only a matter of the commands you use to run the utility software, the difference between the commands can become confusing if you are not on the selected platform.

Most of the examples in this chapter were set up with Oracle 8 for Windows NT, but short notes give commands for other platforms where appropriate. However, one key step for you to understand is how you install Oracle. You will find it easiest to set Oracle up on Windows NT, and you will need to consult your platform-specific documentation for other environments.

Administration Tools

A number of administration tools are available in Oracle, and at first, it can be confusing to figure out which one to use. Unfortunately, you cannot use the same tool for everything. With the introduction of the Windows environment, and spurred on by other database vendors, Oracle has the GUI tools to make life a little easier. At the same time, with the GUI executing all the underlying commands for you, you may not understand exactly what is going on behind the scenes.

What is worse, the GUI tools seldom allow you the same flexibility as the command-line versions. The ideal situation is for you to learn the command-line techniques and then to progress to the GUI tools when you are comfortable with the process. In this chapter, we will look at the command-line techniques and then end with the graphical methods.

Identifying Your Database

You can set up as many Oracle instances as you want on your server, which is useful for separating the processing, especially when you want to set up a test database. Because you cannot enter the name of the database instance that you wish to work on in the administration tolls themselves, you have to define the current database instance before

Continued on next page

you start the tools up. Typically, the name of the instance (or the SID) is held in an operating-system environment variable. In Windows NT, it is stored in ORACLE_SID. You should set this variable before you start any of the tools by typing the following command:

```
C:> SET ORACLE_SID=TEST
```

This sets the instance name to "test." In NT, there is also a default ORACLE_SID in the Registry that you can set with the `regedt32.exe` or `regedit.exe` program, under \HKEY-LOCAL-MACHINE\SOFTWARE\ORACLE.

Take great care with identifying your instance because you are not the only developer who will be testing changes in your production database.

SQL*Plus

SQL*Plus is the workhorse utility for developers and is available on every platform on which the Oracle server runs. It is valuable for creating database objects, setting up users, and granting privileges. However, SQL*Plus has no value for any other database administrative operations. We shall use it extensively in later chapters.

You can start SQL*Plus by typing **c:\> SQLPlus** at the command prompt, or on the Windows platform, you can start it by double-clicking on the application icon. Type **Exit** to exit out of SQL*Plus.

NOTE   To run a script in either SQL*Plus or Server Manager, discussed next, precede the name of the script with "@", for example, `@create_database.sql`.

Server Manager

Server Manager is the utility that you will use most of the time to set up and administer your database. It is available on all platforms and supersedes the SQL*DBA program. On Windows NT, you start the program by typing

```
c:\> SVRMGR30
```

at the command prompt for Oracle8. Type **Exit** to exit out of Server Manager.

NOTE Type SVRMGR23 for Oracle 7.3 on NT and SVRMGRL on other platforms for the Line mode version.

NT Instance Manager

The NT Instance Manager utility is required only in the Windows NT environment, and you mainly use it to create the NT services needed to run Oracle on that platform. You can also use these services to set the password for the internal account as well as for creating and starting up a database. However, for the purposes of this book, we will only discuss the utility used to create services on NT, something that no other tool can do.

You can run the NT Instance Manager in Command-Line mode or as a GUI application. Unfortunately, neither one is a superset of the other. I like to use the Command-Line mode and then only for creating database services. You run the command-line version with the Oradim73 or Oradim80 commands for Oracle 7.3 and 8 respectively. Later in the chapter, we will cover the command-line parameters you must use to run these tools.

NOTE There is also a program called Instance Manager, which comes as an application under Oracle Enterprise Manager. It is a completely different program from the one described here.

Oracle Enterprise Manager

Oracle Enterprise Manager is a full-management tool that comes with the Enterprise Edition version of the Oracle server and is available separately from the standard edition. It is a great tool for beginners and allows you to perform a large number of operations. When you install the NT Oracle Enterprise Edition, the Enterprise Manager is installed, as well. Some setup needs to be done, and this is detailed in the Oracle Enterprise Manager documentation. Make sure you set up a tablespace for the repository that Enterprise Manager requires and create a special user with this tablespace as the default.

When you have set up Enterprise Manager, you will be able to administer many Oracle databases from the same console. It comes with a variety of tools that are useful in monitoring and controlling the health of your database. We will see more of this tool in Chapter 4, *Database Administration*.

However, you can get much more benefit from the Performance Pack, an optional addition to the Enterprise Manager, which provides you with an expert system that analyzes your database and makes recommended changes to improve its performance. Although it will take awhile for you to become familiar with and to set up the information it needs, the Performance Pack can recommend changes that would otherwise take years to figure out.

Your Development Environment

An ideal development environment will run Windows NT and have installed not just SQL*Plus, SQL*Net, or Net8, and the relevant ODBC drivers but also Oracle Enterprise Manager and Oracle Procedure Builder (see Chapter 9, *Introduction to PL/SQL*). Of course, you will also be running the Professional or Enterprise Edition of Visual Basic.

It is possible for you to run the Oracle server on the same machine that you are developing on as long as you are prepared for the performance hit. If you do this, then try to get as fast a machine as possible with at least 128MB of memory. This will make it possible to use a laptop for development, which is especially useful if you are often on the road. One of the beauties of Oracle is that you can develop on your laptop and deploy on a high-end Unix server with few problems. You can even deploy to a mainframe.

Other Utility Programs

In addition to the Oracle utilities mentioned previously, there are a few others you will come across:

> **Export and Import**   These utilities allow you to export selected data from a database and to import the data into the same or another database. We will discuss these features in Chapter 4, *Database Administration*.

> **SQL*Loader**   This utility allows you to efficiently import data from a text file, especially for bulk loading of data. We shall discuss this utility in Chapter 8, *Updating Your Database*.

SQL*DBA   A utility that was previously used for database administration, but since Oracle 7.3, it has been displaced by Server Manager and Enterprise Manager. This utility is no longer included with Oracle installation media.

Oracle Installation

Installing Oracle has not traditionally been the simplest of operations, but with Oracle for NT, installing it is now simpler than many desktop programs. Once you insert the CD, run `setup.exe` and supply the information for which you are prompted. Some CDs, like Oracle8 Enterprise Edition, have autorun for the setup program enabled. This version allows you to install a sample database, and it is worthwhile to do so because you can watch the process in action. Although creating an Oracle database can be a little intimidating at first, you can use the demonstration database for all the practicing you need to do.

TIP	The size of the test database (30MB) is too small for any real-life applications and is also poorly tuned. If any real testing needs to be done, you should create a larger, more functional database. If necessary, get some help from an experienced DBA.

As an alternative to the test database, in Oracle8 you can use the *Oracle Database Assistant*, which is a wizard that prompts you for all the relevant information. (You still need to know what you are doing, however.) Visual Basic does not care what sort of database it is, and the sample database can get you up and running much faster.

Oracle is typically installed in the ORANT directory on Windows NT. In this directory you will find all the programs for Oracle as well as the utility software and sample database files. When you run the install program, you will have to enter your company name and base directory as shown in Figure 3.1. Here, we assume that you choose the default. You will also have to select which products to install (see Figure 3.2). We only need the server products at this point. Finally, you will need to select whether you want a sample database. This sample database is always worthwhile if you have never created an Oracle database before because it gives you something to work from and emulate.

FIGURE 3.1:

Determining where to install
Oracle

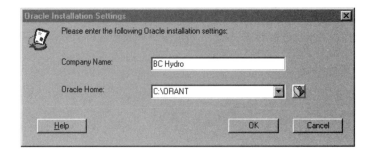

FIGURE 3.2:

Selecting the Oracle product
to install

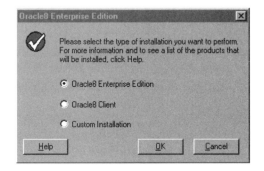

Oracle on Alpha-Based Computers

Currently, Alpha-based computers are the performance leaders as far as NT machines are concerned; you only have to watch a 3-D screen saver to see the difference. Alphas make very powerful servers. But how practical is the NT platform?

There is a special release of Oracle for Alpha-based NT machines. In addition, an emulator called FX32 is available that allows you to run Intel-based code, and this emulator has received favorable reviews. However, you have to be careful about implementing this sort of software.

You can effectively end up with two system directories. From my personal experience, I have discovered how easy it is to completely corrupt the NT system directory, in one case just by installing some ODBC drivers. (Oracle does not produce any designed for the Alpha.) This is not a failing of NT—it could happen on any platform—it is just that there are so many more software choices for the platform.

Continued on next page

My recommendation for installing Oracle on NT is to keep it simple. Do not run other applications on the server as they consume much needed memory, especially GUI-based applications. And do not run an emulator because you will be asking for trouble. Keep the server exclusively for Oracle and maintain it that way.

Services on NT

When you install Oracle, you install executable programs (or *images*) that run the various processes that we saw in Chapter 2, *Oracle Database Architecture*. With Windows NT, these processes are run as separate threads of an NT service. If you use the Oracle Database Assistant, all of the required services will be set up for you. If you do not use the Assistant, you will need to install at least two services, and you do this with the NT Instance Manager. The command that you use is as follows:

```
c:> ORADIM80 -NEW -SID test -INTPWD password -STARTMODE AUTO
-PFILE c:\orant\database\inittest.ora
```

Let's look closely at this line:

- NEW identifies that this is a new service.

- SID is the system identifier that identifies the particular instance (in this case we set the SID to "test").

- INTPWD is the password to the INTERNAL account. You must always enter this password, and you must *always* note it down for your records! With Oracle8, you cannot connect as INTERNAL without the password file that this sets up.

- STARTMODE identifies whether you want the database to be automatically (AUTO) or manually (MANUAL) launched at system start-up.

- PFILE is the Initialization file that you have already set up for this database instance (we will cover this in the next section).

With the NT Instance Manager command successfully executed, you will now have created two new services. For a database called "test," the first service is "OracleServiceTest," which starts the ORACLE80.exe process for the database, and the second service is "OracleStartTest," which ensures that the database is started automatically if the server is ever rebooted. In this way, Oracle can continue running even though a user is not logged on to the server.

NOTE   If the *-STARTMODE manual* parameter is chosen in the ORADIM80 command, then the OracleStartTest service is *not* created.

You should now review the services you have created. These appear under the Services Control Panel. You should see something like the screen shown in Figure 3.3.

FIGURE 3.3:

The Services Control Panel

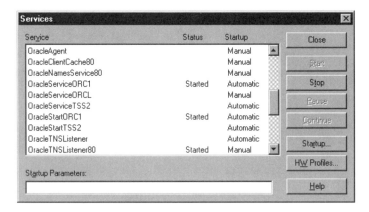

NOTE   On platforms other than Windows NT, you will find that you have to make system start-up procedure changes to ensure that the instance is started on rebooting. Consult your system administrator for the details of how to do this.

Oracle Database Assistant

With Oracle8 for Windows NT, you now have the option to use a wizard called the *Oracle Database Assistant*, which will walk you through all the steps of database creation. You will see the dialog box shown in Figure 3.4, in which you can choose a standard install or a custom database creation. Other platforms, including 7.3 on NT, have sample databases but not the wizard.

FIGURE 3.4:

Deciding what sort of installation to do

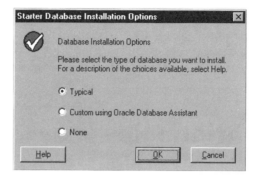

To get a database up and running quickly, the Typical option is the easiest and gives you a sample database called ORCL. If you want something more tailored, then the custom database using the Oracle Database Assistant is a quick way to go. Figure 3.5 gives you an view of one of the many windows you will see when working with the wizard. The wizard will create all the files that you need; you can tailor these files at a later date.

FIGURE 3.5:

A typical window of the Oracle Database Assistant

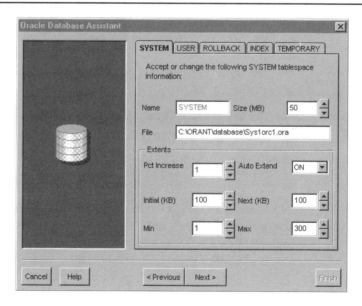

The GUI method appeals to new users of Oracle because it supplies numerous defaults and creates the appropriate files. Several setup functions, however, cannot be done without your manual intervention, and you cannot make intelligent decisions without knowing more about what you are doing. Making those intelligent decisions is the subject of the rest of the chapter.

Initialization Files

Once you have installed Oracle and any required services on your server, you need to plan your database characteristics. To create an Oracle database, you should first define all the parameters you need. Oracle uses a concept familiar to all Windows developers: a text file containing initialization parameters. As with any Initialization file, you can enter a great number of parameters, but we shall stick to the most important ones. This Initialization file is used whenever you start an instance; when you change the parameters, you have to shut the instance down and restart it to implement your changes.

With any Oracle installation, you will find a sample file called `init.ora` that gives you a starting point for your own files. (On NT, look in the `c:\orant\database` directory.) You can edit this file and call it whatever you like, but make sure you've documented it somewhere. The best way is to include the name of your instance in the file name. For example, for a database called "test," name the Initialization file `inittest.ora`.

NOTE   When the STARTUP command in Server Manager is issued without the PFILE option, then the assumed name and location of the Parameter file is `%ORACLE_HOME%\database\init%ORACLE_SID%.ora`.

Now you need to edit the Initialization file. If you review the sample file, you will see many parameters for which there are three options, covering small, medium, and large databases. All but the values for the small databases are commented out with "#".

TIP

When Oracle calls a database "small," you may want to think of it as medium sized. Oracle is designed to handle huge amounts of data (up to many terabytes). You can use the following size guidelines that come with Oracle8 for NT: for Decision Support systems that are heavily read oriented, small is less than 10MB, medium is less than 100MB, and large is greater than 100MB. For an Online Transaction Processing system that is heavily write oriented, small is up to 10 concurrent users, medium is up to 100 concurrent users, and large is over 100 concurrent users. Most users should be using the medium or large database models. When you get to a very large database, it is time for some professional tuning assistance.

There are many possible parameters that you can put in an Initialization file; however, until you are more experienced, it is better to stick to the parameters shown in Table 3.1.

TABLE 3.1:   Suggested Initialization Parameters for a Small Database

Parameter	Description
background_dump_dest	The location of the trace files generated by background processes.
db_name	The name of the database. This is a mandatory parameter of up to eight characters.
db_files	The maximum number of files that the database can have open.
control_files	This parameter defines the number and names of all the Control files. You should specify at least two.
compatible	The version of the server that this database should be compatible with.
db_block_size	The size of Oracle database blocks in bytes. This parameter can only be set at database creation. The default value is 2048, but for more than a very small database or when you have wide columns, you should create a multiple of this number, such as 4096, for a transaction-intensive database. For decision support, Oracle recommends the largest allowable value for db_block_size. This maximum is platform-dependent but will normally be at least 8192.
db_block_buffers	The number of blocks cached in the Database Buffer Cache. Multiply this parameter by db_block_size to get the size of the cache.
db_file_multiblock_read_count	The number of blocks read in one I/O operation. Eight is fine for transaction-intensive operations and 16 for decision support.

Continued on next page

TABLE 3.1 CONTINUED: Suggested Initialization Parameters for a Small Database

Parameter	Description
shared_pool_size	The size of the Shared Pool, which includes the Library Cache and the Data Dictionary Cache. The default is 3,500,000.
user_dump_dest	The location of the trace files generated by Server processes.
log_buffer	The size of the Redo Log Buffer in the SGA in bytes.
log_archive_start	This parameter enables automatic archiving (that is, starts the ARCH background process) if set to true.
log_archive_dest	The directory where archived log files.
log_archive_format	The filename format of the archived Log files.
rollback_segments	The names of the rollback segments, which will be brought online at database start-up.
oracle_trace_enable	The parameter that controls whether the Oracle Trace utility is enabled for the database. Set this to FALSE on NT and Oracle Trace will not be used on the database.

NOTE   The suggested values given for the Initialization Parameter file in Table 3.1 are just that—suggestions. As your database becomes larger and performance more critical, you should invest some time in becoming familiar with changing the parameters to suit your particular database. This process is called *tuning,* and it can be quite complex. In particular, you should take into account not only the database size but also the database activity, whether it is online transaction processing (write-intensive) or decision support (read-intensive).

An example of an Initialization file is shown in Listing 3.1. Most of these parameters have been derived from the suggestions in the default Initialization file (`init.ora`). If you use the sample database or Oracle Database Assistant, then a similar file will be created for you. You can use it as a basis for making changes to tune the database.

Listing 3.1

```
######################################################################
# Example INITtest.ORA file
#
# This file includes the settings you want for a particular Oracle
# instance.
######################################################################

db_name = test
db_files = 100
control_files = (C:\ORANT\DATABASE\ctl1test.ora,
                 D:\ORANT\DATABASE\ctl2test.ora)

compatible = 8.0.3.0.0

db_file_multiblock_read_count =  8
db_block_buffers =  200
db_block_size = 4096

shared_pool_size =  6500000

log_checkpoint_interval = 10000
processes =  50
dml_locks =  100
log_buffer =  8192
sort_area_size = 65536

sequence_cache_entries =  10
sequence_cache_hash_buckets =  10
max_dump_file_size = 10240       # limit trace file size to 5 Meg each
log_archive_start = true         # sets automatic archiving
log_archive_dest = %RDBMS80_ARCHIVE%
oracle_trace_enable = false

# define directories to store trace and alert files
background_dump_dest=%RDBMS80%\trace
user_dump_dest=%RDBMS80%\trace
remote_login_passwordfile = shared
text_enable = true
```

> **NOTE** Parameters enclosed in "%" are read from the Registry in Windows NT or from environment variables defined at the user or system level.

Starting Up and Shutting Down the Database

With our database parameters defined in the Initialization file, we must next learn how to start up and shut down a database. If you did not install the demonstration database, then you will not have anything to start up at this point. However, to create a database you still need the STARTUP command because we need to begin with an instance before we can actually create the new database.

A database instance can be in any one of four states; when you start the instance, it passes through all of them (see Figure 3.6). These states are

SHUTDOWN   Completely shut-down, also called *idle*

NOMOUNT   Processes started and SGA allocated but no file opened

MOUNT   Control files opened

OPEN   All files opened and database fully accessible

FIGURE 3.6:

The possible states of an Oracle database

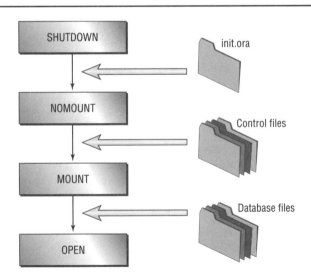

Starting Up a Database

To start up a database, we use the Server Manager utility tool, which is invoked from the command-line prompt (see Figure 3.7). In Windows NT it will be SVRMGR30. Before you can start up or shut down a database, you must connect to the database with the CONNECT INTERNAL or CONNECT/AS SYSDBA commands. You use the STARTUP command with the state you want to take the database to. For example, if you want to open an existing database for general access, you would type

```
STARTUP OPEN PFILE=c:\orant\database\initdemo.ora
```

To start the idle instance before creating a new database, you would type:

```
STARTUP NOMOUNT PFILE=c:\orant\database\inittest.ora
```

The PFILE parameter mentioned in the two examples is defining which Initialization file you want to use for the database. If you leave the PFILE parameter out, Oracle will look for the Parameter file named init%ORACLE_SID%.ora in the directory %ORACLE_HOME%\database. There are similar rules for Oracle on Unix and OpenVMS.

NOTE   In UNIX and OpenVMS, the Server Manager line mode is invoked by *svrmgrl*. Oracle 7.3 for NT uses *svrmgr23*.

You can only use the STARTUP command when your database is shut-down. If you have the database in an intermediate state (NOMOUNT or MOUNT), then you will have to use the ALTER DATABASE command to advance the database to the next state, i.e., from NOMOUNT to MOUNT or from MOUNT to OPEN. For example, you could use

```
ALTER DATABASE OPEN;
```

which advances the database from the MOUNT state to the OPEN state.

TIP   You should keep careful documentation of which Initialization file you use because it can be very confusing if there are several on the disk.

FIGURE 3.7:

Starting up a database
instance

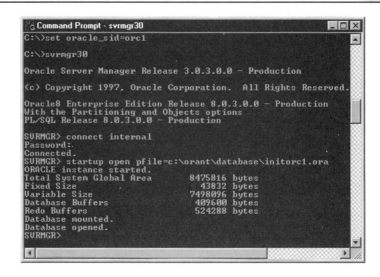

Shutting Down a Database

To shut down a database you use the SHUTDOWN command in Server Manager (see Figure 3.8). You have three options:

SHUTDOWN NORMAL   Shuts down the database when all users have disconnected, and does not allow any new connections in the meantime.

SHUTDOWN IMMEDIATE   Disconnects all users immediately, rolling back any current transactions, and then shuts the database down.

SHUTDOWN ABORT   Shuts the database down immediately without rolling back any transactions. Using this shut-down option leaves the database in a state such that crash recovery will be required on the next start-up; this option should only be used in emergencies.

TIP

I find it convenient to store the STARTUP and SHUTDOWN commands in short script files. Although the commands are only one line long, writing a script file means you do not have to remember or type the Initialization file name, which can become annoying after repeated use. It is also a better way to document your system.

FIGURE 3.8:

Shutting down a database
instance

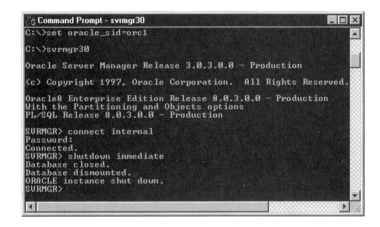

FIGURE 3.8:

Shutting down a database
instance

Creating the Database

Now that you know how to start the instance, you can move on to creating your
new database. As with many aspects of Oracle, there are several ways to do this.
We will cover the most flexible way; that is, we will create a SQL script that will
do the job for us. In this way, we have a record of exactly what we did, which is
useful if we ever need to copy the database to another server or if we have to re-
create it after a disk-drive disaster.

The SQL command we use is CREATE DATABASE, but it is the clauses of this
command that we must pay careful attention to, because once the database is
created, some of the parameters cannot be changed. The most commonly used
parameters are shown in Table 3.2. Other parameters will become more important if you ever create a very large database, but the defaults are quite sufficient
at this point.

NOTE   We will cover SQL in much more detail in Chapter 6, *Implementing a Database*, in
which we create the database tables, and in subsequent chapters in which we create queries and update the database using SQL.

TABLE 3.2: The Most Important CREATE DATABASE Parameters

Parameter	Description
LOGFILE	This parameter allows you to define your online Redo Log files. You must specify at least two groups; you should also have two members in each group. It is useful to distinguish the member and group number (e.g., `log1a.rdo` for the "a" member of the first group and `log2a.rdo` for the "a" member of the second group).
MAXDATAFILES	The maximum number of data files that can ever be opened by your database instance.
DATAFILE	This parameter specifies the files that are used for the system tablespace. If you omit this parameter, a data file will be created in the directory %ORACLE_HOME%\database.
ARCHIVELOG	This parameter specifies that you want archiving enabled. (The default is no archiving.) If you specify this, you must also start the Archiving process in the Initialization file. It is better to configure archiving *after* the database has been created, so do not use this clause in your CREATE DATABASE statement.
CHARACTER SET	This clause specifies the database character set. If omitted, the default is a 7-bit ASCII character set called "US7ASCII," but Oracle recommends that you use "WE8ISO8859P1." You cannot change this default without re-creating the database.

We will create a database called "test" as an example. To do this, we will write the CREATE DATABASE command in a text file called `create_test.sql` as shown in Listing 3.2.

Listing 3.2

```
CREATE DATABASE test
  LOGFILE
    GROUP 1 ('c:\orant\log1a.log', 'd:\orant\log1b.log') SIZE 100K,
    GROUP 2 ('c:\orant\log2a.log', 'd:\orant\log2b.log') SIZE 100K
  MAXDATAFILES 20
  DATAFILE 'c:\orant\system.dbs' SIZE 10M
  CHARACTER SET WE8ISO8859P1;
```

The above command will create a database with two groups of Log files, each of which has two members. A maximum number of 20 data files can be opened by this instance. The system tablespace has a defined data file, and the database has an 8-bit character set. The command also disables archiving when it is created. We will enable archiving for this database in the next chapter.

> **NOTE**
>
> The system tablespace is the heart of the database and is used to hold the data dictionary. It also holds any stored procedures, functions, and triggers. You should *never* create application tables or any other application objects in this tablespace.

Now, we could run the script in Listing 3.2 to create a database, but it is useful to have one script that will do everything, and we still have a few more database objects that we want to create. Next, we need to run two scripts that are provided by Oracle. The first is `catalog.sql`, and it creates the data dictionary in the system tablespace; the second is `catproc.sql`, which installs the objects required by PL/SQL, Oracle's procedural language. These are both added to our `create_test.sql` script as

```
@c:\orant\rdbms80\admin\catalog.sql
@c:\orant\rdbms80\admin\catproc.sql
```

The exact location of these utility scripts will depend on your platform and the version of your Oracle server software. If you have the opportunity to do so, it is also a good idea to enter any other tablespace creation commands into this script file. We will be covering application tablespaces in Chapter 6, *Implementing a Database;* if you know them now, you can enter them in the script.

There are also two other objects you can add to your script: *rollback segments* and a *temporary tablespace,* both of which we'll discuss in the following sections.

Rollback Segments

Rollback segments (groups of extents) are what Oracle uses to store before-image copies of changed objects so that transaction rollback can be performed. When you create a database, the SYSTEM tablespace is created, and it automatically contains a system rollback segment. This rollback segment can grow to have as many extents as that specified in the MAXEXTENTS parameter for the segment. When you implement application tablespaces (and this should be most of time), you should also create two or more application rollback segments. The Oracle server requires the creation of at least one rollback segment outside the SYSTEM tablespace so that DML can occur on these application tablespaces. If you create private segments, then these must be identified in the Initialization file. We create private segments in separate tablespaces as follows:

```
CREATE TABLESPACE rollback01
    DATAFILE 'C:\ORANT\DATABASE\ROLLBACK01.ORA' SIZE 500K REUSE
        AUTOEXTEND ON NEXT 500K MAXSIZE 2M ;

CREATE ROLLBACK SEGMENT r1 TABLESPACE rollback01
    STORAGE (INITIAL 50K NEXT 50K MINEXTENTS 2) ;
```

NOTE

Oracle allows you to create public rollback segments, but this is only recommended for the Oracle Parallel Server configuration.

The rollback segments can be hit hard in an update-intensive database, and ideally, the tablespaces will be on separate disks that no one else uses. A rule of thumb is to have one rollback segment to every four concurrent transactions.

Temporary Tablespaces

Whenever you sort data in the database, Oracle will try to do it in memory. If there is not enough memory to do the sort, Oracle assigns several temporary segments as a working area for the sort. You should have at least one temporary tablespace to hold these segments. If you don't, Oracle will have to use the system tablespace. After the sort, these segments can be freed up. However, this procedure will cause fragmentation to the tablespace and a performance penalty if it occurs in the system tablespace.

To avoid this problem, we add a temporary tablespace with the command

```
CREATE TABLESPACE temporary
    DATAFILE 'C:\ORANT\DATABASE\TEMP.ORA' SIZE 2M REUSE
        AUTOEXTEND ON NEXT 2M MAXSIZE 10M ;
```

Since Oracle 7.3, there is another way in which sort space can be handled. A tablespace can be explicitly designated to contain a single *sort segment*. This is done through the CREATE/ALTER TABLESPACE command, which contains a TEMPORARY clause (not to be confused with the actual name of the tablespace as specified in the example above). For example, we could modify the CREATE TABLESPACE statement by adding the TEMPORARY clause at the end of the statement. This will tell Oracle that this tablespace is to be used for the maintenance of a single segment created on the first sort on disk and dropped at instance shut-down. This single segment is shared among the users whose sort operations are assigned to this tablespace.

WARNING   If you fail to create temporary tablespaces, Oracle will resort to the system table-space to create temporary segments

---

Running the Script

Now that you have all the components to create a database, you can finally run the script (see Listing 3.3). In the example below, I have shown all the components together. When you are learning or testing a script, you may want to try one piece at a time. However, you will find it useful to have it all together in a script file when it is working.

The whole process of running a script can take half an hour or more depending on the speed of your system and the size and complexity of your database. You will notice that the script also includes the SPOOL and SPOOL OFF commands. These commands ensure that all the output messages get routed through to the Spool file, in this case `create_test.txt`. After the Database Creation process has completed, you should carefully scan this file to see whether there are any errors.

WARNING   The CREATE DATABASE statement not only creates the SYSTEM tablespace but also the Control files. You should ensure these Control files do not exist before running the script.

Listing 3.3

```
SPOOL CREATE_TEST.TXT

CREATE DATABASE test
  LOGFILE
    GROUP 1 ('C:\ORANT\DATABASE\TESTLOG01A.LOG',
             'D:\ORANT\DATABASE\TESTLOG01B.LOG') SIZE 100K,
    GROUP 2 ('C:\ORANT\DATABASE\TESTLOG02A.LOG',
             'D:\ORANT\DATABASE\TESTLOG02B.LOG') SIZE 100K
  MAXDATAFILES 20
```

```
    DATAFILE 'C:\ORANT\DATABASE\TESTSYSTEM01.DBF' SIZE 25M
    CHARACTER SET WE8ISO8859P1
    ARCHIVELOG ;

CREATE TABLESPACE test
  DATAFILE 'C:\ORANT\DATABASE\TESTTEST01.DBF' SIZE 1M REUSE
    AUTOEXTEND ON NEXT 1M MAXSIZE 20M ;

CREATE TABLESPACE rollback01
  DATAFILE 'C:\ORANT\DATABASE\TESTROLLBACK01.DBF' SIZE 500K REUSE
    AUTOEXTEND ON NEXT 500K MAXSIZE 2M ;

CREATE TABLESPACE rollback02
  DATAFILE 'C:\ORANT\DATABASE\TESTROLLBACK02.DBF' SIZE 500K REUSE
    AUTOEXTEND ON NEXT 500K MAXSIZE 2M ;

CREATE TABLESPACE temporary
  DATAFILE 'C:\ORANT\DATABASE\TESTTEMPORORY01.DBF' SIZE 2M REUSE
    AUTOEXTEND ON NEXT 2M MAXSIZE 10M ;

CREATE ROLLBACK SEGMENT r1 TABLESPACE rollback01
  STORAGE (INITIAL 50K NEXT 50K MINEXTENTS 2) ;

CREATE ROLLBACK SEGMENT r2 TABLESPACE rollback02
  STORAGE (INITIAL 50K NEXT 50K MINEXTENTS 2) ;

ALTER ROLLBACK SEGMENT r1 ONLINE ;
ALTER ROLLBACK SEGMENT r2 ONLINE ;

rem Ensure that the following line is added to your parameter file
rem after database creation:
rem
rem rollback_segments = (r1,r2)

@C:\ORANT\RDBMS80\ADMIN\CATALOG.SQL ;
@C:\ORANT\RDBMS80\ADMIN\CATPROC.SQL ;

SPOOL OFF
```

TIP	If the script fails anywhere, you can easily recover. Make sure the database is shut-down (assuming it will let you). Then, delete all the files that have been created and start again.

Testing the Database

As soon as your script is completed, you should test the database to ensure every-thing works properly. One area to test includes selecting data from tables. The fol-lowing are some key commands you need to know; we will cover them in more detail in the next chapter.

```
SELECT * FROM v$logile ;
SELECT name from v$controlfile ;
ARCHIVE LOG LIST ;
```

The first two commands should give you similar output to that shown in Figure 3.9. The second tells you the state of archiving, which we will discuss in Chapter 4, *Database Administration.* Another test is to query the data dictionary views dba_tablespaces and dba_rollback_segs.

FIGURE 3.9:

A Server Manager session showing the Log and Control files

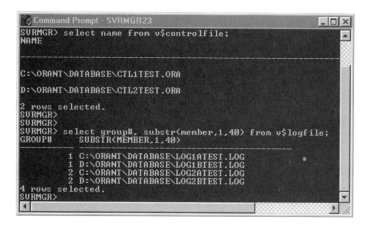

WARNING   Assuming that the output looks reasonable, you should now shut down the database and make a backup copy of all your data files. It is extremely important to start with a good backup.

If you have set up Oracle Enterprise Manager, you can now put it to use. Figure 3.10 shows the sort of information you can get about your database without any difficulty or scripts.

FIGURE 3.10:

A typical Enterprise Manager screen

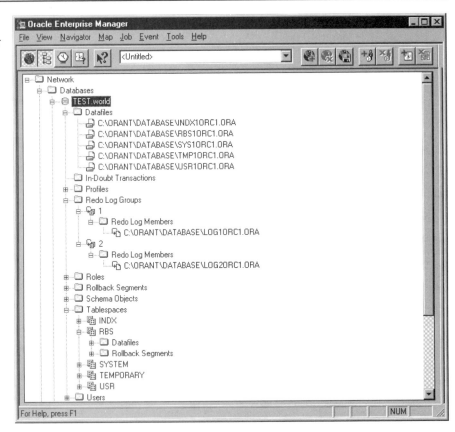

Your Default Users

Now that you have created and tested your database, you automatically have a database with several user accounts already installed. Without these accounts, you would not be able to use it! These default users and the associated passwords are as follows:

SYS   This is the Database Administrator account, and you normally use it to start up and shut down the database. It is also the owner of the Data Dictionary, so you should never use it unless you have to because you could corrupt or destroy the database. The initial password is CHANGE_ON_INSTALL.

SYSTEM   This is the account you should use for general DBA activities. Most installations will create at least one other account with DBA privileges for specific users. The initial password is MANAGER.

SCOTT   This is a demonstration user name that is often set up with an Oracle installation. The initial password is TIGER.

INTERNAL   This is a synonym for the *sys as SYSDBA*. It does not always have a password associated with it, but with the custom install we did, we made sure that there is one.

Do not use any of the above default user accounts for database or Visual Basic development. They should be reserved for database administration only. For development work, you need to set up some new user accounts, which we will cover in Chapter 4.

WARNING   Be aware that every newly created Oracle database contains the SYS and SYSTEM users along with their default passwords as specified previously. Change the passwords immediately!

NOTE   Start-up and shut-down are only possible for users who have the SYSDBA or SYSOPER role. These roles are given through the following command: GRANT SYSDBA TO *user*. This command requires the existence of an external password file. In order for a user (including SYS) to log on with this special role, the CONNECT command must be CONNECT SYS/*password* AS SYSDBA, where *password* is the one set in the external password file. This subtle difference in passwords is initially a difficult distinction to understand.

Configuring the Network

At this point, you have created an active database, and you can start it up and shut it down. To begin any development work, you will need to do two additional tasks. You will need to set up some user accounts to do the development, and you need to configure the network to allow these users to connect to the database from remote machines. We will cover setting up users in the next chapter, but first, we will discuss the network issues.

Server Manager works with a direct connection to the database. This is fine as long as you are on the same machine as the database, but if you need to connect from a remote machine, you need to use the networking capabilities of Oracle. In fact, some local processes, such as SQL*Plus and Enterprise Manager, have to use some features of the network

Oracle uses a multilayered approach to networking. The major layer that we come into contact with is called SQL*Net for Oracle7 or Net8 for Oracle8. When you install the Oracle server, this software is usually installed, as well. When we discuss the client side in Chapter 11, *Client-Side Technology*, we will discuss the layered software in more detail. However, for now we must set up the server with the ability to handle connection requests from remote machines.

Oracle uses the Listener process to listen for incoming requests for connections and hands them off to the appropriate database. This concept is exactly the same as an HTTP listener in a Web server. The Listener process needs a Configuration file called `listener.ora`. Client connection to the database requires a Configuration file called `tnsnames.ora`.

NOTE   The introduction of Oracle8 and Net8 networking software has led to some confusions over which software to run. In simple terms, a SQL*Net client can connect to Oracle7 and 8 databases; however, when you install server software, you must have SQL*Net for Oracle7 and Net8 for Oracle8. Net8 Listeners are backward compatible with SQL*Net 2.3 so you can use them to connect to both Oracle7 and Oracle8 databases.

Tnsnames.ora

The first Configuration file we must deal with is `tnsnames.ora`. This Configuration file is used by the SQL*Net or Net8 client to determine which database you want to connect to. It is similar to the `hosts` file, which is used to resolve hostnames to an IP address. In Chapter 11, *Client-Side Technology,* we will make sure this file is installed on the client database. The file also exists on the server for certain internal-connection requests, however, and this is where it is normally created.

There are a few ways to generate this Configuration file, but it is highly recommended to pick one method and stick to it. Here, we will have a brief review of the Net8 Easy Config tool that is present on Windows NT. For version 7.3 and before, you can use the SQL*Net Easy Config tool.

TIP

Even if your Oracle Server is not based on NT, it is worth running NT for administration, because most of the new tools are being developed for that platform first.

When you run the Net8 Easy Config program, you will see a menu such as that in Figure 3.11. You can choose to create new entries in the Configuration file, delete or modify old ones, or just view the existing entries. Each entry is called a *database alias,* which means it is a pointer to the database that can be used by remote users. It is called an alias because it does not have to be the database *sid*.

FIGURE 3.11:

The Net8 Easy Config program

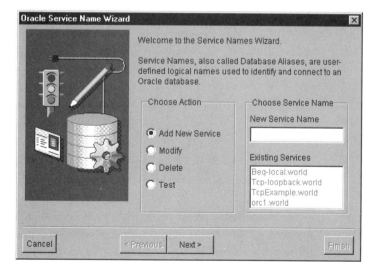

If you view existing database aliases, you will see an alias for the ORCL data-base if you installed the sample database. Each alias must define a network com-munications protocol that describes which protocol is needed to reach it. For example, most of my work is on TCP/IP, so this protocol is mentioned in the Configuration file.

The oddly named *bequeath protocol* is used internally; for example, when the user process is on the machine as the server. It can be seen as an alias on the ORCL server. Any database you want to access from the server with tools such as SQL*Plus will need an entry with this protocol.

With Net8 Easy Config, there is also a window in the wizard that lets you test your connection (see Figure 3.12). This is an efficient way to ensure that you have correctly set up your database aliases, though you can also accomplish this quite easily with SQL*Plus or another tool.

FIGURE 3.12:

Testing your connection

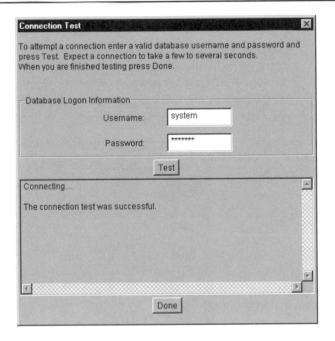

You should also create an entry for any new databases you create and for the network protocol you are running. After this has been done, you should look at the Configuration file for familiarity. An example is shown in Listing 3.4. At the bottom of the listing, you will notice an entry for the test database that we created in the first part of the chapter. The host name is TCCNT01, and its *sid* is "test" as we would expect. It also defines two TCP/IP ports (1521 and 1526) at which to expect Listener processes to be listening. Your tnsnames.ora file will be different from this and depend on the database names, network protocols, and version of your database server.

Listing 3.4

```
# TNSNAMES.ORA Configuration file: C:\ORANT\NET80\ADMIN\tnsnames.ora
# Generated by Oracle Net8 Assistant

Beq-local.world =
  (DESCRIPTION =
    (ADDRESS =
          (PROTOCOL = BEQ)
          (PROGRAM = oracle80)
          (ARGV0 = oracle80ORC1)
          (ARGS = '(DESCRIPTION=(LOCAL=YES)(ADDRESS=(PROTOCOL=BEQ)))')
    )
    (CONNECT_DATA = (SID = ORC1)
    )
  )
Tcp-loopback.world =
  (DESCRIPTION =
    (ADDRESS =
          (PROTOCOL = TCP)
          (HOST = 127.0.0.1)
          (PORT = 1521)
    )
    (CONNECT_DATA = (SID = ORCL)
    )
  )
TcpExample.world =
  (DESCRIPTION =
    (ADDRESS =
          (PROTOCOL = TCP)
          (HOST = Production1)
          (PORT = 1521)
    )
    (CONNECT_DATA = (SID = SID1)
    )
  )
```

```
orc1.world =
  (DESCRIPTION =
    (ADDRESS =
        (PROTOCOL = TCP)
        (HOST = sccnt01)
        (PORT = 1521)
    )
    (CONNECT_DATA = (SID = ORC1)
    )
  )
```

WARNING   Although you can manually edit this file when you become familiar with it, you should avoid doing this if at all possible. Chances are, once manual changes have been made, you will never be able to use Net8Easy Config on it again.

Listener.ora

In addition to and more important than the `tnsnames.ora` Configuration file is the `listener.ora` Configuration file. This is the Initialization file that configures the Listener; this process cannot run without it. The first part of the file (see the example file in Listing 3.5) defines the Listener addresses; that is the servers, protocols, and port numbers where the Listener processes will be listening. It also includes a couple of internal addresses that you should not alter.

The bottom half of the file defines parameters for the listener. The example below shows time outs and a password. This password is used to authenticate access through the *lsnrctl* program. You can even define the ability for pooling or prespawning Server processes here. However, the most important part is the SID_LIST_LISTENER list, which defines the database *sids* it is listening for. To add a new database alias to the list, you can simply use the Notepad accessory and edit it in. Make sure you use exactly the format in the sample file and in the example that follows. Also, any white space must be filled with space characters (ASCII value 32) only. Tabs (ASCII value 9) are not allowed; in fact, they will prevent the Listener process from starting up.

When a client such as Visual Basic specifies a connect string, this string is passed by SQL*Net or Net8 to the listener where it is compared to the *sids* in the list. If a match is not found, then an error will be returned. If a match is made, then a Server process will be created to control the connection between VB and the Oracle server itself.

The actual implementation of the two Configuration files can differ depending on your platform. You should consult your platform-specific documentation if you do not have an NT server for Oracle.

Listing 3.5

```
###############
# Filename......: listener.ora
# Node.........: local.world
###############
LISTENER =
  (ADDRESS_LIST =
       (ADDRESS=
         (PROTOCOL= IPC)
         (KEY= oracle.world)
       )
       (ADDRESS=
         (PROTOCOL= IPC)
         (KEY= ORCL)
       )
       (ADDRESS=
         (COMMUNITY= TCP.world)
         (PROTOCOL= TCP)
         (Host= tssnt01)
         (Port= 1521)
       )
       (ADDRESS=
         (COMMUNITY= TCP.world)
         (PROTOCOL= TCP)
         (Host= tssnt01)
         (Port= 1526)
       )
  )
STARTUP_WAIT_TIME_LISTENER = 0
CONNECT_TIMEOUT_LISTENER = 10
TRACE_LEVEL_LISTENER = ADMIN
SID_LIST_LISTENER =
  (SID_LIST =
```

```
(SID_DESC =
  (SID_NAME = ORCL)
)
(SID_DESC =
  (SID_NAME = ORC1)
)
)
PASSWORDS_LISTENER = (oracle)
```

Operation of the Listener Process

The operation between a user application and an Oracle database can be a little confusing to novices, but familiarity with it is worthwhile. This is especially true when things do not work as they should, for example, when you cannot connect. In these cases, you will have to trace all the links in the chain to find out which one is not functioning.

The diagram in Figure 3.13 should help to explain the Listener process. The way it works in practice is as follows:

1. The DBA starts the Listener Administration program by typing LSNRCTL when the database has been started.

2. The DBA starts up the Listener with the START command. This command spawns a Listener process whose configuration is contained in the `listener .ora` Configuration file.

3. The user application (such as your Visual Basic program) requests a connection to the database over Net8 by calling the Listener.

4. The Listener accepts the connection request, and then creates a Server process to handle the request.

5. With the Server process in place, the connection process is complete, and the VB application can execute queries or update transactions. This user session does not use the Listener again. The Listener is then released and waits for the next connection request.

6. When the VB application closes its database connection, the Server process is terminated (or returned to the pool).

FIGURE 3.13:

FIGURE 3.13:

The operation of the Listener process

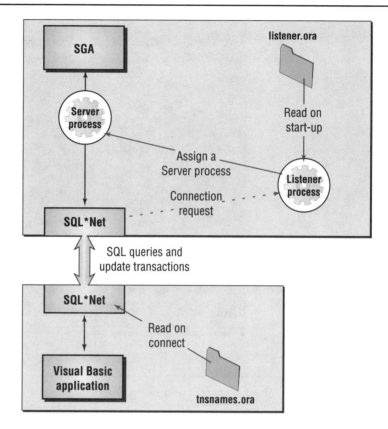

Controlling the Listener Process

Once you have configured your Listener, you are ready to start it (see Figure 3.14). To run the Listener Control program, you type the following command:

```
C:\>lsnrctl80
```

> **NOTE** On all other platforms, including when you run Oracle 7.x under NT, you use the command lsnrctl.

When you are running the LSNRCTL program, you can type the following commands:

STATUS   To show the current Listener status

START   To start the Listener process

SET PASSWORD   To provide a password if required

STOP   To stop the Listener process

HELP   To show the possible commands

EXIT   To exit the Listener Control program

To stop the Listener, you simply type the STOP command as shown in Figure 3.15. However, if the Listener is password protected, you must use the SET PASSWORD command. The password is defined as a configuration parameter in the file listener.ora.

Summary

This has been a fairly brief introduction to creating an Oracle database. We have seen the various administrative tools that Oracle provides for you. We have set up the Initialization Parameter file, set up an idle instance, and then created a script file to create the database. In addition, we looked at the default users for the database and set up the listener to allow us to connect from a remote workstation.

Even in this form it is not a trivial process (Oracle considers database creation an advanced function), but it is one that you can achieve by following the advice laid out in the chapter. If you want to proceed beyond a simple installation, especially when you want to tune the installation for your own requirements, you will have to bring in an experienced DBA or take further training courses yourself.

However, you should be up and running. We will move on to an introduction to the administration of the database so you can ensure that it is reliable and secure. That will set the foundation on which we can build our applications.

CHAPTER
FOUR

Database Administration

- Ensuring That the Backup Procedures Are in Place

- Familiarizing Yourself with Recovery Processes

- Setting Up the Database Security

- Following a Routine of Regular Maintenance Procedures

- Using Oracle Enterprise Manager to Simplify Maintenance Tasks

4

Now that you have set up a new database, or perhaps you are using an existing one at your site or the demonstration database that comes with Oracle, you have to spend some time to make sure it is maintained properly. Maintenance tasks are not the most glamorous to a developer, but if you ignore them, you will eventually lose your database.

Although Oracle is a stable database (you can have the system up and running for months or even years without a problem), one day a disk will crash, and if you have not planned your backup and recovery process, you could lose all your hard-earned data. Despite its stability, Oracle does appreciate the attention of routine maintenance.

Another critical issue is security. There would be no point to building a financial institution full of the latest technology for customers if you forgot to put any locks on the vaults. Someone will find a way to do what they shouldn't whether it is malicious or unintentional.

Therefore, we need to go over the tasks routinely performed by a database administrator (DBA):

- Ensuring that the backup procedures are in place
- Familiarizing yourself with recovery processes
- Setting up the database security
- Following a routine of regular maintenance procedures
- Using Oracle Enterprise Manager to simplify maintenance tasks

NOTE   If your main responsibility is the efficient running of your company's databases, then you should be prepared for two things. First, it can be a full-time job, and you will not have much time to do development, something that can be hard on a Visual Basic developer. Second, you need to get as much training as possible. This chapter is an introduction to what can become a career. A variety of good books devoted to Oracle database management are available, but you should also enhance these with courses.

Backup Procedures

There are a range of environments that use databases. Some are not critical to the success of a business. A typical, noncritical scenario involves a Human Resources department that keeps track of all the educational courses that employees have attended. If this data were to be completely wiped out, the company would survive. Even if the payroll system went down for several days, few people would notice as long as it didn't happen when the paychecks were being cut.

At the other end of the spectrum are systems that are "mission critical." These are systems that a business cannot run without: they *are* the business. An example of a company with this kind of system would be the Web-based bookseller `www.amazon.com`. If Amazon's databases were to go down, then anyone who urgently wanted a book would go elsewhere, along with their business.

If these mission-critical systems fail and the company cannot recover quickly, then new business is lost. If the data is lost, the company loses money as well as the respect of customers who do not get replies to orders they may have made. Anyone who has been at an airport when the booking system "goes down" can attest to the chaos and anger it generates.

Luckily, Oracle is full of methods for ensuring reliable backup and recovery procedures as well as the ability to keep going 24 hours a day. However, these methods are not there by default, and a little bit of knowledge and planning beforehand can save your career. This section will deal with the major ways of making sure that your data is as secure as possible from the effects of hardware failure. These are

- Exporting and importing data
- Mirroring the Redo Logs
- Mirroring the Control files
- Ensuring the archive processes are active
- Doing online backups

Data Export and Import

The simplest method of backing up your database is to do an *export* of the data. This function is exactly the same as the one you would see in Microsoft Access: you are exporting the data from the database to an external file that you can store in a safe place. If you lose one or more data files due to a disk crash, then you can recover by doing an *import* of the whole database, which is the reverse operation to an export.

Unlike a desktop program that has a drop-down menu for imports and exports, you have to run one of Oracle's many utility programs that comes with the database. The Data Manager in Oracle Enterprise Manager is a desktop GUI interface to the export/import utilities. The export utility extracts selected data from the database and writes it to an operating-system file. The import utility can then read an exported file and import the data it contains either into the same database for the purposes of recovery or into a different database; an example of the latter use of import is moving a new table from the development database to the production database.

The Export Utility

The export utility copies selected database objects (or the entire database) to an operating-system file. If you are moving the export to a different platform, you can even specify an alternative to ASCII character format; for example, if you were moving to an IBM mainframe. You run the export utility at the command-line prompt or invoke the Data Manager tool. The actual command differs with each operating system. For example, if you are using Oracle on Windows NT, the commands are

    C:\EXP73

for Oracle 7.3 and

    C:\EXP80

for Oracle 8. In UNIX and Open-VMS, it will typically be "exp".

You can use three methods to export data:

- Interactive session in which you are prompted for all the parameters
- Command-line method in which you supply all the parameters on the line
- Parameter file method

All three modes are viable for doing an export, but I like the flexibility and consistency of using Parameter files. However, the interactive session is fine when you are doing perhaps a one-off backup of a few tables to move from your test database to production. A Parameter file is a text file that you put together with a text editor and contains one keyword/value pair on each line. The most important parameters to a developer are

File   The name of the Export file (defaults to `expdat.dmp`).

Tables   One or more table names that you want to export (comma separated and enclosed in parentheses if there is more than one table).

Indexes   Y or N to flag if you want the indexes saved along with the tables.

Constraints   Y or N to flag if you want the constraints saved along with the tables.

Grants   Y or N to flag if you want to export grants.

NOTE   Some export options are available only through the Command-Line/Parameter file method. For example, direct-path export can be invoked only by passing DIRECT=TRUE through the Command-Line/Parameter file.

When you log on as a user, you will be able to export anything from your own schema. If you need to export the whole database, you will need to specify the following parameter:

FULL=Y

A user who requires the use of this parameter also requires the EXP_FULL_DATABASE role. (A role is a way of providing privileges to a user; we shall discuss this in more detail later in the section, "Predefined Roles.") You will also need this privilege if you export from another user's schema.

WARNING   You can also enter the user name and password in a Parameter file, but you should avoid this whenever possible because it is a security concern: if you leave it out, the system will prompt you. If you run the export in a Batch file, then you will have to hard code the password somewhere. Therefore, try to set the access protection on the Batch file appropriately.

The Export in Practice

To export using a Parameter file, edit a file called `export.par` and enter the following text:

```
FILE=c:\export\movies.dmp
TABLES=(movies, videos, participants)
INDEXES=Y
GRANTS=Y
CONSTRAINTS=Y
```

To execute the file type

```
exp73 parfile=c:\export.par
```

The output is shown in Figure 4.1.

FIGURE 4.1:

The output from an export session

NOTE   The export file is viewable with a text editor, and it is worthwhile just to have a look. If you export a table, the file contains the ASCII text for the CREATE TABLE and CONSTRAINT statements, along with all the data. You may also see privilege grants and other things in the file. In addition, you can copy out a portion of the file to produce a script that re-creates one or more tables. However, do *not* edit the files and save the changes because you will not be able to use it for an import again.

The Import Utility

You will probably do an export on a regular basis if it is part of your backup strategy, which means you will seldom have to do an import. However, you will often use the export as the most convenient method to transfer data from one database to another, and you will then be doing an immediate import of the export file.

To import from a previous export, you use the import utility. Again the command depends on the release you are running; on NT it is

    C:\IMP73

or

    C:\IMP80

As with the export, you can do your import with an interactive session, a command-line statement, or a Parameter file. It is convenient and sometimes necessary to run an import with a Parameter file. The most commonly used parameters used by developers are

File   The name of the export file (defaults to `expdat.dmp`).

Tables   One or more table names that you want to import.

Indexes   Y or N to flag if you want the indexes imported along with the tables.

Grants   Y or N to flag if you want to import grants.

Ignore   Y or N to flag if you want to ignore error messages caused by objects being imported that already exist in the database.

Commit   Y or N to flag if you want to commit the changes more regularly.

As with the export, you can also do a full database import if you use the parameter

    FULL=Y

In this case, the user requires the IMP_FULL_DATABASE role to be granted by the DBA.

TIP   When you import data into your new database, you should be aware that the default is for each database object to be imported as a single transaction. This can put a heavy burden on the rollback segments to the point that the import may fail. To get around this problem, you should use the `COMMIT=Y` parameter. This will ensure that the changes are committed periodically and not kept as a single, huge transaction.

Import in Practice

To import the file, we should first set up a Parameter file, just as we did for the export. However, if it is a one-off situation, you should investigate the interactive mode in which you are prompted for parameters. Create a file, such as `import.par`, as follows:

```
FILE=c:\movies.dmp
COMMIT=Y
IGNORE=Y
TABLE=videos
GRANTS=Y
```

Then, you can run it:

```
IMP73 PARFILE=import.par
```

In this case, we are importing just one table into a different schema. An example is shown in Figure 4.2.

FIGURE 4.2:

The output from an import session

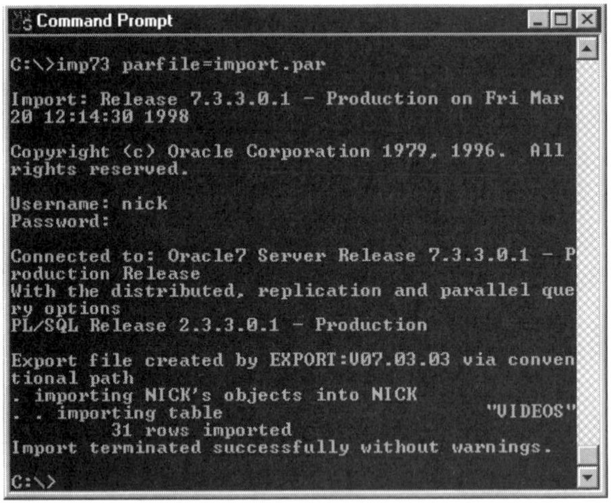

> **TIP** If you are importing a large amount of data, drop the indexes on any tables that are being updated. This will make the import much faster. You should have a SQL script to re-create the indexes once the import is done.

Exports for Backups

You should be aware that an export is not an ideal database backup method. To be completely reliable, the export requires the database to be taken offline. The users are then without access to the data, which may be critical. However, the main problem is the exported backup is only valid at the time you do the export, which means the first time a user changes the data after you run the export, the backup is out-of-date. Another reason exports should not be the primary backup strategy is that the Redo Logs cannot be applied to an export.

TIP   Doing an export is an ideal way to transfer data from one database to another. You can select which schemas and even which tables you want to move.

Mirroring the Redo Logs

Doing a periodic export is certainly better than nothing, but it is best used as a second line of defense should your regular backups fail. The best method for backing up your database is to use a proper strategy of mirroring data files and archiving, which we shall now cover.

As we saw in Chapter 2, *Oracle Database Architecture*, any changes to the database are stored as Redo Log Entries in the Redo Log Buffer and then moved to the Online Redo Log files. Oracle, by default, is set up for a single set of Redo Log files (one member file per group). If you have a disk failure involving these files, you may have to use your export to recover the database, and of course, you will lose any data changed since the export was done.

If you want to run a reliable database, you *must* make sure that you have more than one member file to each Redo Log group. In other words, you must mirror the files. To do this, you add more files to each group; however, you need to find out how many files you have first. The following statement can be entered in a SQL*Plus session if you have the DBA privilege.

```
SELECT GROUP# MEMBER FROM v$logfile;

GROUP#    MEMBER
1         C:\ORANT\DATABASE\LOG1ADEST.LOG
1         D:\ORANT\DATABASE\LOG1BDEST.LOG
2         C:\ORANT\DATABASE\LOG2ADEST.LOG
2         D:\ORANT\DATABASE\LOG2BDEST.LOG
```

You can see that we have only two groups of Redo Log files with one member in each. Estimating the optimum number of groups is a matter of trial and error. If you choose a large number of groups or you make the files too large, then you are wasting disk space. If you make the files too small, then there will be a large number of log switches as the Log Writer process moves from filling one file to the next. If you have too few groups, there may be a time when the Log Writer is waiting for the Archiver process to archive the files. These situations impact the performance of your database.

TIP   Figuring out the optimum number and sizes for the Redo Logs is usually a matter of trial and error. One rule of thumb is to arrange for the log switches to occur about every 15 to 30 minutes. Start with three groups of mirrored files, and check the performance each month. You can get a good idea of the log-switch timing from the times on the Archive files.

Adding New Log Files

If you are setting up a new database, be sure you start with Mirrored Log files. However, if you are taking over a database not set up that way, it is a relatively simple matter to mirror the existing set of Redo Log files. Once you have decided how many groups you want and where you can put the Mirrored Log files, then use the following command to set it up in Server Manager:

```
ALTER DATABASE movies ADD LOGFILE MEMBER
    'd:\redo_logs\log1b.log' TO GROUP 1 ;
```

This command will add another member to the existing Group 1. Because the Mirrored Log files must be the same size, there is no size parameter in the file specification. To create a new group, you use a slightly different command:

```
ALTER DATABASE movies ADD LOGFILE GROUP 3
    ('c:\redo_logs\log3a.log'
    'd:\redo_logs\log3b.log') SIZE 100K ;
```

You should make all of the Log files the same size because making them different only confuses tuning. Figure 4.3 shows the file layout you should achieve when you mirror Redo Log files.

FIGURE 4.3:

The mirrored Redo Log files

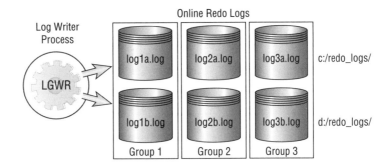

TIP

The Redo Log files are hit fairly hard in an active database. If at all possible, you should try to arrange for each of the sets of members to be on different disk drives. For example, all "a" members should be on one disk, and all "b" members should be on a different disk. They should also be separated from the system and data files. This does mean that you need at least five drives. Many servers, particularly on NT, are set up with just two or three drives, but the performance will be far from optimal.

If the LGWR background process cannot write to any members in a Redo Log group, the instance will crash. If LGWR can write to at least one member of group, then the database will continue to operate, but errors will be generated in the alert log indicating which members failed. This is one reason to check the alert log every day.

NOTE

New Log files can also be added with Backup Manager in OEM.

Mirroring the Control Files

A Control file is the storehouse of many aspects of the database, including its physical structures (such as tables) and the current state of the Redo Log files. The Control files are opened when the database instance is started up and kept open and up-to-date until the instance is shut down. You cannot make a copy of a Control file using an operating-system command like COPY while the instance is running, though there is an SQL command that will let you do this:

```
ALTER DATABASE BACKUP CONTROLFILE TO 'control2.ctl';
```

You should use this only in an emergency because as soon as there are any changes to the database, this backup will be out of date. It is mainly useful if you have a major problem with the database and you are about to shut it down, but you want to make doubly certain that you have a valid Control file.

If you lose your Control file, you are in trouble. Considering how simple the solution is, you should make sure that you always have at least two active Control files on different disks. The extra cautious would perhaps have three. Unfortunately, the Oracle default is only a single Control file.

NOTE   There is little overhead in mirroring the Control files because it is not write-intensive.

If you have not set up your own database, the first thing to check is how many Control files you have and what their names are. You can do this with the following command in Server Manager:

```
SELECT * FROM v$controlfile;
```

```
c:\data\ORA_CONTROL1.CON
d:\data\ORA_CONTROL2.CON
```

If there is only one file you must add a new one. To do this, follow these steps:

1. Shut down the database.

2. Copy the current Control file to a second location, preferably on a different disk.

3. Edit the init.ora file to define the new Control file, for example:

    ```
    control_files=(c:\oradata\test\control1.con,
    d:\oradata\test\control2.con).
    ```

4. Restart the database.

5. Rerun the SELECT command shown above to make sure that you now have more than one Control file.

NOTE   Remember that Control files are opened when the database is started and continually written to any time there is a change. You cannot simply take a copy of the Control file if the database is running.

If you mirror the Control files in this way, and one of them becomes corrupt or is accidentally deleted, you can always use the remaining file as a source for a new copy of the Control file. When a Control file is lost, the database stays up, but no further work can be done once Oracle discovers that the Control file is missing. When you shut the database down, you will not be able to restart it until you have recovered the Control file. If you have lost a disk containing a Control file and just want to get the database up again, you will have to find a different location for the Control file and modify the Initialization file to identify the new location.

Loss of any or all Control files causes Oracle to behave the same way: The database is up, but no changes can be made. If all Control files are lost, there is a way to recover that does not require a full restore from the last cold backup. The CREATE CONTROLFILE statement will create a new set of Control files. The syntax is similar to that of the CREATE DATABASE statement. When you run the command ALTER DATABASE BACKUP CONTROLFILE TO TRACE, a CREATE CONTROLFILE statement is generated by Oracle and placed into the directory represented in the initialization parameter *user_dump_dest*. This statement can be used to re-create the Control files.

Ensuring the Archive Processes Are Active

Now that you have set up your mirrored Redo Log files, you need to ensure that the Archiving processes are active. Without archiving your Redo Log files, media crash recovery to the point of failure is virtually impossible. You have to follow a two-step process here: changing the mode of the database and modifying the Initialization file.

First, we need to change the database so that it has the ability to recover from a disk failure. To do this, you must ensure that a Log file has been archived before overwriting it. Oracle keeps track of all the archived Log files with a sequence number. If you ever need to recover the database, Oracle knows whether any archived files are needed in addition to the current Log files. To put the database in Recovery mode, you use the following command in Server Manager:

```
ALTER DATABASE ARCHIVELOG;
```

To see whether a database is already in Recovery mode you can use the following command from Server Manager *but only when the database is in the MOUNT state of start-up:*

```
ARCHIVE LOG LIST
```

This should show results similar to Figure 4.4. Pay particular attention to the database Log mode and the state of automatic archival.

```
SVRMGR>
SVRMGR>
SVRMGR> archive log list
Database log mode              Archive Mode
Automatic archival             Enabled
Archive destination            C:\ORANT\RDBMS73\
Oldest online log sequence     358
Next log sequence to archive   359
Current log sequence           359
SVRMGR>
```

Setting up the Archive mode of the database is only the first step of the process. If we do not start the Archiving processes, none of the Redo Log files will be automatically archived. Because Oracle will not overwrite an unarchived file in recovery mode the database will eventually hang. To ensure that the archiving takes place, you need to add one or more lines to the Initialization file as shown in this example:

```
log_archive_start = TRUE
log_archive_dest = e:\archives\
log_archive_format = "Movies%S.ARC"
```

The first line is the most important one because it starts the background process for archiving (ARCH) when the database instance is started (see Figure 4.5). The other two optional lines define where the archived files are placed (in this case, in the e:\archives\directory) and override the default file-name specification. It is simpler to leave this last line out, but if you use it, make sure you *never* change it. To make archiving active, you will have to stop an active database and restart it with the new Initialization file.

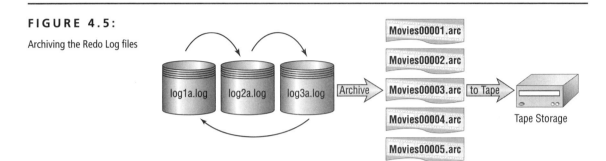

The names of the archived Log files will be derived from the *log_archive_format* parameter in the Initialization file. In the case shown above, the "%S" provides a sequence number so you can tell the order of the archived files, and using this, you would see files such as

```
Movies00001.ARC,
Movies00002.ARC,
Movies00003.ARC,
etc.
```

As we will see in the recovery stage, Oracle uses these sequence numbers to identify exactly which files are needed to recover a crashed database.

If possible, the archives should be on a different disk from any of the Redo Log files, but this is not so important if you ensure that you also back up the database, a task we will cover in the next section. The archives should also be backed up to tape nightly, in case of disk failure. In some environments, you can back up straight to tape. These archived Redo Log files are vital to the recovery process, so you must make *every* effort to ensure the reliability of the files on the mass-storage media.

NOTE   You must keep your archives long enough to recover your most recent backup. I like to keep enough files on disk for the last three backups, just in case.

A good way to test your archiving is to force it to occur. When a Redo Log file fills up, the Log Writer process switches to the next Redo Log file. The following command forces this to happen straight away.

```
ALTER SYSTEM SWITCH LOGFILE ;
```

After you have executed this command, check the archive destination: You should see a new file. If you don't, you will have to review the configuration of the archiving feature.

Just How Many Disk Drives Do You Need?

Several times in this book I mention that Oracle likes as many disk drives as it can get, but how many is that? It is worth looking at an optimal layout for disks in an Oracle database. The general rules are

- The Oracle system software should be on one disk.

- The SYSTEM tablespace should be on a separate disk.

- Redo Log files should be mirrored and each set of members should be on separate disks.

- The rollback segments should be on two separate disks.

- The temporary segments should be on a separate disk.

- The data files and indexes should be separated on different disks.

Control files should be mirrored, but because they are not I/O intensive, they can be put anywhere. Still, this procedure covers nine disks without trying. We may want even more, if our data files grow in size and require throughput.

In practice, this level of separation is seldom achieved, and you will have to get a feel for which are the most intensively used disks. To handle this properly you will need to become familiar with monitoring and tuning an Oracle database, especially before you make a large investment in hardware.

Doing Hot Backups

So far we have set up our database to ensure that the Redo Log files and the Control files are mirrored. The database is also set up to archive the Redo Log files. If (and we should say *when*) a disk crashes, you will now be well prepared to recover the files you have lost. In fact, Oracle will continue running except for recording the problem in the event log. With automated monitoring, you may even be paged.

However, no transactions against the damaged data file will succeed, and the database instance will need media recovery. Oracle does not include mirroring for database files, and if you do not have a RAID box to provide hardware mirroring, you need to have a strategy in place to back up these files periodically. If you have reliable backups (including the archived Redo Log files), you can always recover the database.

A backup of the database files can be very simple. Whichever way you choose to do it, you will be using operating-system commands (whether it is a copy or a sophisticated BACKUP command) to move the data files to an archive disk or to tape. Some environments let you do a backup from the operating system even when the file is open and being written to, but this method should *never* be used because the results will be inconsistent and unreliable, even if you could get them to work.

The simplest way to do a backup is to shut down the database, back up all the files, and then restart the database. This is called a *cold* backup. Depending on the file sizes, this could take an hour or more, so this type of backup is done when there is no activity, particularly overnight.

However, Oracle gives you the ability to use a much better technique, the so-called *hot* backup. By setting each tablespace in turn to a Backup mode, you can copy a consistent view of the tables to your backup disk or tape without shutting the database down. To do this, use the following commands:

```
ALTER TABLESPACE SYSTEM BEGIN BACKUP;
  host operating system copy or backup command
ALTER TABLESPACE SYSTEM END BACKUP;
```

TIP   Any operating-system command can be executed from an SQL script by using the "$" character before the command.

The BACKUP command must be able to operate on an open file. An example production script for OpenVMS is shown below:

```
ALTER TABLESPACE SYSTEM BEGIN BACKUP;
$backup/ignore=(nobackup,interlock)/log -
  oracle_db_0:[TBS]ORA_SYSTEM.DBS; oracle_backup
ALTER TABLESPACE SYSTEM END BACKUP;
```

```
ALTER TABLESPACE ROLLBACK01 BEGIN BACKUP;
$backup/ignore=(nobackup,interlock)/log -
    oracle_db_1:[TBS]ROLLBACK01.DBF; oracle_backup
ALTER TABLESPACE ROLLBACK01 END BACKUP;

ALTER TABLESPACE ROLLBACK02 BEGIN BACKUP;
$backup/ignore=(nobackup,interlock)/log -
    oracle_db_2:[TBS]ROLLBACK02.DBF; oracle_backup
ALTER TABLESPACE ROLLBACK02 END BACKUP;

ALTER TABLESPACE TBS_INDEX BEGIN BACKUP;
$backup/ignore=(nobackup,interlock)/log -
    oracle_db_1:[TBS]TBS_INDEX.DBF; oracle_backup
ALTER TABLESPACE TBS_INDEX END BACKUP;

ALTER TABLESPACE TBS BEGIN BACKUP;
$backup/ignore=(nobackup,interlock)/log -
    oracle_db_2:[TBS]TBS.DBF; oracle_backup
ALTER TABLESPACE TBS END BACKUP;

ALTER DATABASE BACKUP CONTROLFILE TO 'oracle_backup:TBS_1.ctl';
ALTER DATABASE BACKUP CONTROLFILE TO TRACE;
```

WARNING   Windows NT does not allow you to do backups on open files through its operating-system utilities or commands. To get around this, you will have to use the OCOPY73.EXE or OCOPY80.EXE utilities. These do a raw copy, however, and you may find it easier and safer to shut the database down and do a regular copy with NTBACKUP.

This command backs up each of five tablespaces to disk. (There is only one file for each tablespace.) Once you have done the copy, you must end the Backup mode on the tablespace as soon as possible or performance will suffer unnecessarily. The last two lines may be overkill, but they do an online backup of the Initialization file. This file is only read at start up, and it does not change; some DBAs like to be doubly cautious and back up everything, but it is something that is likely never to cause you problems.

Backup Checklist

This is a summary of the points to help you make sure your backups are being done properly:

1. Make sure that your Control file is mirrored.

2. Make sure that your Redo Log files are mirrored.

3. Check that the archiving is working and active.

4. Do a log switch, and check that the Redo Log files are being archived.

5. Take the database down, and do a full backup. This is a vital step because backups previous to ALTER DATABASE ARCHIVELOG cannot be used to achieve complete recovery of a database.

6. Set up a regular batch job to do hot backups and storing of archive Redo Log files to tape.

Recovering a Database

Once you have all the backup processes active and set up properly, you are now prepared for almost any disaster that may strike. Of course, when disaster does strike, usually in the form of a disk crash, it will be at the most inopportune time. If the database is noncritical, you will have time to investigate the problem and, if necessary, bring in a more experienced DBA.

No matter how many databases are mission-critical, the company's business must continue, whether it is an airline-reservation system or an online Web-ordering system. To recover the database, you need to be on the ball; if you haven't set up your backup strategy properly, you are doubling the amount of your stress.

Recovery Fundamentals

In Chapter 2, *Oracle Database Architecture,* we covered the process in which all changes to the database are recorded as Redo Log Entries in the Redo Log Buffer and then get moved to the Online Redo Log files by the Log Writer (LGWR) process.

These files are then archived to disk or tape by the Archiver (ARCH) process. The combination of datafile backups and archived Redo Log file backups gives Oracle what it needs to be able to recover a database to just before the point of failure.

If you lose a disk with a data file belonging to the SYSTEM tablespace on it, you will have to shut down the database manually with the SHUTDOWN ABORT command. Non-SYSTEM tablespaces can be brought offline (and recovered) without affecting the status of other tablespaces. If you lose all members of a Log file group or one of the mandatory background processes is lost, then the database instance will terminate automatically. You must review the situation and try to find the reason for the crash. The most likely scenario is a crashed disk, and this should be fairly obvious by system messages or simply looking at the system. You will have to repair or replace the disk, so it is important to have spare hardware available.

WARNING   I have been in the situation where it is not possible to have a spare for all the types of disks in your installation. A disk crash means that you have to restore your backed-up files to a different disk. This is a more complicated recovery and means you have to rename your tablespace files or create at least an environment variable that points to them. This situation is best avoided until you have more experience as a DBA because to do the process during a high-pressure recovery is not the best time to learn it. You may want to have a friendly DBA available.

The Recovery

If we were to take all those Redo entries and apply them to a healthy backup, we could re-create the database up to the point where it crashed. This is precisely what an Oracle recovery does, and the beauty of it is that most of it is handled automatically (see Figure 4.6). The steps to the recovery of your data are as follows:

1. Ensure that the database is shut down. (Use ABORT if you have to.)

2. Ensure that any hardware failures are repaired.

3. Find your latest database backup, and recover any lost data files.

4. If a Control file was lost, copy the mirrored version to the repaired disk.

5. Make sure you have all the required archived Redo Log files from tape or disk (though Oracle will prompt you if they are not available). It is best if you have room on your archive destination.

6. Start the recovery by typing the following commands in Server Manager while logged on a SYS (or the INTERNAL synonym).

```
SVRMGR> STARTUP MOUNT PFILE=c:\orant\database\inittest.ora
SVRMGR> SET AUTORECOVERY ON
SVRMGR> RECOVER DATABASE ;
```

7. When the recovery has been completed, you can start up the database again with

```
SVRMGR> ALTER DATABASE OPEN;
```

After all the work involved in setting up the database to mirror Control and Redo Log files and ensuring it is archived, it is refreshing to see that the recovery can be accomplished so simply.

FIGURE 4.6:

Recovering a backed-up database from the archived Redo Log files

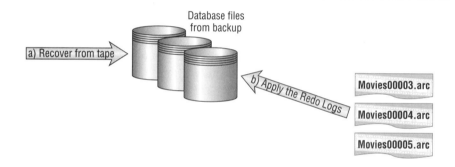

TIP   The more often you do your database backup, the less Redo Log files you will need for recovery, and the faster the process will be.

Setting Up Database Security

In addition to making sure the data is physically secure, the other main area we have to look at is that users are tightly controlled in what they can and cannot do. If users can change data when they should not have access to it, then that data could be more at risk than if it were lost through a hardware failure. Running your business on incorrect data may be worse than having no data at all.

Luckily, Oracle again gives us a range of tools to let us control database security to the level we want. Even if you are not the main database analyst at your site, setting up security will be a joint effort between you as a developer and the DBAs.

There are several key items we need to look at:

- Creating users

- Assigning privileges

- Using roles

- Setting quotas on tablespace usage

- Using profiles to control the consumption of system resources

- Using stored procedures to enhance security

Creating Users

Being a user of the database is like having an account at the bank: you have a name and a password, and without those you can do nothing. However, even with those privileges, what you can do is limited until you either put some money in or arrange for an overdraft: you need extra privileges for any extra capabilities you want.

The same rules apply to a secure database. Although file-based workgroup databases are open to everyone by default and have limited ability to control the actions of users, Oracle allows you to do nothing by default, not even log on! This sort of security is mandatory for a production database. To create a user in the database, you use the CREATE USER command as in the following example:

```
CREATE USER nick
    IDENTIFIED BY ummagumma
    DEFAULT TABLESPACE tbs ;
    TEMPORARY TABLESPACE tbs_temp ;
```

This is really the minimum set of parameters that you should use. If you do not specify the tablespaces, then they will default to the SYSTEM tablespace, something you need to carefully avoid. As mentioned above, this not only does not give the user the right to log on, even if they could, they have no right to use any space. Within the CREATE USER command, you can give the user a *quota* on tablespaces—that is, the amount of disk space they are allowed to use within a tablespace to create database objects, such as tables and indexes. You do this as follows:

```
CREATE USER nick
  IDENTIFIED BY ummagumma
  DEFAULT TABLESPACE tbs ;
  TEMPORARY TABLESPACE tbs_temp
  QUOTA 500K ON tbs ;
```

You can change a user's account attributes at a later time with the ALTER USER command; for example, to change the password and add the quota for another tablespace ("movies"), you would use

```
ALTER USER nick
  IDENTIFIED BY saucerful
  DEFAULT TABLESPACE movies ;
  TEMPORARY TABLESPACE movies_temp
  QUOTA 100K ON movies ;
```

WARNING   Your site standards should require that you modify passwords periodically. In my experience, users uniformly hate this, but this should not be an excuse to forget about it. The chances are that you will not get all users to run a SQL session to change their passwords, and you cannot do it easily from a stored procedure. It will normally be a manual process for the DBA.

TIP   Do not immediately assume that you have to grant the user any quota at all. If you have developed a database and a front-end application, users who are using the application do not need to have any quota on the tablespaces. The quota is enforced only for creating tables, indexes, and so on, and much of the time, end users never have to do this. If they need to create a temporary table, this can always be done from within a stored procedure that is owned in another schema.

Finally, to delete a user from the database, as well as all of the objects in their schema, you use the DROP USER command with the CASCADE option as follows:

```
DROP USER video_user CASCADE ;
```

This situation most often occurs when a user moves to another job, whether inside the company or outside, and it should not be taken lightly. But doing this task is often one of those left until you have more time, and it can get forgotten and pose a potential security problem. Try to get a formal notification from your personnel office, and make it a top priority to drop the user as soon as possible.

What Do You Name a User?

You should adopt any existing site standards. If you do not have any, then consider popular standards, such as the first letter of the first name plus the last name; for example, "nsnowdon" for my name. If you still have two users with the same name, you will have to add a middle initial.

Using Operating-System Authentication

In a networked environment, you typically log on to the network before you run an end-user application. Using Operating-System Authentication, when you try to log on to the database, Oracle checks to see whether you have logged on to the network; if you have and your user name is a valid Oracle user name, then you do not need to provide a password. This is wonderful from an administration point of view in that you do not have to manage passwords for Oracle users because everyone is authenticated by the network logon. However, your aim as a Visual Basic developer is to create end-user applications that run in a client-server mode. By using Operating-System Authentication, anyone who knows what they are doing could conceivably create a user name that automatically gives them access to the database.

WARNING   Operating-System Authentication is too insecure to be used with Oracle in most circumstances. Use Password Authentication for individuals, and change the passwords regularly.

If you insist on using Operating-System Authentication, the process is not difficult. An initialization parameter, *os_authent_prefix*, is added to the beginning of the operating-system user name to produce the Oracle user name. The default string for this parameter is "OPS$", but you can set it to whatever you like, even a blank.

For example, if you are running Oracle on Windows NT and you have an NT network, your network logon name is BMILLS, and you have the default initialization parameter for the prefix "OPS$", then create a new Oracle user account as follows:

```
CREATE USER OPS$bmills IDENTIFIED EXTERNALLY ;
```

The keyword *externally*, instead of the password, indicates the database user will be authenticated by the operating system. If you set the parameter to a blank, then the operating-system user name will be the same as the Oracle user name.

TIP
O/S Authentication gives normal access to the database, not SYSDBA access (that is, start-up and shut-down privileges). If you want to do your administration remotely, you will need to set up a Password file.

Assigning Privileges

You now have set up a group of users who need access to your application. At this time, they only have an account: they cannot actually do anything in Oracle, not even log on. As a DBA, you have to explicitly grant *privileges* to users to allow them to access database objects. You can have as much control over this as you need. The types of privileges you can grant to users fall into two distinct types: *system* privileges and *object* privileges.

System Privileges

The first type of privilege is the system privilege. You need system privileges to execute certain SQL statements rather than access specific objects. An example is the right to drop tables in any schema in the database. There are a large number of system privileges, and they are typically what a DBA will grant to a developer. We will cover some of the more useful privileges from a developer's point of view in Chapter 6, *Implementing a Database*.

Object Privileges

The second type of privilege is the object privilege. Object privileges apply specifically to one type of action on one specific object. For example, if you want a user to have the right to select data from a table, you would grant them SELECT access to that table. That does not give them the right to change anything in that table nor to look at any other table. Object privileges are typically granted by you as the developer to end users. Only the owner of an object may grant access to that object.

There are only a few object privileges, and again, they will be covered in Chapter 6. Object privileges are an important way to secure access to your data, and as we shall see throughout this book, they form a major influence on the design of your application.

Granting Privileges

To grant either system or object privileges to users, you first need the ability to pass on these privileges. There are no special privileges needed to allow a DBA to grant system privileges to developers or to allow developers to grant object privileges on their own schema to end users, but if you want to do more than this, you should read the sections on the GRANT command in the Oracle *SQL Reference* manual.

The GRANT SYSTEM PRIVILEGE command takes the form

```
GRANT privilege TO user_name ;
```

If you want to have the system privilege create tables in any schema, you would use

```
GRANT CREATE ANY TABLE TO jwoods ;
```

The GRANT OBJECT PRIVILEGE command is similar but includes the name of the object that the privilege refers to

```
GRANT privilege ON object_name TO user_name ;
```

So, if you want to grant the object privilege the selection of any data from a particular table, you would use

```
GRANT SELECT ON video_store.movies TO jwoods ;
```

With either of these commands, you can include more than one privilege in one go; to give a user the privilege to do anything to the data in a table, you could use

```
GRANT SELECT, INSERT, UPDATE ON video_store.movies TO jwoods ;
```

NOTE   Certain object privileges, such as INSERT and UPDATE, allow a list of columns that can be affected by the privilege. For example, "GRANT UPDATE (movie_name) ON movies TO jwoods" only allows jwoods to insert a row with a value for ID only.

Figure 4.7 gives you an idea of the number of commands you will need to set up users. For each user, you have to go through the same process. You can put this in a script, which is fine for setting it up in the first place. But it is still a maintenance nightmare, such as when you add a new table to the application: you have to find all the users who should have access to this new table and then add them all.

FIGURE 4.7:

Granting privileges to users

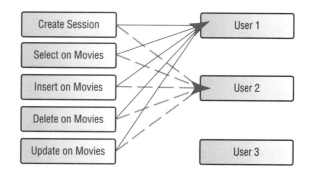

Using Roles

Although it is technically possible to manage every system and object privilege in your database with grants to individual users, this method would rapidly become unmanageable as soon as you had more than a handful of users. If you were to look at the rights you had given to the individuals, you would probably notice that you could sort the privileges into distinct groups.

For example, if you have three separate applications, such as Human Resources, Engineering, and Production, then there are probably more than three types of data access that individuals need: one group would need to update the HR data while others may be allowed to view only part of it. To arrange these privileges into sensible and manageable groups, we can use the concept of a *role*.

A role is a way of collecting several privileges into a single package. If you grant this role to an individual user, they automatically get all the privileges associated with that role (see Figure 4.8). With some careful choice of roles, you should be able to set things up so that each user needs only to be granted three roles at the most.

Using roles is so much more efficient than granting individual privileges that you should think carefully and have a definite reason if you decide to grant privileges to individuals.

When you set up roles for developers, the system privileges that you want to grant to the role are

- Create table
- Create sequence
- Create procedure
- Create trigger
- Create tablespace
- Create view

The object privileges for your end user roles will obviously depend on what tables you have set up and whether you give the users access to the tables through stored procedures or with update privileges.

FIGURE 4.8:

Assigning privileges to roles

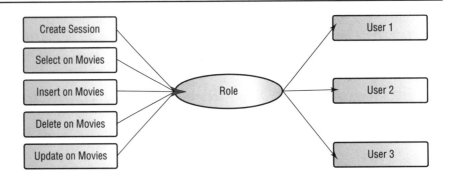

In addition to being able to assign roles to users, Oracle also has the concept of a profile, which describes the user's resource limits, such as maximum CPU time, maximum idle time, and maximum allowable number of reads. You should use these restrictions if the types of queries and transactions placed on the database cause resource shortages.

Predefined Roles

You can make your job a little easier by using *predefined* roles. There are a few roles that you can grant in one easy command. These are shown in Table 4.2.

TABLE 4.2: The Predefined Roles You Can Use

Role	Description
CONNECT	Maintenance privileges
RESOURCE	Developer privileges
DBA	Full DBA privileges
EXP_FULL_DATABASE	Export the full database
IMP_FULL_DATABASE	Import the full database

In a larger installation, you may not want to use the DBA role because you may want to control the tasks that each person can do. For example, you might want one person responsible for doing the backups and maybe another doing tuning. In this case, you will have to create your own roles that have a subset of the DBA privileges.

Stored Procedures to Enhance Security

When you grant privileges, you can control which users are allowed to read or update specific tables or even specific columns. However, this is only a basic level of security. It is without a doubt a vital necessity, but a polished database should impose a finer level of control. We can control *who* updates data but not *how* they can update it. This must be provided by the implementation of business rules.

Business rules need to encapsulate access to the raw data. Current techniques include using middle-tier software components between the client and the database server. However, the easiest way to implement business rules is with stored procedures. Stored procedures are the name given to code that is stored in the database, and you can ensure that the only way to change any data is through these procedures. We will cover this in more detail in Chapter 10, *Creating Stored Procedures*. For now we will just note that you need the execute privilege to use a stored procedure, and as before, this is best achieved through a role (see Figure 4.9).

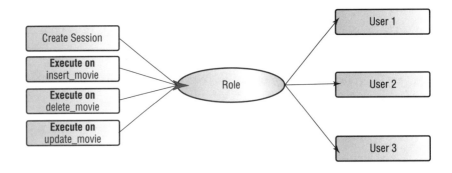

FIGURE 4.9:

Assigning stored-procedure privileges to roles

Regular Maintenance Tasks

You should keep a list of specific maintenance tasks that you carry out on a regular basis. Every DBA will have their own favorite tasks, but the following may be useful as the basis for your own individualized task list.

Daily

- Check any overnight batch jobs to ensure they ran on time and without errors.

- Check your overnight database export.

- Check the hot backup.

- Check the alert logs for any errors.

- Monitor Oracle processes for runaways and resource hogs.

- Monitor space left in data files.

- Monitor tables that may not be able to grow within a tablespace.

- Monitor the performance of overnight batch jobs.

Weekly

- Check Log file sizes.

- Monitor hot tablespaces for free space and correct location.

- Check volume of archives for daily throughput during the week. On databases with heavy transaction activity, this could be a daily task.

- Do a security and user audit.

Monthly

- Check database performance statistics.

- Check fragmentation and chaining of extents.

- Check tablespace growth, and adjust base table size.

Using Enterprise Manager

So far in this chapter, we have seen the SQL commands necessary to administer the database. A thorough understanding of these commands is essential for a professional DBA. However, as with most areas of software design, a GUI software package named Oracle Enterprise Manager (OEM) now comes with the Enterprise edition of Oracle. The software puts a GUI face on all of the SQL commands we have seen in this chapter. The advantage of OEM is that the casual user has a much easier time of doing part-time administration. The downside is, like using a pocket calculator, you forget the manual methods. These manual methods are sometimes indispensable.

Enterprise Manager gives you a point-and-click approach to viewing overall information about the database as well as allowing you to get a more detailed view of the crucial information. Rather than present a full description of the Enterprise Manager, we will briefly visit four of the many capabilities that the product offers you. This should be enough to give you an idea of the possibilities of the software and perhaps even inspire you to buy it.

The first application within Enterprise Manager that we will look at is the Backup Manager (see Figure 4.10). It shows you an overview of the tablespaces and Redo Log groups and lets you control the backups.

FIGURE 4.10:

The Backup Manager
application

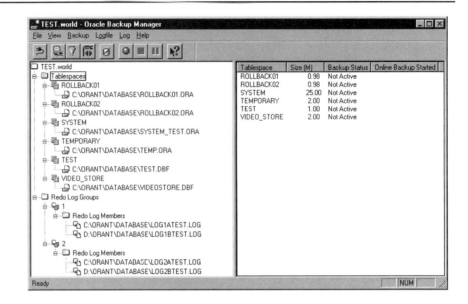

The beauty of the Enterprise Manager is that you can set it up so you can manage
all of your databases on the network from one control panel.

The next application is the Security Manager. It shows you all the users and
roles in your database. The Security Manager also allows you to view which roles
are assigned to which users and which privileges are assigned to which roles and
users. This is a useful feature, but it does much more than that. You can easily create new users (see the Create User dialog box in Figure 4.11) and assign new privileges to the users. By clicking on the Show SQL button, you can see the complete
SQL command that would achieve the same effect from the command-line prompt.

The Storage Manager allows you to view the storage taken by the tablespaces,
data files, and rollback segments. My favorite view is the one shown in Figure 4.12,
and it allows you, at a glance, to see how full the tablespaces are.

FIGURE 4.11:

The Security Manager application

FIGURE 4.12:

The Storage Manager application

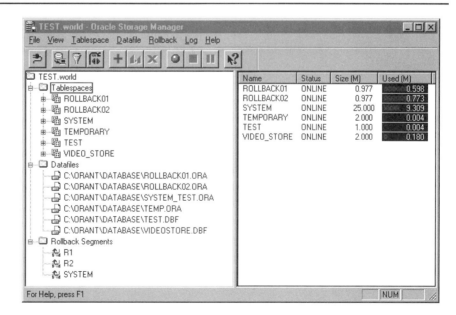

The final example of the Enterprise Manager is actually an add-on. (You have to pay for this feature separately.) It is called the Performance Pack and contains, most notably, an expert system for analyzing the performance of your database. This is the application that makes it possible for you to tune your database without years of tuning experience. Tuning is not to be taken lightly, and you need to have a good grasp of the what the expert system recommends before blindly changing system parameters.

One aspect of the Performance Pack that I regularly use is the Tablespace Manager. It allows you to look inside the tablespace and graphically view the distribution (and perhaps fragmentation) of the tables within that space (see Figure 4.13). Other features allow you to do more automatic management. The Performance Pack is a great addition to a busy DBA's toolkit.

FIGURE 4.13:

The Tablespace Manager in the optional Performance Pack

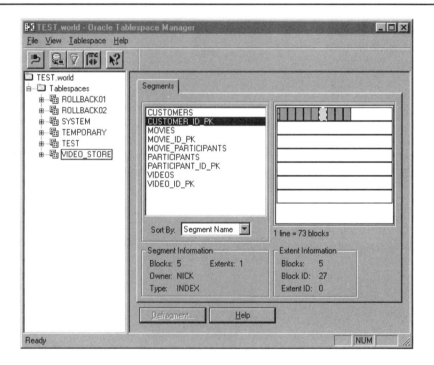

Summary

This chapter has presented an introduction to Oracle database administration. It has covered two major areas: database backup strategies and security. You need to pay special attention to both of these areas to have confidence in the security and reliability of your data. If this becomes a major part of your job, you should get as much training as possible. In this case, you will not only need to have a thorough understanding of all the available tools but also to get experience in areas such as tuning.

This and the previous two chapters are sufficient to provide a basis on which to build applications. If you are working with an experienced DBA, you should have enough knowledge to understand what tasks are being carried out and to provide as much assistance as possible. You may even find some areas that could be improved. We can now work toward building databases with tables, stored procedures, and more, ready for access from your Visual Basic programs.

CHAPTER
FIVE

5

Database Design

- Conceptual Design of the Requirement Specifications

- Logical Design of the Conceptual Model

- Implementation of the Physical Data Tables

When you first start creating databases, there is a temptation to ignore any formal techniques in the design phase. This is especially true when you develop small applications that have a limited data store associated with them or if you are, at heart, a developer who just can't wait to get to coding. The smaller the database, the less important is your design. However, the corollary is also true. As your database grows, any shortcuts you have taken putting it together start to show. At best, they will be embarrassing; at worst, your applications will slow down and the data will become unreliable. Eventually, you will be faced with doing the job properly. And, as you know, the database will keep growing and be used in more ways than you ever dreamed of.

The design of a database is one integrated step in the whole process of system design. How large a part your involvement represents will depend on the environment you work in. At one extreme, you may be responsible for absolutely everything, which can be a daunting task: there is much to learn, most of which you will not be aware of at the beginning. At the other extreme, you may be working in a highly structured and carefully controlled shop with separate teams for database design, maintenance, and implementation, never mind about the development of front-end applications. If you are in this last situation, it is worth understanding as much about the process as possible.

We can split up the process of database design into three distinct phases:

Conceptual Design   Take all the requirement specifications that have come from your interaction with the user communities, and create a design that is independent of any hardware or software concerns. The Entity-Relationship model is the most popular technique in this circumstance.

Logical Design   Map the conceptual model into a logical model suitable for the type of DBMS we are using. You want to ensure the design is a technically sound one with a minimum of data redundancy and maintenance concerns.

Physical Implementation   Implement the physical data tables, and make design decisions to enhance the usefulness of the database with the proposed applications. This is the final phase of creating a database.

You will find that the particulars of these phases differ depending on which methodology you use, but generally, they follow the outline described above and shown in Figure 5.1.

FIGURE 5.1:

The process of creating a database

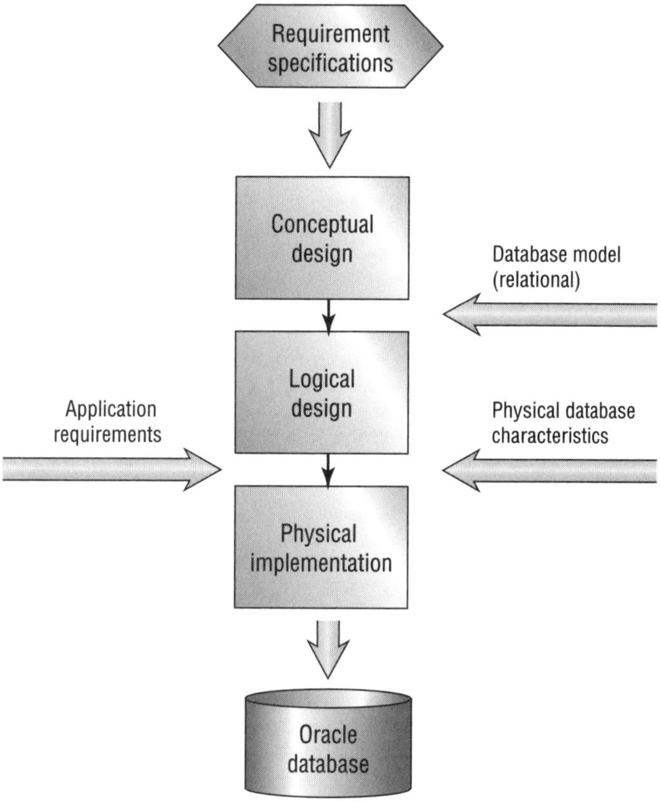

Try to keep these phases in mind as your design proceeds. Even when you have done these steps many times, it is easy to forget one or more parts. This will usually come back to haunt you.

Although the phases are distinct, they're not necessarily following a one-way street. For example, if you know that a particular feature of the physical database will affect your design you can use this information up front in the logical-design phase. This will happen naturally as your experience increases.

In the rest of this chapter we will cover the conceptual design as well as the logical design in greater detail. The practicalities of physical implementation will be dealt with in Chapter 6, when we take the design developed in the first two phases and create an Oracle database that best suits what we have come up with.

The Conceptual Design

To produce a good database design we use a process called *data modeling*. A data model is an abstract representation of a real-world environment that includes objects and their relationships. You could be modeling the business of a corner store or the economy of a country for budget purposes; the process is the same, but the complexity changes. The aim of the model is to represent that environment without any concern for the database technology you are using or the applications that might be run against it.

In the conceptual phase, you will create a model of your environment. You should gather as much information from the users as you can about both the current system and the proposed system, but do not dwell on current implementations too much, such as whether they are computerized or paper based. Rather you should find out what the key processes are and which data flows the system must have. Then, you can figure out exactly what the data items are. A general approach is as follows:

- Define the data requirements
- Prepare data flow diagrams
- Produce state transition diagrams if applicable
- Document the data in Entity-Relationship diagrams
- Complete the diagrams with entity attributes

Of most importance to this chapter are the last two steps. These steps document all the data items we have uncovered in a way that is applicable to creating our database. If you are unfamiliar with the other stages, you should consult one of the many good books on systems analysis.

Entity-Relationship Diagrams

Entity-Relationship diagrams are the accepted way to view the relationships between entities. There have been many different ways to create these diagrams. In this section, we will review what they are in their most basic form.

An *entity* can be considered as a class of real-world objects: for example, they could be jobs, people, or cities. You should be able to uniquely define an entity within the context you are working. You can do this by name, social security number, or some other key item. You can then assign *attributes* to each of the entities. Attributes are additional information you need to keep about an entity, such as a job title or a person's name. In Visual Basic, a comparable operation would be to define classes, each with their own properties that will later appear as rows and columns in a logical database design.

As an example of database design, I will use a simple but familiar case of a video-rental store. The owners have decided to keep information about the movies for rent on a computer in their store so customers can quickly look up any facts that might be available. They have been using spreadsheets to keep track of the videos. Although spreadsheets were initially a cheap solution, they have proven to be a maintenance nightmare and impossible to build an application on top of.

The intention is to provide a realistic situation without too much complexity. This complexity would merely serve to cloud the design issues. It is surprising how many businesses *do* use spreadsheets as their main database.

In this example, after reviewing the business requirements, you can write down various entities you find important, such as

- The movies you want to stock

- The actual video copies of the movies

- The actors

- The directors

- The customers

When you have come up with the entities for your environment, you next determine what are the possible relationships between them, such as

- Actors *star* in movies

- Directors *direct* movies

- The store *has* one or more video copies of each movie

- Each copy of a movie can be *rented* by one customer

TIP   Remember that entities can be described by a noun and relationships by a verb.

The standard technique to diagram the conceptual model is to use rectangles for the entities and diamonds for the relationships. When you have done that, you can then draw lines between the boxes to define where the relationships apply. Finally, you should identify the number of objects of each entity involved in each relationship. For example, many actors can take part in many different movies, but only one customer can rent a specific copy of a movie at a time. This is called the *cardinality* of the relationship, and it is shown in Figure 5.2.

FIGURE 5.2:

Describing the cardinality of relationships

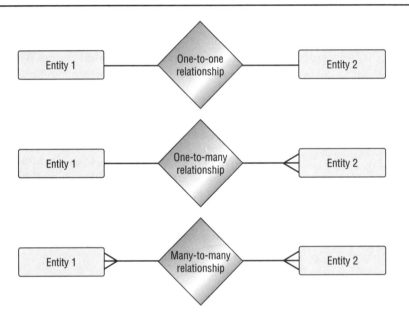

When we apply the diagramming technique to the Movie database, we may come up with a design like the one shown in Figure 5.3. Let's look at the relationships between the entities. These should match up with the business rules that came from our interaction with the users in the requirements specification. Documenting the relationships in this way is an excellent tool for communicating the growing design with your end users. Figure 5.3 shows the following numbered relationships.

1. Each customer can rent several movies.

2. There can be several physical copies (videos) of a movie.

3. Each movie can have several actors, and each actor can star in several movies.

4. Each movie can have several directors, and each director can direct in several movies.

Adding the Attributes

Now that we have our entities laid out, it is time to add in the attributes for each. Attributes can be thought of as items that describe objects in more detail. You have to think of all possible information you might want to keep about any of the entities, such as for movies, you want to know the name, the rating, the length, and perhaps the year it was released. You will, of course, want to know who starred in each film, but this information will be represented by the relationship, not by the entity.

These attributes are often added to the Entity-Relationship diagram in ellipses, but this can rapidly become difficult to comprehend. If you instead display them in the box with the entity, the diagram not only becomes easier to understand but makes the translation to the logical design fairly simple. With all the attributes in place we may see a design like that shown in Figure 5.4. The diagram can have a more complicated layout, but this example is enough to give you a taste for designing a database.

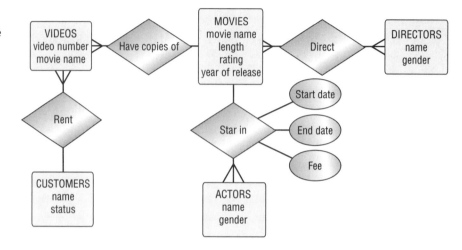

You may often find attributes that apply to the relationship rather than the entities. For example, you may want to know the featured actors who star in a movie,
but you may also want to know what their reported fee was for appearing in it or
when they started and finished work. This information can be added in ellipses
as shown in Figure 5.4.

TIP   The appearance of attributes for a relationship should be a strong indication that
you will have to convert the relationship into an entity. Although we shall do this
procedure in the next section, it could equally be done here.

Reviewing the Design

Now is the ideal time to review what your Entity-Relationship diagrams have
produced, to see how sensible it appears and whether it can be simplified in any
way. To simplify the design, we look to reducing the number of entities, because
more tables means more maintenance and code to update them. To reduce the
number of entities we must combine them.

A commonly used technique is to combine code entities especially if they just
have a short code and a description. The information can be assembled as one
entity, with a new field to define what sort of code each represents. For example,

instead of one entity for the status of a video and another for the ratings of a movie, we could do it all in one as shown in Table 5.1.

TABLE 5.1: Putting Two Code Tables into One

Code Type	Code	Description
RATING	PG	Parental guidance
RATING	PG-13	No children under 13
RATING	NC-17	Adults only
STATUS	RS	Reserved
STATUS	AV	Available
STATUS	RE	Rented

We could then have the first two columns as a key. The decision whether or not to put an index on this table comes in the implementation stage, though with such a small number of codes, an index would not be worthwhile.

Although this is a simple example, we can take it a step further. Are there any other tables that describe the same type of object? In this case, the Directors and Actors tables both describe people and their roles in the movie industry. Combining these into a "participant" entity is quite easy and really only means that we need to add an attribute that defines their role in the movie. They may be an actor or director, but we now open up the possibilities of including other roles, such as producer or screenwriter, without having to create new tables to accommodate them. We have also reduced the maintenance overhead.

The Logical Design

When you have a good conceptual model you can start to convert it into a logical design. The process is one of mapping the entities to the logical model, and ensuring that the relationships between tables can be implemented as combinations of two or more tables.

NOTE   Whereas Oracle7 was a relational database, Oracle8 is sometimes referred to as an object-relational database because it has the capability to store complex data structures in its tables. However, it is not a true object-oriented database and, if the object-relational approach is well received by database users, modeling techniques will be modified to suit it.

When the complexity of the database increases, the chances that any two designers will arrive at the same solution becomes small. This does not matter as long as the guidelines are followed. Business practices seem to change so fast these days that you will probably be making regular changes to the design anyway as time goes on. What is important is that you come up with something that not only handles your data properly but also allows for those inevitable changes as well as growth.

With a database held in a simple spreadsheet layout, you will find that the same piece of information can occur in several different places. When you create a logical design, you are aiming at a database model that contain few, if any, of these data *redundancies*. In this way, your design will not be subject to problems and anomalies when you make changes to the data. The relational model that we use for the logical design was developed by Dr. E. F. Codd in 1970. His model is based upon tables of simple and discrete data with relationships between the tables. Relationships are represented by references in one table to another table, though this does lead to a certain amount of duplication of data because the same key must appear in both tables. Over the last few years, the relational model has become the dominant database-management system, although that model is now being challenged by object-oriented databases as well as hybrids, such as Oracle8.

The phases of logical design include these key tasks:

- Identify the record types (essentially the mapping of entities to tables).

- Identify the fields in those records (column and datatype definitions and so on).

- Identify any data dependencies.

- Normalize the database.

- Identify the keys.

Identifying the Record Types and Fields

The Entity-Relationship techniques described in the section on conceptual design are based on the relational model. Because we also require that the logical model be a relational one, mapping between the conceptual and logical designs is fairly straightforward. Record types are similar to the entities—so much so that most designers can do a one-to-one transfer. The same applies to fields, which should be more or less the same as entity attributes.

Identifying Any Data Dependencies

The entities map directly to the logical model, but the relationships are not mapped. Instead, you have to create additional attributes so that you can implement the relationships as combinations of tables. These new attributes often appear as references from one table to another and can become foreign keys in your physical design.

Watch out for many-to-many relationships because they do not perform well in the SQL environment. The presence of these relationships is a sign that the relationship may have some characteristics of its own. You should consider representing the relationship as a new entity.

For example, in the video-store example we have a many-to-many relationship between movies and directors (more than one director could work on a movie, while a director can also work on many movies). Consider making a new entity called Participant_Assignment with a one-to-many relationship for both the Participant and the Movies tables as shown in Figure 5.5. This step is especially important if you need to store information about the relationship, such as start and end times or payments.

FIGURE 5.5:

The interdependencies of data tables

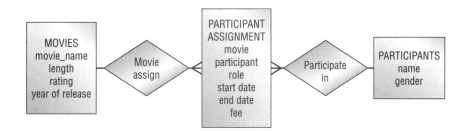

TIP   This conversion of relationships could just as easily occur later in the logical-design phase or in the conceptual design. The important thing is that the steps are all covered, even if you do not rigidly stick to the order shown in this chapter.

Normalizing the Database

Once you define a record layout, you can use the technique of *normalization*. This is the process of breaking down a complex design into a group of simple relationships. Normalization is important for adapting a real-life scenario to something that will fit effectively into a relational database. There is a formal mathematical basis to normalization, but essentially, the process boils down to a commonsense approach to achieving a database that

- Is easy to maintain

- Can be expanded with minimum effort

- Does not include more duplicated data than necessary

- Minimizes inconsistencies in the data

- Minimizes the effect of update and delete anomalies (e.g., does not update all affected records)

Normalization is the outcome of the work originally done by E. F. Codd and is based on a rigorous mathematical theorem, which gives a solid theoretical foundation to the technique. Luckily, we do not need to understand any of the mathematics to normalize a database. Codd proposed three *Normal* forms that defined characteristics of good relational design; these are the First, Second, and Third Normal forms. Codd later coproduced the Boyce-Codd form, which is an enhanced Third Normal Form. Subsequent research has produced Fourth and Fifth Normal Forms; we will briefly discuss these, but to most designers, they are only of academic interest.

So what are we trying to achieve with normalization? The techniques are designed to ensure that your database has the following characteristics.

- All attributes are atomic (indivisible).

- There are no repeating fields.

- There are no partial key dependencies.

- All nonkey dependencies are removed.

The process of normalization is shown in Figure 5.6. Each phase will be described in the sections that follow.

FIGURE 5.6:

The Normalization process

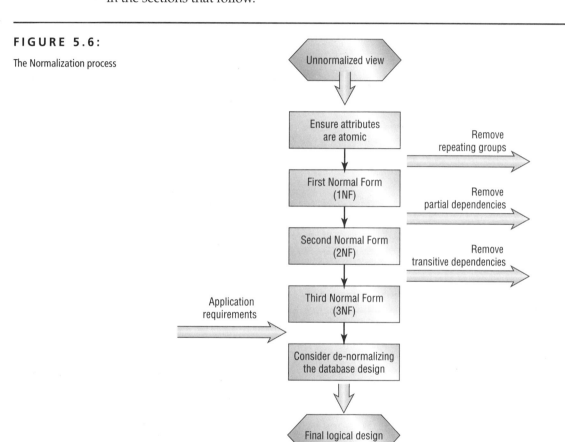

Examples of the desirable database characteristics will make them much easier to understand. We will take the video store example in which the owners want us to set up a small database to track the tapes. In practice, if you go through the process of producing Entity-Relationship diagrams, you should have a relatively normalized database to start from, but for this example, just about every mistake that could be made has been made.

The owner of the video store has set up the data in an Excel spreadsheet. Microsoft unofficially considers Excel to be the most commonly used database. However, its ease of use encourages some pretty sloppy design as you can see in Figure 5.7. One example of this poor design is that each video copy of a movie has the same duplicated information, which makes maintenance difficult (such as if the price changes, you have to find all copies and update them). Another problem is that the actors are in three columns, making it difficult to run queries.

FIGURE 5.7:

An initial logical design for the Movie database

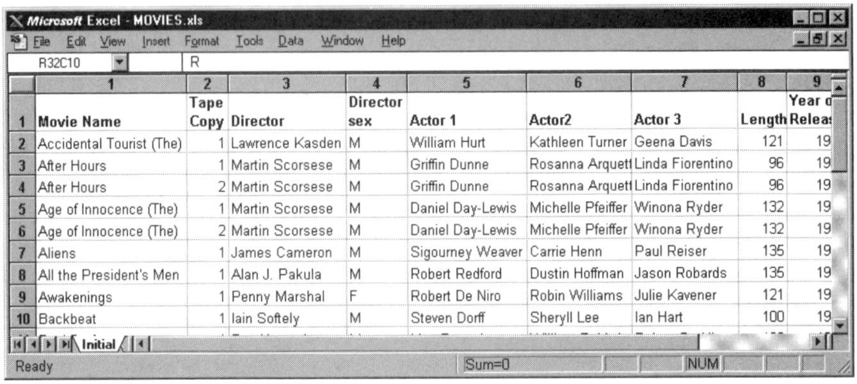

	1	2	3	4	5	6	7	8	9
1	Movie Name	Tape Copy	Director	Director sex	Actor 1	Actor2	Actor 3	Length	Year o Releas
2	Accidental Tourist (The)	1	Lawrence Kasden	M	William Hurt	Kathleen Turner	Geena Davis	121	19
3	After Hours	1	Martin Scorsese	M	Griffin Dunne	Rosanna Arquett	Linda Fiorentino	96	19
4	After Hours	2	Martin Scorsese	M	Griffin Dunne	Rosanna Arquett	Linda Fiorentino	96	19
5	Age of Innocence (The)	1	Martin Scorsese	M	Daniel Day-Lewis	Michelle Pfeiffer	Winona Ryder	132	19
6	Age of Innocence (The)	2	Martin Scorsese	M	Daniel Day-Lewis	Michelle Pfeiffer	Winona Ryder	132	19
7	Aliens	1	James Cameron	M	Sigourney Weaver	Carrie Henn	Paul Reiser	135	19
8	All the President's Men	1	Alan J. Pakula	M	Robert Redford	Dustin Hoffman	Jason Robards	135	19
9	Awakenings	1	Penny Marshal	F	Robert De Niro	Robin Williams	Julie Kavener	121	19
10	Backbeat	1	Iain Softely	M	Steven Dorff	Sheryll Lee	Ian Hart	100	19

With only a few video tapes to look after, the system works fine, and cutting and pasting keeps the data straight. However, the more videos we put into the spreadsheet, the closer we get to chaos.

Ensure Attributes Are Atomic

When normalizing your database design, you should first review each attribute to ensure it is *atomic*. This term refers to an attribute that can't be split up without losing its meaning. Although ensuring atomicity is not strictly a normalization function, it is worth considering because it is working toward the same end: a more functional and flexible design. One example of designing your attributes so that they are atomic is with the actors' and directors' names. The video-store design in Figure 5.7 shows names represented in one field, containing the first, last, and maybe middle name of an actor or director. Although you do not have to, you could consider splitting the names into two or more fields, such as first_name, last_name, and title. Without this step, it will be difficult, for example, to sort on the last_name.

Attributes containing more than one piece of information can also cause problems; there is a tendency to design codes so that they cover multiple attributes.

For example, a Human Resources department may have codes for the status of each employee, such as those shown in Table 5.2.

TABLE 5.2: An Example Of a Badly Conceived Code Table

Code	Description
FTT	Full Time, Temporary
FTR	Full Time, Regular
PTT	Part Time, Temporary
PTR	Part Time, Regular
CON	Contractor

You can easily design these codes into your database, but how do you produce a listing of all the full-time staff? Where do contractors come in? The problem with this layout is that codes have been created without a thought as to how they will fit into a database. For a paper-based system, they work well, but unfortunately, two pieces of information exist for each code. The code describes whether someone is full time or part time, and it describes whether they are a regular staff member or temporary. A contractor code has been added to extend an already poor system.

Keep aware of situations like this, and split them up into two or more fields (in this case "Full Time/Part Time," "Temporary/Regular," and perhaps another field for "On Contract"). Each field then means just one thing, and you can search and sort without problems.

This move toward atomic attributes is a move toward simplicity. You will also come across it in your Visual Basic programs when you are tempted to use one variable to mean more than one thing. I must admit to a great temptation to code-numbering schemes that have some built-in meaning to certain ranges. For example, it is easy to modify an existing application with a variable that is always positive so that a negative value means something a little different. A simple example might be passing a key value to a procedure to delete the row from the database. If you pass a negative value, it means delete the key and all its child rows. This is usually the fastest way to make the change in an application because you do not have to add any new control parameters, but it will mean the most headaches for the future.

TIP	Do not split the fields up more than you have to. You should split fields only to the level that the kind of functionality you want is reached. If you know you will never sort on "last name," then you could keep the name as one field. You would probably never split up an address so that the street and street number were separate, unless you were creating a geographical database.

First Normal Form (1NF)

First Normal Form requires us to remove any repeating fields or groups of fields. In fact, "pure" relational databases discourage any object with its own structure. In the video-store example, it is quickly apparent that each film has two actors. What happens when you want to add another actor? Add another column? Then another and another? In a simple Excel situation this may work, but what if you wanted to search for all the films starring your favorite actor? You would have to search each relevant column of each record, while your query gets more complicated and less suitable to a report generator producing it. Another factor to think about is the wasted space when a film has less actors than the number allowed for in the database.

What we need to do is remove the repeating columns and move them to another table. Let's call this table *Actors*. For the moment, we are going to assume that the film name uniquely identifies the actual film so use the name as the key to the Actors table. Figure 5.8 shows the Movies table without the repeating columns.

FIGURE 5.8:

The Video Store database design with repeating columns removed (1NF)

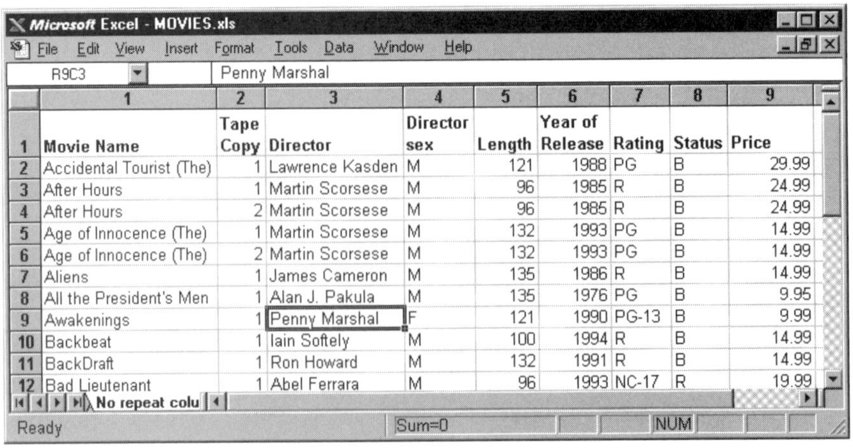

	1	2	3	4	5	6	7	8	9
1	Movie Name	Tape Copy	Director	Director sex	Length	Year of Release	Rating	Status	Price
2	Accidental Tourist (The)	1	Lawrence Kasden	M	121	1988	PG	B	29.99
3	After Hours	1	Martin Scorsese	M	96	1985	R	B	24.99
4	After Hours	2	Martin Scorsese	M	96	1985	R	B	24.99
5	Age of Innocence (The)	1	Martin Scorsese	M	132	1993	PG	B	14.99
6	Age of Innocence (The)	2	Martin Scorsese	M	132	1993	PG	B	14.99
7	Aliens	1	James Cameron	M	135	1986	R	B	14.99
8	All the President's Men	1	Alan J. Pakula	M	135	1976	PG	B	9.95
9	Awakenings	1	Penny Marshal	F	121	1990	PG-13	B	9.99
10	Backbeat	1	Iain Softely	M	100	1994	R	B	14.99
11	BackDraft	1	Ron Howard	M	132	1991	R	B	14.99
12	Bad Lieutenant	1	Abel Ferrara	M	96	1993	NC-17	R	19.99

It is really a restriction (some say a shortcoming) of SQL and relational theory that repeating columns are not allowed. In many cases, data is repetitive, and we have to artificially modify the information to a form that fits the database. A case in point is the entering of Visual Basic class objects into a table. An object may contain one or more collections. To put the collection in a table, we must deconstruct the object and place it among separate tables. To recover the object, we must reconstruct it into the relevant object.

This problem has been solved with object-oriented databases, which can easily represent collections of data just as Visual Basic does. However, object-oriented databases come with their own set of problems. Oracle8 has introduced an object-relational approach that adds some object-oriented capabilities to the relational database structure, but at present, these are not directly available to the Visual Basic developer.

NOTE   Oracle8 now supports repeating columns in the new complex datatypes: Nested Tables and VARRAY.

If you do decide to implement a database design with repeating columns, you will at least be able to deal with the columns in Visual Basic. Although SQL, before Oracle8, has no way of handling an array of attributes, if you read the data into a Visual Basic Recordset, then you can access the fields with an index. We shall discuss how to do this step in Chapter 14, *Data Access Objects*.

If you want to represent an array in a table, it is best to set up one column for each dimension in the array and one column (or more) for the data values (see Figure 5.9). To retrieve the data, simply select with the appropriate subscripts. Although this method will work, you should find an alternative because a table is not an ideal design or implementation.

FIGURE 5.9:

Using a table to represent an array

X	Y	Value
1	1	25
1	2	15
2	2	0

Array(1,1) = 25
Array(1,2) = 15

A final concern regarding the removal of repeating columns is how to produce a report with the data headings going across the page; for example, you want monthly sales figures with the months across the page. Unfortunately, Oracle does not have a cross-tabulation function, so the best options are to put the data in array format in VB code, put it in a stored procedure, or use a report generator that can do this.

Repeating Columns in Real Life

In text books on database modeling, the most popular example of repeating columns is that of Invoices and Line_Items in an invoicing system. In this circumstance, splitting the Invoices up from the Line_Items (a master/detail relationship) is the best thing to do. You will not know how many Line_Items there will be for each Invoice and making room for a high number wastes space in the majority of situations. I should also mention that relational databases have *no* support for handling repeating columns even if you do include them.

But there are cases where you will want to consider them. There is nothing inherently *wrong* with repeating columns as a concept, it's just that the relational model does not handle them well. One situation I have encountered a few times is one where I have to create a database to hold hourly data, with a different value for each hour. Do we normalize the data so that we have one row for each hour, as shown below?

Date	Hour	Value
12/01/98	1	101
12/01/98	2	105
12/01/98	3	116

Or do we put all hours of the day on one row as shown below?

Date	Hour1	Hour2	Hour3	Hour4	etc.
12/01/98	101	105	116	116	
12/02/98	105	106	108	120	
12/02/98	206	206	205	NULL	

Another alternative is to use an object-oriented database that allows structured data. In these situations, some data attributes are not hourly data, and you would see those in a header entity.

Continued on next page

My initial work was with a normalized database. It allowed me to store other information for each hour, such as the user name, the time-stamp of the last update, and a reference to a comments table. From a design point of view, the normalized approach is the best way to go. If you need to collect data more often than once an hour, it is a much more flexible technique. In fact, if you store the data as start time and stop time, instead of hour number, the design is even better, as seen below.

Date	Start	Stop	Value
12/01/98	0	1	101
12/01/98	1	2	105
12/01/98	2	6	116

It is up to you to decide whether you can store the data and time together or separately.

But offset against this improved design is the performance penalty you have to take. Though every case is different, I noticed that it took about twice as long to retrieve the data from a normalized table compared with using a design that kept all the hours together in one record. These are the kinds of decisions you have to make carefully.

As a further note on this topic, if you have a database that tracks data on the basis of time of the day, you have to be prepared for the switch to daylight savings time and back. The best way is to store time in Universal Time (or GMT), though I have successfully stored data as a 25-hour day, allowing for the extra hour. I have even seen some commercial systems ignore the problem entirely, perhaps on the basis that you are not losing *much* data!

NOTE With First Normal Form we have moved from one table (Videos) to two: Videos and Actors.

Second Normal Form (2NF)

To understand the Second Normal Form, we must understand keys. A key is one or more fields that we can use to identify the record. (They do not have to be unique—we shall discuss unique *candidate* keys later on.) When more than one field is combined to create a key, it is called a *composite* key. These fields do not have to be next to each other.

In our video-store example, the most obvious key for the videos is the film name combined with the copy number. With these two fields we can identify any video in our entire stock. You will notice that some of the nonkey fields depend on this entire key, such as date of acquisition and status, while other nonkey fields, such as release year and length, depend only on the film itself. When the attributes depend on only part of the key, this is called a *partial-key dependency*.

Second Normal Form says that we should have no partial-key dependencies. In the video-store example, the date of release and length depend only on part of the entire key: the film name. To conform to 2NF, we must remove these fields to another table, which we will call Movies (see Figure 5.10). The Actors table is already in this form because that is the way we created it.

FIGURE 5.10:

Partial-key dependencies are removed to produce 2NF

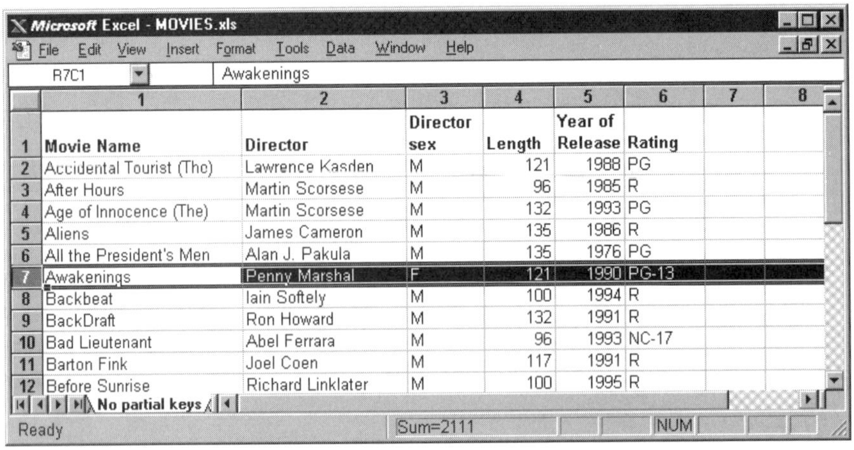

Microsoft Excel - MOVIES.xls

	1	2	3	4	5	6	7	8
	Movie Name	Director	Director sex	Length	Year of Release	Rating		
1	Movie Name	Director	Director sex	Length	Year of Release	Rating		
2	Accidental Tourist (The)	Lawrence Kasden	M	121	1988	PG		
3	After Hours	Martin Scorsese	M	96	1985	R		
4	Age of Innocence (The)	Martin Scorsese	M	132	1993	PG		
5	Aliens	James Cameron	M	135	1986	R		
6	All the President's Men	Alan J. Pakula	M	135	1976	PG		
7	Awakenings	Penny Marshal	F	121	1990	PG-13		
8	Backbeat	Iain Softely	M	100	1994	R		
9	BackDraft	Ron Howard	M	132	1991	R		
10	Bad Lieutenant	Abel Ferrara	M	96	1993	NC-17		
11	Barton Fink	Joel Coen	M	117	1991	R		
12	Before Sunrise	Richard Linklater	M	100	1995	R		

No partial keys   Sum=2111   NUM

Time-Dependent Data

One of the more interesting design problems involves how to handle data that is dependent on time. The example that springs to mind is a stock market–type system in which the price of a commodity can change at any time, but one and only one price applies to your purchase request.

There are, in fact, two separate problems here. The first is that you must keep a local copy of the price on the purchase order because it is going to be almost impossible to find it later on. This is typically done in all purchasing systems because product prices can always change.

The second problem of storing a historical record of the changes is more complex because we have to set up a new table to hold the historical records. We shall see how to get a value for a specific date from this table in Chapter 7, *Queries*. This step is not the simplest of queries, so storing the current price in another table usually gives a performance gain.

NOTE

With Second Normal Form, we have moved from two to three tables: Videos, Actors, and Movies.

Third Normal Form (3NF)

The final form used is the Third Normal Form, and it can be a little more difficult to understand. Technically, all the *transitive dependencies* are removed. To put it simply, we must avoid the situation where changing one nonkey field means that we must change another nonkey field. Another way of looking at it is that every nonkey field must depend entirely on the whole primary key and nothing else.

In our example, we have the gender of the director in the same record as the director. The Gender column is dependent on the Director field, not on the Movie field, so it does not belong in the table. For a 3NF design, we need to take the fields that describe the director out of the table and put them in the Participant table along with a description of their role (see Figure 5.11).

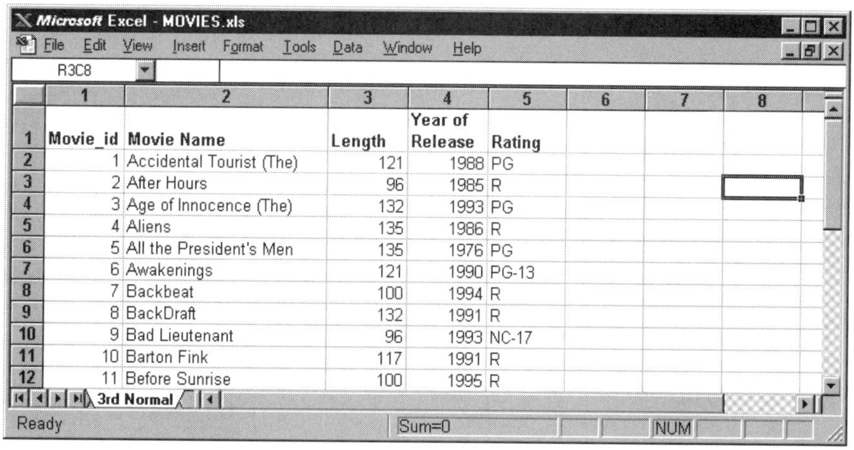

	1	2	3	4	5	6	7	8
1	Movie_id	Movie Name	Length	Year of Release	Rating			
2	1	Accidental Tourist (The)	121	1988	PG			
3	2	After Hours	96	1985	R			
4	3	Age of Innocence (The)	132	1993	PG			
5	4	Aliens	135	1986	R			
6	5	All the President's Men	135	1976	PG			
7	6	Awakenings	121	1990	PG-13			
8	7	Backbeat	100	1994	R			
9	8	BackDraft	132	1991	R			
10	9	Bad Lieutenant	96	1993	NC-17			
11	10	Barton Fink	117	1991	R			
12	11	Before Sunrise	100	1995	R			

FIGURE 5.11: Removing the transitive dependencies, such as the Director field, leads us to 3NF

NOTE

With Third Normal Form, we have moved from three to four tables: Videos, Actors, Movies, and Directors.

Storing Derived Data

If you store any values in your database that are calculated or otherwise derived from another value, then your design will not meet 3NF. However, circumstances arise in which you need to do precisely that. This situation will normally occur when it takes too many server resources to repeatedly calculate a value (usually a total of several detail rows); however, it will also occur whenever the derived value might become impossible to re-create at a later date.

From the performance point of view, almost any master/detail relationship would be a candidate for storing a derived value. In the Movie database where we have a one-to-many relationship between the movies and videos entities, we could perhaps store the total number of videos in the movies entity. This is something that should be well thought out at the design stage. Although it can be added at a later date, this sort of derived value does need to be maintained so that the details that constitute it are always in agreement with the summary value.

In the Video Store database, there will probably not be much call for knowing the total number of video copies of a movie, but in other circumstances, this decision can become critical to performance. The actual improvement you get is difficult to assess as it depends on how often the derived value is updated, how often it is read, and how many records need to be read to calculate the value.

Higher Normalization Techniques

The first three Normal Forms remove most of the redundancies from your design. Research in the 1980s led to several other techniques, which include the Boyce-Codd Normal Form (an enhanced form of 3NF that actually removes all transitive dependencies) and the Fourth (eliminates multivalued dependencies in tables) and Fifth Normal Forms. If you spend most of your time designing databases, then you should research the techniques; however, the situations in which you need to use the higher Normal Forms become progressively less common.

Simplifying the Design

Now that you have completed the normalization phase, we should now review the design to see whether we can simplify it or improve its flexibility. In the first part of the logical-design phase when identifying any data dependencies, we saw that the Actors and Directors tables are very similar in content. We created new tables called Participants for the individuals and Participant_Assignment for their roles in the movies. Despite having the same number of tables, we have significantly improved its flexibility in that it can hold more information about the assignments and can easily hold different roles on the film.

NOTE   At this point, we will add in a Customer table, which was not part of the original spreadsheet. We have now ended up with five tables in our design: Videos, Movies, Participants, Participant_Assignment, and Customer.

De-normalizing the Database

By taking the database design to Third Normal Form, we have moved from one to five tables. We have gone a long way toward a "pure" design, but this could be at the expense of performance. Ideally, any time you select data from the database, you should not have to reference more than three or four tables. Any more is a sign that performance could be suffering, and queries are becoming more complicated.

The solution to the performance problem is to consider undoing one or more normalizing steps or "de-normalizing" the database. This should be done with care, of course. One area you may want to look at is code tables, especially if you use several of them. Using the full name instead of a code might be worth the expense of losing storage space.

Another possibility for improved performance is to use the techniques developed for data warehousing although the idea has been around for years. You can produce a new table or separate database with everything de-normalized. This de-normalized approach should be used only for decision support systems; updates are only done to the base tables, and then every night the de-normalized database can be reloaded with data derived from the updated base tables. This approach is often good enough for reports. You can even maintain the derived data tables in real time, although you must make sure data consistency is maintained.

De-normalizing a database is not something to take lightly. You should be prepared to support your decision to create a database that is not even in First Normal Form. You should document your Third Normal Form and add reasons for de-normalizing it. The main reasons will be flexibility and performance, but you should get some corroboration from tests you have done.

Using Keys

Now that we have our database in normalized form (and in five times as many tables!), we can look at how we distinguish each row of a table. Every row in a relational table must be different, and there should be at least one attribute that can uniquely identify the row. These attributes are called *candidate* keys. Occasionally, you must combine more than one attribute, and this is called a *composite* key (see Figure 5.12).

FIGURE 5.12:

Table design showing candidate and composite keys

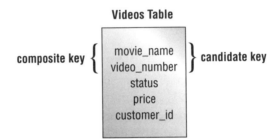

At this stage of the video-store design, we should look for all the candidate keys for the tables. For the Participants table, this could be the name of the actor or director, though in the next section we will cover the reasons for not using a name. In the case of the Videos table we have to decide whether we want to use the movie_name and the video number. A better alternative is to use a unique key for the video and another unique key for the movie.

Primary Keys

When we review all of the candidate keys, we want to select the most appropriate one for the *primary* key. A primary key for a table uniquely identifies each row in a table and cannot be null (that is, it must have a value). Oracle tables can have only one primary key defined, but we can define *unique* keys for the other candidate keys. These unique keys are allowed to be null, but in practice, you will often define them so that they are not null.

TIP   You should design and implement a primary key for every table. Although it may not always be used in queries, Visual Basic can only create updatable Recordsets against tables with primary keys.

Surrogate Keys

What if you cannot find a unique key suitable to be a primary key? This happens more often than you may think, especially when you want to allow for a change in the primary-key value. For example, what would happen if we had a database set up in which the actor's first and last names constitute the primary key. We end up with that value used in every table that refers to the actor. If that actor's name changed, what would we do?

Another problem is that of uniqueness. You have probably noticed this one already: the film name is fine for a key as long as it is unique, but that would rely on Hollywood never doing a remake. We can combine the name with the year, but even then the name is not necessarily unique. And to make matters worse, what if more than one actor has the same name?

> **WARNING** Names are usually a poor choice for a primary key, because they may change and because it is difficult to ensure that they are and will be unique.

One technique that can be used to address these problems is to assign *surrogate* keys. A surrogate key is a unique key we make up and is independent of the data (see Figure 5.13). You will normally use it for a primary key. This technique is used all the time in Microsoft Access with counterfields as well as in a different (and more unwieldy) form available in Oracle: we use sequence generators to provide the value for the primary key. I have had enough primary keys that change that I now make extensive use of sequences. We will deal with them in the next chapter because they are a physical implementation issue.

FIGURE 5.13:

Defining a surrogate key, in this case *movie_id*

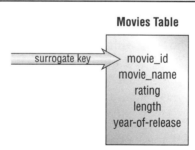

You should also realize there are a few disadvantages with surrogate keys. These include the difficulty of locating a record if you do not know what the key is (there is no way to find it from the data, and you will have to search the whole table); in this case, you may have to put a nonunique index on that attribute. For example, if we are using surrogate keys on the Participants table and this is used as the primary key, then you may also want to put an index on the movie_name attribute so that you can quickly look up personal information. The indexes will also be discussed in the next chapter.

A final problem with surrogate keys is when you have to merge data from two different sources (maybe you are copying the data to a data warehouse or perhaps your company is being merged with another). If two comparable tables use surrogate keys, then there may again be the risk of key duplication.

> **NOTE** Surrogate keys are a commonly used device, even though many designers may never have heard of them. For example, Microsoft Access encourages their use by making the Counter field available. This type of field is simpler to use than creating your own key and indexing it.

Despite any small problems that surrogate keys may have, they have sufficient advantages to recommend them in most situations. When we move on to implementing the database in the next chapter, we will create surrogate keys for all tables. These keys will be used as the foreign-key references in any related tables.

Foreign Keys

A *foreign* key is a reference from a child or detail table (such as the Videos table) back to a row in a parent or master table (such as the Movies table). The table's status as a parent or child is really determined by which side of the one-to-many relationship it is on. (The parent is the "one," the child is the "many.") The child identifies its parent by containing a foreign key, which is an attribute that ties the row in the child with a comparable attribute in the parent table, which must be a primary key. For example, the Videos table should contain a foreign key that holds a value equal to the primary key of the Movies table. It is strange to think about it this way, but a parent object has no idea who is claiming to be its children. The children have to make themselves known.

Oracle has a special constraint to check the validity of this claim. If the claimed parent does not exist, the foreign-key constraint (also called the referential-integrity constraint) will not allow that record to be saved. Conversely, if you try to delete a parent of an existing child, the same constraint will not let you do it. We will cover foreign keys in much more detail in the next chapter.

Automating the Design Process

Up to this point we have dealt with the design as a manual process. You can use any of the desktop tools at your disposal, such as spreadsheets and drawing tools. I believe this is the best way to learn the techniques. However, if you do much design work, you may want to get hold of a tool specifically designed to assist you. These tools are usually called CASE tools (Computer Aided Software Engineering). We are also talking about a significant investment in software.

For users who have purchased the Enterprise Edition of Visual Basic 6, you have access to the Database Designer and Database Diagrams. We will look at this product in the next chapter; however, Figure 5.14 shows you an example of the Video Store database that you can easily obtain with the Database Designer.

FIGURE 5.14:

The relationships in the video_store database as seen through VB6's Data Diagram

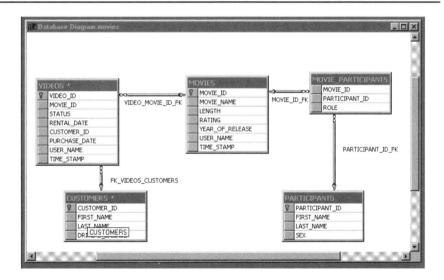

Summary

This chapter has covered the first two steps of database design: conceptual and logical designs. These form the core of data modeling. There are many different ways to do these steps; we have dealt with relational modeling throughout and as a result there is some overlap between the conceptual and logical phases. In practice, the two phases aid each other, and you do not end up duplicating effort, you just end up with a reinforced design.

Whether you start off with spreadsheets or a high-end CASE tool such as Oracle Designer 2000, the important point is to make sure you carry out the design. The investment in time that you make at the design stages will be more than repaid down the road after implementation.

CHAPTER
SIX

6

Implementing a Database

- Create Tablespaces for Your Database.

- Determine the Data Types from the Entity Attributes and Create the Associated Tables.

- Specify Any Constraints for Design.

- Create Any Indexes for Performance Purposes.

- Create Sequences to Provide Unique Values for Key Columns.

- Add Specific Columns to Tables to Assist Auditing Purposes.

- Review Other Schema Objects.

- Create User Access.

- Use Microsoft Database Designer.

Now that you have completed your design work outlined in the previous chapter, you are ready to move on to implementing the physical design of the database. You will be tempted to move straight to this step without understanding the two previous phases: *conceptual* and *logical* design. However, I have invariably found that if you take the short route and skip the design work, it will come back to haunt you.

The main benefit of preparing the groundwork before reaching this stage is to ensure that your database is *designed,* not thrown together. Initially, it will show your client or employer that you have done a professional job; a little bit of paper work can go a long way. However, the main point is that once designed, the physical implementation will be that much better. It will perform better, match the actual business needs more accurately, and in the long run, be cheaper and easier to maintain.

In the previous chapters, we saw the concepts of what constitutes an Oracle database as well as how one is designed. In this chapter, we will implement the Video Store database for which we have already done a conceptual and logical design. Although the design is very simple, the techniques apply to every database you will deal with.

There is more involved in the physical implementation of an Oracle database than you may think, especially if you come from a file-based background, such as Microsoft Access or FoxPro. It is not enough to understand how to add file types to a table with a button click: if you do not follow a deployment strategy, you will end up with a poorly performing database that constantly needs maintenance.

However, these tasks will probably be handled by a database administrator working closely with you, especially in a larger organization where everything is more closely controlled. As your experience grows, you will most likely be given more freedom to control these things yourself. Outlined below are some general steps you should think about when implementing your database.

- Create tablespaces for your database. These are the first logical structures you must set up and assign the physical disk space to hold the rest of the database structures.

- Determine the data types for your tables from the entity attributes that you developed in the conceptual design, and create the associated tables.

- Specify any constraints that your design calls for.

- Create any indexes you need for performance purposes.

- Create any sequences you need to provide unique values for key columns.

- Add specific columns to your table to assist auditing purposes.

- Review other schema objects that you may want to implement.

- Create any users who need access to your data, and grant all necessary privileges for them.

- Use Microsoft Database Designer.

Now, let's examine each of these steps.

Creating a Tablespace

In Chapter 2, we introduced the concept of a tablespace, the largest logical data structure in an Oracle database. Tablespaces store database objects and consist of at least one physical file for each tablespace. You can add more files or make the files grow as required. Tablespaces contain one or more segments, each of which contains a table, index, cluster, or rollback segment or temporary segment.

Tablespaces are used to separate different classes of data; you will probably want to set up one or more tablespaces for each application using the database (see Figure 6.1). The database design should account for the types or classes of data that are going to go into the database and where the best places are for each type. If this is the first time you have used an Oracle database and it is a pilot project, then you should perhaps set up two application tablespaces: one for the data and one for the indexes. When you add new tables, ensure that if these tables belong to a separate application, they are placed in a separate tablespace.

The advantages of using separate tablespaces to segregate your data include the ability to put data on separate disk drives for performance reasons. But often overlooked is the ability to take a tablespace offline while the rest of the database is up and running. For example, if the disk containing the accounting tablespace has failed, we can bring the database up without that tablespace. Try to think of these things beforehand: it is much harder to change the database when it is in production and filling fast with data.

FIGURE 6.1:

Using tablespaces to store database objects

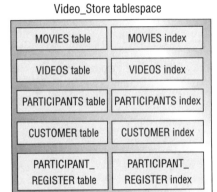

Video_Store tablespace

MOVIES table	MOVIES index
VIDEOS table	VIDEOS index
PARTICIPANTS table	PARTICIPANTS index
CUSTOMER table	CUSTOMER index
PARTICIPANT_ REGISTER table	PARTICIPANT_ REGISTER index

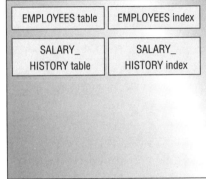

Human Resources tablespace

| EMPLOYEES table | EMPLOYEES index |
| SALARY_ HISTORY table | SALARY_ HISTORY index |

NOTE   Access to tablespaces, like everything in Oracle, is governed by privileges and quotas. We shall discuss this topic later in the chapter in the section "Setting Privileges."

If you have a new user ID, you may not have access to any tablespaces, or more likely, they will be reserved for specific applications. To try out the examples in this chapter, you need access to at least one tablespace, but you should take care not to create any database objects in the SYSTEM tablespace. An experienced DBA would not allow you to create data here anyway, so you will need to get your own tablespace.

To create your own tablespace, you must use the following CREATE TABLE-SPACE statement:

```
CREATE TABLESPACE video_store
    DATAFILE 'c:\database\test.db' SIZE 2M;
```

This command is about as simple as you can get. It identifies

- The tablespace name, which in this case is Video_Store.

- A file that will provide the physical storage; this file will be created automatically. Note that you should enclose file names in single quotes, such as 'c:\database\test.dbf'.

- The file size, which in this case is 2MB. (You can use M for megabytes and K for kilobytes.) Remember to allow space for any indexes as well as expansion beyond the segment's initial extents.

When you create the tablespace, you are not restricted to one file: you can include as many data files as you want in one command, such as

```
CREATE TABLESPACE video_store
   DATAFILE 'c:\database\test.dbf' SIZE 1M REUSE,
  'c:\database\test2.dbf' SIZE 1M REUSE ;
```

In the example, we have defined two data files for the tablespace. We have also used the REUSE option, which will cause Oracle to reuse a data file of the same name if one already exists.

Defining two files is particularly useful when your storage capability is restricted, because you can put the files on different disks; however, you should generally avoid doing this process because it can be a maintenance headache. In times gone by, adding a second file to the tablespace was the only way to get around the problem when a data file became filled, and it is still a viable alternative. To get around this problem, you can now use the AUTOEXTEND option:

```
CREATE TABLESPACE video_store
   DATAFILE 'c:\database\test.db' SIZE 1M AUTOEXTEND ON;
```

WARNING   The AUTOEXTEND option is an attractive but dangerous way to define tablespaces because you lose control of the data file size. The file may expand to consume the whole disk. We will see how to limit the increase a little later in this section.

A decision that you have to make at this point is just how much space you need. Unfortunately this is not a trivial decision, and there is no easy answer. You need to review how many tables and indexes you will be assigning to the tablespace and what their storage requirements are. You need to plan for expansion because any storage area that is dynamically increased when the call comes for more space is inherently less efficient than when planned well from the beginning. If you do get into a storage space problem and end up with a fragmented storage area, you will have to consider exporting the data, recreating the tablespace with a more suitable storage specification, and then importing the data back. This will necessitate the database being down for a length of time depending on how much data you have. When databases grow large, it can take many hours to do an import, so think first!

Once you have determined how large your tablespaces need to be, you next have to grant users the privilege to use it. You do this with the ALTER USER command to give a specific or unlimited quota (the right to use a certain amount of the tablespace storage) to a user as follows:

```
ALTER USER nick QUOTA 500K ON video_store ;
```

or

```
ALTER USER nick QUOTA UNLIMITED ON video_store ;
```

Useful Commands

To list all the tablespaces accessible within your schema, you can use the following command:

```
SELECT tablespace_name FROM  user_tablespaces ;
```

To find the amount of unused space left in your tablespace, use the following command:

```
SELECT SUM (bytes) FROM dba_free_space
  WHERE tablespace_name='TEST';
```

Not all users will have access to this dictionary view, but there is another view called user_free_space to review the objects in your schema.

Optional Parameters

With a test database, the CREATE TABLESPACE command will work fine. However, when you set up a production database, you need to be aware of the optional parameters you can specify. In particular, you should review the following AUTOEXTEND option, which allows your file sizes to grow within operating-system limits and availability.

AUTOEXTEND   The data-file name that this parameter follows can be extended in size automatically (up to operating-system limits or to a value you can define with a MAXSIZE clause). This clause also allows you to switch this feature ON or OFF and define the extent size when the data file is increased. Note that this does not extend quotas.

DEFAULT STORAGE   This parameter specifies the default storage parameters for any object that is created in this tablespace, such as tables and indexes. Generally, you will want to define the storage parameters for each object individually because they will have wildly different storage requirements, but this clause can make it easier to manage if you have many objects with the same requirements. Note that if you omit this clause then the Oracle system defaults will apply.

ONLINE (default)   The tablespace will be immediately available to users.

OFFLINE   The tablespace will initially be unavailable to users.

PERMANENT (default)   The tablespace will be used for permanent objects, such as tables.

TEMPORARY   The tablespace will be used to store temporary objects only, typically as a work area for sorting.

REUSE   This keyword can appear after the DATAFILE clause. If you specify it, then any existing file will be reused (otherwise a new file is created).

TIP

When you set up a real application, you will want to have at least two tablespaces available to you: one for data, the other for indexes. Also consider splitting different application areas, such as Accounting, Human Resources, and Engineering, into different tablespaces. If you leave it until your database grows, it will be much more difficult to split up. To move the tables to a different tablespace, you will have to either do an export and import of the tables or use the "CREATE TABLE AS SELECT *subquery*" command. Either way could take a substantial amount of time to move and re-create indexes, and that will mean these tables will be unavailable to users. It can be done, but it is much better to get it right the first time.

The following is an example of using these parameters to automatically increase the size of your files.

```
CREATE TABLESPACE video_store
    DATAFILE 'c:\database\test.db' SIZE 1M REUSE
    AUTOEXTEND ON MAXSIZE 10M
    OFFLINE ;
```

You will notice that this command also sets the new tablespace to an *offline* status. This means that it will not be available to users. To bring it online you use the ALTER TABLESPACE command shown in the next section.

Related Commands

If you want to remove a tablespace because, for example, you don't need it any longer or want to assign a larger file instead of adding a separate file, then you can drop a tablespace with

```
DROP TABLESPACE tablespace_name ;
```

To do this you should ensure that any segments, such as tables and indexes, have been removed first; however, if you are certain you will not remove anything that is still needed, then you can use

```
DROP TABLESPACE tablespace_name INCLUDING CONTENTS ;
```

NOTE   When you "drop" a tablespace, you are not deleting any files but just the logical structure applied to those files. If you want to remove the files as well, you will have to use operating-system commands.

If you want to alter tablespace properties to do things such as adding a new data file or taking a tablespace online or offline, then you use the following command.

```
ALTER TABLESPACE new_parameters ;
```

WARNING   If you drop a tablespace, an entry will appear in the alert log.

TIP   One technique to make use of when creating tablespaces is to set up one tablespace for large tables and one for small tables. If you look at any existing database, you will probably find you have many small tables, often for code tables or situations where there will never be many rows of data. There will probably also be fewer large tables. If you create separate tablespaces for each type and use an appropriate DEFAULT STORAGE clause, then you can ignore the storage parameters for the tables. In this way, the tables in any tablespace have uniform storage characteristics. We will deal with the STORAGE clause in the next section.

Creating a Table

Once you have set up a tablespace, you can now create the various schema objects in it, such as tables and indexes. You will need to get sufficient privileges to be able to create objects, including a quota. We'll discuss privileges in the "Setting Privileges" section in this chapter.

Assuming that you have the privileges, you may now start by creating one or more tables. In this chapter, we will discuss Oracle7 compatible objects, in particular, *relational* tables as opposed to *object* tables that are now available in Oracle8. Your relational tables have hopefully been designed as entities with attributes. If you are not familiar with these terms, you should review Chapter 5, *Database Design*.

TIP   A relational table is one that has rows of columns, and each column has one particular data type. An object table is similar except that the columns can contain complex or structured data. There are some interesting tools in Visual Basic 6 to handle tables. We will see these at the end of the chapter.

At this point, you need to review the data types that you have designed and decide how you are going to implement them in an Oracle table.

NOTE   The variety of data types in Oracle has increased with Oracle8, but the selection is not particularly rich in comparison with what is available from some other database vendors. On the positive side, the limited choice means that there are limited decisions to make, which is always a benefit.

If you choose to purchase the Objects Option (which is an optional package from Oracle), Oracle8 supplements the normal relational tables that you see in every RDBMS with object tables. Rather than being restricted to columns that contain a single data type, object tables can contain columns with user-defined data types that simulate an object.

Oracle Data Types

There is an obvious temptation to think in terms of Visual Basic data types when you are setting up a table. Although thinking this way will not hurt conceptually (you will, after all, be retrieving these tables into Visual Basic variables anyway), it should not become an overriding factor. Visual Basic has an extremely rich set of data types, whereas Oracle data types are much more restrictive. However, when your Visual Basic program does read the data from Oracle, the information can be interpreted in different ways. For example, a one-digit table column can be used to store and retrieve a Boolean variable.

A table consists of a series of rows, each of which are made up of columns. Oracle7 is restricted to 254 columns, but Oracle8 can have 1,000 columns, which should be enough for most of your requirements! You must first decide how you want to convert the designed-attribute types into the available database types. Using the movies application, you would look at the entities and make a decision about what data types are best suited to the attributes and how large you expect the data values to get. Figure 6.2 gives an example of how this is done for the Movies table.

FIGURE 6.2:

Turning entities into tables

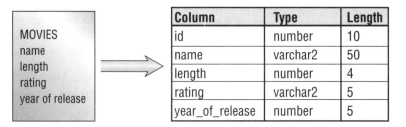

Column	Type	Length
id	number	10
name	varchar2	50
length	number	4
rating	varchar2	5
year_of_release	number	5

The tables represent the entities of the design whereas the columns represent the attributes. Each example of a particular entity is represented by a row in the table. Oracle's available data types are shown in Table 6.1.

TABLE 6.1: Data Types Available when Designing a Table in Oracle 7.*x*

Data Type	Description
CHAR (size)	Fixed-length strings of length *size*. They can be up to 255 bytes long, and the default length is 1.
DATE	General date and time field.
LONG	Variable-length character field up to 2GB in length.
LONG RAW	Variable-length binary data (such as graphics) up to 2GB in length.
RAW (size)	Binary data up to 2,000 bytes in length.

Continued on next page

TABLE 6.1 CONTINUED: Data Types Available when Designing a Table in Oracle 7.*x*

Data Type	Description
NUMBER (size)	Integer with *size* digits.
NUMBER (precision, scale)	Floating point number with precision digits before the decimal point and scale digits after.
VARCHAR2 (size)	Variable-length string of up to *size* characters long with a maximum of 2,000 bytes.
VARCHAR (size)	Same as VARCHAR2 but it is not recommended that you use it.

The most commonly used of these Oracle7 data types are NUMBER, VARCHAR2, and DATE. The only data types that have some restrictions are LONG and LONG RAW. These restrictions include

- You cannot index them.

- You can have only one LONG column per table.

- They cannot be used in SELECT subqueries or clauses, such as WHERE and ORDER BY.

In addition to the above data types, several new data types are available to Oracle8 users. Oracle8 has been designed for scalability: bigger everything is better. The new data types are designed to meet the modern need for larger binary files for sound, video, spatial, and other needs. These new data types are outlined in Table 6.2.

TABLE 6.2: Additional Data Types in Oracle8

Data Type	Description
BLOB	Binary data up to 4GB
CLOB	Single byte character data up to 4GB
NCLOB	Multibyte character code (e.g., Unicode) up to 4GB
BFILE	A reference to a file held external to the database, up to 4GB

These types of data are designed to accommodate the emerging need to store large graphics, video clips, and other multimedia data types.

Long Data Types

If you are going to make much use of large table columns, those over 2,000 bytes or containing raw data, you must be aware that there is no easy way to put data into them or to take it out. As a Visual Basic developer, you will have to resort to the **GetChunk** and **AppendChunk** methods that your data-access method provides. These methods send or retrieve data in "chunks," and you repeat the method until all the data is processed. You cannot send this data through a stored procedure. In fact, you will have to work with an updatable Recordset. A good design is to pull the long columns out of the table altogether and put them in their own table with an appropriate key. You might think of this as "overnormalizing," but there are distinct benefits, including the fact that these large fields will not be pulled into a query unless you want them to be as well as the fact that you can process the other columns with your normal methods (hopefully using stored procedures instead of updatable Recordsets). These tables can be kept in a separate tablespace.

Creating the Table at Last

Now you are finally ready to create a table. Remember from Chapter 2 that a table is a database object in your schema that can be thought of like a spreadsheet. It consists of rows and columns, with each row containing a description of an individual instance of the data, such as in our case, a movie or a video. Each column contains a different kind of data, each with a specific purpose; for example, the name of the movie or its length, which we assigned an appropriate name to. This concept can be directly tied into the creation of our Oracle table.

The simplified syntax for this is

```
CREATE TABLE table_name (
  column1_name data_type <constraint_information>,
 . . .
  repeat for each column
 . . .
) TABLESPACE tablespace_name
STORAGE storage_clause;
```

Each column is defined in turn and is followed by its data type and, optionally, a CONSTRAINT clause. Column definitions are separated by commas and surrounded as a whole by parentheses. The column definitions can be followed by optional parameters. The CONSTRAINT clause limits what data can be placed in the table columns and will be explored in the next section.

Now we take our logical design one entity at a time and turn each into a table. Each of the entity attributes must be changed into a column. It doesn't really matter which order the columns are put in, but you might want to make it a convention that the Key columns come at the beginning and perhaps any Auditing column, such as Time_Stamp or User_Name, come at the end. There are no rules about this, but a uniformity to your physical design can make working with tables much easier.

Once you have figured out the Oracle data type corresponding to each of your attributes, you can write down a script to create the table. An example script is shown in Listing 6.1. I've simplified this bare bones script to create the Movies table by leaving out any constraints, but it does cover the most commonly used optional parameters. We will cover constraints in the section called "Specifying Constraints."

Listing 6.1

```
CREATE TABLE movies (
  movie_id        NUMBER(10),
  movie_name      VARCHAR2(100),
  length          NUMBER(4),
  year_of_release NUMBER(4),
  rating          VARCHAR2(6))
TABLESPACE video_store ;
```

You can see from Listing 6.1 that some data types are easy to determine from the logical design (for example, variable-length character columns only need their maximum length figured out), but others may be a little more difficult. With key values, you will not go wrong with a large field. Up to 10 digits allow a billion records, but remember that among the "used" key values can be records that have been deleted as well as "lost" sequence numbers. A large key also gives you the freedom to fetch the sequence numbers at will without worrying about hitting the maximum value allowed for the key.

One thing you should make note of, when working with Visual Basic as the front end to your database, is that your database will inevitably grow large. If you design it for a smaller number, you may be tempted to develop your code working with an *integer variable* to hold key fields. When you reach over 32,767, you are going to get an overflow situation. Aim big and start off with *long* Visual Basic variable types.

Optional Parameters

Although the examples shown in the previous sections will work, it is important that you specify your requirements for your database in more detail. This step will transform your design from one that is thrown together to one that shows the thoughts of a well-planned design. If you don't think through your database requirements, your physical implementation will suffer.

To create a well-designed database, we must make use of the optional parameters for the CREATE TABLE statement. Listed below are a few of the more important ones. If nothing else, make it a habit to always give some thought to the storage requirements and to the tablespace where the table will be created.

Tablespace This parameter allows you to define in which tablespace you want to create the table. It will allow you to pick a tablespace for design reasons, such as spreading tables over separate disk drives for performance reasons or an application-related tablespace. Although you do not need to define the tablespace (Oracle will use your default tablespace if you leave it out), it is good practice to start using it. A good DBA will educate developers on fundamental database-design considerations.

Storage This parameter allows you to define the initial storage requirements for your table as the way the table can grow; if you omit a storage parameter, Oracle will use the tablespace defaults, which may not be ideal for your requirements. This parameter is covered in more detail below.

Default This parameter allows you to define a default value for a column if an INSERT statement does not provide one. It can be an actual value (such as 100), and it can also be an expression; unfortunately, it cannot be tied to a sequence number. However, this option can be used to set the user name and time stamp for auditing purposes (see the section "Audit Trails" later in this chapter).

NOTE   When creating tables, you can also specify the *AS subquery* clause. This clause lets you create a table that takes not only its column structure but also its data from a SELECT statement. In this case, we do not define any columns because that is done implicitly. An example of this is shown in Chapter 8, *Updating Your Database.*

Other parameters are available for performance tuning and require a deeper understanding of how segments are used. For a list of these parameters, you should check out the *Oracle SQL Reference* manual that ships with Oracle.

Displaying Table Information

To find out what columns are in any table, type

```
DESC table_name
```

To list the tables you have in your schema, use the following command:

```
SELECT table_name, tablespace_name FROM user_tables ;
```

Specifying the Storage Parameters

To accurately specify the storage parameters, you need to evaluate what your current storage needs are, estimate how these needs will grow, and then plan for this growth accordingly. When you are creating a database for test purposes, it probably does not matter how large the tables are. It is more important to be careful with your estimates when you set up a production database, because so many defaults seem to work well at first and because of the storage requirements.

Most techniques to estimate the storage space for a table involve a certain amount of experience and trial and error. If you have the luxury of setting up a prototype database with a sufficiently large amount of representative data, then you can monitor how much storage you have used (Oracle Enterprise Manager is a great tool for this) and make an intelligent guess about how the requirements may grow over the next few months or so. After the prototype stage, you can add up all the table requirements, add some leeway for unexpected volume growth and perhaps new tables, and then you have a better estimate for the tablespace.

The storage parameter not only applies to tables but also to indexes and clusters as well as rollback segments and snapshots. Oracle assigns space in *extents*, which are groups of contiguous data blocks. Before Oracle 7.3, the standard advice given was to store a table in fewer, larger extents. With Oracle 7.3 and later, this is less of an issue; you no longer have a limit to the maximum number of extents, although it is wise to have all of the extents on a tablespace the same size.

The storage parameter is in fact a clause containing several other optional parameters. If you remember from Chapter 2, *Oracle Database Architecture,* each object, such as a table, is held in a logical structure called a segment. Each of the storage parameters is a *segment attribute*. These parameters are listed below in Table 6.3.

TABLE 6.3: Storage Parameters

Parameter	Description
INITIAL	The initial storage allocation for the table in bytes (you can use K for Kilobytes and M for Megabytes).
NEXT	The size of the next extent when the table increases beyond the initial size, in bytes again.
MINEXTENTS	The minimum number of extents that can exist for the table. Ideally, it will be 1, indicating that you have created the initial extent large enough.
MAXEXTENTS	The maximum number of extents that your table can grow to. You can specify a number or use the keyword UNLIMITED to allow your table to grow as needed.
PCTINCREASE	Each time a new extent is added you can automatically increase the size of the most recent extent by the percentage value provided in this parameter. For example, if you specify a value of 100, then each extent added to the table segment will be 100 percent bigger than the previous one.

An example using all of the parameters listed in Table 6.3 is shown in Listing 6.2. The script in Listing 6.2 allows you to create the Movies table that includes all the storage parameters.

Listing 6.2

```
CREATE TABLE movies (
    movie_id        NUMBER(10),
    movie_name      VARCHAR2(100),
    length          NUMBER(4),
```

```
     year_of_release NUMBER(4),
      rating          VARCHAR2(6))
  TABLESPACE video_store
    STORAGE (
     INITIAL 50K
     NEXT   50K
     MINEXTENTS 1
     MAXEXTENTS 4
     PCTINCREASE 100) ;
```

Creating the table in this way specifies that initially 50KB of disk space will be allocated to the first extent of the table segment. Because the minimum number of extents is 1, only the first extent will be allocated. When the time comes for the table to grow beyond this first extent, a 50KB extent will be allocated for the second extent. All subsequent extents will be 100 percent larger than the previous one, so we will see the third being 100KB and the fourth being 200KB, as shown in Figure 6.3. The maximum number of extents is limited to 4 so no more will be created. In reality, of course, you will be using tables much bigger than the sizes shown here.

FIGURE 6.3:

Four extents assigned to the Video_Store tablespace

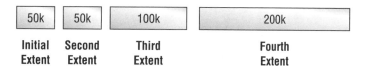

50k	50k	100k	200k
Initial Extent	**Second Extent**	**Third Extent**	**Fourth Extent**

Storage Parameter Hints

For the least amount of disk fragmentation, you should set PCTINCREASE = 0. For best usage, set the Initial extent to a large value, and plan to have no more than about four or five extents. Monitor the usage (the Oracle Enterprise Manager Performance Pack, which comes with the Oracle Enterprise Server and is available separately, is excellent for this use because you have all the information at your fingertips), and when it starts to get full, make the decision whether to extend or reorganize.

It is also a good idea to have all the tables in a tablespace use the same storage parameters. The easiest way to do this is to use the STORAGE clause when you create the tablespace instead of the table.

Continued on next page

Although you should have only a few extents, there is little advantage in specifying a small maximum because that will only restrict storage expansion if you have not estimated properly.

Related Commands

Once you have created a table, your work is not necessarily done. There are many times when you change your design for some reason, usually because the business has changed or you no longer need to keep certain types of data. There are other commands that are closely related to the CREATE TABLE statement that help you maintain your tables. If you no longer need a table, you can drop it with

```
DROP TABLE table_name ;
```

The ALTER TABLE command lets you add new columns, change the data type of existing columns, or add new optional parameters.

```
ALTER TABLE ADD (new_column, new_type) ;
ALTER TABLE MODIFY (existing_column, new_type) ;
ALTER TABLE
   new_parameters ;
```

The following example puts the command to use.

```
ALTER TABLE ADD (user_name VARCHAR2(30)) ;
```

Expect Changes

We all know that change is the only constant in this world, and the world of computers gets far more than its fair share of change. In the old days, this was a well-recognized fact. Making changes to a fixed-length, file-based system was horrendous, so designers would often create records longer than needed to allow for the inevitable changes. Changes being unpredictable, the extra space was often not enough or was in the wrong place.

Times have changed dramatically. With Oracle, it is extremely easy to add a column to a table. You can do it online, and everything may keep working (though this is not guaranteed). However, one thing to keep in mind is that while it is easy to add a column, and changing one is only slightly more onerous, it is next to impossible to remove a column—you have to recreate the table, which is something that is going to take a long time. And there is nothing worse than seeing a table with columns that seemed like a good idea but quickly vanished from usefulness.

Altering Tables in Practice

The biggest problem with altering tables is when it involves an online database. If you can bring the system down, then you can make all your changes, test them thoroughly, and bring the system back up again. If you cannot do this, then once you have successfully run all your changes through your test database, you have to update the production database as quickly as possible. If you add a column to a table, stored procedures that reference that table will be marked as invalid because they have not been recompiled though you can execute them.

The biggest problem is with an INSERT statement that will fail due to the wrong number of columns. If you can't bring the database down to make these changes, then you will have to be aware of this problem and modify and recompile the stored procedures as soon as possible.

If the Visual Basic front end needs updating, then you have a much bigger problem that will need a coordinated plan to update the database, stored procedures, and front end, and you will probably have to bring the database down.

Performing maintenance on redundant columns can be a painful chore. You can put a database into production, but business rules change so quickly these days that there will be a tremendous amount of pressure to make corresponding changes to the database. The truth is that the designer part of us would love to see a good design given the time to settle down, but reality implies a constant change.

TIP
The Database Designer that is part of Visual Basic 6 is an excellent product to make table maintenance much easier. We will cover the product in the last section of this chapter.

Columns will be added and often increased in size. But it is easy to do this. You do not have to specify a 100-character field when 10 will do, especially if it is a fixed-length column. In fact, it is probably better not to use fixed-length columns except when they are small.

At some point you will have to resign yourself to the fact that the table has so many out-of-date decisions affecting its design that it is time to re-create it. At this point, you can use a SQL command, such as

```
CREATE TABLE AS subquery
```

to copy the data you still need to a new table and then drop the old table and rename the new one to the original name (use the RENAME command for this). You might also want to use import and export for this purpose.

WARNING   You can modify a table while it is being used. For example, if you add a column, be aware that any stored procedure that accesses this table will be marked as uncompiled. Interestingly enough, Oracle will still let you execute the procedure, but you take your chances over whether it will work or not. In Oracle 7.3, procedures are automatically recompiled if they are found to be invalid; the recompilation occurs at the next execution. In general, if you have a procedure that deletes a row, then it should probably work, but an insert will fail if you are not entering enough values for each column.

Specifying Constraints

The next step in creating a table is including constraints. Constraints are features that let you restrict the values that can be entered into one or more table columns. They are the most basic way to define rudimentary business rules.

Using constraints, you can set up your database so an end user cannot enter data that does not conform to the rules you want to impose. It does not matter whether they use SQL*Plus or Visual Basic. Only the owner of the table and a user with DBA privileges will be able to bypass the rules (usually by dropping or disabling the constraints).

There are two types of constraints: *column* and *table* constraints, though in most circumstances they serve exactly the same purpose, and there is no operational difference between them. We will review how to use both types, but keep in mind that it usually doesn't matter which you use: just be consistent.

Column Constraints

Column constraints indicate restrictions in the column definition of a table. They are defined as CONSTRAINT clauses that come after the column names.

If you look at Listing 6.2, you will notice that we did not include any constraints. We will now put some in. You do not need to specify a constraint name, but you will reap the rewards later on if you do. However, if you don't, then the system will create a cryptic name for them. The format of the CONSTRAINT clause is

```
CONSTRAINT constraint_name constraint_type
```

The types of column constraints are shown in Table 6.4.

TABLE 6.4: The Types of Column Constraints

Constraint Name	Description
CHECK	Specifies a simple expression (which may include column references) that each row must satisfy.
REFERENCES	Specifies that the value in this column must also appear in the PRIMARY KEY of the referenced (or parent) table. This constraint gives the database its built-in referential integrity. It also means that the row referenced in the parent table cannot be deleted while the row in this table still exists.
NOT NULL	Specifies that the column cannot contain a NULL (the default is that it can). This constraint is implicit if PRIMARY KEY is also specified.
PRIMARY KEY	Defines the column as a PRIMARY KEY, i.e., it is unique and cannot be NULL. An index is automatically created on this column.
UNIQUE	Defines the column as unique, i.e., you cannot enter the same value into more than one row. An index is automatically created on this column.

An example of using all the constraints listed in Table 6.4 is shown in Listing 6.3.

Listing 6.3

```
CREATE TABLE videos (
  video_id  NUMBER(10)
    CONSTRAINT video_id_pk PRIMARY KEY,
  movie_id  NUMBER(10)
    CONSTRAINT video_movie_id_fk REFERENCES movies(movie_id)
      UNIQUE,
  status  VARCHAR2(10) DEFAULT 'available' NOT NULL,
  rental_date    DATE,
  customer_id    NUMBER(10) DEFAULT 0,
  purchase_date  DATE NOT NULL) ;
```

In this case the Video_id column is defined with a PRIMARY KEY constraint, the Movie_id column with a UNIQUE KEY constraint, and a FOREIGN KEY constraint referencing the Movie_id column of the Movies table. There are also some columns with the NOT NULL constraint, which means that whenever you try to insert a new record in the Videos table, the foreign-key designation first checks to ensure that there is a matching record in the Movies table.

NOTE   The CONSTRAINT clause is purely optional; for example, it is possible to define a constraint this way: 'id number(10) PRIMARY KEY'. In this case, Oracle will assign a constraint name of the form SYS_Cnnnn where *nnnn* is some number. However, it is far better to include the CONSTRAINT keyword and a constraint name.

Table Constraints

Table constraints perform the same function as column constraints: they impose restrictions on what you can enter into the columns of the database. However, table constraints appear in the CREATE TABLE statement at the end rather than after each column. This way, they can apply to the table as a whole column as well as individual columns. Table constraints are really only a different way of saying the same thing as column constraints. The only advantage they have is that they allow you to create a composite index; that is, a single index whose definition includes more than one column. The types of table constraints are described in Table 6.5. You will notice that in most cases they are the same as the column constraints except that they include the name of the column (or columns) that they apply to.

TABLE 6.5: The Options for Specifying Table Constraints

Constraint Name	Description
CHECK (condition)	Defines a condition that each row must pass.
FOREIGN KEY ...REFERENCES	Specifies the column(s) that should have a FOREIGN KEY constraint that references a column(s) in another table.
PRIMARY KEY (column)	Specifies the column(s) that should have a primary-key index.
UNIQUE (column)	Specifies that the column(s) should have a unique key.

As an example of using table constraints, consider Listing 6.4. The NOT NULL constraints have been kept as column constraints for simplicity.

Listing 6.4

```
CREATE TABLE movies (
movie_id        NUMBER(10),
movie_name      VARCHAR2(50),
length          NUMBER(3),
rating          VARCHAR2(6),
year_of_release NUMBER(4),
  CONSTRAINT movie_id_pk PRIMARY KEY (movie_id),
  CONSTRAINT movie_rating_chk
    CHECK (rating IN ('G', 'PG', 'PG-13', 'NC-17', 'R'))) ;
```

You will notice that the table constraints appear at the end of the script (though they can appear anywhere) and are separated by commas. We have specified two table constraints: one to define the Movie_id column as having a primary key, and the second defines a CHECK constraint that, in this case, ensures that the rating column value is one of five possibilities.

NOTE

To list the constraints that you have in your schema, use the following command:
`SELECT constraint_name, table_name FROM user_constraints ;`

Implementing Referential Integrity

Relational databases are built upon the relationships among tables. There are many different types of relationships, but one of the most common is the master-detail of, for example, the Movies table to the Videos table. Another common example is the relationship between the Invoice-to-Line-Items tables in a Purchasing database. The master-detail relationships appear as one-to-many relationships in the entity relationship diagram. For every master row, there can be zero, one, or many detail rows.

When we create tables to represent master-detail relationships, we ensure each detail record does not contain any of the data that is common to the master record; the Video table does not have any information about the movie itself, just information regarding the physical tape. If we want to find out which movie it is, we must link the detail table (videos) to the master table (movies) by a column in the detail table; we call the column the *foreign key*, in this case Movie_id (see Figure 6.4). This column refers to the *primary key* in the master table. The process is called *referential integrity*. If there were no matching key in the parent table (perhaps the matching key was deleted or never existed), then the database would lack integrity.

To avoid this situation, we can use constraints to do two things:

1. Stop a detail row from being inserted or updated without a matching parent key.

2. Stop any parent key from being deleted if it still is referred to by a foreign key.

FIGURE 6.4

Referential integrity in practice

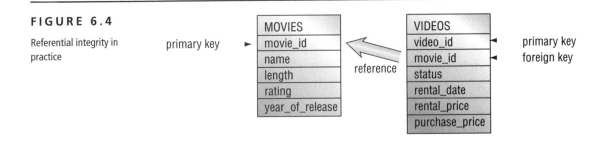

Although we could implement these referential integrity rules in our client code, it is far better to achieve it with constraints. The process can be done once and forgotten about. In Listing 6.3, the foreign-key definition appeared as

```
movie_id  NUMBER(10)
    CONSTRAINT video_movie_id_fk REFERENCES movies(movie_id)
```

in which we define a constraint on the Movie_id column in the Videos table (the foreign key) that refers to the Movie_id column in the Movies table (the primary key). The only decision you have to make here is whether you should give the matching columns the same name. Although it can lead to a little confusion when reading constraints, it usually makes join conditions easier to write.

In practice, whenever you now enter a detail record, the master table is automatically read to find out if the parent key exists. Whenever you delete from the master table, you have to scan for matching foreign keys. Developers will often not put an index on the foreign key (this is not automatic like it is with primary keys). This can slow down deletes because they have to do a full table scan of the detail table to ensure that the master row can be deleted. So, as you can see, automatic referential integrity does not come without a price.

Specifying the Placement of Indexes

By default, any index created with a constraint will be placed in the same tablespace as the table, and the segment will receive a default storage specification. Relying on defaults is not often an optimum situation, and it is best to put indexes in their own tablespace (usually with other indexes). The exact design depends on what data you have and how it is used. However, you can define which tablespace an index will be in as follows:

```
CREATE TABLE videos (
  video_id   NUMBER(10)
   CONSTRAINT video_id_pk PRIMARY KEY
     USING INDEX
       TABLESPACE video_store
       STORAGE storage_clause,
  movie_id NUMBER(10),
  status  VARCHAR2(10) DEFAULT 'available' NOT NULL,
  rental_date     DATE,
  customer_id     NUMBER(10) DEFAULT 0,
  purchase_date   DATE NOT NULL) ;
```

Using Constraints

Indexes will normally speed up SELECT statements but will slow down any inserts, updates, or deletes to your data. Other constraints will also slow down inserts and updates because the constraint will have to be checked first. In the case of referential integrity, extra data reads might end up being done, so you should employ constraints with care. If in doubt, put constraints in only your most important tables. Then, when you have a feel for the data being entered, you can remove some constraints in the most heavily used table and see what effect it has on the performance.

As the PRIMARY KEY and UNIQUE constraints automatically create an index, you will find this can substantially increase the time to save data, because you are saving data to the table as well as the key to the index. To mitigate the effect of this process, you should try to make sure that indexes are placed in a tablespace on a separate disk. You can do this either with the USING INDEX option of the CONSTRAINT clause or, alternatively, with the CREATE INDEX command.

If you are bulk loading information, you may want to disable the constraints or even drop them. You can do this with the ALTER TABLE command as follows:

```
ALTER TABLE DISABLE constraint_name ;
```

or

```
ALTER TABLE DROP constraint-name ;
```

This is one reason that giving your constraints sensible names will pay off.

Creating Indexes

An *index* is a database object that allows you to directly access any particular record in a table. For any tables with more than a few records, an index dramatically improves retrieval time. The alternative way to find a record is to do a full table scan, which on a large table could take minutes or longer and would not make you too popular around the office. The index contains an entry for every value in the indexed column(s); the index is likely to be a unique one but does not have to be. An index can be based on one column, or it can be a *composite* index based on several columns. These columns do not have to be adjacent fields in the table. NULL values are not stored in an index.

A skillfully placed index is vital for performance. Remember that all indexes will impose a small performance penalty on inserts and updates because Oracle will have to read several blocks to find the record you want. If the table is very small or you always need to read the whole table, then an index should not be used.

The easiest way to create an index is to have one created automatically with a constraint, such as PRIMARY KEY or UNIQUE. Ideally, you will set up (at least) one tablespace on a separate disk drive just for indexes. The result is less contention for the disk access compared to reading the index and the data from the same disk (assuming, of course, it is not already in memory).

TIP

If you are doing bulk uploads, such as when you have batch updates or you are importing data into the table, the load will be faster if you drop the index and re-create the index after you have finished. This step has the added benefit of ensuring your index is cleaned up, something you should try to do regularly anyway.

To create an index, use the following SQL statement:

```
CREATE [UNIQUE] INDEX index_name ON
   table_name (column1, column2 . . . )
   [TABLESPACE tablespace_name]
   [STORAGE storage_clause] ;
```

For example,

```
CREATE UNIQUE INDEX video_index ON
   videos (video_id, movie_id)
   TABLESPACE movie_indexes ;
```

NOTE

To find out what indexes you have use the following SQL:

```
SELECT index_name, table_name FROM user_indexes;
```

This example shows why it is important to have your indexes named sensibly. This SQL command will help you find all your indexes, including those created as a result of constraint conditions.

Creating and Using Sequences

In Microsoft Access, there is the Counter field, and in SQL Server, there is the *identity* property for a column. Both the Counter field and the identity property automatically increment the key value whenever you insert a new row into the table. However, Oracle does not implement this automatic key-generating column in any form. Oracle provides *sequences,* which generate an automatically increasing counter which cannot be tied to any table or column; you have to do that part yourself. This means that you must do much more work to get your unique-key value into the table. Although sequences are flexible (they are not restricted to the one function of providing a unique key), there are few other positives. But one positive is that the unique key generation does not cause any locking problems and so is slightly more efficient than a Counter field.

Creating a Sequence

Creating a sequence is simple; here's how:

```
CREATE SEQUENCE sequence_name
```

When you create a sequence, the default is to generate the next 20 numbers in a cache so that when you are ready to use them, one is normally available in memory and does not have to be generated. You can change the number of entries to cache by using the optional parameters described below. The side effect of the cache becomes apparent when you have to restart the database. The cache is lost, and a new set of numbers is generated.

For a sequence number to be useful to you, you need to be able to find what its current value is and be able to get the next available one. You do this with two built-in functions:

```
sequence_name.NEXTVAL
```

which returns the next sequence number and

```
sequence_name.CURRVAL
```

which returns the sequence number retrieved by the most recent call to NEXTVAL by the current session.

These functions are not statements but must be used as a part of a SQL statement. The most common use of a sequence is to generate a unique index, which can be created explicitly in a SELECT statement or implicitly in an INSERT statement. These can be executed in a stored procedure or even as part of a SELECT statement executed from Visual Basic. Examples of each type of use are

```
SELECT my_sequence.NEXTVAL INTO next_sequence FROM dual;
INSERT INTO movies VALUES (
   next_sequence, . . .
```

and

```
INSERT INTO movies VALUES (
   my_sequence.NEXTVAL, 'Movie Name',
   . . .

   ) ;
```

The "dual" table that is used in the first of these examples is available to all users and is just a dummy table. It is mostly used in this kind of statement in which you are not accessing any real data from a table column (NEXTVAL and CURRVAL are called *pseudocolumns*).

Problems Accessing Sequences

When you access a sequence number, it is unique and only available in your session. You cannot get the current value of a sequence in your session until you have retrieved the next value. If you try, you will get the following error:

```
ERROR: ORA-08002: sequence MY_SEQUENCE.CURRVAL is not yet defined
in this session
```

Although no other user will generate the same number from the same sequence, you cannot see what another user's current number is. Depending on your application, this may cause some problems. For example, I had one application that had a screen with the latest values of rows from a few tables. The data had to be current, so one option was to refresh the display every 30 seconds. This step put a fairly heavy load on the server because there were many thousands of rows that had to be periodically read to produce the display, even if the data had not changed.

A better approach was to have some indicator in the database that the data had changed, and then the Visual Basic client had to poll for only one number until, of course, the data did change. The most obvious indicator that rows have been inserted is that the sequence number has increased, but you can only find your own session's sequence number.

Continued on next page

The solution was to save the sequence number in another one-row table every time a new sequence number was generated. The best way to do this step is with a stored procedure. By accepting this slight overhead, the latest number is available to all users. I modified the stored procedures that also updated and deleted rows so that they also incremented the sequence. (You have billions of unique numbers available so a few used for this purpose will not go amiss.)

Now the VB client polls for the sequence number and caches it. When it changes, it knows it is time to refresh the display. I have included a few sequence numbers in this one-row table to monitor all kinds of things, and this has turned an application from having been too slow to an efficient user of database resources.

Optional Parameters

When you create a sequence, there are several optional parameters you can include with the command. Although you will usually find that the defaults are fine, you should be aware of these parameters for special situations. Table 6.6 lists the optional parameters available to you when creating a sequence.

TABLE 6.6: Optional Parameters for Creating a Sequence

Qualifier	Description	Default value
INCREMENT BY x	Successive sequence numbers are generated with an increment of x, in which x can be positive or negative but not zero.	1
MINVALUE x	The minimum value of the sequence.	-10^{26}
NOMINVALUE	The default for the minimum value for a sequence.	1 for ascending and -10^{26} for descending
MAXVALUE x	The maximum value of the sequence.	$+10^{26}$
NOMAXVALUE	Default for the maximum value for a sequence.	$+10^{26}$ for ascending and -1 for descending
STARTWITH x	The first value of the sequence after it is created.	Depends on increment
CYCLE	Cycle the sequence numbers, i.e., start at the minimum number again when the maximum number is reached.	NOCYCLE

Continued on next page

TABLE 6.6 CONTINUED: Optional Parameters for Creating a Sequence

Qualifier	Description	Default value
CACHE *x*	Generate next *x* sequence numbers, and store them in a cache ready for fast access.	20
NOCACHE	No sequence numbers are cached.	
ORDER	Sequences are generated in order of the time of the request.	NOORDER

You will not often find yourself setting up sequences, so it is worthwhile to do it well and to use as many of the optional parameters as appropriate. You should give some thought to how many you want to cache (a higher number if they are constantly in use), and you should always specify the starting number. An example of using the optional parameters is

```
CREATE SEQUENCE my_sequence
    STARTWITH 1000
    INCREMENT BY 1
    CACHE 10;
```

This example creates a new sequence starting at 1,000 and increments by one each time NEXTVAL is used. Oracle generates and caches 10 values ready for the current user.

You should try to tailor the cache size to the frequency of use of the sequence. For example, if there is a constant flow of inserts to the table in question, then set the cache higher, say at 100. On the other hand, if the sequence is used for a table, such as a company table that gets updated less than once a day, then use the NOCACHE option.

Using Sequences in a Replicated Environment

You will not often use an increment greater than one, but there is a case in which it is really valuable. If you are using synchronous replication (that is, two or more synchronized databases), you want to ensure that if two users enter a new record into the database at the same time then there is no conflict over the index values used. Sequences are not synchronized. One way to get around this problem with two databases is to set one sequence starting at 1 and the other starting at 2. If the INCREMENT BY parameter is set to 2, one sequence will generate even numbers and the other odd numbers. You could, of course, expand this to any number of databases.

Maintaining a Sequence

If you use sequences, you must accept that there will sometimes be gaps in the sequence values you use. If you use them for keys and a row is deleted, then the sequence number used for that row will not be reused. When you restart the database, all values that were in the sequence cache disappear and a new cache is created. You could "lose" many numbers this way. The gaps do not cause any technical difficulties with indexes, though some developers fret unnecessarily about the "missing" numbers. Problems may appear only if you are using the sequence-to-generate numbers that dictate there be no gaps (such as invoices). You will have to develop your own number-generation scheme in this case.

TIP   Occasionally, you may want to reset a sequence number, such as after a round of testing on a new database. You will want to start again at 1. To do this, you must drop the sequence and create a new one.

You should note the following two commands for maintaining sequences:

```
DROP SEQUENCE sequence_name ;
```

which allows you to drop the named sequence, and

```
ALTER SEQUENCE sequence_name
   new_parameters ;
```

which allows you to change an existing sequence with new parameters, such as changing the maximum value. Note that you *cannot* change the current value unless you drop and re-create the sequence.

NOTE   To find out which sequences you have created, use the following SQL:

```
NOTESELECT sequence_name FROM user_sequences.
```

You cannot find out how sequences are applied to tables by looking at the database, so try to keep them for special purposes.

Sequences in Practice

Once you have a unique number, you still have to decide exactly how you are going to use it. There are several different schools of thought on applying unique numbers.

One Sequence Fits All

You can create one sequence and use it for everything. This technique is simplest because you only have one sequence to maintain and to provide new values. It is also a method that fits well into an object-based design in which you consider each table another type of object. Each object shares attributes, such as ID number, name, and possibly other characteristics. These attributes can all be held in an object-description table (which in practice will begin to look like a glorified code table).

If you have ever worked with a system using one sequence for everything, you can appreciate that it can be difficult to conceptualize what is going on sometimes, and you always have to link in an extra table to get anything done.

Many Sequences per Table

It is certainly possible to use more than one sequence per table. You can restrict each one to a range, and then they can coexist side by side. The reason sometimes offered for doing this is that one department will have one range (say 1,000 to 1,999) and another department a different range (such as 2,000 to 2,999). However, it can sometimes be difficult to dispel the myth that this procedure enables users to sort out their own information more easily.

In fact, selecting a range in a query can be more difficult than choosing a particular department number in your queries, even if the department number is in the table. If the number is not there, then make sure that you put one in rather than buckle to pressure to dictate the design. This method of putting more than one piece of information (in this case the key and the department number) into a column is bad design and should be avoided at all costs. It will also prove to be a maintenance nightmare.

To Each Table Its Own Sequence

The usual method of handling sequences is to use a separate sequence for the primary key of each table (see Figure 6.5). This procedure tends to be appropriate with most database designs. From a user point of view, it can be much easier to pull out data in an understandable way, but you need to take more care when inserting new records.

You have to make sure that the right sequence is *always* used with the appropriate table. If you don't, then you will eventually get into trouble with trying to use nonunique keys. If you are strict about using stored procedures for any Data Manipulation (DML) statements (INSERT, UPDATE, and DELETE), then you can keep this problem to a minimum. Another thing you should do is to ensure that you use a standard naming convention for the sequence, such as table name plus the word "sequence" (for example, "movie_sequence").

Despite the maintenance headaches that you can get with dozens of sequences, you will find they are more natural and more commonly accepted. The benefits make sequences worthwhile.

FIGURE 6.5:

The preferred way to use sequences

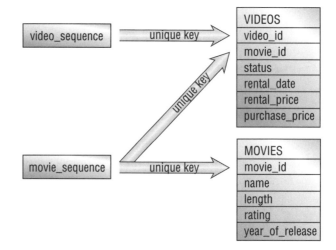

Audit Trails

Now that we have learned how to create a table, let's see how we can enhance our implementation to give us the capability of an audit trail. Oracle does have a built-in auditing capability using the AUDIT SQL command, but that capability is designed to keep track of what statements have been executed or attempted on a schema object. For example, the audit will help you keep track of all operations done on a table, such as who has altered the table, inserted new rows, or deleted or updated the table. Although this is useful to see who is doing what, it is not an audit trail in the sense of keeping track of *how* that data was updated or *which* rows were updated or deleted and with *what* data. Auditing in Oracle records the statements that do the changing rather than the actual values that are changed. To track the changes of values you will have to create your own auditing scheme.

You have to decide how important it is for you to know who is doing what to your data. The scenario is that you come in to work and find out that several rows of data have been deleted in one of your tables, and you know it should not have been done. Although rows are being inserted and deleted all the time, who was involved in these transactions and when? If rogue data was inserted, who did it? What were the previous values; that is, where is the audit trail?

The first aspect of transaction auditing is usually found on all important database tables. In some environments, keeping an audit trail is mandatory. So what is the best way to do it? The easiest way is to add a couple of fields onto the end of each table to contain the name of the user updating the record as well as a time stamp to record when the change was done. These new columns will be User_Name and Time_Stamp. The new table creation script is shown in Listing 6.5.

Listing 6.5

```
CREATE TABLE movies (
  movie_id           NUMBER(10)
    CONSTRAINT movies_movie_id_pk PRIMARY KEY,
  movie_name               VARCHAR2(100) NOT NULL,
  year_of_release    NUMBER(4) NOT NULL,
  rating                   VARCHAR2(6) NOT NULL,
  acquisition_date   DATE NOT NULL,
  user_name          VARCHAR(30)
    DEFAULT USER NOT NULL,
  time_stamp         DATE
    DEFAULT SYSDATE NOT NULL)
TABLESPACE movies ;
```

You must be rigorous about entering values into these fields whenever they are inserted or updated. You can try to do this step in your INSERT statements, but you will have to rely on developers always writing their client code to the same specification. You should then set default values for the columns from USER and SYSDATE as shown in Listing 6.5. In this situation, if a lazy programmer does forget to supply values for these columns, they are automatically filled in.

The best way to get it right is to insert table rows from within a stored procedure. This is a method I highly recommend, and we will cover it in Chapter 8. For now, we will just say that stored procedures should be used for all DML statements: they use the values of USER and SYSDATE functions.

TIP   By adding the User_Name and Time_Stamp columns, you can now keep track of who has last changed the record. I have seen commercial systems in which this was as far as the audit trail went. To do a better job, we have two choices. We either write a trigger (a stored procedure that is executed when a certain change occurs to a table) and save the old data in a special table, or we can create our own code to write to a transaction log.

Other Schema Objects

There are three other schema objects that we must touch on before moving on to other matters, though you can get by without any of them. These are *clusters*, *views*, and *synonyms*. While clusters are a different way of storing one or more tables, views and synonyms are not real objects in the sense of having a data segment with real data associated with them. Instead, they are "virtual" objects in that they refer to other objects. The main reason for this is hiding the source of data from users for security reasons as well as to make data access simpler for performance reasons.

The type of situation that may cause you a problem is when you want to give access to users to some parts of a table but not all parts. For example, you may have a personnel table that also includes employees' salaries. You want users to have access to some of the table (name, ID, start date), but you also want to hide the salaries. This is a perfect situation for using a view. Your front-end Visual Basic code can hide the sensitive data, but that still leaves it open to users writing their own access code or even using a database query. The only way your VB code can duplicate this without a view is to use some of the advanced techniques that we will review in later chapters.

Clusters

Clusters are an alternative way of storing table data. Instead of having one table per data segment, clusters allow you to have one or more tables in the same segment, and more importantly, you can control the way the tables are stored physically in the segment. The main reason for doing this is that you can determine the order in which the rows are physically stored, and then if you select the data from the segment in that order, it should be much faster.

There are two types of clusters the *indexed* and *hash* clusters. The difference is that the former uses an index (see Figure 6.6) while the latter uses a hash algorithm to look up rows stored in the segment. Both types of clusters require a key on the cluster, and this effectively makes a physical table join for you if there is more than one table stored. Despite this seemingly overwhelming advantage, the penalty is often felt when you insert or update data. Clusters do not seem to provide as much performance improvement as you would expect, and they can be safely left as a technique to explore when you have some spare time for tuning.

FIGURE 6.6:

Clusters physically store data by the cluster key

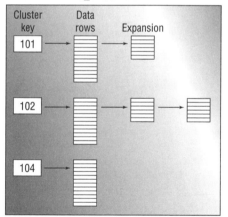

Views

Up to now we have created tables as the store for data. To access all of them, you need SELECT access on each table, and you often have to perform a complex table join to get at the data. An alternative is to create a view or "virtual" table derived from selected columns in one or more real tables.

To create a view, you must have the same privileges on all the tables that comprise the view as you want on your view. However, end users will only need privileges on the view but not on the *base tables* of the view.

A typical statement to create a view is

```
CREATE VIEW video_view
  AS SELECT  movie_name, rating, status
    FROM movies, videos
    WHERE videos.movie_id = movies.movie_id ;
```

The advantage of a view is that the user has no idea what the base tables are or, in the case above, if there are any missing columns. If the AS SELECT subquery involves more than one table, the user does not have to worry about the join conditions, they are declared in the view (see Figure 6.7).

FIGURE 6.7:

The way a view works

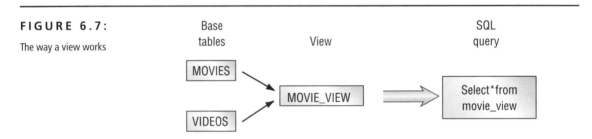

Synonyms

Synonyms are an alternative way of accessing an object. You could think of it as an alias for the object, whether it is a table, view, stored procedure, or another object. Creating a synonym is easy:

```
CREATE SYNONYM films FOR movies;
```

The synonym that you create (films) is a private one and is only available to those users with the privileges. Oracle assumes that the objects you have created the synonym for (in this case, movies) are in your own schema. More useful are public synonyms that are available to all users:

```
CREATE PUBLIC SYNONYM films FOR movies;
```

Views and Synonyms for Visual Basic

The ODBC parser has been notoriously bad understanding views and synonyms. Visual Basic 6 and the latest ODBC drivers from Microsoft appear to be improving this situation dramatically, although you will get the best support from Oracle's data-access technology, which we will see in Chapter 18, *Oracle Objects for OLE*.

Setting Privileges

This chapter has covered many SQL statements for which you will need privileges before you can use them and which you will probably need to pass on to other users. There are two basic types of privileges that can be granted: *system privileges* that allow you to execute specified SQL statements and *object privileges* that are granted for one particular database object, such as a table.

NOTE   Security is a vital aspect to running a database; for a more detailed view you should see Chapter 4, *Database Administration*.

System Privileges

These privileges will have to be granted by the database administrator to the developer. The syntax of these privileges will be

```
GRANT system privilege TO user | role ;
```

A sample of the system privileges that are available to you are listed in Table 6.7. There are over 80 system privileges in all.

The following is an example of using the privileges listed in Table 6.7:

```
GRANT CREATE SESSION TO rjames ;
GRANT CREATE TABLE TO rjames ;
```

TABLE 6.7: System Privileges Required for the Example Database

Privilege	Description
CREATE SESSION	This privilege is required to be able to log in to the database.
CREATE TABLESPACE	Ability to create a tablespace.
CREATE TABLE	Enable user to create a table in their own schema. You must have sufficient quota in the tablespace.
CREATE ANY TABLE	Enable user to create a table in any schema.
INDEX	Ability to create an index on a table in your own schema.
CREATE ANY INDEX	Ability to create an index on a table in another user's schema.
CREATE SEQUENCE	Ability to create a sequence in your own schema.
CREATE ANY SEQUENCE	Ability to create a sequence in another user's schema.
CREATE VIEW	Ability to create a view in your own schema.
CREATE ANY VIEW	Ability to create a view in another user's schema.

Object Privileges

The object privileges shown in Table 6.8 will normally be those that you as a developer pass on to your users so that they can operate on your schema in the database. Remember that you have developed your database in an application schema that no other users can see until you grant them the right to do so.

TABLE 6.8: Sample Object Privileges

Privilege	Description
SELECT	Ability to do a SELECT query, or ability to examine and increment a sequence.
INSERT	Ability to insert data into a table or view.
UPDATE	Ability to update data in a table or view.
DELETE	Ability to delete data from a table or view.

NOTE   The other object privileges are ALTER, INDEX, REFERENCES, EXECUTE, and ALL.

The following is an example of giving object privileges to our Movie database in which the user "rjames" is given the privilege to execute a SELECT and INSERT command against the Movies table.

```
GRANT SELECT ON movies TO rjames ;
GRANT INSERT ON movies TO rjames ;
```

TIP   Granting of privileges is one of the major ways of ensuring that your database is as secure as possible while still allowing users to review and manipulate data. As we shall see in the chapters on stored procedures, the best way to ensure integrity and security of data is to do any database updating through stored procedures. When you use stored procedures, you will need to give EXECUTE privileges to the stored procedures instead of INSERT, UPDATE, and DELETE privileges on the table.

Privileges in Action

Using the built-in security mechanisms in Oracle is vital to create a secure database, but it does not necessarily lead to the kind of applications that we may want to see. For example, if an end user is running one of your front-end applications and half the things they try lead to Oracle error messages, then this will look pretty unprofessional. So while you need the security, how do you supplement it so that it integrates seamlessly into your application?

The route I have followed is to create another table to hold application users. This table holds the valid users of your application (as opposed to everyone who has an Oracle account) and includes some details, such as their names, but its major purpose is to contain indicators to which aspects of the program they can use.

The simplest approach is to duplicate the privileges they have on the tables. For example, if a user does not have the right to change a particular table, then your Visual Basic program will remove the UPDATE option from the menu or, alternatively, give a polite message that they are not allowed to take this action.

Taking this one step further, you can create the kind of security that cannot be done otherwise. For example, if you have a table that contains data that cannot be changed after the end of the business day without special authorization, then include this capability as a flag in your user table.

Continued on next page

The kind of table I have used is

```
CREATE TABLE app_users (
    user_name           VARCHAR2(30)
      CONSTRAINT app_users_pk  PRIMARY KEY,
    first_name          VARCHAR2(20) NOT NULL,
    last_name           VARCHAR2(20) NOT NULL,
    admin_privilege     NUMBER(1) DEFAULT 0,
    schedule_privilege  NUMBER(1) DEFAULT 0) ;
```

Using Microsoft Database Designer

It is important to understand the techniques necessary to create tables and other database schema objects; however, the techniques we have covered so far have involved typing in text into a command-line prompt with SQL*Plus or, preferably, creating a script with an editor. With the release of Visual Basic 6, Enterprise Edition, we now have available the Database Designer, which runs within the Visual Basic environment. The Database Designer can take much of the typing out of creating and maintaining tables, although, as we will see, you still have to know what you are doing and to be aware of the shortcomings.

The first step you should do is create a Data Link. The Data Link is an object independent of the Visual Basic project, but it appears in whichever project you open. Next, open a Data View by selecting Data View Window from the View menu. You will see a window like that shown in Figure 6.8 with no Data Links and no Data Environment Connections.

FIGURE 6.8:

The initial Data View window

To create a new Data Link, right-click on the Data Links folder and choose Add Data Links... from the drop-down menu. You will see the Data Link properties dialog box. Select the Microsoft OLEDB Provider for ODBC Drivers on the first page. On the second page, enter the ODBC Data Source Name and your user name and password (see Figure 6.9). You might as well test your connection by clicking the appropriate button. Assuming that the connection is all right, you can click the OK button and see your new Data Link in the Data View window. The link is called DataLink1, but you can rename it.

FIGURE 6.9:

The second page of the Data Link properties dialog box

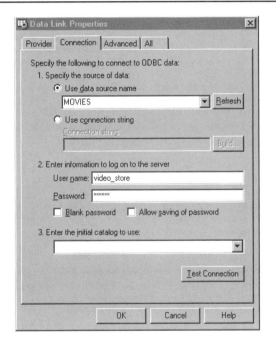

If you now expand the Data Link tree, you will be prompted for a password, and then you will see the Data View window with all of the accessible objects at your fingertips. In Figure 6.10, you can see that the Tables item has been expanded to show all of the tables you have access to.

FIGURE 6.10:

The Data Link makes your tables visible from your Visual Basic environment.

Let us take stock of where we are. The Database Designer allows us access to several types of database schema objects. In this chapter, we will deal with the Database Diagrams and the Tables options. Chapter 9, *Introduction to PL/SQL,* will cover stored procedures and functions in more detail.

Database Diagrams

The Database Diagram option is a way of viewing your database tables graphically. It provides you a view that you may have seen with Microsoft Access, though you can now apply this same capability to Oracle databases. First, you should right-click on the Database Diagram folder and select New Diagram from the drop-down menu.

How do you put tables in your new Database Diagram? This process is simply a matter of drag and drop. Select the table that you want to add the diagram from the Data View window, and drop it on the diagram. In Figure 6.11, you can see that two tables have been dropped onto the diagram: *movies* and *videos*. The system automatically determines whether there are any relationships between the tables using the foreign-key constraints and then draws on the link. Right-click on the diagram, and select Show Relationship Labels to show the relationship constraint, in this case VIDEO_MOVIE_ID_FK. You can now add the rest of the tables, save the diagram, and print it.

FIGURE 6.11:

The Database Diagram being put together

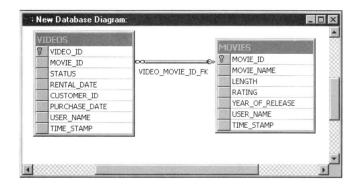

Creating Tables

The Database Diagram feature is a good way to document the relationships among your tables once you have created them. To make the creation phase easier, you can use the second of the design tools. Right-click on the Table folder in the Data View window, and select New Table… from the drop-down menu. Select a new name for the table. Now fill in the descriptions of the columns for your new table. In Figure 6.12, a new table, "Employees," has eight columns set up and ready to go.

FIGURE 6.12:

Creating a database table in Design mode

Design Table:EMPLOYEES

Column Name	Datatype	Length	Precision	Scale	Allow Nulls	Default Value	Comment
ID	NUMBER	22	10	0			Employee id
FIRST_NAME	VARCHAR2	25	0	0			
LAST_NAME	VARCHAR2	25	0	0			
CATEGORY	VARCHAR2	6	0	0			
START_DATE	DATE	7	0	0		(sysdate)	
END_DATE	DATE	7	0	0	✓		
SALARY	NUMBER	22	8	2	✓		
PHTO	LONG RAW	0	0	0	✓		

NOTE

When you are creating a table, notice that numeric columns are given a length of 22. This has nothing to do with the Oracle column length; it is a by-product of the way that ODBC and OLE-DB retrieve information from Oracle.

Before you save the new table, you should set a few properties. Right-click on the table in this design mode, and select Properties from the drop-down menu. You can set several useful properties, such as

- Identify a check constraint (such as the one we set on the rating column in the Movies table).

- Identify which tablespace the table should go in.

- Create indexes on the table.

When you are ready to save this table to the database, you are in for a surprise. You are given the option of saving the script that generates the table to a script file. Figure 6.13 shows you the dialog box where this question is asked. Notice that it shows you the SQL script. This is an excellent learning tool.

FIGURE 6.13:

Saving the table creation script

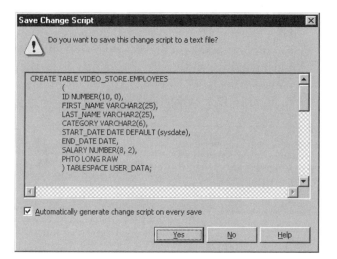

```
Save Change Script                                              ×

  ⚠   Do you want to save this change script to a text file?

  CREATE TABLE VIDEO_STORE.EMPLOYEES
        (
        ID NUMBER(10, 0),
        FIRST_NAME VARCHAR2(25),
        LAST_NAME VARCHAR2(25),
        CATEGORY VARCHAR2(6),
        START_DATE DATE DEFAULT (sysdate),
        END_DATE DATE,
        SALARY NUMBER(8, 2),
        PHTO LONG RAW
        ) TABLESPACE USER_DATA;

  ☑ Automatically generate change script on every save

                          Yes        No        Help
```

WARNING   If you double-click on one of the tables in the Data View window, you will go into display mode instead of design mode; the table will be displayed in a window with all the columns of all the rows. This should definitely be avoided on any large table.

Deleting a Column

One of the best features of the Database Designer is you can delete a column from an existing table. You may have realized that we have not covered how to do this in this chapter. That is because there is no simple way to do it. If you ever have to do it, you will find that it is a multistep process. It is much easier to leave the offending column where it is.

When you are in the Database Designer Design mode, you can highlight a column and hit the delete key. The Designer does all the hard work behind the scenes and creates a script for you that creates a temporary table, uses PL/SQL code to copy the data over to that table, and then creates the new table with all the constraints in place. The script to delete the Salary column is shown in Listing 6.6. The script shows how much work you have just saved yourself. It may not be the best way to do it, but the process gives you the script to modify as you wish.

Listing 6.6

```
CREATE TABLE VIDEO_STORE."Tmp_EMPLOYEES"
    (
    ID NUMBER(10, 0),
    FIRST_NAME VARCHAR2(25),
    LAST_NAME VARCHAR2(25),
    CATEGORY VARCHAR2(6),
    START_DATE DATE DEFAULT (sysdate),
    END_DATE DATE,
    PHTO LONG RAW
    ) TABLESPACE USER_DATA;

LOCK TABLE VIDEO_STORE.EMPLOYEES IN EXCLUSIVE MODE NOWAIT;

DECLARE
    CURSOR datacursor IS SELECT ID, FIRST_NAME, LAST_NAME, CATEGORY,
START_DATE, END_DATE, PHTO FROM VIDEO_STORE.EMPLOYEES;
    datarecord datacursor%ROWTYPE;
BEGIN
    OPEN datacursor;
    LOOP
            FETCH datacursor INTO datarecord;
            EXIT WHEN (datacursor%NOTFOUND);
```

```
                INSERT INTO VIDEO_STORE."Tmp_EMPLOYEES"(ID, FIRST_NAME,
LAST_NAME, CATEGORY, START_DATE, END_DATE, PHTO) VALUES (datarecord.ID,
datarecord.FIRST_NAME, datarecord.LAST_NAME, datarecord.CATEGORY,
datarecord.START_DATE, datarecord.END_DATE, datarecord.PHTO);
    END LOOP;
END;

DROP TABLE VIDEO_STORE.EMPLOYEES CASCADE CONSTRAINTS;

RENAME "Tmp_EMPLOYEES" TO EMPLOYEES;

ALTER TABLE VIDEO_STORE.EMPLOYEES
    MODIFY ID NUMBER(10, 0)
    CONSTRAINT NL_EMPLOYEES_4 NOT NULL;

ALTER TABLE VIDEO_STORE.EMPLOYEES
    MODIFY FIRST_NAME VARCHAR2(25)
    CONSTRAINT NL_EMPLOYEES_3 NOT NULL;

ALTER TABLE VIDEO_STORE.EMPLOYEES
    MODIFY LAST_NAME VARCHAR2(25)
    CONSTRAINT NL_EMPLOYEES_2 NOT NULL;

ALTER TABLE VIDEO_STORE.EMPLOYEES
    MODIFY CATEGORY VARCHAR2(6)
    CONSTRAINT NL_EMPLOYEES_1 NOT NULL;

ALTER TABLE VIDEO_STORE.EMPLOYEES
    MODIFY START_DATE DATE DEFAULT (sysdate)
    CONSTRAINT NL_EMPLOYEES NOT NULL;

CREATE INDEX VIDEO_STORE.IX_EMPLOYEES_ID ON VIDEO_STORE.EMPLOYEES
    (
    ID
    ) TABLESPACE VIDEO_STORE;

COMMENT ON COLUMN VIDEO_STORE.EMPLOYEES.ID IS
    'Employee id';
```

TIP   You will notice that when using the Database Designer, you cannot enter a STOR-
AGE clause. This is not as bad as it might seem because you can set up a DEFAULT
STORAGE clause for your tablespaces.

Summary

This chapter has covered all the aspects of implementing a database from your
logical design. This includes setting up the tablespaces to hold your database
objects and then creating the tables and indexes and other constraints. We then
covered creating and using sequences to give unique keys to your tables. We also
touched on additional fields for your tables to allow a rudimentary auditing system. We next covered the privileges you need to not only create your database
objects but also allow other users to interact with them. Finally, we saw some of
the capabilities of the Database Designer that is part of Visual Basic 6.

Now that you can create a complete database, we will move on to seeing how
we can retrieve data with SQL queries and then make changes to the data in the
database.

PART II

Queries and Stored Procedures

CHAPTER

SEVEN

7

Queries

- An Introduction to SQL

- The Types of SQL Command

- The Basic SELECT Command

- Group Functions

- The GROUP BY Clause

- Selecting Data from More Than One Table

- Subqueries

- Optimizing Your Queries

- Specifying Schemas in Your Queries

The Visual Basic developer has two things to contemplate when dealing with an Oracle database: putting data into the database or retrieving data out of it. A thorough understanding of the ways to do both is vital for providing a user application that can get to the data you want as fast as possible without putting undue strain on the database server and without fetching more data than the minimum needed to do the job.

Chapter 8, *Updating Your Database,* will focus on changing the data in your database, but the main focus of this chapter will be retrieving data from an Oracle database. We will cover

- An introduction to SQL

- The types of SQL command

- The basic SELECT command

- Group functions

- The GROUP BY clause

- Selecting data from more than one table

- Subqueries

- Optimizing your queries

- Specifying schemas in your queries

A SQL Overview

If you have worked on a relational database before, such as Microsoft SQL Server, then you are probably familiar with Structured Query Language, or SQL. SQL was the result of research by Dr. E. F. Codd at IBM in 1971, and the concept was eventually taken up by database companies, the first commercially available being Oracle. SQL was developed into a standard by the American National Standards Institute (ANSI), and it was quickly adopted by most vendors of relational database systems. Its current standard is ANSI SQL-92, however, as you can imagine, each vendor has added their own feature sets to SQL with the aim of distinguishing their product in the market as well as attempting to display the widest range of features.

SQL is a full-featured language but quite different from Visual Basic and C. It is truly the language of relational databases and, according to the original research, should be the only way to interact with the database. In practice, SQL is usually supplemented by other techniques, especially stored procedures. With Visual Basic and C, you can go to great lengths to indicate exactly how everything is done in a procedural way, with each step in the process defined in turn. SQL is not a procedural language—it is often called a *nonprocedural* or *declarative* language. This means that you are declaring *what* you want, not *how* to get it. This concept can take some time to get used to if you have not seen this kind of thing before, but with an open mind, it is quite easy to learn.

SQL includes commands that enter new data into database tables, update or delete the data already there, as well as select specific data from it. It also includes a large number of other commands typically used to create, maintain, and alter objects in the database: we have covered many of these in Chapters 3 through 6. In this chapter, we will be concentrating on the ability to retrieve data by creating queries with the SELECT command.

Query creation with SQL is important to master. It is involved in everything from setting up a data control to some of the most advanced techniques used inside stored procedures now becoming available to Visual Basic developers. We will cover SQL statements that update data in Chapter 8.

Before we get started, a short word on terminology. Users of Microsoft Access and Visual Basic are used to thinking of database tables comprising many records, each record consisting of several fields. Oracle users are used to speaking of a table with rows comprising several columns. There is no practical difference between the two forms of terminology. In this book, the terms *row* and *column* will always be used where appropriate.

Types of SQL Commands

There are several distinct types of SQL commands. In Oracle, there are eight types, as described in Table 7.1.

TABLE 7.1: The Six Basic Types of SQL Statements

SQL Type	Description
QUERY Command	This is the SELECT command and is the only way to retrieve information from the database within the SQL language.
Data Definition Language (DDL)	These commands create, alter, or drop database objects, including tablespaces, tables, and indexes as well as do administrative tasks, such as managing users.
Data Control Language (DCL)	These commands are used to administer privileges granted to users.
Data Manipulation Language (DML)	These commands change data in existing tables (e.g., SELECT, INSERT, UPDATE, and DELETE).
Transaction Control Language (TCL)	These commands control if and when any changes made to the data are made permanent (e.g., COMMIT, ROLLBACK, and SAVEPOINT).
Session Control	These commands control the user's active session.
System Control	These commands alter the active database instance.
Embedded SQL	These commands can be used in a procedural language, such as those provided by the Oracle precompilers for C and PL/I. These can include DDL, DML, and TCL as well as other commands. They are not available to Visual Basic.

In both this chapter and the next, we will be discussing Query and Data Manipulation Language commands. Data Definition Language commands are covered in Chapter 6, *Database Implementation*. Transaction control will be covered in Chapter 8. The remaining types of SQL commands are not normally dealt with by developers, but full details of the commands are in the *Oracle SQL Reference* manual.

The Basic SELECT Command

The easiest way to enter SQL, whether it is for the examples shown in this chapter or for any of the experimentation you want to do, is to use a SQL*Plus session. The SQL*Plus program is available on any platform that Oracle supports and comes as part of the Oracle Server package. However, you can use any tool you have handy, are familiar with, or just prefer over SQL*Plus. If you use a query tool, make sure that it produces Oracle compatible SQL.

SELECT Syntax

The full syntax of the SELECT command is available in a syntax diagram (affectionately called a "railroad" diagram) in the *Oracle SQL Reference* manual. A simplified view of the SELECT syntax diagram follows:

```
SELECT column_list | *
   FROM table_list
   WHERE row_conditions join_conditions subquery
   ORDER BY sort_columns;
```

Next, we will explore the SELECT statement step by step, gradually building up the complexity of the query.

A Simple SELECT Statement

Whether you retrieve rows into a simple Recordset Object with Visual Basic's Data Access Objects or in a sophisticated and controlled way with a stored procedure, you always use the SELECT statement. Although this command can have many parts or *clauses*, the fundamental syntax of the command is as follows:

```
SELECT column_list
   FROM table_name;
```

An example of this is

```
SELECT movie_name, length
   FROM movies;
```

which retrieves the values of the Movie_Name and Length columns from the Movies table. If you are typing this command into a SQL*Plus session, it will typically display the result set on the screen as well as the number of rows found. The convention is to use uppercase for all the SQL keywords and lowercase for everything else. Any SQL statement can appear on one or more lines and is normally terminated by a semicolon. It is good practice to start each new clause on a new line and indent it, though you don't need to do this. If you are entering this clause in a Visual Basic program, then you will be entering it on one line.

The components of the basic SELECT command are as follows:

SELECT   This keyword introduces the command as a query.

column list   A series of column names, each separated by a comma. The columns of the result set will be displayed in the order you enter them in the command (on the screen or in a Recordset if you have retrieved them into your Visual Basic program). You can use an asterisk instead of the column list to select all columns.

FROM   This keyword introduces the names of the tables where the columns are to be found.

table_name   The table from which you want to retrieve the columns.

The result of running the simple SELECT command is shown in Figure 7.1. The SELECT command will retrieve everything you ask for, although in some cases, you may find you get nothing or more rows than you bargained for. If you do not need a specific column, do not request it. Even if you do not access it in a Visual Basic Recordset, it will take a little extra time and put a little extra load on the database server.

FIGURE 7.1:

A simple SELECT command

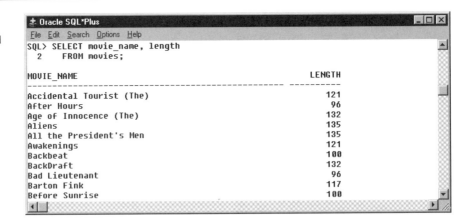

If we had used this SELECT command on a table with duplicated information, then we would have retrieved that duplicated data and wasted resources. For example, the query

```
SELECT movie_id, status
   FROM videos;
```

produces the output shown in Figure 7.2. As you can see, each "movie_id" value can occur several times in the videos table.

Finally, if you want to select all the fields from the table, use an asterisk as in the following example.

```
SELECT * FROM videos;
```

Using Dual

There is a special table in all Oracle databases, called *dual*. It is automatically available to all users. It contains one VARCHAR2 column, called *dummy*, and it has one row with a value of *x*. It proves useful in retrieving information from Oracle that does not actually reside in a real table. For example, to get the clock time for the Oracle server, use

```
SELECT SYSDATE FROM dual;
```

in which SYSDATE is a function that returns the server time and date. In this way, the minimum amount of table processing has to be done. You can find sequence numbers by using the dual table, as well:

```
SELECT my_sequence.NEXTVAL FROM dual;
SELECT my_sequence.CURRVAL FROM dual;
```

Narrowing the Selection

The simple SELECT statements we have seen so far will retrieve all of the rows from the table you are looking at, but most of the time, you will want to use an expression to narrow down the number of rows.

FIGURE 7.2:

Unintentionally retrieving
duplicate data

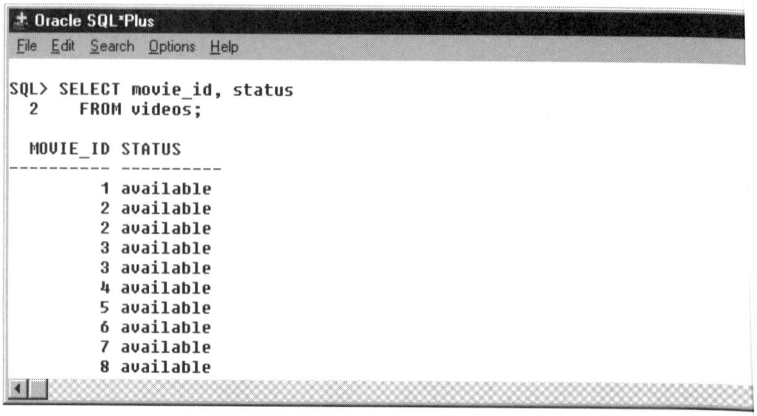

```
± Oracle SQL*Plus
File  Edit  Search  Options  Help

SQL> SELECT movie_id, status
  2    FROM videos;

  MOVIE_ID STATUS
---------- ----------
         1 available
         2 available
         2 available
         3 available
         3 available
         4 available
         5 available
         6 available
         7 available
         8 available
```

SQL gives you the ability to restrict the rows you retrieve to those rows
distinctly different from each other. You do this with the DISTINCT keyw

```
SELECT DISTINCT movie_id, status
  FROM videos;
```

The result of this query is shown in Figure 7.3. If you compare it to Figure
will notice we now do not retrieve any duplicated rows of data. You also
note that although "available" appears multiple times in the status colum
looks at the *combination* of the columns Movie_id and Status when determ
distinct rows.

FIGURE 7.3:

Using the DISTINCT keyword
to eliminate duplicate rows

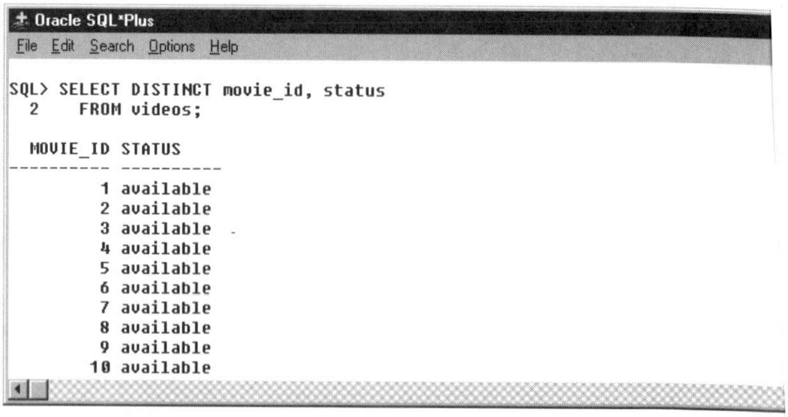

```
± Oracle SQL*Plus
File  Edit  Search  Options  Help

SQL> SELECT DISTINCT movie_id, status
  2    FROM videos;

  MOVIE_ID STATUS
---------- ----------
         1 available
         2 available
         3 available
         4 available
         5 available
         6 available
         7 available
         8 available
         9 available
        10 available
```

To restrict the rows returned, use the WHERE clause followed by a *condition*. A condition is one or more expressions that are either true or false for each row in the table that is being used. Conditions will be familiar to Visual Basic programmers because they are basically an IF statement applied to each row of data. As an example, if you wanted to display all the movies under 100 minutes long, you could type

```
SELECT movie_name
  FROM movies
  WHERE length < 100;
```

You can combine expressions in the condition easily with Boolean operators as follows:

```
SELECT movie_name
  FROM movies
  WHERE length < 100 AND rating ='PG';
```

This last case raises a new issue. When a character column is compared to a string literal, that string must be enclosed in single quotes; in contrast, Microsoft Access uses double quotes. However, you never enclose numeric values in quotes.

The AND and OR operators will be familiar to Visual Basic developers. As in any language, if you use the OR operator and have more than two expressions, you should use parentheses to distinguish exactly how you want the condition to work, as in the following example.

```
SELECT movie_name
  FROM movies
  WHERE length < 90 OR (length < 120 AND rating ='PG');
```

This example finds all movies under 90 minutes as well as those movies under 120 minutes and rated PG (see Figure 7.4).

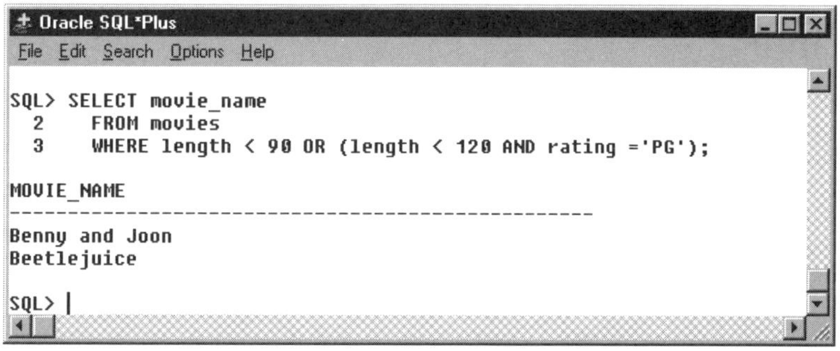

FIGURE 7.4:

Using two operators in the WHERE clause

```
Oracle SQL*Plus                                          _ □ ×
File  Edit  Search  Options  Help

SQL> SELECT movie_name
  2    FROM movies
  3    WHERE length < 90 OR (length < 120 AND rating ='PG');

MOVIE_NAME
--------------------------------------------------
Benny and Joon
Beetlejuice

SQL> |
```

Sorting Your Results

Now that you can select the rows of data you want with the WHERE clause, we will put the rows in the order we want to see them. You may have noticed that up until now you cannot guarantee what order the rows will be in. You cannot even bet on them coming out in the order they went in. To define the order they are retrieved in, you use the ORDER BY clause. The columns specified in the ORDER BY clause do not need to appear in the SELECT column list.

```
SELECT movie_id, movie_name
  FROM movies
  WHERE length < 100 AND rating ='PG'
  ORDER BY length;
```

As you may guess, this SELECT statement will retrieve the movies in ascending order of their length. If you want them in descending order, you need to follow the column name with the keyword DESC as follows:

```
SELECT movie_name
  FROM movies
  WHERE length < 100 AND rating ='PG'
  ORDER BY length DESC;
```

You can specify more than one column for the sort order as long as you separate them by commas.

```
SELECT movie_name
  FROM movies
  WHERE length < 100
  ORDER BY rating, length;
```

This SELECT statement will first sort the rows into groups of their ratings (alphabetically); then, within each group of ratings, they will be sorted by their length (see Figure 7.5).

NOTE   When you have become familiar with the SELECT statement, you will be able to better understand the documentation that comes with Oracle. In this case, you will want to look at the *Oracle SQL Reference* manual. This manual diagrams every aspect of each command in what is called a *syntax*, or *railroad*, *diagram*, which is a series of lines containing all the various options. For the purposes of this chapter, you will meet the various aspects of the SELECT command in increasing order of complexity rather than everything at once.

FIGURE 7.5:

Sorting rows with two
ORDER BY columns

Some Useful Operators

To add the finishing touches to the basic SELECT statement, we must look at the operators you can use in the condition expressions in the WHERE clause. The WHERE clause is the powerhouse behind which records you select. Table 7.2 includes the more common operators, which you will be familiar with because of your VB knowledge.

TABLE 7.2: The Most Commonly Used Operators in SQL

Operator	Description	Example
=	Equality test	SELECT * FROM movies WHERE rating = 'PG';
!= <>	Inequality test (i.e., "not equals")	SELECT * FROM movies WHERE rating <> 'R';
>	Greater than	SELECT * FROM movies WHERE length > 90;
<	Less than	SELECT * FROM movies WHERE length < 120;
>=	Greater than or equal to	SELECT * FROM movies WHERE length >= 90;
<=	Less than or equal to	SELECT * FROM movies WHERE length <=120;
‖	Character-string concatenation (similar to & in Visual Basic)	SELECT first_name ‖ last_name FROM participants;

Continued on next page

TABLE 7.2 CONTINUED: The Most Commonly Used Operators in SQL

Operator	Description	Example
AND	True if both expressions are true. Otherwise it is false.	SELECT * FROM movies WHERE length <=100 AND rating = 'PG';
OR	True if either of the expressions are true. Otherwise it is false.	SELECT * FROM movies WHERE length > 120 OR rating <> 'R';
NOT	Takes the logical opposite of the expression result.	SELECT * FROM movies WHERE NOT rating = 'PG';

Normally, you will use the operators >, <, <+, and >= with numeric data, but they also work with string comparison for character columns. In this case, a string comparison is done the same way as in Visual Basic, where for example, "titanic" is greater than "monty."

In addition to these standard operators, there are some additional comparison operators that you can use in the WHERE clause condition and are available in most relational databases (see Table 7.3).

TABLE 7.3: Additional SQL Operators

Operator	Description	Example
BETWEEN a AND b	Selects rows in which the column value is greater than or equal to a and less than or equal to b	SELECT * FROM movies WHERE length BETWEEN 90 AND 120;
IN	Selects rows in which the column value is equal to any one of a list	SELECT * FROM movies WHERE rating IN ('PG', 'NC-17');
IS NULL	Selects rows in which the column value is a NULL (i.e., undefined)	SELECT id FROM movies WHERE name IS NULL;
LIKE	Case sensitive, character-string pattern matching with wild cards "-" to match exactly one character and "%" to match zero or more characters	SELECT name FROM movies WHERE UPPER(name) LIKE '%JURASSIC%';

Using the LIKE Operator

You can use the LIKE operator for searches using wildcards, but you must be aware that if you use a wildcard at the beginning of the search string, such as in '%JURASSIC', it can place a heavy burden on the server, because no use can be made of any indexes. If your program's main function is to do string searches, you may need to consider using Oracle's Context option. This optional software not only produces an index on *every* word in a document but also allows thematic and proximity searches. This useful feature is becoming more expected of Web sites. The downside is that the index can take up a similar amount of space compared with the original data, but it *is* a scalable solution given sufficient resources, and the index can even be held in a different database from the data.

One excellent use for the Context option is in a Web-based Yellow Pages application. Fast string searches, the ability to look for similar types of words, as well as finding words close to each other are extremely powerful capabilities and may give your application a competitive advantage.

Calculated Columns

So far in this chapter, we have been supplying a list of column names in the SELECT statement that can be returned from the database. You can instead include one or more *calculated* columns that return the value of a calculation between columns, such as the sum of two columns or text values concatenated together. Calculated columns can include operators, such as "+", "-", "*", and "/", as well as standard Oracle functions.

NOTE   The exponential operator is not available in SQL, but it is available in PL/SQL as '**'.

Examples of calculated columns are shown below. The first returns a concatenated column, the second adds 8.5 percent to all prices, and the last adds two days to the rental date to find the return date.

```
SELECT first_name || last_name FROM participants;

SELECT cost * 1.085 FROM videos;

SELECT rental_date + 2 FROM videos;
```

Calculated Column Processing in Practice

In the tests that I have done with calculated columns in SELECT statements, I have found little overall speed difference between returning a concatenated field back to Visual Basic as opposed to doing the calculation in VB itself. To decide where you do the calculation, you should keep in mind the application's architecture and the relative resources available to your servers and clients.

If you are developing a "thin" client—that is, one with a minimum amount of processing—or you have an overly powerful or underworked server, then you will probably do the processing on the server. If you have a traditional client/server architecture that is typical of Visual Basic–to-Oracle processing or your server is lacking horsepower, you will probably find it more efficient to do the calculations on the client.

Oracle-Specific Functions

Oracle includes a large number of functions that operate on columns as does virtually every other RDBMS. However, nearly all databases sport different sets of functions, and even those that have the same functionality can have different implementations. A few Oracle specific functions that need to be picked out for special attention are shown in Table 7.4.

TABLE 7.4: The Most Commonly Used Oracle-Specific Functions

Function Name	Description
SYSDATE	Returns the current server date and time. The default display is in the format 'DD_MON-YY'. To change the format, use the TO_CHAR function.
USER	Returns the user name of the user executing the command.
TO_CHAR()	Converts data to a character format. Useful with dates because it allows you to specify formats different from the default, such as SELECT TO_CHAR(SYSDATE, 'DD-MON-YYYY:HH:MM'), which will add hours and minutes, e.g., 21-JUN-1998:12:01.
TO_DATE()	Converts a character string to a valid date if possible, e.g., TO_DATE('21 January 1998','DD Month YYYY'). The format must match the character string being converted.
CONCAT	Concatenates only two column values; the "ll"operator is more versatile.
UPPER()	Returns a character column in uppercase.

Continued on next page

TABLE 7.4 CONTINUED: The Most Commonly Used Oracle-Specific Functions

Function Name	Description
LOWER()	Returns a character column in lowercase.
INITCAP()	Sets the initial characters or words to uppercase.

Dates in Practice

Displaying dates is another issue that can cause some concern when selecting fields from a database table. Normally, the default format will be used, such as in the following example:

```
SELECT SYSDATE FROM DUAL;
> 12-SEP-1998
```

If you want to display a date column in a different format, especially to uncover the time information, you will have to use the TO_CHAR function, which is similar to Visual Basic's FORMAT command:

```
SELECT TO_CHAR(SYSDATE,'DD-MON-YYYY:HH:MI:SS') FROM DUAL;
> 12-SEP-1998:13:24:43
```

You will encounter an interesting problem when you want to put a date into a WHERE clause. If you do specify a date, then Oracle will search for rows with exactly the same value in the date column. This means Oracle will match the date *and* the time portions of that column. If your date column is entered as date only, such as '12-SEP-98,' then the time portion defaults to 12 A.M. (The time is stored as a decimal portion for the column and the default is zero.)

If you want to search for rows that are stored with date and time, then you have to be more careful; the SYSDATE function, for example, holds both the date and time. If you now try to do

```
SELECT * FROM movies WHERE time_stamp = '12-SEP-98';
```

then it is highly unlikely you will find any rows, because you are looking for values of the Time_Stamp column that has a time of 12 A.M. You can work around this, however, by using the TRUNC function. This function truncates the time portion of the date column. You can now do the SELECT command you want as follows:

```
SELECT * FROM movies WHERE TRUNC(time_stamp) = '12-SEP-98';
```

Note that we will be covering the ways of formatting dates in the Chapter 8, in which it is even more critical to have a full understanding of how Oracle handles dates.

The DECODE Function

The DECODE function is perhaps one of the least understood of all the functions. This predicament is not helped by the fact that the manuals virtually ignore it. The DECODE function is listed only under "decoded expression," but it can be a valuable tool and can contribute to more efficient queries.

The DECODE function is best thought of as a way to convert (or literally decode) one expression into another. These expressions can be numeric or character. You provide an expression (often a column name) you want to convert and a list of search/result pairs to do the decoding, and you follow it with a default value, which is used if there is not a match between the search and result expressions. The following command syntax sums this up:

```
DECODE (expression, search1, result1,
                    search2, result2, (etc)
                    default_value)
```

However, it is much easier to understand this function with an example. If you want to query the Movies table but you want to see a more meaningful version of the code instead of the codes for the ratings, you could do it by creating a new code table and linking it to the Movies table. However, you can also do this without a second table, by using the DECODE function as follows:

```
SELECT movie_name,
   DECODE (rating, 'G','General',
                   'PG','Parental Guidance',
                   'PG-13','No children under 13',
                   'Adults only') rating
   FROM movies;
```

So what actually does this produce? As each row is retrieved, the rating column is first compared to 'G.' If it matches, the SELECT statement retrieves 'General' for that column. If it doesn't match, it is next compared to 'PG' and so on. If there are any rows in which the value of the rating column does not match the three search expressions, then the default value "Adults Only" is returned for that row. The output of this SELECT statement is shown in Figure 7.6.

You can see this is a useful and efficient way to convert these code values into meaningful strings. The only downside is that it works best for a small number of values that need to be decoded. Preferably, the list will seldom change.

FIGURE 7.6:

Using the DECODE function

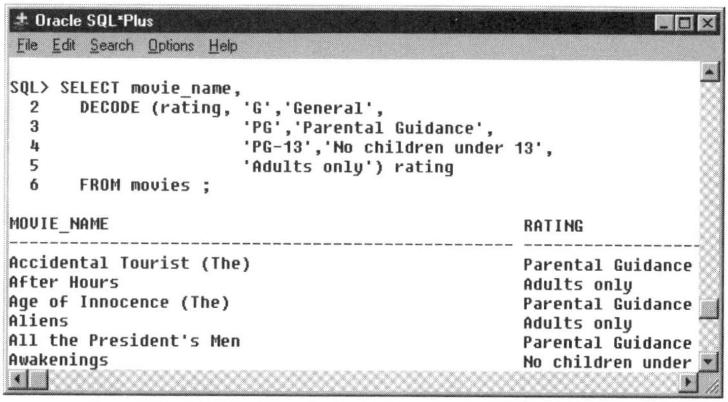

To make the returned values easily visible from Visual Basic, it is best to follow the DECODE function with a column *alias* to give it a useable name. An alias is a string that follows the column name separated only by a space and provides a different name for the column in the result set. In the example of a DECODE function shown above, the alias "rating" is used, which then appears as the column name in the output.

The DECODE Function in Practice

Listing 7.1 shows a more interesting example of how the DECODE function can work. In this situation, we are dealing with a database that holds hourly schedules, with each hour in a separate row. The user really wanted to use the CROSS-TABULATION function that is found in Microsoft Access but is missing from Oracle. CROSS-TABULATION can take the data and create 25 columns, one for each hour (the database allows an extra hour for the long day when the clocks roll back in the fall) and which are named "hour1" to "hour25."

Listing 7.1 emulates a CROSS-TABULATION. There are 25 DECODE statements, each one creating one hourly column in the returned result set, and each calculated in the same way. Each DECODE function checks the value in the hour column for the current record. If it equals the test value (say number one), then the value in the Schedule_Amount column is placed into the return column, which has the alias "hour1." If the test hour does not match, then the default value of zero is returned.

Rather than return all of the rows in this query, the totals for each hour are summed by Schedule_Day and Schedule_Number with a SUM function, and only the totals are returned because a GROUP BY clause is used; in this way the amount of rows returned is many times less than it would have been.

Listing 7.1

```
SELECT schedule_day, schedule_number,
    SUM (DECODE (hour, 1, schedule_amount,0)) hour1,
    SUM (DECODE (hour, 2, schedule_amount,0)) hour2,
    SUM (DECODE (hour, 3, schedule_amount,0)) hour3,
    SUM (DECODE (hour, 4, schedule_amount,0)) hour4,
    SUM (DECODE (hour, 5, schedule_amount,0)) hour5,
    SUM (DECODE (hour, 6, schedule_amount,0)) hour6,
    SUM (DECODE (hour, 7, schedule_amount,0)) hour7,
    SUM (DECODE (hour, 8, schedule_amount,0)) hour8,
    SUM (DECODE (hour, 9, schedule_amount,0)) hour9,
    SUM (DECODE (hour, 10, schedule_amount,0)) hour10,
    SUM (DECODE (hour, 11, schedule_amount,0)) hour11,
    SUM (DECODE (hour, 12, schedule_amount,0)) hour12,
    SUM (DECODE (hour, 13, schedule_amount,0)) hour13,
    SUM (DECODE (hour, 14, schedule_amount,0)) hour14,
    SUM (DECODE (hour, 15, schedule_amount,0)) hour15,
    SUM (DECODE (hour, 16, schedule_amount,0)) hour16,
    SUM (DECODE (hour, 17, schedule_amount,0)) hour17,
    SUM (DECODE (hour, 18, schedule_amount,0)) hour18,
    SUM (DECODE (hour, 19, schedule_amount,0)) hour19,
    SUM (DECODE (hour, 20, schedule_amount,0)) hour20,
    SUM (DECODE (hour, 21, schedule_amount,0)) hour21,
    SUM (DECODE (hour, 22, schedule_amount,0)) hour22,
    SUM (DECODE (hour, 23, schedule_amount,0)) hour23,
    SUM (DECODE (hour, 24, schedule_amount,0)) hour24,
    SUM (DECODE (hour, schedule, sch_amount,0)) hour25
FROM hours_view
GROUP BY schedule_day, schedule_number
```

Group Functions

Although the functions we saw in Tables 7.2 and 7.3 operate on the rows individually, *group* functions act on groups of rows. As such, they can normally return only one row from a single SELECT statement. However, in the next section, you will see that you can group rows with the GROUP BY clause to produce a group function on multiple groups of rows and so return one row from each group. The group functions shown in Table 7.5 will be familiar to programmers who have used products like Excel because they perform a similar function.

You should always consider using functions if at all possible. The natural reaction for a Visual Basic developer is that you can more easily do whatever calculations you want on the PC. However, if you consider doing an average of a column in 100 rows, you would have to pull all 100 rows off the database and then do your calculations. Instead, the use of the AVG function will mean your retrieval will work much faster because only one value needs to be retrieved: the average itself.

TABLE 7.5: The Oracle Functions That Operate on a Group of Rows

Group Function	Description
AVG (col_name)	Returns the average of all the values in the specified column.
COUNT (col_name)	Returns the number of records whose specified column value is not a null. Note the special case of COUNT(*), which returns a count of all the rows, including nulls, in the selected list.
MAX (col_name)	Returns the maximum of all the values in the specified column.
MIN (col_name)	Returns the minimum of all the values in the specified column.
STDDEV (col_name)	Returns the statistical standard deviation of all the values in the specified column.
SUM (col_name)	Returns the sum of all the values in the specified column.
VARIANCE (col_name)	Returns the statistical variance of all the values in the specified column.

The normal way that you will use the group functions is shown in this example:

```
SELECT MAX(length), MIN(length), AVG(length)
   FROM movies;
```

The SELECT statement will display one row giving the maximum, minimum, and average length of all the selected rows. (Figure 7.7 shows the output of the query.) These functions are useful, but they really come into their own when used as the input to other SQL commands, as we shall see later in the section on subqueries.

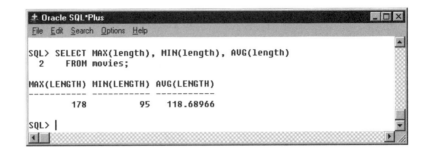

The GROUP BY Clause

In the previous section, we saw how to apply a group function, such as AVG or
SUM, to the group of selected rows all at once. You can also separate the selected
rows into distinct groups and apply the group functions to each of the distinct
groups. Your SELECT command will produce one line of output for each group.
The following example demonstrates this:

```
SELECT rating, AVG(length)
   FROM movies
   GROUP BY rating;
```

The SELECT statement produces a listing of the average length of each type of
rating and displays that average alongside the movie rating as shown in Figure 7.8.
The columns that you include in the GROUP BY clause are used to define the
groups. When any of the columns in this clause changes, a new group is started.
So in this case, a change in the rating column will mark the end of a group.

```
Oracle SQL*Plus
File  Edit  Search  Options  Help

SQL> SELECT rating, AVG(length)
  2      FROM movies
  3      GROUP BY rating ;

RATING AVG(LENGTH)
------ -----------
NC-17           96
PG       121.14286
PG-13    120.57143
R        118.14286

SQL>
```

Problems with GROUP BY

What is not immediately obvious from the example is that although you can display more than just the group function value—in this case, the AVG (length)—the other columns returned must be mentioned in the GROUP BY clause; that means those columns are also used to define the groups, which may not be what you want. This can, in certain circumstances, be frustrating and mean that you have to resort to much more sophisticated SELECT commands or even retrieve all the data and produce the calculations yourself in your Visual Basic application.

We can show this problem in an example using the MAX function. If we want to select the maximum length and name of the movies in each rating category, we cannot type

```
SELECT movie_name, rating, MAX(length)
  FROM movies
  GROUP BY rating;
```

In fact, we will get an error message, referring to the Movie_Name column:

```
ORA-00979: not a GROUP BY expression
```

This is because, although the rating and maximum length can be found, Movie_Name, which is not in the GROUP BY clause, cannot be retrieved. If you want to know the name of the movie that has the maximum length in each rating category, you will have to find a different method. Though it is beyond the scope of this book, those of you wanting to know how to do this in one SELECT statement can investigate the following code:

```
SELECT movie_name, rating, length
  FROM movies
  WHERE (rating, length) IN
    (SELECT rating, MAX(length)
        FROM movies
  GROUP BY rating);
```

The HAVING Clause

A final refinement of the GROUP BY clause is to control exactly which groups are selected for reporting. In the previous example, we listed the maximum length of movies in all ratings groups. If you only want to see those groups where the maximum length of film is over, say, 120 minutes, then you will need to use a new clause: the HAVING clause. This clause functions in a similar way to the WHERE clause except that it operates on groups and not on individual rows. In this situation, we only want to select the groups that have a maximum length over 120 minutes, so we write:

```
SELECT rating, MAX(length)
 FROM movies
 GROUP BY rating
  HAVING MAX(length)> 120;
```

NOTE   Try to remember that the WHERE clause applies to single rows and the HAVING clause applies to groups. They can both appear in the same SELECT statement.

Queries from More Than One Table

If you have a totally de-normalized database, then the preceding sections will satisfy most of your requirements. However, even in a poorly designed database, you will usually have to retrieve data from more than one table, and if you have fully normalized the database (as I certainly hope you have), then you will be combining several tables for nearly *every* query you execute.

To join two or more tables, you need to perform what is called a table join. A join is the term for literally joining together the columns of more than one table. As we have seen in Chapter 5, *Database Design*, the very heart of a relational database is the relations between the tables. These relationships are identified in the tables by means of foreign keys; however, the foreign keys are just a way of ensuring that the database integrity is maintained because it does not implicitly produce a join. To make these relationships functional, you have to put the relationships into your SQL code.

There are several types of joins, and the syntax is worth looking at, especially for those of you familiar with other implementations of SQL, because there are some "regional" differences between vendors.

We have seen previously that the FROM clause in the SELECT command allows us to specify a table from which to retrieve data. In fact, we can specify any number of tables if we separate them by commas. Let's take the example of two tables. If we try

```
SELECT *
 FROM movies, videos;
```

hoping to read all the columns from both tables, that is what we will get. However, we will also get far more than we bargained for. What the command will do is combine every row from one table with every row from the other. If we had one thousand records in each of the two tables, we now have one million combined rows to look through (this is called a *Cartesian* join and should normally be avoided at all costs).

You need to be more careful and exact about what you want. If you want to match rows in the Videos table with those in the Movies table where they have the same movie_id value, then you need to define that with a *join condition* as follows:

```
SELECT *
  FROM movies, videos
  WHERE movies.movie_id = videos.movie_id;
```

This SELECT statement returns rows from the Movies table joined to the Videos table only if there are matching Movie_id columns in each one. All other combinations of rows are ignored.

The query has now introduced a potential problem. In the example, we have two tables, and each has a column called Movie_id that we want to join together. In the WHERE clause, we have to be specific about which table we are talking about, and including the table name is the way we do this. When we want to refer to a column in one particular table, we precede it by its table name separated by a period, for example, `videos.movie_id`. This technique is similar to defining a class property in Visual Basic in which you also have to separate the object name and the property by a period.

Duplicate Column Names

Whenever we return every column from two or more tables, and there are tables containing the same column name (in this case it is Movie_id), you should avoid selecting both. You may find that one of them is not returned, even if you specify it because the Oracle parser does not realize they are different. This can be confusing when you are looking at your Recordset in Visual Basic and wondering why not enough columns have been returned. In the example, you may find you only get first Movie_id column, the one from the movies table and not the videos table.

Continued on next page

This missing column may not be a cause for concern (in our example they are the same value), but it could become more of a problem. It is always better to select only the fields you want, but if you need both occurrences of a column, such as Movie_id, then you should follow at least one with a column *alias*. This is an alternative column name added after the actual column name. For example

```
SELECT movies.movie_id movie_id1,
   videos.movie_id movie_id2
   FROM movies, videos
   WHERE movies.movie_id = videos.movie_id;
```

TIP   It is better to use explicit table references not only to remove ambiguity but also to improve performance because Oracle uses recursive SQL to resolve unqualified column names.

TIP   In addition, try to avoid joining too many tables. Fewer are better because it means less server-side processing, but in any event, try to keep the number of tables to no more than four.

Outer Joins

The type of table join we saw in the previous section is considered a standard join in Oracle, although there really is no defined term. In other environments, this may be called an *inner join*, which means the rows are selected from the first table only if a matching row is available in the second table. In the example, we take every row in the Movie table that has a matching Movie_id column in the Video table.

However, sometimes you want to return all the rows in the first table irrespective of whether there are any matching rows in the second table. This is called an *outer join*. We can produce this in Oracle with the (+) operator. We place the operator in the join condition after the column name of the table. An example will make it clearer.

```
SELECT *
   FROM movies, videos
   WHERE movies.movie_id = videos.movie.id (+);
```

The SELECT statement will select all the rows from the Movies table whether there are matching rows in the Video table or not. If there are matching rows, then those matching rows will be selected. If not, then the values of the "missing" columns will be NULL. Though this is not the standard join, there are many circumstances in which you may need this type of join. For example, we can include the names of all the movies in our query results even if we do not have a video copy of the movie.

NOTE   RDBMS vendors implement table joins in different ways and with different syntax. Oracle does not implement the full SQL-92 syntax for joins. (It does not even have the JOIN clause.) At the other extreme, Microsoft Access has a large number of ways to produce joins, including LEFT OUTER JOIN and RIGHT OUTER JOIN. At least Oracle syntax is simple and can produce most of the required results.

Subqueries

A *subquery* is an interesting variation on the SELECT command and leads to some powerful ways to extract data, although the queries tend to become too complicated to understand and control. A subquery is a query that is placed inside another SQL statement (usually a SELECT, UPDATE, or DELETE command that can also be used with the INSERT command) and is often called a *nested query*.

You use the subquery to extract information from the database that can effectively be passed on as input to another query (the *parent query*). In fact, you can nest SELECT statements several deep, though you have to be careful that you know what you are doing, or you will not get the results you want, and the query could become a resource hog.

There are two distinct types of subqueries: those that return exactly one row, and those that can return zero, one, or more rows. The way you use each type is slightly different and is described in the next two sections.

Subqueries That Return One Value

Most often you will create a subquery that returns only one value. An example is to find all the movies longer than the average length. We could run one query to find the average length and then construct another query, hard-coding this value. However, we can do this all in one go with subqueries:

```
SELECT movie_name
  FROM movies
```

```
WHERE length >
  (SELECT AVG(length)
    FROM movies)
ORDER BY movie_name;
```

The subquery is enclosed in parentheses and returns the average length of all the movies in the Movies table as follows:

```
SELECT AVG(length)
    FROM movies
```

This average value is then passed to the parent query as an actual value (such as 102 minutes). Note that with this syntax, the subquery must return exactly one row, or you will get an error message. The results of the query are shown in Figure 7.9.

FIGURE 7.9:

Using a subquery to find all movies of greater than average length

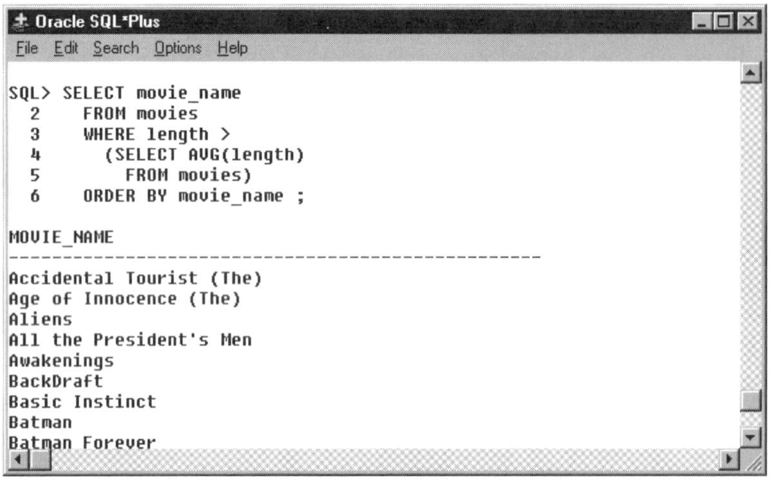

Subqueries That Return More Than One Row

There are times when you need to use a subquery that returns more than one row. You then have to use the subquery with the IN part of the WHERE clause in the parent query. As an example, suppose you want to find all the video copies of movies that are shorter than 90 minutes and available for rent (status = 'available'). The following code will do the job:

```
SELECT video_id, copy_number
    FROM videos
```

```
WHERE videos.movie_id IN
  (SELECT movie_id
     FROM movies
     WHERE length<90)
  AND status = 'available';
```

The subquery first finds the Movie_id values of all the movies that are less than 90 minutes long. In this case, it will return more than one row. The resulting list of Movie_id column values is now passed to the parent query where it is used to see whether there is an available video copy of it. You can achieve the same result with a regular SELECT statement as follows:

```
SELECT video_id, copy_number
  FROM videos, movies
  WHERE videos.movie_id = movies.movie_id
    AND videos.status = 'available'
    AND movies.length < 90;
```

The subquery method is a little simpler but is generally to be avoided because of the performance penalty. However, in some circumstances, there is no practical alternative.

Optimizing Your Queries

It is important to understand how Oracle handles a SQL statement. First, any statement must be parsed into what is called a *parse tree* or *execution plan*. This includes the steps needed to retrieve the data. Oracle arrives at the best execution plan using its *optimizer*.

Oracle has two types of optimizer. One type is called a *rule-based* optimizer and has been around for a long time. A look-up table includes about 20 rules (or access paths) for deciding the best plan for a particular SQL statement. The fastest path is "single row by ROWID," which is a direct route to a row of data. Indexes are high on the list but not at the top.

NOTE   A ROWID is the location or address of an individual row in the Oracle database and does not change for the life of the row. It is represented by the ROWID pseudocolumn, so you can SELECT it from a table, but you will not see it as part of the description.

The second type of optimizer is the *cost-based* optimizer that works on statistics gathered about the data in the tables. Until recently, this optimizer has not had a good reputation, and many developers won't use it. However, it is becoming recognized as the better of the two types. In the cost-based approach, Oracle decides on access paths by using table statistics generated by the ANALYZE statement. You can compute the exact statistics or, for a large table, estimate them. The main thing is to ensure that the statistics are kept up-to-date.

Efficient SELECT Statements

Tuning a database is a wonderful yet totally frustrating experience, especially for those with less knowledge. There is no magical solution, and often trial and error and some intimate knowledge of the application are as much as anyone has. However, there are a few general-purpose hints you may want to consider to improve the performance of your code.

- Place the smallest table last. This is because the order of tables in the FROM clause of the SELECT statement can have some affect on the execution plan. However, the cost-based optimizer may ignore this.

- Construct the WHERE clauses so that the most restrictive condition is last. Again the optimizer may ignore this.

- Try to avoid the use of functions in the query, especially when an indexed column is involved, because the presence of the function will disable the index.

- Review each column in the WHERE clause to determine whether it is suitable for an index. If it is a small table or the SELECT statement retrieves a large amount of data, the index will not be beneficial, and you may even want to stop using it or drop it all together.

- Try to avoid the LIKE function using a wild card at the beginning (for example, `"movie LIKE '%world'"`). The LIKE function may result in an unintended full table scan. Do not use calculations on an indexed column because this will disable the use of the index.

- Consider the use of the DECODE function instead of code tables.

- Do not use more subqueries than necessary.

- Do not request more columns than you need. (The "*" selects all columns and is a bad offender.) If you limit the columns to only those you require, then you can use methods such as GetRows in Visual Basic to improve performance.

- Do not request more rows than you need, so be careful with your WHERE clauses. Also, use Oracle group functions such as AVG and MAX if you only need summaries.

- Keep in mind that you want to avoid physical disk reads and the amount of sorting.

Database Design for Fast SELECT Statements

Although this is not a chapter on database design, it is worth going over some of the decisions made when designing a database that will greatly affect the speed with which SELECT statements are processed. Databases are generally considered to be either Online Transaction Processing applications, with many more writes to the database than reads, or Decision Support in which there are many more reads than writes.

If you want to make your SELECT statements as fast as possible, this will be detrimental to the writes. For example, one of the better ways to improve query times is to use indexes on several columns in a table. I have seen designs like this that are fine for queries but die on the operating table when it is updated.

The most difficult decisions come when you want good performance of both reads *and* writes. This is a compromise between read performance and write performance that you will have to make with as much knowledge of the working application as possible.

The Explain Statement

Although an understanding of the optimizer is useful for anyone needing to produce efficient queries and we can use rules of thumb to improve the performance of our SELECT statements, it is nice to know that there is a tool that we can use to figure out exactly what the optimizer has decided is the best way to get the job done. This tool is the SQL command EXPLAIN PLAN, and it can produce what is called the execution plan that the optimizer comes up with.

Unfortunately the EXPLAIN PLAN command is not an easy-to-use GUI tool. It is in fact a three-step process. The steps are

1. Create a table to receive the execution plan. (You only need to do this the first time you run it.) You create the table with a standard script called

UTLXPLAN.SQL on most platforms. On Windows NT, this file is normally found in C:\ORANT\RDBMSxx\ where *xx* is the server version number, such as 73. You should create this table in your own schema by executing the script from your account.

2. Run the EXPLAIN PLAN command. The way you run this is shown in the script file in Listing 7.2.

3. Run a SQL statement to interpret the execution plan. The standard script is shown in Listing 7.3.

Listing 7.2

```
DELETE FROM PLAN_TABLE;

EXPLAIN PLAN FOR
    SELECT movie_name, video_id
      FROM videos, movies
      WHERE  movies.movie_id = videos.movie_id
      AND videos.status = 'available'
      AND movies.length < 90;
```

Listing 7.3

```
SELECT LPAD (' ',2*level) || operation || ' ' ||
    OPTIONS || ' ' || object_name "Execution Plan"
    FROM plan_table
    CONNECT BY PRIOR id=parent_id
    START WITH id=1;
```

The results of running this script are shown in Figure 7.10. Unfortunately, it is not overly obvious what the output means at this stage. One of the major things you want to look for is how the tables are accessed. This information is available in the TABLE ACCESS lines, which can have the possible values shown in Table 7.6. There are many other pieces of information presented in this output. For a full description, you should see the *Oracle Server Tuning* manual.

In this particular example, Figure 7.10 shows that while the Movies table is accessed by ROWID (that is, an indexed scan), the Videos table undergoes a full table scan.

FIGURE 7.10:

The execution plan for a simple query

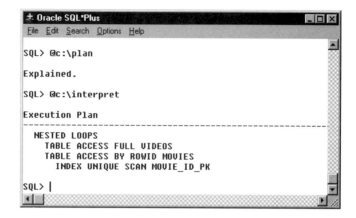

TABLE 7.6: The Various Values for the TABLE ACCESS Lines in the EXPLAIN PLAN Output

Value	Description
FULL	This indicates a full table scan, something that should be avoided unless the table is very small or you really are going to retrieve most of the rows from it.
CLUSTER	With this value, the access will be to a table in a cluster using a cluster index.
HASH	This value again indicates access to a table in a cluster, this time using a hash index.
BY ROWID	This indicates that retrieved rows are accessed directly by ROWID, usually indicating that an index has been used.

WARNING   EXPLAIN PLAN writes rows to the table Plan_Table, but it does not commit those rows. You should use the COMMIT statement if you want to make those changes permanent. However, you should delete all the rows before running EXPLAIN PLAN again, or you will end up with a meaningless mixture of rows.

As an example of a more complex situation, the EXPLAIN PLAN statement shown in Listing 7.4 is taken from a production-database query. For simplicity, the query shows an asterisk for the field names because the actual query has 19 columns specified. The output, shown in Listing 7.5 identifies that two tables are accessed with full table scans. This was to be expected because they are very small look-up tables. The other two tables are accessed by key as designed.

Listing 7.4

```
EXPLAIN PLAN FOR
SELECT  *
  FROM Route_paths, Services, Transactions, Schedules
  WHERE Transactions.Transaction_Date =
    TO_DATE('23-Aug-1998','DD-MON-YYYY')
    AND Schedules.Service_ID = Services.ID
    AND Schedules.ID = Transactions.Schedule_ID
    AND Schedules.Path_Id = Route_Paths.Route_Id
    AND Schedules.type = 'regular'
  ORDER BY path_id, service_id, schedule_id, transactions.id
```

Listing 7.5

```
SORT ORDER BY
  HASH JOIN
    TABLE ACCESS FULL ROUTE_PATHS
    HASH JOIN
     TABLE ACCESS FULL SERVICES
     NESTED LOOPS
       TABLE ACCESS BY ROWID TRANSACTIONS
         INDEX RANGE SCAN IND_TRANS_DATE
       TABLE ACCESS BY ROWID SCHEDULES
         INDEX RANGE SCAN SCHEDULES_ID_PK

10 rows selected.
```

TIP   With almost every Visual Basic screen I create that runs queries, I like to put in a hidden multiline text box that only becomes visible with my user name. Into this text box I place the current SQL query string. Apart from being an excellent debugging tool, this also allows you to copy the query and paste it into an EXPLAIN PLAN statement in a SQL*Plus session.

Specifying Schemas

Much of the chapter up to this point could apply to any relational database. However, when you are accessing data in an Oracle database, there are several things that you need to keep in mind, such as where is the data and do I have the privileges to access it?

If you are accessing the data in your own schema (that is, you are the owner of the tables that you are accessing), then the select statements presented so far will work without any trouble. However, if an end user (probably using your Visual Basic program) wants to access the data store in the applications schema, then we need to define which schema each table is in.

You define where a table is by adding the schema name in front of every table in the FROM clause (separated, as usual, by a period). You do not need to specify the schema anywhere else, such as in the WHERE clause, because Oracle now knows exactly which table you mean. This assumes that you do not have tables of the same name in different schemas that you are accessing at the same time! For example, if the movie database tables are in the movies schema, then for non-schema users you would have to write:

```
SELECT *
  FROM video_store.movies, video_store.videos
  WHERE movies.movie_id = videos.movie_id;
```

It is a good idea to give your tables a short application prefix, in case you ever do have to retrieve data from more than one schema. For example, the Customers table would better be named *Movie_Customers*. Then, if there is another table with customer information in another schema, you will easily be able to distinguish the two tables.

If your tables have the same name, you have to take an additional step. Just as we saw column aliases, you can also have table aliases. You use the same technique of adding a name after the table name as follows:

```
SELECT *
  FROM video_store.movies a, video_store.videos b
  WHERE a.movie_id = b.movie.id;
```

Though using single letters is not the most descriptive alias to give to tables, it is a very common technique. It is also useful to simplify your queries and reduce the amount of typing you have to do.

Problems with Pseudocolumns

You have now seen a large number of ways to select one or more rows of data from your database. The main SELECT command (as opposed to a subquery) identifies a list of column names that will be retrieved. These column names may refer to actual columns or to *pseudocolumns,* such as NEXTVAL and CURRVAL, that retrieve sequence values. The term pseudocolumn also refers to computed columns, such as the average of the values in a column, or the count, or maybe the concatenation of two columns to return them as one. None of these are real, physical columns.

We shall go over the ways of creating and accessing the retrieved data in Visual Basic in later chapters, but you generally create a Recordset by passing a SELECT statement to the server. When you want the actual value from a column in the Recordset, you can refer to it by the column name, which will only work as long as it is a proper column. In the case of pseudocolumns, you have two options:

- Refer to the column by its position in the Fields collection of the Recordset (remembering it is zero-based).

- Add a column alias to refer to it. An alias is a string that you add after the column name in double quotes, such as

```
SELECT first_name || ' ' || last_name full_name FROM customers
```

where the alias *full_name* is returned as the column name.

Summary

This chapter has introduced most of the major features you will use when writing SELECT statements. It has covered basic SELECT statements with filtering and ordering. We have seen how to join two or more tables together and dealt with subqueries. We have also covered some of the Oracle and Visual Basic specific things you need to be aware of. Other features and a richer command syntax await you in the *Oracle SQL Reference* manual.

The examples covered have been simple but complete enough to show most aspects of the SELECT command. As you develop more complex statements, you will usually be adding more column names to select, more tables, and more WHEN clause expressions; the fundamentals will always remain.

CHAPTER

EIGHT

8

Updating Your Database

- A Philosophy of Updating Tables

- Inserting Rows

- Updating Rows

- Deleting Rows

- Transaction Control

- Security Implications

- Database Triggers

- Bulk Loading of Data

- Dates and the Year 2000 Problem

Apart from using queries to retrieve data from the database, the other major task you will have is to write data into the database. You have to be familiar with the process using the Data Manipulation Language SQL commands, such as INSERT, UPDATE and DELETE, and you have to make sure the process is done in a secure, correct, and efficient way.

In this chapter, we will cover the following topics:

- A philosophy of updating tables
- Inserting rows
- Updating rows
- Deleting rows
- Transaction control
- Security implications
- Database triggers
- Bulk loading of data
- Dates and the Year 2000 problem

A Philosophy for Updating Tables

What is the best way to update a table? In the second half of this book, we will be reviewing in great detail the many ways for a Visual Basic developer to select data from tables and make changes to those tables; for now, we will take an overview of the general philosophy behind these processes.

There are several ways to update a table or view from Visual Basic:

1. Use a Data Control.
2. Use an updatable Recordset.
3. Executing SQL statements.
4. Executing a stored procedure.

It would be fair to say that these steps are roughly in order of difficulty. But they are also in inverse order of security and performance, which means there is a trade-off between these features.

Data Controls attract most developers, especially if they are new to database programming. Updatable Recordsets come in a close second. In the Microsoft Access world, Data Controls are not a *bad* alternative. However, once you move to an enterprise environment, you have to be careful that you are using a secure and efficient method of interfacing with the database. You will, after all, be competing with Oracle's own high-end tools, which integrate tightly with the database. You will also have to give privileges to users that will allow them to update your Oracle tables with Microsoft Access, Excel, or the programs the users write themselves. It depends on how much you trust your users!

At a minimum, you should become familiar with executing INSERT, UPDATE, and DELETE statements from Visual Basic: some DBAs consider these statements the "proper" way to do it. However, using these DML statements does nothing for security, which is difficult to enforce. A far more secure method is to do all your updates through stored procedures. This way, you allow users to only have EXECUTE privileges to the procedures rather than access to all the DML statements. If the data is at all valuable, a good DBA would not want it any other way.

WARNING There is one other problem with updatable Recordsets in Visual Basic. When used with Oracle, the ODBC parser simulates the updatable cursor on the client. As a result, you cannot include any Oracle-specific syntax, such as functions. To use this syntax, you must use the SQLPassthrough option. This option, in turn, does not allow the Recordsets to be updatable—you are stuck with read-only.

Whether you execute your DML statements from within Visual Basic or you execute stored procedures, you will need to understand how to use the INSERT, UPDATE, and DELETE commands, which we shall now cover.

Inserting Rows

The SQL INSERT command allows you to insert one or more rows into your table or view. Whenever you are creating a new record, the constraints we encountered in Chapter 6, *Implementing a Database,* must always be observed. If you try to bypass the constraint requirements, then the INSERT will fail.

There are two forms of the INSERT statement: the first allows only one row to be inserted, and the second uses a subquery allowing zero, one, or more rows to be inserted.

NOTE   You can always execute an UPDATE command on any table in your own schema; if you want to work on a table in another schema, then you have to include the schema name, which must precede the table name separated by a period, such as video_store.movies. You also need appropriate privileges to operate on that table.

Single-Row Inserts

There are two basic forms of the single-row INSERT statement. Both use a VALUES clause to list the values we want to insert into the columns of the new row. The syntax of an INSERT statement is

```
INSERT INTO table_name
    VALUES (value1, value2…;
```

The following is a more detailed example of the syntax.

```
INSERT INTO movies
    VALUES (213, 'My New Film', 102, 'PG-13', 1998, USER, SYSDATE);
```

When this statement is executed (see Figure 8.1), you will notice how many rows have been inserted—in this example, only one. The INSERT statement assumes you are entering one value in the VALUES clause for each column in the table. The values must match exactly one for one in data type and number. If you don't match up the values to the columns, then you will see an error message, unless the missing values are at the end and are either NULLs or a DEFAULT value that you have supplied in the table definition.

NOTE   Oracle determines the column order by the relative order of each column in the data dictionary view, DBA_TAB_COLUMNS. This relative order is most easily seen when you execute a DESCRIBE command on the table.

FIGURE 8.1:

A simple INSERT statement

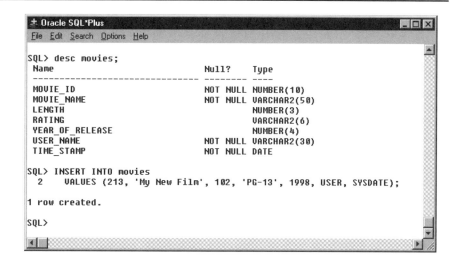

```
Oracle SQL*Plus                                              _ □ ×
File  Edit  Search  Options  Help

SQL> desc movies;
 Name                            Null?     Type
 ------------------------------- --------- ----
 MOVIE_ID                        NOT NULL  NUMBER(10)
 MOVIE_NAME                      NOT NULL  VARCHAR2(50)
 LENGTH                                    NUMBER(3)
 RATING                                    VARCHAR2(6)
 YEAR_OF_RELEASE                           NUMBER(4)
 USER_NAME                       NOT NULL  VARCHAR2(30)
 TIME_STAMP                      NOT NULL  DATE

SQL> INSERT INTO movies
  2     VALUES (213, 'My New Film', 102, 'PG-13', 1998, USER, SYSDATE);

1 row created.

SQL>
```

The second form of a single-row INSERT statement lets you enter a subset of the table columns. Again the values you supply must match the column list exactly. You can specify the columns in any order you want so long as the order of the list in the VALUES clause matches. For example,

```
INSERT INTO movies (movie_id, movie_name, length,
           year_of_release, rating)
   VALUES (214, 'My Other New Film', 102, 1998, 'PG-13');
```

Any missing values will be NULL, unless a DEFAULT value is provided in the table definition. All constraints must be met; if you do not provide a value for a column that is NOT NULL and has no default, the INSERT statement will fail. For example, the INSERT statement in Figure 8.2 has a missing user name and time stamp, which are provided automatically. The SELECT statement, which follows the INSERT, proves that the values of the missed columns have been supplied.

TIP

You can insert a NULL value into a column by specifying "NULL" in the VALUES clause. If you have columns that are likely to be NULL, you should put them at the end of the table; there is no data in a NULL column; however, they will take up one byte to contain the length (in this case a zero).

FIGURE 8.2:

Automatically providing
column values with the
DEFAULT clause

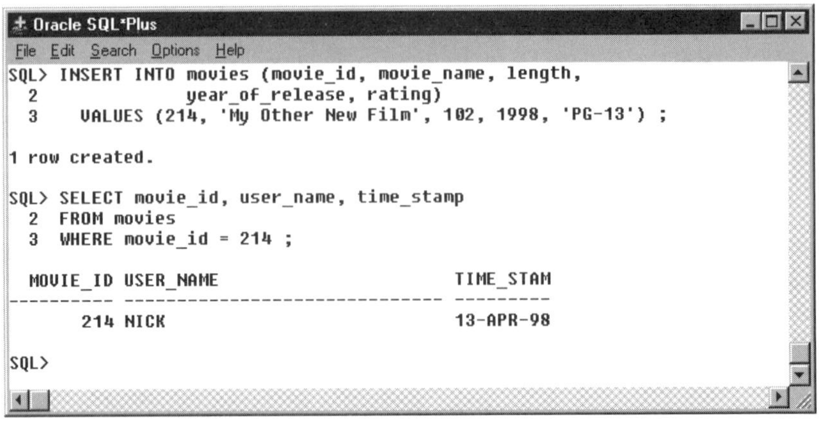

```
Oracle SQL*Plus
File Edit Search Options Help
SQL> INSERT INTO movies (movie_id, movie_name, length,
  2              year_of_release, rating)
  3    VALUES (214, 'My Other New Film', 102, 1998, 'PG-13') ;

1 row created.

SQL> SELECT movie_id, user_name, time_stamp
  2  FROM movies
  3  WHERE movie_id = 214 ;

  MOVIE_ID USER_NAME                        TIME_STAM
---------- ------------------------------   ---------
       214 NICK                             13-APR-98

SQL>
```

When you insert rows of data, you must make sure you know whether a sequence generator is used to generate unique keys (sequences are covered in Chapter 6). Assuming that sequences are used, you will use a slightly different looking INSERT statement:

```
INSERT INTO movies
  VALUES (movie_sequence.NEXTVAL, 'My New Film', 102,
          1998, 'PG', USER, SYSDATE);
```

The new primary key is generated from the sequence with the NEXTVAL function. If you want to find out what number was generated, you will have to use the CURRVAL function of the sequence:

```
SELECT  movie_sequence.CURRVAL from DUAL;
```

Multirow Inserts

Although you will most often use the single-row INSERT command, a form of INSERT that is sometimes overlooked is the ability to insert rows into a table or view that have been retrieved with a subquery. In this way, you could insert a large number of rows in one efficient statement. This step presumes the data is already available in another table; as such, it is often a form used for maintenance or doing data extracts.

```
INSERT INTO new_movies
  SELECT * FROM movies
    WHERE year_of_release = TO_NUMBER (SYSDATE, 'YYYY');
```

The SELECT subquery will retrieve all the movies that were released in the current year and insert them into the table, New_Movies. This subquery will only work if the two tables, Movies and New_Movies, have the same columns and are in the same order. If they aren't, then you will have to specify a column list, such as

```
INSERT INTO new_movies (movie_id, movie_name, length)
  SELECT movie_id, movie_name, length
    FROM movies
    WHERE year_of_release = TO_NUMBER (TO_CHAR(SYSDATE, 'YYYY'));
```

This example is shown in Figure 8.3. It assumes that the table, New_Movies, already exists. If it doesn't, you would be better off using the CREATE TABLE AS SELECT command that you will find later in the chapter in the section, "Bulk Loading of Data."

FIGURE 8.3:

An INSERT statement that inserts more than one row

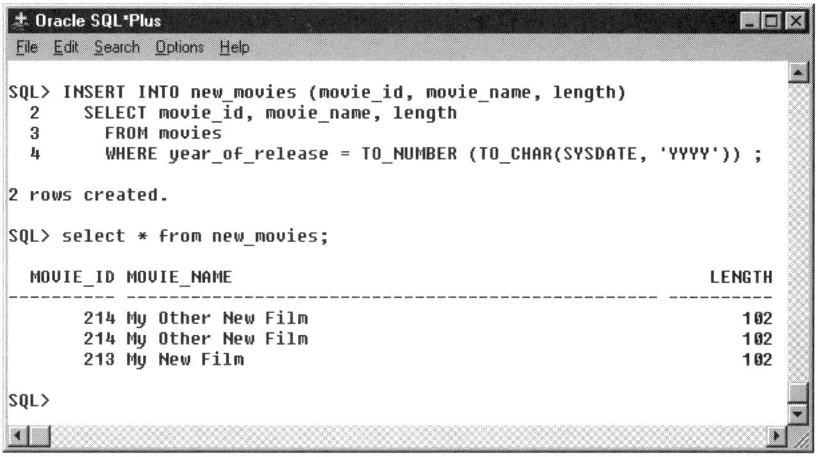

Handling Long Columns

Whatever client-side tools you use, whether it is Visual Basic or even Oracle's own tool set, inserting or updating binary or character data over 2,000 bytes long can be a real hassle. SQL*Plus has a limit of 2,000 bytes for a single quoted text string, such as you would use in an INSERT or UPDATE statement or even a stored procedure call.

Continued on next page

Now you could pass several quoted strings to a procedure and let it put them together into a single column, but that is far from a satisfactory solution and is certainly not scalable or adaptable to binary data.

One of the major problems, whether you use ODBC or an alternative, is binding a large value to a column. What you have to do is move the column in smaller *chunks,* build up the whole column in pieces, and put them together again.

In Visual Basic, you will need to get used to the AppendChunk and GetChunk methods, which we will discuss in Chapter 13, *Visual Basic Design Issues.* There is no alternative if you insist on storing large columns in the database.

Even though you will be able to do an export of these long columns (up to 2GB in Oracle7 and 4GB in Oracle8), it can become impossible to import them back in due to memory constraints and rollback segment restrictions. You would be wise to consider whether the database is the right place to store this data. An alternative is to store the files on disk (perhaps compressed) and store the location of the file in the database.

This method might work well if the files are stored in a place that is mountable by your client PCs, perhaps on a Netware or NT file server. Experience shows that over a network, retrieval of files, rather than long database columns, can show a large performance improvement.

Updating Rows

Once you have inserted data into your tables, you will have to update the information. The UPDATE command allows you to alter one or more columns of one or more rows of data in a table or view. The following is an example of typical syntax:

```
UPDATE table_name
  SET column1 = value1,
      column2 = value2, ….
  WHERE condition_expression;
```

The SET clause has one or more pairs of matched column names and new values, separated by commas.

```
UPDATE videos
  SET status = 'available',
      price  = 29.99
  WHERE movie_id = 1243;
```

The Status and Price columns will be updated by the assigned values for the row with a Movie_id value of 1243. You will normally use a WHERE clause to identify exactly which rows of the table will be affected, as shown in the example; if you don't, then all the rows in the table will be updated.

If any of the rows that you try to update violates a constraint, you will get an error message (see Figure 8.4), and the UPDATE statement will be rolled back.

FIGURE 8.4:

An UPDATE statement violates a constraint.

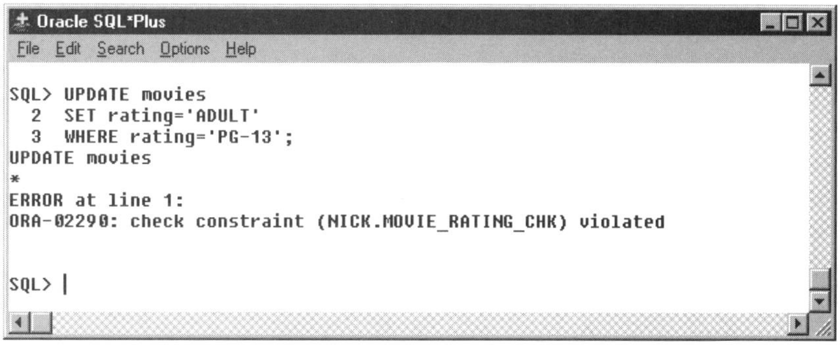

```
± Oracle SQL*Plus                                            _ □ ×
File  Edit  Search  Options  Help

SQL> UPDATE movies
  2   SET rating='ADULT'
  3   WHERE rating='PG-13';
UPDATE movies
*
ERROR at line 1:
ORA-02290: check constraint (NICK.MOVIE_RATING_CHK) violated

SQL> |
```

The new value for a column can be based on the existing value of the same column or a different one, as shown in the following example, in which prices get a 5 percent increase over the board:

```
UPDATE videos
   SET price  = price * 1.05;
```

Substitution Values in SQL*Plus

If you find yourself writing scripts to maintain your data in SQL*Plus, you should become aware of substitution variables. These allow you to run a script that prompts you for values for columns that are used in the script. A substitution variable is indicated by preceding the variable with "&", for example, &rating. By default, SQL*Plus will prompt for a value for the variable with "Enter value for *variable*:" However, you can also use the ACCEPT PROMPT clause to define your own prompt.

Continued on next page

The following code shows how to do this.

```
ACCEPT movie_id PROMPT 'Enter movie id to update: '
ACCEPT RATING PROMPT 'Enter new rating: '
UPDATE movies
  SET rating = '&rating'
  WHERE movie_id = &movie_id;
COMMIT;
```

You have to store this code in a text file, or it will not work properly. In this example, it was stored in c:\orawin95\scripts\update_rating.sql and executed in the example below. You will notice that you get several lines showing the substitutions you made. To remove these, use the SQL*Plus command SET VERIFY OFF.

```
Oracle SQL*Plus                                                      _ □ ×
File  Edit  Search  Options  Help

SQL> @c:\orawin95\scripts\update_rating.sql
Enter movie id to update: 213
Enter new rating: PG-13
old    2:    SET rating = '&rating'
new    2:    SET rating = 'PG-13'
old    3:    WHERE movie_id = &movie_id
new    3:    WHERE movie_id = 213

1 row updated.


Commit complete.

SQL> |
```

Deleting Rows

The final DML statement is the DELETE statement, with which you can delete one or more rows from a table or view. The syntax is

```
DELETE FROM table_name
  WHERE condition_expression;
```

and is illustrated by

```
DELETE FROM videos
    WHERE purchase_date < TO_DATE('01-FEB-1997','DD-MON-YYYY');
```

which will delete all rows in the Videos table where the Purchase_Date is before 1 February 1997 (see Figure 8.5).

FIGURE 8.5:

Deleting rows from a table

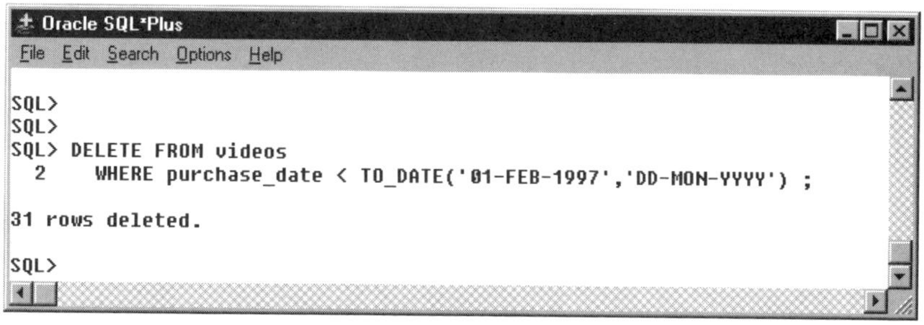

If you do not use a WHERE clause in the DELETE statement, then all the rows in the table will be deleted. You may want to consider an alternative command:

```
TRUNCATE table_name;
```

which basically moves a pointer to the beginning of table; it is a much faster method of deleting all the rows in a table. However, it cannot be rolled back!

Constraints to be wary of include the foreign-key constraint. You can DROP a table with the CASCADE option, which drops all tables that depend on it for foreign keys (a powerful and dangerous option!). However, there is no simple way to do that with the DELETE command. If you want to delete a row from a master-detail relationship, you will find that you have to delete the appropriate detail records first. Deleting a master record and all the child records is an ideal situation to develop into a stored procedure and to do it all with one procedure call. Pass the parent key to the procedure, delete all detail records with that key, and follow it up with a delete for the master record with that key. We will discuss this step in Chapter 10, *Creating Stored Procedures*. An alternative is to use the ON DELETE CASCADE option when defining a foreign-key constraint in the detail table. When the parent row is deleted, any child rows are also deleted.

If you do try to delete a row that is referred to in a referential integrity constraint, you will get an error message, as shown in Figure 8.6.

FIGURE 8.6:

Violating referential integrity

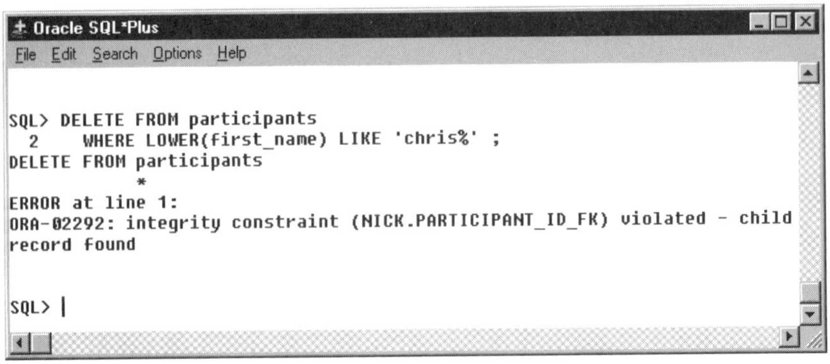

If you want to delete from a view, there are additional restrictions. The view must not contain the following:

1. A join condition.

2. Any group operator, such as GROUP BY or DISTINCT.

Transaction Control

Whenever you use an INSERT, UPDATE, or DELETE statement in Oracle, you make a change to the database, but this change is not, by default, made permanent. The changes are considered part of a transaction, which can be thought of as way to combine several changes, usually related, that will succeed or fail as a group. If even one of the changes fails, all the changes in the transaction should fail. When the transaction is committed, all the changes are made permanent at the same time.

The classic example of a transaction is in an accounting system. When you move money from one account to another, you are in fact doing two operations: taking money out of one account and placing it in another. If the first operation worked but not the second, then the money would be lost forever. If the first failed and the second worked, you could create money! A transaction wraps these two operations together so that they both work or neither work.

Oracle is a transaction-based system: by default, Oracle does not make permanent any changes to the database until the outstanding transaction is committed. A user need not explicitly issue the COMMIT statement. For example, a DDL statement will cause an implicit COMMIT. However, as we start to look at the way Visual Basic handles this through ODBC (starting in Chapter 11, *Client-Side Technology*), we will find that an *Autocommit* mode is sometimes imposed.

Within Oracle, you will need to know several transaction control commands, and these are shown in Table 8.1.

TABLE 8.1: The Transaction Control Commands

Transaction Control Command	Description
COMMIT	Makes all the outstanding data changes permanent.
ROLLBACK	Discards all the outstanding changes and ends the transaction.
SAVEPOINT name	Sets a named marker in the current transaction.
ROLLBACK TO SAVEPOINT name	Discards the outstanding changes made because the named marker was declared.

Oracle starts a transaction for you when you execute your first INSERT, UPDATE, or DELETE command either at the start of your session or immediately after the end of the previous transaction. The transaction ends when you do one of the following:

- Issue the COMMIT or ROLLBACK statement.

- Execute a Data Definition Language statement, such as a CREATE TABLE statement (DDL commands are themselves transactions).

- Exit your SQL*Plus session or your Visual Basic application (in this case, the transaction is committed).

- Abnormally terminate your SQL*Plus session or your Visual Basic application (in which case, the transaction is rolled back).

NOTE   It is important to be aware of the automatic transaction feature of Oracle. It is different from Microsoft SQL Server and, therefore, different from ODBC, both of which require you to explicitly request a transaction. If you forget to commit your changes, the problem may not be evident for some time, but you will end up with users seeing data that is different from the changes, and eventually, you will not be able to update the locked rows.

Due to Oracle's concurrency features, which we covered in Chapter 2, *Oracle Database Architecture,* any changes you make within an uncommitted transaction are not visible to any other user except yourself. A feature of making changes to tables in an Oracle database is that any data rows that you have altered are now locked, and no other user can change the rows. Therefore, it is vital that transactions are kept as short and fast as possible. Although it may prove to be inconvenient to developers who are not familiar with the locking schemes of Oracle, the locking model is a vital component to the enforcement of data integrity.

Transaction Control in Action

We have reviewed the various commands that you can use for transaction control, and we will now look at how you will use them in practice. If you are using updatable Recordsets or the Data Control in Visual Basic, you will allow the changes to be automatically committed, or you will be using the BeginTrans, CommitTrans, and Rollback methods that Data Access Objects provides for transaction control.

Within SQL, whether executed from SQL*Plus, a stored procedure, or Visual Basic, the situation you will most often encounter is the simple COMMIT statement with a ROLLBACK command in case of errors. This is illustrated in the following script:

```
   insert new rows
   update rows
 COMMIT;
```

If you execute this from SQL*Plus, any errors will be written to the screen, so you can follow the error with the ROLLBACK command. When you use a stored procedure to change data, you will have to add a ROLLBACK command in the Exception handler. If you trap the errors in Visual Basic, you will want to use the Rollback method to rollback the transaction.

A more complicated and less common method for controlling a transaction is to use *savepoints*. Savepoints are a way of marking a spot in the middle of a long transaction, and they give you the ability to rollback just to that point. The following conceptual script illustrates this method:

```
insert new rows
update rows
SAVEPOINT phase1-complete;
insert new rows
update rows
SAVEPOINT phase2-complete;
delete rows
update rows
ROLLBACK TO phase2_complete;
COMMIT;
```

The ROLLBACK TO phase2_complete command is executed after an error is found in the most recent update of rows. This means that the changes to the rows that were deleted and updated after the last savepoint are rolled back. This ROLL-BACK command is followed by a COMMIT command, which means that all changes before the phase2_complete savepoint are committed.

Security

To be able to use any of these DML statements on a table that is not in your own schema, you will need the appropriate privileges. These are summarized in Table 8.2.

TABLE 8.2: Privileges to Execute DML Statements

DML Statement	Privilege Required
INSERT	INSERT ON *table_name* TO *user_name*
UPDATE	UPDATE ON *table_name* TO *user_name*
DELETE	DELETE ON *table_name* TO *user_name*

As an example of granting the right to a user to insert rows into the Movies table, you would use

```
GRANT INSERT ON movies TO jsmith;
```

Although you can grant these privileges on all tables to a user, it is much more secure to deal with it on a table-by-table basis. This is not difficult because you will probably use *roles* most of the time anyway; roles were covered in Chapter 4, *Database Administration*.

You can restrict the columns of a table that you can insert or update by following the privilege with a list of columns in parentheses as follows:

```
GRANT UPDATE (movie_name, movie_length) ON movies TO jsmith;
```

> **TIP** As mentioned throughout this book, it is much more secure to give only EXECUTE access to users, so they can execute a stored procedure, rather than give the INSERT, UPDATE, and DELETE privileges, which give the user the ability to bypass any business rules you have in the database.

Database Triggers

Whenever you use one of the DML statements that we have covered, you must be aware that it could activate a *database trigger*. You can assign a trigger (a piece of PL/SQL code that we will cover in the next two chapters) to a table that will be executed, or *fired,* when a user performs an INSERT, UPDATE, or DELETE on the table. The trigger can be set to fire before or after the DML statement is executed or before or after each row is altered. A trigger is similar to an event being triggered in a Visual Basic control.

Triggers seem like a great idea to set up an auditing scheme, and they can certainly provide that capability by automatically moving deleted or updated rows into an audit table; they can also cascade changes from one table to others in the database (perhaps keeping a summary table up-to-date); however, you should take care when using them for the following reasons:

1. The trigger actions are committed whether the regular action is committed or rolled back.

2. The more triggers you have, the more chance they can fire each other and cascade the effects with a potentially dangerous effect.

3. The presence and effect of a trigger are not readily apparent to every developer.

4. An audit scheme based on triggers is auditing at the lowest level and will result in huge audit files; auditing at a higher transaction level can often be a more useable alternative.

Bulk Loading of Data

When we create our database tables, we need to fill them with data. We have covered the normal techniques for doing this with SQL commands. If we have our Visual Basic program already prepared, we can also use that to manually enter data. However, there may be a faster way. It is not likely with a new table that the data already exists in another table or perhaps in another database, but if it does, we can use the IMPORT utility mentioned in Chapter 4. However, we will discuss some alternatives in the next few sections.

CREATE TABLE AS Subquery

The first way to bulk load data into a table is with the CREATE TABLE AS *subquery* SQL command. This command is the simplest way, but it assumes the data is in *some* form already in the database. For example, if you wanted to create a table that contained the combined data from the Videos and the Movies tables, we could do something like this:

```
CREATE TABLE movie_videos
  AS SELECT videos.video_id, videos.movie_id, status, movie_name
    FROM movies, videos
      WHERE videos.movie_id = movies.movie_id;
```

You can add the usual optional parameters to this command, such as defining the storage parameters and the tablespace. Would you often use this? Well, that depends on what you want to achieve. The subquery can be very useful when reorganizing tables, but it can also be useful to create temporary tables or a denormalized database against which reports could be run.

SQL*LOADER

The CREATE TABLE method of loading a table assumes that you already have the data in a table; however, you may often find yourself wanting to move data from a desktop application to Oracle. When you want to bring in data from an external source, you will have to make use of a utility package that does this job well. Although there are alternatives, you have one available with the database, and that is the SQL*LOADER utility program.

The SQL*LOADER utility program, which you run outside of the Oracle environment, is designed to work with two types of input files, which are familiar to Visual Basic developers. You can load up a fixed-format file or a comma-delimited, variable-length file with text enclosed with double quotes. This process can, for example, be an export from Microsoft Excel or Access or even from a Visual Basic Print statement. The comma-delimited file is the easiest to work with. You run the SQL*LOADER program from a Control file, which instructs the SQL*LOADER program to load the data you want into which table you want, and it provides a few control parameters. An example Control file is shown in Listing 8.1. The syntax is reasonably self-explanatory but is documented in the *Oracle Utilities* manual. Note that the script indicates that fields are terminated by X'09', which is a tab character. (The data was exported from Microsoft Excel.)

Listing 8.1

```
LOAD DATA
INFILE *
APPEND
INTO TABLE movies
FIELDS TERMINATED BY X'09'
(movie_id, movie_name, length, year_of_release, rating)
BEGINDATA
1    Accidental Tourist (The)    121    1988    PG
2    After Hours                  96    1985    R
3    Age of Innocence (The)      132    1993    PG
4    Aliens                      135    1986    R
5    All the President's Men     135    1976    PG
6    Awakenings                  121    1990    PG-13
7    Backbeat                    100    1994    R
8    BackDraft                   132    1991    R
9    Bad Lieutenant               96    1993    NC-17
```

You must now run the SQL*Loader program and specify the Control file. The command to run the Control file differs depending on what platform you are on. For Oracle 7.3 on Windows NT, you would type

```
c:> SQLLDR73  control=control_file.ctl
```

You would then be prompted for your user ID and password. A Log file will be created called `control_file.log`, and this will detail any errors encountered in the load.

Entering data, like we did with the example Control file, is called the *conventional-path* load. It creates INSERT statements for each line of data. It is no faster than if you wrote a program to do it yourself (if you can run the program on the server and avoid network delays). An alternative method, called the *direct-path* load, writes straight to the table in the internal format and is many times faster than the conventional-path load. However, you need exclusive access to the table, so it is not suitable for an online database. You should use the direct-path load when you are creating a database or when you can run with no users updating the tables for the duration of the load.

Database Design for Fast Updates

In Chapter 7, *Queries,* we saw some tips for designing a database to provide the fastest retrieval of data, something that is required in a Decision Support System. However, in an Online Transaction Processing System, you want fast updates. Unfortunately, these two types of systems require different environments; everything that makes queries faster will tend to make updates slower.

There are a few important concepts that you need to keep in mind to make updates faster:

- Do not use more indexes than you have to. In some cases I have seen, going from one to two indexes can almost double the time for an INSERT statement.

- If you are using referential integrity between tables, make sure you create an index on the column referred to. This conflicts with the previous tip, so you will have to experiment.

- In WHERE clauses, specify the primary key for the table where possible.

- Ensure that the writes-to-disk are spread evenly over the available disk drives. Ideally, you should have more, smaller drives rather than few, larger drives so that the writes are spread as thinly as possible.

- Keep transactions as short as possible. Otherwise, rows of data will be locked for longer than necessary. If you need huge transactions, try to do them when the system is little used, such as at night.

Roll Your Own

If a conventional load with the SQL*Loader utility is just executing INSERT statements, then it may occur to you to write your own program to do this. Creating your own application for this purpose has the obvious disadvantage of taking time to write but has distinct advantages to it as well. Apart from the fact that an application like this is a great project to hone your Oracle skills, it also gives you much more control.

Dates and the Year 2000 Problem

Dates are an interesting data type especially with the Year 2000 problem so close. As a recap, this problem is due to the fact that for years, databases were designed with a six character date field in one of several formats. The most useful was 'yymmdd,' which gives a date string, such as '980327'; with this format, you could at least do a simple chronological sort on it. However, how is the next century represented in this format? Most designers never thought their programs would survive this long, and storage space was at a premium.

Visual Basic 5 and Oracle no longer have problems with dates, but that does not mean you cannot create some of your own. Both products are properly aware of leap years when calculating date differences, so you no longer have to code in that complexity.

Leap Year Rules

If a year is evenly divisible by 4, then it is a leap year except

if the year is evenly divisible by 100, then it is not a leap year except

if the year is evenly divisible by 1000, then it is a leap year.

So the year 2000 is a leap year, whereas 1900 was not.

Oracle's default date format is 'DD-MON-YY,' for example '27-MAR-98,' but what happens if you enter '27-MAR-01'? You will get 1901 when you probably meant the year 2001. When you enter a value in this format, Oracle always assumes the current century, so if you want to enter a date in a different century, you have a problem.

An alternative Oracle format is 'DD-MON-RR.' The 'RR' format causes Oracle to interpret the date as a result of the combination of the current date and the entered date. It makes the assumption that

1. If the current date is in the first half of a century and the entered year is from 0 to 49, then the current century will be assumed for the entered year; if the entered year is from 50 to 99, then the previous century will be assumed for the entered year.

2.   If the current date is in the last half of a century and the entered year is from 0 to 49, then the next century will be assumed for the entered year; if the entered year is from 50 to 99, then the same century will be assumed for the entered year.

This works fine in *some* circumstances, though it will obviously cause headaches towards 2050, and you have to read the rules several times to figure it out. It is not the best technique to use.

WARNING   Note that the default date format *can* be changed by a system parameter, but do this with caution because your code may not be easily transferable from one Oracle instance to another. It is also best not to rely on it being in any particular format.

There are several ways to avoid the date format problem. The best way is to explicitly format the date string before it is entered into the database and to format it with a four-digit year. For example, in Visual Basic, you can let the user enter a date and then immediately redisplay it:

```
Format (my_date, "dd-mmm-yyyy")
```

To pass it to the database in a DML statement, such as an INSERT, you need to use an Oracle function, TO_DATE.

```
TO_DATE (date_string, 'DD-MON-YYYY')
```

The TO_DATE function takes the first argument (*date_string*) and converts it to a date in Oracle's internal format, assuming that it is in the format provided by the second argument ('DD-MON-YYYY'). This formatting can become a little annoying at times, so Listing 8.2 shows a Visual Basic function that achieves this for you:

Listing 8.2

```
Public Function OracleDate(inDate as Date) As String

'    Return the date in the form suitable for Oracle stored procedures

     OracleDate = "TO_DATE('" & Format(inDate, "dd-mmm-yyyy") & _
                  "','DD-MON-YYYY')"
End Function
```

NOTE   To specify a 3-character month string, you use 'MON'; Visual Basic uses "mmm".

A date column also stores time in hours, minutes, and seconds. (In fact, these are stored as the decimal portion of the date value.) If you just enter a date, then the time defaults to 12:00 A.M. To enter a date and time into your database, you will need to use an extended format.

```
TO_DATE (date_string, 'DD-MON-YYYY:HH24:MI:SS')
```

This is even worse to code in Visual Basic, so Listing 8.3 shows a VB procedure that will do the work for you.

Listing 8.3

```
Public Function OracleDateTime(inDateTime as Date) As String

'    Return the date and time in the form suitable
'    for Oracle stored procedures

     OracleDateTime = "TO_DATE('" & _
       Format(inDateTime, "dd-mmm-yyyy:hh:mm:ss") & _
       "','DD-MON-YYYY:HH24:MI:SS')"
End Function
```

TIP   When entering a date column for a time stamp, you can use the system date and time with the SYSDATE function.

Summary

In this chapter, we have covered the major ways to enter, update, and delete rows of data in the tables in our databases. These techniques are provided by the DML statements available in SQL and are fairly standard across different RDBMS systems. We have also covered how to understand and handle transactions in Oracle, an important concept to grasp because it is quite different from other systems.

With the additional section on bulk loading of data into your database tables, you have covered everything you need for your development. Our coverage of the philosophy for updating data will hopefully encourage you to use a technique that is efficient and secure.

CHAPTER

NINE

9

Introduction to PL/SQL

- Stored Procedures

- Packages

- Tools for Creating Stored Procedures, Including SQL*PLUS, Visual Database Tools, and Oracle Procedure Builder

- Error Handling in PL/SQL

Databases originally appeared with a single purpose in mind: they were designed to store data. This is not a strange concept to anyone who has grown up with products such as Microsoft Access or FoxPro. Even in a product like Access, the designers realized that storing objects not strictly data items improves the functionality of the product enormously. In an Access database, for example, we can store not only tables but also queries, forms, reports, and code modules. The alternative would be to distribute and store them locally to all interested users.

With the more enterprise-oriented products like Oracle, adding extra features gave a competitive advantage and provided a better fit with the requirements of an enterprise. The most commonly added feature is the ability to execute code on the server to manipulate the data before it is read or saved. This feature is called a stored procedure and is the subject of this and the next chapter.

The topics we will cover in this chapter are

- Stored procedures
- Packages
- Tools for creating stored procedures, including
  - SQL*PLUS
  - Visual Database Tools
  - Oracle Procedure Builder
- Error handling in PL/SQL

PL/SQL as an Extension of SQL

Structured Query Language (or SQL) is a set of commands that enable you to manipulate data in a relational database. SQL is a nonprocedural language (often called a descriptive language), which means you describe what result you want rather than explain exactly how to do it. For example, there are no loops or IF-THEN-ELSE constructs in SQL.

Although SQL is powerful and easy to use, it is similar to Visual Basic programming when you only use the mouse. You can make attractive forms (and even create some rudimentary data-entry systems with the Data Control), but to make a really useful application in Visual Basic, you have to add code to more closely define what you want and how to do it. SQL is the same, and each relational database vendor has come up with their own extensions to SQL. For Oracle, the extension is called PL/SQL, the PL standing for *procedural language.*

Various Oracle products include PL/SQL engines, which perform the same role as the Visual Basic run-time interpreter. Unfortunately, even though PL/SQL is based on the programming language ADA, it does not have much in common with languages like Basic and is slowly being supplemented with Java. But PL/SQL is where most of the work is at the moment and where you need to devote your energy. On the positive side, there are not too many constructs to learn.

Stored procedures are not attached to any database objects, such as tables or sequences. Procedures are only attached to the schema in which they were created. However, there is some dependence on these other objects. For example, if a stored procedure refers to a table that is subsequently altered, the stored procedure will be marked as an invalid compilation, although you may still be able to execute it. In the case of a DELETE statement, the stored procedure will probably still work, whereas an INSERT statement could fail if the number or type of columns has been altered. We shall see how this process works in the next few sections.

Stored Procedures

A stored procedure is a block of code that is stored in the database and performs varied functions usually involving reading data from or writing data to the database. Procedures can be called by applications external to the database (Visual Basic programs, for example) and can allow data to be passed back and forth between them and the application in the form of parameters. Stored procedures are created and entered into the database interpreter as text, but after being compiled, they are stored in the database in an internal format called *p-code.*

We usually use the term *stored procedure* generically though it should strictly apply to procedures, which is the same concept as the Visual Basic subroutine. Oracle uses the term *subprogram,* which refers not only to procedures but also to *functions* and *triggers.* Functions are perhaps a lesser used and somewhat overlooked PL/SQL subprogram type that perform the same role as a function in

Visual Basic. Triggers are subprograms that are literally "triggered" to execute when you insert, update, or delete a row in a table, much like an event.

Stored procedures and functions are stored in a user's schema, and the owner or the DBA will arrange for other users to have permission to execute them if that is the requirement of the application. The best way to set up stored procedures is to create an application schema (that is, a schema that does not belong to a real user) in which all the procedures are stored for that application. You do not need privileges for triggers; in fact, you can't stop them triggering because that will happen automatically unless they are disabled.

The Advantages of Stored Procedures

Stored subprograms have many advantages for the database and application designer. Although the stored subprograms are usually the last thing that a Visual Basic programmer wants to learn about, they may also be the only way you can interact with the data.

The advantages of stored procedures are listed below.

Reduced data flow   Executing code on the database server means there is no increase in network traffic apart from sending a few parameters back and forth. In a file-based system such as Access, some operations require the client program to pull in all the records to search for just a few. This can lead to systems that are totally unscalable.

Reduced code flow   If you have a complex piece of code, it would be inefficient of network resources to transfer it to the database every time you wanted to execute it. Storing it in the database solves this problem.

Improved performance   Executing the code in the database means that it will execute as fast as possible. Although the code does not go through an optimizer in the VB sense of the word, it is parsed, and an execution plan is in place that would otherwise have to be done at run time.

Enforce business rules   By giving users the privileges to execute a stored procedure, they can indirectly manipulate data through the procedure; however, you can ensure they do not have any privileges to access the base tables themselves. Ensuring that no user can bypass the business rules is mandatory in an enterprise installation, but this also gives you a means to allow the user to access certain information that only the owner of the schema would have.

Simplify data access   Stored procedures can process the data before it is returned to a user's application. This technique can hide any complications in the database layout and even make it more secure. Unfortunately, from a Visual Basic programmer's point of view, this feature is not as advanced as in, say, Microsoft SQLServer and Sybase. The ability to return records from a stored procedure is developed in a different form and is most beneficial for users of Oracle's Developer 2000 product range, but this situation is slowly changing as we will see in the later chapters of the book.

Improved memory utilization   If the same stored procedure is executed by more than one user, Oracle needs to allocate memory for only one copy of the procedure. All users can then share this copy. This means that Oracle can make efficient use of whatever memory you have available.

Portable   You can move PL/SQL code around platforms. This is of great interest to users of Oracle's Developer products because the same code can be moved between the tiers of an application. (This is called *application partitioning*.) You can also move your procedural code to other Oracle database server platforms.

Procedure Structure

The most common subprogram you will create is a stored procedure. A PL/SQL stored procedure is defined with a procedure header in the same way that a Visual Basic procedure is defined with a SUB statement. PL/SQL is called a *block* structured language. A block is defined by a declaration section, a BEGIN and END statement, and an optional error-handling EXCEPTION block (see Listing 9.1). Each block can contain other PL/SQL blocks within it.

Listing 9.1

```
declarations
.  .  .  .
BEGIN
.  .  .  .
PL/SQL statements
EXCEPTION
     .  .  .  .
Error handling PL/SQL statements
END;
```

This block structure applies to all PL/SQL code whether it is a stored procedure, function, trigger, or anonymous code block. A typical procedure is shown in Listing 9.2.

NOTE   An *anonymous* code block is a term you will often come across. A stored subprogram is a *named* block of code, named, of course, with the procedure name, but you can also string together code in a block without a stored name. This so-called anonymous block might, for example, be submitted from Visual Basic. It must be surrounded by BEGIN/END statements. We shall cover this topic in Chapter 14, *Data Access Objects,* when we call stored procedures from Visual Basic. Triggers are also defined with an anonymous PL/SQL block.

Listing 9.2

```
PROCEDURE movie_insert (
  p_movie_name        IN VARCHAR2,
  p_length            IN NUMBER,
  p_rating            IN VARCHAR2,
  p_year_of_release   IN NUMBER
  ) IS

/* This procedure inserts a new movie in the MOVIE table*/

/* Declare local variable */
v_id    NUMBER(10);

BEGIN

  SELECT movie_sequence.NEXTVAL INTO  v_id FROM dual;

  INSERT INTO movies VALUES (
    v_id, p_movie_name, p_length, p_rating, p_year_of_release,
    USER, SYSDATE);

END movie_insert;
```

A few things you should note from this example are

- The procedure header includes the keyword PROCEDURE and the procedure name (movie_insert), a list of typed parameters in parentheses, and the keyword IS, which introduces the body of the procedure.

- The convention followed is that SQL and PL/SQL statements are in upper-case while the rest of the code is in lowercase.

- Comments can be included in the code surrounded by the delimiters /* and */.

- Any procedure-wide variables should be defined next.

- All statements in PL/SQL can be multiline and must be terminated by a semicolon just as in the C language.

- The code body is defined as one or more blocks, which are bound by BEGIN and END statements.

- All procedure and function definitions must be terminated by an END statement.

Nested Blocks

Stored subprograms are block-based, and you can also have *nested blocks*. Nested blocks means that each block may contain one or more other blocks. They also enable long procedures to be broken down into shorter, self-contained units and encourage better programming techniques. An example of this nested structure is given below.

```
declarations
. . . .
BEGIN

    DECLARE
    Local declarations
    . . . .
    BEGIN
        PL/SQL statements

        . . . .
    EXCEPTION
        . . . .
        Error handling PL/SQL statements local to the block
    END;
PL/SQL statements

    . . . .
EXCEPTION
    . . . .
```

Continued on next page

```
        Error handling PL/SQL statements
        END;
```

The big advantage of using nested blocks is that the exception handling is self-contained. Whenever there is an exception in a block, the EXCEPTION handler is executed, and program control leaves the block. By using nested blocks, when control falls out of a block after an error, control then passes to the outer block.

Function Structure

The second type of stored subprogram is the function. Functions are defined in much the same way as procedures, but they include a return value and its data type in the heading as shown in Listing 9.3.

Listing 9.3

```
FUNCTION GET_MOVIE_ID
    ( p_movie_name IN VARCHAR2) RETURN NUMBER

IS

v_movie_id   number(6);

BEGIN
  SELECT movie_id INTO v_movie_id FROM movies
    WHERE movie_name = p_movie_name;
  RETURN v_movie_id;

EXCEPTION
  WHEN OTHERS THEN
      RETURN -1;
END;
```

Trigger Structure

The final subprogram type is the trigger. This subprogram is quite unlike any Visual Basic construct. It cannot take any parameters, because it is not called; it is triggered by a change in a row of a table. The trigger has to include information identifying what kind of action it will trigger on (such as insert and update in the example) as well as whether it is triggered before or after the event and whether it is for each row or each transaction.

Another major difference from procedures is that the trigger has available the old version of the data row as well as the new version (available with the *old* and *new* bound records), which means you can check the column values before updating the rows with new values. You could, for example, check to see whether a numerical value changes by more than a certain percentage. Listing 9.4 gives an example of a trigger.

Listing 9.4

```
TRIGGER check_movie_length
BEFORE
INSERT OR UPDATE OF length ON movies
FOR EACH ROW
/*  The DECLARE statement can go here. */
BEGIN
  IF :new.length > 200 THEN
    RAISE_APPLICATION_ERROR(-20009,
'The film ' || :new.movie_name || cannot be over 200 minutes.');
  END IF;
END;
```

Procedure Parameters

The only input to and output from a stored procedure is passed via parameters, which you include in parentheses after the procedure name. When you define a procedure, you include *formal* parameters for use within the procedure. When you call it, you pass *actual* parameters to the procedure. You will notice from the examples above that the formal parameters in the procedure have a specific format. In a similar way to Visual Basic, you specify each parameter with its name and data type. In between these you can include an optional mode keyword that defines whether it is an input or output parameter or whether it shares both of these characteristics. If you omit it, then the default is IN. The possible values are shown in Table 9.1.

TABLE 9.1: The Possible Parameter Modes

Mode	Description
IN	The parameter is an input-only parameter and can only be passed to the stored procedure. The value cannot be changed. This type is the default. It is also the most efficient. The actual parameter may be a constant or a variable.
OUT	The parameter is an output-only parameter. You cannot pass a value to the stored procedure with this parameter type, just return a value. The actual parameter must be a variable.
IN OUT	The parameter is capable of passing a value to the stored procedure and returning an altered value to the calling procedure. The actual parameter must be a variable.

You will achieve a small improvement in performance if you can avoid using more parameters than necessary. Be especially careful that you do not pass the user name, time, or some other value that can be easily found from inside the procedure.

Packages

Just as we might group Visual Basic procedures and functions into a class module, we can also group PL/SQL procedures and functions into *packages*. Typically, you will use a package to group together code that has a central theme whether it is all the procedures that apply to a particular table or all the procedures that apply to a particular department, such as Human Resources or Engineering. You may also want to package all your utility code together.

In addition to this organizational benefit, there are two other reasons for using packages. First, when Oracle pulls one of the procedures into the SGA memory, it pulls in the whole package. Chances are you will need more than one procedure from the package that is already in memory; this obviously improves performance.

The second reason for using packages is that this is the only way you can use a user-defined data type as a parameter to a procedure. The more advanced techniques that we will see in Chapter 10, *Creating Stored Procedures*, require packages.

Creating a Package

A package is similar to a C module: it consists of a specification (or header) and a body (the actual code). Together they form the package. To create a package, we create the specification and body separately. In Procedure Builder, when you create a new object, you select "Package (Spec)" for the header and "Package (Body)" for the body.

The body consists of all the PL/SQL code for the procedures and/or functions that comprise the package. The specification consists of the PROCEDURE statements from the body and any user-defined type definitions used in the formal parameters and any others you want to make available to the package as a whole. The next chapter will describe several packages, which should make it easier to follow.

> **TIP**
>
> When you define a package, make sure the procedures' definitions are exactly the same in both the specification and body. If you don't, this oversight can cause confusing error messages.

Built-In Packages

In addition to creating your own packages, many prebuilt packages come with Oracle. These prebuilt packages provide powerful capabilities to PL/SQL users for everything from locking the database tables to communicating with outside processes through what are called pipes; they even include packages for creating HTML. Table 9.2 contains a brief description of some of the available built-in packages. You should at least be aware of these packages because they can add another dimension to your applications.

TABLE 9.2: Prebuilt Packages

Package	Description
DBMS_ALERT	Enables asynchronous signaling of events (similar to events in Visual Basic).
DBMS_DDL	Allows Data Definition Language (DDL) commands, such as altering and compiling procedures.
DBMS_DESCRIBE	Describes the arguments of a stored procedure.
DBMS_JOB	Schedules PL/SQL procedures at predefined intervals. Useful for housekeeping routines.

Continued on next page

TABLE 9.2 CONTINUED: Prebuilt Packages

Package	Description
DBMS_LOB	Provides packages for manipulating large objects (Oracle8 only).
DBMS_LOCK	Gives access to Oracle lock management for the development of sophisticated locking schemes.
DBMS_OUTPUT	Produces terminal output via a buffer.
DBMS_PIPE	Communicates between different processes on the same computer.
DBMS_SESSION	Allows control of an application's session characteristics.
DBMS_SQL	Allows execution of dynamic SQL. This is Data Definition Language (DDL) and Data Manipulation Language (DML) commands that are not parsed until run time.
DBMS_TRANSACTION	Provides transaction control similar to the SQL equivalents.
DBMS_UTILITY	Provides a variety of utility procedures, such as compiling procedures and analyzing tables.
UTIL_FILE	Opens, closes, reads, and writes operating-system files.
UTIL_HTTP	Sends URL request to a Web site and receives reply.

NOTE   In theory, the only input to and output from SQL databases should be by SQL. PL/SQL itself violates this rule, but as you can see from the packages that are available, there is functionally an alternative route to the database. Extensions such as these are present in nearly every RDBMS and add to the functionality.

Tools for Creating a Stored Procedure

There is a variety of tools for entering PL/SQL procedures and functions into the Oracle database. In this chapter, we will deal with three of the most important:

- SQL*Plus
- Visual Database Tools
- Oracle Procedure Builder

Whichever one you choose is a personal decision, but you should be familiar with the capabilities of all three so you can make a decision based on the capabilities versus cost.

SQL*Plus

SQL*Plus is fundamentally an environment for writing SQL statements and viewing the results. The SQL*Plus program is available on every platform that Oracle is available on (which covers most of today's platforms). For example, in the Windows 95 environment, you can create a session by running

```
C:\ORAWIN95\BIN\PLUS33W.EXE
```

or a similarly named executable, depending on which version of the software you have. Note that the connection to the database is via SQL*Net and has nothing to do with any ODBC sources you have set up.

SQL*Plus, however, is more than merely a way to enter SQL statements. In addition to having the capabilities of providing a simple report generating program (you may want to investigate the formatting capabilities in the *Oracle SQL*Plus Users Guide*), it can also be used to create, alter, and execute stored procedures.

You can easily create a SQL script file to create a stored procedure in any editor on your server. You can invoke an editor from the SQL> prompt. The command you type is dependent on the platform, but it must be preceded by a dollar character. For example, if you are using Windows 95 or NT, you can type

```
SQL> $notepad
```

which will, of course, run the notepad editor. If you follow it with a file name you will begin editing that file. The only differences in the actual script from what we have seen in the previous section are that we must now start with the keywords CREATE OR REPLACE and finish the script with a forward slash as in the example in Figure 9.1.

FIGURE 9.1:

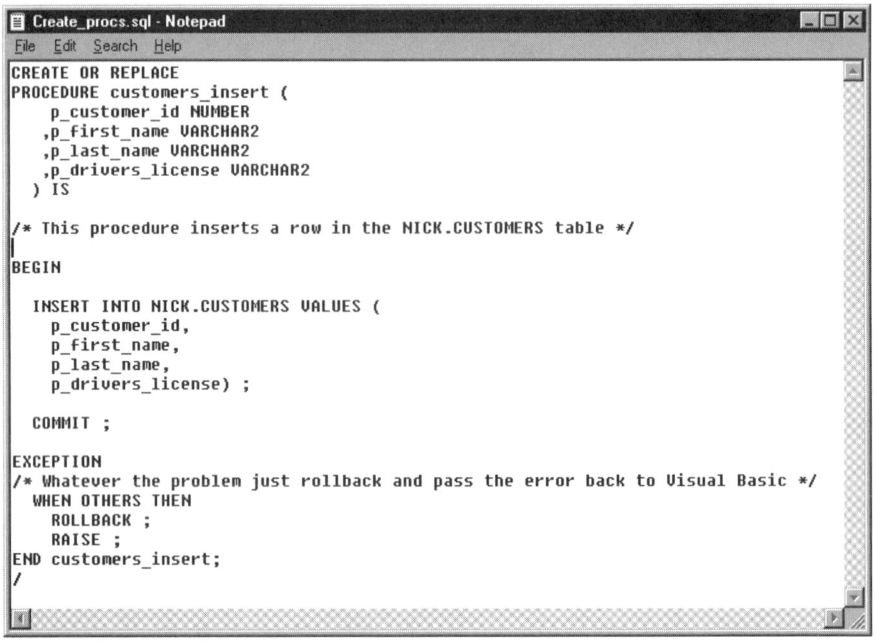

Create_procs.sql - Notepad

File Edit Search Help

```
CREATE OR REPLACE
PROCEDURE customers_insert (
    p_customer_id NUMBER
   ,p_first_name VARCHAR2
   ,p_last_name VARCHAR2
   ,p_drivers_license VARCHAR2
  ) IS

/* This procedure inserts a row in the NICK.CUSTOMERS table */

BEGIN

  INSERT INTO NICK.CUSTOMERS VALUES (
    p_customer_id,
    p_first_name,
    p_last_name,
    p_drivers_license) ;

  COMMIT ;

EXCEPTION
/* Whatever the problem just rollback and pass the error back to Visual Basic */
  WHEN OTHERS THEN
    ROLLBACK ;
    RAISE ;
END customers_insert;
/
```

Creating a stored procedure script in Notepad

Executing the Script

We can now execute the script file from our SQL*Plus session to create the stored procedure. For example, if the script file is `create_proc.sql`, then we execute it by preceding the name with the "@" character.

```
SQL> @c:\scripts\create_proc.sql
```

NOTE

Including the "OR REPLACE" part of the command is not strictly necessary the first time you create a stored procedure, but you may as well include it for consistency.

Creating a stored procedure is an easy process, but the user friendliness ends there. If there are any errors in our code, we get a reasonable error message but only a reference to a line number. When you run the script to create the procedure, you may get a message that says there have been some errors found when PL/SQL compiled it. If this is the case, you can view the errors by typing

```
SHOW ERRORS;
```

In the above example, the table, My_Table, did not exist, and so the result is shown in Figure 9.2.

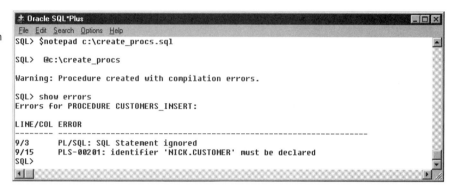

Executing the Stored Procedure

To execute a stored procedure from a SQL*Plus session, use

```
EXEC procedure_name (arguments);
```

If you are in Server Manager you will have to use the full keyword, EXECUTE. If the procedure requires OUT or IN/OUT parameters, then you will have to declare these parameters before calling the routine. Do this with the SQL*Plus VARIABLE command to declare a *bind* variable as follows:

```
VARIABLE user_id NUMBER
```

or

```
VARIABLE user_name VARCHAR2(25)
```

When you call the stored procedure you must precede the bind variable with a colon. To see what value has been returned, use the PRINT command. The SQL*Plus session output shown in Figure 9.3 makes this easier to understand.

FIGURE 9.3:

Executing a stored procedure
from SQL*Plus

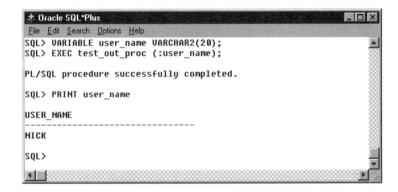

You can do exactly the same thing to test out a function, as shown in Figure 9.4.

FIGURE 9.4:

Executing a function in
SQL*Plus

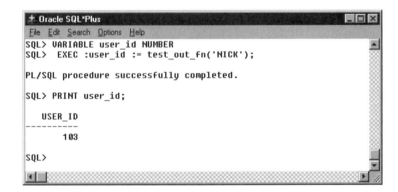

Debugging Your Procedure

When you are working with PL/SQL, debugging your code is limited to the equivalent of Debug.Print statements in Visual Basic. In PL/SQL, you can make use of a special packaged procedure, DBMS_OUTPUT, and within the procedure, you use the PUT_LINE procedure.

```
DBMS_OUTPUT.PUT_LINE (message);
```

For example, to output the value of a variable count, you can type

```
DBMS_OUTPUT.PUT_LINE ('The value of variable count is ' || count);
```

This procedure places the message in a buffer. To see the message, type the following SQL*Plus command before you run the procedure:

```
SET SERVEROUTPUT ON;
```

Unfortunately, the output is only displayed on the screen when the procedure has finished. By default, this output buffer can hold only 2,000 bytes, which can get used up quickly if you are doing much debugging. You can increase this amount by using the following SQL*Plus command:

```
SET SERVEROUTPUT ON SIZE 10000;
```

In fact, you can set the size up to 1,000,000 characters.

TIP   Whichever tool you use, make sure that you always enter your code into a script file, especially if it is more than one line long. This way, you have the source at hand to edit and reuse as the program develops.

Visual Database Tools

Visual Database Tools is a relative newcomer to the tool set for developing Oracle stored procedures. The tools are quite revolutionary in that they show Microsoft's support for Oracle despite the continued rivalry. Visual Database Tools has some nice features and comes as part of the Visual Interdev package and also with the Enterprise edition of Visual Basic. In Visual Basic 6, the tools have been integrated into the development environment, although they can be a little clumsy to use. We first saw this tool set in Chapter 6, *Implementing a Database*. The tools were available with Visual Basic 5, but their operation with Oracle has vastly improved.

Starting Up

To be able to use the Visual Database Tools from Visual Basic, there are two ways to do this. You can go through the Data Environment if you have one already, as long as it is tied to the project. The following method uses a Data Link, which is independent of the project, making it great for development.

1. Open a new or existing VB6 project. (You can create a link even if you don't open a project.)

2. Select the Data View window from the View menu. The Data View window will be displayed on the right-hand side.

3. Right-click on Data Links, and select Add a Data Link.

4. Complete the Data Link properties. (When filling in these properties, you will quickly realize this is a tool designed for ActiveX Data Objects.) You must first select the OLE DB provider. On the Connection Tab, select the data-source name from the drop-down box, and then fill in your name and password. Note that you should use the Microsoft OLE DB Provider for ODBC Drivers, although the OLE DB Provider for Oracle also seems to work well.

5. Click on the Test Connection button to make sure everything is OK.

6. Click on OK to create the connection.

This process adds a Data Link to your environment. Explore the new Data View window, and see how many stored procedures and functions you have access to in your database Data View (see Figure 9.5).

FIGURE 9.5:

The layout of Visual Database Tools

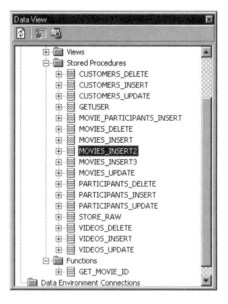

Entering a Script

To enter a new stored procedure, right-click on the Stored Procedures area of the Data View window, and select New Stored Procedure. You will see a new window that operates much like Notepad, except that it color codes the text according to its meaning: comments are in green, strings are in blue, and normal text is in black. Keywords appear in a variety of colors. You can now enter the code of your procedure (see Figure 9.6). The procedure editor gives you the format of a procedure to start with, which makes it easier to use.

FIGURE 9.6:

Entering a script in Visual Database Tools

When you have finished entering the subprogram, you can save it (click the Save To Database button), and the procedure will be compiled and saved to the database. If the compile fails, then error messages will be returned in an error box and, obviously, not stored on the server. When you have a clean compile, you can go on to the testing phase. There is no indication in the window if the existing procedures have been compiled successfully. You can edit procedures by double-clicking on the name in the navigator tree list.

Executing a Procedure

To execute a procedure, you unfortunately have to switch over to Visual Studio.

1. Start up Visual Studio 6.

2. Select a new data project.

3. Select the ODBC data source.

4. Log on to Oracle.

5. Open up your connection in the Data View window to display all the available stored procedures and functions.

6. Right-click on a stored procedure and select Execute.

To test the stored procedure, there is a grid, which shows the procedure's required parameters, their names, and types, with space to enter new values (see Figure 9.7). Note that you do not surround literals with single quotes. When you execute the procedure, you will see a text window with the procedure actually executed and a list of any output parameters along with their values. The only strange thing is that the environment cannot tell how many rows have been affected. (This is something we will see throughout the ODBC/OLE-DB methods.) However, the ease of use makes up for having to go to Visual Studio instead of the Visual Basic Data View. This process also works well for testing functions.

FIGURE 9.7:

Executing a stored procedure in Visual Database Tools

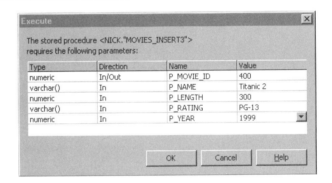

NOTE   The Visual Studio Data View is a different product from the Visual Basic Data View. The editors use different color-coding schemes, and as we saw in the example, several features are missing from the VB version. If you are going to open Visual Studio anyway, then this is the environment to work from.

Summary of Visual Database Tools

It is encouraging to find Microsoft supporting PL/SQL generation in this way, and Visual Database Tools has some nice features. It is much easier to use than SQL*Plus, but it lacks some important qualities.

On the plus side, Visual Database Tools is an easy-to-use interface that can be used for different databases. It is simple to run a stored procedure: you do not have to remember any syntax to execute it and passing parameters is easy. You do not have to define an output parameter, and its value automatically appears in the output window; this is a very nice feature. The environment appears to be more user friendly to Oracle users than previous versions.

However, Visual Database Tools does lack some serious features, which we will see in Oracle Procedure Builder, most notably the ability to debug a procedure. It is doubtful if this ability will ever be built into a Microsoft product. Visual Database Tools is also missing the ability to handle packages, which form the basis of serious PL/SQL applications.

Oracle Procedure Builder

Oracle Procedure Builder comes as part of the Oracle's Developer 2000 suite of application development tools, but it is also available as a separate package. If your company is not using Developer 2000, this alternative provides a cost-effective tool, quite apart from the fact that it is the only full-featured development environment available for PL/SQL. It is relatively easy to install from CD using the standard Oracle install program, `orainst.exe`.

When you run Oracle Procedure Builder, you must first use the File ➤ Connect menu option to connect to the database, with your user name, password, and the name of the database, in the normal way. If you have not set up your client and server for connections, then see Chapter 11, *Client-Side Technology*. When you have connected to the database of choice, you will see a screen like the one shown in Figure 9.8.

The features that Procedure Builder presents are listed below.

- View all objects visible to the user, including subprograms and tables.

- Create and edit procedures and functions.

- Create and edit packages.

- Run stored subprograms on the server.

- A local PL/SQL engine (interpreter) that includes the following:

  - The ability to set breakpoints in the code.

  - The ability to see the values of all variables at a breakpoint.

  - The ability to step through the code line by line.

FIGURE 9.8:

The Oracle Procedure Builder work area

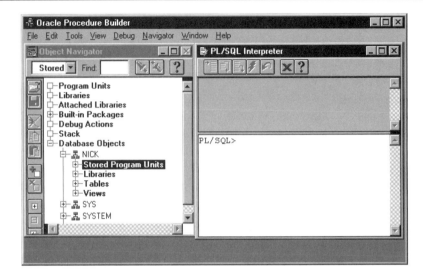

NOTE   The name of Oracle Procedure Builder is likely to change soon to Application Builder for PL/SQL. This reflects the direction toward including other languages, such as Java, in the Oracle database.

Using Procedure Builder

Procedure Builder is a powerful environment for developing, testing, and maintaining Oracle stored procedures and functions. This section will give you an introduction to using it; you will cover enough to produce production-level procedures. However, because the environment is so large, you should be aware that there are many more capabilities that will not be covered.

There are three main windows you will be using in Procedure Builder. If these are not visible when you boot up the program, you can bring them up from the Tools menu. Each of the windows will be covered in the normal order that you need them.

The Object Navigator

The Object Navigator window is the starting point for any of your operations and is shown in Figure 9.9. It is always present in the application. It presents you with a tree-like outline of all the objects you have access to. The top-level objects are called nodes, and the nodes you have access to are shown in Table 9.3. In Figure 9.9, you can see that the Database Objects node has been expanded to show the subprograms.

FIGURE 9.9:

The Object Navigator window

TABLE 9.3: The Layout of the Procedure Builder Navigator Window

Node	Description
Program Units	Displays procedures that are stored locally. These are used to run in the debugger and can later be transferred to stored procedures in your database.
Libraries	Allows you to create and modify libraries of procedures. These will not be dealt with in this book.
Attached Libraries	Allows you to attach and detach existing PL/SQL libraries.
Built-in Packages	Allows you to review which built-in packages are available.
Debug Actions	Allows you to control the actions of the debugger.
Stack	Used in Debug mode, this allows you to view the values of all the variables currently in the scope of the executing program unit.
Database Objects	Allows you to view the various database objects you have access to, such as tables, procedures, and triggers. If you view the list of stored program units, an asterisk alongside the name indicates that the code is in an uncompiled state and needs your attention.

Creating a Local Program Unit

The first type of PL/SQL procedure we will create is a program unit, which is code that is held on your workstation, not on the database server. When you exit Procedure Builder, you lose the code, so if you want to keep it you must move it into a stored procedure, a process we will see later in the chapter in the section, "The Stored Program Unit Editor." An alternative way to retain program units is to use Edit/Export. The reason we need local program units at all is that this is the only way to use the debugger.

WARNING   Program units in Procedure Builder version 1.*x* cannot support advanced functionality, such as PL/SQL Cursors or tables. This functionality is provided in version 2.

To create a program unit, use the following steps.

1. Click on the Database Objects node.

2. Click on the Create button: Procedure Builder will display a dialog box for you to identify the type of code you want to create. Your choices include Procedures, Functions, Package Specs, and Body (see Figure 9.10).

FIGURE 9.10:

Selecting which type of code object to create

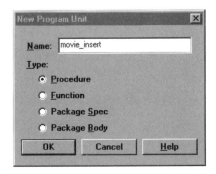

3. Click on Procedures, and fill in the name for your PL/SQL unit. In this case we will enter **movie_insert**. Notice that there is an asterisk after the program-unit name in the name text box. This means the unit has not been compiled.

4. Enter your procedure, and click on the Compile button at the top of the window.

5. Review any error messages; these will appear in the lower half of the window as shown in Figure 9.11. If you click on any error message, the cursor will be placed in the offending line in the upper half of the window. In this case, the problem is that movie_sequence_id was not defined. (The wrong name had been used.)

FIGURE 9.11:

Error messages after a compile is executed

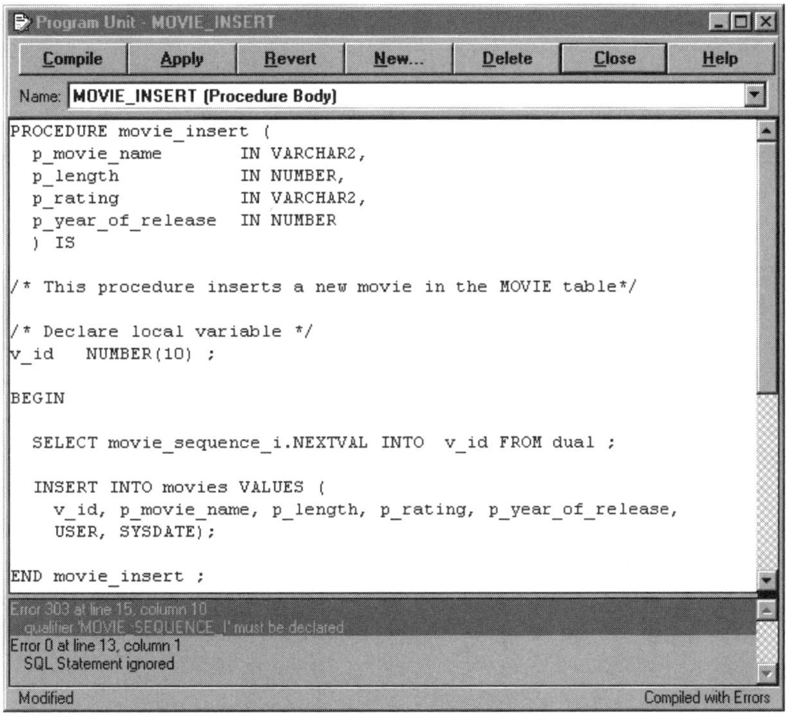

```
Program Unit - MOVIE_INSERT

  Compile    Apply    Revert    New...    Delete    Close    Help

Name: MOVIE_INSERT (Procedure Body)

PROCEDURE movie_insert (
  p_movie_name       IN VARCHAR2,
  p_length           IN NUMBER,
  p_rating           IN VARCHAR2,
  p_year_of_release  IN NUMBER
  ) IS

/* This procedure inserts a new movie in the MOVIE table*/

/* Declare local variable */
v_id   NUMBER(10) ;

BEGIN

  SELECT movie_sequence_i.NEXTVAL INTO  v_id FROM dual ;

  INSERT INTO movies VALUES (
    v_id, p_movie_name, p_length, p_rating, p_year_of_release,
    USER, SYSDATE);

END movie_insert ;

Error 303 at line 15, column 10
  qualifier 'MOVIE_SEQUENCE_I' must be declared
Error 0 at line 13, column 1
  SQL Statement ignored

Modified                                    Compiled with Errors
```

6. When the code compiles cleanly, the asterisk in the name text box will disappear. You can now run your program unit.

You will notice there is no horizontal scroll bar in the editor. This seems to be a bizarre inconvenience; the only way around it is to use the mouse to highlight text moving off the window edge and forcing a horizontal scroll. However, it does encourage you to produce short lines of code!

WARNING   Local program units are local procedures that are not stored on the Oracle server. Once you terminate Procedure Builder, the program unit will be lost if you have not saved it with Edit/Export.

Running the Code with the PL/SQL Interpreter

Now that you have created a program unit, the best way to test it is with the PL/SQL Interpreter, which allows you to not only run the code but also debug it. If the PL/SQL Interpreter is not visible, select it from the Tools menu.

The PL/SQL Interpreter again presents us with a split screen. If you have a program unit in the Program Unit Editor, then the code will automatically appear in the upper half of the window as shown in Figure 9.11. If it doesn't, then close the Program Unit Editor, and open it up again by double-clicking on your program in the Object Navigator.

To execute a procedure from Procedure Builder, you enter the procedure name in the bottom half of the PL/SQL Interpreter window and include any parameters.

```
PL/SQL> movie_insert ('My Next Movie', 105, 'PG-13', 1998);
```

You can see the results of this in Figure 9.12.

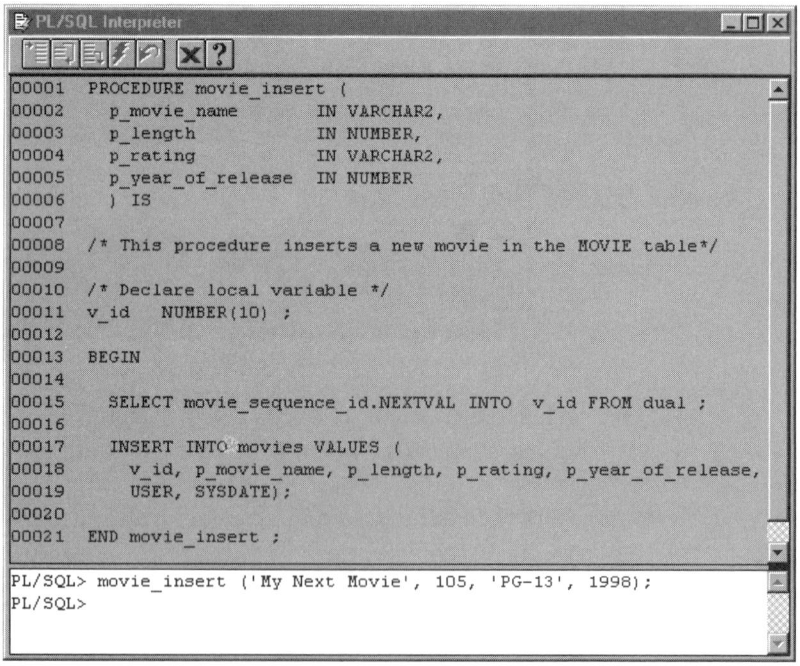

FIGURE 9.12:

Executing a program unit in the PL/SQL Interpreter

Handling Output Parameters

We have seen that input parameters can be dealt with by including them in the procedure call; however, output parameters are more difficult to deal with. If you have output parameters, then you need to create a local variable with the CREATE command. Then, after the procedure has completed, you can view the value with TEXT_IO.PUT_LINE as follows:

```
PL/SQL> .CREATE NUMBER out_parm1
PL/SQL> .CREATE CHAR out_parm2
PL/SQL> test_proc (in_parm, :out_parm1, :out_parm2);
PL/SQL> TEXT_IO.PUT_LINE (TO_CHAR(:out_parm1));
PL/SQL> TEXT_IO.PUT_LINE (:out_parm2);
```

The same approach can be taken with functions:

```
PL/SQL> .CREATE NUMBER return_val1
PL/SQL> :return_val1 := test_function ('My Movie');
PL/SQL> TEXT_IO.PUT_LINE (TO_CHAR(return_val1));
```

In each case, note the use of the colon before the variables. This colon indicates that you are dealing with a bind variable, that is, a variable that the output parameters and return values can be bound to. You should also note that to print out a numeric value you first need to convert it to a character string with the TO_CHAR function.

WARNING In the versions of Procedure Builder before version 2, you must use IN OUT parameters instead of OUT parameters for this to work.

Debugging Your Procedure

Unless you are one of those rare people who never makes a mistake, you will have grown used to the incredible debugging facilities now available in Visual Basic. I cannot remember how I survived without them, and if I use a programming environment that does not provide such a state-of-the-art feature, I am disappointed. The truth is Procedure Builder does not provide this level of debugging. On the other hand, the alternatives (SQL*Plus and Visual Database Tools, for example) provide no debugging at all.

To create a debugging session for a Program Unit, we take up where we left off in the section, "Running the Code with the PL/SQL Interpreter." There are two main features of the debugger: breakpoints and checking the values of variables.

To create a breakpoint, look in the upper half of the PL/SQL Interpreter window: here you can see the source code that you are executing. If you double-click on any line of code, a breakpoint will be set there; you can tell because the line number changes to a "B" followed by the breakpoint number. You will also notice that this is reflected as a message in the lower half of the window (see Figure 9.13).

FIGURE 9.13:

Setting the procedure breakpoints

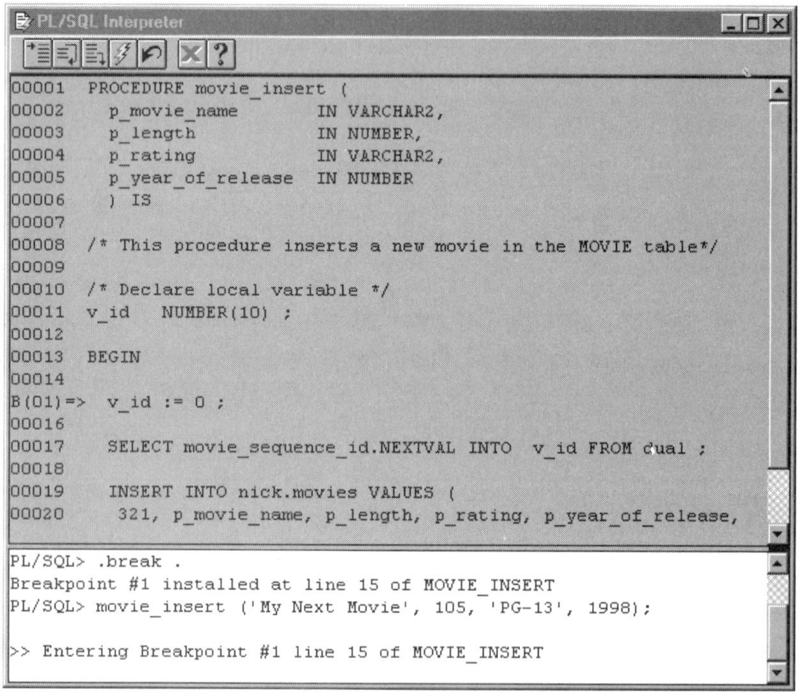

```
PL/SQL Interpreter                                          _ □ ✕

00001    PROCEDURE movie_insert (
00002      p_movie_name        IN VARCHAR2,
00003      p_length            IN NUMBER,
00004      p_rating            IN VARCHAR2,
00005      p_year_of_release   IN NUMBER
00006      ) IS
00007
00008    /* This procedure inserts a new movie in the MOVIE table*/
00009
00010    /* Declare local variable */
00011    v_id    NUMBER(10) ;
00012
00013    BEGIN
00014
B(01)=>   v_id := 0 ;
00016
00017       SELECT movie_sequence_id.NEXTVAL INTO  v_id FROM dual ;
00018
00019       INSERT INTO nick.movies VALUES (
00020        321, p_movie_name, p_length, p_rating, p_year_of_release,

PL/SQL> .break .
Breakpoint #1 installed at line 15 of MOVIE_INSERT
PL/SQL> movie_insert ('My Next Movie', 105, 'PG-13', 1998);

>> Entering Breakpoint #1 line 15 of MOVIE_INSERT
```

WARNING   You have to double-click on an executable PL/SQL statement. This means that you cannot set a breakpoint on a SQL statement, such as INSERT. If you do, you will get a **PDE-CBR001** message. If this is a problem, put in a dummy line such as the one shown on line 15 in Figure 9.13.

When you start up the program in the normal way, you can use the toolbar at the top of the PL/SQL Interpreter to:

- Step Into a subprogram call.

- Step Over a subprogram call.

- Step Out of a subprogram to the calling program.

- Go (that is, execute the program until the next breakpoint is encountered).

- Reset to alter the debug level.

When the executing program reaches a breakpoint, you can view the values of all the variables in the *Stack*. The Stack is one of the nodes in the Object Navigator, and it displays the current value of every variable in the program (see Figure 9.14).

FIGURE 9.14:

The Stack allows you to monitor the values of all variables in the program.

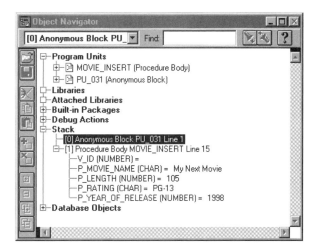

The Stored Program Unit Editor

Once you have tested your code in the debugger, you can now store it on the database server as a stored procedure. To do this step, you will have to cut and paste the code from the Program Unit Editor into the Stored Procedure Editor. You create a new stored procedure in just the same way as we created a program unit, except this time we click initially on the Stored Procedures level under the Database Objects node in the Object Navigator.

The layout of the Stored Procedure Editor is slightly different from the Program Unit Editor. As you can see in Figure 9.15, the main difference is that you now use a Save button instead of a Compile button.

NOTE   You can use the Stored Program Unit Editor as your only working environment if you want but remember that you cannot use the debugger on your code.

FIGURE 9.15:

The Stored Program Unit Editor is similar to the Program Unit Editor.

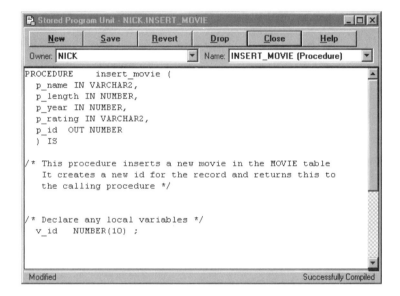

```
PROCEDURE     insert_movie (
  p_name IN VARCHAR2,
  p_length IN NUMBER,
  p_year IN NUMBER,
  p_rating IN VARCHAR2,
  p_id  OUT NUMBER
  ) IS

/* This procedure inserts a new movie in the MOVIE table
   It creates a new id for the record and returns this to
   the calling procedure */


/* Declare any local variables */
  v_id   NUMBER(10) ;
```

Where Is Your Code Stored?

One of the strange things about stored programs is if you edit a working procedure and it does not compile, the previous working procedure still works. This feature is helpful if you have to make changes to a live database. It also lets you realize that the source code is stored separately from the compiled code.

To find the source code, you can look in a special view called USER_SOURCE. View it with the following statement:

```
SELECT name, text FROM user_source
   ORDER BY name, line;
```

Continued on next page

> If you are anything like me, this information can be harmful to your free time; you could envisage writing your own editor with just the features that you want. A Visual Basic program that can test out all your procedures…

Error Handling in PL/SQL

Stored procedures have only one form of error handling, which is through a block of code initiated in a similar way to Visual Basic's "On Error Goto" error handler. In this case, the equivalent of the GOTO statement is automatically invoked if we provide an EXCEPTION handling block. This is a block of code that is defined by the EXCEPTION keyword; an example is shown in Listing 9.5. We say that PL/SQL *raises an exception* when an error is encountered.

Listing 9.5

```
/* This is the EXCEPTION block */
EXCEPTION
  WHEN NO_DATA_FOUND THEN
    code := 1;
  WHEN VALUE_ERROR THEN
    code := 2;
  WHEN OTHERS THEN
    code := 99;
```

If any errors occur in the procedure, control is automatically passed to this EXCEPTION block, and you can decide how you want to proceed. One of the normal things to do is to test for various possible errors and then provide code to handle the required course of action for each. Before we can do this, we must first look at the built-in error types; these are shown in Table 9.4.

TABLE 9.4: The Built-in Error Types in PL/SQL

Exception	Description
CURSOR_ALREADY_OPEN	An attempt was made to open a cursor that is already open. Close it first, or use a different one.
DUP_VAL_ON_INDEX	An attempt was made to save a record with a unique key that already exists.

Continued on next page

TABLE 9.4 CONTINUED: The Built-in Error Types in PL/SQL

Exception	Description
INVALID_CURSOR	An invalid operation on a cursor.
INVALID_NUMBER	Error in a string-to-number conversion because the string does not represent a valid number.
LOGON_DENIED	Invalid user ID or password when logging on (typically not applicable to VB program calls).
NO_DATA_FOUND	The result of a SELECT INTO statement has returned no rows.
NOT_LOGGED ON	Invalid user ID or password when logging on (typically not applicable to VB program calls).
PROGRAM_ERROR	A problem internal to Oracle.
ROWTYPE_MISMATCH	A cursor assignment where the cursors are of different types.
STORAGE_ERROR	Memory error.
TIMEOUT_ON_RESOURCE	Time-out when waiting for a system resource.
TOO_MANY_ROWS	The result of a SELECT INTO statement returns more than one row.
VALUE_ERROR	There has been some arithmetic or conversion error. This may also be due to column size being exceeded.
ZERO_DIVIDE	Divide by zero error.

NOTE After testing a return code with WHEN…THEN, you *must* have at least one executable line of code. If you want to ignore the error, you will still have to put a line of code there even if it does not do much.

One thing you must be aware of is that if you do not trap the error with the EXCEPTION block, then the error will be sent back to the calling routine (again very similar to the way Visual Basic works). This would mean that you have to handle the error in VB, and this may involve executing some more SQL or perhaps another PL/SQL procedure to rollback a partial transaction. This is not the most efficient way of doing things.

On the other hand, if we do trap the error in PL/SQL, then the calling procedure is not aware that any error has occurred. Luckily, we can resignal the error so that the calling program knows it has occurred, and notify the user (typically with some kind of message box). In the calling program, you can rest assured that even though an error has occurred, it has already been dealt with, and you do not have to take any corrective action except notifying the user. This resignaling of the error message is achieved simply by the RAISE statement.

```
EXCEPTION
  WHEN OTHERS THEN
    ROLLBACK;    /* Rollback changes if situation warrants it */
    RAISE;       /* Notify the calling routine */
```

You should consider this approach as a *minimum* when detecting errors. Add a ROLLBACK statement to undo any data that has been inserted, updated, or deleted, and then you can write the Visual Basic code to inform the user that no data was saved due to the error.

TIP   You should make a habit of ensuring that all stored procedures called from external routines, such as Visual Basic, handle their own error conditions internally and gracefully. In this way, you will not have to provide complex error handlers in every application that makes use of them. And remember that *any* procedure you write can have an error.

Enhancing the Error Message

A stored procedure will return an Oracle error message to your VB code, in which you will need a routine to handle it (see Chapter 13, *Visual Basic Design Issues*, for more information). However, this limits your error detection to predefined error messages and only Oracle defined numbers. You may want to send back your own messages that may be more specific than the default messages.

For example, if you are trying to update a record with a certain ID and find that the record is not available, you can return the default Oracle error message, saying that a record was not found. Because this will be in "Oraclese," a more sensible message can let the user know that the ID was not found and give them a few more details, including, perhaps, the ID itself. The users of your application will surely prefer this method of finding out about an error!

To return your own error message, use the following statement:

```
RAISE_APPLICATION_ERROR (error_number, error message, flag);
```

The error number must be between -20000 and -20999, and the message is a string up to 2,048 characters. The flag is optional and not often used: by default it is FALSE and means that your message replaces all other error messages. If TRUE, it will be added to any other error messages returned to the calling procedure.

An example of defining your own error message is

```
IF value > test_value THEN
RAISE_APPLICATION_ERROR
(-20001, 'The value was greater than ' || TO_CHAR (test_value));
END IF;
```

If you make much use of this error handling technique, you should keep track of your error conditions by saving them in a small table with an error code to use in the procedure as well as the associated error number and message. This can then be used across the whole database. An alternative approach is to store the error numbers and messages as constants in a package header. This way, the constants are available throughout the package. Whichever means you choose, you should ensure that the use of error numbers is strictly controlled.

TIP   It is a good idea to not only describe errors with as much detail as possible but also give an explanation of what it means and offer some course of action to follow, even if is just to contact your local DBA.

Summary

This chapter has introduced us to the basics of PL/SQL and given enough examples to get us started. We have reviewed the different ways to create stored procedures, and I hope you will be encouraged to get Oracle Procedure Builder to make this task easier. We have also introduced error handling in sufficient detail for you to develop an initial approach before you code any procedures. We will look into situations that give rise to errors in the next chapter.

Hopefully, the chapter has also given you enough reasons to convince you that stored procedures are the way to go and are not something to be frightened of. However, there is much more that you can do with stored procedures, and the next chapter will take you through some more basics and through to the more advanced features that can really make your Visual Basic programs powerful.

CHAPTER
TEN

10

Creating Stored Procedures

- PL/SQL Data Types

- Declaring Variables

- Statements and Assignments

- Flow Control Statements

- Using SQL Statements in PL/SQL

- PL/SQL Cursors

- User-Defined Data Types, Including Records, PL/SQL Tables, and Cursor Variables

- Using Triggers

- Providing a Transaction Audit

- Procedures and Visual Basic

After the introduction to stored procedures in the previous chapter, we are now ready to learn the intricacies of writing in PL/SQL. Until recently, there was a limited amount of use that Visual Basic developers could make of stored procedures. Although you could encapsulate business rules to control the input of data (this should be your standard way of altering data), you could not return data to your application, apart from stored-procedure output parameters. In the last year or so this has begun to change, and perhaps Visual Basic has had something to do with it.

The areas that we will be covering are

- PL/SQL data types

- Declaring variables

- Statements and assignments

- Flow control statements

- Using SQL statements in PL/SQL

- PL/SQL cursors

- User-defined data types, including records, PL/SQL tables, and cursor variables

- Using triggers

- Providing a transaction audit

- Procedures and Visual Basic

PL/SQL Data Types

Inside a stored procedure or function, you can define one or more variables whose scope is limited to the procedure in the same way that Visual Basic variables are declared. You define PL/SQL variables in the declarative section of a block at the beginning of the procedure, which is the normal practice in VB.

We covered the available data types for columns in database tables when defining a table (see Chapter 6, *Implementing a Database*), but we have to learn a different set here. Although some of the names are the same, the definitions are not always identical. In addition, several new definitions are peculiar to PL/SQL and have no matching type in the database.

Scalar Data Types

The first and simplest data type available to PL/SQL developers is the scalar type. The term *scalar* is given to simple data types that have only one value. To the Visual Basic developer, this means types such as Integer or String. The alternative to scalar types are composite or user-defined data types. VB developers will be familiar with these types as they are equivalent to arrays or to structures defined with the TYPE statement. Table 10.1 lists the scalar data types that are available in PL/SQL.

TABLE 10.1: The Scalar Data Types in PL/SQL

Variable Type	Description
BINARY_INTEGER	Signed integer variables. They use less storage than numbers.
BOOLEAN	Stores TRUE, FALSE, and NULL.
CHAR(n)	Fixed-length character string variables, n characters long where n can be up to 32,767.
DATE	Standard Oracle date field, holding data, and time.
LONG	Variable-length character string variables up to 32,760 bytes. Note the difference from the corresponding column type, which can hold up to 2GB.
LONG RAW	Binary variables up to 32,760 bytes. Again, this is less than the column type, which can hold up to 2GB.
NUMBER(n)	Integer variable up to n digits long.
NUMBER(m,n)	Fixed-point decimal value with m digits before the decimal point and n digits after.
PLS_INTEGER	Signed integers from -2147483647 to +2147483647.
RAW	Binary variables storing up to 32,767 bytes.
VARCHAR2(n)	Variable-length character variables of maximum length n where n is up to 32,767 bytes.

You can also use various subtypes of the NUMBER data type; these subtypes are described in the *Oracle PL/SQL User's Guide and Reference*. However, these subtypes do not give much advantage to a developer except to identify what data type the designer was thinking of.

WARNING   The PL/SQL data types can typically hold more data than will fit into the similarly typed database column. For example, VARCHAR2 can be up to 32,767 bytes in PL/SQL but can hold only 2,000 bytes in the database.

User-Defined (Composite) Variables

User-defined data types are types that you define in your code and include more than just one (scalar) value; for example, a *record* is equivalent to a user-defined structure that a Visual Basic developer creates with the TYPE statement. There are three user-defined data types, and they are detailed in Table 10.2. We will deal with each of these user-defined types later in this chapter because they provide much needed features for the developer.

TABLE 10.2: User-Defined Data Types in PL/SQL

Variable type	Description
Cursor	An explicit pointer to a record in a result set.
Record	The Record type allows you to define your own combination of data types. This type is similar to a structure in C or a user-defined type in VB.
PL/SQL table or collection	This is a recent addition to the data types and solves a deficiency in PL/SQL. It functions like a database table, though it is much more similar in function to a Visual Basic collection. You can also use these as arrays.

Declaring Variables

In PL/SQL, you *must* declare all the variables that you want to use in your procedure. This declaration of variables comes at the beginning of a code block after any header and before the first BEGIN statement. It can also occur in the declaration part of any nested block. As with Visual Basic, you include every variable

name and follow it with its data type. For example, you may see the following
command sequence:

```
PROCEDURE test (p_val NUMBER) IS

    v_customer_name   VARCHAR2(50);
    v_customer_number NUMBER(10);

    BEGIN
    etc.
```

This code fragment declares two variables, one of type VARCHAR2(50) and the
other of type NUMBER(10). You can declare all the variables you want to use in
the procedure whether they are scalar types, such as NUMBER, or the more complex types, which we will see in the rest of this chapter.

You can also define an initialization value for the variable in the declare statement by using the standard assignment operator:

```
v_total_amount      NUMBER (5,2) := 0;
v_data_found BOOLEAN := FALSE;
```

Variable Naming Conventions

Several accepted standards for naming variables are available in Visual Basic. Most of the
examples I have seen make no attempt to duplicate these naming conventions in a stored
procedure. Most of you will probably produce far less PL/SQL code than Visual Basic code,
so it is probably not too important.

However, it would be good practice to come up with some site specific naming conventions of your own. At a minimum, I would suggest differentiating between input parameters (which I prefix with "p_") and locally declared variables (which I prefix with "v_"). The
advantage of this is that it lessens the likelihood of trying to assign a value to an input-
only parameter, though this does often appear as a compile-time error.

Using %TYPE and %ROWTYPE

The use of standard data types is in PL/SQL is similar to those used in Visual
Basic. In PL/SQL, you also have the option of declaring variables of a type

similar to an existing data type in a database table or of one that has already been defined. You can do this with the %TYPE attribute. The following example shows a new variable, movie_length, defined as the same type as the length column in the Movies table, and a variable average_length defined as the same type again.

```
movie_length        movies.length%TYPE;
average_length      movie_length%TYPE;
```

Why use this data type? Well, if you decide to change the precision of a table column from NUMBER(2) to NUMBER(5), you will not have to change every single procedure used in this column. We can simply define a variable of the same type as the column, whatever it is: when the column changes, the procedure should still work. Of course, if we changed NUMBER columns to VARCHAR2 columns, it is not likely that the procedure will work without data-type conversion errors.

We can take this a step further and define composite variable types of the same structure as a table row with the %ROWTYPE attribute, such as the following example.

```
video_record videos%ROWTYPE;
```

This type defines a composite variable "video_record" with the same structure as the Videos table, which means the variable contains one field for every column in the videos table. You can access these fields by prefixing them with the variable name. For example,

```
video_record.status
```

accesses the status field to let you use it or assign it a value.

We will see the benefit of this process later in the chapter when we cover cursors.

Declaring Constants

As every seasoned developer knows, it is far better to use constants rather than hard-coding values with literals such as 3.14159 or 'RESERVED,' especially if they are likely to be used in more than one place. It may be a little more work up front, but it pays off in the long run with ease of maintenance.

Declaring a constant in PL/SQL is similar to declaring a variable except the keyword CONSTANT is added. For example, we could declare

```
pi               CONSTANT  NUMBER(6,5) := 3.14159;
reserved_rating CONSTANT CHAR(8) := 'RESERVED';
```

You use the constants in the same way you would a variable except you cannot assign it a new value.

Ideally, you will build your stored procedures into a package and add the constant declarations to that package. In this way, the constants are available throughout the package.

TIP   Using constants is an ideal way to handle error numbers and messages. You can organize your messages across the package to avoid any reuse of the same error number and to reduce maintenance.

Statements and Assignments

PL/SQL consists of statements like any other procedural language; each statement is terminated by a semicolon, so naturally, they can span more than one line of code. A side-effect is that this method of marking the end of a statement lets you format the code so it easy to read.

Assignments take a little more getting used to. Instead of the "=" that we use in Visual Basic, we must use the variant ":=" that is more familiar to Pascal programmers.

```
v_value_1  := 10;
v_complete := FALSE;
v_name     := 'unknown';
v_name_2   := v_name;
```

Flow Control Statements

Once you have your variables defined you need to become familiar with flow control before you can create more than a simple program. Two basic concepts are missing from SQL but are absolutely necessary for procedural programming: decision flow control and loops. These concepts are the foundation of procedural programming and the most basic feature that PL/SQL brings to SQL.

Decision Flow Control

The first flow control statements you need are for decision control. Decision control of the flow for program statement execution is the familiar IF…THEN statements. Luckily, the concept of these statements is close to what you are used to in Visual Basic, so a brief overview should suffice. There are three forms of the IF…THEN statements that we shall review, with an example of each.

IF…THEN

Use the IF… THEN statement for a simple decision process. For example, to set a variable *movie_type* according to the movie's length, use the following statements.

```
movie_type := 'short';
IF movie_length < 120 THEN
  movie_type := 'long';
END IF;
```

IF…THEN…ELSE

The second form of the decision statement is IF…THEN…ELSE and is useful for a choice of two different outcomes. A practical example is to set a variable message depending on the *movie_rating* variable.

```
IF movie_rating = 'G' THEN
  message := 'Suitable for children';
ELSE
  message := 'Not suitable for children';
END IF;
```

The IF…THEN structure can include any number of statements, including another IF…THEN statement.

IF…THEN…ELSIF

Finally, the most complex of the decision statements is used when there are more than two alternatives. It is a much better choice than nesting IF statements. Unfortunately, PL/SQL does not implement the SELECT…CASE statement that we see in other languages. The following example shows how to set the *rating_description* variable depending on the *movie_rating* variable. If the translation is always the same, it might be better to store the translation in a code table in the database.

```
IF movie_rating = 'G' THEN
    rating_description := 'General';
ELSIF movie_rating = 'PG' THEN
    rating_description := 'Parental Guidance';
ELSIF movie_rating = 'PG-13' THEN
    rating_description := 'No children under 13';
ELSE
    rating_description := 'Adults only';
END IF;
```

NOTE   PL/SQL uses "ELSIF" rather than the more sensible spelling "ELSEIF," which Visual Basic developers are used to. However, the compiler is kind enough to point this one out for you.

Figure 10.1 shows a completed procedure in Oracle Procedure Builder that includes many of the features we have seen so far. To make the example useful, we have to cheat a little and include the SELECT...INTO command, which we will discuss later in the section "Using SQL Statements in PL/SQL."

FIGURE 10.1:

A complete procedure

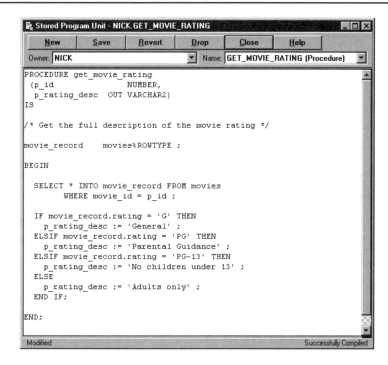

Loops

Loops are the second fundamental control structure in any language; PL/SQL has three types. Loops are of most use when scanning though a *PL/SQL table* (discussed in the section "PL/SQL Tables and Collections") and when reading through the results of a cursor created with a SELECT statement. This section gives examples of the basic loop to calculate the sum of the squares from 1 to 10.

LOOP... END LOOP

The LOOP...END LOOP construct is a continuous loop much like a DO...LOOP construct in Visual Basic. There are three ways to get out of this loop: use the EXIT, EXIT...WHEN, or RETURN statements. (RETURN exits the whole procedure.)

```
LOOP
  sum := sum + (i * i) ;
  i := i + 1;
  IF i > 10 THEN
    EXIT;
  END IF;
END LOOP;
```

An alternative version of this loop uses the EXIT...WHEN statement. It has exactly the same effect as putting the EXIT statement in an IF block, as in the previous example. It is a much cleaner way of ending the loop.

```
LOOP
  sum := sum + (i * i) ;
  i := i + 1;
  EXIT WHEN i = 10;
END LOOP;
```

WHILE...LOOP

The WHILE...LOOP construct is very close to the WHILE...DO statement in Visual Basic. It operates in much the same way as the previous examples.

```
i := 1;
sum_square := 0;
WHILE i < 10 LOOP
  sum_square := sum_square + (i * i);
  i := i + 1;
END LOOP;
```

FOR...LOOP

The final form of the loop is the FOR...LOOP and is similar to the FOR...NEXT loop in Visual Basic. This loop operates for a range of integers.

```
sum_square := 0;
FOR i IN 1..10 LOOP
  sum_square := sum_square + (i * i);
END LOOP;
```

An example of a completed procedure is shown in Figure 10.2.

FIGURE 10.2:

A function with a loop construct

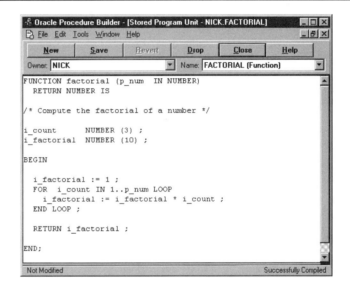

TIP

Although procedures can do all the processing that functions can, functions have one advantage: they can be used anywhere that a standard Oracle function can (assuming you have the right privileges). A great use of this feature is being able to call the function from within a SQL statement.

Using SQL Statements in PL/SQL

For PL/SQL to be of any use to us, we need to do more than sum variables and use loops—we need to interact with the database. PL/SQL is an extension to SQL, and as such, you can include SQL commands seamlessly into your code. However, not all SQL commands can be used in this way. Two types of commands are of interest here: those that update data, and those that just retrieve it.

Update Statements

You can use the INSERT, UPDATE, and DELETE statements in exactly the same way you would in a normal SQL statement, as we covered in Chapter 8, *Updating Your Database*. Listing 10.1 shows you a short procedure to illustrate how you can incorporate an INSERT statement.

Listing 10.1

```
PROCEDURE movie_insert(
  p_movie_id IN NUMBER,
  p_name          IN VARCHAR2,
  p_length        IN NUMBER,
  p_rating        IN VARCHAR2,
  p_year          IN NUMBER) IS

/* Insert a new movie into the database */

BEGIN
  INSERT INTO movies VALUES (
    movie_sequence_id.NEXTVAL, p_name, p_length, p_rating, p_year,
    USER, SYSDATE);
  COMMIT;

EXCEPTION
/* Whatever the problem just rollback and
   pass the error back to Visual Basic */
  WHEN OTHERS THEN
    ROLLBACK;
    RAISE;
END movie_insert;
```

The procedure, movie_insert, is designed to insert a new record into the movies table. All the required data is passed to the procedure as parameters. The procedure uses the INSERT command and follows it up with a COMMIT command to ensure that the change is made permanent. The EXCEPTION block handles any errors encountered while saving the data. Although the ROLLBACK may not be necessary in this case, because an error implies that the new record has not been inserted, it is good practice to cover all bases.

Using a stored procedure, the application developer does not have to write any code to handle a sequence. In addition to this ease of use, it also slightly improves efficiency.

Procedures in Action

Ideally, for the greatest security of your data, you should create three separate procedures for each table that the end users will have access to: one for each of the INSERT, UPDATE, and DELETE functions.

If you have many tables, you probably do not relish creating three procedures for each. However, this task can be handled by a short Visual Basic program. We will cover this in Chapter 14, *Data Access Objects*.

Using SELECT INTO

As mentioned before, Oracle has no direct way to return the result set from a SELECT statement in a stored procedure. If you include a simple SELECT statement in your PL/SQL code, you will get a compile error. However, you can use the SELECT INTO statement, a variation on the standard SELECT that allows data to be read into one or more simple or compound variables. The syntax of the SELECT statement is

```
SELECT column_list | *
  INTO variable_list | record_variable
  FROM table_list | subquery
  WHERE condition
```

The column list in the SELECT INTO statement must match the variable list; that is, there must be one matching variable for each column to be read into. The SELECT statement must also only return one row, otherwise an error will be returned. As an example, we will use the SELECT INTO statement to read the name of a movie whose ID we already know.

```
SELECT movie_name
   INTO v_name
   FROM movies
   WHERE movie_id = p_id;
```

Another use for the SELECT INTO statement is to find and store the next available sequence number, which we can access from the Dual table.

```
SELECT movie_sequence.NEXTVAL
   INTO next_sequence
   FROM dual;
```

In a procedure that generates a new key value with a sequence, it would be useful to be able to pass the sequence number back to the calling procedure, which may be Visual Basic. Typically, you will want to use the number as the input to another procedure to create a master/detail relationship. For example you can insert a new movie and use the key value from the sequence number as an input parameter for inserting a row into the videos table.

To retrieve the sequence number, you could define parameter *p_movie_id* with IN OUT mode and then set its value to *movie_sequence.NEXTVAL* before using it as a value for the INSERT statement (see Listing 10.2). However, to make use of this from Visual Basic, you will need to be using something more advanced than Data Access Objects (DAO), which cannot retrieve an output parameter from a stored procedure. Instead, you will have to use one of the more advanced techniques: Remote Data Objects, Active Data Objects, or Oracle Objects for OLE.

Listing 10.2

```
PROCEDURE movie_insert2(
   p_movie_id IN OUT NUMBER,
   p_name          IN VARCHAR2,
   p_length        IN NUMBER,
   p_rating        IN VARCHAR2,
   p_year          IN NUMBER) IS

/* Insert a new movie into the movie table
   If the formal parameter, p_movie_id is zero it is assigned
```

```
        from the next available sequence number
*/

BEGIN

  IF p_movie_id = 0 THEN
    SELECT movie_sequence_id.NEXTVAL INTO p_movie_id
      FROM dual;
  END IF;
  INSERT INTO movies VALUES (
    p_movie_id, p_name, p_length, p_rating, p_year, USER, SYSDATE);

  COMMIT;

EXCEPTION
/* Whatever the problem just rollback and
   pass the error back to Visual Basic */
  WHEN OTHERS THEN
    ROLLBACK;
    RAISE;
END movie_insert2;
```

You can see this being executed in Oracle Procedure Builder in Figure 10.3. Notice how we create a new variable *movie_num* and set its value to 0. We execute the procedure, passing *movie_num*, plus all the other new values. When the procedure returns, we examine the value of *movie_num* with the TEXT_IO.PUT_LINE procedure and see its new value, 220. Two things to notice are that you should use the colon in front of the bind variables and that you should convert a numeric return value to character with the TO_CHAR function before trying to display it.

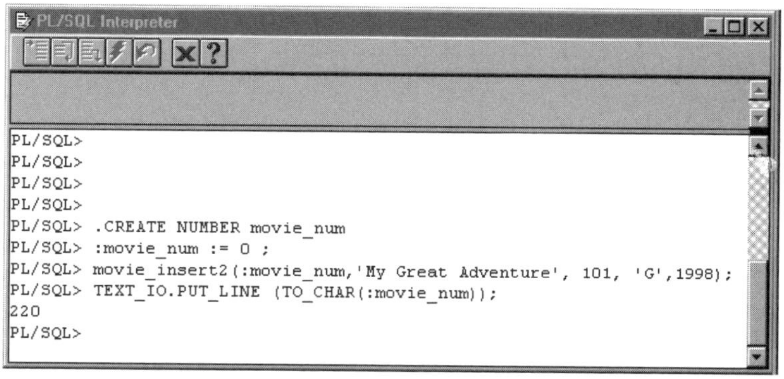

FIGURE 10.3:

Executing the movie_insert2 procedure

```
PL/SQL>
PL/SQL>
PL/SQL>
PL/SQL>
PL/SQL> .CREATE NUMBER movie_num
PL/SQL> :movie_num := 0 ;
PL/SQL> movie_insert2(:movie_num,'My Great Adventure', 101, 'G',1998);
PL/SQL> TEXT_IO.PUT_LINE (TO_CHAR(:movie_num));
220
PL/SQL>
```

If you are not using a data-access method in your Visual Basic code that lets you read output parameters from stored procedures, don't despair. You have several alternatives. You can do everything from within a single stored procedure, such as inserting the master row as well as the detail rows. Although this works in some well-defined situations, you will usually have to resort to using a SELECT statement from VB to read the next available sequence number and pass it to all the stored procedures that need it.

The structure of the stored procedure in Listing 10.2 gives you the best of both worlds: if you pass a zero for the *p_movie_id* parameter, then the procedure will create a new value. If you pass a nonzero value, it will use that.

TIP

Do not be afraid of making your code look easy to read and, well, attractive. One of the easiest things to do is to include plenty of white space, that is, blank lines to split up different areas of code. You can line up parameters or variable declarations with spaces or tabs. There is no version control in PL/SQL, so it is wise to always keep a running history of changes in the comments at the start of the procedure.

Exceptions in SELECT INTO

In the next section we will see *cursors,* memory areas that point to and retrieve data from a result set that can consist of zero, one, or more rows of data. The SELECT INTO statement uses what is called an *implicit* cursor (it is implicit because you do not need to define it; that is done for you automatically), and it must produce only one row. If no rows or more than one row is returned, then an exception is raised, and any action you want to code will have to be placed in the exception block. The possible errors are detailed in Table 10.3.

TIP

Because a SELECT INTO must always produce one and only one row in its result set, you will find it more flexible to use explicit cursors instead.

TABLE 10.3: Errors That Can Be Returned from a SELECT INTO Statement

Error	Description
TOO_MANY_ROWS	More than one row was returned by the SELECT INTO statement.
NO_DATA_FOUND	No rows were returned by the SELECT INTO statement.

An example of trapping these exceptions is shown in Listing 10.3. We select the Movie_id column from the Movies table and place into a local variable, *v_movie_id*. The SELECT INTO must return one and only one row. If it returns zero or more than one, then the EXCEPTION block is activated. We can check for any specific error to, for example, tailor our error message.

Listing 10.3

```
FUNCTION get_movie_id (p_movie_name VARCHAR2)
 RETURN INTEGER
IS

v_movie_id     NUMBER(10);

BEGIN
  SELECT movie_id INTO v_movie_id
    FROM movies
    WHERE movie_name = p_movie_name;

  /* . . . . */

  RETURN v_movie_id;

EXCEPTION
  WHEN NO_DATA_FOUND THEN
/*  Ignore the NO_DATA_FOUND error (PL/SQL needs some statement)*/
    v_movie_id := 0;

  WHEN OTHERS THEN;
/*  Pass other errors back to Visual Basic */
    ROLLBACK;
    RAISE;
END get_movie_id;
```

The SELECT INTO statement can be used to retrieve several variables in one go but can also be used with a record variable. We will see an example of this when we move on to the section, "User-Defined Data Types," later in the chapter.

PL/SQL Cursors

You will come across the term *cursors* several times in this book, but unfortunately, the term really means something different each time. In this chapter, I will use the term *PL/SQL cursor* to distinguish it from client-side cursors, though be aware that Oracle documentation just calls them cursors. PL/SQL cursors are considered a static type of cursor, which means you define them with a SELECT statement that is fixed (in a similar way to a Visual Basic constant). Later on in the chapter, we will see cursor variables that have more flexibility than PL/SQL cursors.

As we saw in the Chapter 2, *Oracle Database Architecture*, Oracle is memory-based, and one of the uses for that memory is the Shared Pool, which, among other things, holds SQL statements in the Shared SQL Area. Each user also has a Private SQL Area, which holds user-specific information. Within this private area, there is again a subdivision that stores the results of an SQL query. A PL/SQL cursor lets you set this up as a named area and access the information in it. If you think of this area as a grid with all the rows and columns that have been retrieved, then the PL/SQL cursor acts as a pointer to the current row. Unfortunately, you can only move forward with the cursor, that is, you can move to the next record but not the previous one. This forward-only feature of Oracle cursors is a fundamental one; the ability to scroll through result sets that most Visual Basic developers are used to is only available through client cursors, as we will see in Chapter 11, *Client-Side Technology*.

There are several steps to using a PL/SQL cursor, which we shall now cover. You can see an overview of the process in Figure 10.4.

FIGURE 10.4:

The process of using a PL/SQL cursor

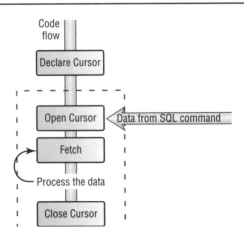

PL/SQL cursors are almost invaluable in PL/SQL programming, but until recently, you have not been able to pass them back to Visual Basic. The only way to do it now is to set up a cursor variable and access it with Oracle Objects for OLE.

Declaring a PL/SQL Cursor

Before you can use a PL/SQL cursor, you must first declare it; you will normally do this along with the other declarations at the beginning of your code block. To define the PL/SQL cursor, we must do it with a SELECT statement:

```
CURSOR video_cursor
  IS SELECT *
    FROM videos
    WHERE status = 'available';
```

This code sets up a cursor called *video_cursor* as a pointer to a structure that corresponds to the column list in the SELECT statement. You can also declare a cursor with one or more parameters. This allows you to open the cursor with different conditions. The following is an example of opening this kind of cursor.

```
CURSOR video_cursor (v_status)
  IS SELECT *
    FROM  videos
    WHERE status = v_status;
```

When you open the PL/SQL cursor, you pass a value for this parameter, in this case, *v_status*.

Opening and Closing a PL/SQL Cursor

Once you have declared a cursor, you need to explicitly open the cursor before we can see any data. No result set has been created at this point. To open a cursor, we use the OPEN statement, and to close it, we use the CLOSE statement.

```
OPEN video_cursor;
PL/SQL statements . . .
. . .
CLOSE video_cursor;
```

To open a cursor with parameters, you pass the parameter values in the OPEN statement:

```
OPEN video_cursor('available');
```

NOTE   You should close the PL/SQL cursor as soon as possible because the SGA memory
allocated to it cannot be released until then.

Fetching a PL/SQL Cursor

With the OPEN statement, we now have the result set in memory. The only way we can access it is to use the FETCH statement, which literally fetches the next row of the result set into local variables. The syntax of this statement is shown below.

```
FETCH cursor_name | cursor_variable_name
   INTO variable_list | record_name;
```

The example in Listing 10.4 opens a PL/SQL cursor, fetches the first row of data into the variables, and closes the cursor. The variables are then available for you to use as you wish.

Listing 10.4

```
OPEN video_cursor;
FETCH video_cursor
  INTO v_video_id, v_movie_id, v_status, v_rental_date,
    v_customer_id, v_purchase_date
CLOSE video_cursor;
```

NOTE   There is no way to move backward in a result set with a PL/SQL cursor.

Error Conditions for PL/SQL Cursors

You need to be aware of several conditions when processing a PL/SQL cursor. You know that you will probably hit the end of the result set at some point; there may not be any rows in the result set. If this condition raised an exception, then the current block of code would be exited, and you would find it difficult to produce any useful programs. Instead, you must test for one of several failure conditions. These conditions are available as *cursor attributes* and are outlined in Table 10.4.

TABLE 10.4: Attributes of a Cursor after a Fetch Operation

Cursor Attributes	Description
%FOUND	This attribute is NULL before the first FETCH and TRUE if the most recent FETCH found a row. It is FALSE if the FETCH did not find a row.
%ISOPEN	This attribute is TRUE if the PL/SQL cursor or cursor variable is open; otherwise, it is FALSE.
%NOTFOUND	This attribute is the opposite of %FOUND; that is, it is TRUE if the last FETCH failed to find a row and FALSE if it did find a row.
%ROWCOUNT	This attribute contains the number of times a row has successfully been fetched. It is zero before the first FETCH.

To use these PL/SQL cursor attributes, we place them next to the cursor name.

```
video_cursor%NOTFOUND
```

If a cursor-error condition has been encountered but your code tries to access the variable that has been read in from a PL/SQL cursor, then this action *will* raise an exception, normally an INVALID_CURSOR. You will then have no choice but to handle the error in the EXCEPTION block.

PL/SQL cursor attributes are normally used in IF statements as follows:

```
OPEN video_cursor;
LOOP
  FETCH video_cursor INTO v_status;
  EXIT WHEN video_cursor%NOTFOUND;
  . . .
END LOOP;
```

PL/SQL Cursors in Action

So how do PL/SQL cursors fit into the structure of a procedure? You will use them to get a result set from the database and then loop through the rows one by one and process them in any way you wish. The truth is you could do any of this processing in your Visual Basic code, so why go to the trouble of writing a procedure in an unfamiliar language?

Doing your processing in a stored procedure has real advantages. You dramatically reduce the amount of data that has to be transferred across the network. You will also find that processing data on the same machine it resides on is far more efficient. In addition, it is much easier for developers to call an existing stored procedure rather than rewrite the processing in each new client application they write. You will find these advantages for any middle-tier code. Although all the excitement currently surrounds ActiveX components, you should always remember that stored procedures perform this same role, though maybe to a somewhat limited extent.

You nearly always want to process the whole result set, and to do this step, you must loop through the cursor and look at each row in turn. To show this interaction, we will create a procedure to count the numbers of videos in various status groups (such as "rented," "available," etc.) and for a particular rating. One way is to pull all the records back into Visual Basic and count them (remember that the COUNT function only returns one value per SELECT statement). Using a PL/SQL cursor allows us to produce the results on the server and ship only a few values over the network rating. Listing 10.5 shows how to define the PL/SQL cursor, open it, and loop through all the rows, and then process each row in turn, and exit after the last row.

Listing 10.5

```
PROCEDURE count_avail_movies (
    p_rating    IN VARCHAR2,
    p_avail     OUT NUMBER,
    p_rented    OUT NUMBER,
    p_reserved OUT NUMBER)

IS

/* Count the number of videos in the three categories
   available, rented and reserved, for the specific rating
```

```
     that is passed as an input parameter to the procedure */

v_status   VARCHAR2(10); /* input field for the FETCH */
v_avail    NUMBER(5);    /* We need these counters as */
v_rented   NUMBER(5);    /*  we are using OUT parameters */
v_reserved NUMBER(5);    /*  not IN OUT  */

/* Set the cursor to define the subset of data we want to look at */
CURSOR video_cursor
  IS SELECT status
    FROM videos, movies
    WHERE videos.movie_id = movies.movie_id
      AND rating = p_rating;

BEGIN
  v_avail := 0;
  v_rented := 0;
  v_reserved := 0;

/* Loop through all the rows in the result set that the cursor
   points to and add up the numbers of videos in the various
   categories. */

  OPEN video_cursor;

  LOOP
    FETCH video_cursor INTO v_status;
    EXIT WHEN video_cursor%NOTFOUND;
    IF v_status = 'available' THEN
      v_avail := v_avail + 1;
    ELSIF v_status = 'rented' THEN
      v_rented := v_rented + 1;
    ELSIF v_status = 'reserved' THEN
      v_reserved := v_reserved + 1;
    END IF;
  END LOOP;

  CLOSE video_cursor;

  p_avail  := v_avail;
  p_rented := v_rented;
  p_reserved := v_reserved;
```

```
EXCEPTION
/* Whatever the problem just rollback and pass
   the error back to Visual Basic */
  WHEN OTHERS THEN
    ROLLBACK;
    p_avail   := 0;
    p_rented  := 0;
    p_reserved := 0;
    RAISE;


END;
```

Figure 10.5 shows how we can execute and test this procedure in Oracle Procedure Builder.

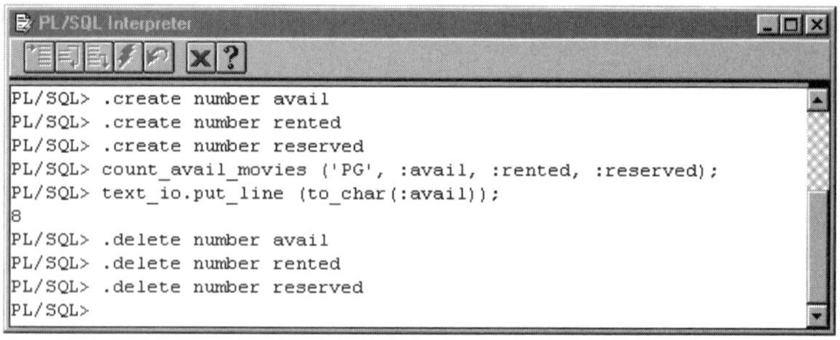

FIGURE 10.5:

Executing the count_
avail_movies procedure

PL/SQL Cursor Loops

A special form of the FOR…LOOP statement can make working with PL/SQL cursors much easier. It will automatically handle the OPEN, FETCH, and CLOSE statements for you and loop through every available row. You do not even need to check for an end-of-loop condition. You can't find a better deal for the money! If we modify Listing 10.5 to use this technique, we would see the following code:

```
. . .
FOR video_record IN video_cursor LOOP
  IF v_status = 'available' THEN
    v_avail := v_avail + 1;
  ELSIF v_status = 'rented' THEN
    v_rented := v_rented + 1;
```

```
      ELSIF v_status = 'reserved' THEN
        v_reserved := v_reserved + 1;
      END IF;
  END LOOP;
    . . .
```

Note that the *video_record* variable is implicitly declared as a record of exactly the same type as the cursor (in this case, only one variable).

User-Defined Data Types

A valuable extension to the variable types we have seen so far is called *the user-defined data type*: this is the ability to group more than one scalar value into a single type. PL/SQL has three different user-defined data types, and a familiarity with them can help you not only make the most of writing stored procedures but also add to the arsenal of tools at your disposal as a Visual Basic developer. The three composite data types we shall review are

- Records

- Tables or collections

- Cursor variables

Records

A record is a user-defined composite data type. It is a grouping of related data (fields) in a defined structure. A record is almost identical to a structure in Visual Basic that you get when you use the TYPE statement, but it is perhaps a little more powerful. In the first part of this chapter, we saw how to define a record with the %ROWTYPE attribute. To use a record, we must first define the data type for the new record in the declaration section of the procedure and then declare a variable of that type.

NOTE   This is the only time the terms *record* and *field* are used in SQL or PL/SQL. They are quite distinct from the rows and columns in a database table, although records are often used to define a structure that a database row can be read into.

To define the new data type we use the TYPE statement.

TYPE *record_type* IS RECORD (*field_list*);

The *record_type* defines the new user type you can then use to declare your variables, and the *field_list* is a list of field names and their data types. For example, you could declare

```
TYPE movie_record IS RECORD (
    movie_id    NUMBER(10),
    movie_name  VARCHAR2(50),
    rating      VARCHAR2(10));
```

which is a structure called movie_record and consists of three fields, movie_id, movie_name, and rating.

You use these in the same circumstances as you would in Visual Basic. It ties together variables that naturally form a logical group and keeps them in a physical structure you can use throughout the program. To reference any particular part of the record, just prefix the variable name with the record name, separated by a period.

```
movie_record.movie_id := 1234;
```

Records are an important way to make your code easier to write and, even more so, easier to read and, therefore, maintain. However, you cannot return a record structure to your Visual Basic code.

TIP

If you use the %ROWTYPE attribute when defining a RECORD, you do not have to define a user type. It is implied when you use the attribute. For example, `movie_record movies%ROWTYPE;` defines a record structure of the same type as a row in the movies table.

PL/SQL Tables and Collections

A structure that is missing from SQL and from earlier versions of PL/SQL was the array. There still is no actual array, but this is no longer a concern because we have the PL/SQL table.

The term *collection* is more accurate because it operates more like the collections you see in Visual Basic and other object-based languages rather than a regular array. The table is more strongly typed than a Visual Basic collection (where you can, by default, add almost any data type), and it has no bounds. One way to view the PL/SQL table is as two columns. The first column holds the index as a primary key, and the second column holds the value. Figure 10.6 shows the way a PL/SQL table is constructed and used.

FIGURE 10.6:

The way a PL/SQL table works

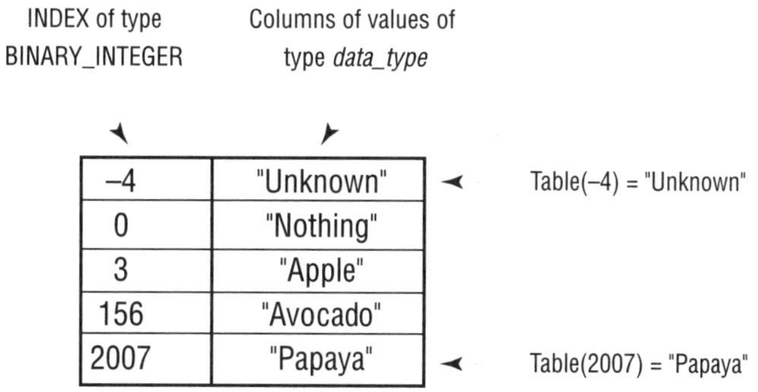

INDEX of type BINARY_INTEGER	Columns of values of type *data_type*	
−4	"Unknown"	Table(−4) = "Unknown"
0	"Nothing"	
3	"Apple"	
156	"Avocado"	
2007	"Papaya"	Table(2007) = "Papaya"

NOTE Oracle8 has expanded the concept of tables into collections, which encompass the tables dealt with here as well as *arrays*. These new array data types are not currently accessible to Visual Basic developers.

Declaring a PL/SQL Table

To declare a table, we again have to define a user type first. In this case, it takes the form

```
TYPE table_type IS TABLE OF data_type
   INDEX BY BINARY INTEGER;
```

You then use the type *table_type* to define subsequent variables in the normal way.

```
TYPE movie_name_type IS TABLE OF VARCHAR2(50)
   INDEX BY BINARY INTEGER;

movie_names movie_name_type;
```

To use this in your procedure, you can reference it like you would an array in Visual Basic, with its index.

```
movie_name := movie_names(i);
```

PL/SQL uses this index (*i* in this case) to access the data by using it as the primary key to find the row in the table and then using the value column to return the value. When you assign a value to an indexed row that does not yet exist, a new row is created and the value assigned. There is no need to have the index increasing. In fact, a table allows you to efficiently represent a *sparse array*, that is, an array with few-and-far-between elements. Elements of the table that have not been assigned are considered undefined and it is an error to try to access the value.

Using a PL/SQL Table

To show a simple example of using tables, let's first fill a table with all the movies that contain a certain word (see Listing 10.6). We must first declare the cursor we are going to use to retrieve the result set; notice the way the WHERE clause uses a complex LIKE statement. Next, we declare a table to receive the film names as well as a counter. Finally, we loop through the result set incrementing the counter for each new row and putting the movie name into the table. That's all there is to it.

Listing 10.6

```
PROCEDURE get_movies (
  p_word   IN VARCHAR2)
IS

/* Put movies containing a certain word into a a PL/SQL table */

  CURSOR movie_cursor IS
    SELECT movie_name
      FROM movies
      WHERE LOWER(movies.movie_name) LIKE
        '%' || LOWER(p_word) || '%';

  TYPE movie_name_type IS TABLE OF VARCHAR2(50)
    INDEX BY BINARY_INTEGER;
  movie_names      movie_name_type;

  v_count     NUMBER(5);


BEGIN
  v_count := 0;
  OPEN movie_cursor;
  LOOP
```

```
      v_count := v_count + 1;
      FETCH movie_cursor INTO movie_names(v_count);

      EXIT WHEN movie_cursor%NOTFOUND;
   END LOOP;

END get_movies;
```

Returning a PL/SQL Table to the Calling Procedure

The only problem with Listing 10.6 is it does not accomplish anything! For the table to be useful, we need to return it to the calling procedure. Let us suppose you want to return a table from a stored procedure with the names of the stars who have been in at least two movies (see Listing 10.7). What is important from a Visual Basic perspective is that we must pass to the procedure a parameter containing the largest number of records we want to allow; in other words, what is the largest number of values we want to receive back from the procedure?

NOTE   PL/SQL tables are probably the most advanced technique you will encounter when communicating between Oracle and Visual Basic, but they are well worth the effort to master. To retrieve a table into Visual Basic, you will have to use Remote Data Objects (RDO), Active Data Objects (ADO), or Oracle Objects for OLE (OO4O). We will go over the appropriate techniques in the relevant chapters.

To pass a table to a procedure as a parameter, we need to define the new data type in a package. This is the only way for Oracle to know what the user-defined type is *before* it executes the procedure. The process is similar to the TYPE statement in Visual Basic in which we define a variable type before passing a variable of that type to a subroutine. The two parts of the package (specification and body) are shown in Listing 10.7.

Listing 10.7

Package Spec

```
PACKAGE movie_package IS
/* Define the table type */
TYPE char_table_type IS TABLE OF VARCHAR2(50)
```

```
                INDEX BY BINARY_INTEGER;

     /* Define the procedures in the package body */
     PROCEDURE get_stars (
       p_table_size        NUMBER,
       p_stars          OUT char_table_type);

     /* any other package definitions */

     END movie_package;
```

Package Body

```
     PACKAGE BODY movie_package IS
     PROCEDURE get_stars (
       p_table_size        NUMBER,
       p_stars          OUT char_table_type)
     IS

        /* Return a PL/SQL table with all the stars who have
           been in at least two movies.
           The table will only hold a certain number of
           entries, up to the limit defined by p_table_size. */

        CURSOR star_cursor IS
          SELECT first_name || ' ' || last_name
            FROM participants, movie_participants
            WHERE participants.participant_id =
                    movie_participants.participant_id
              AND role = 'A'
            ORDER BY last_name;

        v_name                VARCHAR2(50) := '';
        v_last_name           VARCHAR2(50) := '';
        v_num_found           NUMBER(3) := 0;
        v_table_row           NUMBER(2) := 0;

     BEGIN

        OPEN star_cursor;
        LOOP
      FETCH star_cursor
        INTO v_name;
```

```
          EXIT WHEN star_cursor%NOTFOUND OR
             v_table_row >= p_table_size;

          IF v_name = v_last_name THEN
             v_num_found := v_num_found + 1;
          ELSE
             v_num_found := 1;
          END IF;

          IF v_num_found = 2 THEN
             v_table_row := v_table_row + 1;
             p_stars (v_table_row) := v_last_name;
          END IF;

          v_last_name := v_name;

       END LOOP;
       CLOSE star_cursor;

    END get_stars;

  END;
```

The code in Listing 10.7 is one of the most complicated examples in this chapter and deserves a closer look. The first part defines the package specification. It defines the user-defined data type *char_table_type* as a table of VARCHAR2(50) variables. With the table defined, it can be used as a parameter to the procedure. The package specification also defines the procedure *get_stars*.

The second part of the package is the body, which includes any procedures and functions. Remember that the procedure header specified in the package body must exactly match the header in the package specification. The procedure *get_stars* first defines a cursor that selects actors' names from the participants list and orders them by name. It opens the cursor and loops through it, fetching each row in turn until either the end of the result set or the maximum table size is reached, whichever comes first. Processing is simple. It notes when two or more successive records are for the same actor and adds them to the table.

Implicit Loops for Tables

Tables can be successfully integrated into the implicit loop for a cursor to make your code much simpler.

```
v_video_row := 0;
FOR movie_rec IN
  (SELECT movie_name FROM movies ORDER BY movie_name) LOOP
  v_video_row := v_video_row +1;
  video_table(v_video_row) := movie_rec.movie_name;
END LOOP;
```

In the example, the FOR…IN…LOOP statement first does a SELECT to create a result set. It then creates a loop variable, *movie_rec*, which it automatically defines as being a record of the same type as the result set (in this case, only one column). Now it loops through the code, incrementing the counter *v_video_row* and then assigning the Movie_Name of the current row to the table Video_Table. As you can see, much can be accomplished in a few lines of code.

WARNING   When you access a table entry, make sure it has been previously defined. Make sure you have assigned a value for the index you have used before you try to use it anywhere else. If you don't, then accessing the table entry will raise an exception. Some versions of PL/SQL have not handled the exception gracefully, which can make debugging very difficult.

Cursor Variables

Finally, we come to the latest and greatest of the user-defined data types: the cursor variable. These variables first appeared in PL/SQL version 2.3, along with Oracle 7.3. They have much in common with PL/SQL cursors, but whereas those cursors are declared along with a query, cursor variables are only assigned a value (that is, they are associated with a query) at run time. The Oracle documentation compares a PL/SQL cursor to a constant and a cursor variable to a variable. Each has its place, but the introduction of cursor variables will probably supplant the use of PL/SQL cursors because the former really has no disadvantages.

One advantage of a cursor variable is its flexibility, in that you can not only assign a SELECT statement to it at run time but you can reassign it at any time. But perhaps the biggest advantage is that, by defining the cursor variable as a formal procedure parameter, you can return a result set from a stored procedure. What you are actually passing is a pointer to the result set, not the result set itself. Cursor variables are most useful for passing result sets between PL/SQL procedures, but it is now possible to use it from Visual Basic.

Cursor variables, along with PL/SQL tables, are among the most sophisticated ways of interacting with Oracle. However, in most of the situations you will encounter, cursor variables will mainly be used to return a result set to your calling procedure, pure and simple. There will be no processing, because you cannot change the values in the result set.

The effect of cursor variables is to emulate a SELECT statement from a stored procedure, so the advantages are similar to views. You are hiding query complexity and restricting the user from accessing all columns of a base table. The end user cannot even find out which table, or tables, is supplying the data. By delaying the assignment of the query string until run time, you can make the result set dependent on the user name, date, or whatever you wish: another powerful tool to add to your belt.

NOTE
Before you rejoice too much, you should note that to retrieve a cursor variable into a Visual Basic program, you need to use Oracle Objects for OLE (version 2.1 or higher). The cursor variable is not part of the ODBC specification and probably never will be because it is passing back a pointer, not a result set. On the brighter side, the advent of OLE/DB providers may well make this capability more available to us.

Declaring a Cursor Variable

Perhaps the most difficult part of using a cursor variable is how to define and declare it. As with any other user-defined data type, you have to define the type you want first and then declare a cursor variable of that type. The following example is a definition of a cursor variable type.

```
TYPE movie_cv_type AS REF CURSOR RETURNS movies%ROWTYPE;
```

The declaration starts in the normal way with the TYPE keyword and the name of the cursor variable type that we want to define. In this case, it is *movie_cv_type*. The next part "AS REF CURSOR" means that this new type references a cursor. Finally, "RETURNS movies%ROWTYPE" defines the data type that the cursor is going to refer to. This part is actually optional; if you leave it out (*weak typing*) it provides more flexibility but also more chance of raising an exception. It is also probably less efficient than the *strong typing* shown above. In the example, we are declaring that the cursor will point to a structure defined by the row type of the Movies table.

Next, we can declare a cursor variable of this new user-defined type.

```
movie_cv      movie_cv_type;
```

Opening a Cursor Variable

Because the query that a cursor variable uses is not predefined, it has to be defined when we open it. Instead of the OPEN statement, we now use the OPEN...FOR statement. The syntax of this statement is

OPEN *cv_name* FOR *select_query*;

This opens the cursor variable, *cv_name*, and assigns it a result set, *select_query*.

```
OPEN movie_cv FOR
   SELECT * FROM movies
     WHERE year_of_release < 1990;
```

Note that you must make sure that the type of structure the cursor variable points to is exactly the same as the structure of the result set we assign to it with the OPEN statement. In this case, we have assured this by pointing the cursor variable to a row of the Movies table and using "SELECT *" in the query, so we know they will match up. If we wanted to select only certain columns, we would have to define a RECORD structure of this type and then point the cursor variable to it.

Fetching Records

Although the main benefit of cursor variables for the Visual Basic developer will be to return a result set to Visual Basic, cursor variables are also useful as a more flexible version of the PL/SQL cursors. They can be processed in much the same way with the FETCH command in a loop. For example,

```
FETCH movie_cv INTO movie_rec;
```

will work just as well for either kind of cursor.

Closing the Cursor Variable

Whenever you close a cursor variable, the result set is no longer defined. It is good practice to explicitly close any result set when it is no longer used, but this will happen automatically when the procedure ends, unless you declare it as a parameter with IN OUT mode.

```
CLOSE movie_cv;
```

Passing Cursor Variables

Perhaps the most important aspect of cursor variables is that they can pass result sets back to your Visual Basic program, but how precisely do we do that if the variable goes out of scope (becomes undefined) when the procedure ends? The answer lies in defining the cursor variable as a formal parameter to the procedure with IN OUT mode.

NOTE   You can define cursor variables as IN mode parameters, but that is of little use unless you are passing between PL/SQL procedures.

To pass any user-defined data types to a procedure, they need to be part of a package. The package will define the TYPE for the cursor variable. Listing 10.8 gives an example of a packaged procedure that passes a cursor variable back to a calling procedure. The procedure body only opens the cursor variable with a SELECT statement. Whatever rows are selected are returned in the cursor.

Listing 10.8

Package Spec

```
PACKAGE movie_package IS
/* Define the cursor variable type */
TYPE movie_cv_type IS REF CURSOR RETURN movies%ROWTYPE;

/* Define the procedures in the package body */
PROCEDURE get_old_movies (
  p_year      NUMBER,
  old_movies IN OUT movie_cv_type);

/* Add any other package definitions here */
```

```
   END movie_package;
```

Package Body

```
PACKAGE BODY movie_package IS
PROCEDURE get_old_movies (
  p_year     NUMBER,
  old_movies IN OUT movie_cv_type) IS

  /* Return a cursor variable with all the records
     released prior to the passed year */

  BEGIN

    OPEN old_movies FOR
      SELECT * FROM movies
        WHERE year_of_release < p_year
        ORDER BY year_of_release;

  END get_old_movies;

  END;
```

That's all there is to it; we just open the cursor variable with a SELECT statement. We do not close it because it would then become undefined and useless to our Visual Basic program. This is a simple example, but you can get much more creative. You can use cursor variables in the same way that PL/SQL cursors can be used, but a cursor variable is the only real way to return a result set from a stored procedure to a calling routine.

Error Conditions

The problems that you can encounter with cursor variables are exactly the same as with static PL/SQL cursors. Refer to the section "Error Conditions for PL/SQL Cursors" for further details.

Using Triggers

We have spent most of the chapter on procedures at the expense of triggers. Triggers are similar to event handlers in Visual Basic. When a particular registered action occurs, the trigger is executed; the user has no control over it. You should keep any triggers as simple and short as possible. The Visual Basic developer will find that the most obvious application of triggers is the ability to apply audit information to rows, but triggers are also used in everything from validation routines to Oracle's own support for database replication.

As an example of the use of a trigger, imagine that we have a Visual Basic updatable Recordset. (We will see more about these in Chapter 14, *Data Access Objects*.) If you have the audit information on your table rows and columns, such as Time_Stamp and User_Name, then you do not want the VB application to have to provide these. If you set a trigger on the table, then you can automatically provide these column values.

To set up an audit control trigger with Oracle Procedure Builder, do the following steps.

1. Under Database Objects in the Object Navigator, select Tables.

2. Click the table you want to create the trigger on (remember that these are bound to tables), and select Triggers. In Figure 10.7, we chose the Movies table.

3. Click the New icon on the left side of the Navigator and you will see a dialog box for entering the trigger information (see Figure 10.7).

4. Click the New button at the bottom of the dialog box.

5. Click the Before button for the Triggering option, and check UPDATE and INSERT for the Statement options. For the UPDATE, you should check all the columns you want to cause a trigger.

6. Ensure the "For Each Row" option is checked.

7. Give the trigger a sensible name, such as "**movie_audit**".

8. Fill in the Trigger Body, as shown in Listing 10.9.

FIGURE 10.7:

The Trigger screen in Procedure Builder

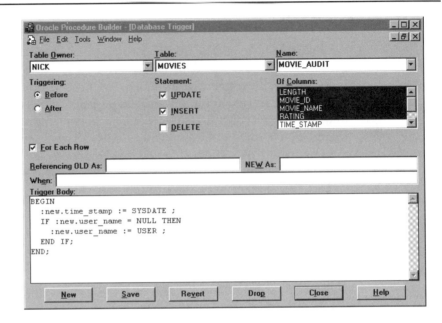

Listing 10.9

```
BEGIN
:new.time_stamp := SYSDATE;
IF :new.user_name = NULL THEN
  :new.user_name := USER;
END IF;
END;
```

Any time a user inserts a new row or updates one of your selected columns, the trigger body will be fired. The firing of this trigger ensures there is a valid time stamp and user name. There is an IF clause for the User_Name column that only updates if the incoming value is NULL. This clause allows you to specify the value in the Visual Basic code, but you may not want to provide this information.

Note that you can theoretically use this same technique to provide a primary key from a sequence generator if one is missing. Although this sounds like binding the sequence number to the table, the technique has some great limitations for Visual Basic developers. The ODBC cursors for updatable Recordsets are based on key: the cursors need to have access to the key to update, and they will fail with a NULL value. You could do a major kludge here and set the key to a particular value, such as 0, and convert it to a valid key in the trigger. However, then your Recordset falls out of synchronization with the database, and you have to refresh. This nullifies the benefit of an updatable Recordset. In Chapter 18, *Oracle Objects for OLE,* you will see the only way to successfully use this technique from Visual Basic.

NOTE   The new counter field value is available in Access as soon as you execute the AddNew method, but this feature is not available with Oracle tables.

Providing a Transaction Audit

Finally, we will look at a way to use stored-procedure techniques to store a log of what actions users have executed. In Chapter 6, *Implementing a Database,* we dealt with the creation of tables and the benefits of adding a time stamp and a user name to the table to trace who made the last change to the data row. You should consider adding this basic level of tracking to any table that contains transaction data. You might not want to add it to code tables.

One improvement to consider is adding a table to store an audit trail for any stored procedure that has been successfully executed. This step is relatively easy. First, we must set up the table that will store the information:

```
CREATE TABLE procedure_audit (
  audit_id   NUMBER(10),
  procedure_name     VARCHAR2(50),
  procedure_parameters VARCHAR2(300),
  time_stamp        DATE,
  user_id                VARCHAR2(20));
```

Now in each procedure, we can add a statement that saves all the relevant information to the table, as shown in Listing 10.10.

Listing 10.10

```
PROCEDURE my_proc (
  p_param1   NUMBER,
  p_param2   VARCHAR2,
  p_date     DATE) AS
  v_1  varchar2(80);
BEGIN
/*  . . . */
/*  PL/SQL statements */
/*  . . . */

/* Add the procedure audit trail */
  INSERT INTO procedure_audit VALUES (
    audit_sequence.NEXTVAL,
    'my_proc',
    TO_CHAR(p_param1) || ', ''' ||
    p_param2 ||
    ''',TO_DATE(''' || TO_CHAR(p_Date,'DD-MON-YYYY') ||
    ''',''DD-MON-YYYY''),',
SYSDATE, USER);

  COMMIT;

EXCEPTION
/* Whatever the problem just rollback and pass
   the error back to Visual Basic */
  WHEN OTHERS THEN
    ROLLBACK;
    RAISE;

END my_proc;
```

This procedure is not as complicated as it first looks. We are inserting a new record into the audit table, so we need to provide values for the four fields. The ID comes from the next available sequence number with audit_sequence.NEXTVAL. The procedure name comes next and has to be tailored for each procedure you write. You provide a string that contains all the parameters in the same format you use to call the procedure. This will cause you the most difficulty because it is difficult to make sure you have exactly the right format. The rules to apply are as follows:

- Numeric values can appear as they are except for the first one, which should be converted to a character value.

- Character values must be surrounded by single quotes.

- Dates must be first converted into a character string so you know exactly what format you have, they must be put into a TO_DATE function, and they will then appear in the parameter string as it does in your VB code.

    ```
    . . . ,TO_DATE('21-OCT-1998','DD-MON-YYYY'), . . .
    ```

- Each variable must have a comma.

- Finally, you should include the time stamp and user ID. These are provided by Oracle built-in functions, so they are easy to use.

What does this process give us? It gives a table with an audit record for every procedure we have applied it to. We have a trail of every procedure that has been called, what parameters were passed, who did it, and when.

NOTE   Because this technique is time consuming, it has been included in the sample Visual Basic example program in Chapter 14, *Data Access Objects*.

In addition to providing an audit trail, the log also allows for the possibility to re-create data if it has been unintentionally deleted. We must have a system to select all the associated audited transactions and simply reexecute them, one by one in their original order. Finally, the log allows you to duplicate this information on another instance of Oracle or even a different database.

NOTE   If your application allows users to update rows rather than just insert and delete (some transactional applications take this course), then you should consider having four audit columns. These columns should identify the user who created the row and the time it was done as well as the user and time when it was last updated.

Procedures and Visual Basic

We have seen the various techniques you can use when creating stored procedures in PL/SQL, but how useful are they to Visual Basic developers? The only way to pass data from a stored procedure to any other procedure, whether it is internally to another PL/SQL procedure or function or externally to a program built in Visual Basic, is through parameters. PL/SQL does not return a result set in the way Microsoft SQL Server and Sybase do.

In later chapters we will cover the various ways to access data with stored procedures, but the summary of features shown in Table 10.6 will give you a head start.

T A B L E   1 0 . 6 : Accessing Stored Procedures from Visual Basic

Data Access method	Capabilities
Data Controls	Not possible
Data Access Objects (DAO)	Can use IN mode scalar parameters only
Remote Data Objects (RDO)	Can use IN and OUT scalar parameters and PL/SQL tables with the latest drivers
ActiveX Data Objects (ADO)	Can use IN and OUT scalar parameters and PL/SQL tables with the latest drivers
Oracle Objects or OLE (OO4O)	Can use IN and OUT scalar parameters, PL/SQL tables, and cursor variables

Because this area of Oracle and Visual Basic communication has changed so much over the last year or so, you should make sure you have at least Oracle 7.3 and either the latest ODBC drivers or the latest version of OO4O. It is highly likely that additional features will be made in the next year or so.

Summary

This chapter has covered all the aspects of PL/SQL procedures that a Visual Basic programmer needs to know. After looking at the data types and declarations, we went on to flow control with IF...THEN structures and loops. The basic PL/SQL operations were then enhanced with some advanced features, including PL/SQL Cursors and Cursor Variables and PL/SQL Tables. These are the features that let you return complex data types back to your calling Visual Basic application. The chapter showed a typical use of a trigger and then provided an example of how auditing can be done in a stored procedure. We finished up with a look at what PL/SQL features are currently available from the different access methods we will be looking at in the second half of the book.

PART III

Data-Access Technology

CHAPTER

11

Client-Side Technology

- The Software Layers

- The Network Software

- The ODBC Standard

- Universal Data Access and OLE-DB

- Cursors

- Connections

- Alternative Access Methods

One of the most difficult things to figure out is how your Visual Basic program actually communicates with Oracle, specifically, the networking aspects, such as setting up Net8 and SQL*Net, and what ODBC provides for Oracle users. This chapter will explore the software components involved in moving SQL commands and result sets over the network as well as how to set up this process so it works smoothly. The topics we will cover are as follows:

- The software layers
- The network software
- The ODBC standard
- Universal Data Access and OLE-DB
- Cursors
- Connections
- Alternative access methods

The Software Layers

First, we will do an overview of exactly what is going on when we want to communicate with Oracle from our Visual Basic program. If you look at Figure 11.1, you will see many layers of software involved in the process. In this chapter, we will look at the setup of the processes that run on the client machine and see how to set them up. At this point in time, ODBC, as the de facto standard, is the most important interface between Visual Basic and SQL databases such as Oracle. However, with Visual Basic 6, we are starting the move toward a new technology called OLE-DB, which will steadily be growing in importance. OLE-DB started off as an interface between VB and the ODBC drivers, but gradually more and more native OLE-DB interfaces are becoming available.

The software layers used in between Visual Basic and Oracle are described in the next few sections.

FIGURE 11.1:

The software layers involved between Visual Basic and Oracle

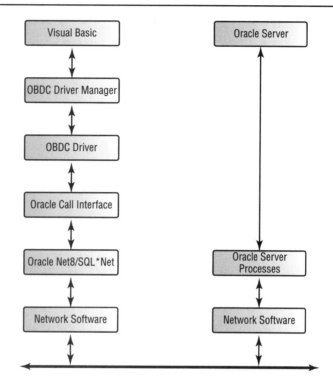

The ODBC Driver Manager

The ODBC Driver Manager is the first layer of software an application will access if using the ODBC route. The Manager is supplied in the file ODBC32.DLL. The Driver Manager loads the correct ODBC Driver Dynamic Link Library (DLL) into memory. If you are using Data Source Names (DSNs), the Driver Manager will find the correct ODBC Driver from the entries in the Registry. It will then call some initialization routines to set the driver up. When you are executing SQL commands, the Driver Manager will route the calls to the correct entry points in the ODBC driver as well as validate some of the parameters.

The ODBC Driver

ODBC drivers are software products that form a database-specific link between the application and the database. They are loaded and controlled by the ODBC Driver Manager and, in the case of the 32-bit Oracle driver from Oracle (Inter-solv), reside in a file called SQO32_XX.DLL, in which XX is the version of the database, such as 73 or 80. The ODBC driver that comes with Visual Basic 6 is in the file MSORCL32.DLL. ODBC drivers typically process the ODBC function calls at a low level and are responsible for moving SQL commands from the application to the database and moving results back from the database to the application.

The functions of the ODBC driver include

- Establishing the connection
- Client-cursor management
- Translation of commands and data formats to suit a particular database
- Error-code management

The driver must communicate with any required database-specific software layers, which in the case of Oracle, comprise the Oracle Call Interface and the networking software, either Net8 for Oracle8 or SQL*Net for previous versions of the database.

The OLE-DB Layer

The OLE-DB layer provides an improved interface to the Oracle database as well as other databases. We shall discuss it in detail later in the chapter. Whereas with ODBC we used the ODBC driver and Driver Manager, with OLE-DB we use a *data provider*. Oracle developers can use two techniques: one with the ODBC data provider that interfaces with the existing ODBC drivers (MSDASQL.DLL), and one that is a native driver to bypass ODBC and communicates directly with the Oracle Call Interface layer (in file MSDAORA.DLL).

The Oracle Call Interface

The Oracle Call Interface (OCI) is an Application Programming Interface (API) for accessing the Oracle Server. It comes on the same CD as your Oracle networking software and is provided in the file ORAXX.DLL. In many ways, it is similar to the ODBC API except that the OCI is specific, not only to Oracle but also to the programming language that it is called from. The OCI is a native interface to Oracle whether you use ODBC, OLE-DB, Oracle Objects for OLE, or another package.

The OCI is a full-featured API capable of all functionality present in the Oracle Server, including parsing and executing SQL statements, transaction control, and executing PL/SQL statements. Just like the ODBC API, it is implemented at a low level, with about three dozen API function calls, and is a complex environment in which to work.

NOTE   The OCI performs a similar role to the db-library used with SQL Server.

Net8 and SQL*Net

Net8 and SQL*Net are the software layers on a client machine that enable both client/server and server/server access to Oracle8 and Oracle7 databases, respectively, across any network. As a Visual Basic developer, you will mainly be aware of these products as a requirement for providing a route from your Visual Basic application to the network via the OCI layer. However, the layers also provide a communication route for other network applications, such as the Network Listener. We will see more of the layers in the section "Setting Up Net8 and SQL*Net."

The Network Software

When you install Net8 or SQL*Net, you are prompted for the network protocol you will be using, and the appropriate networking software is then installed on the client machine. The aim of Oracle's networking strategy is to build a common, or heterogeneous, transport layer on which to run software. The result is that the Oracle server and client software can run on top of any network protocol and on platforms from PCs to IBM mainframes.

This network software actually consists of several layers:

- The Transparent Network Substrate (TNS), which is the foundation for the common network protocol and which is independent of any base-network protocol stack.

- The Oracle Protocol Adapter, which is a platform-specific software layer that interfaces between the TNS and the base-network protocol.

- The Network Specific Protocol Stack, which is the base-level protocol, such as TCP/IP, DECnet, and SPX/IX.

This same networking structure is found on all clients and servers; they may run the same network, as with a small installation, or they may run different protocols, effectively performing the same job as routers and bridges.

The Listener Process

The Listener process runs on the database server and waits for connection requests from applications such as your Visual Basic program. We introduced the Listener in Chapter 2, *Oracle Database Architecture,* and configured it in Chapter 3, *Creating a Database.* If you use the Multithreaded Server on UNIX or OpenVMS, then the Listener process will arrange for your connection to be made through a Dispatcher process; the Multithreaded Server is a more efficient way to handle a large number of connection requests; however, you should be aware that it can prove difficult to configure and get working well.

Server Processes

We also encountered Server processes in Chapter 2, in which we described them as the server-side processes set up for each user connection (for the Dedicated Server mode) or for a group of connections (for the Multithreaded Server mode).

Setting Up Net8 and SQL*Net

Assuming that the Listener software has been set up on the server (see Chapter 3, *Creating A Database*), we are ready to set up the client machine to connect to it. All the communication is done either through OC or Oracle's own networking software, called Net8 for Oracle8 and SQL*Net for previous versions of the Oracle server. Net8 is the next major release after SQL*Net 2.3. As you can see in Figure 11.2 on the server, you need Net8 to access an Oracle8 database and SQL*Net to access an Oracle7 database, although it is possible for a Net8 listener to connect users to an Oracle7 database. On the clients, you have more freedom; you can generally use SQL*Net or Net8 to connect to Oracle7 or Oracle8. Because of this situation, it is most sensible to use SQL*Net on client machines until the time when there are technical advantages to using Net8 for the Visual Basic developer. At that point, you will have to decide whether to put both software types on your clients (they coexist peacefully) or upgrade everything to Oracle8 and Net8. Whether you choose to go with Net8 or stick to SQL*Net, the two technologies are fairly similar. You can install them by selecting the product from the list in your Oracle Install program.

FIGURE 11.2:

Using Net8 and SQL*Net

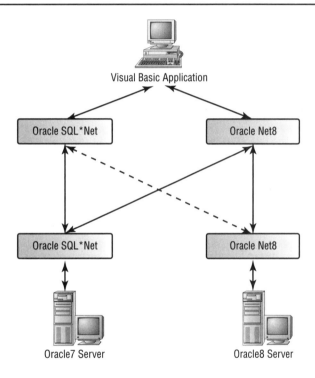

To set up the networking, you need to copy the `tnsnames.ora` file from your server to your client. If you are running Windows 95, then you will copy this file to `C:\ORAWIN95\NETWORK\ADMIN` for SQL*Net or `C:\ORAWIN95\NET8\ADMIN` for Net8. If you run Windows NT clients, you will use the equivalent `ORANT` directories for your `tnsnames.ora` file. That's all you have to do. However, you should ensure that all servers you need access to are defined in the `tnsnames.ora` file.

If they are not, then you should go back to the Easy Config program and define them before you copy it to your PCs (see Chapter 3, *Creating a Database*).

TIP

Although Oracle Corporation does not recommended you edit the `tnsnames.ora` file manually, I have to admit that on the client machine and in a development mode I am constantly editing the file with Notepad. Once you get a feel for Notepad and make small changes, editing is quite easy and convenient. However, the chances are that once you have done this, you will no longer be able to go back to the Easy Config program because it will not recognize the format of your file any more. A final point to note here is that if you do manually edit the `tnsnames.ora` (or the `listener.ora`) files, be careful not to include any tab characters because SQL*Net/Net8 will not function properly.

Making a Connection

When things go wrong, you will find that you need to understand how Net8 or SQL*Net knows where to make the connection. For this process, you need to understand the use of the `tnsnames.ora` file. Understanding this file is also useful knowledge when it comes to setting up the ODBC Data Source Name, which we shall discuss later in the section, "Setting Up an ODBC Data Source." Listing 11.1 shows the format of the `tnsnames.ora` file.

Listing 11.1

```
service_name
  (DESCRIPTOR=
    (ADDRESS_LIST=
      (ADDRESS=
        (COMMUNITY=community)
        (PROTOCOL=protocol)
        (protocol specific information)
        )
      )
    (CONNECT_DATA=
      (SID=sid)
      (GLOBAL_NAME=global_database_name)
      )
    )
```

Several values must be provided in the `tnsnames.ora` file:

service_name   The name of the service you want to give to this database connection. The service name is also called the *database alias*. If you used one of the Easy Config programs to set it up, this is the name you will have supplied.

NOTE   Service name causes a great deal of confusion. Many developers think it is the name of the database, but it doesn't have to be. Unfortunately, both Oracle and ODBC logon prompts a variety of terms, such as *database name, connect string, database, service,* and so on. The term *database alias* is the most descriptive and meaningful.

---

community   The community name defines a selected part of the network; that part must use the same network protocol throughout, but the selection of the various parts is up to you. If you have only one network, then you can keep just one community name and use the default name, which is WORLD.

protocol   The protocol is the network protocol that is used to find the database server; for example, it may be "TCP."

protocol-specific information   For each different protocol you will see different information required to find the server. With TCP/IP, you will need to provide the Host and the Port information.

SID   The SID is the System Identifier for the Oracle database. It is the value you set up in the ORACLE_SID environment variable in Windows NT or in ORA_SID on the UNIX and OpenVMS platforms. The SID should uniquely define your database on the network.

global_database_name   This is a name you can use to distinguish the database in a multidatabase environment. You get the name by using the db_name parameter in the Initialization file combined with the community name separated by a period, for example, "movies.world". If you only have one database, you can safely ignore this field.

As an example of how the service description works in practice, Listing 11.2 shows a portion of the `tnsnames.ora` file that we saw in Chapter 3. The listing shows a service name of `orcl.world`. In this case, for the Listener to find the database on the network, it needs to use the TCP/IP protocol and look for a host named SCCNT01 (which is defined in the `hosts` file) with the Listener process listening on port 1521. The System Identifier (SID) it wants to connect to is ORC1.

Listing 11.2

```
orc1.world =
  (DESCRIPTION =
    (ADDRESS =
          (PROTOCOL = TCP)
          (HOST = SCCNT01)
          (PORT = 1521)
    )
    (CONNECT_DATA = (SID = ORC1)
    )
  )
```

So, armed with this information, let us now look at how the correct database is found when you make a connection request from your Visual Basic program.

1. You request a connection from your Visual Basic program that identifies a service name. (This will often be through an ODBC or OLE-DB Data Source Name but may be a direct reference to the Service Name if you are using Oracle Objects for OLE.)

2. Net8 or SQL*Net looks in the `tnsnames.ora` file for the service name (ORC1.WORLD).

3. Net8 or SQL*Net finds the network address where the Listener process is listening, as SCCNT01 on port 1521. The name SCCNT01 is looked up in the client's `hosts` file to find its matching IP address, or it may also be resolved by a DNS server.

4. The connection request is passed to the Listener process to set up the connection.

5. Assuming that the Listener has been set up with the required SID from the SID_LIST in the `listener.ora` file and assuming that the Listener is running, then the connection through to the database is made.

NOTE   The port specified for the Listener is the listening port, not the port that the actual connection will be made on. A new port is allocated for this purpose.

Testing Your Network Setup

When you set up a client machine ready to connect to Oracle, you should take an orderly approach to testing everything out. The first order of the day should be to test out the server connectivity to ensure that first the Listener with its `listener.ora` file and then the `tnsnames.ora` file are working properly. Once they are and you have copied over the `tnsnames.ora` file to the client, then and only then should you test out the connection from your client PC.

The easiest way to test your connection on both the client and the server is with the SQL*Plus program. When you run this program, you should get the familiar logon screen as shown in Figure 11.3. Fill in the details of your user name, password, and the connection string. This last field is the service name (or database alias) that identifies the database you want to connect to. This name must be the service name, one of those that you set up in the `tnsnames.ora` file.

FIGURE 11.3:

The familiar SQL*Plus logon dialog box

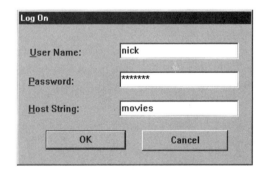

Potential Problem Areas

If you set up your networking software correctly, then you should have no problems; however, human errors will creep in. If you cannot connect with your SQL*Plus application, then you should review the possible causes.

- Ensure that your database is up and running.

- Ensure that the Listener is up and running. Do a STATUS command in the Listener, and check that it is waiting for connection requests on your database alias (see Chapter 3).

- Ensure that the server name is set up in your `hosts` file on your client machine. This file maps network addresses to the server name. For example, in the

TCP/IP world it will consist of entries mapping IP addresses to the server name, such as

```
42.52.50.85    movies
```

- If the server name is set up, try to detect it with the PING program. This program broadcasts a request to the server to see whether it is communicating. Figure 11.4 shows an example of this in action, finding a server called *movies* on a TCP/IP network. If you do not get a reply, then you should consult your network administrator.

- Another pitfall can occur when you manually modify the `tnsnames.ora` file. If the file contains tab characters, the SQL*Net/Net8 client will not be able to read `tnsnames.ora`.

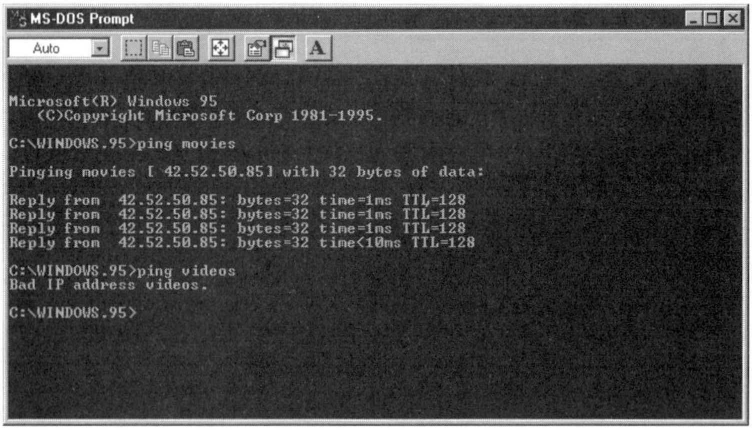

FIGURE 11.4:

Using the PING program to detect a server

Failover Capabilities

Oracle has plenty of scope for creating a database with high availability. The options include having databases running in Hot Standby mode, running Oracle Parallel Server (OPS), or one of the Oracle Advanced Replication options. The result is if one server goes down, there will be another you can connect to. Setup and administering these environments is an advanced function beyond the scope of this book, but you may work in a shop where this has already been done. But to make use of alternative databases, your Visual Basic application must know where that alternative database is. You do this in the `tnsnames.ora` file.

The `tnsnames.ora` is defined with an ADDRESS_LIST with a specific ADDRESS of your database as you saw in Listing 11.2. You can have an ADDRESS_LIST with several addresses in it as shown in Listing 11.3. When your Visual Basic application tries to connect to Oracle, Net8/SQL*Net will attempt the first address. If it has no luck there, it will try the next and so on.

Listing 11.3

```
orc1.world =
  (DESCRIPTION =
    (ADDRESS =
          (PROTOCOL = TCP)
          (HOST = sccnt01)
          (PORT = 1521)
    )
    (ADDRESS =
          (PROTOCOL = TCP)
          (HOST = sccnt02)
          (PORT = 1526)
    )
    (CONNECT_DATA=
      (SID=ORC1)
      (GLOBAL_NAME=ORC1.WORLD)
    )
  )
```

Although specifying multiple addresses sounds ideal, there is a minor glitch; actually, it can be a major problem in practice. When Net8 hands off the connection issue to the Listener process, Net8 forgets about it, thinking that its job is done. If the Listener process is up and running but the Oracle instance is not, then the connection request gets lost. You have to make sure the Listener is down before you will fail over to the next database. To get around this problem, you should take an additional course of action in conjunction with using multiple addresses. When your Visual Basic application makes the connection, it should test the connection with a simple SELECT statement. (I find that SELECT * FROM GLOBAL_NAME is ideal because it lets you know you are connected as well as what database you are connected to.) If this connection fails now or at any other time, you should be prepared to reconnect to an alternative database.

TIP   In UNIX (with *cron*) and OpenVMS (by submitting a job), you can easily set up a process to periodically monitor the database and bring down the Listener process if the Oracle instance has crashed.

ODBC

ODBC is currently the major technique for communicating between Visual Basic and remote relational database management systems such as Oracle. ODBC has become an industry standard with most of the database vendors fully supporting it. In fact, failure to produce an ODBC driver can have a decided impact on the financial viability of a product.

In addition to providing access to relational databases, there are ODBC interfaces available for a large range of other applications from desktop applications, such as Microsoft Access and Excel (which is to be expected), to applications you would not normally associate with databases, such as Visio.

There are some applications whose data source is proprietary and whose data format is nowhere near that of a relational database. You can sometimes find ODBC drivers for these applications, but they come at a premium price. What is worse, you now have even more software layers. For this reason, a movement away from ODBC to OLE-DB should bring many performance and feature improvements.

WARNING   Take great care when installing commercial applications that support ODBC. In at least one case I have encountered recently, the application overwrote the ODBC Driver Manager and the Oracle driver without informing the user. The ODBC Driver Manager ceased to be useable, and a Visual Basic application on this machine no longer worked. If you install ODBC commercial applications, make sure to do it on a test machine first!

In this section, we will delve closely into ODBC. The areas we will cover are

- The origins of ODBC
- ODBC drivers
- ODBC driver categories
- ODBC conformance levels
- Selecting an ODBC driver
- Setting up an ODBC data source
- Testing your ODBC connection

The Origins of ODBC

ODBC stands for Open Database Connectivity and was created as an architecture to provide a way for application programs (such as Visual Basic) to communicate with different vendors' databases. It was created by a consortium, called the SQL Access Group, that had representatives from most of the database vendors, including IBM, Sybase, Microsoft, Oracle, and Digital Equipment Corporation. By 1990, they had thrashed out a slimmed-down, SQL-based, call-level interface model. In the succeeding years, it has been enhanced considerably.

The ODBC interface is usually thought of as a set of API calls, but it does standardize more than just that. For example, the data types and error codes are generally standard across RDBMS implementations, though it is surprising how many differences there can be between ODBC drivers. The ODBC API can be used even from Visual Basic, but Microsoft has spent much energy on providing more practical methods of using it. These methods will be the focus of much of the rest of this book.

As far as the client machine is concerned there are several layers of software that you unknowingly use, and these are shown in simplified networking view in Figure 11.5.

FIGURE 11.5:

The ODBC view of your Oracle connection

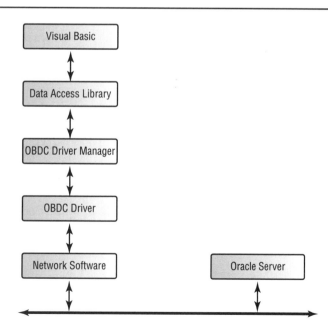

ODBC Drivers

One of the more confusing aspects of ODBC is to find out exactly what works with your driver and your database. As a reader of this book, you probably noticed most of the literature is written either from a SQL Server point of view or, just as bad, from a generic point of view. Let's take a look at what type of features ODBC can present to a developer and then see what applies to Oracle and why.

ODBC Driver Categories

Three categories are used to define an ODBC driver. These categories are based upon the architecture that the driver supports.

Single Tier   Single-tier drivers are built for databases that cannot process SQL statements. These are normally file-based systems, such as Microsoft Access and Foxpro, but also include Excel. These databases are passive: they do not have any actively running software. It is up to your ODBC driver to know how to get data out of the database and where and how the locking feature works. The driver takes a SQL command and converts it into a series of API calls appropriate to the database.

Two Tier   Two-tier ODBC drivers are for true client/server environments: they are designed for active databases that communicate by SQL. There is often some translation and parsing of the SQL commands you send to it before it reaches the database. This is necessary because databases often have their own dialects of SQL. This translation will occur when you pass a query from Visual Basic to Oracle. If you want to use any Oracle-specific syntax, then you must bypass this translation and parse and pass the SQL statements straight through to the database. You use the SQLPassThrough option to do this, which we will cover in detail in later chapters. A typical two-tier ODBC driver sends data from the application to the database. The client machine will run the application, the ODBC driver, and Driver Manager, while the server will be on a separate machine and have the Oracle Server running. Both machines will run compatible networking software.

Three Tier   A much less common type of ODBC driver is the three-tier, or multitier, driver. This driver is typically used when there is some kind of gateway between the database server and the client.

NOTE   As far as this book is concerned, we are only interested in two-tier drivers. Note that despite their name, they can just as easily be used in a multitier Visual Basic architecture. In this case, there is a two-tier link between the database and the middle-tier components.

ODBC Conformance Levels

In addition to the number of tiers that an ODBC driver is designed for, the drivers are also categorized according to their *conformance* level. The conformance level is a measure of how much of the ODBC API specification the driver supports. There are three levels to be aware of:

Core level   The driver must allow you to connect to a database, prepare and execute SQL statements, retrieve result sets from queries, use COMMIT and ROLLBACK statements for transaction control, and retrieve errors.

Level 1   The driver should allow everything at the core level as well as provide driver-specific dialog boxes for connecting to the database, the ability to get and set connections, and the ability to obtain driver and data-source information.

Level 2   The driver should allow everything at the previous two levels as well as allow you to list and browse the capabilities of data sources, retrieve result sets in different formats, and provide scrollable cursors. It should also allow you to retrieve extra catalog information from the database.

If an ODBC driver is advertised at a specific level, then it must provide *all* the features of that level. This does not mean that a level 1 driver, for example, cannot provide some level 2 features. In fact, most do provide a scrollable cursor. Because of this, level 1 drivers have been used for some sophisticated development and should not be ruled out.

Although the conformance levels are quite specific, this conformance does not always translate into practice. There have been many drivers that were advertised as level 2 but did not live up to this in practice. This was not a problem until developers were given tools, such as Remote Data Objects (RDO), that require a level 2 driver for their more advanced features. If you select the wrong driver, you are likely to see the dreaded "Driver not capable" message.

TIP   You should aim to get hold of relatively recent ODBC drivers. These are most likely to have the highest conformance levels and enable you to use the most features from Visual Basic. But make sure you test them on a test machine before putting them into production.

Selecting an ODBC Driver

Now that we have found out what types of ODBC drivers there are and what their capabilities are, it is time to select one for working with your Oracle database. One of the most frustrating aspects of ODBC is finding a driver that does what you want. Many drivers claim high compatibility to the various conformance levels, but each new driver has slightly different capabilities or, what is worse, affects the capabilities of those you last installed on your machine. Given the speed with which things change, it is difficult to be definitive on which drivers to use and which to avoid. It is certainly simpler to stick to those drivers that come either from Oracle (via Intersolv) or from Microsoft and learn to understand and live with their peculiarities.

My recommendation is to stick to either one of these companies' ODBC drivers but be careful before you upgrade. Do not get copies of all the latest versions and blindly install them without allowing for the fact that they may interfere with each other. If you have a test machine, then install any new driver on that and make sure it works as advertised and does not destructively interfere with other drivers. Sometimes the only way to get out of a situation like this is to reformat the hard drive and start again.

One particular case in point is the driver that came as part of MDAC 1.5, the Microsoft Data Access Components, that provides features for ADO (Active Data Components). The new driver exposed a bug in RDO 2.0, which was not fixed until Visual Basic 6.0.

NOTE   More time and effort seems to have been applied to the Microsoft ODBC driver.

Sources of ODBC Drivers

Several possible sources of ODBC drivers are available for Oracle; however, unless you want to pay for a third-party driver, your choices really boil down to two: one from Microsoft and one from Oracle.

Microsoft ODBC Driver

The Microsoft ODBC driver is available with Visual Basic, though you will find this driver can become out-of-date fairly quickly. The version that comes with Visual Basic 6 is preferable to previous versions.

Oracle ODBC Driver

The Oracle ODBC driver is actually developed by Intersolv. It is packaged with several Oracle products including the servers. Again these packaged drivers are likely to become out-of-date quickly, and it is best to download the latest version from the Web. Just be prepared to test the driver out fully before it goes into production. The URL is

```
www.oracle.com/products/free_software/index.html
```

You should use the Oracle8 drivers if you plan on installing Net8 and version 8 or higher of the Oracle Call Interface. Otherwise, use the Oracle7 drivers and SQL*Net.

Setting Up an ODBC Data Source

Having selected your driver, it is now time to install it and set up a data source. To do this, you use the ODBC Data Source Administrator program (ODBCAD32.EXE), which should be present on your machine as the Control Panel, "32bit ODBC." To run this on Windows 95 or NT, you should use the following steps:

1. Click the Start button, and select Settings ➤ Control Panel.

2. Double-click "32bit ODBC."

You will now see a window such as the one shown in Figure 11.6. You will notice several tabs. These tabs are described in Table 11.1.

FIGURE 11.6:

A login window for the
Microsoft ODBC driver

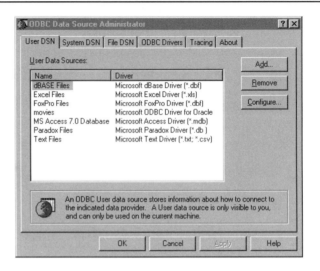

TABLE 11.1: The Options of the ODBC Data Source Administrator

Tab Heading	Description
User DSN	This heading lists the Data Source Names set up for the current user.
System DSN	This heading lists the Data Source Names set up for the system rather than an individual user.
File DSN	This heading lists the file-based data sources.
ODBC Drivers	This heading lists the ODBC drivers that are installed on the local machine.
Tracing	This heading controls whether the ODBC driver manager traces the SQL calls.
About	This heading lists the version and file name for all the key ODBC dlls. You should note down this information for your documentation because drivers can be overwritten by other software.

NOTE   If you are running a Windows NT client application that accesses the ODBC driver and the application needs to run as a service, then you should set up a System DSN. It will be able to run even though no user is logged on.

To add a new DSN for Oracle, we must first make sure that the Oracle driver is installed. You can see the drivers that have been installed on the ODBC Drivers tab. If it is not installed, you will have to get the driver software from your vendor of choice and install it. When you have installed the driver, then you should select the User DSN tab and click the Add button. This button allows you to add a new Data Source Name. When you click the Add button, you will see a list of all the available drivers. Select the one you want, and double-click it. Now you must fill in a description of the DSN you want to set up (see Figure 11.7). There are usually three or four fields you have to fill in.

Data Source Name   You can give the data source any name (DSN) you want, though you should obviously make it meaningful. You can set up any number of DSNs for the same ODBC driver. In practice, it is simplest to use the same name you used for the Oracle database service name.

Description   Use any description that you want here. Your users will hopefully never see this field, so you can leave it blank if you want, though it might help you to differentiate if you have set up many DSNs.

User Name   This is the user name you want to appear in the logon dialog box by default. The user can override this field when they log on.

Server   This is the Oracle service name or database alias name we saw in the section "Setting Up Net8 and SQL*Net," and it must match the name you set up in the `tnsnames.ora` file. Remember that the main function of this setup is to provide information to convert the DSN to a database service name. These names can all be the same if you wish (and this is the simplest thing to do), but they do not have to be the same. Note that this field may be called something different (such as Connect) depending on the make and version of the driver.

FIGURE 11.7:

Setting up the ODBC Data Source Name

Data Source Name:	MOVIES	OK
Description:	Movies test database	Cancel
User Name:	Nick	Help
Server:	movies	Options >>

NOTE   To install an Oracle ODBC driver, you need to have all the required networking software already present. Without this software, you will get an error message.

Creating an ODBC Connection String

A connection string is a string that includes sufficient information for your Visual Basic application to make a connection to the Oracle database. The string is passed to the ODBC Driver Manager, which then takes responsibility for making the connection. You will normally have to use this connection string when you first connect to the database with an OpenDatabase or similar method. You will also use it for Data Controls in the Access property.

There are several optional parts to the connect string, and the possible data can differ for different ODBC drivers. The string itself is made up of keyword and value pairs separated by semicolons. The possible keywords are shown in Table 11.2.

TABLE 11.2: The Keywords in an ODBC Connect String

Keyword	Description
ODBC	Identifies the string as an ODBC connection string. This keyword has no associated value.
DATABASE	The database name. This keyword is mainly useful for identifying the .mdb file in an Access database, and Oracle users should ignore it.
UID	The default user name for the data source.
PWD	The password for the default user name. Including this value is a security concern and should be avoided.
DSN	The data source name that you have set in the ODBC administrator application. In Oracle, this name is converted into a database alias.
LOGINTIMEOUT	The time in seconds that the login will be attempted before timing out. The default is 20 seconds. Note that this information can also be stored in the Registry.

NOTE

When you use OLE-DB, you will have other parameters available to you. This topic is covered in Chapter 17, *ActiveX Data Objects*.

In theory, you do not need to provide any of these keywords; the ODBC Driver Manager will prompt you for the missing values at run time. In practice, however, this will not make your end users too happy. You should identify the DSN so the users will not have to worry about which database they are connecting to. An example of your connect string might be

```
strConnect = "ODBC;DSN=Movies"
```

When the application is run with this connect string, the user name and password will be prompted for in a login dialog box as shown in Figure 11.8. Note that each ODBC driver can have its own login window, so you may see some variation.

FIGURE 11.8:

A login window for the Microsoft ODBC driver

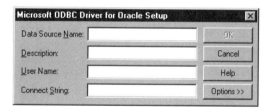

If you are in the process of developing your application, you will probably not want to keep entering the same information into the login box, so you can hard code your user name and perhaps even your password into the connection string. You should be aware that hard coding this information is a potential security issue. An example of a string with these keywords is

```
strConnect = "ODBC;DSN=Movies;UID=nick;PWD=ummagumma"
```

Assuming that the user name and password is valid, you should not see the logon window at all.

Your Own Logon Dialog Box

Many ODBC drivers present a dialog box that prompts for more than just the user name and password. Some drivers prompt you for the Data Source Name, as well. This information can be totally confusing to users and can even lead them to log on to the wrong database. One release of an ODBC driver I used prompted the Data Source Name each time a connection was made. Because Visual Basic programs can use more than one connection, this led to the interesting scenario of being able to run the Visual Basic application with two connections, each unintentionally to a different database!

At this point, I started to bypass the default logon box entirely. It is only displayed if there is any information missing, and it is a simple task of creating a dialog box in VB that prompts for the user name and password and then does the logon. If you are using a multitier architecture, you will need to use this technique anyway, otherwise the logon box would appear on a component server.

Testing Your ODBC Connection

Once you have set up Net8 or SQL*Net, fully tested it, and then installed and configured your ODBC driver of choice, your next step should be to test the driver by opening a connection to the database. You can do this with a Visual Basic application, but the simplest method is to use a small application designed for the purpose, called ODBCT32.EXE, shown in Figure 11.9.

FIGURE 11.9:

The ODBC test program

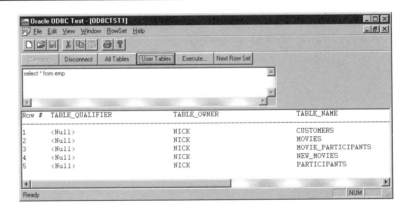

To use the ODBC test program, you must first connect to the Oracle database. To do this step, click the Connect button and select one of the SQL data sources. The source will be the same DSN that you set up in the previous section. Once you have selected the DSN, you will see the familiar logon dialog box that we saw in Figure 11.8.

A simple test of your configuration is to display the tables that you have access to. You can do this step by clicking the User Tables button. This leads you to the display that we saw in Figure 11.9. The tables displayed are the ones you have in your schema. By default, you will only see five rows displayed, which is really all you need to check the connection, but you can use the RowSet menu option to change this number. You can also execute SQL commands against the database. However, this tool is not a replacement for SQL*Plus; it only has a limited range of commands that you can execute, so it is not an administrative-quality tool.

Potential Problems with the ODBC Setup

As mentioned earlier in this chapter, you need to take a stepwise approach to setting up and testing your connection to the database. Testing your ODBC setup should come after you have tested the server and the client-networking installation. It is surprising how many people want to skip steps, but the methodical approach will be the best in the long run.

The next thing to check is whether you are running compatible software. The main concern is that you are running all 32-bit software or all 16-bit software. Unfortunately, a 32-bit ODBC driver cannot talk to a 16-bit version of SQL*Net.

If every step in the chain up to this point is working, then the main problem you will find is either the ODBC installation has not been done properly or you have set up the ODBC Data Source Name to the wrong Oracle service name. These should be double-checked. If there is still a problem, you should first go back to test out the network software again, and if that fails, you should reinstall the ODBC software.

WARNING   One recent problem I have encountered has been with the Oracle Installer. Older versions can overwrite OCX and DLL files. The installer does this without notifying you and can overwrite files with older versions. The giveaway is that you can no longer make connections after installing some new software. The only way out is to uninstall the software and start again.

OLE-DB

The latest alternative to ODBC from Microsoft has come about for two major reasons. The first is the need for a Component Object Model–based, data-access technology, which will make it possible for the technology to become cross-platform rather than being confined to a Windows environment. To make your data-access method useable across different platforms requires that Component Object Model (COM) is widely available across platforms. The distributed version of COM (DCOM) is currently in competition with CORBA (Common Object Request Broker Architecture) from a consortium of vendors (excluding Microsoft). Only time will tell how these two products fare or whether they will merge in some form.

The second desire for movement away from ODBC is that, although ODBC was designed as an access method for relational databases (such as Oracle and SQL Server), there is a need to be able to access data sources other than relational sources. Each source, whether it is an e-mail system, an object-oriented database, HTML files, or an office workflow system requires its own access methods and new ways to link the various data sources together. The ODBC architecture is insufficient for efficiently accessing the wide variety of data sources, and Microsoft has put together plans to phase it out and gradually replace it with a Universal Data Access technology (UDA) as part of the Distributed Network Architecture plans for the next few years.

There are two fundamentally different approaches to accessing different types of data sources. One approach is to bring all the data into the database, which requires the database be extensible with a large variety of tools for accessing and processing the data. This naturally is Oracle's approach, and the database is already capable of handling spatial, graphic, video, and audio data as well as advanced text-handling capabilities (the Context option allows thematic and proximity searches as well as full distributed indexes). This universal approach fits in well with a data-warehouse environment in which your enterprise data is completely pulled into the database periodically.

The alternative approach is to build a toolset that provides the same capabilities of universality but is external to the individual data sources. This approach needs to be a layered one with interoperable components that provide an interface to the data sources as well as allow processing and querying of the data once it is presented in a unified manner. Microsoft has taken this approach. Although these are two competing techniques, this does not rule out the possibility of them working together. In fact, the component approach can complement the database approach and provide any missing capabilities you feel you need. As an Oracle user, you can get the best of both worlds.

The UDA is designed for improved performance and scalability as well as flexibility and the improved stability of a simpler system with less parts to fail. The important part of the UDA to us as Oracle and Visual Basic developers is that the ODBC layer will be replaced with OLE-DB, an architecture consisting of a set of system-level data-access interfaces. OLE-DB is not conducive to access from Visual Basic, but then it is not really intended to be. Though they were available with MDAC 1.5, Visual Basic 6.0 provides us with the new models of ActiveX Data Objects (ADO) and Remote Data Services (RDS). We will cover these models in detail in Chapter 18. Visual Basic 6 also provides a native OLE-DB provider.

OLE-DB is a set of component-based interfaces for data management (see Figure 11.10). These are based on COM and consist of three categories of interface:

- **Data providers**   These are the interfaces to the actual data source; for example, they will expose the rows and columns of your Oracle tables. Whatever data source you use, the data will be exposed as rowsets to the components that use them. The data providers take over the role of both the ODBC Driver Manager and database-specific drivers.

- **Data consumers**   Any component that accesses the data from a data provider is considered a data consumer. In this case, ActiveX Data Objects fulfills that role.

- **Service components**   These are components that provide some kind of processing capability to the system, such as a query processor, cursor manager, or a transaction management system. A query processor would not normally be required if you were only accessing data from an Oracle database because the native query processor would be much more efficient. However, when using data sources without their own query processor or when linking data from Oracle and another data source, then this capability becomes more important.

Initially, the only data provider available for OLE-DB was an ODBC provider. This led to the unusual situation in which an extra interface was created on top of ODBC with marginal benefits. In fact, some changes in performance can be seen already, and they are not all bad. In time, a large number of native data providers will give improved functionality and performance. The area of data providers is going to see a lot of change over the next couple of years.

FIGURE 11.10:

ODBC data providers for OLE-DB will be replaced with native providers.

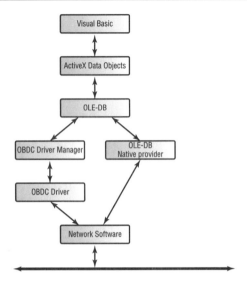

OLE-DB Cursors

In the next section, "Cursors," we will see a generic view of cursor implementation. In many ways, the techniques are just the same in OLE-DB as they are in ODBC except now they are present in service components, not in the ODBC drivers. These service components are added to the data providers to improve the functionality. For example, Oracle has a forward-only rowset cursor, often dubbed the *firehose* cursor. As we saw with ODBC cursors, many users expect more capabilities than the firehose cursor provides. To achieve the familiar backward- and forward-scrolling cursor, the cursor service provider (the *Cursor Manager*) has to provide the same techniques as ODBC to buffer the data in client memory.

This Cursor Manager does not handle the fetching, refreshing, and updating of data; these functions are performed by another service component, called the *synchronization service*. The component architecture means the different components can run on different tiers. Because of this ability, it is now possible to disconnect the cursor from its synchronization process and make use of the disconnected Recordsets that come with Remote Data Services.

NOTE	The OLE-DB native provider for Oracle supplied with Visual Basic 6 supports only the forward-only cursor.

Cursors

The concepts surrounding cursors can be shrouded in mystery to the uninitiated. One problem is that every database vendor has an RDBMS with different capabilities and different ways of doing things. Another is that we encounter cursors on the server side as well as cursors on the client; these are quite separate things.

Whether you are talking about server-side cursors or those on the client, they have some features in common. We all know the concept of a cursor indicating our current position in a text document. In database terminology, a cursor is no different; it is a pointer to our current position in a result set, which is a set of rows and columns retrieved from the database.

When you retrieve data from Oracle with a SELECT statement, the database first allocates part of the Shared SQL Area for the SQL to be parsed, and an execution plan is created. Any data that is not in the Oracle Server memory is pulled in, and the result set is created and returned to the user, one row at a time. If we ignore the concepts of cursor variables, there is no server-side *cursor* as such. The rows are simply returned one by one, with no going back. When the last value is retrieved, the area of memory holding the result set is reclaimed by the system. If you need to see a previous value, then you have to reexecute the SELECT statement. This becomes clear when you use cursors in PL/SQL.

NOTE   A quick note on terminology. A *result set* is the term normally given to the set of rows that is returned from Oracle to Visual Basic. It consists of one or more rowsets, each representing one row. When the data gets into Visual Basic, it is called a *Recordset* by Data Access Objects and a *rdoResultset* by Remote Data Objects.

The Oracle Server's unidirectional cursor is an important concept because it is quite different from what most developers are used to and have come to expect from Visual Basic. We are used to seeing a result set and scrolling backward and forward through it, happily changing any value we want. We should note here that Oracle is not particularly different in this respect from most of the other major RDBMS. Where does the difference come from? Well, the *Cursor Manager* provides for this extra functionality, and scrolling is one feature usually handled on the client, not the server, although there is a limit as to what can be expected. The Cursor Manager typically provides up to four types of cursor originally found in the

ODBC specification: static, dynamic, keyset, and mixed, with the now common addition of the firehose cursor. This model is basically followed by other access techniques (ActiveX Data Objects and Oracle Objects for OLE), though not all cursor managers provide all the cursor types.

> **NOTE**   I use the term *Cursor Manager* generically here. In ODBC, this function is performed by the ODBC driver or Driver Manager. In OLE-DB, the function is provided by a service component called the Cursor Manager, and with Oracle Objects for OLE, the cursor capability is provided as part of the in-process server. All of them pull query results into some form of Recordset.

Static Cursors

The static cursor is the simplest form of cursor. The rows of the returned result set, including any keys and all the values, are fixed when the client-side cursor is created. The cursor library that creates the cursor effectively reads all the values and caches them in memory on the client machine so we can easily scroll backward and forward as easily as moving up and down the rows in a spreadsheet. The problem with the static cursor is that it *is* static; that means while we are scrolling around the cursor, our Recordset is quite oblivious to any changes that have occurred in the database. Rows could have been deleted or values could have been changed by other users, but this will not be reflected in our data. You cannot even change the values in your own Recordset, so it can produce only a read-only cursor. The static cursor's consistency is very high (the result set is consistently the same); concurrency is high because of Oracle's exceptional concurrency. However, you may find that the data becomes out-of-date quickly.

> **NOTE**   The snapshot-type cursor in Data Access Objects is basically a static cursor.

Dynamic Cursors

At the opposite end of the spectrum from static cursors are dynamic cursors. These cursors point to a set of data that is dynamically kept up-to-date, which means that the cursor accurately represents any changes you have made to the data as well as all the changes that all other users have made and committed. Dynamic cursors are difficult to implement and generally rely on server-side cursor availability, such as that provided by Microsoft SQL Server. As you can imagine, the consistency of the data is poor; you cannot rely on anything remaining the same for long, although the data is as up-to-date as possible. Dynamic cursors are the most costly type to use from a client and a server resource point of view. If you remember back to Chapter 2, *Oracle Database Architecture*, you will see that Oracle represents a highly consistent view of data, and this does not lend itself to producing dynamic cursors. As a result, these cursors are not available to Visual Basic developers who work with Oracle.

Keyset Cursors

Keyset cursors are a halfway house for cursors. They have a static representation of the rows in a result set (stored with a unique key value in the *keyset*), but the row values are fetched only just before they are needed. The keyset is a set of pointers to the actual rows in the Oracle table. As such, they represent a significant resource requirement both on the server and the client. Although there are many different implementations of keyset cursors, they generally allow you to see the latest values of rows, including committed updates from other users. The keyset cursor is the only way to get an updatable cursor with Oracle; however, its functionality must be simulated by the cursor library, and this makes it particularly inefficient. You do not have the option of putting it on the server.

NOTE   A dynaset-type cursor in Data Access Objects is similar in concept to a keyset cursor.

WARNING   When data is updated or deleted by another user, it is often referred to as being "dirty." The Oracle driver does not allow you to see the change, so if it is important to your application, you will want to ensure your code detects any changes to a row it is about to alter. Detecting changes reduces the benefits of updatable Recordsets, and users have to accept the error messages that can result from such a situation.

Mixed Cursors

Mixed cursors share the characteristics of dynamic and keyset cursors. They are similar to keyset cursors in that they do have a keyset to store the unique keys of the result set, but the keyset is only a subset of the whole result set. In other words, the cursor knows about some of the rows in the result set but not all. If you direct it to fetch data for a row that is not in this limited keyset, then it has to fetch the row dynamically. Once again, these are not available for Oracle users.

Firehose Cursors

One further thing should be pointed out in this section on cursors. With some data-access models (particularly RDO and ADO), you will find another alternative form of cursor: the forward-only cursor. This cursor is normally used in a read-only mode but can sometimes be updatable. Strictly speaking, the forward-only cursor is not a cursor at all but merely a direct transfer of result-set rows from the Oracle Server to the client. The forward-only cursor is simple to implement and uses resources efficiently. Although you may start off with updatable cursors for small applications, the greater the load on the database, the more you will have to rely on this simple cursor. It is a sensible idea to use the forward-only cursor for all new development work. It will take a little getting used to, and you will have to design your applications differently, but you will be ready for the high end. We will see this approach taken in the chapter on specific data-access techniques, starting with Chapter 14, *Data Access Objects*.

How Cursors Work

Whichever type of cursor you decide to use, it is useful to have a general understanding of how they work because it can help you appreciate the performance issues of using cursors. As we mentioned previously, the data returned from the Oracle Server is a forward-only cursor. The rows retrieved are stored in a buffer on the client (see Figure 11.11). This buffer is created and maintained by the cursor manager. Sufficient rows of data are read from the server into the cursor buffer. If there are enough rows in the result set, then the buffer will be filled, and no more rows will be read at that time. The buffer effectively forms a window onto the buffered data. When you scroll forward past the end of the buffer, another row (or more than one row) is read from the server. Meanwhile, the result set on the Oracle Server is left in a "pending" state and cannot be closed until the last row has been read, thereby consuming valuable system resources.

FIGURE 11.11:

The cursor model reads rows into a buffer.

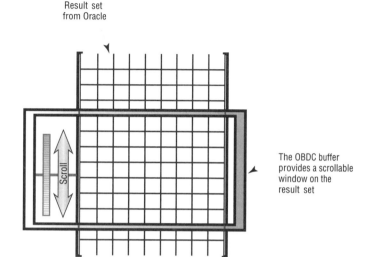

So what happens if you want to scroll backward? Well, the relevant data in the buffer may be lost, and the query has to be executed again! You will not notice this because the Cursor Manager will manage it for you. However, this feature is one reason why a forward-only Recordset is a far more efficient Visual Basic technique than a scrollable cursor. If you are using a keyset cursor and there is insufficient memory to hold the keyset, then part of it will be swapped out to disk.

One final point is worth noting here. Because the ODBC driver manages the cursor, if you use the pass-through option so you can use Oracle-specific code, then you bypass the Cursor Manager. The resulting Recordset becomes read only.

Choosing a Cursor

You will often have the task of choosing a cursor type, in particular for Remote Data Objects (RDO) and Active Data Objects(ADO). As you can see from the notes above, you really have only one choice for an updatable cursor with Oracle: the keyset cursor. However, with ADO, you have access only to the forward-only cursor. As with many aspects of using Oracle from Visual Basic, you do not have much choice; just make sure you know which one *is* your only choice. Read-only cursors will give you a much better and more scalable design; static cursors will give you all the features you would expect, such as updatability; or for the utmost in performance, use the forward-only read-only cursor.

Cursors in Action

When you create an updatable Recordset (what used to be called a *dynaset*), the driver reads in only the key values for the rows. (Oracle Objects for OLE reads in the ROWID.) When you want to retrieve the whole row, the Cursor Manager reads the appropriate columns. When you update or delete a row, the Cursor Manager effects this change in the database. (In the case of OLE-DB, this change is done through the synchronization service.) Of course, being a relatively "dumb" cursor, the keyset cursor will not inform the application of any changes that other users have made to the records in the Recordset until you refresh it. You may end up trying to update a row that someone has just deleted. In practice, this is always a potential problem and something you should plan for.

When you create a read-only Recordset (what used to be called a *snapshot*), all the data is read into client-side memory (within practical limits). You will normally find that this type of Recordset is much faster than the updatable type, though this depends on the size of the Recordset. Of course, memory requirements can be high, and with a large enough Recordset, you may find that the driver has to reread some parts of the data with a potentially heavy performance impact. For this reason, you should try to avoid having BLOB-type data in a read-only Recordset.

WARNING   For updatable Recordsets to work in Visual Basic, the rows have to be accessible by key. If you do not have a unique or primary key on a table, the driver will not be able to find the row it is looking for, and the Recordset will become read-only!

Connections

We tend to treat a database connection as simply a link to the database, but in reality, this is an area you will need to give some thought to, especially as you develop applications that are used by more and more people. Scalability starts to become important. According to the vendor, Oracle8 is capable of supporting up to 10,000 concurrent connections, and some say even more, but there are some issues and features of the database that you should be aware of.

Connections and Sessions

There are two terms that you should be able to distinguish: *connection* and *session*. A connection is the communication pathway between the Server process Oracle has created and the database itself. On the other hand, a session is the communication between the remote application (such as your Visual Basic program) and the database, which uses a particular connection.

The terminology is somewhat unfortunate because Microsoft uses the term *connection* to refer to what Oracle calls a session. Oracle Objects for OLE uses the term *correct* when you create a session (see Chapter 18). However, because we are working in a Microsoft environment, using the term *connection* for both situations does not seem to cause any problems, and we shall continue to do that in future chapters.

Multiple Connections

If you monitor the processes on your server, you will notice there is often more than one connection per user. This is because data-access methods prior to Remote Data Objects are not connection oriented and usually demand more than one connection. Data Access Objects is relatively frugal when working with Oracle but requires a separate connection for execution of SQL or stored procedures. Oracle supports something called *pending result sets*, which means the same connection can support several result sets that have not been closed, though it is preferable to avoid this. If you insist on using this capability, you will at least be in a better situation with Oracle compared to other databases, such as SQL Server, which can end up requiring many connections, especially when the result sets are large.

The worst offender for connection usage is the Data Control, which, by default, requires a separate connection for each control. This function is incredibly wasteful of resources (each connection has its own Private SQL Area in the memory of the server), and it means it can take a long time to get connected. Luckily, there is a technique for sharing connections among Data Controls, which we shall see in Chapter 14, *Data Access Objects*.

NOTE   Oracle is licensed on the basis of users, not connections. As a result, you do not have any licensing issues with multiple connections for an application. However, if you use the Multithreaded Server, then there are more users than connections.

DSN-less Connections

We have seen how to put together a connection string in the previous sections. There are downsides to this method, such as having to create the data source in the ODBC administrator program for every PC; the method also has a small hit on the Registry as the relevant information is read in. However, this is not the only way to create the connection. You can now bypass this process by using a *DSN-less* connection. This is achieved by specifying all the required information, including the name of the ODBC driver, when you connect. We shall see this in Chapter 16, *ODBCDirect,* and in subsequent chapters.

Closing an ODBC Connection

It can come as a bit of a surprise when you are using the JET engine to access Oracle (or any other ODBC database for that matter) and you find it difficult to close a connection. This step can become apparent when you run a Visual Basic application that prompts you for your user name and password. If you stop the application and restart it, you will not be prompted a second time. What is happening is JET will keep the connection open even though you might do everything you can think of to close the database; it does this for the efficiency of not reconnecting repeatedly. This can be a problem if you change back and forth from test to production by altering the service name in the DSN definition.

If you want to ensure that the connection is closed, you will have to wait for the number of seconds defined in the ConnectionTimeout parameter in the Registry. The default value is 600! However, you can change this default value by changing the ConnectionTimeout value to a small number, such as 1. An alternative is to quickly restart your Visual Basic environment.

Take care making any changes to the Registry. If you are not confident making this change, then export the Registry to file before changing it, because if you do the wrong thing, you may find it next to impossible to recover. I personally do not like having to resort to manually making Registry changes; it can be quite impractical when you have many client machines to worry about. If you absolutely must do it, then consider writing a program to make these changes for you rather than doing it manually.

ODBC Connection Pooling

A recent addition to ODBC's capabilities is called *connection pooling*. This is the ability of an ODBC Driver Manager to share ODBC connections, so long as they are using the same ODBC drivers. The feature has come with the ODBC Driver Manager version 3.0 and above and is independent of the actual driver.

The ability to share database connections is most important when you have a component architecture in which you have a large number of components on a single machine wanting to make and break connections repeatedly to the same database. (Components cannot share a connection concurrently.) Due to the high overhead of making a connection to Oracle (and other databases), there has to be some way to avoid the constant start up and shut down of Server processes.

If you are using Microsoft Transaction Server (MTS), you do not need to worry about connection pooling because this feature is built-in. However, at the time of this writing, Oracle's support for MTS is less than enthusiastic; Oracle is pushing somewhat similar architecture with the Oracle Application Server.

If you do want to pursue this, there are a couple of articles in the Microsoft Knowledge base, which you may want to review (Q169470 and Q164221). You may also want to consider whether the benefits of Oracle's Multithreaded Server (which also has the MTS acronym) or Prestarted Connections are of any benefit. We shall cover these in the next few sections.

Oracle Multithreaded Server

When you start off working with Oracle, you will probably be using the dedicated server architecture that we saw in Chapter 2. However, in Chapter 3, we saw the configuration you need to make to run the Dispatcher processes used by Oracle Multithreaded Server. This architecture allows you to share a connection between many users and is a major reason Oracle is able to support such a large number of concurrent sessions. In practice, getting MTS to work has been difficult, and you should consider it an advanced feature. The version of MTS in Oracle8 has been much improved; however, you should only consider using it when you need hundreds of concurrent connections or more. MTS is recommended only for OLTP use.

If you are working with a large number of concurrent connections, you may also want to explore a feature of Oracle8 called *Connection Manager,* which allows multiplexing that is similar to ODBC connection pooling.

Prestarted Connections

If you are not using Oracle Multithreaded Server, then when you make a connection request the Listener process will start up a new dedicated Server process for you. This can take a second or so to accomplish. Oracle has the ability to create *Prestarted Connections* for you.

You can set up Prestarted Connections by providing extra parameters in the `listener.ora` file. When the Listener process is started on the database server, a certain number of connections are created but are not used by any sessions. When you start up your Visual Basic application, the Listener will search for an available (unused) connection from the pool. When it has finished with the connection, it will be returned to the pool.

The effect on a Visual Basic application depends on what technology you are using, but it will probably not be as much as you might think. You only need to consider this technique when you have a large number of simultaneous connections, for example, in an Internet application.

TIP   Before you consider using Prestarted Connections, you should ensure that your connection time really is slow. To test the connection time, you should use SQL*Plus on the server. Do not use a Visual Basic program because you have no idea how much overhead is involved. For example, with Data Access Objects, all the descriptions of the available tables are downloaded to the client, and this can make the connection appear to take much longer than it really does.

Alternative Access Methods

There is no doubt that Microsoft techniques, including ODBC and OLE-DB, dominate the interaction between Oracle and Visual Basic. However, there are a couple of other routes that can be used: the Oracle precompilers and Oracle Objects for OLE. Although the precompilers will probably not entice many Visual Basic programmers, you should become familiar with Oracle Objects for OLE because it enables you to extract as much functionality out of the database as possible.

Oracle Precompilers

It is possible to write applications that access the OCI API by using the provided low-level function calls; this process is similar to writing to the ODBC API. What is probably little known to Visual Basic developers is that Oracle has five programming-language precompilers that run on a variety of platforms. (A precompiler processes your code before it is passed to a compiler.) These precompilers enable you to use *Embedded SQL*, in which the precompiler takes your code and converts the Embedded SQL into direct calls to the Oracle Call Interface. The available precompilers are Pro*C/C++, Pro*Cobol, Pro*Fortran, and Pro*ADA; Pro*PL/1 is available on fewer platforms. Although the OCI is available for the same languages, using these precompilers is far easier than writing to the OCI.

> **NOTE**   You can theoretically access the OCI from Visual Basic; however, the data structures are hard to program, and VB's garbage collection may make this unreliable or impossible. I cannot imagine anyone trying this.

Oracle Objects for OLE

The final alternative to using ODBC is an Oracle product that has been out for a few years called Oracle Objects for OLE (OO4O). The name is a little unfortunate because the term OLE is giving way to COM (Component Object Model). OO4O is a dll that runs in the same process as your Visual Basic application and provides a direct link to the Oracle Call Interface. OLE is easy to master for anyone who has done much database programming in Visual Basic, because it uses the same object model as the familiar DAO and RDO. We will see more about OO4O in Chapter 18, *Oracle Objects For OLE*. The in-process server provides a direct link to the Oracle Call Interface and must provide all the features, such as cursors, the OCI does not have.

Summary

This chapter has covered the background material you should have to understand how your Visual Basic applications actually connect to Oracle. We covered both the Oracle networking software and Microsoft's ODBC architecture in enough detail for you to install, configure, and test both aspects. We also covered OLE-DB, the latest technology that has much promise in terms of functionality, performance, and overall ubiquity. This information is also important for you to be able to produce an efficient communication channel between Visual Basic and the database.

Building on this foundation, we can now move on to the various ways that you, as a Visual Basic developer, can access the data in your Oracle database.

CHAPTER

TWELVE

12

Accessing Oracle from Visual Basic

- The JET Database Engine

- Remote Data Objects

- ODBCDirect

- The ODBC API

- ActiveX Data Objects

- Oracle Objects for OLE

- Exporting an Access Database to Oracle

There is a large number of ways to access Oracle databases from Visual Basic, and each has both advantages and disadvantages. Although you can select the most suitable access method for your circumstances, you first have to be aware of what the various methods are. If there were just two or three methods, it would be relatively easy to cope with; but in reality, there are many methods to choose from, and the number keeps increasing each year. What is even worse is that the details and capabilities of each method seem to change every few months. Such is the effect of a highly competitive market.

This chapter will give you an overview of the various methods you can currently use. I will go out on a limb and suggest the number of methods will probably stabilize for a couple of years now that we have the OLE-DB standard from Microsoft. However, before we rejoice too much, let me add that the details of those methods appear to be going through a period of almost constant change.

In the next few sections, we will take an overview of the following methods, comparing the techniques and features of each method. The various topics we will cover are

- The JET database engine

- Remote Data Objects

- ODBCDirect

- The ODBC API

- ActiveX Data Objects

- Oracle Objects for OLE

- Exporting an Access database to Oracle

For each of the data access types, we will review the features as well as look at code fragments that compare how the individual techniques can be used to connect to an Oracle database and create a Recordset. The fastest Recordset cursor has been set up in each case, because this is the preferred method of retrieving data from an Oracle database. Most of the techniques will be examined in much more detail throughout the rest of the book, but this chapter will give you a quick summary to help you decide on the techniques that are most useful in your situation.

The JET Engine

JET is where it all started. Visual Basic 3 was a real step forward in database access and provided easy data access to Microsoft Access and other file-based ISAM databases, such as FoxPro. To access these databases, you use the JET (Joint Engine Technology) database engine. Many programmers wrongly consider this engine part of Visual Basic, but the truth is the required drivers for JET come with VB as do many other drivers; there is no real integration between VB and JET. If you don't include the right references in your Visual Basic project, your application will not recognize any of the database objects.

To use the JET database engine, Data Access Objects (DAO) provides an object-based approach represented by a hierarchy of objects, such as the database itself, and sets of retrieved records called *Recordsets*. A Recordset exposes the properties and methods that allow us to define the details of the link to the objects as well as navigate and update the records. The JET engine has its own query and result-set processors, so it knows how to read data from the database files and also how to handle file locking when more than one user is involved. However, the query processor also causes the software to be large, with nonstandard handling of SQL, and to be relatively slow. What is worse, JET cannot take advantage of the advanced features of a remote active database it may be attached to (such as Oracle). To use these advanced features, you have to bypass the JET engine, which we shall cover in later chapters.

However, the JET engine is important in that it provides an object hierarchy upon which all others are based, though, as we will see, sometimes the property names have been changed for less than obvious reasons. A recent approach with ADO is to simplify the data-access process considerably as well as expand it to be able to access data from all possible sources, not just databases.

Many, if not all Visual Basic programmers, cut their teeth on Access databases. Visual Basic even provides the Data Manager tool Add-In to let us create the databases without buying the Access product. Your knowledge of Access is directly applicable to moving up to a more serious database, such as Oracle. However, you must not let it limit your thinking. The jump to an external database using ODBC is not as scary as you may think. By following the relatively simple steps outlined in this book, you should be able to move to Oracle quite easily. To become an expert, of course, will take much time and experimentation.

Although you may not often use JET in production applications, you should be aware of the following techniques.

- Linking tables to the Access database

- Using Data Controls

- Using Data Access Objects

Linked Tables

One of the simplest ways to get started with Visual Basic and Oracle is to use *linked* tables (what used to be called *attached* tables). Using linked tables is more of a setup method than an access method, which makes Oracle tables available to the standard DAO techniques. (We will cover DAO techniques in the next section.) You can also use the forms and queries of the Access application itself as an alternative to using Visual Basic.

To use linked tables, we create an Access database and use the capabilities of Access to link or attach a table from an external source, such as Oracle, to an Access table. What actually happens is the Oracle database structure is embedded in the Access table, enabling the JET engine to know how to reach and handle the data. The JET engine is interpreting any requests and sending them off to Oracle. This process provides a certain amount of efficiency because when you use a data-access technique, such as Data Access Objects, all the table definitions are loaded up into memory. Having these definitions in an Access database saves time and server resources (so long as the definitions do not change!).

This knowledge of the Oracle table structure in the Access database enables you to link tables from different sources, such as Oracle, Microsoft SQL Server, and Sybase, and run queries against them all at the same time. Although this may sound promising, it really is not a recommended method because it has considerable drawbacks:

- In addition to the lack of JET performance against remote databases, linked tables can take considerable resources from your client workstation.

- There is a lack of features, such as executing stored procedures.

- Linked tables need setting up on each client PC and must be updated whenever structural changes are made to the database.

- You are restricted to the nonstandard SQL syntax of Access.

Linking an Oracle Table to Access

The first thing we will do is link an Oracle table to an Access database. We will use Access 97 here, but the techniques work just as well if you are still using a 16-bit version of Access 2.0. The steps are fairly straightforward:

1. Create a new Access database (.mdb file).

2. Select File ➤ Get External Data ➤ Link Tables... menu option.

3. At the bottom of the Link dialog box in the "Files of Type" combo box, select "ODBC Databases."

4. Specify the name of the Oracle table you want to link to (see Figure 12.1). This step will typically be under the Machine Data Source tab.

5. Log on to the database with your Oracle user name and password.

6. Select one or more tables to attach to the Access database.

7. Close the dialog box.

The tables will appear in the Access Database window as shown in Figure 12.2.

FIGURE 12.1:

Selecting a Data Source to attach to your Access database

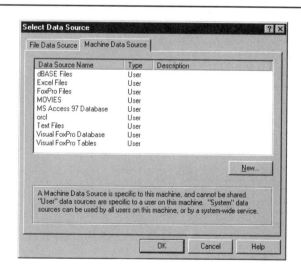

FIGURE 12.2:

The Access database with six Oracle tables attached

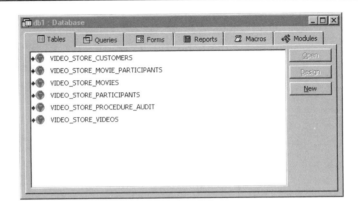

NOTE To remove the attached table, select the table, and hit the delete key or use the Edit ➤ Delete menu option.

We can now either use the linked tables in Access as we would any other database, including the standard Access JET engine, or we can use Visual Basic to access the linked table as if it was an Access database.

The limitations of linked tables are substantial. You will not be able to use any specific Oracle features, such as functions or stored procedures, which can be a real handicap. The lack of performance is also a great penalty. With the available techniques these days, why go through the JET engine at all? There are no advantages for a production environment, though as with Data Controls, you can use them for prototypes or administrative tools that will not get heavy use.

Typical Code

When you use linked tables, you are interfacing with Access as far as the application is concerned. As a result, the typical code you see in Listing 12.1 will be more or less identical to what you would write if you were working with a normal Access database using DAO. The Data Source Name (DSN), in this case "movies," refers to the Access database file `movies.mdb`. The code creates a Database object and then opens a Recordset against it.

Listing 12.1

```
Private Sub FetchAttached()

    Dim dbMovies As Database
    Dim rsMovies As Recordset
    Dim strSQL As String
    Dim iField As Integer

    ' Connect to the database
    Set dbMovies = Workspaces(0).OpenDatabase("", False, False, _
        "DSN=movies;UID=video_user;PWD=ummagumma")

    ' Run the query
    strSQL = "SELECT * FROM movies ORDER BY movie_id"
    Set rsMovies = dbMovies.OpenRecordset(strSQL, dbOpenSnapshot)

    ' Display the fields
    While Not rsMovies.EOF
        For iField = 0 To rsMovies.Fields.Count - 1
            Debug.Print rsMovies(iField)
        Next ' iField
        rsMovies.MoveNext
    Wend

    Set rsMovies = Nothing
    Set dbMovies = Nothing

End Sub
```

Data Access Objects

Data Access Objects (DAO) have been the mainstay of Visual Basic's database capabilities for a good long time. In its current incarnation (version 3.51), we have quite a different product from where we started. DAO is the main technique to deal with Access databases through the JET engine drivers, but it is also capable of dealing with other local data sources, such as Excel files. In addition, Microsoft added the ability to link to ODBC data sources, a feature that was being requested by more and more users. Figure 12.3 gives an overview of the software layers used with this approach. We will examine DAO in more detail in Chapter 14, *Data Access Objects.*

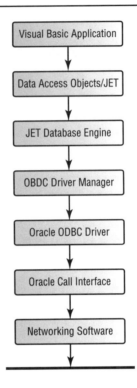

FIGURE 12.3:

The software layers used for accessing Oracle through DAO

DAO is probably one of the main reasons ODBC became more popular. The only alternative at the time was to program to the Application programming Interface (API), which, as we shall see, is a time-consuming and complex technique few programmers have the enthusiasm to become familiar with and few project managers have the resources for.

Features

- You can purchase Data Access Objects, version 3.51, which is currently available in 32-bit code. However, it is still available in 16-bit form for those running Visual Basic 4 or previous versions.

- You can read and write to database tables.

- You can access different databases at the same time, even joining tables from databases as diverse as Oracle, JET, and Microsoft SQL Server.

- You can use the SQLPassThrough option to bypass the JET engine. Queries are then sent directly to Oracle, though Recordsets created this way are read-only.

- You can call stored procedures, but you cannot retrieve any output parameters.

Typical Code

The code you can see in Listing 12.2 is almost identical to that in Listing 12.1. However, in this example, the ODBC keyword has been used in the connection string, and now the DSN refers to a registered ODBC database name.

Listing 12.2

```
Private Sub FetchDAO()

    Dim dbMovies As Database
    Dim rsMovies As Recordset
    Dim strSQL As String
    Dim iField As Integer

    '   Connect to the database
    Set dbMovies = Workspaces(0).OpenDatabase("", False, False, _
        "ODBC;DSN=movies;UID=video_user;PWD=ummagumma")

    '   Run the query
    strSQL = "SELECT * FROM video_store.movies ORDER BY movie_id"
    Set rsMovies = dbMovies.OpenRecordset(strSQL, dbOpenSnapshot)

    '   Display the fields
    While Not rsMovies.EOF
        For iField = 0 To rsMovies.Fields.Count - 1
            Debug.Print rsMovies(iField)
        Next ' iField
        rsMovies.MoveNext
    Wend

    Set rsMovies = Nothing
    Set dbMovies = Nothing

End Sub
```

Data Controls

Perhaps the most appealing thing about Visual Basic to the beginner is the Data Control and associated bound controls. The Data Control is a simple drag-and-drop control that enables direct access to one particular table in the database. You drag the control to a form and specify the data source and table. You then have a link to any Oracle table in a matter of minutes. Once you have done this process, you can drop a variety of other controls on the same form. These controls allow you to bind their displayed value to a specific column in the selected table through the Data Control. Run the project the form is in, and every time the navigation buttons are used to change the current record, any bound controls on the form will change their displayed values to match the new current record. If you enter a new value in the bound control and move to the next record, the value in the database will be updated automatically.

This is true codeless programming. No one can deny the appeal of codeless programming to programmers who are just starting out and especially to those who are in a rush to produce professional-looking code. An even greater appeal is that many new controls take data binding one step beyond a simple text box for updating a field or two. For example, there are sophisticated grid controls that allow you to display and update records from linked tables. This is programming at its easiest. If you review computer magazines, you will have the impression it is the only accepted method of programming. Who would program any other way? Bound controls are state-of-the-art industry standards and the best way to go—or so you may think.

Although Data Controls are beneficial in small work-group situations with an Access database and can be ideal when you are prototyping an application, when I am involved in an enterprise database (company wide and where data security and integrity are important), bound controls should not be used.

The World of Data Controls

You can use many Data Controls to connect to an Oracle database. We have the familiar Data Control provided with every version of Visual Basic; then there is the Remote Data Control that comes along with Remote Data Objects. Oracle Objects for OLE also has a "drop in" replacement for the Data Control. ActiveX Data Objects, the latest technology from Microsoft, takes this concept several steps further and provides the Remote Data Services Data Control, which can provide disconnected operation over the Internet.

Continued on next page

Apart from a brief mention in this chapter, Data Controls of all stripes have been omitted from this book. There are many reasons for this.

- Data Controls are generally easy to use and have extensive coverage in many other books.

- Oracle environments tend to be strictly controlled from a security aspect, and you will not be able to use the updating feature of a Data Control. Without this feature, the main reason for using them disappears.

- Oracle is a high-end database, and most developers cannot even consider the performance hit and locking issues that are incurred with Data Controls.

- Data Controls are generally not useable in a multitier environment, so they have limited scalability.

- Data Controls tend to be generic and do not support Oracle-specific features or syntax (with the exception of the Oracle Objects for OLE Data Control).

- Data Controls cannot access stored procedures.

- Data Controls do not make good use of server resources, such as ODBC connections (again with the exception of the Oracle Objects for OLE Data Control).

Remote Data Objects

With the growing use of DAO, it was becoming obvious the performance problems and lack of features of DAO could only be addressed by writing low-level code to the ODBC API. However, this method was not the simplest task and, if you did not write your code well, would result in a poor performing and fragile application. So Microsoft produced Remote Data Objects (RDO), a "wrapper" around the API encapsulating many of its features and providing the performance improvements many developers had been clamoring for. RDO came into being with version 1.0 appearing with the Enterprise Edition of Visual Basic 4. A much-improved version came along with Visual Basic 5, although only minor modifications were made for the release of Visual Basic 6. Figure 12.4 gives an overview of the software layers RDO uses to communicate with your Oracle database. If you compare this to Figure 12.3, you will see JET has been completely pulled out of the loop. We will examine RDO in more detail in Chapter 15, *Remote Data Objects*.

FIGURE 12.4:

The software layers used by Remote Data Objects

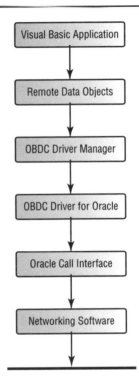

Features

- RDO is available only in 32-bit form and comes only with the Enterprise Edition of Visual Basic.

- RDO 2.0 is the current version, with a minor upgrade for Visual Basic 6.

- RDO has a connection object to allow better use of ODBC connections, compared to DAO/JET.

- RDO leads to much lighter weight client code because it does not have the JET engine that DAO carries.

- RDO provides access to remote SQL databases at almost the same speed as well-written ODBC API calls.

- RDO supports the rdoQuery that sets up an object for retrieving result sets and calling stored procedures.

- RDO supports a Parameters collection for running parameterized rdo-Queries. Parameters also allows you to return output parameters from stored procedures.

- RDO can process asynchronous queries.

- RDO has a full event model.

- RDO contains the UserConnection Designer, which is a graphical tool used to make accessing data a simpler process.

NOTE   RDO should not be a deciding factor in the purchase of the Enterprise Edition of Visual Basic. This version should instead be purchased based on your need to produce multitier applications with one or more logical tiers created as remotely running components.

Typical Code

With RDO, the object model is more biased toward relational databases, such as Oracle and Microsoft SQL Server. The terminology changes to rdoResultsets instead of Recordsets and rdoColumns instead of Fields. As you can see in Listing 12.3, we set up an rdoConnection object to handle all communication with a database rather than the database object of DAO/JET that creates more than one connection to a single database. The other major thing to notice is we have a larger variety of options for creating our rdoResultsets, which can become confusing.

Listing 12.3

```
Private Sub FetchRDO()

    Dim rsMovies As rdoResultset
    Dim strSQL As String
    Dim iColumn As Integer
    Dim strConnection As String
    Dim cn As rdoConnection


    ' Connect to the database
    With rdoEngine
        .rdoDefaultCursorDriver = rdUseClientBatch
        .rdoDefaultLoginTimeout = 1
    End With
```

```
        strConnection = "DSN=movies;UID=video_user;PWD=ummagumma"
        Set cn = rdoEngine.rdoEnvironments(0).OpenConnection _
            ("", rdDriverNoPrompt, False, strConnection)

'       Run the query
        strSQL = "SELECT * FROM video_store.movies ORDER BY movie_id"
        Set rsMovies = cn.OpenResultset(strSQL, rdOpenForwardOnly, _
                        rdConcurReadOnly)

'       Display the fields
        While Not rsMovies.EOF
            For iColumn = 0 To rsMovies.rdoColumns.Count - 1
                Debug.Print rsMovies(iColumn)
            Next ' iColumn
            rsMovies.MoveNext
        Wend

        Set rsMovies = Nothing
        Set cn = Nothing

End Sub
```

ODBCDirect

ODBCDirect is somewhat of an oddball in this list. It is effectively part of RDO because it is a wrapper on top of the RDO wrapper. However, its object model is basically that of DAO. The software layers DAO uses (see Figure 12.5) show this contorted route. ODBCDirect has been downplayed by everyone as an undesirable hybrid. However, it is part of DAO 3.51 and is much more powerful than DAO/JET itself. Performance for ODBCDirect is almost as good as RDO despite the extra layer of software. It has been particularly useful for using inside applications, such as Microsoft Excel, where you cannot use RDO for license reasons. However, this usefulness will give way to the use of ActiveX Data Objects (ADO).

FIGURE 12.5:

The software layers used by ODBCDirect

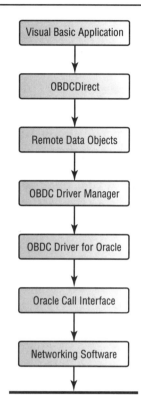

Features

- ODBCDirect is available only with 32-bit DAO version 3.1 and above.

- ODBCDirect uses the DAO model, so the learning curve is easy for developers already working with Microsoft Access.

- ODBCDirect has a Connection object, so you do not incur DAO/JET's use of multiple database connections.

- The memory footprint is greater than RDO but less than DAO/JET.

- ODBCDirect supports QueryDefs, which is the equivalent of rdoQueries.

- ODBCDirect supports some of RDO's feature set, including return parameters from stored procedures.

- ODBCDirect supports asynchronous operation.

- ODBCDirect does not expose RDO's events.

- ODBCDirect is an ideal way to write code that has to switch back and forth between an Oracle and an Access database.

Typical Code

As you can see in Listing 12.4, the object model ODBCDirect uses is the same as DAO/JET except for a couple of differences: ODBCDirect supports a Connection object and RDO's greater number of options for creating result sets. The Connection object is a great improvement compared to DAO's requirement for multiple connections. The code first creates a Connection object in an ODBC workspace and then creates a Recordset against the connection.

Listing 12.4

```
Private Sub FetchODBCDirect()

    Dim cn As Connection
    Dim rsMovies As Recordset
    Dim strSQL As String
    Dim strConn As String
    Dim iField As Integer

    '   Connect to the database
    DBEngine.DefaultType = dbUseODBC

    strConn = "ODBC;DSN=movies;UID=video_user;PWD=ummagumma;"

    Workspaces(0).DefaultCursorDriver = dbUseNoCursor
    Set cn = Workspaces(0).OpenConnection("movies", dbDriverNoPrompt, _
            False, strConn)

    '   Run the query
    strSQL = "SELECT * FROM video_store.movies ORDER BY movie_id"
    Set rsMovies = _
        cn.OpenRecordset(strSQL, dbOpenForwardOnly, 0, dbReadOnly)

    '   Display the fields
    While Not rsMovies.EOF
        For iField = 0 To rsMovies.Fields.Count - 1
            Debug.Print rsMovies(iField)
```

```
        Next ' iField
        rsMovies.MoveNext
    Wend

    Set rsMovies = Nothing
    Set cn = Nothing

End Sub
```

The ODBC API

ODBC is implemented in Windows as most things are, with its own Application Programming Interface (API). The ODBC API provides a way to get down to low-level function calls with a C language interface (see Figure 12.6). The API bypasses most of the overhead associated with the higher-level interface normally presented to VB and should, accordingly, provide a much higher level of performance. This method is familiar to Windows programmers who can squeeze the last drop of performance from an API to get to functions that would remain unavailable to other programmers. In fact, there were not many alternatives before Visual Basic.

FIGURE 12.6:

The software layers used by the ODBC API

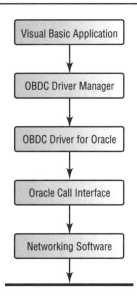

Features

- ODBC API is available as 16- or 32-bit API calls.

- ODBC API supports any function ODBC can support, which includes any of the features you can use in other data-access methods:

  - Retrieval of result sets

  - Calling stored procedures

  - Retrieval of output parameters from stored procedures

  - Asynchronous operation

  - Event handling for database access

Disadvantages

This book will not cover ODBC API programming in any detail. Although there are many development shops that still use the ODBC API for communicating with remote databases (because it has historically been faster and more feature capable), there are fewer reasons for doing so, especially as you now have ActiveX Data Objects for performance and Oracle Objects for OLE for support of all the features the Oracle server can produce. There are significant disadvantages to using the ODBC API, and these are listed below.

- ODBC API requires far more code to be written than any other method available, with the associated maintenance concerns.

- The code can take much longer to write and test.

- Error handling is restricted to in-line return-code management.

- Comparatively few developers are fully conversant with the API, which poses long-term maintenance difficulties.

- The ODBC API no longer has sufficient performance advantages to make it a viable development project, especially compared to a forward-only, read-only Recordset in ADO.

- The ODBC API's long-term future is now in doubt with the introduction of OLE-DB.

Typical Code

For an example of the kind of program you will have to write with the ODBC API, look over the code in Listing 12.5. This code shows how much more work you have to do, calling API functions for everything. We first create a connection handle and make the connection (a handle is a pointer to an object and is fundamental to working with the ODBC API). Next, we create a SQL-statement handle and execute the statement. We retrieve the fields in the result set and finally close the connection and all the handles we have used.

Listing 12.5

```
Private Sub FetchOdbcApi()

    Dim henv As Long
    Dim hdbc As Long
    Dim hstmt As Long
    Dim rc As Integer
    Dim strConnect As String
    Dim connectOut As String * 255
    Dim connectOutLen As Integer
    Dim strSQL As String
    Dim rCols As Integer
    Dim sValue As String * 101
    Dim iCol As Integer
    Dim lValueLen As Long
    Dim ivalueLen As Integer
    Dim strfield

    rc = SQLAllocEnv(henv)
    rc = SQLAllocConnect(ByVal henv, hdbc)

    connectOutLen = 0
    connectOut = String(255, 0)
    connect = "dsn=movies;uid=video_user;pwd=ummagumma"
    rc = SQLDriverConnect(hdbc, Me.hWnd, connect, Len(strConnect), _
        connectOut, 255, connectOutLen, SQL_DRIVER_COMPLETE)

    rc = SQLAllocStmt(hdbc, hstmt)

    strSQL = "SELECT * FROM video_store.movies "
    rc = SQLExecDirect(hstmt, strSQL, Len(strSQL))
    rc = SQLNumResultCols(hstmt, rCols)
```

```
        Do
            rc = SQLFetch(hstmt)
            If rc = SQL_SUCCESS Or rc = SQL_SUCCESS_WITH_INFO Then
                sValue = String(101, 0)
                For iCol = 1 To rCols
                    rc = SQLGetData(hstmt, i, SQL_C_CHAR, sValue, 100, _
                        lValueLen)
                    If lValueLen > 0 Then
                        strfield = Left(sValue, lValueLen)
                    Else
                        strfield = ""
                    End If
                    Debug.Print strfield
                Next
            End If

        Loop While rc = SQL_SUCCESS

        rc = SQLFreeStmt(hstmt, SQL_CLOSE)
        rc = SQLDisconnect(hdbc)
        rc = SQLFreeConnect(hdbc)
        rc = SQLFreeEnv(henv)

    End Sub
```

NOTE

The sample code in Listing 12.5 has been simplified for the purposes of the example. In particular, the error checking has been removed.

As you can see, calling the API does not come without significant effort on your part. If you are used to programming with DAO, you may be shocked to find how much it does for you behind the scenes. You have to understand exactly what low-level functions are being executed and to allow for all eventualities. The learning curve can be many times longer than with any other access methods. Though many programmers have become experts in these techniques, the advantages of writing to the API that once existed are lessening every month.

The reason for the change in the ODBC API's importance is that with the introduction of RDO, we have a thin wrapper layer on top of the API, one that masks off all the intricacies. The advantages of RDO over DAO is that the performance is almost as good as the API. The data-access methods in RDO are written by development teams who fully understand how to optimize the access of data, and the code produced with them can be as fast as, or faster than, the typical API code we may write. With ADO, we now have the capability of a high-level interface, which, in the right circumstances (forward-only, read-only cursors), can be considerably faster than the ODBC API. As a result, this book will not cover the ODBC API in detail; if you insist on using it, there are several resources available to you, including the ODBC API Developers Kit from Microsoft.

NOTE   Given the current availability of RDO and ADO and the move by Microsoft toward the new standard of OLE-DB, I cannot imagine a situation in which a new project should be started by coding in the ODBC API. Having a batch of expert API programmers would be tempting, but severe long-term maintenance problems will still occur. Die-hard API programmers may well disagree, but the cost to a project in terms of implementation time, maintainability, and durability are probably more than any project manager is willing to accept.

ActiveX Data Objects

ActiveX Data Objects (ADO) is the latest and current Microsoft data-access standard, so its terminology may be less familiar to you than the others. As we saw in Chapter 11, *Client-Side Technology*, ADO is a data consumer for an OLE-DB provider. The use of OLE-DB means we have a vast array of potential data sources; we are no longer restricted to the traditional sources, such as relational databases, but we now have access to everything from text files and e-mail systems to a nuclear-power station monitoring system.

As an Oracle user, you are mainly interested in that one data source. You can access Oracle through the OLE-DB provider for ODBC as well as a native provider that has been released for Visual Basic 6. You can see these alternative routes in the software layers shown in Figure 12.7.

FIGURE 12.7:

The software layers used
by ADO

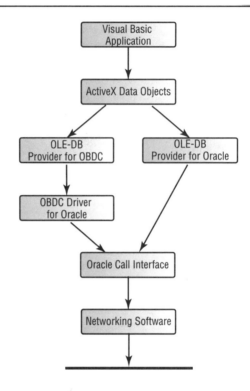

ADO has been around for some time. Originally released as part of Microsoft Data Access Components (MDAC), ADO 1.5 became the core data-access technique for use with Active Server Pages (ASP). ASP is a server-side scripting language that provides Microsoft Internet Information Server (IIS) the ability to produce active Web pages much more efficiently than using CGI scripting, which is the traditional approach. Within the ASP framework, ADO provides an efficient and scalable method of accessing data sources from within a Web page. ADO is also eminently suitable for application components that run under Microsoft Transaction Server (MTS). We will cover ADO in detail in Chapter 17, *ActiveX Data Objects*.

Features

- ADO is available in only 32-bit form.

- The current version is ADO 2.0 and is released with Visual Basic 6.

- ADO leads to much lighter weight client code and is suitable to Web development in which it is already a standard for Active Server Pages.

- ADO has a Connection object and allows you to create a connection through a Recordset or Command object.

- ADO has fast access to Oracle, especially with the native OLE-DB provider. A forward-only, read-only cursor can be twice as fast as RDO.

- ADO gives the developer access to many advanced features in the database, such as retrieving PL/SQL tables (through the correct ODBC driver).

- ADO supports the Command object to set up an object for retrieving result sets and calling stored procedures.

- ADO supports a Parameters collection for running parameterized Command queries. Parameters also allows you to return output parameters from stored procedures.

- ADO can process asynchronous queries.

- ADO has a full event model.

- The Data Environment is an ADO-based graphical tool used to make accessing data a simpler process.

Typical Code

Listing 12.6 shows a typical piece of code for accessing a Recordset from ADO. In this case, the OLE-DB native provider for Oracle is used, and the Recordset defaults to forward-only, read-only. The code creates a connection to the Oracle database and then creates a Recordset. After walking through the Recordset, the code closes the Recordset and the connection.

Listing 12.6

```
Private Sub FetchADO()

    Dim cn As Connection
    Dim rsMovies As ADODB.Recordset
    Dim strConn As String
    Dim iField As Integer

'   Connect to the database
    Set cn = New ADODB.Connection
```

```
With cn
    .CursorLocation = adUseClient
    .Provider = "MSDAORA"
End With
cn.Open "source=movies;user id=video_user;password=ummagumma;"

' Run the query
Set rsMovies = New ADODB.Recordset
rsMovies.Open "SELECT * FROM video_store.movies", cn

' Display the fields
While Not rsMovies.EOF
    For iField = 0 To rsMovies.Fields.Count - 1
        Debug.Print rsMovies(iField)
    Next ' iField
    rsMovies.MoveNext
Wend

Set rsMovies = Nothing
Set cn = Nothing

End Sub
```

Oracle Objects for OLE

Although Microsoft has provided us with a myriad of data models whose names confuse us (never mind trying to compare which one is the best to use in each circumstance), Oracle Corporation has provided us with one basic model, Oracle Objects for OLE (OO4O). It is an in-process OLE server (comes in dll form) that provides an object hierarchy remarkably similar to DAO yet does not use the ODBC standard; it talks to Oracle by the Oracle Call Interface, a native-code driver (see the software layers in Figure 12.8). It is unfortunate that this product is that it is not more widely used. You will not get more overall functionality with any other product when accessing Oracle databases, and it is a mature and stable product. OO4O will not be useful if you have to access other databases, so keep that in mind if you have a multivendor database site.

Unlike the other database-access technologies, OO4O has more frequent updates, and you should try to get hold of the latest versions, which often represent minor bug fixes as well as feature and performance enhancements. The most recent improvements in versions 2.2 and 2.3 have been to make the product more compatible with Web-based environments and useable in MTS. Version 2.3 also supports a Connection Pool Management facility. This feature allows you to create a pool of frequently used objects, such as OraDatabase objects, so in an environment in which users are continually connecting and disconnecting (such as a Web application), the objects can remain open and active and not continually reconnected.

Generally, OO4O is the data-access method in which you will find the most support for features of the Oracle database. It is also the product that will probably be the first to support the object-relational features of Oracle8. However, there is a wide range of functionality we will see in Chapter 18, *Oracle Objects for OLE*.

FIGURE 12.8:

The software layers used by OO4O

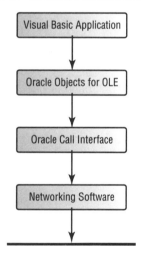

Features

- You can download Oracle Objects for OLE from the Oracle Web site or find it on your Oracle server disk.

- OO4O is available in 16-bit and 32-bit versions (though the latest methods are restricted to 32-bit). The current version is 2.3.

- OO4O has easier setup with direct access to the database alias name.

- OO4O has the object hierarchy familiar to DAO and RDO users.

- OO4O supports retrieving and updating result sets through the *dynaset* object.

- OO4O supports a connection-based Parameters collection, which become SQL and PL/SQL bind variables.

- OO4O can call stored procedures with parameters, enabling you to use input and output parameters.

- OO4O can retrieve PL/SQL tables.

- OO4O can retrieve result sets from stored procedures (via PL/SQL cursor variables).

- OO4O does not support asynchronous operation or events.

- The OO4O Data Control makes use of shared connections.

NOTE   It should be pointed out that while you can only access Oracle databases with OO4O, it is theoretically possible to access other SQL databases, such as Microsoft SQL Server, through one of Oracle's gateway products. This combination should be used only as a last resort because you will lose much functionality with the database behind the gateway, and performance will be less than impressive.

Typical Code

In OO4O, the connection is much simpler (and less feature rich). You simply enter your user name, password, and the database alias. The object model is similar to that of DAO, with the noticeable difference that all objects are preceded by "Ora". The code creates an OraSession object and an associated OraDatabase object. It then creates an OraDynaset to hold retrieved result sets. Finally, the OraDynaset and OraDatabase objects are closed.

Listing 12.7

```
Private Sub FetchOO4O()

    Dim OraSession As Object
    Dim OraDatabase As Object
    Dim rsMovies As Object
```

```
Dim strSQL As String
Dim iField As Integer


'   Connect to the database
Set OraSession = CreateObject("OracleInProcServer.XOraSession")
Set OraDatabase = OraSession.OpenDatabase("beq-local", _
                    "video_user/ummagumma", ORADB_DEFAULT)

'   Run the query
strSQL = "SELECT * FROM video_store.movies ORDER BY movie_id"
Set rsMovies = OraDatabase.CreateDynaset(strSQL, ORADYN_READONLY)

'   Display the fields
While Not rsMovies.EOF
    For iField = 0 To rsMovies.Fields.Count - 1
        Debug.Print rsMovies(iField)
    Next ' iField
    rsMovies.MoveNext
Wend

Set rsMovies = Nothing
Set OraSession = Nothing

End Sub
```

Comparison of Object Models

Although we shall go into the object models used by the various data-access techniques in Chapters 14 to 18, this is a good place to compare the different objects
the object models expose to developers. Table 12.1 gives an overview of the major
objects in each of the five models we will look at in detail. Because there is not a
one-to-one correspondence between object models, the table is mainly for comparison purposes. However, you can see that ADO has the simplest model of all,
dispensing with much of the setup that dominates the majority of the methods. It
also becomes immediately clear DAO/JET has the least functionality, and many
of the more interesting features of the other methods are missing.

TABLE 12.1: Comparing the Major Objects of the Various Data Access Models

DAO/Jet	RDO	ODBCDirect	ADO	OO4O
DBEngine	rdoEngine	DBEngine	N/A	OraClient
Workspace	rdoEnvironment	Workspace	N/A	OraSession
Database	N/A	Database	N/A	OraDataBase
N/A	rdoConnection	Connection	Connection	OraConnection
N/A	rdoQuery	QueryDef	Command	OraSQLStmt
N/A	rdoParameter	Parameter	Parameter	Parameter
Recordset	rdoResultset	Recordset	Recordset	OraDynaset
TableDef	rdoTable	TableDef	N/A	N/A
Field	rdoColumn	Field	Field	OraField
N/A	N/A	N/A	Property	N/A
Error	rdoError	Error	Error	LastServerError

Exporting an Access Table to Oracle

When you first start working with Oracle, you may well have the task of migrating an existing database to Oracle. I have come across several cases in which a Microsoft Access table is migrated from a work group situation (or maybe a prototype) up to a corporate database. Although Microsoft SQL Server has many upsizing wizards to handle this situation, we have to do a little more thinking when moving up to Oracle.

Microsoft Access Export

One possibility for moving a database from Access to Oracle is to use the Access export facility. The basic process is as follows:

1. Start the Access database you want to export from (such as NWIND.MDB).

2. Select the Tables tab, and click the table you want to export. In this example, the Orders table was chosen).

3. Select File ➤ Save As/Export menu option.

4. Select "To an External File or Database," and click OK (see Figure 12.9).

5. Ignore all but the bottom of the dialog box (most of which is devoted to exporting to another Access database), and in the "Save Table 'Orders' in" dialog box, select the Save As Type as "ODBC Databases."

6. Specify the name of the Oracle table you want to export to (see Figure 12.10).

7. Select your ODBC data source, that is, the Oracle database. (In this case, Movies was selected because it already exists.)

8. Enter your user name and password. The table will be created in the default schema for the user name you choose, and the export will proceed.

FIGURE 12.9:

The export "Save As" dialog box

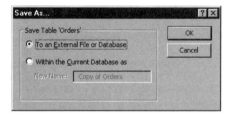

FIGURE 12.10:

Specifying the Oracle table to receive the Access export

TIP

In Oracle, the names of all objects are stored in capital letters. This can cause a problem if your access table or field names contain mixed lower- and uppercase letters or, even worse, a space. To use them in Oracle, you will have to enclose the name in double quotes. A much better solution is to change the Access table and column names to uppercase and no embedded blanks prior to exporting them. Then the transition is a little smoother.

WARNING   In the sample export shown previously, the table "Orders" was specifically chosen to work. Some of the other tables do not work because they try to create a table with more than one LONG column. This is an Oracle limitation. However, if you were to create a matching table in Oracle, you could use VARCHAR2 columns in place of memo fields and be successful with your export.

Although I have not covered it here, you can also import an Oracle database into Access. I expect there are fewer cases in which this method is valuable or even viable compared to exporting.

Viewing an Exported Table in Oracle

To ensure that the exported table is as it should be, you can see what tables you have in your Oracle database by entering the following command in an SQL*Plus session:

```
SELECT table_name FROM user_tables;
```

Then, for each table you are interested in, you can ensure their structure is correct by displaying it with

```
DESC table_name
```

If you have made a mistake or the structure is not correct, then drop the table as follows:

```
DROP TABLE table_name;
```

When you review what a typical export from Microsoft Access will accomplish, you will see it leaves a lot to be desired. In the following example, I created a table in Access with nine different column data types. I then exported it to Oracle and looked at the resultant table that was created. As you can see in Figure 12.11, the translation of data types is often unusable. At best, it can produce a poor database implementation.

FIGURE 12.11:

The structure of a table exported from Access to Oracle

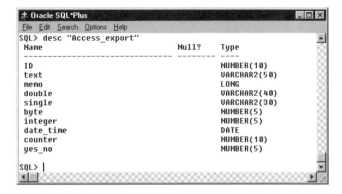

A much better solution for exporting Access databases to Oracle is to use the Oracle Export Wizard for Access that we will see in the next section. If you want to export data from another desktop application, you may be tempted to write your own code that can make more intelligent decisions about how to convert Access data types to Oracle. However, I recommend you become familiar with the SQL*Loader utility program in Chapter 8, *Updating Your Database,* because the program is a more efficient method for taking data from a desktop application into Oracle.

Oracle Export Wizard

A better alternative to the Access export function we saw previously is the Oracle Migration Wizard for MS Access. This product comes with the Oracle Server, so if you have Oracle, you should have this wizard. The product allows you to export the database definition or include all of the data.

The wizard is supplied as part of the Oracle Server software for NT without additional charge. The software used for these examples is for Oracle 7.3. You can start up the wizard by selecting it from the Programs ➢ Oracle Tools for NT option of the Start Menu.

1. Build up a list of Access databases to export. Start off with one small Access database until you have gone through the process successfully at least once (see Figure 12.12).

2. Next, you have an opportunity to customize the conversion of Access data types to Oracle data types. You will find the defaults are good enough for most circumstances.

3. You will now have the opportunity to customize the data object names. The Table names, Column names, and Index names are all pretty straightforward, and you can usually accept what the wizard comes up with. You should give some thought, however, to the Username and Tablespace Name tab (see Figure 12.13). The wizard will create a new user, tablespace, and associated file for you, and this is your chance to change it.

4. The following page of the wizard allows you to change migration options if you so wish.

5. You must next decide whether to migrate the structure or the structure and the data of the selected database.

6. Enter the user name and password for the migration process. You need administrative privileges to be able to create the tablespaces, new users, and other database objects; use the SYSTEM account if you do not have any other users with DBA privileges set up.

7. When you click OK, the process will start. Expect this to take several minutes for a small database or much longer if you have a large database to migrate.

8. When the process is complete, you have the option of reviewing a variety of reports, such as a log of any errors, SQL scripts to create the database objects, table descriptions, and so on.

FIGURE 12.12:

Building up the list of Access databases to export

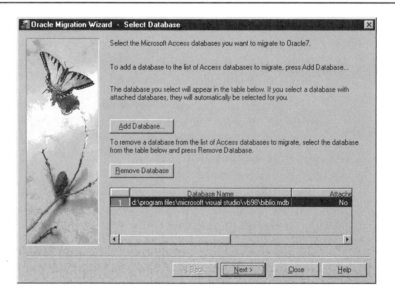

FIGURE 12.13:

Changing the default names
and properties created for the
Oracle database objects

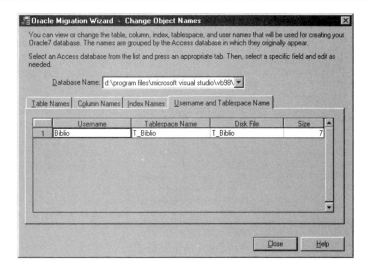

If you try this, you will notice the NWIND.MDB database is exported properly. The reports are excellent as is the tool. Several other benefits include

- Managing referential integrity.

- Allowing you to use Access forms, and reporting to work the new Oracle database.

- Working with databases with attached tables.

- Working with Access 2.0 (16-bit) and Access 7.0 (32-bit).

Summary

I have presented several different methods for accessing data from Visual Basic. We have barely mentioned other lesser-known methods. So which do you use? That is, in fact, a $64,000 question: the answer is perhaps more difficult and important given today's software-development costs. If you have the time, become familiar with as many of these techniques as possible. You may find that performance, capabilities, or even political concerns have an overriding influence. And personal likes and dislikes will also come into play. It can often be a personal decision, but don't base it on fear or ignorance of one or more of the products. Table 12.2 presents a personal summary of the products.

TABLE 12.2: The Available Technologies for Accessing Oracle Databases from Visual Basic

Technology	Opinion
Data Controls	Data Controls are an easy way to get started but have such great drawbacks that their use for anything but a short learning exercise or prototyping should be discouraged.
DAO	DAO provides good access to the basics of Oracle but will give you none of the benefits of the advanced Oracle features that are now available. Do not start a new project with DAO.
RDO	RDO is a step up from DAO and was the recommendation of Microsoft until the recent appearance of ADO.
ODBCDirect	ODBCDirect is also a step up from DAO and is valuable for providing an ODBC interface without the expense of RDO. With ADO, the popularity of ODBCDirect will probably wane.
ADO	ADO is now the flagship product from Microsoft, and the company has finally given a serious amount of thought to catering to Oracle databases. It is fast, powerful, and suitable for high-end databases as well as Web programming.
ODBC API	The ODBC API is a powerful but complicated programming technique that obtains its benefits at the expense of a great deal of complex development. It is only recommended if you are already using the API.
OO4O	Oracle Objects for OLE is the flagship product from Oracle and supports more of Oracle's capabilities than any other product. It is a stable and mature environment that will eventually be expanded to cover Oracle's object-relational features.

So which do we choose? If you have a current investment in software and developer experience, it is not worth changing the approach already chosen just for the sake of it. Chapters 14 to 18 will take you through the capabilities of your current technology and help you to wring the most functionality from it. These chapters will also pave the way for technologies you have not yet thought about or have not yet used.

When you are starting up new development projects, you should use ADO if you want to access more than just Oracle or you want to remain a Microsoft shop on the client side. You should use OO4O if you want to get the maximum functionality from your Oracle database, and you know you will never change to another database; OO4O is especially important if you know you will want to use new Oracle database features, which will take a long time to get into an OLE-DB provider (if they ever do). Combine either of these two selected technologies with a component-based methodology, and you are ready for whatever comes up.

Should you ever change your technology? The answer is probably yes, although choosing when that will be is a much more difficult decision. You should be aware of the features of each of the technologies and realize that moving between any of them is not a trivial thing to do (even between DAO/JET and ODBCDirect, if you want to make the move worthwhile). Plan your development now, keeping in mind that you will eventually change; an object-based approach should keep the turmoil to a minimum.

CHAPTER

THIRTEEN

13

Visual Basic Design Issues

- Logging On to the Database

- Views, Synonyms, and Schemas

- Cursor Selection

- Querying the Database

- Updating the Database

- Transaction Control

- Locking Issues

- Using BLOB-Type Data

- Error Handling

Now that we know the techniques for accessing data in an Oracle database from within your Visual Basic application, we should have a quick look at the types of things that we want to do with whichever method we select. We need to become familiar with several basic design issues, and these are outlined in the next few sections. These issues include

- Logging on to the database

- Views, synonyms, and schemas

- Cursor selection

- Querying the database

- Updating the database

- Transaction control

- Locking issues

- Using BLOB-type data

- Error handling

The Architecture Issue

One aspect of design that is beyond the scope of this book is architecture. In your future work, you should aim to design around the idea of components. In the simplest sense, your design can be represented in Visual Basic by individual classes that *encapsulate* access to certain types of data. For example, you could have one class that handles the saving of data to and retrieval of data from the Movies table. You do not have to separate this class off into a dll; you can run it inside the main client program, and it will still be a tiered design. As long as you have the correct design, you can easily scale it up and place the components on another machine at a later date. You will find that your Oracle application will sooner or later require this architecture, so you should design the application with this in mind at the beginning.

Logging On to the Database

Whenever you access an Oracle database, your application has to go through the logon process. This process does not necessarily mean you will see a logon screen, but you can normally provide the user name and password in the application code. This is obviously not the most secure situation, but if you decide that this is the best way to run your code, then you should use the operating-system security to ensure that your Visual Basic application code, and hence the password, is not available to outsiders.

NOTE   You may want to embed a generic user name and password in your application code when writing data-access components that run in the middle tiers of a multi-tier application. These components can then be shared between different users. Again, make sure your code is protected.

However, you will normally be presented with a logon window by the ODBC Driver Manager. The exact layout of the window can differ between vendors. The Microsoft ODBC Driver for Oracle Connect window is shown in Figure 13.1.

FIGURE 13.1:

The Oracle logon window

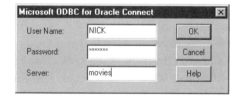

To log on to Oracle, you will have to enter your user name and the password given to you by the DBA. Sometimes you will be given the opportunity to enter a different connect string from the one you set up with your ODBC connection or, even more confusing, from the one you defined in your code. These situations are best avoided because, in the majority of cases, you will only confuse end users.

One way to avoid the logon window is to create your own logon window as shown in Figure 13.2. You can easily convert a text box into a password box by specifying the *password* property as "*". There are a few advantages to this:

- You can pass the user name and password to a middle tier for actually logging on. If you want the middle tier to log on for you, you must either have a fixed user name and password or pass the information to the components. You cannot have a middle-tier component directly prompt for any user information.

- Your own logon screen allows you to trap the password because in Oracle7, it cannot be found any other way. This method can, for example, allow you to write code for users to update their own passwords, which ensures the new password is different from the existing one.

FIGURE 13.2:

The Movies application logon window

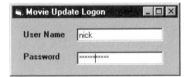

> **NOTE**
>
> One reason I needed this trapping of the user name and password was when one of my applications had to send data from the database to another server via FTP. Even though this was taking place in a secure site, I had to have another logon to the FTP server. To avoid the outrage of the users, I made sure that the two servers allowed the same passwords so, using the cached value, there was no need to manually log on a second time.

One way to improve the overall usefulness of the main application window is to include a status bar with relevant information. At a minimum, I like to include the user name, when they logged on, and in an environment where it is possible to access more than one Oracle instance, I include the instance service name. A nice touch is to add the version of the application being run. If you are using a minimal approach to error messages (see the section "Error Handling" in this chapter), then you can also put error messages in the status bar, perhaps in a red color so they stand out. Your main application window will start to look a little like Figure 13.3. To find these status bar values, use the code shown in Table 13.1.

FIGURE 13.3:

The main application window with status bar

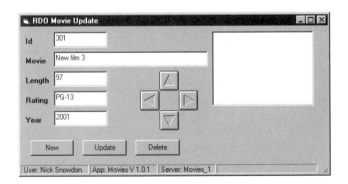

TABLE 13.1: Finding Application and Database Information for the Status Bar

INFORMATION	HOW TO GET IT
Application version	`App.Major & "." & App.Minor & "." & App.Revision`
User name	`SELECT USER FROM dual;`
Database name	`SELECT * FROM global_name;`

Views, Synonyms, and Schemas

Access to views, synonyms, and schemas has been a big problem for the Microsoft data-access methods, and these problems have typically revolved around the peculiarities of the ODBC drivers available. I should point out that Oracle Objects for OLE, which we will cover in Chapter 18, has none of these issues. We should expect no less because it is Oracle's own access method.

However, the problem remains that many installations use views or synonyms to hide the base tables of all queries. If you do not use synonyms, then you must be able to define schemas because your code points to exactly which Schema objects (such as tables or stored procedures) you want to access.

The good news is the ODBC driver for Oracle that comes with Visual Basic 6 and the latest data-access methods seem to have solved most of these problems, and you can quite happily use views, synonyms, and schemas in every aspect of ODBC access. The native OLE-DB provider for Oracle that comes with Visual Basic 6 does not have any problems either.

However, there appears to be a problem accessing PL/SQL packages through ODBC. If you currently need packages, you might need an older ODBC driver, or you might need to switch to ADO or OO4O. Remember that to specify a stored procedure in a package, you should use the *schema.package.procedure* syntax rather than the normal *schema.procedure*.

NOTE   One peculiarity here is with DAO/JET. To use schema names in a query without SQLPassThrough, you have to enclose both the schema and table name in square brackets, such as `SELECT * FROM [video_store.movies]`.

Cursor Selection

Throughout the second half of this book, you will find a pervasive theme about cursors. When you execute a query, Oracle provides result sets that are forward-only and read-only. Any scrollable or updatable cursors are implemented on the client side. If you use these additional features, your application is prone to display increasingly out-of-date information and will be more liable to update conflicts. Consequently, the application will not be scalable. You should aim for as little interaction with the data as possible and get in and out of the Oracle Server quickly. Transactions should be fast to reduce locking situations. Thus, we have a premise for the ultimate cursor.

The Ultimate Cursor

The ultimate cursor design for performance and scalability is no cursor. You should select the forward-only, read-only cursor. If you want scrollability, you can put all the data into a control, such as a grid or a spreadsheet. Whenever an update is needed, you use a stored procedure or some form of middle-tier component. The UPDATE command can also update the grid if you wish. This technique will effectively duplicate an updatable result set. If you requery the result set instead of updating it, you have come close to duplicating a dynamic cursor. The overhead should not be too high so long as the result set is small, which it should be anyway.

Communication between components should be as efficient and simple as possible, especially because we may be moving the representation of many rows and columns. The variant array is the best solution. It is a read-only method, but the array fits in with the ultimate design. Variant arrays are flexible and adaptable to any design whether you are using a single-tier approach or Microsoft Transaction Server.

Querying the Database

There is little use for a database application that cannot read data from the database. You will normally retrieve data from Oracle with SQL Queries, which were covered in some detail in Chapter 7, *Queries*. However, now that we are moving on to Visual Basic, we need to put our SQL queries into our Visual Basic code.

This process is usually done with statements that create Recordsets (or rdoResultsets in RDO and OraDynasets in OO4O). Using Recordsets is an easy way to create an object that gives us access to all the data in our query.

The creation of simple Recordsets is as far as DAO will take us, but RDO can also easily retrieve result sets from stored procedures. This feature, which goes back to the days when Microsoft SQL Server and Sybase were the same product, is borne of the fact that any SELECT statement in a stored procedure returns the result of that SELECT in a Recordset *by default*. This feature is further exploited in RDO by allowing you to retrieve more than one rdoResultset from a stored procedure at the same time. Unfortunately, Oracle does not actually allow the SELECT statement in a stored procedure (though there is the limited SELECT INTO version as we saw in Chapter 10, *Creating Stored Procedures*). As a result, there is no simple way to return a result set from a stored procedure with Oracle, and the multiple rdoResultset is out of reach.

NOTE   The latest versions of the ADO and OO4O allow you to simulate the returning of result sets, though the technique is more complicated. See Chapter 17, *ActiveX Data Objects,* and Chapter 18, *Oracle Objects for OLE,* in which the vastly different approaches are explored.

One thing you must remember is SELECT strings for queries are seldom completely hard-coded. You will usually build them up piece by piece. Creating the string can sometimes take many, many lines, and it is better to break up the strings into separate statements rather than use continuation lines excessively (see Listing 13.1). The main thing to keep in mind is that you are usually creating a string using Oracle syntax. You must ensure that values coming from Visual Basic text boxes, list boxes, and the like are treated as the correct data type. In particular, you must enclose character strings in single quotes, making sure that single quotes within a string are converted to two single quotes and that dates are converted to the correct format (see Chapter 7, *Queries,* for more information and a couple of Visual Basic functions for formatting dates).

Listing 13.1

```
' Set up the SQL string
strSQL = "SELECT * FROM movies "
strSQL = strSQL & " WHERE rating = '" & cmbRating.text & "'"
strSQL = strSQL & "  AND year > " & txtYear
strSQL = strSQL & "  ORDER BY movie_name"
```

Once you have put together a SELECT statement string, remember that the exact same string should work in a SQL*Plus session. I find it useful to place a multiline scrolling text box on any form that executes a query. This text box is normally invisible. As part of the application's preferences, I allow the user to switch on the debugging output of which this text box is one source. In this case, the text box will become visible on the form. You should also make sure you can copy the string into the Windows clipboard. Then, you could run the exact query in SQL*Plus and use it to show an execution plan. It is a tool like this that will make you the envy of those working with Oracle Developer 2000.

FIGURE 13.4:

Showing the SQL string on a form in Debug mode

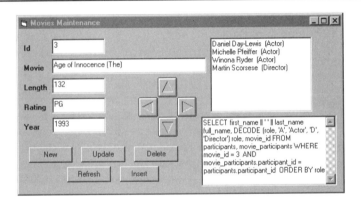

The code you execute might look something like Listing 13.2 (in this case, it is for RDO). Notice that the SQL string is also placed on the clipboard so that it is even easier to put it in another application or analysis tool.

Listing 13.2

```
Set rsParticipants = cn.OpenResultset(strSQL, rdOpenStatic, _
                     rdConcurReadOnly)

txtSQL = strSQL
If bDebug Then
'    Display the SQL string if in debug mode
     txtSQL.Visible = True
     Clipboard.SetText strSQL    ' For the really lazy !
Else
     txtSQL.Visible = False
End If
```

If you are working in the development environment, you can simply write the SQL string to the watch window with `DEBUG.PRINT`; however, the text box method is much more flexible.

A real advance in using SQL commands is to set up an object that can handle the query, parse it locally, and enable you to parameterize it. Most of the data-access methods allow you to do these steps, and you should make full use of the features. These objects are

- QueryDef (ODBCDirect)

- rdoQuery (RDO)

- Command (ADO)

- OraSQLStmt (OO4O)

Each of the following relevant chapters details the techniques, which you should use for any SQL command you execute more than a few times.

Updating the Database

When updating your Oracle database, you will have to spend some time during the application-design phase deciding how you want to handle this process. The topic is dealt with from an Oracle point of view in Chapter 8, *Updating Databases*, but it is more important at this point to decide exactly how you want to deal with ease of use versus security.

The ease of updating a database certainly comes with the Data Controls and associated bound controls, and it's almost as easy with updatable result sets. There are two better ways to solve this problem, but they both involve more work on your part. The first way to do your updates is by executing INSERT, UPDATE, and DELETE SQL statements from the Visual Basic application (this could be at the client level or in the middle tier of a multitier application), but the most secure is to do all updates through stored procedures.

If you have an established enterprise database environment with a high emphasis on security, it is very likely that the only updates you will be allowed to do are through stored procedures. If you are setting up a new environment and you care about the security of your data, then you should spend time learning how to write stored procedures (see Chapters 9 and 10) and rigorously implement them. Chapter 14, *Data Access Objects*, includes a short application, which eases the pain of creating a PL/SQL procedure for every operation on every table.

Transaction Control

We have seen how Oracle handles transaction control in Chapter 8, *Updating Your Database*, but Visual Basic, through ODBC, can handle this task, as well. The two methods are fundamentally different, however. By default, ODBC and Visual Basic run in Autocommit mode, meaning that any change is automatically committed to the database as soon as it occurs. The reason for this ODBC behavior is that it is the default mode for Microsoft SQL Server databases. You will recognize this feature if you have used updatable result sets. If you use the Update method, the change is immediately committed. You do not have anything further to do.

Whichever method you choose, make sure you place only the minimum number of DML statements into the transaction necessary to support the business rules. Any more and you unnecessarily lock too many rows.

Using Visual Basic to Control Transactions

To implement transaction control in Visual Basic, you need to make use of three commands, which are the same for all the different data-access methods we discuss in this book:

BeginTrans   Marks the beginning of a transaction.

CommitTrans   Commits the changes to the database (executes the Oracle COMMIT command).

Rollback   Rolls back any uncommitted changes (executes the Oracle ROLLBACK command).

NOTE   The BeginTrans method is somewhat artificial as far as Oracle is concerned. It is better to think of it as switching the Autocommit off rather than taking a positive action.

These three commands are only of any use with updatable result sets. Although the result set will show the changes, they will not be visible to any other users until the CommitTrans method is executed. The main feature missing from the transaction control method is the inability to nest transactions in the same way as Oracle's SET TRANSACTION command does.

A simple example of how to control transactions from the user interface is shown for DAO in Listing 13.3. Two buttons control the start and end of the transaction. In reality, you will probably code the transaction inside the application in a place appropriate to the business rules. Notice you have to be careful about which object is the one you use for transaction control; in this case, it is the current workspace. In RDO, it will be the Connection or Environment objects and the Connection object in ADO.

Listing 13.3

```
Private Sub cmdTransaction_Click(Index As Integer)
    If Index = 0 Then
        Workspaces(0).BeginTrans
    Else
        Workspaces(0).CommitTrans
    End If
End Sub
```

If you are doing many repetitive updates—for example, importing a file of data into the database—you may find that combining a query-type object with transaction control can dramatically improve your execution time. For example, a group of rdoQueries can be made several times faster, simply by including them in a transaction.

Using Oracle to Control Transactions

As you will see throughout the book, updatable result sets tend to be restricted in use to low-end, low-volume systems. However, as you move up the ladder toward high-throughput enterprise systems, you will be forced to move toward the optimum situation of forward-only, read-only result sets. You will probably be doing updates by stored procedures.

All of the data-access technologies we cover in this book allow you to execute SQL statements from Visual Basic via an Execute method. This method is discussed in each relevant chapter. With any of these methods, if you take the stored procedure route (or even execute DML statements INSERT, UPDATE, and DELETE from Visual Basic), you will have a few alternatives for controlling transactions:

- Include a COMMIT statement in every stored procedure.

- Pass a flag to the stored procedure that indicates if the changes should be committed. This is more flexible than the previous method but requires you to pass an extra parameter.

- Execute a COMMIT or ROLLBACK SQL statement from Visual Basic. This is easy to do, but it requires an extra round-trip over the network.

- If you use an anonymous PL/SQL code block to update your data, you can include a COMMIT statement along with your INSERT, UPDATE or DELETE statement. Chapter 15, *Remote Data Objects*, covers this topic.

You need to carefully think about how you want to control your transactions. DAO and the Oracle database do not explicitly commit after a SQL statement is executed, but RDO and ADO, for example, commit by default. If you are going to use these technologies and still want to use the transaction control techniques shown above, you will have to use the BeginTrans method before you execute your DML statements. In this way, you can not only use explicit transaction control but you can also use more sophisticated Oracle techniques for nested transactions with the SAVEPOINT SQL command.

Using a Transaction Server

The final technique for transaction control is to use a Transaction Processing Monitor. The one most in the news for Visual Basic developers is Microsoft Transaction Server (MTS); however, these systems have been in place for decades and were used in mainframe systems, such as CICS.

If you are developing an application of any major size, you should be developing with an object-oriented approach and creating software components that encapsulate a small and discrete amount of functionality. The Visual Basic documentation is very good on this topic. Microsoft proposes a *services*-based architecture, which is not really any different than a multitier architecture, but the service terminology is less likely to confuse developers into thinking every tier has to be on a separate machine.

In the Microsoft view of the world, there are several service layers we need to be aware of, and the middle-tier services will all be written in Visual Basic and run on a Windows NT server under MTS. The services layers are

1. User services: the GUI interface, which should be thin (but not dumb).

2. Business services: this is where you put your business rules, such as when a movie becomes overdue or when charging for an overdrawn account.

3. Data services: these services provide the interface to the data source. Often they will be combined with the business services but do not have to be. These data-service components can use stored procedures or SQL commands, but the transaction control is managed through MTS, not directly by the application.

On the opposing front, the Oracle view of the world is quite happy with this services model, but the middle-tier services are usually written in PL/SQL as stored procedures and can be moved onto another server under the Oracle-application Web server. These services will eventually be written in Java.

Both Microsoft's and Oracle's preferred methodologies are somewhat difficult to implement at the present time. Oracle is XA-compliant, a requisite for working with Microsoft Transaction Server, but there are many issues to be careful of. MTS is beyond the scope of this book; however, there are notes in the VB6 documentation that will assist you. The Oracle Application Server may soon support Visual Basic (via COM).

Locking Issues

Oracle has a very good locking scheme, which we covered in Chapter 2, *Oracle Database Architecture* and which takes care of most of the situations you are likely to encounter. However, you should be aware of exactly how locking affects your application and what decisions you must make that will affect the locking that does take place.

First, a quick recap of Oracle's locking strategy: whenever you do an update or delete, an *exclusive lock* is placed on the affected row or rows. Other users can still read those affected rows, but they cannot alter them until the first user commits the changes. The data other users retrieve is based on the values that were current before the rows were updated and locked. When you select data rows from the database, you get a consistent view that does not include any rows with exclusive locks in any uncommitted transactions in the system. Reading a row doesn't put any kind of lock on the row.

With a read-only scrollable cursor, every selected column of every selected row is, as much as possible, pulled into memory on the client machine. This Recordset is a snapshot of the data and will never include any changes made to records by other users that were committed after you created your Recordset. To see any changes, you will have to rebuild the Recordset (usually with the Refresh method). If you take this read-only approach, then the only way to update the data is by executing SQL statements or calling stored procedures; these are features all of the data-access technologies allow you to do, some better than others. However, one thing is sure: you do not have to worry about locking. There is no way to tell whether you are reading a row someone has a lock on.

With an updatable Recordset, you have a few more issues to consider. You will be storing all the keys to the rows of the result set in memory on your client. With ODBC, as you access the data rows, the actual current data is pulled in from the database by the unique key. This does not lead to a consistent view of the database (a snapshot at one point in time). OO4O on the other hand pulls all the data into a local cache at the time you run the query. This is a consistent view. It is up to you to decide which route is preferable.

Whether you use ODBC or OO4O, any changes you make to the data are first reflected in the Recordset when you execute the AddNew or Edit methods and then typically made permanent in the database when you use the Update method. When you make changes to the data, you have to consider whether you want to lock the affected row when you do the AddNew or Edit (*optimistic locking*) or whether you want to leave the lock until the Update (*pessimistic locking*).

Optimistic locking is normally the default locking scheme, and the data-access method will take care of that for you. This scheme is also Oracle's natural locking scheme. If you try to update a row that someone else has locked, you may find your application hangs until that lock is released. How the data-access method you are using reacts to this situation can vary, and you should experiment because this situation is likely to be a problem.

Pessimistic locking against Oracle databases is more difficult to achieve than optimistic locking. This is because pessimistic locking relates to the situation in which Microsoft SQL Server locks a page (which can contain many rows of data) as soon as you execute the Edit method. There is no page locking in Oracle (which does not need it) and no natural equivalent of pessimistic locking. If you are using read-only Recordsets, you do not have the option of automatically locking the row anyway. If you want to lock the specific row when you start the Edit rather than at the

Update method, then you will have to do this step manually. To do this manually, you need to use a more advanced form of the SELECT SQL statement. This statement accesses one or more rows and readies them for update. This statement places an exclusive lock on the rows, so make sure you do not hold the lock for too long. The statement is shown in Listing 13.4 and must be executed as a normal SQL command. Notice the NOWAIT option is included, so your application does not hang waiting for someone else's lock to be resolved; instead, the command immediately fails if a lock occurs.

Listing 13.4

```
strSQL = "SELECT * FROM movies WHERE movie_id = 132" & _
         " FOR UPDATE NOWAIT
```

You should use caution with the SELECT FOR UPDATE command because it may interfere with the normal working of whichever data-access method you are using. Try to restrict its use to read-only Recordsets.

NOTE   In comparison to the ODBC locking method, OO4O only has pessimistic-type locking in the OraDynasets. OO4O includes a SELECT FOR UPDATE command internally as soon as the Edit method is executed.

Using BLOB-Type Data

The term *BLOB* is given to data larger than normal and usually binary in nature. (BLOB is an acronym for Binary Large Object.) Oracle does not use this term but prefers the term *LOB*. Handling large columns in Oracle, especially when they contain binary data, is not a trivial matter. Large columns may be easier to handle in Visual Basic than Oracle, but they still require some careful planning. Luckily, there are techniques common to all the data-access methods you will see in this book: these are the GetChunk and AppendChunk methods.

GetChunk   Read a block of data from the table column.

AppendChunk   Append a block of data to the table column.

There are several good examples of using AppendChunk and GetChunk in the Visual Basic help files that apply to Oracle, among other databases. The major practical problem is that large amounts of data are moved between the application and the database, and the variables used for this purpose must be large enough to contain the whole column value. If BLOBs were handled in the same way as ordinary columns, then vast amounts of memory would be required to hold the bound variables.

NOTE   RDO allows you to determine the maximum column size that can be bound to the rdoColumn object. You can retrieve this size from the BindThreshold property of the rdoQuery object.

There are situations when reading and writing BLOBs is a worthwhile pursuit. However, rather than running headlong into this activity without thinking about it, you should consider why you are storing BLOBs in the database in the first place. Are you storing images for delivery to a Web browser? Is it a glorified filing system for Word documents? I have even seen BLOBs used for storing application .exe files.

In many cases, the database is used to store these files because the capability is there. Once you have your Oracle hammer, everything begins to look like a nail. The alternative is to store the files as files! If you need a reference to the file, simply store the file's fully qualified name (on a common network file server), and program your application around it. You will achieve *far* better performance.

This is not to say you shouldn't store BLOBs in your database. Some of the new tools that Oracle provides, such as the ConText option for indexing every word in a text document or the amazing Image Processing options that allow you to scan stored images for colors and textures, demand that the data be stored in the database. But even Oracle has allowed for storing very large files externally: Oracle8 introduced the new data type BFILE, which allows up to 4GB of binary data to be held outside of the database.

WARNING   One thing to keep in mind when dealing with binary data is Visual Basic uses Unicode strings that take up two bytes per character. Because Oracle is expecting raw data with single-byte encoding, you will end up with bizarre problems if you hold the binary data in strings. Instead, you should use byte arrays.

Error Handling

Whenever you start to design an application around a database, you are dealing with different types of errors from what you would normally encounter. Even more than usual, you need to adopt a standardized approach to error handling and ensure that your application can cope with an error in *any* module; something will always happen where you never thought it could. This section will cover the basics.

Trapping Errors

Visual Basic provides us with a few statements that allow us to choose the type of error handling we want to invoke. In other languages you may have seen return codes that you can test and exception handling where you can jump to an error-handling routine. Visual Basic provides both of these techniques. In practice, you may use more than one of these statements in a single procedure. It is up to you as the developer to understand all the different techniques and implement them as you think works best. The error-trapping statements are

On Error Goto label   The most commonly used error-trapping technique is *exception handling*, which means to jump to a piece of code that handles the error (see Listing 13.5). There is an unwritten convention that error-handling code such as this will be at the end of the procedure or function; you will usually precede it with an Exit Sub statement so your code will not execute it.

On Error Resume Next   This is an alternative to the exception-handling technique that switches error trapping off. If you do this, the onus is on you to check every time to ensure there are no errors. You will normally do this with the Err object.

On Error Goto 0   This statement is a bit of an oddity because it switches the error trapping to its default condition. In other words, after this statement, any errors will not be trapped in the current procedure and, if left unhandled, will eventually cause the application to abort with its familiar message box. This statement is necessary when you want to intentionally pass any errors back to their calling procedures, because any error that is not handled is passed back up the call stack.

Resume Next   This statement resumes execution after an error has occurred at the next line after the one that caused the error. It is perfect for finding out where the error actually did occur when you are debugging your application.

Raise   You should use the Raise method to create an error event. The type of place to use this statement is in a component where you do not want any interaction with the user to take place. If you raise a new error (for example, in the error-handling code), it will be passed back to the calling procedure to be handled there. An example of this is shown in Listing 13.5.

Default Behavior   The default behavior in any error situation is for Visual Basic to notify the user of the error with a message box and shut down. You should make it a point of honor that this will never happen to one of your applications.

Listing 13.5

```
Private Sub Demo ()

'    Application code

     Exit Sub

ErrorHandler:
     Err.Raise Err.Number, "ErrorDemo: Creating Recordset", _
               Err.Description
End Sub
```

Error Trapping in the Development Environment

More than once I have seen a programmer use the On Error Resume Next statement without effect. You should be aware that you can set error-trapping characteristics in the development project. To do this procedure, go to General in the Tools ➤ Options menu. If you have Break on All Errors selected, this will bypass all your error trapping (see Figure 13.5).

FIGURE 13.5:

Make sure the application
does not stop on all errors.

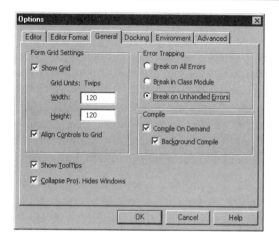

Developing an Error Message

An often-used technique in error handling is to display a message of what went wrong and include the error description. This message could be something as simple as a missing file, or it could be a complex message from Oracle. If you simply give the user this kind of message, they will usually be confused and probably intimidated. A much better solution is to provide a message that indicates

1. What went wrong, in simple terms

2. What they can do about it

3. Who to consult for assistance if the problem persists

A better design approach is to try to avoid error messages from ever happening. This usually involves good all-around design. The easiest way to do this is to restrict the information users can enter into your application. You should make full use of list boxes, check boxes, and option boxes. If at all possible, try to avoid combo boxes that allow the user to enter their own strings. However, you also should make it as easy as possible for a user to add a new value to a list box; they should not have to cancel a data-entry form to navigate a series of data-maintenance menus.

For a more subtle example of avoiding error messages, you should look at how users get access to the various parts of your application. If your business rules detect security violations, then they will raise an error condition. For example, if a user gets access to the Human Resources data-entry forms and tries to update them, your stored procedures would detect a security violation and raise an error condition. This security validation is vital, but wouldn't it be a big improvement to disable the menu item or form button that started the operation? You still need the back-end check, in case someone found a way around your code, but your application begins to look more polished and easy to use. Ideally, the user should never be in the situation in which they can cause a business-rule violation.

The big problem is knowing what operations each user is allowed to do. The technique I try to adopt is to have one table in the database that defines what privileges each user has. When the application is started, these tables are scanned to detect the user's privileges, and the forms and menus are adjusted accordingly. It is relatively quick to disable controls and menus or even make them invisible.

WARNING   Never put any error handler that requires user interaction into a component. You should either handle the error completely in the component or raise the error to the user-interface tier.

Error Windows or Status Lines?

There is a move away from using an Error window (whether it is a MsgBox statement or your own form) and toward using other techniques that do not interfere with the flow of using the application. The irony of this change is that not too long ago, when the only game in town was a dumb terminal, the status line was about the only way to notify a user of any errors. To a certain extent, a Web browser still operates in that mode.

Still the psychology of this move to status lines is quite understandable: having to click the OK button on an error window can become annoying. And how many times do you click a message box without even reading the message? I know I am not alone in doing that!

However, think twice before abandoning the error window completely. It has become a standard feature of Windows applications and users do not normally expect to have to keep an eye on a status bar. You might be able to compromise by putting business-rule violations in the status bar and system errors in an error window.

Logging Errors

Although errors resulting from a user violating business rules do not need to be retained, you should make a point of setting up a system to log all other errors, those you might think of as "serious" errors. These will usually be errors that come back from Oracle as well as errors "internal" to the application (a polite way of saying programming errors).

There are a variety of accepted methods to implement logging:

- Log to a file local to the user's computer.

- Log to a file on the network.

- Log to the database.

- Log to the user's Registry.

- Install an e-mail–based system.

E-mail Logging

I have found an e-mail–based system to be highly attractive. It gives fast notification of the error details to the developers. I have often corrected an error in the database before any users contacted me. Another advantage to this approach is users often do not like reporting errors because they feel responsible for "damaging" the program or do not want to appear stupid. The downside with e-mail is that it does not provide a historical record, so you may wish to combine it with another approach.

The amount of data you want to log is usually a personal decision, but you should consider the following list that has proved useful.

1. Data and time when the error occurred

2. The error number

3. The error message

4. The error source (which should identify the application, module, and procedure)

5. The Oracle user name

6. The application version number

7. The database name and version number if available

Oracle Errors

Throughout the rest of the book, you will see in each of the data-access methods specific collections used to report any errors from ODBC. For example, it may be the Errors or rdoErrors collections. If you just use the Err object from Visual Basic, then you will normally get only error number 3146, which means that there is an ODBC error. You will find that the error collection contains its most useful information in the first Error object (for example, Errors(0).Description). The form of this error message returned from ODBC is as follows:

[*vendor*] [*ODBC_component*] [*data_source*] *message*

An example is shown below:

```
S0022: [Microsoft][ODBC driver for Oracle][Oracle]ORA-00904: invalid
column name
```

The main thing to note with ODBC or OO4O is that the Oracle error message (in this case "ORA-00904: Invalid column name") will not mean much to the user, so your error-handling strategy must include presenting this message in a more satisfactory way. The best way to resolve the problem is simply to tell the user that there is an internal error and that they should contact a technical support person as soon as possible. Make sure the full error message is available somehow from the application: a "More Information" button works well.

TIP Some errors are "Application specific" and differ depending on which ODBC driver you use. To be proactive, find as many of the expected error messages from your ODBC driver as you can before you put your program into production. This applies especially to errors involving incorrect logon credentials and detecting an Oracle instance that has become unavailable.

Summary

In this chapter, we have covered some of the design issues you will find in Visual Basic, whichever data-access method you choose to use. We have covered how to create a more acceptable way to log on to the database compared with simply presenting the default ODBC Driver Manager dialog box. In addition, we discussed the process of selecting data from a database and updating it, including transaction control and any locking issues. We covered the use of BLOB-type data in the database and the preferable approach of storing data on a file server. We finished up with a brief look at error handling.

In the next few chapters, we will look in detail at each of the data-access methods that you as a Visual Basic developer have available.

CHAPTER
FOURTEEN

14

Data Access Objects

- The DAO Object Hierarchy

- Accessing a Database

- Creating Recordsets

- Executing SQL Commands

- Calling Stored Procedures

- Error Handling

- Putting It All Together

- Viewing and Using the Structure of a Database

- Drawbacks to DAO

Data Access Objects (DAO) is the name given to the object model for the JET engine. DAO has been around for years and has experienced many changes, but it is still a model designed for dealing with databases such as Microsoft Access. The ability to access ODBC data sources was added to DAO (and without that it would not appear in this book). DAO has also followed Visual Basic's lead by becoming, along with VB5, a 32-bit-only access method. If you want to access a 16-bit database, you will have to dig out your old versions.

Although DAO has the weakest functionality of any of the data-access techniques, it is the most widely known. It also exists in other environments, such as Microsoft Excel. If you have an application running satisfactorily in DAO, then you will probably not want to consider changing it. However, if you are creating a new project, you should give careful thought to using ODBCDirect, Remote Data Objects (RDO), or even better, ActiveX Data Objects (ADO). If you have an immediate need and DAO developers at hand, you may be happy with DAO for the time being, but you should gradually move away from this data-access model to ADO. You will have a learning curve, but you will be better off in the long run.

On the positive side, despite being limited to a JET database model, there is still a surprisingly large functionality for the Oracle user in the DAO model, and with the move to version 3.5, the performance in certain areas has become quite acceptable.

The topics we will cover in this chapter include

- The DAO object hierarchy

- Accessing a database

- Creating Recordsets

- Executing SQL commands

- Calling stored procedures

- Error handling

- Putting it all together

- Viewing and using the structure of a database

- Drawbacks to DAO

The DAO Object Hierarchy

Throughout the remaining chapters of this book, as we look at the various ways of interfacing with Oracle from Visual Basic, we will see an object-based approach to the techniques discussed. This means that under the top-level object of the DAO model, there is a hierarchy of other objects and their collections, each with their own properties and methods, that allows you to access the data in your database. The object-based model has proven easy to use and adaptable. In the case of DAO, the object hierarchy is shown in Figure 14.1. The higher-level objects in the hierarchy are then described individually.

FIGURE 14.1:

The Data Access Objects object hierarchy

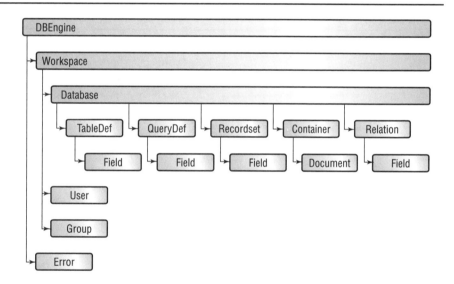

DBEngine

The top-level object in the DAO object hierarchy is the DBEngine. There can be only one DBEngine object, and it contains all the other objects in the hierarchy. You do not create the DBEngine object, because it is available to you by default, and you cannot create another one. The objects under the DBEngine are collections of objects, so for example, Errors is a collection of the Error objects. The DBEngine object contains the Workspaces and Error collections.

Workspace

Most of the DAO hierarchy lies under the Workspaces collection. A Workspace is an organizational structure that allows you to group database connections into a named area or session. You will need more than one workspace if you want to access groups of databases in different ways, such as one group through the JET engine and another through ODBCDirect (which we will cover in Chapter 16, *ODBCDirect*). In general though, you will probably be quite happy using the default Workspace called Workspaces(0) as we shall see in the next section. This Workspace is automatically opened as soon as you reference it and stays open until the end of your application. Under the JET engine, a Workspace object contains the Groups, Users, and Databases collections.

TIP   If you are only accessing one database, then you should use only the default Workspace. This step keeps your code shorter and easier to maintain.

Groups and Users

In a JET database, such as Microsoft Access, you may define workgroups consisting of Groups, Users, and their associated permissions for accessing the database. These objects are mainly used for Access databases in which the permissions are stored in the `system.mdw` file. Groups and Users have no value to an Oracle database user.

Database

The Database object is the most important object we will be dealing with because it allows us to interface with the database, view its structure, retrieve and update Recordsets from it, and execute SQL commands against the database. The Database object forms the basis of the rest of this chapter.

Accessing a Database

You may have noticed that if you choose the standard Exe project in Visual Basic, the Data Control is in the project by default; one click and you can put it on a form. If you are using VB6, do not choose the Data Project because this will add a reference to the ADO library. To make use of the Data Access Object library, you need to do a little more work. You have to add the library reference to the project. If you don't do this, your code will not run. To add the reference, use the following steps:

1. Choose Project ➤ References to open the References dialog box as shown in Figure 14.2. You will see a list of all the object libraries you can reference in your application.

2. Check the option labeled Microsoft DAO 3.51 Object Library (or 3.5 for VB5).

3. Click OK.

FIGURE 14.2:

The References dialog box with the DAO library checked

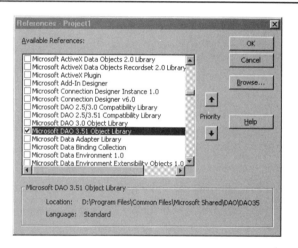

When you have added the reference to it, the DAO library is available to your project. This library exposes all the methods and properties you need to create workspaces, open databases, and create Recordsets.

The first thing we will do is open our example Video Store database. To do this step, we use the OpenDatabase method. This method is part of the Workspace object, but thankfully, we can use the default Workspace without having to worry about creating a new one. The method returns a reference to a Database object, so we have to use the Set command. This command assigns an object reference to a Database-type object variable.

The syntax of the OpenDatabase command is

```
Set database = _
    workspace.OpenDatabase (dbname, options, read-only, connect)
```

The OpenDatabase method has the following arguments:

dbname   The Data Source Name (DSN) for your Oracle database that you set up in the ODBC Driver Manager. This information is usually supplied in the connect property, so you can leave this field blank.

options   Set this argument to False (the default) if you want to open the database in Exclusive mode; the alternative is Shared mode. This option really refers to a JET database, and for your Oracle database, you should always specify False. Note that for the ODBCDirect database, which we shall cover in Chapter 16, there is a different set of options.

read-only   Set this argument to True if you want the database to be read-only; otherwise, set it to False, which is the default, so you can read and write to the database. This kind of security is application-specific and should supplement—but not replace—Oracle security.

connect   This is the connect string you need to connect to your Oracle database. This string is covered in Chapter 12, *Accessing Oracle with Visual Basic*.

We can now put this information together and proceed to connect to our database, as shown in Listing 14.1.

Listing 14.1

```
Private dbMovies As Database

Private Sub ConnectToDatabase ()

'   Declare and open a database using the default workspace.

  Set dbMovies = Workspaces(0).OpenDatabase _
      ("", False, False, "ODBC;DSN=movies;")
End Sub
```

Where to Keep the Database Object

When you create a Database object, you want that object to be available throughout the program. A standard practice in client-server applications is to open a connection to the database when the application starts up and close the connection when the application closes. In Listing 14.1, we ignored this issue by simply defining the Database object, dbMovies, in the same procedure as we created the object.

In reality, there are at least three different ways to handle where to put the Database object:

- Define the Database object as a global variable in a program module, and refer to it throughout the program. This is the simplest approach.

- Follow an object-oriented approach, and store the Database object in a private variable in a class, which can be referenced by other classes.

- Open and close the database connection when you need it; this step is high in overhead but may work if you make few connections and you set up the server so the connections are fast (perhaps using prestarted Server processes or connection pooling). This is a typical approach for middle-tier components that service requests from a Web server. DAO overhead is too high for this method. If this is the solution you need, you should be using ActiveX Data Objects, where connect times can be much faster.

Database Object Properties

Once you have connected to the Oracle database, you can access several methods for more information. You probably won't use them much, but you may want to find more details about how the database connection can be used. The more common properties are shown in Table 14.1.

TABLE 14.1: The Properties of the Database Object

Property	Description
Connect	The actual connect string used.
Name	The name of the database, as provided in the OpenDatabase method.
QueryTimeout	The timeout period in seconds for any queries.

Continued on next page

TABLE 14.1 CONTINUED: The Properties of the Database Object

Property	Description
RecordsAffected	The number of records affected by the most recent Execute method on the database. This property does not provide useful information for Oracle users.
Transactions	Indicates if transactions are allowed on the database.
Updatable	Indicates if the database is updatable.

Creating Recordsets

Now that we have opened a Database object for our Video_Store application, we next need to be able to pull in data from the database. For example, we might want to run a query to retrieve all the videos we have for rent. When Oracle executes a query like this, it makes the result set available to our Visual Basic application. In DAO, the object we need to create to accept this data is called a *Recordset*. We create a new Recordset object with the OpenRecordset method of the Database object. The method adds a new Recordset to the Recordsets collection. The OpenRecordset command creates a reference to the new Recordset object, so we must assign it to a Recordset variable with the Set command.

The syntax of the OpenRecordset method is as follows:

```
Set recordset = _
    database_object.OpenRecordset (source, type, options, lockedits)
```

The method has the following arguments:

source This is a string that represents the source of the data for the new Recordset. It will typically be a SQL statement enclosed in double quotes, such as `"SELECT * FROM videos WHERE status='A'"`. Do not include a semicolon at the end of the line. Note that you can't use an Oracle table name in this field.

type An optional constant that indicates the type of Recordset to open, as specified in Table 14.2.

options   An optional combination of constants that specify characteristics of the new Recordset. You can use one or more of the constants defined in Table 14.3. If you use more than one, you can add them together. Several more constants are defined in the help files, but these do not work with Oracle.

lockedits   An optional constant that determines the locking for the Recordset. You can choose one of the constants outlined in Table 14.4.

TABLE 14.2: The Possible Constants of the Type Argument of the OpenRecordset Method

Constant	Description
dbOpenDynaset	This constant opens a dynaset-type Recordset object, which is updatable. It is similar to an ODBC keyset cursor.
dbOpenSnapshot	This constant opens a snapshot-type Recordset object, which is not updatable. It is similar to an ODBC static cursor.
dbOpenForwardOnly	This constant opens a forward-only cursor, which, as its name implies, only supports the MoveNext method. Other Move methods result in a trappable error.
dbOpenTable	This constant opens a table-type Recordset object (not available with Oracle).

TABLE 14.3: Possible Constants for the Options Argument of the OpenRecordset Method

Constant	Description
dbAppendOnly	This constant allows users to append new records to the Recordset but not to edit or delete existing records (updatable Recordsets only).
dbSQLPassThrough	This constant passes a SQL SELECT statement straight through to Oracle, bypassing the JET query processor. This creates a read-only Recordset, but you will need to use the dbSQLPassThrough option if you want to use Oracle-specific syntax, including functions and schemas.
dbInconsistent	This constant refers to the ability to update Recordsets from table joins such that the join condition no longer holds. Recordsets from table joins in Oracle are not updatable, so this constant is unusable.
dbConsistent	This constant implies table-join conditions must remain in updatable Recordsets. Again, this constant is unusable with Oracle.

TABLE 14.4: Possible Constants for the Lockedits Argument of the OpenRecordset Method

Constant	Description
dbReadOnly	This constant prevents users from making changes to the Recordset. Though Oracle primarily controls whether you can alter the data, this option lets you enforce read-only. It also means there is less overhead accessing the data. You can use *dbReadOnly* in either the options argument or the lockedits argument but not both. If you try to use it for both arguments, a run-time error occurs.
dbOptimistic	This constant has optimistic locking, which implies the page (the row in Oracle's case) containing the record is not locked until the Update method is executed. This is the default for ODBC sources, such as Oracle.
dbPessimistic	This constant has pessimistic locking, which implies the page that the record is on is locked when you invoke the Edit method. Pessimistic locking does not work against an Oracle database.

NOTE
The tables of argument values above have been simplified to remove any options not applicable to Oracle. In the Visual Basic documentation, you will find a variety of other constants only applicable to JET databases.

When you create a Recordset from an Oracle database, the major decision you will have to make is whether you want the Recordset to be updatable or read-only. Once you have decided this, there are only two variations of the OpenRecordset method you need to consider, and we will see both of these in the next few sections.

Creating Updatable Recordsets

Updatable Recordsets are Recordsets you can read and write to. Of course, to make this work, you will need select, insert, update, and delete privileges on all the tables you want access to. You will be used to working with these types of Recordsets if you have done much work with Microsoft Access or have used the Data Control. The following code shows how you would create an updatable Recordset.

```
Dim rs as Recordset
Set rs = dbMovies.OpenRecordset _
        ("SELECT * FROM [video_store.movies]", dbOpenDynaset)
```

This example opens a new Recordset based upon the SQL query.

```
SELECT * FROM [video_store.movies]
```

Notice that you do not include the semicolon at the end of the SQL statement. Remember that any changes to the data rows represented in the Recordset by other users will not appear in the Recordset until you refresh it. The only problem with this process is the possibility other users may have changed the same records you want to change, or worse still, the records may have been deleted from the database.

Later in the chapter in the section "Putting It all Together," we will see an example of a form with an updatable Recordset.

TIP

One of the major problems with using updatable Recordsets with DAO is that JET is processing your query requests, and JET does not recognize Oracle syntax. In the case of updatable Recordsets, if you use an application schema (and you certainly should), then you need to enclose the table names in square brackets, as in [video_store.movies].

Creating Read-Only Recordsets

The alternative to updatable Recordsets is read-only Recordsets, but why would you choose something you cannot update? There are three major advantages of the read-only Recordset:

- They are more efficient from the server and client point of view.
- You can use the SQLPassThrough option and make use of Oracle syntax, including schema names.
- They lead to a more scalable architecture.

The efficiency of being a read-only Recordset comes from the fact that the ODBC cursor used is very simple, with no need for update capability. However, as all the data in the Recordset is stored on the client machine in memory, you should make sure you only include columns in the SELECT statement you absolutely need. If you can use the forward-only cursor, you will gain even more efficiency at the expense of being able to move around the data (though you can always effectively duplicate the use of a cursor yourself, for example, in a read-only grid).

TIP   Despite the theoretical advantages of the slower cursors in DAO, in tests over thousands of rows, I have found it difficult to quantify a real performance increase. The moral of this issue is to experiment with your environment.

With snapshots, you must also be careful not to include data from LONG RAW columns or BLOB-type columns. Remember the cursor reads all the data into memory, and you could have disastrous consequences if you do this with huge amounts of binary data. If your application allows you to, you should pull in the long fields only when you need to. An example of this application is when you are displaying employee data but only pulling in an image of a particular employee when the relevant button is clicked. Including the image column as part of the Recordset means all the images are pulled into memory. This is not a problem if there are only a few records in the Recordset, but it could become a significant resource problem. In these circumstances, it might actually be more efficient to use an updatable cursor.

NOTE   For a discussion on ODBC cursors, see Chapter 11, *Client-Side Technology*.

Despite the advantages of read-only Recordsets, you cannot update the records in them; this is fine in certain circumstances (for example, where you want to fill a data-bound list box used for data-entry choices) but otherwise using read-only Recordsets demands a totally different approach to application design. If you take the approach that all inserts, updates, and deletes to the database should be done by executing DML statements or, even better, through stored procedures, then this read-only approach is the way to go. In many environments, especially toward the high end, you simply do not have the option of an updatable cursor, and you have to use the single, most efficient method that is available.

NOTE   In Chapter 15, *Remote Data Objects*, we will see a technique that does in fact allow you to update the data with DML statements or stored procedures and, at the same time, have the changes reflected in the updatable result set.

Later in the chapter in the section, "Putting It All Together," we will see an example of a form with a read-only Recordset that allows updates through stored procedures.

A Personal Approach to Recordsets

In my applications, I tend to use the read-only approach to Recordsets. The data retrieved can be displayed in a Visual Basic form in a variety of ways, such as text and combo boxes or perhaps in a grid or spreadsheet control. When a user updates any of the data, this update is done by calling stored procedures. We will see how to do this a little later in the chapter.

This is not a particular hardship because, unless you are using data-bound controls, you will have to code procedures to do this anyway. It's just that with an updatable Recordset, you could use the AddNew, Edit, and Update methods of the Recordset.

Once stored-procedures have been written, you have much more control of the process. For those of you who are daunted by the task of having to write stored procedures to insert, update, and delete on every table in your database, we will be developing a DAO program to help automate this process toward the end of the chapter.

We can now put this information into practice and create a read-only Recordset. A sample piece of code is

```
Dim rs as Recordset
Set rs = dbMovies.OpenRecordset ("SELECT * FROM video_store.movies", _
         dbSQLPassThrough, dbOpenSnapshot)
```

You will notice we have the dbOpenSnapshot constant in the lockedits argument as you would expect, but we also have the dbSQLPassThrough constant in the options argument. The dbSQLPassThrough constant implies that the SQL command used for the source of the Recordset bypasses the JET query processor and is passed straight to Oracle. Not only does this bypass any parsing that JET wants to do to our query, including joins for a potential performance gain, but we can use Oracle syntax instead of JET syntax. This is especially useful when we want to use Oracle functions, such as TO_DATE to convert dates to an Oracle format. It also means we can use schemas in our queries. The only downside of this option is that the Recordset is now going to be read-only—but because that's what we want anyway in our example database, there is no harm done.

Whether we use updatable or read-only Recordsets, the ODBC driver for Oracle provided with VB6 allows us to use public and private synonyms and views. This feature is a real improvement over some older drivers that had particular difficulty with this capability. However, the ability to handle PL/SQL packages appears to have been lost. If this is important to your development, you may have to switch to ActiveX Data Objects of Oracle Objects for OLE.

JET Engine Syntax

The JET query processor has it own individualistic syntax for many SQL commands (such as joins and date delimiters). In many cases, you can use the JET syntax instead of the Oracle syntax and get by without the dbSQLPassThrough option; however, you have to learn two dialects of SQL. You can also use escape sequences in the ODBC parser to make your query database-specific, but this method seems like a lot of trouble for someone who is happy with the way Oracle does things!

Recordset Properties

Once you have opened a Recordset, there are several properties you have access to. A few of the more important ones are shown in Table 14.5. We will see how to use many of them in the next section.

TABLE 14.5: Selected Recordset Properties

Properties	Description
AbsolutePosition	This property moves the Recordset to a particular record number.
BOF	This property is True if you have moved before the first record in the Recordset.
Bookmark	This property points to a record in the Recordset.
Bookmarkable	This property indicates if you can use Bookmarks on this Recordset.
CacheSize	This property indicates the size of the record cache. The default is 0.
CacheStart	This property indicates the Bookmark of the start of the record cache.
EditMode	This property indicates the state of editing of the current record.
EOF	This property is True if you have moved past the last record in the Recordset.
LockEdits	This property reflects the LockEdits parameter in the OpenRecordset method.

Continued on next page

TABLE 14.5 CONTINUED: Selected Recordset Properties

Properties	Description
Name	This property is the source string that created the Recordset.
NoMatch	This property indicates there was no match found for one of the Find methods.
RecordCount	This property indicates the number of records in the Recordset. This value is normally relatively meaningless until the Recordset has been fully populated, for example, with a MoveLast method.
Transactions	This property indicates if the Recordset supports transactions.
Type	This property indicates the value of the type parameter in the OpenRecordset method.
Updatable	This property indicates if the Recordset is updatable.

Exploring the Recordset Methods

Once you have opened a Recordset, there are several methods you have access to. You can use these to control how your data is pulled from the server, to change values in the Recordset, to move through the Recordset, and to find records matching particular criteria.

Populating the Recordset

One thing you never had to think about in the old days was populating the Recordset. *Populating* is when the rows are pulled from the Oracle server into the Recordset. This is generally done one row at a time, not all at once. The rows are retrieved when they are accessed but not before they are required. As a result, the process can make many trips over the network with all the attendant inefficiencies.

Although you can still use the default method of Recordset population, you also have the option of more control. DAO now provides a cache that stores records in a buffer in memory on the client machine; however, this process only works with dynasets. You can fill this by explicitly defining how many records you want to retrieve in one go with the CacheSize property and then actually filling the cache with the FillCache method. The other property of note here is the CacheStart property, which defines a bookmark in the Recordset. The FillCache method fills the cache starting at this bookmarked record.

As an example of filling the cache, the following code sets the bookmark to the current record, then sets the cache size to 100 records, and finally, fills the cache with up to 100 records.

```
With rsMovies
    .CacheStart =.Bookmark
    .CacheSize = 100
    .FillCache
End With
```

Although this method will only work with updatable Recordsets, there is an another possibility when you are happy with a read-only situation. This alternative is to use the GetRows method, which we will cover a little later in the chapter. With both of these methods, you can expect a reasonable increase in the speed of the Recordset population. The improvement depends on many variables, but you might get your data speed up to twice as fast.

Changing the Current Record

When you first create a Recordset, it is always positioned on the first record. There are four methods typically used to move around a scrollable Recordset as shown in Table 14.6. Note that for a forward-only Recordset, you can use only the MoveNext method. You can execute these methods from code, but most applications provide a GUI interface in the form of buttons.

TABLE 14.6: The Recordset Move Methods

Recordset Method	Description
MoveFirst	This method moves the current record to the first record in the Recordset.
MoveLast	This method moves the current record to the last record in the Recordset.
MoveNext	This method moves the current record to the next record in the Recordset.
MovePrevious	This method moves the current record to the previous record in the Recordset.

When you use these methods, you should be aware of the consequences of reaching the end of the Recordset and of the Recordset being empty. With MoveNext, you should check for the EOF property (end of file), and with MovePrevious, you should check for the BOF property (beginning of file). If you try these Move methods when EOF or BOF are True, you may end up with an invalid current record.

NOTE   If both EOF and BOF are True, then the Recordset is empty.

If you look at the RecordCount property, you will see a value, but it will probably not accurately reflect the number of records in the Recordset. The value will not be a reliable number until you have moved to the end of the Recordset with a method, such as MoveLast.

Accessing the Fields of a Recordset

Whether you are using an updatable or read-only Recordset, you will want to look through the data and pick out particular fields. To do this you must understand the Recordset object a little more. As you can see from Figure 14.1, the Recordset object itself contains several other objects, one of which is the Fields collection. A Field is the JET mapping of an Oracle column. To find the value of any field in the current record of the Recordset, you can reference it in one of two ways: by index (ordinal number) or by name. The syntax for this is

```
Fields(0)
```

or

```
Fields("name")
```

TIP   An alternative but less intuitive form of the syntax for accessing a field by name is
`Fields![name]`.

When we put this collection together to fill a list box, we can use the code shown in Listing 14.2. Yes, there are data-bound ways to do this step, as well, but the listing illustrates the point.

Listing 14.2

```
Public sub FillListBox (ListBox as control)

'    Fill a list box with movie names
'    Ignore error trapping

     Dim rs As Recordset
```

```
Set rs = dbMovies.OpenRecordset _
    ("SELECT movie_name FROM video_store.movies", dbOpenSnapshot, _
    dbSQLPassThrough)

ListBox.Clear
While NOT rs.EOF
    ListBox.AddItem rs("movie_name")
    rs.MoveNext
Wend
ListBox.ListIndex = 0   ' Display the first item

Set rs = Nothing

End Sub
```

If there is any possibility of a field being NULL, you should take care of the potential error condition by ensuring the problem is handled. For a character field, you should concatenate the field to an empty string, and for a numeric value, you should add an empty string and then convert it to a numeric.

```
strName = "" & rsMovies("Movie_Name")
```

or

```
iMovieID = Val("" & rsMovies("Movie_Id"))
```

Differences between JET and Oracle

One thing you need to keep in mind is the difference between the way JET likes to return fields to you and the way Oracle will return them when you use the dbSQLPassThrough option. This difference becomes important when you return fields from more than one table with a join condition.

If you use an updatable cursor (that is, you go through JET to retrieve the data records), then the columns used to link the tables together in the join condition are each returned with their column name preceded by the table name and separated by a period. For example, if the Recordset SOURCE statement is

```
SELECT * FROM movies, videos

    WHERE movies.movie_id = videos.movie_id
```

Continued on next page

then JET will return a field called *movies.movie_id* as well as one called *videos.movie_id*. The other fields will not have the table name prefix, so they will be *movie_name*, *rating*, and so on.

Now when you have a read-only Recordset and use the dbSQLPassThrough option, Oracle will return the fields it wants to return. In this case, you will get just the one join field *movie_id*. If you need to get them both for any reason, then you will have to use column aliases as we saw in Chapter 7, *Queries*.

So beware that these two methods can give different field names as well as a different number of fields in the Recordset, all from the same query.

Changing the Records and Values in a Recordset

There are a few methods we can use to change the records and their values in the Recordset, assuming you are using an updatable cursor. First, you should navigate to the record you want to change with the Move methods and then use the following editing methods:

AddNew Adds a new record to the Recordset but not to Oracle. To make the change permanent, you have to use the UPDATE command.

Edit Puts the current record into Edit mode, meaning you can change any of the values.

Update Saves any changes you have made to the Oracle server, assuming all constraints are met.

Delete Deletes the current record. You do not use the Update method after a Delete.

If you have executed the AddNew or Edit methods, you can change any of the fields in the Recordset. You do this as follows:

```
rsMovies ("Name") = "The Wonderful World of Oracle"
```

JET will first do its own validation. This procedure is not sophisticated, but it will check, for example, that you don't assign a character string to a numeric field. If you try something like that, you will get the trappable error "Data type conversion error."

When you have made all the changes you want (perhaps by referring to a text field on the input form), you can use the Update method. If there are any constraint problems, such as an invalid key or a rating that is not part of the defined list, then you will get back a trappable error.

If the Oracle row you are trying to update is already locked by another user, then your application will hang until that lock is freed up. The JET engine does not handle this situation gracefully, and if this is likely to be a problem, you may want to consider using the SELECT FOR UPDATE NOWAIT syntax we saw in Chapter 13, *Visual Basic Design Issues*. This is normally where you want pessimistic locking.

When you add a new record to the Recordset, you have to make sure all the required fields (that is, those that have a NOT NULL constraint on them) do in fact have a valid value. Finding these values can be a problem, especially if you use sequences for the primary key. You should really read the key value from the database with a SELECT statement before you update the Recordset, but this step is a nuisance. However, you could do this step by passing a dummy value and setting it to a valid key with a trigger on the table, but doing this is even more messy and leaves your Recordset with an invalid value. But if you stick with read-only Recordsets, use stored procedures, or execute some SQL code to update the data and then refresh the Recordset, you will have a better overall system.

Finding a Particular Record

The final thing we will look at for Recordset methods is how to find a record that matches the criteria you set down. There are four methods and a property you need to be aware of, and these are shown in Table 14.7.

TABLE 14.7: Methods and Properties Used to Find Records

Method / Property	Description
FindFirst	This method finds the first occurrence of the search string in the Recordset.
FindLast	This method finds the last occurrence of the search string in the Recordset.
FindNext	This method finds the next occurrence of the search string after the current record.
FindPrevious	This method finds the previous occurrence of the search string before the current record.
NoMatch	This property indicates no match was found for the Find commands.

You can use these methods simply by providing a search string. Note that the search string must be in JET syntax. Apart from that restriction, you can usually use the same criteria you would use in the WHERE clause of a SELECT query. The following example illustrates this point.

```
rsMovies.FindFirst "rating = 'PG-13'"
If rsMovies.NoMatch Then
    MsgBox "No matching records were found for the rating PG-13"
End If
```

You should note these Find commands are not a substitute for creating a well-written SELECT query in the first place. If you use FindNext and FindPrevious, then this use is a sign you should probably incorporate the search criteria into your Recordset source query.

Closing a Recordset

A Recordset will automatically be closed as soon as it goes out of scope; for example, if you define it in the Form_Load event, it will be closed as soon as the Form_Load event is exited. However, if you declare the Recordset as a form-level variable, then you may find it does not go out of scope and may be left open. It is good practice to close the Recordset as soon as you have finished with it. This ensures the Private SQL area in the Oracle server and any memory taken by ODBC cursors is released as soon as possible. To close the Recordset, you need to set it to "Nothing" as follows:

```
Set rs = Nothing
```

An alternative is to use the Close method:

```
rs.Close
```

As we saw in the section "Populating the Recordset," Oracle has a forward-only retrieval of rows from the Private SQL area in the server. This memory is only released when the last row is read in or when the Recordset is closed. If you need to keep the Recordset open, then you should move to the last record in the Recordset as soon as you can.

Using the GetRows Method

When we looked at populating a Recordset, we saw that DAO, by default, reads one record at a time as it is needed. We also saw how to populate the Recordset explicitly using the FillCache method to more efficiently read more than one row at a time. We must now touch on one more method because it is particularly efficient but does not actually read the data into a Recordset. The GetRows method of the Recordset object fills what is called a *variant array* by reading a large number of rows from Oracle all in one go.

A variant array is not an array of variant data elements but rather a single-variant data type. Variants are designed to take any types of data whether they are integers, character strings, or more complex types. When you use them, implicit conversion routines change the data type to match the situation it is in (assuming that is possible). For example, if you assign a variant to an integer variable, the variant's value is converted to the integer type. This conversion allows us to define an array within a single data type. This might seem like a fine point to argue, but it is important: the variant array not only encapsulates the results from the query in a neat parcel but you can also efficiently pass variant arrays between components, even if you use them in something like Microsoft Transaction Server. (You only have to marshal one variable over DCOM.)

NOTE Because the variant array does not use a cursor, it is not updatable.

To use the GetRows method, you first have to decide how many rows you want to retrieve in one go. You can retrieve a portion of the entire result set or the whole thing. You can request more rows than are there, and only those rows that exist will be brought over. If you request a portion of the result set, you can repeatedly fetch more until there are none left. DAO will automatically size the variant array and let you retrieve the number of rows and columns represented in the array. Once you have your variant array filled, it is a simple matter to loop through it and retrieve the values you want. Listing 14.3 gives an example of creating a Recordset, pulling the data into the variant array, and then looping through the values. For the sake of an example, we will pull the data into VB in blocks of 100 records. With a sufficiently capable machine, you can happily pull in thousands of records in one go for a substantial boost in performance.

Listing 14.3

```
Private Function ReadData() As Integer

'   Read in the data into a variant array

    Dim varRecords As Variant    ' The variant array
    Dim iNumRecords As Integer   ' The number of records
```

```
Dim iNumCols As Integer      ' The number of rows
Dim iRecNo As Integer        ' Record counter
Dim iColNo As Integer        ' Column counter
Dim rsMovies As Recordset
Dim strSQL As String

strSQL = "SELECT * FROM video_store.movies ORDER BY movie_id"
Set rsMovies = dbMovies.OpenRecordset(strSQL, dbOpenDynaset)

varRecords = rsMovies.GetRows(100)
iNumRecords = UBound(varRecords, 2) + 1
iNumCols = UBound(varRecords, 1) + 1

' Process each record
For iRecNo = 0 To iNumRecords - 1

    ' Process each column
    For iColNo = 0 To iNumCols - 1

        MsgBox varRecords(iColNo, iRecNo)
    Next
Next

End Function
```

> **TIP**
>
> To get the best efficiency from the GetRows method, you should create a Recordset that has only those rows and columns you actually want. If you only want a few of the rows, then you may find another method faster.

Executing SQL Commands

Using updatable Recordsets may be as far as you want to go at the moment, but there will be occasions when you want to execute some SQL code that does something a little more active. In Microsoft terminology, these are Action Queries, which are SQL statements that insert, update, or delete data. In Oracle terminology, these are the Data Manipulation Language (DML) statements we first saw in Chapter 8, *Updating Your Database*.

To execute a SQL statement from Visual Basic, we use the Execute method of the Database object as shown in the following syntax:

```
database_object.Execute source, options
```

The arguments for the Execute method are

> **source**   A SQL string that defines the single DML statement we want to execute.

> **options**   One or both of the constants that define the characteristics of the Execute method as shown in Table 14.8. As a matter of course, you should always use at least the dbSQLPassThrough option.

TABLE 14.8: The Constants of an Execute Method

Constant	Description
dbSQLPassThrough	This constant executes a SQL pass-through query; for example, one that is passed through to the Oracle query processor, bypassing the JET engine.
dbFailOnError	This constant rolls back updates if any errors occur. It is better to manage transaction failure with stored procedures if at all possible.

An example of executing SQL commands is shown in Listing 14.4.

Listing 14.4

```
Private Sub DeleteMovie(iMovieId As Integer)

'   Delete a movie

    On Error GoTo ErrorHandler
    dbMovies.Execute "DELETE FROM video_store.movies WHERE id=132", _
                     dbSQLPassThrough
    Exit Sub

ErrorHandler:
    MsgBox "Error deleting movie id = " & iMovieId & " : " & _
           Errors(0).Description

End Sub
```

TIP Do not include the semicolon at the end of the SQL statement, even with the SQLPassThrough option.

Anytime you execute a DML statement, it will become part of a transaction. There is no automatic committing of changes when you use this method, so you must be prepared to explicitly commit them. However, this is easy, as Listing 14.5 shows. Unfortunately, you cannot combine SQL commands in the same call.

Listing 14.5

```
Public Sub Commit()

'    Commit any outstanding updates in the database

    On Error GoTo ErrorHandler
    dbMovies.Execute "Commit", dbSQLPassThrough
    Exit Sub

ErrorHandler:
    msgBox "Error committing changes : " & Errors(0).Description
End Sub
```

WARNING Do not mix the explicit execution of a COMMIT statement with the DAO transaction commands BeginTrans and CommitTrans because these two types of transaction control commands will be on different connections.

Calling Stored Procedures

You will eventually want to execute Oracle stored procedures from within Visual Basic. If you thought you could call a stored procedure using the syntax for executing SQL that we saw in the last section, you would be partly right. However, there are some limitations and one little trick you should be aware of.

The Execute method of the Database object executes an anonymous code block, that is, a block of code that is not stored with a name. To execute a stored procedure, we have to wrap the call in BEGIN and END statements just as we saw when looking at PL/SQL in Chapter 10, *Creating Stored Procedures*. This effectively converts the stored-procedure call to an anonymous PL/SQL code block. A practical example of this is shown in Listing 14.6. This code executes the stored procedure movies_insert2 in the video_store schema. You first have to build up the SQL string that contains the command to be executed, and this must include all the parameters.

Listing 14.6

```
Private Sub MovieInsert(iMovieId As Integer, strMovieName As String, _
          iLength As Integer, strRating As String, iYear As Integer)

'    Insert a new movie into the database

     On Error GoTo ErrorHandler
     Dim strSQL As String

     strSQL = "BEGIN video_store.movies_insert2 ("
     strSQL = strSQL & iMovieId & ", '" & strMovieName & "', "
     strSQL = strSQL & iLength & ", '" & strRating & "', " & iYear
     strSQL = strSQL & "); END;"

     dbMovies.Execute strSQL, dbSQLPassThrough
     Exit Sub

ErrorHandler:
     MsgBox "Error inserting movie : " & Errors(0).Description
End Sub
```

The kind of SQL string this gives you is:

```
BEGIN video_store.movies_insert (321,
     'Retirement Home for Software', 55, 'R', 1995); END;
```

The stored procedure that is actually executed here is shown in Listing 14.7.

Listing 14.7

```
PROCEDURE movies_insert2(
  p_movie_id  IN NUMBER,
  p_name      IN VARCHAR2,
  p_length    IN NUMBER,
  p_rating    IN VARCHAR2,
  p_year      IN NUMBER) IS

/*  Insert a new movie into the movie table
    If the formal parameter, p_movie_id is zero it is assigned
    from the next available sequence number
*/
v_movie_id  NUMBER(6);

BEGIN

  IF p_movie_id = 0 THEN
    SELECT movie_sequence_id.NEXTVAL INTO v_movie_id FROM dual;
  ELSE
    v_movie_id := p_movie_id;
  END IF;

  INSERT INTO movies VALUES (
    v_movie_id, p_name, p_length, p_rating, p_year, USER, SYSDATE);

  COMMIT;

EXCEPTION
/* Whatever the problem just rollback and
   pass the error back to Visual Basic */
  WHEN OTHERS THEN
    ROLLBACK;
    RAISE;

END movies_insert2;
```

TIP   If you are using sequence numbers for your primary keys, then you should create a stored procedure that manages the retrieval of the next sequence value. In this case, you do not need to pass a key value to the procedure; however, I like to pass a 0 to indicate the procedure should create a sequence number. Although this is unnecessary in DAO, it paves the way for retrieving the assigned key with the other technologies.

You will almost always have to include the schema name in your SQL strings (in this case, we have used video_store). This schema name will normally be the owner of the base tables and probably be application specific. To be able to execute the stored procedure, you obviously need the privileges to do so. If you do not have the Execute privilege, you will see the misleading error message:

```
[Microsoft][ODBC driver for Oracle][Oracle]ORA-06550: line 1, column 7:
PLS-00201: identifier 'VIDEO_STORE.MOVIES_INSERT2' must be declared
ORA-06550: line 1, column 7:
PL/SQL: Statement ignored
```

This error message is also possible if you have specified the wrong name for the stored procedure.

There is no way to return any output parameters, and you also cannot execute stored functions. If you want more advanced functionality, you will have to use one of the other methods outlined in the later chapters of this book.

NOTE   Data Access Objects creates a second connection (or session) to Oracle to execute the SQL statements (including stored procedures). It can be disconcerting to users to have the application lock up while this second connection is made, so if possible, you should force this connection to be made at start-up. A call to the COMMIT command would do the job.

Error Handling

In addition to the familiar Err object, DAO provides us with the Errors collection for data-related errors. You will need this collection to make sense of the errors returning from Oracle, otherwise you will just have the familiar error number

3146. The Errors collection consists of Error objects whose properties are outlined in Table 14.9. Each Error object has information in it, but the only useful object is the first one in the collection, Errors(0).

TABLE 14.9: The Properties of the Error Object for DAO Errors

Property	Description
Number	The valid number (a long integer).
Description	A string containing a description of the error.
Source	The name of the object that raised the error.
HelpFile	The full file name of the Visual Basic Help file.
HelpContext	The Help file context ID for the error number.

Chapter 13, *Visual Basic Design Issues,* gives an overview of what to expect from Oracle errors retrieved in ODBC and how to use them. You will typically use the error number and description properties either in a message box or preferably in your own error-handling routine.

Putting It All Together

In the previous sections, we have seen a variety of techniques, properties, and methods; in this section, we will use this information to provide a small form that allows us to view and update the Movie database. We will take two fundamentally different approaches to this procedure. In the first example, we will use an updatable Recordset that is typical of the way a Microsoft Access form would be used. In the second example, we will use a read-only Recordset and call stored procedures to do the updates. The first approach is suitable for small applications, but the second approach becomes a necessity as the application is scaled up. Both of the solutions use the same form as shown in Figure 14.3.

FIGURE 14.3:

The Movie database
update form

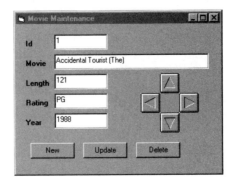

The code common to the program is shown in Listing 14.8. We will use this code in other chapters, but it will not be repeated. The main routines are

- Form_Load contains the OpenDatabase statement.

- ShowNewRecord displays blank data fields.

- ShowRecord displays the data of the current record.

- Picture1_Click controls the navigation around the RecordSet.

Listing 14.8

```
' Movie Maintenance form
' Nick Snowdon   June 1998

Option Explicit

Private dbMovies As Database
Private rsMovies As Recordset
Private rsParticipants As Recordset
Private strMode As String


Private Sub Form_Load()

'   Connect to the database
    Set dbMovies = Workspaces(0).OpenDatabase("", False, False,
                   "ODBC;DSN=movies;")

'   Ensure the recordset is up to date
    RefreshRecordset
End Sub
```

```
Private Sub ShowNewRecord()

'   Show a new blank record
    Dim iField As Integer

    For iField = 0 To 4
        txtMovie(iField) = ""
    Next                    ' iField

End Sub


Private Sub ShowRecord()

'   Show the current record
    Dim iField As Integer
    On Error GoTo ErrorHandler

'   Take care of the situation if there is no current record
    If rsMovies.BOF And rsMovies.EOF Then
        ShowNewRecord
        Exit Sub
    ElseIf rsMovies.BOF Then
        rsMovies.MoveFirst
    ElseIf rsMovies.EOF Then
        rsMovies.MoveLast
    End If


'   Display the fields
    For iField = 0 To 4
        txtMovie(iField) = "" & rsMovies(iField)
    Next ' iField
    Exit Sub

ErrorHandler:
    If Err.Number = 3146 Then
        MsgBox Errors(0).Description
    Else
        MsgBox Err.Description
    End If
End Sub
```

```
Private Sub lstRatings_Click()
    RefreshRecordset
End Sub


Private Sub Picture1_Click(Index As Integer)

'    Navigation controls

    Select Case Index
        Case 0                   ' Top of recordset
            rsMovies.MoveFirst
        Case 1                   ' Previous record
            If Not rsMovies.BOF Then
                rsMovies.MovePrevious
            End If
        Case 2                   ' Next record
            If Not rsMovies.EOF Then
                rsMovies.MoveNext
            End If
        Case 3                   ' Bottom of recordset
            rsMovies.MoveLast
    End Select

    ShowRecord

End Sub
```

Listing 14.9 shows the following routines used in the updatable Recordset implementation:

- RefreshRecordset, which regenerates the Recordset with different criteria if that is required. In the updatable version, it is only called once. You should not code it in the Form_Load event though, because you may want to refresh it with additional criteria at some point.

- cmdAction_Click, which includes the AddNew, Edit, Update, and Delete methods being used to change data.

Listing 14.9

```
Private Sub RefreshRecordset()
'    Ensure the recordset is up to date

    Dim strSQL As String

    strSQL = "SELECT movie_name, length, rating, year_of_release, " & _
             "movie_id FROM video_store.movies "
    strSQL = strSQL & " ORDER BY movie_id"
    Set rsMovies = dbMovies.OpenRecordset(strSQL, dbOpenDynaset)
    ShowRecord

End Sub


Private Sub cmdAction_Click(Index As Integer)

'    Execute the require action - insert, update or delete.

    Dim iField As Integer

    On Error GoTo ErrorHandler

    If Index = 0 Then                ' Add a new record
        rsMovies.AddNew
        ShowNewRecord
        strMode = "Add"

    ElseIf Index = 1 Then            ' Update the record
        If strMode <> "Add" Then
'           You should not lock this if you are using transactions and
'           then only for edits of existing records.
            dbMovies.Execute "SELECT * FROM movies WHERE movie_id = " _
            & rsMovies(4) & " FOR UPDATE NOWAIT", dbSQLPassThrough

            rsMovies.Edit
        End If

        For iField = 0 To 2
            rsMovies(iField) = "" & txtMovie(iField)
```

```
            Next      ' iField
            rsMovies(3) = CInt(Val(txtMovie(3)))
            rsMovies(4) = CInt(Val(txtMovie(4)))

            rsMovies.Update
            strMode = ""

        ElseIf Index = 2 Then            ' Delete the record
            rsMovies.Delete
            ShowRecord
        End If


        Exit Sub

    ErrorHandler:
        If Err.Number = 3146 Then        ' ODBC Error
            If Errors(0).Number = 54 Then   ' Locked
                MsgBox "The record is currently locked: ORA-00054"
            Else
                MsgBox Errors(0).Description & ": " & Errors(0).Number
            End If
        Else                             ' Non-ODBC error
            MsgBox Err.Description
        End If
        rsMovies.CancelUpdate            ' Ensure update is canceled
        strMode = ""
    End Sub
```

Listing 14.10 shows the following routines used in the read-only Recordset implementation:

- RefreshRecordset, which regenerates the result set when required. In the read-only version, it needs to be called every time a stored procedure is used to update the base tables.

- cmdAction_Click, which includes the stored procedure calls for procedures *movies_insert2, movies_update,* and *movies_delete.*

Listing 14.10

```
Private Sub RefreshRecordset()
'    Ensure the recordset is up to date

     Dim strSQL As String

     strSQL = "SELECT movie_name, length, rating, " & _
              "year_of_release, movie_id FROM video_store.movies "
     strSQL = strSQL & " ORDER BY movie_id"
     Set rsMovies = dbMovies.OpenRecordset(strSQL, dbOpenSnapshot)
     ShowRecord

End Sub

Private Sub cmdAction_Click(Index As Integer)

'    Execute the require action - insert, update or delete.

Dim strSQL As String

     On Error GoTo ErrorHandler

     If Index = 0 Then              ' Add a new record
         ShowNewRecord
         strMode = "Add"

     ElseIf Index = 1 Then          ' Update the record
         If strMode = "Add" Then
             strSQL = "BEGIN video_store.movies_insert2 (0,"
             strSQL = strSQL & "'" & txtMovie(0) & "', " ' Movie Name
             strSQL = strSQL & txtMovie(1) & ", "        ' Length
             strSQL = strSQL & "'" & txtMovie(2) & "', " ' Rating
             strSQL = strSQL & txtMovie(3)               ' Year
             strSQL = strSQL & "); END;"
             dbMovies.Execute strSQL, dbSQLPassThrough

         Else
             strSQL = "BEGIN video_store.movies_update ("
             strSQL = strSQL & rsMovies("movie_id") & ","
             strSQL = strSQL & "'" & txtMovie(0) & "', " ' Movie Name
```

```
                strSQL = strSQL & txtMovie(1) & ", "         ' Length
                strSQL = strSQL & "'" & txtMovie(2) & "', " ' Rating
                strSQL = strSQL & txtMovie(3)                ' Year
                strSQL = strSQL & "); END;"
                dbMovies.Execute strSQL, dbSQLPassThrough
            End If
            strMode = ""
            RefreshRecordset

        ElseIf Index = 2 Then             ' Delete the record
            dbMovies.Execute "BEGIN video_store.movies_delete (" & _
                rsMovies(4) & "); END;", dbSQLPassThrough
            RefreshRecordset
        End If


        Exit Sub

    ErrorHandler:
        If Err.Number = 3146 Then          ' ODBC Error
            If Errors(0).Number = 54 Then    ' Locked
                MsgBox "The record is currently locked by another user :
    ORA-00054"
            Else
                MsgBox Errors(0).Description & ": " & Errors(0).Number
            End If
        Else                                ' Non-ODBC error
            MsgBox Err.Description
        End If
    End Sub
```

Viewing the Structure of a Database

There are many times you will want to find out more about the structure of your Oracle database. Though you can use SQL*Plus to get this information, if you can view it from VB, it not only makes your code adaptable to other database vendors but it also enables you to automate several processes. We shall put this into practice at the end of this section.

To look at the structure of a database, we need to first look at the objects, collections, and properties that exist in our DAO hierarchy. Because the Visual Basic Help files include a large number of properties, we will select the most important ones to review here. Figure 14.4 shows the relevant structures and properties.

FIGURE 14.4:

The Tabledefs collection hierarchy and the most important properties

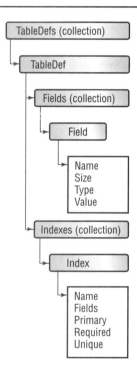

Accessing Collections

It is important to understand the various ways to access collections because they form the basis of how we work with database structures. There are three ways to access any item in a collection:

- By ordinal number, to index the object, such as `dbMovies.Tablesdefs(2)`
- By object name, such as `dbMovies.Tabledefs("movies")`
- By looping through the collection with the FOR EACH statement, such as

```
For Each tbl In dbMovies.Tabledefs
```

TableDefs

Just as every object under the DBEngine object can be a collection or object, TableDefs is a collection of TableDef objects. The TableDef object is a representation of the Oracle tables in the database we have opened and have access to. The collection is filled with information when you connect to the database. Yes, this extra database access is an overhead, but it only happens once per connection. This situation is fortunate because the database access can add several seconds to your connection time.

To find out as much as possible about the tables at our disposal, we have to look into this object closely. The only property that is of much use to an Oracle user is the Name property. This enables us to find out the names of all of the tables accessible to our user name. We can use this property as shown in Listing 14.11.

Listing 14.11

```
Dim tbl As TableDef

For Each tbl In dbMovies.TableDefs
    Debug.Print tbl.Name
Next
```

What does this code do? First, it declares a variable of type TableDef. Then, it loops through each TableDef in the TableDefs collection and prints out its name. Simple stuff, really.

Fields

Of more interest than the table names are the fields that exist in the table. Each Tabledef object contains a Fields collection, which in turn contains one or more Field objects. The important properties of the Field object are shown in Table 14.10.

T A B L E 1 4 . 1 0 : The Properties of the Field Object that Apply to Oracle

Property	Description
Name	The name of the field.
Size	The size of the field in bytes.

Continued on next page

TABLE 14.10 CONTINUED: The Properties of the Field Object that Apply to Oracle

Property	Description
SourceField	The field name from an attached table (if applicable).
SourceTable	The name of the attached table (if any).
Type	A number representing the field type interpreted by JET. This needs to be interpreted before it is useful against an Oracle database.
Value	This is the default property but is only relevant when you use it referring to a Recordset. For the Tabledef object it is meaningless.

You can track these quite easily with the sample code in Listing 14.12.

Listing 14.12

```
Dim fld As Field
Dim tbl As TableDef

For Each tbl In dbMovies.TableDefs
    For Each fld In tbl.Fields
        Debug.Print fld.Name, fld.Type
    Next
Next
' Or ...
Debug.Print dbMovies.TableDefs("Movies").Fields("movie_name").Type
```

You could get carried away at this point and start a little application that displayed all the data associated with your database. You can even use DAO to alter your tables if you have the required permissions to do so. However, there are many other professionally written tools that do this process better, so there is not much point in doing it yourself; even SQL*Plus can give you a reasonable view of your database.

So you might ask why would you want to use this information at all. Well, we can, for example, use the information to create SQL scripts that do more than just add a field to a table or create a new table. You will see an example in the section, "A Practical Application of TableDefs," that takes this to a new level.

Indexes

Just as you can look at the various fields you have in a table, you can also view the indexes on it. Each TableDef object can have an associated Indexes collection with one or more Index Objects in it. You should check the Count property of the Indexes collection to ensure an index actually exists before you try to access it. It seems you cannot get all the information on an Oracle table you might want, but this should come as no surprise. Table 14.11 covers the important properties for Oracle users.

TABLE 14.11: Some Important Properties of the Index Object

Property	Description
Fields	This property is a string that includes all the field names that make up the index. These names are also available separately in the Fields collection under the Index object.
Foreign	This property indicates if the index is a foreign key (not available).
Name	This property gives the name of the index. (This is the Oracle constraint name.)
Primary	This property indicates if the index is a primary key (not available).
Unique	This property indicates if the index is a unique key. An Oracle primary key will have the unique property set to True.

There is a Field object under the Index object, but it is not a true Field object. It only has a Name property available. To find the object's Type property, for example, you must refer back to the Field object under the Fields collection. The following code does this:

```
StrIndexName = tbl.Indexes(0).Fields(0).Name
Debug.Print tbl.Fields(strIndexName).Type
```

A Practical Application of TableDefs

As promised in Chapter 8, *Updating Your Database,* we are now going to use the information we have covered in the preceding chapters to create a useful utility program, which will scan all the tables in our database and create a script with up to three stored procedures for each table: one to insert, one to update, and one to delete rows of data. This approach can save hours of work compared to the hand-coding approach.

You should treat this code as a start for your own ideas. For example, the Insert procedures it creates include parameters for the unique keys. If you use sequences (and you should), then you may want to modify the example so that you remove the key field and instead set the value from the appropriate sequence.

There is only a simple form for the CreateProcs application, and this is shown in Figure 14.5. As you can see, you enter the schema name as a filter so that you are not processing every single table you have access to. You can check the option to include the Create or Replace syntax, which you will need if you are going to execute the output script from a SQL*Plus session. Finally, you can click an option to include the audit scripting in each procedure.

FIGURE 14.5:

The CreateProcs form

The main loop of the program is shown in the CreateProcs procedure (see Listing 14.13). It loops through all the tables in the TableDefs collection, and it will include any table the user has access to, not just those in their own schema. To reduce the amount of processing, you can enter your schema name on the form; if the table name includes the entered schema, then the table will be processed.

Listing 14.13

```
'    Process each table in the collection

For Each tbl In dBTss.TableDefs

    iNumFields = tbl.Fields.Count    ' Number of fields in table

    If InStr(tbl.Name, UCase(txtSchema) & ".") And _
        iNumFields > 0 Then

'           Find a unique index if one exists
            iIndexes = tbl.Indexes.Count
            Set fldUnique = Nothing
            If iIndexes > 0 Then
                For Each idx In tbl.Indexes
                    For Each fld In idx.Fields
                        Set fldUnique = fld
                        Exit For
                    Next
                Next
            End If

'           Create the header
'           Create the SQL command
'           Create the audit
'           Create the footer

        Else
            txtMessages.Text = "Ignoring table " & tbl.Name
        End If
        DoEvents
    Next tbl
```

The first thing the processing loop does is to look for a unique key because DAO does not allow us to detect the PRIMARY KEY constraint. This unique key will be used in creating the update and delete stored procedures. Once the unique key is found, the loop calls procedures to create the stored-procedure headers, bodies, and footers. In Listing 14.13, these calls are only represented by comments to simplify the code.

The code to create a stored procedure header is shown in Listing 14.14. In this procedure, we include formal parameters for each column in the table, except the user name and the time stamp. The delete stored procedure is dealt with a little differently because it only has one formal parameter. The unique key will be used to identify the row to delete.

Listing 14.14

```
'    Create the header for a stored procedure.

Print #1, "PROCEDURE " & LCase(RemoveSchema(tbl.Name)) & _
          "_" & strType & " ("

' Write out one parameter for each field except
' user_name and time_stamp
iField = 0
For Each fld In tbl.Fields
    If fld.Name <> "USER_NAME" And fld.Name <> "TIME_STAMP" Then
        iField = iField + 1
        If iField > 1 Then
            Print #1, "    ,p_" & LCase(fld.Name) & _
                " " & FieldType(fld.Type)
        Else
            Print #1, "    p_" & LCase(fld.Name) & _
                " " & FieldType(fld.Type)
        End If
    End If
Next fld
Print #1, "  ) IS "
```

To write out the formal parameters, we must know the data type of each column. This poses a small difficulty as the ODBC types do not have a one-to-one conversion to Oracle data types. The code in Listing 14.15 does this conversion for us.

Listing 14.15

```
Function FieldType(intType As Integer) As String

'    Convert the field type to an Oracle column type
```

```
Select Case intType
    Case dbByte
        FieldType = "NUMBER"
    Case dbInteger
        FieldType = "NUMBER"
    Case dbLong
        FieldType = "NUMBER"
    Case dbSingle
        FieldType = "NUMBER"
    Case dbDouble
        FieldType = "NUMBER"
    Case dbDate
        FieldType = "DATE"
    Case dbText
        FieldType = "VARCHAR2"
    Case dbLongBinary
        FieldType = "RAW"
    Case dbMemo
        FieldType = "VARCHAR2"
    Case Else
        FieldType = "Unknown"
End Select

End Function
```

Finally, the results you have been waiting for are shown in Listing 14.16. The output is a PL/SQL procedure you can put straight into Oracle Procedure Builder. Actually, if you are creating many procedures, the application has a check box for adding a CREATE or REPLACE statement at the front of each procedure and follows each with a forward slash. In this way, you can execute the whole output file in a SQL*Plus session.

NOTE   If you have tables with raw data columns, you will not be able to use DAO to call them. You will have to use one of the other data-access libraries.

Listing 14.16

```
PROCEDURE customers_delete
  ( p_customer_id NUMBER
  ) IS

/* This procedure deletes a row in the NICK.CUSTOMERS table */

BEGIN

  DELETE FROM NICK.CUSTOMERS
    WHERE customer_id = p_customer_id;


/* Add the procedure audit trail */
  INSERT INTO procedure_audit VALUES (
    audit_sequence.NEXTVAL,
    'customers_delete',
    p_customer_id
    ,SYSDATE, USER);
  COMMIT;

EXCEPTION
/* Whatever the problem just rollback and pass the error back to Visual
Basic */
  WHEN OTHERS THEN
    ROLLBACK;
    RAISE;
END customers_delete;
```

Even if you do not plan to use this exact method, it is an idea worth keeping in mind, because there are countless other similar ideas that can make your job a lot easier.

Drawbacks to DAO

DAO is an aging technology. You should accept that whatever experience you have with DAO is becoming less important. It is still used for a huge number of applications, but there are definite disadvantages compared to the more recent technologies.

- DAO has a weak object model with the lowest level of functionality of all of the data-access technologies.

- DAO was designed for JET and is not tuned for ODBC data sources.

- You cannot retrieve output parameters from stored procedures.

- DAO is not a technology adaptable to a wide range of types of data sources.

- The technology has reached the end of the road and will not be upgraded further.

Summary

This chapter has covered all the major features of using DAO with Oracle. This includes creating database connections, retrieving read-only and updatable Recordsets, executing SQL statements, and calling stored procedures. We covered practical examples of the two major ways of using DAO to view and update data. We finished with an overview of the database structure and the use of this information to produce a script to create stored procedures.

Despite the functionality you can extract from DAO, it is a limited and somewhat artificial object model when applied to an Oracle database. The rest of the data-access technologies that we will move on to provide better functionality and move closer to the way Oracle actually works.

PART IV

Advanced Oracle Techniques

CHAPTER

FIFTEEN

15

Remote Data Objects

- The RDO Object Hierarchy

- Databases and Connections

- Working with rdoResultsets

- Executing SQL Commands

- Using rdoQuery Objects

- Calling Stored Procedures

- Asynchronous Operation

- Retrieving PL/SQL Tables

- Error Handling

- The Disadvantages of RDO

- The Future of RDO

So far, we have seen how Data Access Objects can be used to access your Oracle database. As you saw, DAO is not an ideal model because it does not give you access to the full functionality of Oracle. However, this fact does not take anything away from DAO, because in its latest incarnation (version 3.51 and ODBCDirect), it runs acceptably fast. Many good applications have been written using it. However, DAO was never really designed for intelligent remote databases; it was designed for the JET database engine, and it grew from there.

At its lowest level, ODBC is implemented as an Application Programming Interface (API); to make ODBC more available to the majority of programmers, Microsoft originally provided the DAO model, which hid the complexity of the API but at the expense of functionality. Remote Data Objects 1.0 (RDO) came about in VB 4.0 as a wrapper on top of the ODBC API to take care of all the gritty details and to open up all the power of the ODBC driver to the developer. Then, with VB 5.0, came RDO 2.0, which brought a more stable and rich environment. RDO gets as much functionality out of the ODBC architecture as we can expect. You should note that RDO only works in a 32-bit environment, and it has only had a minor revision for Visual Basic 6.

One point of issue you must be aware of is that RDO is only available with the Enterprise Edition of Visual Basic, so there is the associated extra licensing cost. You can only use RDO in the development environments, such as VB and VC++; you do not have this option if you are a Microsoft Office developer. In this case, you have to use a different technique, such as what we will discuss in Chapter 16, *ODBCDirect*, or Chapter 17, *ActiveX Data Objects*.

Although RDO is an enormous playing field, we will be concentrating on the topics you need to produce acceptable applications with Oracle. The topics we will cover are

- The RDO object hierarchy

- Databases and connections

- Working with rdoResultsets

- Executing SQL commands

- Using rdoQuery objects

- Calling stored procedures

- Asynchronous operation

- Retrieving PL/SQL tables

- Error handling

- The disadvantages of RDO

- The future of RDO

The Object Hierarchy

The RDO object hierarchy is noticeably different from the one we saw in Chapter 14, *Data Access Objects*. It obviously has more complexity, and some of the terminology has changed, as shown in Figure 15.1. There is a good reason for this (well, it seemed like a good idea at the time): it comes closer to the terminology of the ODBC API and the relational database model that ODBC was designed to interface with. However, from a developer's point of view, it merely makes it more confusing. This is unfortunate because with ActiveX Data Objects, we have now moved away from looking at relational databases as the foundation of everything and moved back to the term *Recordset*. Luckily, developers get regular exercise at dealing with the changing names of familiar objects.

FIGURE 15.1:

The RDO object hierarchy

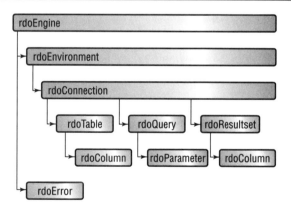

rdoEngine

The rdoEngine object is the top-level object in the RDO hierarchy. There is only one rdoEngine, and it may contain one or more rdoEnvironments in a collection. The rdoEngine is used to define the rdoEnvironments you want to create; however, you cannot create a new rdoEngine. The rdoEngine contains the rdoEnvironments and rdoErrors collections.

rdoEnvironments

An rdoEnvironment object is a grouping of one or more remote database connections that all fall under the same transaction scope. That means that if you are using transaction control from RDO (that is, you are using BeginTrans, Commit-Trans, and RollbackTrans) and commit the changes, then all the changes in the same environment but on different connections will be committed at the same time. It is effectively the same as a DAO Workspace, but you have more control of it. As with DAO, most of the time we can accept the default environment, rdo-Environment(0), which will not be created until you first reference it.

rdoConnections

An rdoConnection object represents a connection to a particular remote database, such as your Oracle database. An rdoConnection contains the rdoQueries, rdo-Resultsets, and rdoTables collections. Connections are the first level of the hierarchy in which you actually have to start doing something; you can accept the default environment and ignore the rdoEngine, but you have to pay more attention with connections. We will cover these in the next section. Note that you can also use the transaction control methods with the rdoConnection object, and this is perhaps the more usual way to use them.

rdoResultsets

An rdoResultset is the group of rows returned from a query and is the equivalent of a Recordset in DAO. We will look at using rdoResultsets in depth later in the chapter. A single rdoResultset can hold more than one related group of rows. Handling multiple result sets in a single rdoResultset object is a feature that is designed for use with SQL Server, but it can be made to work with Oracle, as you will see in the section "Retrieving PL/SQL Tables." We will leave it to Chapter 17, *ActiveX Data Objects*, to put this technique into practice. Most of the time, you will only have a single Oracle result set in your rdoResultset object.

rdoQueries

An rdoQuery is an object that achieves two major purposes. First, it is a way of preparing a SELECT query with parameters so that you do not have to re-create it each time you change one or more of the parameter values. If you use it several times, it is a way of avoiding the repeated parsing of the statement that ODBC has to do each time you run it. The second major use of rdoQueries is to call stored procedures and retrieve output parameters.

rdoTables

An rdoTable is the representation of a base table in the Oracle database. There is one rdoTable in the rdoTables collection for every Oracle table you have access to. (You might be surprised how many tables this covers if you have developer privileges.) It is directly comparable to the TableDef object in DAO. Some databases allow you to use an rdoTable as the basis for a query, but this does not apply to Oracle. Although DAO allows you to add, modify, and delete tables, RDO does not have this capability. However, this is not the preferred way to modify the database structure anyway.

Databases and Connections

To make use of any of the features of Remote Data Objects, we first have to set up a reference in our application to the RDO library in our current project. We do this process with the following steps:

1. Choose the Project ≻ References to open the References dialog box, as shown in Figure 15.2. You will see a list of all the object libraries that you can reference in your application.

2. Check the option labeled Microsoft Remote Data Object 2.0.

3. Click OK.

FIGURE 15.2:

The References dialog box with the RDO library checked

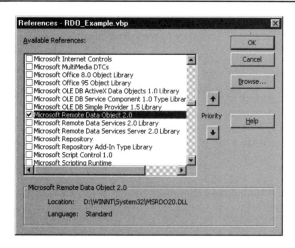

There are two ways to create a connection to your database: the short way and the long way. To pursue the short route, you should jump straight to the section, "Creating a Connection." The long way achieves the same result but allows you to have more control over the environment you create.

If you accept the default environment, you can happily ignore the rdoEngine object. However, if you want full control over any rdoEnvironment objects you subsequently create, you can use properties to set the default values. Table 15.1 shows the defaults you can set. When you are working with Oracle, you will find that the ClientBatch cursor driver is the best option for updatable rdoResultsets because it performs far better than the other cursors. You will have to explicitly set this cursor driver because it is not the default. The other properties of the rdoEnvironment are of limited use.

TABLE 15.1: The rdoEngine Properties You Can Use to Set the Default rdoEnvironment Features

Property	Description
rdoDefaultCursor	This property is the default cursor driver. The possible values you can select are shown in Table 15.2.
rdoDefaultUser	This property is the default Oracle logon user name.
rdoDefaultPassword	This property is the password associated with the rdoDefaultUser.
rdoDefaultErrorThreshold	This property is the filter on error-severity codes. Meaningless in an Oracle environment.
rdoDefaultLoginTimeout	This property is the maximum time allowed to try to make connection with the database.
rdoVersion	This property indicates the version number of the RDO library.

TABLE 15.2: The Possible Default Cursor-Driver Library Options in the rdoEngine Object

Constant	Value	Description
rdUseIfNeeded	0	This constant is the default value. The ODBC Driver Manager selects which cursor-driver library to use. In the case of Oracle, it will select the ODBC cursor library (rdUseOdbc).
rdUseOdbc	1	This constant uses the ODBC cursor library on the client machine.
rdUseServer	2	This constant uses server-side cursors. Not available for Oracle.

Continued on next page

TABLE 15.2 CONTINUED: The Possible Default Cursor-Driver Library Options in the rdoEngine Object

Constant	Value	Description
rdUseClientBatch	3	This constant uses the ClientBatch cursor library that was developed for FoxPro and is significantly faster than the rdUserOdbc option. Use this for updatable rdoResultsets.
rdUseNone	4	This constant indicates the cursor will be a forward-only, read-only, one-row-at-a-time cursor. This constant is not really a cursor at all, but it matches the way Oracle produces the result set, making it very efficient.

Remember that the options shown in Table 15.2 are for selecting the cursor-driver library, not the cursor itself. However, as Oracle developers, we have a limited and simple choice. If you are sure you will not need any updatable result sets in your application, then choose *rdUseNone*; otherwise, you should select *RdUseClientBatch*, which is considerably faster than *rdUseOdbc*.

The example in Listing 15.1 shows how to use the properties of the rdoEngine to set up connections that you subsequently make. In this case, we are setting the default user information. Assuming it is correct, there will be no errors or need for the Driver Manager to prompt for information. This information would probably come from your own logon dialog box. In reality, you will probably define user information when you create the connection, although this is a good place to set the values if you intend to connect to several database instances at the same time. The code also defines the cursor-driver library and the time-out period for making the connection.

Listing 15.1

```
With rdoEngine
    .rdoDefaultCursorDriver = rdUseClientBatch
    .rdoDefaultUser = "video_user"
    .rdoDefaultPassword = "ummagumma"
    .rdoDefaultLoginTimeout = 5
End With
```

Creating an rdoEnvironment Object

You will probably not need to create an rdoEnvironment object because the default object is often sufficient. However, if you want to use ODBC transaction control for different databases or you want to have connections for different users, then you need to be able to create your own environments.

To create an rdoEnvironment object, you use the following syntax:

```
Set env_variable = rdoCreateEnvironment (name, user, password)
```

The object has the following arguments:

name   A string that uniquely identifies the rdoEnvironment object.

user   A string that identifies the owner of the new rdoEnvironment object.

password   A string of up to 14-characters long that contains the logon password for the new rdoEnvironment object.

rdoCreateEnvironment is probably one of the least important methods and can normally be forgotten. However, Listing 15.2 shows an example of setting up the environment. The User and Password arguments become the default values for this environment in cases where they are not supplied in the connect string. After you execute this, you will have two environments (including the default) logging on to more than one user ID but with the possibility of different transaction scopes in each environment.

Listing 15.2

```
Dim en As rdoEnvironment
Set en = rdoCreateEnvironment("Env2", "JOE", "saucerful")
```

Creating a Connection

The basis of working with RDO is the connection to your Oracle database. Creating the rdoConnection object is the one thing you must do before you can proceed. Unlike the JET engine under DAO, we now have control of the connections and can make better use of the resources available to us. It really is not much different from opening a database in DAO except that we have a slightly different paradigm. The main thing we have to worry about is the database connection string.

Because RDO is an object-based system, when we open a connection to a remote database, we are actually creating an object that represents that connection. The normal way to create the Connection object is first to declare an object of the correct type and then to use the OpenConnection method to create the object. The OpenConnection syntax is

```
Set connection = environment.OpenConnection(dsName, prompt, readonly,
connect, options)
```

The various arguments for the OpenConnection method are as follows:

dsName   You use this argument to provide the registered Data Source Name (DSN) for the connection. You will often pass this DSN in the connect string, and if you do, you must set a zero-length string ("") as the dsName field. The main advantage of passing a dsName value is that you can identify the connection with it.

prompt   This argument controls how the ODBC logon dialog box will be shown. The possible values are shown in Table 15.3. You should aim to select a prompt argument that causes the users the least amount of confusion while still allowing them to connect to any database they need to. If possible, the ODBC logon dialog box should be avoided entirely.

readonly   You should set this argument to False if you intend to use updatable result sets on this connection, otherwise set it to True.

connect   This argument holds the ODBC connect string we saw in Chapter 11, *Client-Side Technology*. If you supply a value in the string for the *dsName* argument, then you must not define the DSN field in the connect string.

options   The only important option for Oracle users is the *rdAsynchEnable* constant, which means the connection will be made asynchronously. Once this connection process is started, you get control back in your application to continue processing. You will have to check for a successful completion of the connection process before using the connection (for example, you can use the Connect event). Because you will normally be connecting at start-up and connections do not take too long, this option is not as important as when you create rdoResultsets asynchronously.

TABLE 15.3: Possible Values for the Prompt Parameter

Constant	Value	Description
rdDriverPrompt	0	The ODBC Driver Manager displays the Data Sources dialog box and builds up a connection string from the data supplied.
rdDriverNoPrompt	1	The ODBC Driver Manager uses the connection string you have provided in the *dsName* and connect arguments. If you have not supplied enough information, then you will get a trappable error.
rdDriverComplete (default)	2	If the connect argument includes the DSN, then it will be used to connect, otherwise the Data Sources dialog box is displayed.
rdDriverCompleteRequired	3	This constant is the same as rdDriverComplete except that only information required to logon can be entered.

TIP

As mentioned in Chapter 13, *Visual Basic Design Issues,* allowing a user to see any of the ODBC Driver Manager logon dialog boxes is not the best solution. You should create your own logon dialog box for user name and password and use the rdDriverNoPrompt constant to connect. If your data services are on a middle tier, then this kind of approach is mandatory.

Listing 15.3 shows the procedure ConnectToDatabase, which connects to the database through the default environment. In this case, we have supplied all the logon parameters needed so the rdDriverNoPrompt is used. This causes the Driver Manager to fail if the parameters are wrong and is better than showing the user the Driver Manager or Driver dialog boxes.

Listing 15.3

```
Dim cn As rdoConnection

Private Sub ConnectToDatabase ()

'    Declare and open a connection to the database

    Dim strConnection As String
```

```
        strConnection = "DSN=movies; UID=video_user; PWD=ummagumma;"

        Set cn = rdoEngine.rdoEnvironments(0).OpenConnection _
            ("movies", rdDriverNoPrompt, False, strConnection)
    End Sub
```

Creating Stand-Alone Connections

An alternative way to create a connection is with a *stand-alone* connection. To do this, you create the Connection object by declaring it *New* as in

```
    Dim cn as New rdoConnection
```

or

```
    Set cn as New rdoConnection
```

Now you have an object you can manipulate with properties, such as Connect, until you are ready to actually connect to a database with the EstablishConnection method.

DSN-less Connections

The traditional way to make a connection with an ODBC data source is through a registered Data Source Name (DSN). First, you have to set a DSN up for every client machine that runs your application. Then, when your application runs, the application has to look up the DSN in the Registry and find out which ODBC driver to use. This takes a little time.

With RDO 2.0, you can create a connection without a DSN, the so-called DSN-less connection. To do this, you have to specify the name of the ODBC driver in the connect string after the DRIVER keyword. You must make sure you specify the exact name for the driver (which you can find out from the ODBC Admin program) and include it in braces. As an example, suppose you want to connect to the Movie database in the most efficient way. Listing 15.4 shows an alternative to the ConnectToDatabase procedure that does this through a DSN-less connection. In this example, we also use the ClientBatch cursor library.

Listing 15.4

```
Dim cn As rdoConnection

Private Sub ConnectToDatabase()

    Dim strConnection As String

    With rdoEngine
        .rdoDefaultCursorDriver = rdUseClientBatch
        .rdoDefaultUser = "video_user"
        .rdoDefaultPassword = "ummagumma"
        .rdoDefaultLoginTimeout = 1
    End With

    strConnection = "SERVER=movies;" & _
                    "DRIVER={Microsoft ODBC for Oracle};"

    Set cn = rdoEngine.rdoEnvironments(0).OpenConnection _
            ("", rdDriverNoPrompt, False, strConnection)

End Sub
```

You should notice in Listing 15.4 that we have specified a default user name and password at the rdoEngine level, so we do not have to duplicate it in the connection string. We must also specify the DSN parameter in the connection string as a zero-length string. However, we do have to specify two new items:

Driver   The exact name of the ODBC driver that you want to use, as shown in the ODBC administration program. The name is not case sensitive, but in must be included in brackets.

Server   The Oracle Service name that you want to connect to; that is, the name that appears in tnsnames.ora.

As mentioned before, the DSN-less connection is an efficient way to connect to the database, although the error messages you receive can be more than a little cryptic. If you do have errors, double-check the names of the server and driver.

rdoConnection Properties

The rdoConnection object has a good number of properties, and these are shown in Table 15.4. Most of them are informational only and probably won't get much use. There are two properties worth pointing out. You can use StillExecuting to see if an asynchronous query on the connection is still executing. (A better way to do this is with the Connect event, which we shall cover in the next section.) The other important property is the QueryTimeout property, which lets you avoid any queries taking more than their fair share of server resources.

TABLE 15.4: The rdoConnection Properties

Property	Description
AsyncCheckInterval	This property shows the number of milliseconds between checks to see if an asynchronous operation is complete (default 1000 ms).
Connect	This property shows the connection string used to make the connection.
CursorDriver	This property shows the number referring to the cursor driver used.
LoginTimeout	This property shows the timeout period (in seconds) for making the connection.
LogMessages	This property enables ODBC trace logging.
Name	This property shows the name of the connection.
QueryTimeout	This property shows the timeout period (in seconds) for the query on this connection.
LastQueryResults	This property refers to the last rdoResultset.
RowsAffected	This property shows the number of data rows affected by the last Execute method. Oracle does not return the values.
StillConnecting	This property indicates an asynchronous connection request is still underway.
StillExecuting	This property indicates an asynchronous Execute method is still underway.
Transactions	This property indicates if the connection supports transactions.
UpdateOperation	This property indicates whether you can use the Update method or whether you must use the Delete and Insert methods instead.

rdoConnection Events

Three events are fired when you make a connection (see the top of Table 15.5). You will probably not use these events often, but you might need them if you are carefully controlling your logon environment. For example, the BeforeConnect event lets you test and even change the connect string before the connection is made. The Connect event lets you test the connection and retry it if any problems have occurred (perhaps an ideal spot for failing over to another data source if one exists). It is also useful if you are using an asynchronous connection because it flags the completion of the process (successfully or otherwise). The only thing you cannot do is to stop the connection process, short of terminating the application. The second half of Table 15.5 shows events that will fire when you are executing a query.

> **NOTE**   The QueryComplete event fires for any query completion, not just asynchronous queries.

TABLE 15.5: The rdoConnection Object Events

Event Name	Description
BeforeConnect	This event is fired before RDO attempts to connect to the Oracle database.
Connect	This event is fired after RDO has completed the connection operation, even if it is unsuccessful.
Disconnect	This event is fired after a connection to the database has been closed.
QueryComplete	This event is fired when a query run on this connection is completed.
QueryTimeout	This event is fired after the QueryTimeout period is reached.
WillExecute	This event is fired before the query is executed, allowing you to check or change the query or even cancel it.

We cannot use the events in Table 15.5 like we do the events from most of the other objects we use, such as a timer or a text box. The RDO library is an ActiveX object, and we have to take some special steps to make our application aware of the events. The first thing we must do is declare our objects, such as the rdoConnection object, with the WithEvents keyword. This declares that the object can respond to the events from RDO (see Listing 15.5). Note that you cannot use the New keyword in the same declaration as WithEvents.

With the declaration complete, we now have to create a procedure that will be called by the event. To do this step, we create a procedure with the rdoConnections name and add on the event name from Table 15.5, separated by an underscore. For example, if the connections name is *cn*, then to receive the QueryComplete event, we create a procedure cn_QueryComplete.

Listing 15.5

```
Private WithEvents cn As rdoConnection


Private Sub cn_Connect(ByVal ErrorOccurred As Boolean)

    If ErrorOccurred Then
        MsgBox "You encountered an error trying to connect !"
    Else
        MsgBox "You have connected !"
    End If
End Sub
```

When you use the WithEvents keyword, you should use the drop-down boxes for events in the Editor window to show the exact form of the event procedure. If your procedure and its ActiveX definition do not match exactly, you will get a compiler error. This is a good opportunity to use the Object Browser available under the View menu to show the possible events and their required parameters. Figure 15.3 shows the Object Browser being used to show the Connect event.

FIGURE 15.3:

The Object Browser displaying the Connect event

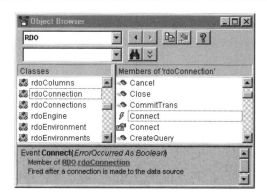

Working with rdoResultsets

Retrieving rows of data from your Oracle database is the most fundamental operation you will carry out. Each data-access method has its own particular way of doing the retrieval, and in RDO, the operation is performed by the OpenResultset method of the Connection object. The syntax of this command is as follows:

```
Set rs = cn.OpenResultset (source, type, locktype, options)
```

The arguments to this method are outlined below:

> **source**   The source argument defines how the result set is created. This will normally be a SQL string that is hard-coded or built up by the program (the OpenResultset method also works against the rdoQuery, which we will see later in the chapter). Note that the source cannot be an Oracle-stored procedure because Oracle cannot return result sets from stored procedures, though you may wish to investigate the section "Retrieving PL/SQL Tables" later in the chapter.

> **type**   This argument defines the type of cursor you want to create. Table 15.6 lists the available types of cursor.

> **locktype**   This argument defines the concurrency model that controls the locking aspects of the rdoResultset. The various locktypes are listed in Table 15.7.

> **options**   The only options you can choose are rdAsynchEnable, which allows you to create your result set without waiting for it to complete (which we will see later), and rdExecDirect, which is a SQL Server–only parameter for controlling temporary stored procedures.

NOTE   Control of the QueryTimeout value is done through the rdoConnection object, not the rdoResultset object.

TABLE 15.6: The Possible Values for the Type Parameter

Constant	Value	Description
rdOpenForwardOnly	0	This constant opens a forward-only rdoResultset object. It is generally associated with a read-only rdoResultset and is the most efficient cursor. (This is the default value.)
rdOpenKeyset	1	This constant opens a keyset rdoResultset. It is the type you will normally use for an updatable Resultset.
rdOpenDynamic	2	This constant opens a dynamic rdoResultset object, which is not available to Oracle users.
rdOpenStatic	3	This constant opens a static rdoResultset object. It is the type you will normally use for read-only but scrollable data.

TABLE 15.7: The Possible Values for the Locktype Parameter

Constant	Value	Description
rdConcurReadOnly	1	This constant defines a read-only rdoResultset. (This is the default value.)
rdConcurLock	2	This constant defines pessimistic concurrency (lock on Edit method).This is not effective with Oracle, and you may be warned of an update conflict.
rdConcurRowVer	3	This constant defines optimistic concurrency based on the Time_Stamp column (not available with Oracle).
rdConcurValues	4	This constant defines optimistic concurrency based on row values.
rdConcurBatch	5	This constant defines optimistic concurrency using Batch mode updates (needs the ClientBatch cursor driver). Status values are returned for each row successfully updated.

All the information needed to describe how to return a set of data can be confusing, especially if you are new to the environment. Exactly which combination of options are the ones to use with Oracle? Luckily, Oracle cannot support many of the options that are available, and so we can reduce everything to a couple of simple possibilities: updatable result sets and read-only result sets.

NOTE Notice that with RDO, we do not have any need for SQLPassThrough to be specified. There is no local processing with RDO and thus no need for the option. All SQL statements are processed by the back-end database.

Creating Updatable Result Sets

The most obvious way to update data is with the updatable rdoResultset object. As you will recall from the discussion on ODBC cursors in Chapter 11, *Client-Side Technology*, we are pretty much restricted to using a keyset cursor. The example in Listing 15.6 shows the most common way to do this. You should make sure that you use the ClientBatch cursor library when you set up the rdoEngine object because it is far more efficient at supporting any scrollable cursors than the default ODBC cursor library.

Listing 15.6

```
Dim rs as rdoResultset
Dim strSQL as string


strSQL = " SELECT * FROM video_store.movies WHERE rating = 'G'"
Set rs = cn.OpenResultset (strSQL, _
                           rdOpenKeyset, _
                           rdConcurValues)
```

This example opens the rdoResultset with the source query set in the *strSQL* string. We open a keyset cursor to allow us to update the data, and we use the *rdConcurValues* locktype argument for optimistic updating. You could use the rdConcurBatch concurrency type, which basically waits until you execute the BatchUpdate method before it communicates any changes to Oracle. You can also use the *rdConcurReadOnly* model with a keyset cursor, but that would just be a waste of resources.

NOTE Remember that the rdoResultset will not be updatable if there is no unique key on the table or if you are using a read-only cursor. If you have insufficient privileges to update the data, you will get an error message back from the Update method.

Creating Read-Only Result Sets

The updatable cursors we saw in the previous section are not an efficient way to update data in your Oracle database. The cursor itself takes resources on the client machine (memory and processing), but it also takes resources on the server. It is also not a scalable methodology. A better approach is to use the cheapest cursor possible. The cost of the cursor is defined in terms of the resources it uses. With RDO, we can use either a read-only cursor or a forward-only cursor. If you look at Table 15.6 and Table 15.7, you will notice that RDO defaults to the cheapest type of cursor support, the forward-only.

Scrollable Result Sets

To create a fully scrollable (that is, backward as well as forward), read-only rdoResultset object, we must use the right combination of options: these are the static cursor and the read-only concurrency model. An example of how you do this is shown in Listing 15.7. You can use the Clientbatch cursor library in this situation because it gives you more efficient scrolling cursors than the ODBC cursor library.

Listing 15.7

```
Dim rs as rdoResultset
Dim strSQL as string

strSQL = " SELECT * video_store.movies WHERE rating = 'R'"
Set rs = cn.OpenResultset (strSQL, _
                    rdOpenStatic, _
                    rdConcurReadOnly)
```

Forward-Only Result Sets

The cheapest cursor model is the forward-only, read-only cursor. This cursor is the cheapest because this is precisely the way Oracle returns the rows of your SELECT statement to you, with no scrolling back and no update capability. There is no need to cache anything on the client, though your application may duplicate this functionality by placing the data in a grid or some similar control. The example in Listing 15.8 shows how to do this. In this case, you do not need a scrolling cursor library, and it would be a waste of resources to request one (assuming you do not use scrolling cursors anywhere else in your application). When you create your rdoEngine object, you should specify the rdUserNone option.

Listing 15.8

```
Dim rs as rdoResultset
Dim strSQL as string

strSQL = " SELECT * video_store.movies WHERE rating = 'R'"
Set rs = cn.OpenResultset (strSQL, _
                           rdOpenForwardOnly, _
                           rdConcurReadOnly)
```

It may seem a little pedantic going over these examples that differ by only one line, but it shows the whole range of possible cursor types you have to work with in RDO. Creating the rdoResultset object need not get any more complicated.

NOTE   As an Oracle user, you can forget everything that you have heard about retrieving multiple result sets with RDO. Multiple result sets are a feature of SQL Server in which a SELECT statement in a stored procedure sends back the associated result set to the calling program. Oracle does not work this way: you cannot even retrieve a single result set from Oracle unless you use Oracle Objects for OLE (see Chapter 18). You can, however, now duplicate this effect by retrieving a PL/SQL table into one or more rdoResultsets. We will cover this later in the chapter. It's a lot more work, but it's at least possible.

The ClientBatch Cursor Library

We have mentioned the ClientBatch cursor library a couple of times, but it does deserve some special attention. It was created by the FoxPro team specifically for Visual Basic and presents a much faster cursor library than the default ODBC library. Although the Client-Batch cursor library comes at the expense of a slightly larger footprint, you should always use this library if you use scrollable result sets, whether they are updatable or not.

However, the capabilities of the library go much further than a performance gain. As its name suggests, you can use the library to do *batch* updates of changes. This means that rather than a row-by-row update as you would normally expect, you can save up all your updates to the Oracle database and do them together. Do not confuse batch updates with transaction control, which you may still need to use in addition to the batch updates.

Continued on next page

Using batch updates can mean saving your changes for minutes or even hours, which can cause a lot of problems when it comes time to do the update. It is certainly not a method suitable for a highly changing environment, and it is not scalable; however, you may find situations where it is appropriate. If you do use it, then you have to ensure that you set it up properly, and you should keep these points in mind:

- Define the ClientBatch cursor library for the connection before you set up a rdo-Resultset.

- Select the rdConcurBatch concurrency model.

- Use the BatchUpdate method to save any batch changes.

- Resolve any update collisions or errors.

There is much work to be done in getting batch updates to work, particularly when it comes to resolving collisions and error. It is wise to take a leaf out of the replication-design book and try to design so that there is little or no possibility of update conflicts. Designing this way can be a complex matter, but it can be done; for example, a Human Resources database has a single user responsible for updating which users have access to selected views, or perhaps a single user has control of a specific subset of the data in a certain time range. Only you can tell if your application fits these requirements.

Using rdoResultset Events

Just as with the rdoConnection object, the rdoResultset object exposes events that you can use with the WithEvents keyword in the rdoResultset declaration. These events are outlined in Table 15.8. All the events put more control over the operations of the rdoResultset into your hands.

TABLE 15.8: The Events Triggered When You Use an rdoResultset

Event Name	Description
Associate	This event is fired after a new connection is associated with the object.
Dissociate	This event is fired after the connection is set to nothing.
ResultsChange	This event is fired after the current rowset is changed. This only applies to multiple result sets used to retrieve PL/SQL tables.
RowStatusChange	This event is fired after the current rowset has been changed by an Edit, Delete, or AddNew method.

Continued on next page

TABLE 15.8 CONTINUED: The Events Triggered When You Use an rdoResultset

Event Name	Description
RowCurrencyChange	This event is fired after the current row pointer is changed.
WillAssociate	This event is fired before a new connection is associated with the object (allows you to cancel the operation).
WillDissociate	This event is fired before the connection is set to nothing (allows you to cancel the operation).
WillUpdateRows	This event is fired before an update to the database occurs.

There are two important sets of events here. Firstly, four events are linked to running dissociated rdoResultsets. A dissociated rdoResultset is where you set up a stand-alone rdoResultset object (with the New keyword), populate it, and then close the connection with the Set cn = Nothing statement. The rdoResultset will stay alive, ready for you to reconnect by setting the ActiveConnection property. This is mainly useful if you are running in ClientBatch mode and for keeping any changes until you reconnect and make the changes in the database with the BatchUpdate method (typical of techniques used with a Web interface).

The second useful event is WillUpdateRows. This event is triggered before RDO tries to send changes to the Oracle database with the Update method. The event gives you the opportunity to use your own methods to update the data, in particular with a stored procedure. This becomes a useful feature to allow you to handle updates with a read-only result set, because you can supply a return code to indicate successful completion, and you do not have to refresh the result set.

None of these events are available by default. You have to declare the rdoResultset with the WithEvents keyword and code it as we saw in Listing 15.5 when we did the same thing for the rdoConnection object.

Exploring rdoResultset Methods and Properties

RDO was built after DAO and, apart from using "rdoResultset" rather than the "Recordset" of DAO, it uses the same method names. An object-oriented designer would say that this exhibits polymorphism in which the same method name can be applied to different objects and produce potentially different effects. We will see the same applies to ActiveX Data Objects and Oracle Objects for OLE. Although it is good to know there is a theoretical reason for naming the methods the same, a more pragmatic view would be, why name the methods anything different? The term *rdoResultset* is the only thing to get left out of this concept.

Populating the rdoResultset

As with DAO, an rdoResultset is never fully populated with data until you get to the last row. With any scrollable cursor, it should be your aim to get to the end of the result set or, even better, to close the result set as soon as possible. Because Oracle can support pending result sets (that is, result sets that have not been closed), this is not a particularly serious problem, but you should try to close the them as soon as possible. RDO is inherently more efficient at populating a result set compared to DAO, and there are no FillCache methods.

Changing the Current Row

You can use the DAO Move methods that we first saw in Table 14.6 to move the current row in the rdoResultset. The BOF and EOF properties of the rdoResultset should be tested as you did with DAO. The major difference from DAO is that RDO allows you to use the MoveLast method asynchronously. In this case, you can arrange for a Completion event from the rdoResultset when the move is complete. This is useful for large rdoResultsets that take a long time to populate; however, it is a warning sign that you may have result sets that are too large. Note that if you have forward-only cursors, you can only use the MoveNext method.

Accessing the Fields of a rdoResultset

The DAO Recordset has the Fields collection, whereas the rdoResultset has the rdoColumns collection. The main use for this collection is to review the data in the result set, but we shall see later that it can also be used to view the structure of the database table. Sometimes, you will need the kind of information that this collection can give you to use rdoQueries and other objects. For example, you can check the ChunkRequired property to see if you need to use the GetChunk and AppendChunk methods on a long, binary data column.

As with DAO, to find the value of any column in the current row of the rdoResultset, you can reference it by index (ordinal number) or by name. The syntax for this is

```
rs (iCol)
```

or

```
rs ("name")
```

Once again, as with DAO, we will use this information to fill a list box. In this version, we will use the slightly more efficient method of using WITH...END WITH to refer to the rdoResultset, as shown in Listing 15.9. Yes, there are data bound ways to do this method, but the listing illustrates the point.

Listing 15.9

```
Public Sub FillListBox(ListBox As ComboBox)

'    Fill a list box with movie names
'    Ignore error trapping

     Dim rs As rdoResultset
     Dim strSQL As String

     strSQL = "SELECT movie_name FROM video_store.movies"
     Set rs = cn.OpenResultset(strSQL, _
                          rdOpenForwardOnly, _
                          rdConcurReadOnly)

     ListBox.Clear
     With rs
         While Not .EOF
             ListBox.AddItem rs("movie_name")
             .MoveNext
         Wend
     ListBox.ListIndex = 0   ' Display the first item
     End With

     Set rs = Nothing

End Sub
```

Changing the Rows and Values in a rdoResultset

Following again the lead of DAO, we use the AddNew, Edit, Update, and Delete methods on an updatable rdoResultset if we want to change the row values in the rdoResultset. We will see an example of this later in the chapter in the section "Putting It All Together."

Finding a Particular Row

One thing you will encounter with RDO is that it does not support any of the Find methods. This will be annoying to those of you raised on updatable Record-sets in DAO/JET, but it is all part of the sleek and slim profile represented by RDO.

It does not have anything in particular to do with being connected to a remote database. As we mentioned in the last chapter, if you use any of the FIND commands, it indicates that you should have selected a smaller result set in the first place. If you find the command hard to give up, note down the criteria you use for the FIND statement and build a new rdoResultset around it. Strangely enough, Oracle Objects for OLE, in contrast, presents a much richer FIND capability than RDO.

Fetching Multiple Rows

RDO contains the GetRows method we saw in the previous chapter. This method allows you to pull multiple rows from the Oracle database into a variant array. It is one of the most efficient methods used to retrieve data if you need all the rows and columns.

Closing a rdoResultset

The rdoResultset should be closed as soon as possible, and you should do this step by explicitly setting the object to Nothing, such as

```
Set rs = Nothing
```

or you can use the Close method.

Using rdoQuery Objects

Creating rdoResultsets with the static SQL strings as we saw in the previous section works fine but only up to a point. Have you ever looked at the queries in your code and noticed that you often execute the same query with only a small change in the WHERE clause between each one? For example, you might code

```
SELECT * video_store.movies WHERE rating = 'PG-13'
```

and then later run more or less the same query with

```
SELECT * video_store.movies WHERE rating = 'G'
```

You certainly have code that builds up much more complex queries than this piece by piece, each time through. This may require substantial processing to put the query together. But there are several problems with this process. First, building the query can become complex and make your code difficult to read. Second, RDO, ODBC, and Oracle must parse the query each time you execute it.

The rdoQuery object can provide a good solution to this problem, although, as we shall see in the next section, it is even more important in executing stored procedures. rdoQueries are a more sophisticated way of communicating with ODBC and the database, and they make use of ODBC's parameter capabilities.

NOTE   RDO does not use Oracle bind parameters. Only Oracle Objects for OLE can use them, and we will see this in Chapter 18.

First, we shall look at how to use the rdoQuery in a simple way with what could be called a hard-coded SQL string that we have used so far with the OpenResultset method. We need to use the CreateQuery method of the rdoConnection object, which has the following syntax:

```
query = cn.CreateQuery (name, query_string)
```

Name is an arbitrary name for the query, and *query_string* defines the SQL string. We now use the OpenResultset method of the Query object to retrieve the result set from Oracle. The syntax of this method is the same as for the rdConnection object, except that in this case, we do not provide the SQL string (see the section "Working with rdoResultsets," earlier in the chapter). To create the query and use it to produce the result set, we can use the OpenResultset method, as shown in Listing 15.10.

Listing 15.10

```
Dim qy As rdoQuery
Dim rs As rdoResultset
Dim strSQL As String

strSQL = "SELECT * FROM video_store.movies WHERE rating = 'PG-13'"
Set qy = cn.CreateQuery("query1", strSQL)
Set rs = qy.OpenResultset(rdOpenForwardOnly, _
                          rdConcurReadOnly)
```

I prefer to leave the query name blank, especially while developing the code. If you specify the name, then you cannot re-create the query. In a production environment, you do not want this to happen anyway, but leaving the query name blank means that you can reexecute the query creation (by moving the current-program-line pointer backwards) and fix any problems you might have found.

To improve on the simple example shown in Listing 15.10, we introduce the concept of *query parameters*. To find out what you should use as a parameter, you must look at your code to find which values change. In the example above, it is the Rating column, but in a complex query, you could end up with many values that could change. There is one rdoParameters collection for each rdoQuery, and these collections provide a way to set up a query independent of these values in the WHERE clause, and you provide only the values that change just before you execute the query.

For ODBC to know where in the query these parameters should go, we use a question mark in the SQL string as a placeholder for the parameter. This is the syntax that the ODBC API uses internally. In our example, we would use

```
strSQL = "SELECT * video_store. movies WHERE rating = ? "
```

Now we have to provide a value for this placeholder, and for this, we use the parameters collection. We do not have to create or add Parameter objects to the collection, because RDO creates them for us when we create the query. All we have to do is provide a value for them. Listing 15.11 shows an example of how we would do this in a query with two parameters: one a string and one a number. Notice that you have to get the order of the parameters correct and that they are numbered consecutively from zero.

Listing 15.11

```
Dim qy2 As rdoQuery
Dim rs As rdoResultset
Dim strSQL As String

strSQL = "SELECT * video_store. movies WHERE year_of_release > ? "
strSQL = strSQL & " AND rating = ? ORDER BY movie_name"
```

```
Set qy2 = cn.CreateQuery("", strSQL)
qy2.rdoParameters(0) = 1995
qy2.rdoParameters(1) = "PG-13"
Set rs = qy2.OpenResultset(rdOpenForwardOnly, _
                            rdConcurReadOnly)

While Not rs.EOF
    MsgBox rs(1)
    rs.MoveNext
Wend
Set rs = Nothing
```

If you want to change any of the parameters, you do not need to rebuild the query, you just change the parameters you want and then use the Requery method of the rdoResultset, and the work is done. However, make sure you do not re-create the query variable a second time unless you know why you are doing it.

The rdoQuery object sports a variety of properties, and these are shown in Table 15.9. These properties are particularly useful for creating stand-alone rdoQueries in which you set up the object and then provide the properties, the last of which will be setting the ActiveConnection to a valid rdoConnection.

TABLE 15.9: RdoQuery Properties

Property	Description
ActiveConnection	This property returns or sets the active connection for this query object. You need this if you have created a stand-alone rdoQuery object.
BindThreshold	This property indicates the largest column to be automatically bound. The default value is 1024, and for anything greater than the threshold, you must use the GetChunk and AppendChunk methods.
CursorType	This property returns or sets the cursor to use for the query. This is the same cursor selection that we saw in Table 15.6.
KeysetSize	This property indicates the size of the keyset buffer used when creating cursors.
LockType	This property returns or sets the concurrency model, which sets the Locking method for the query.

Continued on next page

TABLE 15.9 CONTINUED: RdoQuery Properties

Property	Description
MaxRows	This property indicates the maximum number of rows to be returned by a query.
Prepared	This property indicates if the rdoQuery object should be prepared by the ODBC SQLPrepare function. With SQL Server, you can use this property to create a temporary stored procedure on the server, but this has no effect on an Oracle database.
QueryTimeout	This property indicates how long the ODBC Driver Manager waits before timing the query out and firing the QueryTimeout event.
RowsAffected	This property indicates how many rows are affected by an action query.
RowsetSize	This property determines how many rows are buffered internally when building a cursor. RowsetSize must be "1" for a forward-only cursor.
SQL	This property contains the SQL string that forms the source of the query.
StillExecuting	This property indicates if the query is still executing.
Type	This property indicates what type of query it is (such as a select query or stored procedure).
Updatable	This property indicates whether the result set generated by an rdoQuery can be updated.

NOTE   The MaxRows property will restrict the number of rows returned from the Oracle results via ODBC but will not have any affect on the Oracle query at all. If you want to restrict the number of rows, then use the Oracle syntax in your WHERE clause, `WHERE rownum < 500`, or something similar.

The easiest way to set up an rdoQuery is to create one particular procedure in your module to initialize all the queries to be used in the module. You should then declare the rdoQuery object as a private, module-level variable, so that it is available throughout the module. Remember that you should create the query only once, although you execute it many times. Try to avoid defining the queries in a Form_Load event, but by all means, call the query initialization procedure from there. You should not need to make the rdoQuery object available outside of the module, class, or form. If you do, then you have probably not encapsulated the data access properly in your design, and you should review the situation.

NOTE   The rdoPreparedStatement object is obsolete and was replaced by rdoQueries in Visual Basic 5. You should convert over to rdoQueries as soon as you have a chance.

Executing SQL Commands

You can execute SQL commands in exactly the same way as with DAO, but this time, we use the Execute method of the rdoConnection object rather than the Database object. You will normally use this method to run the INSERT, UPDATE, and DELETE commands and perhaps the COMMIT and ROLLBACK commands for transaction control. (Note that RDO has an autocommit on every database access including executing SQL commands, so the extra COMMIT is not by default required in this case.) Listing 15.12 shows an example of how to do this with RDO. You can only include one SQL command at a time, and you do not include a terminating semicolon. (However, see the sidebar "Anonymous PL/SQL Code Blocks" later in the chapter for a better way to do this.)

Listing 15.12

```
Dim strSQL As String

strSQL = "DELETE video_store.movies WHERE movie_id = 303"
cn.Execute strSQL

strSQL = "COMMIT"
cn.Execute strSQL
```

NOTE   Remember that if you execute these commands, the deleted row will still be in any current rdoResultset until it is refreshed.

There are a couple of options you can use with the Execute method that differ considerably from DAO. These are shown in Table 15.10.

TABLE 15.10: The rdoConnection Execute Method Options

Constant	Value	Description
rdAsyncEnable	32	This constant executes the SQL command asynchronously.
rdExecDirect	64	This constant bypasses creation of a stored procedure to execute the query. Does not apply to Oracle.

If you choose to use the asynchronous option, then you will need to check for completion of an event as we will see in the section, "Asynchronous Operation," later in the chapter.

> **NOTE**
>
> Even though a tool like SQL*Plus will inform you of the number of rows affected by your DML "Action" statement, there is no mechanism for Oracle to return this value to ODBC. As a result, the RowsAffected property will always be zero.

Calling Stored Procedures

In the previous section, we saw how to execute a SQL statement in RDO. What we are actually doing is executing an anonymous PL/SQL code block (in this case, just one statement), and this is the way you can execute a stored procedure as we saw in Chapter 14, *Data Access Objects*. However, as with DAO, we are restricted to a hard-coded or built-up SQL statement, with no way of retrieving output parameters. But with any technology later than DAO, we can make use of the output parameters, and this provides us with a fundamental improvement in the way we can use stored procedures.

You need to ensure you have the right ODBC driver to ensure you can retrieve output parameters and to define your procedures with a schema. The ODBC driver that comes with Visual Basic 6 satisfies these requirements, though many others do not (including the VB5 version). The only thing that is currently lacking with the Visual Basic ODBC driver is that it does not support PL/SQL Packages.

To make use of output parameters, we once again visit the rdoQuery object that we saw earlier in the chapter. We use the same parameter placeholders (the question mark) and the rdoParameters collection. By default, any parameter is an input parameter, which was fine for a SELECT query, but to use parameters with stored procedures that have directions other than input, we have to ensure that the correct direction is set for each one. Luckily, you can do this with the Direction property of each parameter. Overall, there are four properties to the Parameter object, and these are shown in Table 15.11.

TABLE 15.11: The Properties for the Parameter Object

Property	Description
Direction	This property shows the direction of the parameter, as shown in Table 15.9.
Name	This property shows the name of the parameter. (It can be left blank.)
Type	This property shows the data type for the parameter.
Value	This property shows the actual value of the parameter.

NOTE   Notice that Value is the default property of the Parameter object, so you do not have to define it. You will also find that the Parameters property of the rdoQuery object is the default, so you do not have to define that either.

Take a look at the stored procedure you want to execute, and find each parameter (the formal arguments) and the mode of each. Remember that if your stored procedure does not specify a mode, then it defaults to IN. Table 15.12 shows the conversion from PL/SQL mode to RDO parameter direction constant.

TABLE 15.12: The Modes for RDO Parameters

PL/SQL Mode	RDO Parameter Constant	Description
IN	rdParamInput	Input value only
IN OUT	rdParamInputOutput	Input and Output value
OUT	rdParamOutput	Output value only

TIP   RDO 2.0 seems to be quite successful at determining the direction and data type of the parameters by itself, so you can often leave this direction property out. However, if you use LONG- or RAW-type data, then you will have to declare these yourself.

As an example, we will improve on the code to execute the stored procedure that we saw in the previous chapter (see Listing 14.7). First, we are going to improve the stored procedure. We will use the PL/SQL procedure *movies_insert3* (see Listing 15.13), which inserts a new movie record, sets the key value from an Oracle sequence, and then returns that value to us via an IN OUT mode parameter. The advantage of this is that you could then use the value as the foreign key to another INSERT statement, for example, one that stores data for video copies of a movie. The example actually allows you to pass your own key value and creates a new one only if you pass zero. This gives a little more control in advanced applications, such as replication in which one database instance already has a row with a certain key and you want to duplicate that in a second instance.

Listing 15.13

```
PROCEDURE movies_insert3(
  p_movie_id IN OUT NUMBER,
  p_name     IN     VARCHAR2,
  p_length   IN     NUMBER,
  p_rating   IN     VARCHAR2,
  p_year     IN     NUMBER) IS

/*  Insert a new movie into the movie table
    If the formal parameter, p_movie_id is zero it is assigned
    from the next available sequence number.
*/

BEGIN

  IF p_movie_id = 0 THEN
    SELECT movie_sequence_id.NEXTVAL INTO p_movie_id FROM dual;
  END IF;

  INSERT INTO movies VALUES (
    p_movie_id, p_name, p_length, p_rating, p_year, USER, SYSDATE);

  COMMIT;

EXCEPTION
/* Whatever the problem just rollback and
   pass the error back to Visual Basic */
  WHEN OTHERS THEN
```

```
        ROLLBACK;
        RAISE;

    END movies_insert3;
```

To execute this stored procedure, we have to set up an rdoQuery to execute it. We must set up one parameter placeholder for each parameter in the stored procedure. We cannot hard-code any of the parameters because ODBC expects one placeholder for each parameter. Because all parameters default to IN direction, you can explicitly define the direction of OUT and IN OUT parameters, though in this case, RDO successfully detects the right directions. Make sure you get the definition exactly right. This time around we will handle queries with a little more care and create a *CreateQueries* procedure that is called at a module level to create any rdoQueries the module will use (see Listing 15.14). When compared with creating a SELECT-type query, we have to use a slightly different syntax, including curly brackets and the CALL keyword, but we must still keep the ODBC parameter placeholders.

Listing 15.14

```
    Dim qyMovieInsert as rdoQuery

    Private Sub CreateQueries()

    '    Set up any queries required in this module

        Dim strSQL As String

        strSQL = "{call movies_insert3 (?, ?, ?, ?, ?) }"
        Set qyMovieInsert = cn.CreateQuery("", strSQL)
    End Sub
```

Now when we actually get around to executing the stored procedure, we need a Visual Basic procedure to make the call. Listing 15.15 shows one way to do this. Notice that the procedure is much simpler and cleaner than hard-coding the parameters in a SQL string, and it also retrieves a useful piece of information.

Listing 15.15

```
Private Sub MovieInsert(iMovieId As Integer, _
    strMovieName As String, _iLength As Integer, _
    strRating As String, iYear As Integer)

'   Insert a new movie into the database

    qyMovieInsert(0) = 0
    qyMovieInsert(1) = strMovieName
    qyMovieInsert(2) = iLength
    qyMovieInsert(3) = strRating
    qyMovieInsert(4) = iYear

    qyMovieInsert.Execute
    MsgBox "The movie_id used was " & qyMovieInsert(0)
End Sub
```

WARNING   With the version of RDO 2.0 that came with Visual Basic 5, you could not include a schema in front of the procedure names. The revised RDO 2.0 library that comes with Visual Basic 6 fixes this problem. However, this has come at the expense of no longer being able to work with packages.

The Anonymous PL/SQL Code Block

We first encountered this strange beast in Chapter 9, *Introduction to PL/SQL*. An anonymous PL/SQL code block is simply an unnamed group of PL/SQL commands in a block structure, defined by a BEGIN and END keyword. It is considered unnamed in comparison with stored procedures and functions, which are named. You can execute anonymous code blocks through ODBC, and that is how we execute stored procedures.

If we take this train of thought a step further, the code within the block can be used for more than a single SQL statement call. The example is to include a COMMIT statement after a DML statement, such as DELETE.

```
strSQL = "BEGIN DELETE FROM movies WHERE id = 123;"
strSQL = strSQL & "COMMIT; "
strSQL = strSQL & "END; "
```

Continued on next page

> There may not be many occasions when you can use this particular technique because RDO includes an automatic commit on every database action unless you are using BeginTrans/CommitTrans transaction control from Visual Basic.

Calling PL/SQL Functions

Something that is often forgotten about in the excitement over stored procedures is that RDO can execute PL/SQL functions just as easily as stored procedures. You cannot execute a function through the JET engine because you cannot retrieve output parameters, which is the basic mechanism of a function. To call a function, you use the same rdoQuery syntax that we saw for stored procedures, except now we include the return value in the definition string. We must also make sure to define the direction of this first parameter as *rdParamReturnValue*. Listing 15.16 shows a simple PL/SQL function, and Listing 15.17 shows the Visual Basic code that calls the function and displays the return value.

Listing 15.16

```
CREATE OR REPLACE FUNCTION GET_MOVIE_ID
    ( p_movie_name IN VARCHAR2 ) RETURN NUMBER

IS

/* Function to return the id for a movie name */

v_movie_id   number(6);

BEGIN
  SELECT movie_id INTO v_movie_id video_store.movies
    WHERE movie_name = p_movie_name;
  RETURN v_movie_id;

EXCEPTION
  WHEN OTHERS THEN
    RETURN -1;
END;
```

Listing 15.17

```
Dim qy1 As rdoQuery
Dim strSQL as String

strSQL = "{ ? = call video_store.get_movie_id (?) }"

Set qy1 = cn.CreateQuery("", strSQL)

qy1.rdoParameters(0).Direction = rdParamReturnValue
qy1(1) = "Awakenings"

qy1.Execute

MsgBox "The id for the movie is " & qy1(0)
```

Asynchronous Operation

The capabilities that RDO brings to Visual Basic developers are extremely power-ful. Given the restrictions of working with ODBC, it is difficult to imagine many improvements that could have been made to RDO. Along with the ability to return output parameters from stored procedures, the ability to execute certain operations asynchronously is one of the most exciting features, and RDO 2.0 has these features in abundance.

With DAO/JET, if you do anything that involves Oracle, whether it is executing a stored procedure or running a query, your application will block (lock up the application) until the action is complete. That is not to say that other applications also lock up, because they don't, but a well-designed application from a user's point of view will never block for more than one second.

Asynchronous operation implies that you start a database operation and then continue with local processing, periodically checking to see if that operation has completed or, preferably, acting on an event that indicates the operation has com-pleted. This event-driven solution became available in Visual Basic 5 and RDO 2.0. You can use asynchronous operation with the following methods:

- OpenConnection
- OpenResultset

- Requery

- MoveLast

- Execute

In each case, you set the rdAsyncEnable constant in the options parameter. Listing 15.18 shows an example of how you would do this.

Listing 15.18

```
Private Sub RefreshRecordset()
'    Ensure the recordset is up to date
'    If the selection box is not set to "ALL" then add a WHERE clause

     Dim strSQL As String

     strSQL = "SELECT movie_name, length, rating, year_of_release, " & _
              "movie_id FROM video_store.movies ORDER BY movie_id"
     Set rsMovies = cn.OpenResultset(strSQL, rdOpenKeyset, _
                    rdConcurRowVer, rdAsyncEnable)

End Sub
```

The ShowRecord procedure call has to move out of this procedure and be executed when the operation is complete.

Checking for Completion

One way to know when the asynchronous operation has completed is to periodically check the StillExecuting property of the object. You can do this in a loop with a DoEvents statement in the middle, but this really does not buy you much in terms of performance. In fact, the overhead of checking may slow down the whole operation. However, at least you can do other things in your program, such as preparing a form. An example of coding the DoEvents statement is

```
While cn.StillExecuting
    DoEvents
Wend
```

A better approach to checking for completion is to put the check in a Timer event, as shown in Listing 15.19. With this method, you have to be careful to remember to disable the timer at design time and enable it straight after you use the CreateResultset method.

Listing 15.19

```
Private Sub Timer1_Timer()

'   This timer event is used to check for completion
'   of the CreateResultset method

    If Not cn.StillExecuting Then
        Timer1.Enabled = False
        ShowRecord
    End If
End Sub
```

Using Events

Although you can use the StillExecuting property, RDO 2.0 offers to do most of the work for you by providing a full event-driven model. By declaring the object, whether it is an rdoConnection or rdoResultset, with the WithEvents keyword, you make the events available to your application. Listing 15.20 shows an example of using events with the rdoResultset that we saw created asynchronously in Listing 15.18.

Listing 15.20

```
Dim WithEvents rsMovies As rdoResultset

Private Sub cn_QueryComplete(ByVal Query As RDO.rdoQuery, _
        ByVal ErrorOccurred As Boolean)

'   Process the QueryComplete event

    ShowRecord

End Sub
```

Asynchronous Operation in Practice

When you use the asynchronous features of RDO or one of the other object models, you need to take more care in your design. You can now let your users continue doing other work while the database action is taking place, but you must take care that your application does not lose track of what it is doing. Users do not want every operation to be submitted and then minutes later get a message box indicating that it has finished. This may work for large Batch-type jobs, but for smaller tasks, it can quickly become overwhelming.

To make practical use of asynchronous operations, you should have something useful that the application or the user can do in the meantime. Here are a few suggestions:

OpenConnection Although your connect time using RDO should be very short, you can still use the connection time to asynchronously do all the local setup processing that is needed. This is especially valuable if you need to make several connections at the same time.

OpenResultSet A typical operation is to put an OpenResultset method in a Form_Load event or preferably a procedure called from the Form_Load event. The form will not display until the result set is fully populated, possibly delaying the form by a few seconds. With asynchronous operation, you can display the form very quickly, but disable data-related functions until the Completion event. This can give your application the illusion of speed that can sometimes be more important than real speed.

MoveLast Populating an rdoResultset can take a noticeable amount of time, especially if you have used the slower ODBC cursor library. This process may only take a second or so, but even if you have no other processing to do in the meantime, you can make your form appear almost instantaneously.

The Biggest Asynchronous Gain

Although I try to work with small result sets, I have come across operations, such as importing data from a large file, that can take an inordinate amount of time because the import requires a great deal of validation and cross-referencing to existing rows. This kind of import can take 10 minutes, but there are situations where it may take an hour or more

Continued on next page

and should really be run in batch while the system is offline (the old overnight runs). However, the days of the database being asleep overnight are becoming much rarer, and using asynchronous operation means that your Visual Basic program can control a medium-size job without locking up the user's application. For jobs longer than a few minutes and those run regularly, you need to place them on a server designed for the purpose, otherwise, you run the risk of losing track of the job if a user terminates the application.

WARNING   Take care with asynchronous operations because they can lead to effects you do not expect. For example, the cn_QueryComplete event fires whenever *any* query completes, not just an asynchronous query. If you have a regular query executed in the event, you will end up with an endless loop.

Retrieving PL/SQL Tables

One of the recent advances made available to us with RDO (as well as with ActiveX Data Objects) is the ability to access PL/SQL tables. We first saw these in Chapter 10, *Creating Stored Procedures*, where they were a kind of dynamic array, based on a table. We can now pull these tables into a result set in an ODBC-based system. In effect, this puts the lie to the assertion that Oracle cannot return a rdoResultset from a stored procedure; however, it is not as simple a task as with Microsoft SQL Server. The system, however, is dependent on the ODBC driver required. (For example, Microsoft ODBC Driver for Oracle 2.0 was required for VB5.) Due to constant changes in the capabilities of the ODBC drivers, you may want to try your luck with PL/SQL tables, but the operation is more reliable with ADO. Given the right combination of components, you can retrieve PL/SQL with RDO, but we will leave the discussion until Chapter 17, *ActiveX Data Objects*. If you wish to try retrieving PL/SQL tables with RDO, you should see the ADO version because the syntax is more or less the same.

Error Handling

Whereas DAO provides the Errors collection for data errors, RDO provides us with the rdoErrors collection. You use this collection in exactly the same way that you would the Errors collection. You should refer back to Chapter 13, *Visual Basic Design Issues*, for an overview of handling errors in a database environment.

TABLE 15.13: The Properties of the rdoError Object for RDO Errors

Property	Description
Number	This property shows the valid number (a long integer).
Description	This property shows a string containing a description of the error.
Source	This property shows the name of the object that raised the error.
SQLRetcode	This property shows a completion code for the statement executed.
SQLState	This property exposes internal ODBC error codes.
HelpContext	This property shows the Help file context ID for the error number.
HelpFile	This property shows the full file name of the Visual Basic Help file.

Putting It All Together

With your transition to RDO, you are likely to be moving away from updatable result sets and toward using read-only result sets with stored-procedure calls to update. Another possibility is you have built middle-tier components to do the updating via SQL commands (in this way, you can give INSERT, UPDATE, and DELETE privileges to your carefully controlled components). For this section, we will view the process of using stored procedures, because it demonstrates the more complex techniques; however, both updatable result sets and SQL commands can be built in quite easily now that we have covered the principles.

We will take the opportunity to improve upon the DAO example by displaying the participants in the movie that is being reviewed. You can see the form in Figure 15.4.

FIGURE 15.4:

The RDO movie update form

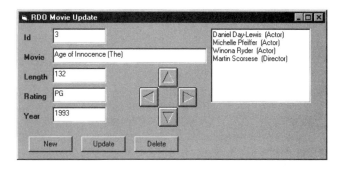

Much of the code is the same as we saw in Chapter 14, *Data Access Objects,* but it includes the techniques we have covered in this chapter. One particular point to note is the query that pulls out the participants (actors and directors) associated with the displayed movie. It is interesting because the query is a little more complicated than we have seen in most of the chapter. Creating a query to handle the process is an excellent way of hiding the complexity of the SQL statement. Listing 15.21 shows the code for the *CreateQueries* procedure, which first sets up the Movies_ Insert3 query and then sets up an rdoQuery to retrieve the list of participants for the movie. This listing includes one parameter for the Movie_Name; it also includes a DECODE function that converts the participant code to a more meaningful name. For more information on creating SQL queries, see Chapter 7, *Queries.*

Listing 15.21

```
Private Sub CreateQueries()

'   Set up any queries required in this module

    Dim strSQL As String
    On Error GoTo ErrorHandler

'   Set up the query to call the insert stored procedure.

    strSQL = "{call video_store.movies_insert3 (?, ?, ?, ?, ?) }"
    Set qyMovieInsert = cn.CreateQuery("", strSQL)


'   Set up the query to select the participants.
```

```
    strSQL = "SELECT first_name || ' ' || last_name full_name,"
    strSQL = strSQL & " DECODE (role, 'A', 'Actor', 'D', 'Director') _
            & "role, movie_id"
    strSQL = strSQL & " FROM video_store.participants, " & _
                        video_store.movie_participants"
    strSQL = strSQL & " WHERE movie_id = ? "
    strSQL = strSQL & "  AND movie_participants.participant_id =" & _
            " participants.participant_id"
    strSQL = strSQL & "  ORDER BY role"

    Set qyParticipants = cn.CreateQuery("", strSQL)

    Exit Sub

ErrorHandler:
    If Err = 3146 Then
        MsgBox "Error creating query : " & rdoErrors(0).Description
    Else
        MsgBox "Error creating query : " & Err.Description
    End If

End Sub
```

Viewing the Structure of a Database

Just as we saw with DAO, you can view the structure of any tables you have access to. The main difference between DAO and RDO is that you cannot alter the database structure with RDO commands. Even DAO is not recommended for this purpose, and DBA's everywhere will be happier that users no longer have this ability to change the database structure.

rdoTables

The rdoTables collection contains one rdoTable object for every Oracle table you have access to. This does not imply you can update those tables, but it does let you look at their structure. The types of things we can do with rdoTables are the same things we did with TableDefs in DAO, so I will give a fairly brief overview of the object hierarchy.

You can view which Oracle tables you have access to with the code in Listing 15.22, which loops through all of the rdoTable objects.

Listing 15.22

```
Dim tbl As rdoTable

For Each tbl In cnMovies.rdoTables
    Debug.Print tbl.Name
Next
```

rdoColumns

DAO has Field objects, whereas RDO has rdoColumn objects. The important properties of the Field object are shown in Table 15.14.

TABLE 15.14: The Properties of the rdoColumns Object That Apply to Oracle

Property	Description
AllowZeroLength	This property indicates if NULLs are allowed in the column.
Attributes	This property returns a list of attributes about the column. This is mainly useful to SQL Server users.
BatchConflictValue	This property returns the current database value (use this when using batch updates).
ChunkRequired	This property indicates you must use the GetChunk and AppendChunk methods.
KeyColumn	This property indicates if this is a unique key.
Name	This property shows the name of the field.
OrdinalPosition	This property shows the position of the column in the rdoColumns collection.
OriginalValue	This property shows the value of the column when the result set was first populated.
Required	This property indicates if the NOT NULL constraint has been set.
Size	This property shows the size of the field in bytes.

Continued on next page

TABLE 15.14 CONTINUED: The Properties of the rdoColumns Object That Apply to Oracle

Property	Description
SourceColumn	This property shows the column name from the source table.
SourceTable	This property shows the name of the attached table (if any).
Status	This property indicates if the column value has been altered.
Type	This property shows a number representing the column type interpreted by RDO. This needs to be interpreted before it is useful against an Oracle database.
Updatable	This property indicates if the column can be updated.
Value	This property shows this is the default property but is only relevant when you use it referring to a result set.

You can list column properties quite easily; for example, the sample code in Listing 15.23 lists the Type property. If you need to interpret the column type in terms of Oracle, use the function shown in Listing 15.24.

Listing 15.23

```
For Each tbl In cn.rdoTables
    Debug.Print ""
    Debug.Print tbl.Name
    For Each col In tbl.rdoColumns
        Debug.Print col.Name, FieldType(col.Type)
    Next
Next
```

Listing 15.24

```
Private Function FieldType(intType As Integer) As String
'   Convert the rdoColumn type to an Oracle column type

    Select Case intType
        Case rdTypeINTEGER
            FieldType = "NUMBER"
        Case rdTypeDECIMAL
            FieldType = "NUMBER"
        Case rdTypeNUMERIC
            FieldType = "NUMBER"
```

```
        Case rdTypeREAL
            FieldType = "NUMBER"
        Case rdTypeDOUBLE
            FieldType = "NUMBER"
        Case rdTypeDATE
            FieldType = "DATE"
        Case rdTypeCHAR
            FieldType = "CHAR2"
        Case rdTypeVARCHAR
            FieldType = "VARCHAR2"
        Case rdTypeLONGVARBINARY
            FieldType = "RAW"
        Case rdTypeTIMESTAMP
            FieldType = "DATE"
        Case Else
            FieldType = "Unknown"
    End Select

End Function
```

Indexes

RDO does not keep a separate collection for Indexes. However, this is not a great inconvenience because you can always use the KeyColumn property of the rdo-Column object.

Disadvantages of RDO

RDO has been the flagship technology for accessing data from ODBC data sources. It has been designed around the ODBC API, which is not a perfect fit with Oracle; although there are great improvements over DAO, some features are not available to Oracle users because Oracle architecture is quite different from SQL Server. As you have seen in this chapter, every effort is being made to fit Oracle into the mold, and it will take ADO some time to catch up; however, there are still some deficiencies with RDO we should note:

- You cannot retrieve PL/SQL cursor variables from stored procedures.

- RDO is considered old technology by Microsoft and will not have any more development work done on it, only minor bug fixes.

- RDO is dependent on ODBC drivers and the incompatibility problems they always seems to create.

- RDO does not support Oracle bind parameters.

- RDO is not as fast as ADO, especially when you use the OLE-DB provider.

The Future of RDO

There has been some speculation as to the future of RDO now that Active Data Objects (ADO) is coming onto the scene. Where should you put your development effort? The truth is that although ADO will have features that RDO will never have, ADO also will probably never have all the capabilities of RDO. To a certain extent the two complement each other, and it will be a good long time before RDO is abandoned by developers.

Microsoft will be supporting RDO for a while, at least as long as developers are actively using it; however, any improvements will be minimal. If you have a substantial investment in your RDO applications, you should be wary about porting them to ADO, at least until we get a hoped-for set of conversion wizards. For all foreseeable new development work, you should seriously consider moving to ADO.

Summary

In this chapter, we have covered RDO in enough detail to make connections with the Oracle database, retrieve result sets from Oracle tables, and use the rdo-Connection object to execute SQL commands and call stored procedures. We saw features that have a substantial functionality gain compared to using the JET engine in DAO, including the ability to return output parameters from stored procedures as well as create rdoResultsets from stored procedures that return PL/SQL tables. Asynchronous operation was also discussed along with its advantages. After touching on error handling with RDO, we saw an example of putting these techniques together.

Until the arrival of ADO, RDO was the state of the art as far as data access was concerned. Because of its licensing issues, some of the features were made available to other environments, such as Microsoft Excel via ODBCDirect, which we shall now take a brief journey through.

CHAPTER

SIXTEEN

16

ODBCDirect

- Viewing ODBCDirect Object Hierarchy

- Accessing a Database

- Creating Recordsets

- Using QueryDefs

- Calling Stored Procedures

- The Drawbacks to ODBCDirect

ODBCDirect is the name given to one part of DAO 3.51, a part that gives you access to some of the features of Remote Data Objects that we covered in Chapter 15. It sits between what I will call DAO/JET and RDO in that it has the same object model of the original DAO but with RDO-type extensions. Visual Basic loads up the RDO 2.0 library for ODBCDirect instead of the JET engine so you cannot access the JET database with ODBCDirect; at the same time, you cannot access the full functionality of RDO 2.0. Because of these issues, ODBCDirect has been somewhat difficult to categorize; however, just like with music, even if you cannot put a label on it, that does not mean you cannot enjoy it fully.

ODBCDirect was initially a part of DAO 3.1 as a downloadable add-on. It became fully available with Visual Basic 5. Being based on RDO, ODBCDirect is available only in a 32-bit form, so those of you still in the 16-bit world will not have an easy upgrade from your JET environment.

ODBCDirect can do almost everything that DAO/JET can do for remote databases but with a smaller footprint. Although you cannot use it to link heterogeneous databases together, you can now get finer control of cursors, access to stored-procedure output parameters, queries, asynchronous capabilities, and control of your connection usage. All this and some improvement in performance, as well.

NOTE If you really need to link different databases together, you can purchase one of the Oracle gateway products, which makes other database products almost as easy to access as Oracle. Of course, there are penalties in performance and capabilities as well as price.

ODBCDirect raised much excitement when it was first introduced in early 1996, but marketing strategies have really downplayed it to the status of an also-ran. RDO was available up to VB5 in the Enterprise Edition only, but with VB6, it is now also available in the Professional Edition; ODBCDirect is available with the Professional Edition and is also available for other VBA environments, such as Excel. In fact, this is the market where it was originally targeted. Although ADO duplicates and improves on all of ODBCDirect's functionality and will be replacing it in most cases, ODBCDirect still provides a relatively straightforward upgrade route from DAO compared with RDO or ADO.

The topics this chapter will cover are

- Viewing ODBCDirect object hierarchy

- Accessing a database

- Creating Recordsets

- Using QueryDefs

- Calling stored procedures

- The drawbacks to ODBCDirect

NOTE   Most of the topics covered here are the direct equivalent of DAO/JET methods or those from RDO. We will not cover them in great detail, but we will go over the salient points and differences.

The ODBCDirect Object Hierarchy

Strictly speaking, the ODBCDirect object hierarchy is much the same as the DAO hierarchy that we saw in Chapter 14, *Data Access Objects*. Naturally, this is what you would expect. However, as you can see in Figure 16.1, there is the addition of a few collections and objects. Specifically, the new model includes the Connection, QueryDef, and Parameters collections and objects. We will introduce these new items in this section and go into them more deeply in the rest of the chapter.

FIGURE 16.1:

The ODBCDirect object hierarchy

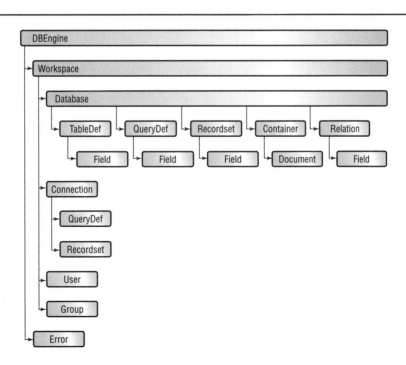

DBEngine

The top-level object in the ODBCDirect object hierarchy is the DBEngine, just as it was with the DAO/JET hierarchy. When you use the ODBCDirect option, you will use more DBEngine properties than we did when working through JET. As before, the DBEngine object contains the Workspaces and Error collections.

Workspace

The Workspaces collection becomes a more important organizational structure now because it is the only way that you can control which type of environment you want to work with: JET or ODBCDirect. It also gives you the capability of working with both environments at the same time. Instead of just containing the Databases collection, it now includes the Connection object, which provides most of the new features. Under ODBCDirect, a Workspace object contains Connections and Databases collections.

Database

The Database object is the most important for JET, but to make the best use of ODBCDirect, you will want to migrate away from it and toward the Connection object. However, in the meantime, you can still use the Database object in exactly the same way that we did with JET. In fact, the ODBCDirect team has made the Connection object used by the Database object available to your application, but this will not let you make the best use of the Connection your application creates.

Connection

By setting up your Workspace with the correct options, you make the Connection object available to your application. This is the object that will give you the ability to select cursors, use asynchronous techniques, and use QueryDefs (the equivalent of RDO's rdoQuery objects).

Accessing ODBCDirect

Just as we saw in Chapter 14, you must make the DAO 3.51 library available to your application by checking it in the References option of the Project menu in Visual Basic. If you use the default Workspace, you will get the JET engine, so the first thing we need to access ODBCDirect is a new Workspace. We do this with the CreateWorkspace method of the DBEngine object, which has the following syntax:

```
Set workspace = CreateWorkspace(name, user, password, type)
```

This method has the following arguments:

> **name**   The name of the Workspace. You can use a null string for the name if you are only going to create one new Workspace.
>
> **user**   The default user name for the Workspace. This name is used if the connection string does not provide a UID value.
>
> **password**   The password for the default user name. This password is used if you do not include a PWD field in the connection string.
>
> **type**   The type of Workspace you want to create. The choices are shown in Table 16.1, and as you can see, you should use *dbUseODBC* to access the ODBCDirect model.

TABLE 16.1: The Types of DAO Workspace That You Can Create

Constant	Description
dbUseJet	This constant creates a Microsoft JET Workspace.
dbUseODBC	This constant creates an ODBCDirect Workspace.

The type argument was added specifically for ODBCDirect. It is optional, and if you leave it out, it will default to the JET Workspace. Listing 16.1 shows an example using the CreateWorkspace method.

Listing 16.1

```
Private wks As Workspace

Private Sub ConnectToDatabase()

'    Connect to the Oracle database via ODBCDirect

    Set wks = CreateWorkspace("WKS", "", "", dbUseODBC)

End Sub
```

The ODBCDirect Workspace can be created another way, and you may find it easier. The DefaultType property of the DBEngine object controls the type of Workspace that is created after the property is set. If you set this before referring to Workspaces(0), then the default will become an ODBCDirect Workspace the first time you reference it. In this case, you can avoid the CreateWorkspace method entirely. The following line demonstrates this.

```
DBEngine.DefaultType = dbUseODBC
```

Because this is the simplest method to move from a JET environment, we will use it to create a Workspace from now on. One further thing you have to do before you can leave the Workspace object is to set the DefaultCursorDriver property just as we did with RDO. You must do this before you create any connections. The possible cursor drivers are shown in Table 16.2.

TABLE 16.2: The Possible Values for DefaultCursorDriver

Constant	Description
dbUseDefaultCursor (Default)	For Oracle databases, this constant defaults to the ODBC cursor library.
dbUseODBCCursor	This constant uses the ODBC cursor library. It is preferable to use the client-batch cursor library.
dbUseServerCursor	This constant uses server-side cursors. Not available for Oracle users.
dbUseClientBatchCursor	This constant uses the client-batch cursor library. This option is the fastest scrollable cursor driver and is required for batch updates.
dbUseNoCursor	This constant uses a forward-only, read-only (firehose) cursor.

NOTE   It is important not to confuse these options for the DefaultCursorDriver with the cursor types themselves. The cursor drivers are just the library that makes the different types of cursors available. The main reason for defining this option is to select a more efficient cursor library for whatever circumstances we have. We still have to define the cursor when we create the Recordset.

Let's now put this together and produce a procedure that will give us the correct environment for using ODBCDirect. Listing 16.2 shows how to do this procedure; the only thing we have left to add to this is to create a connection, which we shall look at next.

Listing 16.2

```
Private Sub ConnectToDatabase()

'   Connect to the Oracle database via ODBCDirect

    DBEngine.DefaultType = dbUseODBC
    Workspaces(0).DefaultCursorDriver = dbUseClientBatchCursor

End Sub
```

Making the Connection

Having laid the groundwork for the connection environment, we next have to create the actual connection (or possibly more than one connection if you are dealing with multiple databases). You have a choice, and you have to decide which route to follow. You can continue with the DAO/JET format and use the Database object in the same way as we saw in Chapter 14, or you can follow the new route, via the Connection object. The Connection object is more suitable for remote databases, such as Oracle; this is the route we will follow for the rest of this chapter. Without it, you will not be able to use QueryDefs or asynchronous operations.

The Connection object is the functional equivalent of the Database object we used in DAO/JET. JET creates and handles any connections it needs behind the scenes, whereas ODBCDirect exposes connections to your application so that you have more precise control. This is a definite advantage because although JET tries to use connections as efficiently as possible, it does not fully understand the capabilities of all the back-end databases it might have to deal with. The result is that we can do everything we need to with one connection per database, whereas JET needs at least two. The only reason not to use the Connection object is if you want to write code that you can use to switch back and forth between Oracle and JET. This is not too likely.

Access and Oracle

There is a temptation to use a Microsoft Access database to prototype applications. This is understandable because you can build the database from Visual Basic with the Visual Data Manager (VisData). This is especially useful if you do not yet have an Oracle installation or have not committed to any particular database vendor. The temptation is particularly great when you use ODBCDirect because it gives you the opportunity to write an application that handles both environments, perhaps checking which kind of Workspace you are in before you execute any commands.

However, due to the great differences between the JET syntax and the Oracle syntax, you may have to rewrite a large amount of code. Although Oracle has a good upsizing wizard for converting the database, you should at a minimum use the ODBC driver for Access if you insist on going this route. But it is much better to get hold of a trial copy of Oracle (for a nominal distribution charge) and develop using that for the prototyping phase. If you use the table creation tools now available in Visual Basic 6, you can get by for a while with only a limited amount of Oracle experience.

To create a connection, we use the OpenConnection method, which has the following syntax:

```
Set connection = workspace.OpenConnection (name, options, readonly,
connect)
```

The arguments for the OpenConnection method are:

name   You use this argument to provide the registered Data Source Name (DSN) for the connection, or if you provide the DSN in the connect string, you can provide an arbitrary name for the connection.

options   This argument is a combination of the RDO prompt argument (for determining whether and how the ODBC Driver Manager prompts for connection information) and the argument to specify asynchronous operation. The possible values are shown in Table 16.3. *dbDriverNoPrompt* is recommended so that there is no chance a user will see the Driver Manager prompts.

readonly   You should set this argument to False if you intend to use updatable Resultsets on this connection; otherwise, set it to True. As elsewhere, this argument simply reinforces Oracle security, it does not replace it.

connect This argument holds the ODBC connect string that we saw in Chapter 11, *Client-Side Technology*. If you do not include the UID or PWD fields, then the defaults will be taken from the Workspace object.

TABLE 16.3: The Possible Values for the Options Argument

Constant	Description
dbDriverNoPrompt	The ODBC Driver Manager uses the connection string provided in the *name* and *connect* properties. Insufficient information will cause a trappable error. This is mandatory if you wish to work with Microsoft Transaction Server.
dbDriverPrompt	The ODBC Driver Manager displays the ODBC Data Sources dialog box, which displays any relevant information supplied in *name* or *connect* arguments.
dbDriverComplete (Default)	If the *connect* argument includes all the necessary information to make a connection, the ODBC Driver Manager uses it. Otherwise, it behaves as it does when you specify *dbDriverPrompt*.
dbDriverCompleteRequired	This constant behaves like *dbDriverComplete* except the ODBC Driver disables the prompts for any information not required to complete the connection.
dbRunAsync	This constant executes the OpenConnection method asynchronously. This constant may be added to any of the other *options* constants.

Just as we saw with RDO, there is a complex set of choices to be made here, but in practice, we can reduce this to a smaller range. Listing 16.3 include codes for the three possible scenarios: updatable cursors, read-only cursors, and firehose cursors. These do not create the cursors themselves, but you need to set them so you can accommodate all the types of Recordsets you want to set up on the connection. In other words, if you plan to create even one updatable Recordset, then you will have to set up the Connection accordingly.

Listing 16.3

```
Private cn As Connection


Private Sub ConnectToDatabase()

'   Connect to the Oracle database via ODBCDirect
```

```
    Dim strConnection As String

    On Error GoTo ErrorHandler

    DBEngine.DefaultType = dbUseODBC

    strConnection = "ODBC;DSN=movies;UID=video_user;PWD=ummagumma;"


'   Choose one of the following connections ......

'   Prepare connection for scrollable updatable cursors
    Workspaces(0).DefaultCursorDriver = dbUseClientBatchCursor
    Set cn = Workspaces(0).OpenConnection("", dbDriverNoPrompt, _
            False, strConnection)

'   Prepare connection for scrollable read-only cursors
    Workspaces(0).DefaultCursorDriver = dbUseClientBatchCursor
    Set cn = Workspaces(0).OpenConnection("", dbDriverNoPrompt, _
            True, strConnection)

'   Prepare connection for firehose cursors
    Workspaces(0).DefaultCursorDriver = dbUseNoCursor
    Set cn = Workspaces(0).OpenConnection("", dbDriverNoPrompt, _
            True, strConnection)

    Exit Sub

ErrorHandler:
    If Err = 3146 Then
        MsgBox Errors(0).Description
    Else
        MsgBox Err.Description
    End If

End Sub
```

Creating Recordsets

Once we have set up the environment with the correct cursor libraries and ensured that we are using ODBCDirect, we can now move on to creating a Recordset. This is another one of those points where you have more options than you really want, particularly when it comes to selecting cursors. The syntax of the OpenRecordset method is as follows:

```
Set recordset = _
    database_object.OpenRecordset (source, type, options, lockedits)
```

This method has the following arguments:

source   This is a string that represents the source of the data for the new Recordset. It will typically be a SQL statement enclosed in double quotes, such as "SELECT * FROM videos WHERE status='A'". Do not include a semicolon at the end of the line.

type   An optional constant that indicates the type of Recordset to open, as specified in Table 16.4.

options   An optional combination of constants that specify characteristics of the new Recordset. You can use one or more of the constants defined in Table 16.5. If you use more than one, you can add them together. More constants are defined in the Help files, but the others do not work with Oracle.

lockedits   An optional constant that determines the locking for the Recordset. You can choose one of the constants outlined in Table 16.6.

T A B L E   1 6 . 4 :   Constants for the OpenRecordset Type Argument in an ODBCDirect Workspace

Constant	Description
dbOpenDynamic	This constant opens a dynamic Recordset object, which is similar to an ODBC dynamic cursor.
dbOpenDynaset	This constant opens a dynaset Recordset object, which is similar to an ODBC keyset cursor.
dbOpenSnapshot	This constant opens a snapshot Recordset object, which is similar to an ODBC static cursor.
dbOpenForwardOnly	This constant opens a forward-only (firehose) Recordset.

NOTE
I have been unable to find any difference between the *dbOpenDynamic* and *dbOpenDynaset* options for the Recordset cursor type. Both detect updates and deletes committed by other users, and neither detect inserts. You might as well stick to dynasets, which is more of a DAO standard.

TABLE 16.5: Possible Constants for the OpenRecordset Options Argument in an ODBCDirect Workspace

Constant	Description
dbRunAsync	This constant runs an asynchronous query.
dbExecDirect	This constant runs a query by skipping SQLPrepare and directly calling SQLExecDirect. This is designed for SQL Server and has no effect when you are using an Oracle database.

NOTE
SQLPassThrough is not available (or required) in ODBCDirect.

TABLE 16.6: Possible Constants for the OpenRecordset Lockedits Argument in an ODBCDirect Workspace

Constant	Description
dbReadOnly	This constant prevents users from making changes to the Recordset. Though Oracle primarily controls whether you can alter the data, this option lets you enforce read-only. It is the default for ODBCDirect Workspaces.
dbOptimistic	This constant uses optimistic locking, which implies the page (the row in Oracle's case) containing the record is not locked until the Update method is executed. This is the default for ODBC sources such as Oracle.
dbPessimistic	This constant uses pessimistic locking, which implies that the page the record is on is locked when you invoke the Edit method. Pessimistic locking does not work against an Oracle database.
dbOptimisticValue	This constant uses optimistic concurrency based on row values.
dbOptimisticBatch	This constant enables batch optimistic updating.

Putting all these options together again, we come up with our three favorite ways to open a Recordset: the updatable, read-only, and firehose cursors. Listing 16.4 shows a procedure that includes all of these three types.

Listing 16.4

```
Private rsUpdatable As Recordset
Private rsReadOnly As Recordset
Private rsFirehose As Recordset
Private rsMovies As Recordset


Private Sub CreateRecordsets()

    Dim strSQL As String

    strSQL = "SELECT movie_name, length, rating, year_of_release, " & _
             " movie_id FROM video_store.movies ORDER BY movie_id"

    Set rsUpdatable = _
        cn.OpenRecordset(strSQL, dbOpenDynaset, 0, dbOptimisticValue)

    Set rsReadOnly = _
        cn.OpenRecordset(strSQL, dbOpenSnapshot, 0, dbReadOnly)

    Set rsFirehose = _
        cn.OpenRecordset(strSQL, dbOpenForwardOnly, 0, dbReadOnly)

'   Select one recordset to work with
    Set rsMovies = rsUpdatable

End Sub
```

NOTE   The DAO documentation indicates that you can define a query string with more than one SELECT statement in it. Although this works for SQL Server, you cannot do this for Oracle.

When you work with ODBCDirect Recordsets, you have pretty much the same set of methods that you used with DAO/JET. There are a couple of exceptions:

- ODBCDirect cannot use the Find methods, even with a scrollable cursor. This is because RDO does not support Find.

- You cannot use the FillCache method. This is because the RDO engine behind ODBCDirect is much more efficient than DAO and has a reasonable CacheSize to start with. (It defaults to 100 rows.) You can only adjust the CacheSize property if you use QueryDefs.

Using QueryDefs

Although creating Recordsets with the methods explained in the previous section work well, it can be difficult to code and cumbersome when you want to use queries that differ by only a few values each time. To improve on this situation, we can use QueryDefs. QueryDefs are the direct equivalent of the rdoQuery objects we saw in Chapter 15, *Remote Data Objects*. They allow you to define and "prepare" a SELECT-type query with parameters and, as we shall see in the section "Calling Stored Procedures," give us the power of output parameters that comes from RDO.

To create a QueryDef object, use the CreateQueryDef method, which has the following syntax:

```
Set querydef = object.CreateQueryDef (name, SQL_string)
```

The arguments are

name   An optional name for the QueryDef object. As with rdoQueries, there is limited value in providing a name.

SQL_string   The text of the SELECT query (or stored procedure definition).

The query strings you define are exactly the same as what we saw with rdo-Queries. You identify any parameters in the string with ODBC placeholders (the "?"). Of course, you do not have to use parameters if you don't want to; a query will work just as well without them, but then you lose the real power of the Query-Def. An example of a parameterized QueryDef is shown in Listing 16.5. It is almost identical to the code used for RDO. Notice that when you open a Recordset against the QueryDef, you use the same arguments as the OpenRecordset method of the Connection object except for the query string.

Listing 16.5

```
Private qy1 As QueryDef

Private Sub CreateQuery1()

    Dim rs As Recordset
    Dim strSQL As String

    strSQL = "SELECT * FROM video_store.movies WHERE "
    strSQL = strSQL & " year_of_release > ? "
    strSQL = strSQL & " AND rating = ? ORDER BY movie_name"

    Set qy1 = cn.CreateQueryDef("", strSQL)
    qy1.Parameters(0) = 1995
    qy1.Parameters(1) = "PG-13"
    Set rs = qy1.OpenRecordset(dbOpenForwardOnly, 0, dbReadOnly)

    While Not rs.EOF
        MsgBox rs(1)
        rs.MoveNext
    Wend

'   Close the Recordset
    Set rs = Nothing

End Sub
```

TIP   To run a query again after changing the parameter values, use the Requery method.

QueryDef Properties

The QueryDef object has a variety of properties that allow you to find out specific information about the object and set a couple of tuning parameters. As you can see in Table 16.5, several of the parameters are simply not available to Oracle users. The confusing thing is that the Visual Basic Help files are written from a SQL Server point of view, and you will not get error messages from setting them. Just don't expect them to have any effect.

The major properties you want to make note of are the *CacheSize* to tune the number or records pulled over the wire in one go (especially if you use large Recordsets), the *ODBCTimeout* period to ensure that queries do not last too long (a simple way to cut down on queries from hell), and *StillExecuting*, which is the only way you will be able to detect that the Recordset has been created if you are using asynchronous operation.

TABLE 16.7: QueryDef Properties

Property	Description
Connect	This property indicates the connection string for the QueryDef.
CacheSize	This property indicates the number of records cached locally. Use this to tune the Recordset.
MaxRecords	This property indicates the maximum number of records that will be returned.
Name	This property indicates the name of the QueryDef if you defined it.
ODBCTimeout	This property indicates the time in seconds allowed for the query before being timed out.
Prepare	This property controls whether a temporary stored procedure should be prepared (has no effect on an Oracle).
RecordsAffected	This property indicates the number of rows in the database affected by the last Execute method (not applicable to Oracle).
SQL	This property indicates the SQL source string.
StillExecuting	This property indicates if an asynchronous query is still being created.
Type	This property identifies the type of QueryDef, such as a SELECT statement, stored procedure call, or DML statement.
Updatable	This property indicates if the Recordset can be updated.

Calling Stored Procedures

Although ODBCDirect can execute SQL commands and stored procedure calls in exactly the same way that DAO/JET can, the real power is in executing stored procedures with parameters in the same way that RDO does. Naturally, ODBCDirect suffers the same advantages and disadvantage as RDO because RDO is the route through to the ODBC API. Listing 16.6 shows how to set up a QueryDef to execute a stored procedure with an output parameter. It is almost identical to the RDO code that we saw in Listing 15.14. In fact, it is so similar we can use the Visual Basic procedure MovieInsert that we saw in Listing 15.15 to execute this ODBC-Direct version.

Listing 16.6

```
Private qyMovieInsert As QueryDef


Private Sub CreateQuery2()

'   Set up any queries required in this module

    Dim strSQL As String
    On Error GoTo ErrorHandler

'   Set up the query to call the insert stored procedure.

    strSQL = "{call video_store.movies_insert3 (?, ?, ?, ?, ?) }"
    Set qyMovieInsert = cn.CreateQueryDef("", strSQL)

    Exit Sub

ErrorHandler:
    If Err = 3146 Then
        MsgBox "Error creating query : " & Errors(0).Description
    Else
        MsgBox "Error creating query : " & Err.Description
    End If

End Sub
```

Asynchronous Operations

The final feature we will briefly look at is using asynchronous operations. You will remember from Chapter 15, *Remote Data Objects*, that certain operations can be run asynchronously; that is, you set them running and carry on with other processing. You have to code around the problem of checking when the operation has finished. Asynchronous operation is again a feature made possible by RDO, but the design team has made available only the StillExecuting property associated with asynchronous operations. Unfortunately, the events that come with RDO 2.0 are not available in ODBCDirect.

You can use asynchronous operations with the following ODBC methods:

- OpenConnection
- OpenRecordset
- Requery
- MoveLast
- Execute

In each of these cases, you can specify the dbRunAsync constant for the options argument. Listing 16.7 gives a short example of creating a Recordset asynchronously. In this case, we use the cheap and nasty way to detect that the operation has completed. If you look back to Chapter 15 in the section, "Asynchronous Operation," you will find details of using the timer event to detect that the operation has completed; that is the preferred method.

Listing 16.7

```
Private Sub CreateAsynchRs()

    Dim strSQL As String

    strSQL = "SELECT movie_name, length, rating, year_of_release, " & _
        " movie_id FROM video_store.movies ORDER BY movie_id"

    Set rsMovies = _
        cn.OpenRecordset(strSQL, dbOpenDynaset, dbRunAsync, _
            dbOptimistic)

    If rsMovies.StillExecuting Then
        DoEvents
    End If

End Sub
```

Drawbacks to ODBCDirect

Although ODBCDirect is a great improvement on DAO/JET, it has never caught on to any great extent and will probably slowly disappear as ADO becomes available for all development environments. The disadvantages for ODBCDirect are much the same as with RDO except that the list is a little larger.

- You cannot retrieve PL/SQL cursor variables from stored procedures.

- Like DAO and RDO, ODBCDirect is considered old technology by Microsoft and will only be upgraded with minor bug fixes.

- ODBCDirect is dependent on ODBC drivers and the incompatibility problems that they always seems to create.

- ODBCDirect does not support Oracle bind parameters.

- ODBCDirect is not as fast as RDO or ADO.

- ODBCDirect does not expose the RDO events, so you must use polling to check for completion of asynchronous events.

- You cannot create stand-alone objects with ODBCDirect.

Summary

In this chapter, we have covered the main improvements that moving to ODBC-Direct will provide for you over DAO. These include the Connection object for tighter control of connections with your Oracle database, a larger array of cursors when creating Recordsets, the use of QueryDefs for queries with parameters, and stored procedures with output parameters. Finally, we touched on the asynchronous capabilities of ODBCDirect.

CHAPTER
SEVENTEEN

17

ActiveX Data Objects

- The ADO Object Hierarchy

- Connecting to Oracle

- Working with Recordsets

- Dissociated Recordsets

- Using the Command Object

- Executing SQL Commands

- Calling Stored Procedures

- Asynchronous Operation

- Retrieving PL/SQL Tables

- Error Handling

- Using the Data Environment

- Drawbacks to ADO

The data-access technologies we have seen so far in this book are all based on ODBC. As we saw in Chapter 11, *Client-Side Technology*, ODBC was created to tackle the problem of interfacing to relational databases, such as SQL Server and Oracle, in a generic way. However, there is a need to pull data from more than just relational databases; you may need data from flat-file systems, spreadsheets, e-mail, a workflow system, or perhaps even a high-speed data-collection system in a physics laboratory. Although Oracle's answer to this is to pull everything into a universal database, Microsoft has decided that it is better to provide access to each of the raw data sources by a powerful, fast, and generic method. This led to the creation of OLE-DB and with it, ActiveX Data Objects (ADO), which makes it possible for Visual Basic developers to make best use of the OLE-DB engine.

ADO is a 32-bit-only interface that is based on COM and OLE automation, and as such, it can move data to any environment that supports both of these. In truth, there is not much alternative to using a Microsoft Windows environment because that is the only environment supporting Visual Basic.

ADO is where all of Microsoft's development effort will be placed for the next few years, where any new and exciting capabilities will be born. It is also fast becoming the de facto access technique for the Web. But ADO really made its mark as the data-access technique of Active Server Pages (ASP), a scripting environment that provides a very powerful and efficient way of responding to Web requests for active information and a far better solution to the problem than the all-pervasive CGI scripting (which does not lend itself to scalable situations). With the release of Visual Basic 6, ADO 2.0 is poised to become more widespread, not just for Internet programming but in more traditional client-server and multi-tier development as well.

In this chapter, we will be covering the following ADO topics:

- The ADO object hierarchy
- Connecting to Oracle
- Working with Recordsets
- Dissociated Recordsets
- Using the Command object
- Executing SQL commands
- Calling stored procedures
- Asynchronous operation

- Retrieving PL/SQL tables

- Error handling

- Using the Data Environment

- Drawbacks to ADO

The ADO Object Model

ADO is a departure from the DAO lineage, which even Oracle Objects for OLE follows. As we saw with RDO, there is a risk that as the feature set becomes richer, the object model becomes more complicated. In ADO, the aim has been to produce an object-based system that is simpler to use but does not mask the advanced features developers need when dealing with systems such as Oracle. The result is the trimmed-down hierarchy that you can see in Figure 17.1. The complexity tends to be hidden in the Property objects.

FIGURE 17.1:

The ActiveX Data Objects object hierarchy

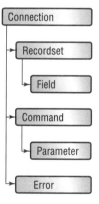

Figure 17.1 represents the actual hierarchy of ADO, but there is an alternative way of looking at it. In all the other data-access techniques, you have to start off by creating a connection to the database, then accessing the database you want, and building a Recordset of some kind. ADO allows you to bypass the creation of the higher-level objects and start immediately with the Recordset. We will take a good look at this capability, but for now, we must note that this feature leads to a different view of the object model, one based more on the practical use we can

make of the objects. There are many complex ways to show this process, but Figure 17.2 lays it out in its simplicity, showing that the three major objects can be considered on par with each other.

FIGURE 17.2:

The practical object model for ActiveX Data Objects

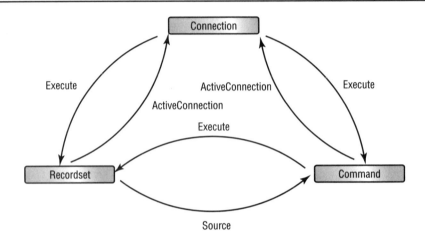

One of the beauties of ADO is there are only seven important objects in the whole system. These objects are introduced next.

Connection

At the top of the ADO hierarchy is the Connection object. Although you can create other objects independently of the Connection object and of each other, you really cannot do anything without a Connection object. It is the sole access point to your data source. With ADO, the Connection is made through an OLE-DB provider (the equivalent of the ODBC driver and Driver Manager), and this provider can connect directly to the Oracle OCI interface (a so-called *native* provider) or through ODBC. The capabilities of the Connection depend on which provider you use. The Connection object is usually associated directly with the Recordset object.

Recordset

The Recordset object is the next most important object in the model and is usually the center of all the action that takes place in your interaction with the database. A Recordset receives the result sets returned from queries to the Oracle database and allows you to manipulate them. With an ODBC provider, you will have access to scrolling and updatable Recordsets. You can create a stand-alone Recordset independently of a Connection, though you will have to associate it with a Connection to actually communicate with the database.

Command

The Command object is an object that allows you to maintain and store queries and Parameter collections and to execute stored procedures with input and output parameters. It is similar to an rdoQuery in RDO. You can execute a command on a Recordset without creating a Command object though one will be created implicitly. The power of the Command object comes with all of the new properties available from ADO and the OLE-DB provider you use.

Parameter

The ADO model includes a collection of parameters just as RDO does for each rdoQuery. You have the option of creating the Parameters collections or leaving it to ADO to create them. This is a trade-off between simplicity and efficient programming. ADO does allow you to have more control over the individual parameters, and this is a recommended technique for efficient programming.

Field

The Field object represents a single column in a Recordset. When dealing with Oracle, each Field will map to one column in a row in the query result set. It contains more information than RDO or DAO and almost as much information as you will see from OO4O. Each Field is held in a Fields collection within each Recordset.

Error

The Error object is similar to what we have seen with DAO and RDO. It is held in the Errors collection and represents the most recent data-access error, in our case representing the message returned from the Oracle Server or some intermediate point along the way. The Errors collection can hold more than one error returned from the same call to Oracle.

Property

As we mentioned in the introduction, although the object hierarchy has been flat-tened, much of the power and flexibility of ADO has been placed into the Prop-erty objects. These allow you to specify the values of a variety of aspects of the interface. Although these properties are normally the ones built into ADO, there is also the possibility of other properties specific to the OLE-DB provider that you are using. This will allow the effectiveness to be increased for a particular data source with just a change in the provider's capabilities; the object model does not need to change at all.

Connecting to Oracle

As we go through the capabilities of ADO, we will find that you can create any of the three major objects (Connection, Recordset, and Command) independently of the others. This can simplify your code to a certain extent because you can create in one line of code what would take several lines in any other data-access tech-nique. However, one thing to keep in mind is that simplicity and effectiveness are often diametrically opposed goals. A good recommendation is to become familiar with all the techniques for making a connection, such as creating an explicit con-nection, as well as their advantages, and then you can resort to the simpler tech-niques with the full knowledge of what you might be giving up.

To make use of any of the features of ActiveX Data Objects, we first have to set up a reference in our application to the ADO library in our current project. We do this through the following steps:

1. Choose the Project ➢ References to open the References dialog box as shown in Figure 17.3. You will see a list of all the object libraries that you can reference in your application.

2. Check the option labeled Microsoft ActiveX Data Objects 2.0.

3. Click OK.

FIGURE 17.3:

The References dialog box
with the ADO library checked

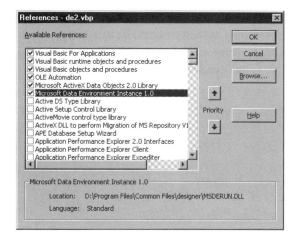

The first thing we will do is create a Connection object explicitly; in other words, we will write the code to create a Connection object rather than do it implicitly through the Recordset or Command objects. In this way, we can create one Connection object for each database that we access and use that connection for all interaction with the database. As we shall see later, if we implicitly create a connection, then we will get a new and different connection to the database each time.

If you look at Table 17.1, you will see the various methods that you can use with the Connection object.

TABLE 17.1: The Connection Object Methods

Method	Description
BeginTrans, CommitTrans, RollbackTrans	These methods control transactions from ADO. Note an autocommit is the default event for the Command object.
Cancel	This method cancels execution of an asynchronous Execute or Open method.
Close	This method closes the connection and any associated Recordsets.
Execute	This method executes the specified SQL query or command.
Open	This method opens a connection to the specified database.
OpenSchema	This method returns a Recordset detailing database information, such as Tables and Columns.

In this section, we will look at the Open method, which allows us to set up a new connection to the Oracle database. We come up immediately against ADO's flexibility, which can also be a source of confusion. We can specify the description of the connection we want to make with properties, a connection string, or both. Let's take this one step at a time.

In ADO code, we typically create a stand-alone object, set its parameters, and then open it. We create the Connection object with one of two methods:

```
Dim cn As New ADODB.Connection
```

or

```
Private cn As ADODB.Connection
Set cn = New ADODB.Connection
```

NOTE   When we are using ADO, the declarations seem a little more complicated as the variable types are referenced through the ADODB-type library.

Despite the fact that it is an extra line of code, I like to use the second form of declaration, the explicit creation as opposed to the implicit creation. Among other advantages, the second method gives you the opportunity to use the WithEvents keyword; it also gives you explicit control over the creation of an object.

At this point, we have a stand-alone connection, but we cannot use it for data access because it is not yet open. We set the connection's properties before opening it. The available properties are shown in Table 17.2. Using the values in this table gives us much more control over the connection than when we create a connection implicitly with the Recordset object. As you can see, some properties are more important than others, especially for Oracle users.

TABLE 17.2: Connection Properties

Property	Description
Attributes	This property defines whether a CommitTrans or Rollback starts a new transaction (see Visual Basic Help file for constants).
CommandTimeout	This property shows the time to wait for a command to finish (default is 30 seconds).
ConnectionString	This property shows ADO-specific arguments. If you supply other arguments in this string, they are sent to the provider (for example, to the ODBC driver).

Continued on next page

TABLE 17.2 CONTINUED: Connection Properties

Property	Description
ConnectionTimeout	This property shows the time to wait for a connection to finish (default is 15 seconds).
CursorLocation	This property uses *adUseClient* to specify client-based cursors and *adUseServer* for cursors on the server or the provider. For Oracle, you should use *adUseClient*.
DefaultDatabase	This property shows the default database when the provider can use more than one database per connection.
IsolationLevel	This property shows the level of isolation of transactions for the connection.
Mode	This property sets or returns access permissions; ignore this property for Oracle databases.
Provider	This property shows the name of the OLE-DB provider. (This can also be set in the ConnectionString property.)
State	This property indicates whether the connection is open (*adStateClosed*) or closed (*adStateClosed*).
Version	This property shows the ADO version number.

If we use some of the more important properties of the Connection object, we can start to build up our ConnectToDatabase procedure (see Listing 17.1). As you can see in the listing, we create a new stand-alone Connection object, *cn*, with a time-out value of three seconds and a client-based cursor (which is the only one currently available for Oracle), and then we specify the native OLE-DB provider for Oracle ("MSDAORA").

Listing 17.1

```
Private cn As ADODB.Connection

Private Sub ConnectToDatabase()
'    Connect to the Oracle database

    Set cn = New ADODB.Connection
    With cn
        .ConnectionTimeout = 3
        .CursorLocation = adUseClient
        .Provider = "MSDAORA"
    End With

End Sub
```

Now that we have a stand-alone Connection object, we are ready to open that connection. The Open method has the following syntax

```
connection.Open ConnectionString, UserID, Password, OpenOptions
```

with the following optional arguments:

ConnectionString   This string contains connection information. Any information in this argument will override the ConnectionString property settings.

UserID   This string contains the Oracle user name. If supplied, this argument will override the user name in the *ConnectionString* argument.

Password   This password is for the supplied user name. If supplied, this argument will override the password in the *ConnectionString* argument.

OpenOptions   This argument should be set to *adConnectAsync* for the connection to be opened asynchronously.

There are obviously many different ways to fill in this information, especially as each successive line or argument can override previous values. Select one particular method, and stick to it as a site standard. If you do otherwise, when you maintain someone else's code, you are going to be chasing down the reasons your connection does not work properly. We will look at two ways to make a connection, one using each of the available OLE-DB providers: the provider for ODBC and the native provider for Oracle.

OLE-DB Provider for ODBC

ADO would have been of little use to anyone had there not been an OLE-DB provider for you to use in your environment. The simplest way for Microsoft to produce an OLE-DB provider was to come up with a provider for ODBC. This OLE-DB provider for ODBC ("MSDASQL") is the default provider. Although an OLE-DB provider introduces yet another layer between your code and Oracle, it does have some advantages. It exposes all of the functionality of ODBC, and as we shall see later, it surprisingly gives us better access to features and sometimes better performance than RDO.

Because the ODBC provider is the default provider, we do not have to specify it at all. If we also consider that OLE-DB will also pass along any parameters it does not recognize further down the chain (in this case, the ODBC Driver), we can use exactly the same connect string that we used for ODBC as follows:

```
cn.Open "DSN=movies;uid=video_user;pwd=ummagumma;"
```

Finally, we will put this together in our ConnectToDatabase procedure (see Listing 17.2). We will use the ODBC provider for much of this chapter partly due to the extra functionality that we want to look at but also because it is more mature and less error prone than the native provider.

Listing 17.2

```
Private cn As ADODB.Connection

Private Sub ConnectToDatabase()
'    Connect to the Oracle database

    Set cn = New ADODB.Connection
    With cn
        .ConnectionTimeout = 3
        .CursorLocation = adUseClient
    End With
    cn.Open "DSN=movies;UID=video_user;PWD=ummagumma;"
End Sub
```

We can also use a DSN-less connection with ADO just as we did with RDO. Listing 17.3 gives an example of how to do this. Remember that the advantages of DSN-less connections are that you do not have to create the DSN (the registered Data Source Name) on each client machine and that it is also a little faster because it does not have to access the Registry to find out which Oracle service name to access. ADO is fast at making connections, but there is nothing wrong with making ADO even faster.

Listing 17.3

```
Private cn As ADODB.Connection

Private Sub ConnectToDatabase()
'    Make a DSN-less connection to the Oracle database
```

```
Dim strConnection As String

Set cn = New ADODB.Connection
With cn
    .ConnectionTimeout = 3
    .CursorLocation = adUseClient
End With

strConnection = "SERVER=movies;" & _
                "DRIVER={Microsoft ODBC for Oracle};" & _
                "UID=video_user;PWD=ummagumma;"

cn.Open strConnection
End Sub
```

Native OLE-DB Provider for Oracle

Although the OLE-DB provider for ODBC was the first to arrive (and the most important provider to the acceptance of ADO), Visual Basic 6 was released with native OLE-DB providers for Oracle and SQL Server among others. If OLE-DB really does become as accepted a standard as ODBC, we shall see much more movement in this area with hopefully very interesting repercussions. For the moment, though, we have a native provider that comes between the ADO data-consumer level and the Oracle Call Interface. It does not have much functionality compared to the ODBC provider, but in a high-end system, you are probably not using much of this functionality (such as scrollable, updatable cursors) anyway.

To use the OLE-DB provider for Oracle we need to specify the provider name ("MSDAORA") as well as the rest of the connection information. The following line shows an example of this.

```
cn.Open "Provider=MSDAORA;Data Source=movies;" & _
        "User Id=video_user;Password=ummagumma;"
```

In this string, notice four keyword value pairs similar to those used in ODBC.

Provider   We include the provider name here, although we could just as easily specify this with the provider property of the Connection object.

Data Source   This keyword specifies the Oracle service name (database alias).

User Id   This keyword specifies the user name for the connection.

Password   This keyword specifies the password for the connection.

NOTE   Notice that the *User ID* and *Password* keywords are different from ODBC, which typically uses *UID* and *PWD*.

Listing 17.4 shows an example of making your connection using the native OLE-DB provider for Oracle. The main points to notice are that we define the provider name and that we must ensure that the connection string is defined with the proper keywords.

Listing 17.4

```
Private cn As ADODB.Connection

Private Sub ConnectToDatabase()
'    Connect to the Oracle database

    Set cn = New ADODB.Connection
    With cn
        .ConnectionTimeout = 3
        .CursorLocation = adUseClient
        .Provider = "MSDAORA"
    End With
    cn.Open "Data Source=movies;User Id=video_user;Password=ummagumma;"

End Sub
```

WARNING   Early versions of the OLE-DB provider for Oracle have not proven very stable. In particular, be careful to make sure you code the connection string properly, otherwise you may notice your application hang.

Connection Events

One of the weak spots of ADO 1.5 compared to RDO was that its event handling was minimal. With ADO 2.0, released with Visual Basic 6, there is an event model to rival, if not improve on, RDO 2.0. As you can see in Table 17.3, these events give you great control over the operation of your data interface. Most of these events trigger even if the operation is not successful. Although several events will have minimal appeal to Oracle users, a few will prove useful in the same way as they did for RDO.

TABLE 17.3: The ADO Connection Events

Event	Description
BeginTransComplete	The BeginTrans operation has completed.
CommitTransComplete	The CommitTrans operation has completed.
ConnectComplete	The Connection operation has completed.
Disconnect	The Disconnect operation has completed.
ExecuteComplete	A command Execute method on this connection has completed.
InfoMessage	An information message has been added to the Errors collection (SQL Server only).
RollbackTransComplete	The RollbackTrans operation as completed.
WillConnect	This event is triggered before a connection attempt starts.
WillExecute	This event is triggered before the execution of a query on this connection.

To use events with ADO, you need to use the same techniques we saw with RDO. You have to first declare any object with the WithEvents keyword if you want to use their events. An example of such a declaration is shown in the following line:

```
Private WithEvents cn As ADODB.Connection
```

If you use the WithEvents keyword, you cannot use the New keyword in the same declaration; you will have to use the Set command to create the new object as we have done in the last few examples. This restriction is enough to enforce the declaration style throughout your application.

NOTE   You must use the WithEvents keyword for object declarations at the module level, not the Sub level.

In Listing 17.5, you can see a more complete example of using events. The code defines the connection *cn* using WithEvents. Then, in the Form_Load event handler we create a new stand-alone Connection and open it. Once you have declared any object using WithEvents, you can then use the Visual Basic drop-down boxes to create the required events for you with the correct syntax (see Figure 17.4). This technique is much easier than trying to code the events by hand, because you not only have to get the event name right (with the object and the event name separated by an underscore) but you also have to get the format of the event arguments correct, as well.

Listing 17.5

```
Private WithEvents cn As ADODB.Connection

Private Sub Form_Load()
    Set cn = New ADODB.Connection

    cn.ConnectionTimeout = 4
    cn.CursorLocation = adUseServer
    cn.Open "DSN=movies;uid=video_user;pwd=ummagumma;", "", "", _
            adConnectAsync
End Sub


Private Sub cn_ConnectComplete(ByVal pError As ADODB.Error, _
            adStatus As ADODB.EventStatusEnum, _
            ByVal pConnection As ADODB.Connection)

    If adStatus = adStatusOK Then
        MsgBox "Connected OK"
    Else
        MsgBox "Error connecting " & pError.Description
    End If
End Sub
```

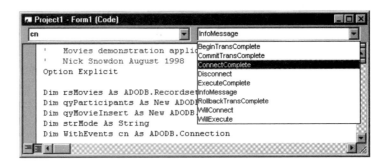

The ConnectComplete event that you see in Listing 17.5 is typical of ADO events in that it provides more information than the equivalent RDO events. The information includes an Error object to describe the reason for any failure to connect, a Status object, and the connection that the event occurred on. The Status object is interesting in that it gives us a number of possible status values:

adStatusOK   The status if the connection was successful.

adStatusErrorsOccurred   The status if the connection failed.

adStatusCancel   The status if the connection was canceled in the Will-Connect event.

adStatusUnwantedEvent   Set this status to avoid any other event messages.

Working with Recordsets

As we saw with DAO, we need to create Recordsets to handle the output of SELECT queries to the Oracle database. With ADO, we now have several ways to do this, and we shall look at all of them. However, if you have worked with any of the other data-access methods, the most familiar way will be to use the Open method, which also gives us the most control over the creation of the Recordset.

We again use the technique often seen in ADO, which is to create a stand-alone Recordset object with the New keyword as follows:

```
Set rs = New ADODB.Recordset
```

This does not contain any records. We cannot do anything with it until we use the Open method, which has the following syntax:

```
rs.Open Source, ActiveConnection, CursorType, LockType, Options
```

The method has the following optional arguments:

Source   This argument is a SQL SELECT string.

ActiveConnection   This argument can either be an active Connection object, or it can be a *ConnectString* argument with enough information to make a new connection.

CursorType   If we are working with the ODBC data provider, we can use the ADO cursor provider to give us a choice of four cursors (see Table 17.4).

LockType   The argument gives the type of locking we want. The choices are shown in Table 17.5.

Options   This argument gives the possible options you can include with the Open method, as outlined in Table 17.6.

TABLE 17.4:   The Possible Values for the CursorType Parameter

Constant	Cursor type
adOpenForwardOnly	Forward-only cursor (default)
adOpenKeyset	Keyset-driven cursor
adOpenDynamic	Dynamic cursor
adOpenStatic	Static cursor

TABLE 17.5:   The Available Values for the Locktype Parameter

Constant	Locking type
adLockPessimistic	Pessimistic concurrency (irrelevant to Oracle)
adLockOptimistic	Optimistic concurrency using row values
adLockReadOnly	A read-only Cursor (default)
adLockBatchOptimistic	Defers any updates until you use the BatchUpdate method

TABLE 17.6: The Possible Options for the Open Method

Constant	Description
adCmdText	The *Source* string contains a SQL command, such as a SELECT statement.
adCmdTable	The *Source* string contains the name of a table to be retrieved. (ADO creates a SQL query.) Using this option is not recommended because it can pull in too many records.
adCmdStoredProc	The *Source* string contains the name of a stored procedure (not applicable to Oracle).
adCmdUnknown	This constant indicates that the type of command in the *Source* argument is not known. Using this option is inefficient.
adExecuteAsync	This constant indicates that the *Source* string is created asynchronously.
adFetchAsync	This constant indicates that ADO should read the number of records in Cache-Size first and then fill the rest asynchronously.

As with RDO and DAO, we really have a limited number of different types of Recordset to open, depending on whether we want the Recordset to be updatable, scrollable, or forward-only. The default ADO cursor is forward-only and read-only. This is the cheapest (most efficient) cursor, because there is no need to cache data, and it is in line with the way that Oracle wants to return the result set. If you need the scrollable or updatable features of a Recordset, then you have no choice but to choose the OLE-DB provider for ODBC; the native provider is strictly a forward-only, read-only cursor. Listing 17.6 gives an example of each type of Recordset: scrollable and updatable; scrollable and read-only; and forward-only and read-only. In the last case, you do not have to enter the arguments for Cursor-Type and LockType because they will default to the required values.

Listing 17.6

```
Private WithEvents rs1 As ADODB.Recordset
Private WithEvents rs2 As ADODB.Recordset
Private WithEvents rs3 As ADODB.Recordset


Private Sub CreateRecordsets()

'   Create three types of Recordset
```

```
'   Scrollable and updatabable
    Set rs1 = New ADODB.Recordset
    rs1.Open "SELECT * FROM movies", cn, adOpenKeyset, adLockOptimistic

'   Scrollable and read-only
    Set rs2 = New ADODB.Recordset
    rs2.Open "SELECT * FROM movies", cn, adOpenStatic, adLockReadOnly

'   Forward-only and read-only
    Set rs3 = New ADODB.Recordset
    rs3.Open "SELECT * FROM movies", cn, adOpenForwardOnly, _
            adLockReadOnly


End Sub
```

Should Your Recordset Create a Connection?

There is a variation on a theme of how we have been creating a Recordset. You have probably heard the hype about being able to create a Recordset and automatically create a connection. You can do this by passing the connection string instead of the Connection object (*cn* in the examples). The following code shows an example of doing this:

```
Dim rs4 As New ADODB.Recordset
rs4.Open "SELECT * FROM movies", _
    "DSN=movies;uid=video_user;pwd=ummagumma;"
```

Although this code is a stylish way to create a Recordset (and gives the impression that ADO is not a hierarchical system), you should keep in mind that this will always create a new Connection object even if the connection string is exactly the same as a previously used one. So where would you use this technique? Limit it to situations in which you create only one Recordset in the application. This may be a Web-based retrieval of a small amount of data, but even then, you should try to keep one connection for all requests. One of the reasons for moving away from DAO is to get better control of connections, not worse control. Use this technique sparingly.

Other Ways to Create Recordsets

The Open method on the Recordset object is the best way to create a Recordset. The reason for this is that you can include not only the type of cursor but also the locktype (concurrency). However, we cannot move on until we mention two other methods that can produce a Recordset as the output. These methods are

- Connection.Execute

- Command.Execute

Each of them produces a Recordset with a static, forward-only cursor. In many cases, this situation may be what you want, but this limitation is something you should keep in mind.

Exploring Recordset Methods and Properties

Although you create your Recordset with the Open method, you have a similar range of methods to use with the Recordset that we saw with RDO. This section details many of the different operations you will want to perform and the section, "Putting It All Together," later in the chapter, puts most of these operations into a more complete example.

Populating the Recordset

Whenever you open a Recordset, ADO will populate it (that is, fill it with actual data) up to the value of the CacheSize property. The default value of this property is 1, so only one record is read from the Oracle result set. It is cached locally in the client memory. Whenever you move to a different record, ADO will first check the cache to see if it is there; if not, then it will again fill the cache.

It is clear that the default CacheSize of 1 is rarely going to be efficient. Each new record read in means another trip over the network, which will increase overhead. Instead of this default, you should always specify a value more in keeping with the number of Records you typically expect to read. Keep in mind that the penalty is more client-side memory is required.

You will have to experiment with different values of CacheSize. Listing 17.7 shows a test procedure I have used to time the effects. In reality, the benefits depend on your hardware and network. If you try this on a heavily loaded network, the effects of a higher CacheSize will be more dramatic. Even if you only have a few records, you should probably use a CacheSize of more than 1 because it will ease the load on your network. When you get up to hundreds of records, you should definitely be tuning the parameter as well as looking for why you need that many records.

Listing 17.7

```
Private Sub TestCache(iCacheSize As Integer)

    Dim StartTime, EndTime
    Dim rs As ADODB.Recordset

    Set rs = New ADODB.Recordset

    rs.CacheSize = iCacheSize

    StartTime = Timer
    rs.Open "SELECT * FROM customers", cn
    While Not rs.EOF
        rs.MoveNext
    Wend
    EndTime = Timer

    MsgBox "Time for CacheSize = " & iCacheSize & " is " & _
        EndTime - StartTime & " seconds. " & _
        rs.RecordCount & " records"
End Sub
```

NOTE   If you use a record cache with a forward-only Recordset, it is possible to move backward in the Recordset up to the limit of the cached records. This is not a recommended practice because it means the query may have to be reexecuted.

Fetching Multiple Rows

As we saw with RDO and DAO, we can use the GetRows method of the Recordset to pull a large number of rows into a variant array (see Chapter 14, *Data Access Objects*, for further details of variant arrays). In ADO, the GetRows method has become a little more flexible and powerful. The syntax of the method is as follows:

```
variant_array = rs.GetRows(Rows, Start, Fields)
```

It has the following optional arguments:

Rows   This argument shows the number of rows to retrieve. The default is *adGetRowsRest*, which pulls in all the rest of the available rows.

Start   This argument shows a bookmark to where the record retrieval should begin.

Fields   This argument is a new feature allowing you to specify a variant variable that contains details of one or more fields that you want to retrieve. You can specify either field names or field ordinal positions.

NOTE   Being able to specify the fields that you want with the GetRows method seems like a great idea; however, it is poor practice to actually use it. You should always specify only the fields you want in the SQL SELECT statement. Let the Oracle database do as much of the filtering as possible.

Listing 17.8 shows an example of using the ADO GetRows method. Notice that you only need declare the variant array as *variant*. ADO will take care of ensuring the array is the correct size. The example specifies two values for the GetRows parameters, but because these are defaults anyway, they could have been left out. Finally, notice how you use the Ubound function to determine the number of records and fields in the variant array and how they are both zero-based, so you have to add 1 to each of the values.

Listing 17.8

```
Private Sub GetRsRows()

'   This procedure is an example of using GetRows.

    Dim rs As ADODB.Recordset
    Dim vArray As Variant

    Set rs = New ADODB.Recordset

    rs.Open "SELECT * FROM movies", cn, adOpenForwardOnly, _
            adLockReadOnly
    vArray = rs.GetRows(adGetRowsRest, rs.Bookmark)

    MsgBox "There are " & UBound(vArray, 2) + 1 & " records" & _
            " and " & UBound(vArray, 1) + 1 & " fields."
End Sub
```

Changing the Current Row

ADO is much like DAO and RDO in that it has the four Move methods you would expect: MoveFirst, MovePrevious, MoveNext, and MoveLast. It also has an additional method, Move, with the following syntax:

> *rs*.Move *NumRecords, Start*

NumRecords is the number of records you want to move, and the value can be positive for a forward direction and negative for a backward direction. *Start* gives you the opportunity to indicate where you want to begin. The default is the current direction (*adBookmarkCurrent*), although you can also choose *adBookmarkFirst* or *adBookmarkLast* to start at the beginning of the Recordset or the end.

As with the other data-access methods, you should check the BOF and EOF properties of the Recordset to ensure that you are accessing a valid record. If both of these properties are true, then you have an empty Recordset.

Accessing the Fields of a Recordset

As with DAO, there are three simple ways to reference a field in a Recordset *rs* once you have created it: by ordinal number, by name, or with the ! syntax. Examples of these methods are as follows:

```
rs(1)
rs("movie_name")
rs!movie_name
```

WARNING   Take care when you use a field number such as *rs(1)*. The fields are stored in the same way they are in the base table, not in the SELECT statement, as they are in every other data-access method. It is best to retrieve the field values by the name of the field.

Once again, if there is a danger of the field containing a NULL value, then you should concatenate a zero-length string to the field when you assign it to a variable.

Listing 17.9 once again shows the FillListBox procedure, this time written for ADO. In this case, we let the Recordset simply default to forward-only and read-only, although we could have explicitly defined these characteristics with the correct arguments in the Recordset Open method.

Listing 17.9

```
Public Sub FillListBox(ListBox As ComboBox)

'   Fill a list box with movie names

    Dim rs As ADODB.Recordset
    Set rs = New ADODB.Recordset

    rs.Open "SELECT * FROM movies", cn

    ListBox.Clear
    With rs
        While Not .EOF
            ListBox.AddItem rs("movie_name")
            .MoveNext
        Wend
    ListBox.ListIndex = 0   ' Display the first item
    End With

    Set rs = Nothing

End Sub
```

Changing the Rows and Values in a Recordset

If you are using an updatable Recordset, then when you have moved to the row you want to change, you can set the values in the same way as we have seen with DAO and RDO. Updating an existing record is, however, a little different in ADO than in the other techniques, and it is actually less of a hassle to code because the Edit method no longer exists. ADO automatically takes care of this for us and maintains the editing status in the *EditMode* property of the Recordset. (You will recall from the examples for DAO and RDO that we maintained this status explicitly in the code.) The EditMode property can have one of three values as shown in Table 17.7.

TABLE 17.7: The Possible Values for the Recordset EditMode Property

Constant	Description
adEditNone	This constant shows no editing is in progress.
adEditInProgress	This constant shows data in the current record has been changed but not saved.
adEditAdd	This constant shows you have used the AddNew method, and the record has not been saved.

As you can imagine, this new property means that you can go straight in and make changes to a record without having to use the Edit method. (It is a wonder that this technique never appeared when RDO was released.) After the changes have been made, you can use the Update method to save the changes to the database.

Although you can use both the AddNew method to add a new record to the Recordset and Update to save it to the database, these two methods have an expanded syntax. They both allow you to include a list of field names and values to the method calls. How useful these additions prove to be, only time will tell, but because you will have to create the variant arrays that hold both the field names and their values, it is probably more trouble than it is worth. It certainly becomes less obvious what is going on in your code.

For an example of using these methods, see the section,"Putting It All Together," later in the chapter.

Finding a Particular Row

Once again, as with RDO, there are no Find methods in ADO. A much better way to do the same thing is to tighten up your WHERE clause when you create the Recordset.

Closing a Recordset

As with all data-access techniques, if your aim is for a scalable application architecture, you should endeavor to close any Recordsets as soon as you practically can. To do this, you can use the Close method on the Recordset or set it equal to Nothing to entirely remove the object from memory. The latter method is the preferred one if you are not going to reuse the Recordset.

Recordset Events

As you might expect in a data-access method that supplies you with a highly event-driven model, the Recordset object is no different and supplies you with a wide variety of events (see Table 17.8). These events are mainly useful when you are using an updatable cursor.

TABLE 17.8: The Available Recordset Events

Event Name	Description
EndOfRecordset	You have attempted to move beyond the last record.
FetchComplete	An asynchronous Recordset open has completed.
FetchProgress	This event reports the progress of an asynchronous Recordset open.
FieldChangeComplete	The value of a field has been changed.
MoveComplete	The current record has changed.
RecordChangeComplete	One or more records have been changed and saved to the database (such as with an AddNew or Update method).
RecordsetChangeComplete	The Recordset has been changed (such as with a Resync or Close method).
WillChangeField	The value of a field is about to be changed.
WillChangeRecord	One or more records is about to be changed and saved to the database.
WillChangeRecordset	The Recordset is about to be changed.
WillMove	The current record is about to be changed.

TIP

As you can see from the events listed in Table 17.8, you can code a large number of events. If you review the Visual Basic Help files, you will find that each of the events can also supply a large amount of information about the incident that caused the event to trigger. Some of these events can be useful; for example, *WillChangeField* can be used to code data-validation routines, and *EndOfRecordset* can be used to add a new record if you go beyond the end of the Recordset.

You should, however, be wary of all the power that these events give you and try to use them only to solve some otherwise difficult problems. If you get carried away with using events, your application will become needlessly complicated and difficult to maintain. Keep in mind that just because the ADO model gives you access to everything you can think of, you do not have to use all of that power at every opportunity.

The Command Object

With the Open method that we used to create a Recordset, we passed a string that defined the SELECT statement we wanted to run. There was nothing else we could do with it: we couldn't, for example, use parameters with it as we could with rdo-Queries when we use Remote Data Objects. To get this extra functionality and the improved coding techniques that come with it, we have to use the third of the major ADO objects, the Command object.

The Command object is below the Connection object in the ADO hierarchy, though once again we can create a stand-alone Command and only associate it with a Connection when we want it to do something. In fact, because there is no equivalent of the rdoCreateQuery method, we have no choice but to create stand-alone Command objects and then set their properties. The first thing to look at is what properties you can use for the Command object. Luckily, there are not many of them (see Table 17.9).

TABLE 17.9: The Possible Properties for the Command Object

Property	Description
ActiveConnection	This property shows the connection you want to use for the command or a string that defines a new connection.
CommandText	This property shows the text of the command, such as a DML statement or a stored-procedure call.
CommandTimeout	This property shows the number of seconds before a command timeout (default is 30).
CommandType	This property shows the type of statement that the *CommandText* property represents. See Table 17.10 for a list of the possible values.

Continued on next page

TABLE 17.9 CONTINUED: The Possible Properties for the Command Object

Property	Description
Prepared	This property determines if the statement in the *CommandText* property is held by the data provider in compiled form. This is not relevant to Oracle users.
State	This property indicates the state of the Command object. This property is of more use for Recordsets, but it can, for example, include *adStateExecuting* if you have executed your command asynchronously. The value of this property may be the sum of several values.

TABLE 17.10: The Possible Constants for the CommandType Property of the Command Object

Constant	Description
adCmdText	CommandText contains the complete text of a query.
adCmdTable	CommandText is a table name whose columns are all returned. (The SQL is created for you.)
adCmdStoredProc	CommandText is a stored-procedure name.
adCmdUnknown	The type of command in the CommandText property is unknown (default). ADO may have to interrogate the database to fill in the missing information.

WARNING   Do not use any command that uses *adCmdTable* because it returns the whole table. Most Oracle database tables are far too large to make this practical or wise.

ADO makes it simple to use any of its features. One way it does this is by supplying any of the information you did not provide. For example, if you do not indicate which type of *CommandText* property you are using, ADO can find out. However, it may have to make a trip to the data server *every* time it needs to find this missing information. It is much better practice to supply all of the information at design time. So let's now do just that. Listing 17.10 shows an example of a new procedure called CreateCommands, which sets up any Command objects in the current module. You can call this procedure from the Form_Load event.

Listing 17.10

```
Private cmd As New ADODB.Command

Private Sub CreateCommands()

    Dim rs As ADODB.Recordset

    With cmd
        .ActiveConnection = cn
        .CommandType = adCmdText
        .CommandText = _
"SELECT * FROM video_store.movies WHERE rating = 'G'"
    End With

'   Test it out for the sake of the example.
    Set rs = cmd.Execute
    MsgBox rs(1)
End Sub
```

The example in Listing 17.10 supplies the connection, the text of the command to be executed, and the type of the command. In this case, the command executes a SELECT statement, so we use the CommandType property *adCmdText*. Notice that you can easily use the schema name with the query. However, as it stands, this example is not very exciting because we cannot change the query in any way, though we can change one or more of the command properties and easily refresh the Recordset with the Execute method.

Command Parameters

There are only two methods for the Command object and the previous section showed us one, the Execute method. The second method allows us to add a parameter to the parameters collection. We have already seen parameters in both ODBCDirect and RDO. They allow us to store a value that will be inserted into the query or stored-procedure call at the time the command is executed. For example, we can put together a query that uses a parameter, and then we can repeatedly refresh the Recordset (with the Resync method), changing the parameter value or values each time we execute the Command.

Before we look at using parameters, we must first create them. We do this with the CreateParameter method of the Command object. It creates an ordered collection of parameters. The syntax for the CreateParameter method is as follows:

```
Set parameter = command.CreateParameter (Name, Type, Direction, Size,
Value)
```

The method has the following optional arguments:

Name   This argument indicates the name of the parameter object.

Type   This argument indicates the parameter data type. See the Type property in the Visual Basic Help file for a full list of data types. The types you are likely to work with in Oracle are shown in Table 17.11.

Direction   This argument indicates the direction of the parameter. See Table 17.12 for valid settings as well as how they tie up with the Oracle PL/SQL mode.

Size   This argument indicates the maximum length for the parameter value in characters or bytes.

Value   This argument indicates the parameter value. You will usually supply this value just before you execute the command.

Note that these arguments are all optional because you can either provide them with the parameter (see Table 17.13) or, in some cases, leave them out.

TABLE 17.11: The Data Types Typically Used with an Oracle Database

Basic Oracle Data Type	ADO Parameter Data Type
DATE	adDate
LONG	adLongVarChar
LONG RAW	adLongVarBinary
NUMERIC	adNumeric
RAW	adVarBinary
VARCHAR2	adVarChar

TABLE 17.12: The Direction Argument of the CreateParameter Object

Constant	PL/SQL Mode	Description
adParamUnknown		This constant indicates parameter direction is un-known. For reasons of efficiency, you should not use this constant.
adParamInput (default)	IN	This constant indicates an input parameter.
adParamOutput	OUT	This constant indicates an output parameter.
adParamInputOutput	IN OUT	This constant indicates the parameter is for both input and output.
adParamReturnValue	OUT	This constant indicates a return value.

TABLE 17.13: The Command Parameter Properties

Property	Description
Attributes	This property indicates if the parameter can contain signed numbers, null values, and RAW data.
Direction	This property defines the direction of the parameter (input, output, or both) as shown in Table 17.12.
Name	This property defines an arbitrary name for the parameter (can be a zero-length string).
NumericScale	This property defines the number of decimal places for a numeric parameter.
Precision	This property defines the maximum number of digits in a numeric parameter.
Size	This property defines the maximum length of a variable-length parameter, such as adVarChar.
Type	This property defines the parameter data type that we saw in Table 17.11.
Value	This property defines the value of the parameter. This can be changed and the command executed again.

Now that we have seen all the technical descriptions of the Parameter objects it is time to put them all together. We deal with a SELECT query with parameters in this section and move on to other uses for parameters in the next few sections.

When we deal with queries, as we saw in the last section, you can create the Command object this way:

```
With cmd
    .ActiveConnection = cn
    .CommandType = adCmdText
    .CommandText = _
        "SELECT * FROM video_store.movies WHERE rating = 'G'"
End With
```

As we have seen in with ODBCDirect and RDO, you can use parameters in this query instead of hard-coding the value "G." Just as in the ODBC methods, we must use parameter placeholders to identify where the parameter should be in the query, and just as before, we use the question mark.

We put all this together in an example in Listing 17.11, which contains a procedure CreateQueryCommand that would typically be called from a Form_Load event or the Initialization event of a Class. Because we want the command and its parameters to be available throughout the module, we declare them at the module level. In the procedure, we have many different ways to code the same thing. Because the Command object does not have events of its own, there is no need to use the WithEvents keyword, so we use the New keyword in the Dim declaration.

Listing 17.11

```
Private qy1 As New ADODB.Command
Private pYear As New ADODB.Parameter
Private pRating As New ADODB.Parameter

Private Sub CreateQueryCommand()

    Dim qy1 As New ADODB.Command
    Dim strSQL As String

    Dim pYear As New ADODB.Parameter
    Dim pRating As New ADODB.Parameter

    strSQL = "SELECT * FROM movies WHERE year_of_release > ? "
    strSQL = strSQL & " AND rating = ? ORDER BY movie_name"
```

```
        With pYear
            .Direction = adParamInput
            .Type = adNumeric
        End With

        With pRating
            .Direction = adParamInput
            .Type = adVarChar
            .Size = 6
        End With

        With qy1
            .CommandText = strSQL
            .CommandType = adCmdText
            .ActiveConnection = cn
            .Parameters.Append pYear
            .Parameters.Append pRating
        End With

    End Sub
```

After we have set up the SELECT statement in a string with the embedded parameter placeholders, we set up the details of the two required parameters: pYear and pRating. We could have used the CreateParameter method here, but ADO will handle this for us automatically. You must provide sufficient information for the parameters to be valid, though you will not get any error messages until you try to append the parameter to the command. You should use the WITH…END WITH syntax when you have more than one property to set, because it is slightly faster and much more readable.

The final action in Listing 17.11 is to set up the command itself. Up to this point, it is a stand-alone object. Now we add the important information, such as the ActiveConnection, that the command is going to run on and then append the parameters.

Once you have created a command like this, you need to execute it to make sure it is working properly. Listing 17.12 shows a procedure TestQueryCommand that not only tests the command but also shows how you would normally run it. You provide values for all the parameters, and then you execute it to return a Recordset. Remember that the parameters are defined at the module level.

Listing 17.12

```
Private Sub TestQueryCommand()

    Dim rs As New ADODB.Recordset

    pRating = "PG-13"
    pYear = 1992

    Set rs = qy1.Execute

    While Not rs.EOF
        MsgBox rs(1)
        rs.MoveNext
    Wend
    Set rs = Nothing

End Sub
```

NOTE The Recordset that is returned from the Execute command is restricted to a static, forward-only cursor.

When you are entering your code, Visual Basic offers you an incredibly large amount of help. For example, in Figure 17.5, you can see that you do not even have to remember which keyword to use for your data type; a drop-down menu supplies this for you.

FIGURE 17.5:

Using Visual Basic's IntelliSense features to make coding simpler

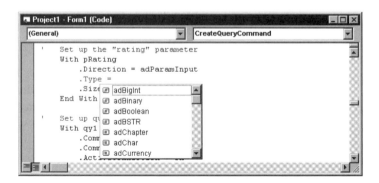

Once you have played with parameters for a while, you will realize there are an endless number of ways to code a procedure like this. The main thing is that when you have found a style you like, stick to that style, with the aim of improving the look and maintainability. A more condensed version of Listing 17.11 is shown in Listing 17.13. It does the same thing but uses the CreateParameter method to create a parameter, and the Append method to add it to the collection all in one line. To execute the command, you will need to use a procedure like the one shown in Listing 17.14. Because the parameters were not created as objects, we must refer to them through their position in the parameters collection.

Listing 17.13

```
Private qy2 As New ADODB.Command

Private Sub CreateQueryCommand2()

    Dim strSQL As String

    strSQL = "SELECT * FROM movies WHERE year_of_release > ? "
    strSQL = strSQL & " AND rating = ? ORDER BY movie_name"

    With qy2
        .CommandText = strSQL
        .CommandType = adCmdText
        .ActiveConnection = cn
        .Parameters.Append .CreateParameter _
            (, adNumeric, adParamInput)
        .Parameters.Append .CreateParameter _
            (, adVarChar, adParamInput, 6)
    End With

End Sub
```

Listing 17.14

```
Private Sub TestQueryCommand2()

    Dim rs As New ADODB.Recordset
```

```
qy2(1) = "PG-13"        ' Rating
qy2(0) = 1992           ' Year

Set rs = qy2.Execute    ' Create the Recordset

End Sub
```

Executing SQL Commands

There will be many times that you need to execute SQL commands. You will normally want to execute the DML commands INSERT, UPDATE, and DELETE; however, you are not limited to those three. Because updatable Recordsets are not a scalable design, hopefully, all of your updates will be done with SQL or, even better, as we shall see in the next section, with stored procedures.

To execute a simple SQL commands, you use the ADO Connection object. The example (see Listing 17.15) deletes a row from the Movies table. Notice that there is an implicit Commit done on this command just as there is with RDO. If you want it to be part of a transaction, you will have to use the BeginTrans/CommitTrans methods.

Listing 17.15

```
Dim strSQL As String

strSQL = "DELETE FROM movies WHERE movie_id = 303"
cn.Execute strSQL
```

Using the Connection object for executing SQL commands is fine, but we need to use the Command object to use the power of parameterized commands. We can use exactly the same syntax we saw in the previous section (see Listing 17.16). The main difference now, and it is a small one, is that the command does not return a Recordset. We do not Set a Recordset object, we merely execute the command as you can see in Listing 17.17.

Listing 17.16

```
Private Sub CreateQueryCommand3()

    Dim strSQL As String

    strSQL = "DELETE FROM movies WHERE movie_id = ?"

    With qy3
        .CommandText = strSQL
        .CommandType = adCmdText
        .ActiveConnection = cn
        .Parameters.Append .CreateParameter _
            (, adNumeric, adParamInput)
    End With

End Sub
```

TIP

The procedure TestQueryCommand3, in Listing 17.7, uses the BeginTrans and CommitTrans methods of the Connection object to control the committing of changes to the database. If you have many changes within the transaction, you will notice a distinct performance improvement, but this will be at the expense of rows being locked for the duration of a longer transaction.

Listing 17.17

```
Private Sub TestQueryCommand3()

    cn.BeginTrans
    qy3(0) = 71            ' Movie_id
    qy3.Execute            ' Delete the movie
    cn.CommitTrans

End Sub
```

Calling Stored Procedures

All of the data-access methods you can use from Visual Basic allow you to execute stored procedures, and all of them except DAO/JET allow you to return output parameters. You can execute stored procedures with the Begin/End syntax of the anonymous PL/SQL blocks that we saw in previous chapters. A much better way, however, is to use the Command object for all your procedure calls.

As we saw in Tables 17.9 and 17.10, we can define the CommandType of the Command object as *adCmdStoredProc*. This means that in the CommandText property we only have to enter the name of the stored procedure; we do not have to enclose it in Begin/End statements, and we do not even have to enter a text string with parameter placeholders. We do, however, have to make sure that all of the parameters are correctly appended to the Command Parameter's collection and that they are correctly defined and in the right order.

As an example of how to do this, we will use the stored procedure, *movies_insert3*, that we saw in the Chapter 15, *Remote Data Objects*, in Listing 15.13. The set up and execution of the stored procedure is quite different in ADO compared to RDO. Listing 17.18 shows you how to set up the command. The only disadvantage to the techniques that ADO uses is that we have a substantial amount of code to create with each stored procedure we want to execute. We will see in the section, "Using the Data Environment," how to make this whole job much easier.

Listing 17.18

```
Private Sub CreateQueryCommand4()

    Dim strSQL As String

    With qy4
        .CommandText = "video_store.movies_insert3"
        .CommandType = adCmdStoredProc
        .ActiveConnection = cn
        .Parameters.Append .CreateParameter _
            (, adNumeric, adParamInputOutput)
        .Parameters.Append .CreateParameter _
            (, adVarChar, adParamInput, 50)
        .Parameters.Append .CreateParameter _
            (, adNumeric, adParamInput)
```

```
            .Parameters.Append .CreateParameter _
                (, adVarChar, adParamInput, 6)
            .Parameters.Append .CreateParameter _
                (, adNumeric, adParamInput)
        End With

    End Sub
```

Listing 17.19 shows the way that we can execute the stored procedure that was set up as a command in Listing 17.18. Because we have not created stand-alone parameters, we must again refer to them by their position in the Parameters collection, both for input values and output values.

Listing 17.19

```
    Private Sub TestQueryCommand4()

        qy4(0) = 0              ' Movie_id
        qy4(1) = "A short about shorts"
        qy4(2) = 33
        qy4(3) = "G"
        qy4(4) = 1999
        qy4.Execute
        MsgBox "The id used for the movie was " & qy4(0)
    End Sub
```

Calling PL/SQL Functions

Once again, we cannot leave stored procedures without touching on how to call PL/SQL functions. Just as we did with RDO, we will produce some code that calls the function, GET_MOVIE_ID, that we saw in Listing 15.16. There really is not much difference between calling a function and a stored procedure; the only thing we have to remember is that the first parameter in the collection must be the return value of the function, and we must code with the type *adParamReturnValue*. Everything else works as you would expect (see Listing 17.20).

Listing 17.20

```
Private Sub TestFunctionCall()

    Dim qy As New ADODB.Command

    With qy
        .CommandText = "video_store.get_movie_id"
        .CommandType = adCmdStoredProc
        .ActiveConnection = cn
        .Parameters.Append .CreateParameter _
            (, adNumeric, adParamReturnValue)
        .Parameters.Append .CreateParameter _
            (, adVarChar, adParamInput, 50)
    End With


    qy(1) = "Awakenings"

    qy.Execute

    MsgBox "The id for the movie is " & qy(0)

End Sub
```

Retrieving PL/SQL Tables

In Chapter 15, we mentioned that you could retrieve PL/SQL tables into Recordsets. Unfortunately, there is no other way to retrieve PL/SQL tables without going to Oracle Objects for OLE, so if you are going to use Microsoft technology, you should become familiar with this method. Converting a PL/SQL table to a Recordset is a little unusual and makes use of enhancements to the ODBC driver, but at the present time, this feature is not available through the native OLE-DB provider for Oracle.

Because the technique we must use is different from a normal stored procedure or function call and because we need to use a PL/SQL package, we cannot use the easy-to-use syntax we saw in the section "Calling Stored Procedures"; instead, we must revert back to the placeholder syntax and Call statement that we saw in Chapter 15. The most important part of the technique is to define the command string. Here are two different formats for the syntax:

```
{call package.proc ({RESULTSET max_recs, table1, table2 …})}

{call package.proc({RESULTSET max_recs, table1}, { RESULTSET max_recs,
table2}, …)}
```

Both of these need some careful attention. The first form is the simplest to define and, in some ways, is the most powerful. The code calls a packaged procedure (*package.proc*) that has as its formal parameters, one or more PL/SQL tables, named table1, table2, and so on. You will remember from Chapter 10, *Creating Stored Procedures,* that a PL/SQL table is really a simple collection. When the PL/SQL table reaches Visual Basic, it becomes a zero-based array (that is, the index starts at zero). The first technique combines any number of PL/SQL tables into a single Recordset and places elements from each table into successive fields of the Recordset. You need to make sure all the tables have the same number of elements. You must define the maximum number of elements in the table in the *max_rec* argument so that the correct storage space can be reserved and used. The keyword RESULTSET must be used to indicate to the ODBC driver that you want it to convert the data it retrieves into a Recordset (the naming convention stems back from the RDO implementation).

NOTE The table name that you use in the command string must be the same name defined in the packaged procedure.

The second form of the syntax is a little more lengthy, but it allows you to pull each PL/SQL table into its own part of the Recordset. (This is the only way that you will ever be able to access multiple Recordsets from a single stored procedure in Oracle.) The downside of this second technique is that each Recordset will only have one field. However, this result is the intention of the table mechanism and is the way Oracle Objects for OLE handles it.

One final note before we get down to using the techniques. In addition to the syntax that you can see above, we can also add parameter placeholders (the "?") in the call string just as we did with other procedure calls. This is important because many times a stored procedure will need to be passed the maximum number of records that you want to retrieve; the *max_recs* argument in the procedure call is only to let ODBC know what is going on, and the value never reaches PL/SQL.

We will now put these details into action as we execute the example of retrieving a PL/SQL table we saw in Chapter 10, (see Listing 10.7). The design of our call string must exactly match that of the procedure itself. In the case of the *get_stars* procedure in the package *movie_package,* we have the following header:

```
PROCEDURE get_stars (
  p_table_size     NUMBER,
   p_stars         OUT char_table_type)
```

We need to create one command parameter to input the maximum table size. The setup of the Command object in this instance is shown in Listing 17.21. This listing shows how to set up the Command object with one input parameter and one output table. Notice that in this case, we have set up the command so that it can only receive a maximum of 20 records. However, the stored procedure needs to know how many records to actually return, and it uses the input parameter for this purpose. If the value of the input parameter were greater than 20, we would get a run-time error. You should also be aware that neither of these numbers can ensure that you will get that number of records returned; there may be insufficient records that fit the criteria.

Listing 17.21

```
Private Sub TestPLSQLTable()

    Dim qy As New ADODB.Command
    Dim rs As ADODB.Recordset
    Dim strSQL As String

'   First, set up the command object
    strSQL = "{call movie_package.get_stars " & _
            "(?, {RESULTSET 20, p_stars})}"
    With qy
        .CommandText = strSQL
        .CommandType = adCmdText
        .ActiveConnection = cn
        .Parameters.Append .CreateParameter(, adNumeric, adParamInput)
    End With
```

```
'    Define the maximum number of records that we want back
'    and execute the stored procedure to return the Recordset.
     qy(0) = 5

     Set rs = New ADODB.Recordset
'      rs.CursorType = adOpenStatic
'      rs.LockType = adLockReadOnly
     Set rs = qy.Execute
     While Not rs.EOF
        MsgBox "Star name is  " & rs(0)
        rs.MoveNext
     Wend
     rs.Close
     Set rs = Nothing
End Sub
```

Putting It All Together

In this section, we will look at some of the code for the movie application that we first introduced in Chapter 14. Several of the procedures for this version of the application will be exactly the same as the Chapter 14 example, although some have already been provided in this chapter. The main differences come in the CreateQueries procedure, which is called in the Form_Load event (see Listing 17.22), and the cmdAction procedure, which reacts to the user clicking on the New, Update, and Delete buttons.

Listing 17.22

```
     Private Sub CreateQueries()

'    Set up any queries required in this module.

     Dim strSQL As String

'    Set up the query to call the insert stored procedure.

     With qyMovieInsert
```

```
            .CommandText = "video_store.movies_insert3"
            .CommandType = adCmdStoredProc
            .ActiveConnection = cn
            .Parameters.Append .CreateParameter _
                (, adNumeric, adParamInputOutput)
            .Parameters.Append .CreateParameter _
                (, adVarChar, adParamInput, 50)
            .Parameters.Append .CreateParameter _
                (, adNumeric, adParamInput)
            .Parameters.Append .CreateParameter _
                (, adVarChar, adParamInput, 6)
            .Parameters.Append .CreateParameter _
                (, adNumeric, adParamInput)
        End With


    '   Set up the query to select the participants.

        strSQL = "        SELECT first_name || ' ' || last_name full_name,"
        strSQL = strSQL & "    DECODE (role, 'A', 'Actor', 'D', 'Director')"
        strSQL = strSQL & "    role, movie_id "
        strSQL = strSQL & " FROM video_store.participants, "
        strSQL = strSQL & "    video_store.movie_participants"
        strSQL = strSQL & " WHERE movie_id = ? "
        strSQL = strSQL & "    AND movie_participants.participant_id = " & _
                          "        participants.participant_id "
        strSQL = strSQL & "    ORDER BY role"

        With qyParticipants
            .CommandText = strSQL
            .CommandType = adCmdText
            .ActiveConnection = cn
            .Parameters.Append .CreateParameter _
                (, adNumeric, adParamInput)
        End With

    End Sub
```

In Listing 17.22, we create two command objects. The first is *qyMovieInsert*, which we saw earlier in the chapter. In a production system, you would create a Command object similar to this for every stored-procedure call that you made.

This could be a substantial amount of code, but it makes calling the stored procedures much easier. The second Command object is *qyParticipants,* which is a somewhat complex SELECT statement with parameters. This Command object is executed each time the current movie record changes, so you can display the appropriate participants in the movie. Using a parameterized query is the most efficient way to do this.

Listing 17.23 shows the cmdAction_Click procedure, which reacts to requests for insert, update, and delete functions. For the example, we have two ways of doing this. The insert function is performed by a Command object, although the update function is performed by a hard-coded SQL string. In reality, we would set up Visual Basic calls for both of these operations (probably in a movie class module) so you would move this complexity out of the main GUI front-end code, as we did with the movie_insert procedure earlier in the chapter.

Listing 17.23

```
Private Sub cmdAction_Click(Index As Integer)

'   Execute the require action - insert, update or delete.

    Dim iField As Integer
    Dim strSQL As String

    If Index = 0 Then            ' Add a new record
        ShowNewRecord
        strMode = "Add"

    ElseIf Index = 1 Then              ' Update the record
        If strMode = "Add" Then
            qyMovieInsert(0) = 0
            qyMovieInsert(1) = txtMovie(0)
            qyMovieInsert(2) = CInt(txtMovie(1))
            qyMovieInsert(3) = txtMovie(2)
            qyMovieInsert(4) = CInt(txtMovie(3))
            qyMovieInsert.Execute
            RefreshRecordset

        Else
'       Use a conventional inline call here
            strSQL = "BEGIN video_store.movies_update ("
```

```
            strSQL = strSQL & " rsMovies("movie_id") & ","
            strSQL = strSQL & "'" & txtMovie(0) & "', " ' Movie Name
            strSQL = strSQL & txtMovie(1) & ", "          ' Length
            strSQL = strSQL & "'" & txtMovie(2) & "', " ' Rating
            strSQL = strSQL & txtMovie(3)                ' Year
            strSQL = strSQL & "); END;"
            cn.Execute strSQL
        End If
        strMode = ""
        RefreshRecordset

    ElseIf Index = 2 Then              ' Delete the record
        cn.Execute "BEGIN video_store.movies_delete (" & _
                   " rsMovies("movie_id") & "); END;"
        RefreshRecordset
    End If

End Sub
```

Asynchronous Operation

With ADO 2.0, we finally have an event-driven model that can rival, and maybe even surpass, RDO. We have seen the events that ADO exposes in Tables 17.3 and 17.8 for the Connection object and the Recordset object respectively. You can specify the asynchronous option for the following methods:

OpenOptions argument of the Connection.Open method

Options argument of the Recordset.Open method

You should refer to Chapter 15 for a deeper discussion of using asynchronous operations and events; the RDO techniques work in similar manner to those of ADO.

Looking at the Database Structure

As we have done in the last few chapters, understanding the database structure we are dealing with is occasionally useful. With ADO, there is no equivalent to the Tabledef we see in DAO or the rdoTable of RDO. We have a Fields collection under the Recordset object. ADO contains many attributes about the Fields of a Recordset in the Field object properties (see Table 17.14).

TABLE 17.14: The Command Parameter Properties

Property	Description
ActualSize	This property indicates the actual size of the field.
Attributes	This property indicates if the parameter can contain signed numbers, null values, and RAW data.
DefinedSize	This property indicates the size of the field as defined in the database. This may differ from the ActualSize value, for example, for VARCHAR2 columns.
Name	This property contains an arbitrary name for the parameter (can be a zero-length string).
NumericScale	This property shows the number of decimal places for a numeric parameter.
OriginalValue	This property shows the original value of the field when you populated the Recordset.
Precision	This property shows the maximum number of digits in a numeric parameter.
Type	This property shows the parameter data type that we saw in Table 17.7.
UnderlyingValue	This property shows the current committed value in the database.
Value	This property shows the current value of the field in the Recordset.

If you want to examine the data types that the Field object has, you can use a procedure such as that in Listing 17.24.

Listing 17.24

```
Private Function FieldType(intType As Integer) As String
'    Convert the ADO field type to an Oracle column type
```

```
Select Case intType
    Case adInteger
        FieldType = "NUMBER"
    Case adDecimal
        FieldType = "NUMBER"
    Case adNumeric
        FieldType = "NUMBER"
    Case adSingle
        FieldType = "NUMBER"
    Case adDouble
        FieldType = "NUMBER"
    Case adDate
        FieldType = "DATE"
    Case adChar
        FieldType = "CHAR2"
    Case adVarChar
        FieldType = "VARCHAR2"
    Case adLongVarChar
        FieldType = "LONG"
    Case adLongVarBinary
        FieldType = "LONG RAW"
    Case adVarBinary
        FieldType = "RAW"
    Case adDBTimeStamp
        FieldType = "Date"
    Case Else
        FieldType = "Unknown " & intType
End Select

End Function
```

The OpenSchema Method

As you can see from the information available for Fields, as described above, ADO does not by default present you with much information about the database objects to which you have access. This is actually a good design decision compared, in particular, to DAO/JET, which brings in everything it can about the database objects when you first connect to the database. Much of the time this information, which takes a significant amount of time and resources to collect, is never used, and this will happen for every connection that is made.

ADO has an alternative that is very powerful. It lets you use the OpenSchema method against the connection to pull in every conceivable bit of information about the database objects. The name *OpenSchema* is a little misleading from an Oracle point of view, because it does not retrieve just one schema in which the database objects are found, it retrieves every schema object you have access to. This information is almost certainly going to be vast, so you should be prepared to sift through what you retrieve.

The OpenSchema method has the following syntax:

```
Set rs = cn.OpenSchema (QueryType, Criteria, SchemaID)
```

The OpenSchema method has the following arguments:

QueryType   This argument shows the type of information you want to retrieve. There are 30 different types; a few of the more useful are shown in Table 17.15.

Criteria   You can use this argument to define a subset of all the attributes that can be returned about the schema object. This is optional; if you omit it, you will retrieve all the attributes in the Recordset.

SchemaId   An object GUID used only for nonstandard OLE-DB-provider schema information.

TABLE 17.15: Possible QueryTypes for the OpenSchema Method

QueryType	Description
adSchemaColumns	Table and column information (use this with care because you can get a lot of information back)
adSchemaForeignKeys	Foreign keys
adSchemaIndexes	Indexes
adSchemaPrimaryKeys	Primary keys
adSchemaProcedureParameters	Procedure name and parameter types
adSchemaTables	All the tables you have read access to

If you use these query types, you will find there is often a field for "Catalog" description. This is a Microsoft SQL Server convention and does not apply to Oracle. One good feature is you can retrieve Oracle stored procedures that exist inside packages as well as functions, although you cannot retrieve the package headers.

> **WARNING** If you use the OpenSchema method, you will find that only a subset of the Query-Types work with the Microsoft ODBC driver. For full coverage, you should use the native OLE-DB provider.

Error Handling

Whenever you use a data-access method, whether it is ADO or another method, you then have the possibility (some would say the probability) of error messages due to your interaction with the data source rather than just the usual Visual Basic programming errors. Just as the other methods provide an additional collection for holding these data-access errors, so ADO has the Errors collection. This collection consists of one or more Error objects, each with the properties shown in Table 17.16. Because the collection holds errors that have been encountered on the data source, the collection is dependent on the Connection object for that data source.

TABLE 17.16: The Properties of the ADO Error Object

Property	Description
Description	This property gives a description of the error.
HelpContext	This property gives the Help file context ID for the error number.
HelpFile	This property gives the full file name of the Visual Basic Help file.
NativeError	This property gives the error number from the data source.
Number	This property gives a unique error number. This is of little use.
Source	This property gives the name of the ADO object that triggered the error.
SQLState	This property gives a five-character string to ANSI standards holding the error code from the OLE-DB provider.

You can loop through the Errors collection with the following code:

```
Dim Error As ADODB.Error
For Each Error In cn.Errors
    Debug.Print Error.Description & Chr(9) & Error.NativeError
Next
```

You will usually find it is the first error object in the collection that is the only one worth looking at. For example, the following code

```
Debug.Print "Description " & cn.Errors(0).Description
Debug.Print "NativeError " & cn.Errors(0).NativeError
Debug.Print "Number      " & cn.Errors(0).Number
Debug.Print "Source      " & cn.Errors(0).Source
Debug.Print "SQLState    " & cn.Errors(0).SQLState
```

can give you the output shown below:

```
Description [Microsoft][ODBC driver for Oracle][Oracle]ORA-00904:
invalid column name
NativeError 904
Number      -2147217900
Source      Microsoft OLE DB Provider for ODBC Drivers
SQLState    S0022
```

As usual, the main item of interest is the description. This should be parsed to extract the most useful information, in this case, `invalid column name`. ADO has the NativeError property that shows the actual Oracle error number (904 here). In DAO, this value was held in Errors(0).Number.

ADO can return error messages you can trap normally. These are errors not triggered by the data source. In addition, you will find that events return error messages.

Using the Data Environment

When you have written code to deal with stored procedure calls for a while, you will start to think that there must be a better way than having to type in so much information every time you want to run the procedure. You need a more automated approach. You can achieve this goal of little code writing with data wizards that create a form with data-bound controls bound to a selected Recordset, but this is not a scalable approach.

In previous versions of Visual Basic, RDO could use the UserConnection object to make using stored procedures and queries easier. Visual Basic 6 has been released with the Data Environment, which is a large and complex ActiveX designer aimed at simplifying the tasks developers have to contend with. In this section, we will take a short look at the Data Environment to make it easier to call stored procedures. The designer is capable of much more, but at this point, you should tread very carefully with it because of its complexity and stability problems, which can cause you more trouble than is worthwhile.

With the Data Environment designer you create a Data Environment object that handles all of the access to the database for you (or as much of it as you want it to). For example, you can design into the Data Environment the capability to handle stored-procedure calls, taking all of the hard work out of it. You can create Recordsets, drop the fields or the whole Recordset onto a form, and have an instant data maintenance form. However, unless you are using updatable Recordsets, you will still have a lot of work to do to get your application up and running (such as calling stored procedures).

We will create a new Data Environment and set it up to execute a stored procedure. If you use this method in a practical situation, you might set a Data Environment object up for each database area. In the example, we will set up an environment for the Movie database. Because the Data Environment is a little different from the normal Visual Basic operations, we will take it a little more slowly.

We will start off by creating a new project, which we will call DeDemo. If you click the Project ➤ Add Data Environment menu option, a new object will be added to your project (see Figure 17.6). The name of the object and the file it is stored in will be DataEnvironment1 by default; however, we will be sure to change both of these names. If you look at your project window, you will also see that the designer has been added to your project.

FIGURE 17.6:

The new Data Environment object

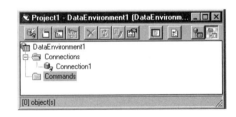

The first thing I like to do is rename the DE (Data Environment) object so that any subsequent work does not have to be modified if we change the name. To do this, click once on the DE window, hit the F4 button to show the properties, and then change the name (in this case, I have called it Movies). It is a sensible idea to now save the DE to file. You can do this by making sure the DE is highlighted, then using the File menu, and selecting the option to save the file. As with all designer files, this will get a .dsr extension. If you intend to make much use of DEs, you should set up a special folder for them where they can be easily shared.

In Figure 17.6, you should have noticed that we have two types of folders in the DE: Connections and Commands. There is a Connection object in the DE by default because without one, you cannot do anything; however, this Connection object needs setting up with the relevant properties.

Right-click Connection1 (you can rename it if you wish), and then select Properties from the pop-up menu. The window you now see will resemble the one you used to create a Data Link (see Figure 17.7). Select your OLE-DB provider, and enter your connection information (user name, password, and either service name for the native provide or the DSN for an ODBC data source). Now that we have a valid data connection, we do not need to define the connection string anywhere in code; this is one of the things that is hidden in the DE.

FIGURE 17.7:

Creating the data connection

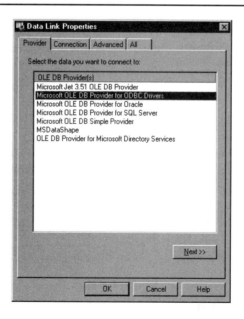

WARNING   You should remember that every Data Environment has its own connection. If you use more than one DE or you create another connection using the more traditional approach we have been using up to now, then you could end up with multiple connections to the same database.

To be able to do anything with the DE, we need to add at least one Command object. You can do this by right-clicking any object in the DE window and selecting "Add Command" from the pop-up menu. A new command will appear in the DE window under the Commands folder. This is equivalent to a stand-alone Command object; until we set its properties, it can do nothing. Right-click the Command object, and select "Properties…" from the pop-up menu. This is where things get interesting (see Figure 17.8).

FIGURE 17.8:

The Command object
properties

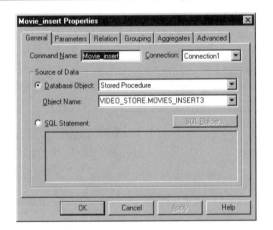

At this point, we must give a name to the Command object; the example shows movie_insert. We must set the connection for this command, and that is the one we created at the beginning of this example (Connection1). Next, we must select what type of command we want to create. We have a choice between executing a stored procedure (or function) and creating a Recordset from a SQL statement. In the example, we are using the stored procedure movies_insert3, in line with the example we have used in this and other chapters. A quick look at the Advanced tab will show you that the DE has interrogated the database, knows that it does not return a Recordset, and has created the stored procedure call with parameter placeholders (see Figure 17.9). If we were creating a SQL statement command, then we could have some control over the resultant Recordset on this page of the properties dialog box.

FIGURE 17.9:

The Advanced tab on the Command properties designer

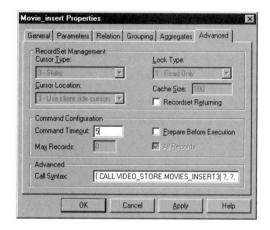

When we finally click OK, we have set the DE up with its first Command object. The next thing is to see how to incorporate it into our project. The DE object is an ActiveX control, and we must create an instance of it in code to be able to use it (just as you would create an instance of a class). We can do this with the following line of code:

```
Private DE As New Movies
```

This declares a new Data Environment (DE) as an instance of the Data Environment that we set up and called Movies. Now we want to see some code to execute it (see Listing 17.25). Notice that the working part of this code is one line, and we do not have to do any query setup at all. You cannot make calling a stored procedure any easier. In the call, you could pass actual values for all of the input parameters, but for the input/output parameter (the first one), you need to define it as a variable so the DE has something to pass the value back to.

Listing 17.25

```
Private Sub MovieInsert(iMovieId As Integer, strMovieName As String, _
          iLength As Integer, strRating As String, iYear As Integer)

    DE.Movie_insert iMovieId, strMovieName, iLength, strRating, iYear

    MsgBox "The movie id used was " & iMovieId

End Sub
```

WARNING   There are serious problems with the Data Environment that indicate it is not yet a solid product and show its lack of maturity. From the Oracle standpoint, it does not support packaged procedures, and you really should be trying to use these as often as possible not only from the maintenance point of view but also because they tend to be more efficient. However, for returning Recordsets, the environment still has it share of problems. The best advice is to experiment when you have plenty of spare time and do not rely on the Data Environment yet for your most demanding production work.

Drawbacks to ADO

ADO is currently the pinnacle of the Microsoft technologies. ADO 2.0 is much more mature than version 1.5, especially with the event models. However, there still are a few things missing from this technology.

- You cannot retrieve PL/SQL cursor variables from stored procedures.

- You cannot use Oracle bind parameters.

- The Data Environment is relatively immature with its share of problems.

- The Data Environment does not support Oracle packaged procedures.

Summary

This chapter has covered ActiveX Data Objects from the point of view of an Oracle user. We have seen the ADO model, which is much flatter than the models of the other data-access techniques discussed in this book. We have seen how to create a connection with the Oracle database using both the OLE-DB provider for ODBC as well as the native OLE-DB provider for Oracle. We used the ODBC driver because it is a little more powerful and stable than the native provider.

We next moved on to the various ways of building Recordsets and saw how to manipulate them. We also covered how to use the events that Connections and Recordsets provide for us. After Recordsets, we dealt with the Command object as well as how to produce parameterized queries and call stored procedures and functions with input and output parameters. We saw how to retrieve PL/SQL tables from stored procedures into Recordsets and then briefly covered ADO error handling and the structure of the database. We finished off with a look at how to use the Data Environment to execute stored procedures with a minimal amount of Visual Basic code.

Oracle Objects for OLE

All of the Visual Basic techniques we have examined so far have been Microsoft-provided technologies. There are a number of other methods, the most popular of which is Oracle Objects for OLE (OO4O). OO4O is the Oracle Corporation's answer to DAO, upon which it was modeled; it has changed considerably since its first appearance for Visual Basic 3. As we have mentioned in previous chapters, none of the ODBC access methods truly allows the developer to use all the features of the Oracle server. Over the last few years as new capabilities have been added to Oracle, such as returning PL/SQL tables and cursor variables from stored procedures, OO4O has been enhanced with matching features. Generally, these features do not sit well with the ODBC specification, although it is likely that OLE-DB may one day have the capabilities. As an additional boost to the product, OO4O is likely to be the first data-access method to handle Oracle's object-relational extension, although that is currently something we can only look forward to.

OO4O is now a 32-bit-only data-access method and is fully thread-safe for use in Microsoft Transaction Server (MTS) and Internet Information Server (IIS). OO4O is also different from the other access methods in that it is an in-process OLE server. This is the same kind of in-process server that you can create as a dll with the VB environment, though in this case, it is developed in C++. COM is used to move data back and forth between your application and OO4O, so you have to be careful in the way you handle the data.

OO4O, as you would expect, displays the kind of integration with Oracle that RDO displays with SQL Server; in fact, the integration is tighter, to the point where OO4O almost becomes an extension of the Oracle server.

The topics we will cover in this chapter include

- The OO4O object hierarchy
- The early binding issue
- Accessing a database
- Creating OraDynasets
- Using parameters
- Executing SQL commands
- Calling stored procedures
- Retrieving cursor variables and PL/SQL tables

- Using OraSQLStmts

- Viewing and using the structure of a database

- The drawbacks to OO4O

The Oracle Objects for OLE Object Hierarchy

As with all of the other various ways of interfacing Visual Basic with Oracle, OO4O exposes an object model that makes it easy to understand and to manipulate the data. A quick glance at the object hierarchy (see Figure 18.1) shows its heritage as a derivative of DAO but with a few extensions added. The terminology is DAO-like, which makes it easy for a new user to adapt to OO4O. The higher-level objects in the hierarchy are detailed below; the rest of the chapter is devoted to exploring the lower levels where most of the work is done.

FIGURE 18.1:

The Data Access Objects object hierarchy

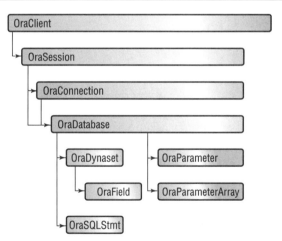

OraClient

The OraClient object is a little different as far as hierarchical diagrams go: although it is the top-level object in the diagram, OraClient really represents only the working environment for the workstation that OO4O is run on. It can be thought of as representing the in-process server. Although it contains the OraSession objects, it has no methods, so it can safely be ignored.

OraSession

In contrast to the OraClient object, the OraSession object is the practical top-level object in the hierarchy as far as the application is concerned. You can create new session objects by a direct call to the in-process server (via the CreateObject automation method) as opposed to an OO4O method call. The OraSession provides a transaction-level object (that is, it supports BeginTrans and CommitTrans); if you need more than one transaction scope, you will need to create another OraSession. It also contains the OraDatabase objects and the OraConnection objects.

OraConnection

The OraConnection object is a representation of the actual connection between the OraDatabase object and the Oracle server. In practice, it only supports the CommitTrans and RollbackTrans methods, which are better handled by the OraSession object. We will not deal with the OraConnection object, and it can safely be ignored.

OraDatabase

The OraDatabase object represents one single session with a database. It is similar to a session anywhere else in the Oracle domain, with a user name and password. In previous versions of OO4O, sessions could be shared if the user name and password were identical, but in version 2.2 and above, the OraDatabase has a single Session object. Each OraDatabase can contain one or more OraDynasets for retrieving rows from the database.

The Early Binding Issue

When you call any property or method in an ActiveX component (such as OO4O), Visual Basic has to determine what arguments are required for the call. The method it uses to do this depends entirely on the way you declare the object. With versions of OO4O prior to 2.2, you would typically declare the OO4O objects "As Object".

This is a generic data type and means that Visual Basic must find out which OO4O object type it really is by referring to the type library and which arguments are required for the call at run time. This is called *late binding* and requires extra overhead compared with properly declaring the alternatives.

With OO4O 2.2, you can declare your objects with their true type. This declaration enables Visual Basic to look up the object type and the argument information at compile time and makes the process faster at run time. This process is called *early binding* and requires that you incorporate a new reference into the project. To add this reference, you should follow these steps:

1. Choose Project ➤ References to open the References dialog box as shown in Figure 18.2. You will see a list of all the object libraries you can reference in your application.

2. Check the option labeled OracleInProcServer 2.2 Type Library.

3. Click OK.

FIGURE 18.2:

The References dialog box with the Oracle In-Process Server Type Library checked

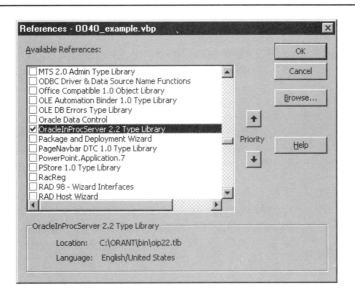

| TIP | If you are declaring objects and find that the Auto List Members feature does not provide any Oracle-specific objects, you have not included the Oracle In-Process Server reference. |

WARNING   If you are working with Visual Basic 6, you may encounter difficulties getting early binding to work. If so, you will have to switch back to late binding and declare your objects simply "As Object". Because of this problem, all the examples in this chapter use late binding.

Accessing a Database

Accessing a database with OO4O is the easiest way to access an Oracle database with Visual Basic, even though it looks complicated at first. The best part is that the code is nearly always the same, and you only need a little information to make the connection. To create an OraSession object, you have to call the Visual Basic CreateObject method, which creates a new OraSession object and sets its reference to the object variable you have declared. This code will always be the same regardless of how many sessions you create; you just assign different object variables.

The first operation you will always have to do is create an OraSession. This is done simply by the following code:

```
Dim OraSession As OraSession
Set OraSession = CreateObject("OracleInProcServer.XOraSession")
```

You can also create a *named* session with the CreateNamedSession method; however, most developers simply place the CreateObject code straight into their applications. This technique creates an object that represents a session ready to be connected to the database.

As you can see from the OraSession methods in Table 18.1, the OraSession object is the key to working with OO4O. Its main function is to create database connections as well as the transaction control commands.

TABLE 18.1: The OraSession Methods

Method	Description
BeginTrans	This method begins a transaction.
CommitTrans	This method commits a transaction.

Continued on next page

TABLE 18.1 CONTINUED: The OraSession Methods

Method	Description
ConnectSession	This method returns a reference to the session with the supplied name.
CreateNamedSession	This method creates a session with a supplied name.
LastServerErrReset	This method resets server error information.
OpenDatabase	This method opens an OraDatabase object.
ResetTrans	This method rolls back all outstanding transactions.
Rollback	This method rolls back a transaction.

Once you have created a session, whether it is the default session or you have decided to create a named session, you can now move to create a connection to the database. To open a database connection within the session, you use the OpenDatabase method of the OraSession object. The syntax for this is

```
Set oradatabase = orasession.OpenDatabase (database_name,
                          connect_string, options)
```

The method has the following arguments:

database_name   This argument defines the Oracle SQL*Net/Net8 service name.

connect_string   This argument defines the user name and password to connect to your Oracle database. These two values are entered together separated by a forward slash. (This will also work with SQL*Net/Net8.)

options   This argument sets the options for the database (see Table 18.2). Notice that OO4O considers the options to be data-access *modes*, a term unique to OO4O.

TABLE 18.2: The OpenDatabase Method Options

Constant	Value	Description
ORADB_DEFAULT	0	Visual Basic Mode (Default). With the AddNew and Edit methods, if you don't provide values for a field, the values are set to NULL regardless of the column DEFAULT constraints. This mode also locks or waits for a lock with the Edit method.

Continued on next page

TABLE 18.2 CONTINUED: The OpenDatabase Method Options

Constant	Value	Description
ORADB_ORAMODE	1	Oracle Mode. This constant allows a database to set the default column values with AddNew or Edit and fetches the values actually used.
ORADB_NOWAIT	2	Lock No-Wait Mode. This constant does not wait for any locks held by other users to be released (causes ORA-54 errors).
ORADB_NO_REFETCH	4	Oracle Mode (No Refetch). This constant is similar to Oracle Mode, but the data is not refetched to the local cache after inserting or updating rows.
ORADB_NONBLK	8	Nonblocking Mode. This constant has no effect in a 32-bit environment.

TIP

To be able to include the constants in Table 18.2, you must include the file ORACONST.TXT in your project.

To put the OpenDatabase method into practice, Listing 18.1 shows a procedure, which can be easily modified to fit any scenario you have. You just have to change the database service name as well as the user name and password for your particular situation.

Listing 18.1

```
Dim OraSession As Object
Dim OraDatabase As Object

Sub ConnectToDatabase()


'  Create the OraSession Object
   Set OraSession = CreateObject("OracleInProcServer.XOraSession")

'  Create the OraDatabase Object by opening a connection to Oracle.
   Set OraDatabase = OraSession.OpenDatabase("movies", _
                     "video_user/ummagumma", ORADB_DEFAULT)

End Sub
```

When should you use the options in Table 18.2? The ORADB_ORAMODE option is useful if you use triggers to assign key values from sequences. In fact, this is the only practical way to combine sequences with updatable *dynasets* (see the section, "Making Use of Triggers," later in the chapter). Again, if you are using updatable dynasets, then the ORADB_NOWAIT option is the only way you can avoid blocking your application when it encounters a lock on a row; you will have to trap for the possible error, but you should be doing that anyway.

NOTE OO4O has OraDynaset objects derived from the original Dynaset object in DAO. The term *dynaset* is often used generically to indicate updatable result sets, although OO4O uses the term for read-only result sets, as well.

However, for a truly scalable and secure application, you should just use the default (ORADB_DEFAULT) and use SQL or stored procedures to update and modify your data. In this case, you will create your dynasets with ORADYN_NOCACHE and ORADYN_READONLY options to simulate the firehose cursor available in the ODBC and OLE_DB technologies.

Database Object Methods

Once you have connected to the Oracle database, you will need several methods to retrieve data from Oracle. The list of available methods, shown in Table 18.3, includes four methods to create OraDynasets, Oracle's answer to DAO's Record-set. We will cover two of those methods in detail in this chapter; the other two are variations on a theme that allows you to customize the operating parameters. The rest of the other OraDatabase methods allow you to execute SQL statements and create stored queries. As you can see, the Database object is the center of activity in OO4O.

TABLE 18.3: The OraDatabase Methods

Method	Description
Close	This method closes the database.
CreateCustomDynaset	This method creates a dynaset with tuning parameters.
CreateDynaset	This method creates a dynaset.
CreatePLSQLDynaset	This method creates a PL/SQL dynaset (from a cursor variable).

Continued on next page

TABLE 18.3 CONTINUED: The OraDatabase Methods

Method	Description
CreatePlsqlCustomDynaset	This method creates a PL/SQL dynaset with tuning parameters.
CreateSQL	This method creates an OraSQLStmt object.
ExecuteSQL	This method executes a SQL command.
LastServerErrReset	This method resets the last server error.

Creating OraDynasets

Now that we have opened up a Database object for our application, we can create an OraDynaset to hold the results of any queries we want to execute. The OraDynaset object can hold the results from any valid query, such as all the G-rated movies shorter than 120 minutes. You create a new OraDynaset object with the CreateDynaset method of the Database object. As with the other data-access technologies, the method creates a reference to the new OraDynaset object, so we must assign it to an OraDynaset variable with the Set command.

> **NOTE**
>
> Oracle Objects for OLE only includes dynasets, which are comparable to the same thing in DAO. There is no equivalent of the snapshot.

The syntax of the CreateDynaset method is as follows:

```
Dim OraDynaset As Object
Set oraDynaset = oraDatabase.CreateDynaset(source, options)
```

This method has the following arguments:

> **source**   This argument is a string that represents the source of the data for the new OraDynaset. It will typically be a SQL statement enclosed in double quotes. Do not include a semicolon at the end of the line.
>
> **options**   This argument is an optional combination of constants that specify characteristics of the new OraDynaset. You can use one or more of the constants defined in Table 18.4.

TABLE 18.4: The Possible Values for the CreateOraDynaset Options Flag

Constant	Value	Description
ORADYN_DEFAULT	0	This constant shows the default behavior.
ORADYN_NO_AUTOBIND	1	This constant stops the binding of parameters to the query. Use this value if your query does not use parameters.
ORADYN_NO_BLANKSTRIP	2	This constant stops trailing blanks from being stripped from character-string fields.
ORADYN_READONLY	4	This constant sets the dynaset to be read-only.
ORADYN_NOCACHE	8	This constant stops creation of a local dynaset data cache. It gives a faster but forward-only cursor.
ORADYN_ORAMODE	16	This constant produces Oracle Mode. It allows the database to set the default column values with AddNew or Edit and fetches the values actually used by the Oracle database.
ORADYN_NO_REFETCH	32	This constant is like Oracle Mode, but data is not refetched to the local cache after inserting or updating rows.
ORADYN_NO_MOVEFIRST	64	This constant avoids a MoveFirst on dynaset creation; in other words, the dynaset is not populated. This constant is useful if you are only going to insert new records. BOF and EOF are both TRUE.
ORADYN_DIRTY_WRITE	128	This constant ensures Update and Delete will not check for read consistency.

One interesting point in the dynaset creation options is the dirty writes. Normally, when you try to update the dynaset, OO4O will check to ensure that the data in the cache is still the same as the data in the database; in other words, that the data is consistent. If the data has changed, then you will get the error message "OIP-4119 data has been modified." If you use the ORADYN_DIRTY_WRITE option, there will be no consistency check and, therefore, no error message. This option is useful for times when the data is changing rapidly.

Pessimistic Locking

Although some developers may bemoan the fact that pessimistic locking is not generally available in Oracle, it is no panacea. Pessimistic locking refers to the situation in which a row that you want to edit is locked as soon as you execute the Edit method. Unlike some databases that can only lock pages containing the row, Oracle locks only the particular row. In OO40, there is no equivalent to the lockedits argument that you see in the Microsoft methods. The updatable OraDynaset always uses pessimistic locking; it is done by executing an internal SELECT FOR UPDATE command.

Unfortunately, pessimistic locking invariably increases the amount of time that the row is locked. The worst-case scenario is if you execute an Edit and then leave the Update until the user has finished data entry. In this case, the user could end up locking the row for a coffee break, overnight, or even a weekend. This is something you must program around at all costs. The preferable way is to avoid updatable dynasets altogether and, instead, execute DML statements or stored procedures to alter your data.

Listing 18.2 shows an example of creating an OraDynaset and writing out some of the field values. The source for your SQL string can be any valid Oracle SQL query, and you can include views and synonyms.

Listing 18.2

```
Private Sub OpenDynaset()

    Dim dynMovies As Object

  ' Create the OraDynaset Object.
    Set dynMovies = OraDatabase.CreateDynaset _
        ("SELECT movie_id, movie_name FROM video_store.movies", _
         ORADYN_DEFAULT)

    If Not dynMovies.EOF Then

      ' Display the first record.
        MsgBox dynMovies.Fields("movie_id").Value & " : " & _
               dynMovies.Fields("movie_name").Value
        MsgBox "Updatable = " & dynMovies.Updatable
    End If
End Sub
```

Oracle Objects for OLE has no problems handling any Oracle-specific features, such as schema names, simple views (one table), and synonyms. The moment you make use of more complex SQL features, such as column aliases or table joins, then the Oracle result set, and therefore also your dynaset, will be read-only.

One interesting thing you can do is to include functions and calculations in your query. For example, if you use

```
SELECT year_of_release + 2 FROM movies
```

you can actually refer to the field

```
dynMovies.Fields("year_of_release + 2")
```

though you must make sure that the spelling is exactly right, down to the last space. This technique works because Oracle, by default, names any complex column with the name specified in the query. This field will not be updatable.

The OraDynaset is more liberal over its requirements for updatable result sets compared with ODBC methods. ODBC requires that the result sets have a unique key, whereas the CreateDynaset method always adds the ROWID to the list of columns requested, if it is available. In this way, the result set can almost always be updatable even without a unique key.

TIP

If you want to modify the cache and fetch parameters, you can make use of the CreateCustomDynaset method. See the section, "Tuning the OraDynaset," for more information.

Making Use of Triggers

When you use the equivalent of an updatable dynaset in the other data-access methods, you are in trouble if you use sequences to generate primary keys for your tables. This is because the primary key cannot be NULL (by definition), so when you use the Update method, you must provide a value for it; however, you do not know what that value is unless you first execute another SELECT command to find it, such as

```
SELECT MyTable.NEXTVAL FROM dual
```

One solution to this problem is to pass a dummy value in the update (such as a zero) and then put the real value into the table by a trigger. The trouble is that the dynaset would have a zero in it while the corresponding column in the database would have the actual number used. You would not be able to update that record again without refreshing the dynaset.

OO4O has a different take on this and is designed with this sequence problem in mind. If you use the right option (ORADYN_ORAMODE), you can ensure that whenever you use the AddNew or Edit methods, any default values used by the database or assigned by triggers will be refetched from the database into the dynaset. Listing 18.3 shows the code you can type into a SQL*Plus session to create a trigger on the Customers table. This code checks for a new record being inserted. If the Movie_id of the new record is zero, then it substitutes in a value from the sequence generator.

Listing 18.3

```
CREATE OR REPLACE TRIGGER video_store.customer_insert
  BEFORE
  INSERT
  ON video_store.customers
  FOR EACH ROW
  WHEN (NEW.customer_id = 0)

  DECLARE
    v_id  NUMBER(6);

  BEGIN
    SELECT CUSTOMER_SEQUENCE_ID.NEXTVAL INTO v_id FROM dual;
    :NEW.customer_id := v_id;
  END;
```

Once you create a trigger, you can then write your code with the knowledge that whenever you add a new record to the dynaset with a Movie_id of zero, not only will the next valid sequence number be used for the primary key but the number that is used will appear in the dynaset. The code in Listing 18.4 shows this effect. In the example code, we use a message box to show which sequence number has been used. Notice that you have to ensure you are at the right record. The AddNew method adds a new record onto the end of the dynaset, therefore we do a MoveLast to display the correct value.

Listing 18.4

```
Set dynMovies = OraDatabase.CreateDynaset _
        ("SELECT * FROM video_store.customers WHERE last_name = " & _
        " :cust_name", ORADYN_ORAMODE)

dynMovies.AddNew
dynMovies.Fields("customer_id") = 0
dynMovies.Fields("first_name") = "Mark"
dynMovies.Fields("last_name") = "Berry"
dynMovies.Fields("drivers_license") = "1243886-12"
dynMovies.Update

dynMovies.MoveLast
MsgBox dynMovies.Fields("customer_id")
```

Fetching values produced by the database does require an extra round-trip over the network. This is how the updatable dynaset works anyway, so the additional overhead is low. However, if this overhead is a concern, you can always use the ORADYN_NO_REFETCH constant to avoid the trip back to the server.

Tuning the OraDynaset

OO4O is the most tunable of all the data-access methods, and this can be quite confusing for newcomers. There are two fundamentally different types of parameters for tuning, namely the *cache* and *fetch* parameters. These parameters can be set in the Registries as shown in Figure 18.3.

FIGURE 18.3

Tuning the dynaset in the Registry

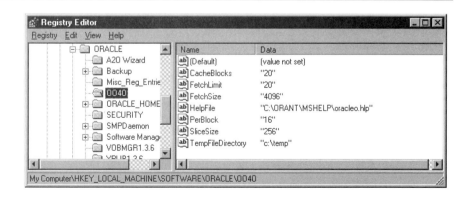

The cache is an area of memory that caches dynaset data locally on the client machine; there is one cache for each dynaset. The cache is populated when data is required if it is an updatable dynaset; if it is read-only, then the whole result set is brought into the cache. This parameter can create a great demand for memory if you are bringing over large amounts of data, and it can easily exceed your memory availability. OO4O provides an overflow mechanism by moving data from the cache to local data files when new data has to be brought in.

Although the ODBC methods do a certain amount of caching for you, the local caching of all the data in your dynaset means that you have more issues of memory management. However, OO4O gives you the cache parameters to help you tune your application. There are three cache parameters:

SliceSize The minimum number of bytes used to store an individual field. If all of your fields are short, you should reduce the default, which is 256.

PerBlock The number of slices per memory or file block. This normally represent the number of fields per block. The block size is (SliceSize * PerBlock).

CacheBlocks The maximum number of blocks held in memory.

If you multiply all these values together, you will arrive at (256*16*4096) = 80KB. This is not much memory by today's standards. Assuming you do not keep too many dynasets open concurrently, you should certainly increase the cache size, particularly with the CacheBlocks parameter.

NOTE   You can switch off the cache entirely with the ORADYN_NOCACHE option. In this case, you will get a forward-only cursor.

The second type of dynaset tuning involves the fetch parameters. Using these is much simpler than cache tuning. There are two fetch parameters:

FetchLimit The number of rows, which are read in from the Oracle result set into the cache in one go. You should make sure the cache is large enough to hold the FetchLimit. The default value is 20, which is generally never high enough. This parameter is a trade-off between reducing the number of network round-trips and increasing the memory requirements for the application.

FetchSize The size of the buffer for LONG and LONG RAW columns.

There are no easy rules for any particular dynaset, and the best action is probably trial and error. One thing is for sure: as with tuning any system, only change one value at a time, and test its affect.

TIP
The Registry settings for the tuning parameters are the defaults for any Ora-Dynaset created. To override these values, you can use the CreateCustomDynaset and CreatePlsqlCustomDynaset methods. You can also use several of the dynaset properties we will see in the next section, though in this case, any changes you make will only take affect when you refresh the dynaset.

OraDynaset Properties

There are a large number of properties, as you can see from Table 18.5. Most of the properties are the direct equivalents to the properties of the same name in DAO. The only real differences are the six additional properties for setting the cache and fetch characteristics.

TABLE 18.5: The OraDynaset Properties

Property	Description
BOF	This property flags the beginning of file. The value is True if you have moved before the first record in the Recordset.
Bookmark	This property holds a pointer to a record in the Recordset.
BookMarkable	This property indicates if you can use Bookmarks on this Recordset.
CacheBlocks	This property sets or returns the maximum number of blocks in the cache.
CacheChanged	This property indicates if cache parameters have been changed.
CacheSliceSize	This property sets or returns the size of each slice.
CacheSizePerBlock	This property sets or returns the number of slices per block.
Connection	This property returns the OraConnection object for the dynaset.
Database	This property returns the OraDatabase object for the dynaset.
EditMode	This property indicates the state of editing of the current record.
EOF	This property flags the end of file. The value is True if you have moved passed the last record in the Recordset.

Continued on next page

TABLE 18.5 CONTINUED: The OraDynaset Properties

Property	Description
FetchLimit	This property sets or returns the Fetch Array size (the number of rows retrieved in one go).
FetchSize	This property sets or returns the Fetch Array buffer size.
Fields	This property represents a collection of the fields associated with the dynaset.
LastModified	This property returns a Bookmark to the last modified row.
NoMatch	This property indicates no match was found for a Find method.
Options	This property returns the options flag used for dynaset creation.
RecordCount	This property contains the number of records in the dynaset.
RowPosition	This property contains the current row number in the dynaset.
Session	This property returns the OraSession object for the dynaset.
SQL	This property contains the query string for the dynaset.
Transactions	This property indicates if you can use transactions (always True).
Updatable	This property indicates if the dynaset is updatable.

Another interesting point to note is that the RecordCount property actually gives you the total number of records in the dynaset, even if you use the ORADYN_ NOCACHE option. This is unusual because none of the other methods we cover in this book can do this. The RecordCount in ODBC methods is a local count of the records that have populated the Recordset. In the case of OO4O, the number of records is picked up from the Oracle Server, just as you would see in a SQL*Plus session.

Exploring the OraDynaset Methods

Now that you have opened an OraDynaset, you can use a variety of methods to manipulate the records and columns in the dynaset. These methods include moving through the dynaset, changing column values, and finding records matching particular criteria. OO4O supports a wide and rich set of methods compared to other data-access technologies, with ADO in particular being trimmed down rather than enhanced. This extra functionality in OO4O is mainly due to the tight integration with the Oracle Server and the flexibility it has by only having to communicate with one RDBMS.

Populating the OraDynaset

Populating a dynaset is similar to most of the other data-access technologies. Data is pulled from the server in a Fetch Array, the size of which is determined by the FetchLimit property that we saw in the section, "Tuning the OraDynaset." This property defines the maximum number of rows pulled over to the client in one go and with one network excursion. This data is brought into the cache. When you try to access data that is not in the cache and not in the backup files, then the next set of rows must be brought over.

The main difference between an updatable dynaset and a read-only dynaset is that the SELECT statement you use to create an updatable dynaset is modified to include the ROWID pseudocolumn. For example, if your statement was

```
SELECT movie_id, movie_name rating FROM video_store.movies
```

it would now become

```
SELECT ROWID, movie_id, movie_name rating FROM video_store.movies
```

You can see in this situation that if you have a table join, you would not have a unique ROWID, and the dynaset would not be updatable.

One alternative to this scenario of populating the OraDynaset is when you use the ORADYN_NOCACHE option, you get a forward-only dynaset with no cache. You can also avoid populating the dynaset at all by using the ORADYN_NO_MOVEFIRST option. In this case, you do not bring any rows over from the database, so it is a little faster. This option is most useful if you do not want to see any of the existing data and only want to add new records.

Changing the Current Record

When you first create a dynaset, it is usually positioned on the first record (although you can avoid this by using the ORADYN_NO_MOVEFIRST constant in the CreateOraDynaset *options* flag). There are eight methods typically used to move around a scrollable dynaset as shown in Table 18.6. You can execute these methods from code or from buttons on a GUI interface. Note that several of them can be used with an offset number of rows.

TABLE 18.6: The Recordset Move Methods

Method	Description
MoveFirst	This method moves to the first record in the Recordset.
MoveLast	This method moves to the last record in the Recordset.
MoveNext	This method moves to the next record in the Recordset.
MoveNextn	This method moves *offset* records forward, where offset is the argument to the method.
MovePrevious	This method moves to the previous record in the Recordset.
MovePreviousn	This method moves *offset* records backward.
MoveRel	This method moves *offset* records from the current position (backward or forward).
MoveTo	This method moves to the row number *offset*.

As with DAO, you should check for the EOF property (end of file) when you use MoveNext, and you should check for the BOF property (beginning of file) when you use MovePrevious. If you try these Move methods when EOF or BOF are True, you may end up with an invalid current record. If the Recordset is empty, then both BOF and EOF will be True.

Accessing the Fields of an OraDynaset

To access the fields of an updatable or read-only OraDynaset, you can adopt one of two different techniques. The first technique is similar to DAO in that you use the dynaset's Fields collection. To find the value of any field in the current dynaset, you can reference the field by index (ordinal number) or by name. With OO4O, you have to include the property name "Value". The syntax for accessing a field is

```
OraDynaset.Fields("movie_id").Value
```

or

```
OraDynaset("movie_id").Value
```

Versions of OO4O prior to 2.2 were notoriously slow at retrieving field values in this way because of the repetitive access to the Fields collection. With any version of OO4O, you should use the second available technique and set up a Field object for each field you want to retrieve as shown in the code in Listing 18.5.

Listing 18.5

```
Dim fld1 As Object
Dim fld2 As Object
Set fld1 = OraDynaset.Fields(0)
Set fld2 = OraDynaset.Fields(1)

'   Now use the temporary objects
MsgBox fld1.value
MsgBox fld2.value
```

Of course, there is some overhead when creating these temporary objects, and you need to use this technique only when you are walking through a large number of records. If you have several fields, you should declare an array of Field objects rather than each one separately.

```
Dim flds(10) As Object
Set fld(0) = OraDynaset.Fields(0)
Set fld(1) = OraDynaset.Fields(1)
```

To fill our familiar list box, we could use the code shown in Listing 18.6. As you can see, this uses a read-only and forward-only (no cache) dynaset, since we want to avoid the overhead of a scrolling, updatable cursor.

Listing 18.6

```
Public Sub FillListBox(ListBox As Control)

'   Fill a list box with movie names
'   Ignore error trapping

    Dim rs As Object
    Dim fld As Object

    Set rs = OraDatabase.CreateDynaset _
        ("SELECT movie_name FROM video_store.movies", _
         ORADYN_READONLY + ORADYN_NOCACHE)

    Set fld = rs.Fields(0)
```

```
ListBox.Clear
While Not rs.EOF
    ListBox.AddItem fld.Value
    rs.MoveNext
Wend
ListBox.ListIndex = 0   ' Display the first item

End Sub
```

Changing the Records and Values in an OraDynaset

There are a few methods that we can use to change the records and their values in
the dynaset, assuming you are using an updatable dynaset. First, you should navigate to the record you want to change with the Move methods and then use the
following editing methods:

AddNew   This method adds a new record to the OraDynaset but not to
the Oracle database. To make the change permanent, you have to use the
Update method.

Edit   This method puts the current record into edit mode, meaning you
can change any of the values.

Update   This method saves any changes you have made to the Oracle
database, assuming that all constraints are met.

Delete   This method deletes the current record. You do not use the
Update method after a Delete.

If you have executed the AddNew or Edit methods, you can change any of the
fields in the OraDynaset. The following is an example of this technique.

```
OraDynaset("movie_id").Value = "The Wonderful World of Oracle"
```

OO4O does not do any validation when it comes to specifying new values for
fields (in comparison to JET, which does some rudimentary field-type checking).
You will find the field validation is done by Oracle when you use the Update
method, so it is good practice to ensure you do as much validation with Visual
Basic as you can. If there are data validation problems or any constraint problems, such as an invalid key, or if there is a character value when you need a
numeric one, then you will get back a trappable error.

When you use the Edit method, OO4O tries to put a lock on the affected row with an internal SELECT FOR UPDATE command. If another user has an outstanding lock on the same row (an uncommitted change), then your application will block. However, it will gracefully recover when the lock is released. Of course, this could be a long time if you do not write your application keeping this in mind. Unfortunately, locks like this leave open the possibility of a user putting a lock on a database row and going home for the night.

TIP
Rather than letting your application block when it is trying to access a locked record, you should use the ORADB_NOWAIT option of the CreateDatabase method and trap any resulting errors.

When you add a new record to the dynaset, you have to make sure all the required fields (that is, those that have a NOT NULL constraint on them) have a valid value. This can be a problem, especially if you use sequences for the primary key. If you use updatable dynasets, then you should read the section, "Making Use of Triggers," earlier in the chapter. However, if you stick with read-only dynasets, you can use stored procedures or execute some SQL code to update the data and then refresh the dynaset. By doing so, you will have a better overall system.

Finding a Particular Record

The final thing we will look at for OraDynaset methods is how to find a record that matches the criteria you set down. It is a little strange that OO4O supports such a rich Find environment, whereas the Oracle server does not support a FIND command; and data-access methods, such as RDO and ADO, have dropped Find entirely. OO4O was based on DAO/JET, which used the JET engine to do all the Find processing. In OO4O, the processing of the FIND command is also handled locally, and you can use any syntax in the FIND clause that you would use in a WHERE clause in a SELECT statement. This includes

- Normal conditional statements, such as "Movie_Name = 'Awakenings'"
- Oracle functions, such as "LENGTH(Movie_Name) < 100"
- Subqueries

There are four Find methods and one property you will make use of for the Find function, and these are all shown in Table 18.7. Notice they are completely compatible with DAO.

TABLE 18.7: Methods and Properties Used to Find Records

Method/Property	Description
FindFirst	This method finds the first occurrence of the search string in the dynaset.
FindLast	This method finds the last occurrence of the search string in the dynaset.
FindNext	This method finds the next occurrence of the search string after the current record.
FindPrevious	This method finds the previous occurrence of the search string before the current record.
NoMatch	This property indicates that no match was found for the FIND commands.

As with DAO, you should use these commands sparingly because they are an indication that you have extracted more data from the database than you currently need. This may be acceptable if you have a read-only result set that is relatively static. Otherwise, consider putting the FIND clause into the WHERE clause of your initial SELECT statement. If you do decide to use the Find methods, then Listing 18.7 gives you an example of how they work. Notice that after a successful match, you can execute a FIND command with no FIND clause.

Listing 18.7

```
Dim strSearchClause As String

strSearchClause = "LENGTH(movie_name) < 100 "

rsMovies.FindFirst strSearchClause

If rsMovies.NoMatch Then
    MsgBox "Couldn't find movie "
Else
    MsgBox "Movie ID for 'Titanic' is " & rsMovies("movie_id").Value
End If
```

> **NOTE**
> OO4O uses a local parser for interpreting the FIND clauses; this saves an extra round-trip to the server. In the current versions of OO4O (at least up to version 2.3), you should avoid any clause that includes an embedded single quote; otherwise, the parser will give you an error message.

Closing a Dynaset

The other data-access methods provide a Close method to close a Recordset object; the Close method in OO4O is only provided so that you can easily translate you code from DAO to OO4O with a minimum amount of fuss. The Close method does not actually do anything; the dynaset is automatically destroyed as soon as it goes out of scope.

Using Parameters

Before we go any further, we must look at the OraParameter collection. Although you can write entire applications without worrying about parameters, you will not be operating much above the level of DAO/JET. The use of parameters gives OO4O more functionality than any of the other data-access methods. In OO4O, you set up a single OraParameters collection for each Database object. This is in comparison to say, RDO, where there is one Parameter collection for each rdoQuery.

As you saw in Chapter 9, *Introduction to PL/SQL,* Oracle allows you to set up bind variables that you can use for input and output variables to stored procedures. When you have created a bind variable, you can use it in a SQL statement by preceding it with a colon. For example, instead of the following line

```
DELETE FROM  movies WHERE movie_id = 9;
```

you could set up a bind variable ID, assign it a value, and then type

```
DELETE FROM  movies WHERE movie_id = :id;
```

Oracle substitutes the value of the bind variable into the SQL statement at run time. The advantage of using bind variables is that Oracle only has to parse the statement once; subsequent executions of the statement can make use of the Shared Pool and simply bind the new variable values without reparsing the statement. In this way, bind variables are potentially faster than when the SQL is hard-coded, at least at the first execution.

NOTE
Technically, SQL bind parameters only represent IN mode parameters. If you use IN OUT mode parameters, these are PL/SQL bind variables. The Oracle Server takes care of binding the variables.

OO4O allows us to do exactly the same thing as SQL. First, you must create the parameters for the OraParameters collection with the Add method as follows:

```
OraDatabase.OraParameters.add Name, InitialValue, Type
```

0040 has the following arguments:

Name   This argument defines an arbitrary but unique name for the parameter, which you must supply.

InitialValue   This argument defines the value you first give to the parameter.

Type   This argument defines the Parameter mode. The possibilities are shown in Table 18.8.

T A B L E   1 8 . 8 : The Possible Type Constants for the OraParameters Collection

Constant	Value	PL/SQL Mode
ORAPARM_INPUT	1	IN
ORAPARM_OUTPUT	2	OUT
ORAPARM_BOTH	3	IN OUT

There is one other thing we must do before we can use parameters: we must provide the *server type* for each parameter. The server type defines the data type of each bound parameter. To define the type, we must use the *ServerType* property of the Parameter object with the values shown in Table 18.9. Even with this type defined, you must still be careful to ensure that you have the correct data types specified. If you don't, it can sometimes be difficult to find out why the parameter substitution is not working as it is supposed to.

TABLE 18.9: The Possible Constants for the ServerType Property

Constant	Value	External Data Type
ORATYPE_VARCHAR2	1	VARCHAR2
ORATYPE_NUMBER	2	NUMBER
ORATYPE_SINT	3	SIGNED INTEGER
ORATYPE_FLOAT	4	FLOAT
ORATYPE_STRING	5	Null Terminated STRING
ORATYPE_VARCHAR	9	VARCHAR
ORATYPE_DATE	12	DATE
ORATYPE_UINT	68	UNSIGNED INTEGER
ORATYPE_CHAR	96	CHAR
ORATYPE_CHARZ	97	Null Terminated CHAR
ORATYPE_CURSOR	102	PL/SQL Cursor

Although the main use of these parameters is with stored-procedure calls and the OraSQLStmt object, we can also use the input parameters with any SQL statement. Listing 18.8 gives a couple of examples of how to do this. The code first adds a new parameter, Cust_id, with a default value of 6 and then sets its data type. The second example works in a similar way, but this time it sets a character-string parameter, Cust_name, with a default value of "Berry".

Listing 18.8

```
'    Customer_id parameter
    OraDatabase.Parameters.Add "cust_id", 6, ORAPARM_INPUT
    OraDatabase.Parameters("cust_id").ServerType = ORATYPE_NUMBER

    Set dynMovies = OraDatabase.CreateDynaset _
("SELECT * FROM video_store.customers  " & _
        " WHERE customer_id = :cust_id", ORADYN_ORAMODE)


'    Customer_name parameter
```

```
OraDatabase.Parameters.Add "cust_name", "Berry", ORAPARM_INPUT
OraDatabase.Parameters("cust_name").ServerType = ORATYPE_VARCHAR

Set dynMovies = OraDatabase.CreateDynaset _
  ("SELECT * FROM video_store.customers " & _
    "  WHERE last_name = :cust_name", ORADYN_DEFAULT)
```

In this kind of simple case, you may also find that you do not need to provide the *ServerType* property because it works fine without it. If you need to prepare parameterized queries, such as those shown above, then you should review the section "Using OraSQLStmts" because it describes a more efficient way to use SELECT queries.

After you have executed a command that uses parameters, you can change the values of one or more of these parameters and either reexecute a stored procedure or re-create a dynaset. You can set or retrieve the value of a parameter by referring to the Value property as follows:

```
OraDatabase.Parameters("cust_name").Value = "Gilmour"
```

When you have finished with a parameter, you should clean up by deleting it from the OraParameters collection with the Remove method.

NOTE   If you are retrieving CHAR or VARCHAR output variables longer than 128 bytes, then you must set the MinimumSize property of the parameter to a value large enough to contain the value.

WARNING   Because the OraParameters collection is attached to the Database object, OO4O has no way of telling which of the parameters is supposed to be bound to any particular SQL query or stored procedure. Oracle, by default, tries each and every parameter in the collection to see if it needs to be bound. If you have a large number of parameters, this process can cause a significant loss of performance, although this only occurs the first time you execute the SQL statement. To avoid attempting to bind unneeded bind variables, use the ORADYN_NO_AUTOBIND option when creating a dynaset without parameters or disable each of the unwanted parameters with the AutoBindDisable method.

Executing SQL Commands

To achieve better scalability and security, you will move away from updatable result sets and toward executing SQL commands and eventually stored procedures. For the DML commands, INSERT, UPDATE, and DELETE, you need a new method. OO4O is no different from the other data-access methods in that it has an Execute method, although in this case, it is called ExecuteSQL.

One feature of the ExecuteSQL command that is a refreshing change is that you can retrieve the number of rows affected by the command. As you know, you cannot retrieve this number with the ODBC-based methods. The ExecuteSQL syntax is

```
rowcount = oradatabase.ExecuteSQL (sql_statement)
```

where *sql_statement* is a valid SQL command. This includes groups of commands and stored-procedure calls wrapped in the BEGIN and END statements of an anonymous PL/SQL block. An example of using this command is shown in Listing 18.9.

Listing 18.9

```
Dim iRowCount As Integer

iRowCount = OraDatabase.ExecuteSQL( _
    "DELETE FROM customers WHERE customer_id < 100")
MsgBox iRowCount & " customers deleted!"
```

WARNING   The ExecuteSQL method executes an automatic COMMIT command, which may not be what you would expect. Although superficially useful, this can adversely affect any other transactions that are going on. (When you commit on the Ora-Session object, everything gets committed.) Luckily, you can (and should) include the ExecuteSQL method in a transaction. This also improves performance noticeably.

Calling Stored Procedures

The move from executing a standard DML statement, such as INSERT, UPDATE, or DELETE, to executing a stored procedure is really quite small. In fact, you could simply execute the stored procedure by enclosing it in the BEGIN and END keywords as we did for all the other data-access methods. For example, the code in Listing 18.10 works fine just as it did in DAO.

Listing 18.10

```
Private Sub MovieInsert(iMovieId As Integer, strMovieName As String, _
            iLength As Integer, strRating As String, iYear As Integer)

    '   Insert a new movie into the database

    Dim strSQL As String

    strSQL = "BEGIN video_store.movies_insert2 ("
    strSQL = strSQL & iMovieId & ", '" & strMovieName & "', "
    strSQL = strSQL & iLength & ", '" & strRating & "', " & iYear
    strSQL = strSQL & "); END;"

    OraDatabase.ExecuteSQL strSQL

End Sub
```

However, this limits us to input parameters only, and we have to build up the query each time. If you have a procedure with 15 parameters, this is a lot of extra work. Instead of this hard-coded approach, we can use parameters for input values and to retrieve any output values. First, let us set up a Visual Basic procedure to create any parameters required in this module. This procedure is shown in Listing 18.11.

Listing 18.11

```
Private Sub CreateParameters()

    '   Create the database parameters
    '   Notice that this works without defining ServerType
```

```
        OraDatabase.Parameters.Add "movie_id", 0, ORAPARM_BOTH
        OraDatabase.Parameters.Add "movie_name", "", ORAPARM_INPUT
        OraDatabase.Parameters.Add "length", 0, ORAPARM_INPUT
        OraDatabase.Parameters.Add "rating", "", ORAPARM_INPUT
        OraDatabase.Parameters.Add "year", 0, ORAPARM_INPUT
    End Sub
```

Now let us use these parameters in a procedure to insert the data into the database. Listing 18.12 shows you how this is done. Notice we are not creating a query object like we did with an rdoQuery, but we are re-creating the statement each time. We can get around this problem with the OraSQLStmt object, which we shall see later.

Listing 18.12

```
Private Sub MovieInsert(iMovieId As Integer, _
            strMovieName As String,_iLength As Integer, _
            strRating As String, iYear As Integer)

'    Insert a new movie into the database

    OraDatabase.Parameters("movie_id").Value = 0
    OraDatabase.Parameters("movie_name").Value = strMovieName
    OraDatabase.Parameters("length").Value = iLength
    OraDatabase.Parameters("rating").Value = strRating
    OraDatabase.Parameters("year").Value = iYear

    OraDatabase.ExecuteSQL "BEGIN movies_insert3 (:movie_id, " & _
                    ":movie_name, :length, :rating, :year); END;"

    MsgBox "The movie_id used was " & _
        OraDatabase.Parameters("movie_id").Value

End Sub
```

One advantage of OO4O when executing stored procedures is that you can use a bind variable wherever you want in the query. With ODBC and OLE-DB, you have to have one Parameter object for every formal parameter in the stored procedure.

Retrieving Cursor Variables

We first encountered cursor variables in Chapter 10, *Creating Stored Procedures*. They are one of the most sophisticated ways to retrieve data from an Oracle database and the one feature that gives lie to the notion that Oracle cannot return a result set from a stored procedure. Well, Oracle certainly can, but the process is not trivial, and it is not available through ODBC methods, nor is it currently available through OLE-DB.

A cursor variable is a pointer to an open PL/SQL cursor on the server that is passed back from the stored procedure. The cursor is kept open on the server until it has been finished with. It is fundamentally a read-only, forward-only cursor, as are all Oracle result sets; the client-side scrolling capability is available through OO4O, but it remains read-only.

To access a cursor variable, you need to use a special method, the Create-PLSQLDynaset method, which has the following syntax.

```
Set OraDynaset = CreatePLSQLDynaset(SQLStatement, CursorName, Options)
```

The following list contains the method's arguments:

SQLStatement   This argument contains an Oracle PL/SQL stored procedure or an anonymous PL/SQL code block.

CursorName   This argument contains the name of the cursor created in the PL/SQL stored procedure.

Options   This argument contains a flag indicating the status of any optional states of the dynaset. You can combine options by adding them. The possible constants that you can use are shown in Table 18.10. These are a subset of the options for the CreateDynaset method.

TABLE 18.10: The Options Constants for the CreatePLSQLDynaset Method

Constant	Value	Description
ORADYN_DEFAULT	0	This constant accepts the default behavior.
ORADYN_NO_BLANKSTRIP	2	This constant stops trailing blanks from character-string data from being stripped off.
ORADYN_NOCACHE	8	This constant stops the creation of a local dynaset data cache. This cursor is more efficient but forward-only.
ORADYN_NO_MOVEFIRST	64	This constant avoids a MoveFirst method on the dynaset at creation. BOF and EOF are both TRUE. This constant is of little value because we are creating a read-only dynaset.

To bring the method to life and to demonstrate its finer points, we will look at a simple situation in which you want to retrieve a result set based upon the following query:

```
SELECT * FROM movies WHERE year_of_release = 1995
```

As we have seen before, we can treat the *year_of_release* value as a bind variable, [:year], so we end up with

```
SELECT * FROM movies WHERE rating = :year
```

First, we must create a stored procedure that can return a cursor variable based on this query. We created this stored procedure in Chapter 10, Listing 10.8. Now we can get around to creating an OO4O program to read the cursor variable in. Remember that the stored procedure must be created in a package to be able to return the result set. Refer back to Chapter 10 for a refresher on how this works.

In the *movie_package* package, we have a procedure with the following definition:

```
PROCEDURE get_old_movies (
  p_year              NUMBER,
  old_movies IN OUT movie_cv_type);
```

Now that we have our stored procedure we must set up the CreatePLSQLDynaset method in our application. Listing 18.13 shows how this is done. Notice that we create only one parameter for the query; the other bind variable, *Old-Movies*, is implicitly declared in the CreatePLSQLDynaset statement and is automatically converted into the dynaset.

Listing 18.13

```
Dim OraSession As Object
Dim OraDatabase As Object

Private Sub GetOldMovies(iYear As Integer)

    Dim OraDynaset As Object


    '  Create the year_of_release parameter
    OraDatabase.Parameters.Add "year", 0, ORAPARM_INPUT
    OraDatabase.Parameters("year").ServerType = ORATYPE_NUMBER

    OraDatabase.Parameters("year").Value = iYear

    '  Create OraDynaset based on the "OldMovies" cursor

    Set OraDynaset = OraDatabase.CreatePLSQLDynaset _
     ("Begin movie_package.get_old_movies(:year, :OldMovies); end;", _
      "OldMovies", 0&)

    If Not OraDynaset.EOF Then

      '  Display the first record.
      MsgBox OraDynaset.Fields("movie_id").Value & " : " & _
             OraDynaset.Fields("movie_name").Value
    End If
End Sub
```

The procedures you write that make use of cursor variables will typically be quite simple. You do not have the option of building a result set of your own making; instead, it will be the outcome of the SELECT statement. In the case shown above, we passed a variable used in the WHERE clause of the SELECT statement. In practice, you can add whatever you like to the WHERE clause, whether it is dependent on the user, the day of the week, or anything else. Using cursor variables is more flexible than using a view, but they have the same advantage of hiding the base table from the user.

TIP   If you want to modify the cache and fetch parameters, you can make use of the CreatePlsqlCustomDynaset method.

Calling PL/SQL Functions

Calling PL/SQL functions is often ignored. In fact, PL/SQL functions are just as easy as calling stored procedures, but you have to be aware of a couple of things. First, you must set up an output parameter to hold the return value, and second, you must use PL/SQL assignment syntax to set the return value to your bind variable. This is shown in Listing 18.14. This Visual Basic procedure calls the get_movie_id function with one input parameter. You can see the original PL/SQL function in Listing 15.6.

Listing 18.14

```
Private Function GetMovieId(strMovieName As String) As Long

'    Find the ID for the supplied movie name

'    First set up the parameters
     OraDatabase.Parameters.Add "movie_name", 0, ORAPARM_INPUT
     OraDatabase.Parameters.Add "movie_id", 0, ORAPARM_OUTPUT

'    Now set the value and execute the function
     OraDatabase.Parameters("movie_name") = strMovieName
     OraDatabase.ExecuteSQL "BEGIN :movie_id := nick.get_movie_id " & _
                            "(:movie_name); END;"

'    Finally print out the return value
     MsgBox "Movie ID is " & OraDatabase.Parameters("movie_id").Value
     GetMovieId = OraDatabase.Parameters("movie_id").Value
End Function
```

Retrieving PL/SQL Tables

In addition to the cursor variables we have just seen, Chapter 10 also introduced PL/SQL tables. You will recall these are effectively collections in PL/SQL and are represented as a zero-based array (in other words, they start with element zero) in OO4O. This is the usual way of working with them in PL/SQL anyway, so this should cause no problems.

Before we can make use of PL/SQL tables, we must first look at a different kind of parameter that we can add to the OraParameters collection. This new object is called a *Parameter Array,* and we add the array to the collection with the AddTable method rather than the Add method we used for normal (scalar) parameters. The form of the AddTable method is

```
OraDatabase.Parameters.AddTable Name, Type, ServerType,
                            ArraySize, ElementSize
```

This method has the following arguments:

Name   This argument provides an arbitrary but unique name for the parameter array, which you must supply.

Type   This argument defines the mode this parameter represents. The possibilities are the same as those shown in Table 18.8.

ServerType   This argument defines the data type for the elements of the parameter array that is going to be bound to the database (see Table 18.9).

ArraySize   This argument defines the number of elements in the parameter array up to a maximum buffer size of 32K. This figure is used by OO4O to determine memory requirements as well as by the stored procedure as a limit to table size.

ElementSize   This argument defines the maximum size of the character fields that will be retrieved in the table (leave the argument out for numeric data).

To put this method into action, we will execute another of the examples we used in Chapter 10, in this case, Listing 10.7. The layout of the procedure we want to execute is

```
PROCEDURE get_stars (
  p_table_size      NUMBER,
  p_stars        OUT char_table_type)
```

This procedure exists in the package *movie_package*. As you can see, it is expecting to receive the maximum size of the table in the first parameter; this size is used to place a limit on the number of values returned when the stored procedure builds the PL/SQL table. To retrieve the table *p_stars,* we need to add a parameter array to the Parameters collection. This step is done in the first part of Listing 18.15.

Listing 18.15

```
Private Sub GetStars(iNumStars)

    Dim iStar As Integer

'   First set up the parameters
    OraDatabase.Parameters.AddTable "GetStars", ORAPARM_OUTPUT, _
                            ORATYPE_VARCHAR2, iNumStars, 30
    OraDatabase.Parameters.Add "NumStars", 0, ORAPARM_INPUT


'   Set the maximum table size required and retrieve the table
    OraDatabase.Parameters("NumStars").Value = iNumStars
    OraDatabase.ExecuteSQL "BEGIN movie_package.get_stars " & _
                            "(:NumStars, :GetStars); END;"

'   Now we will print out the results
    For iStar = 0 To iNumStars - 1
        Debug.Print OraDatabase.Parameters("GetStars").get_Value(iStar)
    Next

End Sub
```

Notice in Listing 18.15 that we have specified that the table is an OUT mode parameter. Once we have executed the stored procedure, we can retrieve the values from the table in Visual Basic by using the Get_Value property. If we had designed the stored procedure so that the PL/SQL table was IN or IN OUT mode, we could have passed data to the procedure by using the Put_Value property.

One ability that would be useful is to return a table of a complex data type rather than the simple scalar types we are restricted to. This would enable us to return a Record structure back that would be more powerful than a cursor variable, because we could construct its content field by field, row by row. Although this capability would be incredibly powerful, it does not look as though this feature will appear any time soon. PL/SQL tables can be a useful tool just as they are and are occasionally used by built-in PL/SQL. They are also a worthy tool to add to your arsenal.

Using OraSQLStmts

Just as we saw with rdoQueries and QueryDefs in previous chapters, OO4O gives us the opportunity to create an object that defines a SQL statement. The advantage of this technique is that it is parsed by the Oracle server only once and can be reused many times. Using this object is obviously going to be somewhat more efficient than creating the SQL statement afresh each time. The way to do this step is with the CreateSQL method as follows:

```
Set orasqlstmt = oradatabase.CreateSQL(sql_statement, options)
```

The arguments for this method are

sql_statement   This argument defines a valid SQL statement and is not limited to SELECT queries.

options   This argument describes which options you want to use. You can select either or both of those shown in Table 18.11.

TABLE 18.11: The Possible Values for the Options Argument in the CreateSQL Method

Constant	Value	Description
ORASQL_NO_AUTOBIND	1	This constant stops parameter binding. Use this option if the statement does not include parameters because it will be more efficient.
ORASQL_FAILEXEC	2	This constant raises an error and does not create a SQL statement object if the statement raises an error.

To use the OraSQLStmt object, we have to create the SQL string, as shown in Listing 18.16. This SQL statement can contain any number of bind variables in this case, one for every argument in the stored procedure. Next, and preferably in another part of the program, we assign values to the parameters and refresh the OraSQLStmt. This Refresh method executes the SQL statement, binding the latest values of the parameters.

Listing 18.16

```
        Private ostMovieInsert As Object

    '   Set up an OraSQLStmt for the insert

        strSQL = "BEGIN movies_insert3 (:movie_id, " & _
                 ":movie_name, :length, :rating, :year); END;"
        Set ostMovieInsert = OraDatabase.CreateSQL(strSQL, 0)


    '   Assign values to the parameters and refresh the OraSQLStmt

        OraDatabase.Parameters("movie_id").Value = 0
        OraDatabase.Parameters("movie_name").Value = "Movie Name"
        OraDatabase.Parameters("length").Value = 122
        OraDatabase.Parameters("rating").Value = "G"
        OraDatabase.Parameters("year").Value = 1998

        ostMovieInsert.Refresh
```

Batch Updates

An interesting use of parameter arrays is with a so-called *batch update*. We have already seen that you can bind parameters to, say, an INSERT statement as follows:

```
iRowCount = OraDatabase.ExecuteSQL( _
    "INSERT INTO movies VALUES (:movie_id, :movie_name, " & _
    ":length, :rating, :year, USER, SYSDATE) "
```

If you have to execute this many times in a row, you will have the overhead of a network round-trip for each row you want to insert. An additional problem with OO4O is that being an ActiveX control, you have more overhead than with other methods, such as RDO. Without an efficient object like an rdoQuery, the performance can be quite poor. However, OO4O has one trick up its sleeve, which is you can not only use bind parameters in the INSERT statement but also parameter arrays. Using this technique, you can set up an array of 10 or 100 rows to be inserted and can execute them all in one call. The performance increase can be substantial.

As an example of a batch insert, we will set up some code to enter dummy data into the Customer table. We will enter 500 rows and compare the technique, speed-wise, to using individual inserts. Listing 18.17 shows the code that performs both of these tasks and times the two. The code consists of several parts. First, the data-base connection is set up. Then, the OraSQLStmt for the repetitive insert and its associated parameters are created. Next, the statement is run 500 times by refresh-ing the OraSQLStmt. The second half of the code consists of creating Parameter Arrays and then running the test, which fills the Parameter Arrays with 500 records (remember they are zero-based) and, finally, executes the INSERT statement.

Listing 18.17

```
Private OraSession As Object
Private oraDatabase As Object

Private Sub Form_Load()

'   Test repeated inserts against batch inserts

    Dim StartTime, EndTime
    Dim i As Integer
    Dim strSQL As String
    Dim ostInsert As Object
    Dim OraPArray1 As Object
    Dim OraPArray2 As Object
    Dim OraPArray3 As Object
    Dim OraPArray4 As Object

'   Connect to the database
    Set OraSession = CreateObject("OracleInProcServer.XOraSession")
    Set oraDatabase = OraSession.OpenDatabase("beq-local", _
                    "video_user/ummagumma", 0)

'   Set up an OraSQLStmt and associated parameters
    strSQL = "INSERT INTO customers VALUES(:id, :first_name, " & _
        ":last_name, :license)"
    Set ostInsert = oraDatabase.createsql(strSQL, 0)

    oraDatabase.Parameters.Add "id", 0, ORAPARM_INPUT
    oraDatabase.Parameters.Add "first_name", 0, ORAPARM_INPUT
    oraDatabase.Parameters.Add "last_name", 0, ORAPARM_INPUT
```

```
oraDatabase.Parameters.Add "license", 0, ORAPARM_INPUT

oraDatabase.executesql ("DELETE FROM  customers")

'   Start the first test
StartTime = Timer
For i = 1 To 500
    oraDatabase.Parameters("id") = i
    oraDatabase.Parameters("first_name") = "Peter"
    oraDatabase.Parameters("last_name") = "Richards"
    oraDatabase.Parameters("license") = "123456ABCDEF"
    ostInsert.Refresh
Next
EndTime = Timer

MsgBox "Normal inserts " & EndTime - StartTime & " seconds"


'   Set up the parameter arrays
oraDatabase.Parameters.AddTable "ids", ORAPARM_INPUT, _
  ORATYPE_NUMBER, 500
oraDatabase.Parameters.AddTable "first_names", ORAPARM_INPUT, _
  ORATYPE_VARCHAR2, 500, 25
oraDatabase.Parameters.AddTable "last_names", ORAPARM_INPUT, _
  ORATYPE_VARCHAR2, 500, 25
oraDatabase.Parameters.AddTable "licenses", ORAPARM_INPUT, _
  ORATYPE_VARCHAR2, 500, 20

Set OraPArray1 = oraDatabase.Parameters("ids")
Set OraPArray2 = oraDatabase.Parameters("first_names")
Set OraPArray3 = oraDatabase.Parameters("last_names")
Set OraPArray4 = oraDatabase.Parameters("licenses")


oraDatabase.executesql ("DELETE FROM  customers")

'   Start the second test
StartTime = Timer
For i = 0 To 499
    OraPArray1.put_Value i + 1, i
    OraPArray2.put_Value "Stanley", i
    OraPArray3.put_Value "Matthews", i
    OraPArray4.put_Value "123456ABCDEF", i
```

```
        Next
        oraDatabase.executesql ("INSERT INTO customers VALUES" & _
            "(:ids, :first_names, :last_names, :licenses)")
        EndTime = Timer

        MsgBox "Normal inserts " & EndTime - StartTime & " seconds"

    End Sub
```

You will probably notice that this test is not entirely fair to the second case because we should really have removed or disabled the first set of parameters. However, this particular test shows that the repetitive inserts took 8.875 seconds while the batch insert took 0.871 seconds. A gain of this magnitude was on a single machine where network speed was not an issue. Although an rdoQuery, for example, is an efficient method for doing this kind of operation, nothing can compare with the speed of a batch insert. Not every situation will be suitable for using batch inserts, but if you have the opportunity, make use of them.

Error Handling

The error-handling capabilities of OO4O are different from the other data access methods. OO4O runs as an in-process server and is susceptible to automation errors, particularly the dreaded error number 440, which descriptively means "OLE Automation Error." There is no Error collection from which you can retrieve a good description of what has occurred, but you need to check the LastServerError property of the session or database to find out the error raised by the in-process server. To return a textual message from an error, you use the LastServerErrText property of the database or session.

An interesting variation on the error information is that OO4O passes back to the client application the position in the SQL string where it detected the error. You may have noticed this feature in SQL*Plus; if you type an invalid SQL command, then SQL*Plus will not only give you an error message but also indicate the position in the string where it occurred with an asterisk. This is a useful tool for debugging, but there is not much use for it in a production environment. If you want to use this feature, check out the LastServerErrPos property.

The final error-handling feature is resetting the error with the LastServerErrReset method.

Putting It All Together

In this section we again look at our simple movie application, this time built around the features of OO4O. The example application uses many of the features we have discussed in this chapter. One of the more interesting procedures is CreateParameters (see Listing 18.18), which sets up the parameters for the Movie-Insert procedure. It then sets up a dynaset with a parameter to retrieve the participants in the current movie. This parameter is set each time a new movie is displayed on the form and the dynaset is refreshed so that the new parameter is used to produce the records. We finally create an OraSQLStmt to handle the inserts with the parameters we have previously set up.

Listing 18.18

```
Private Sub CreateParameters()

'    Create the database parameters
'    Notice that this works without defining ServerType

    Dim strSQL As String


    OraDatabase.Parameters.Add "movie_id", 0, ORAPARM_BOTH
    OraDatabase.Parameters.Add "movie_name", "", ORAPARM_INPUT
    OraDatabase.Parameters.Add "length", 0, ORAPARM_INPUT
    OraDatabase.Parameters.Add "rating", "", ORAPARM_INPUT
    OraDatabase.Parameters.Add "year", 0, ORAPARM_INPUT

    OraDatabase.Parameters.Add "find_movie_id", 7, ORAPARM_INPUT


'    Set up a forward-only dynaset to show participants

    strSQL = "SELECT first_name || ' ' || last_name full_name,"
    strSQL = strSQL & " DECODE (role, 'A', 'Actor', 'D', 'Director') "
    strSQL = strSQL & " role, movie_id"
    strSQL = strSQL & " FROM participants, movie_participants"

    strSQL = strSQL & " WHERE movie_id = :find_movie_id "

    strSQL = strSQL & "  AND movie_participants.participant_id = "
    strSQL = strSQL & " participants.participant_id"
```

```
        strSQL = strSQL & "  ORDER BY role"

        Set rsParticipants = OraDatabase.CreateDynaset _
                             (strSQL, ORADYN_READONLY + ORADYN_NOCACHE)


    '   Set up an OraSQLStmt for the insert
        strSQL = "BEGIN movies_insert3 (:movie_id, " & _
                 ":movie_name, :length, :rating, :year); END;"
        Set ostMovieInsert = OraDatabase.CreateSQL(strSQL, 0)

    End Sub
```

In Listing 18.19, you can see the code for the cmdAction_Click procedure, which processes the user's request to add, update, or delete a record. The Add method uses an OraSQLStmt to handle the stored-procedure call, although the Update and Delete functions use hard-coded calls. In practice, you would set up one OraSQLStmt object for every stored procedure and function call you used in your application.

Listing 18.19

```
    Private Sub cmdAction_Click(Index As Integer)

    '   Execute the required action - insert, update or delete.

        Dim iField As Integer
        Dim strSQL As String
        Dim iRowCount As Integer

        If Index = 0 Then                ' Add a new record
            ShowNewRecord
            strMode = "Add"

        ElseIf Index = 1 Then            ' Update the record
            If strMode = "Add" Then
                OraDatabase.Parameters("movie_id").Value = 0
                OraDatabase.Parameters("movie_name").Value = txtMovie(0)
                OraDatabase.Parameters("length").Value = CInt(txtMovie(1))
                OraDatabase.Parameters("rating").Value = txtMovie(2)
                OraDatabase.Parameters("year").Value = CInt(txtMovie(3))
```

```
                ostMovieInsert.Refresh
                RefreshRecordset

            Else
            '   Use a conventional inline call here
                strSQL = "BEGIN movies_update ("
                strSQL = strSQL & rsMovies("movie_id").Value & ","
                strSQL = strSQL & "'" & txtMovie(0) & "', " ' Movie Name
                strSQL = strSQL & txtMovie(1) & ", "          ' Length
                strSQL = strSQL & "'" & txtMovie(2) & "', " ' Rating
                strSQL = strSQL & txtMovie(3)               ' Year
                strSQL = strSQL & "); END;"
                iRowCount = OraDatabase.ExecuteSQL(strSQL)
            End If
            strMode = ""
            RefreshRecordset

        ElseIf Index = 2 Then          ' Delete the record
            strSQL = "BEGIN movies_delete (" & rsMovies(4).Value & ");
    END;"
            iRowCount = OraDatabase.ExecuteSQL(strSQL)
            RefreshRecordset
        End If

    End Sub
```

Viewing the Structure of a Database

OO4O gives you one collection that itemizes all the fields in a dynaset. Creating a dynaset is the only way to see the structure. This is different from ODBC methods, which allow you to see the structure of any table you have access to. In OO4O, you use the OraFields collection, which consists of a series of OraField objects. Each of these objects has the properties shown in Table 18.12. As with every other data-access method apart from JET, there is no way to alter the structure of a table. Even with JET, this is ill-advised, so the omission of this feature is not a problem.

TABLE 18.12: The Properties of the OraField Object

OraField Property	Description
OralDataType	This property returns the Oracle internal data-type code (see Table 18.13).
OraMaxDSize	This property returns the Oracle maximum display size.
OraMaxSize	This property returns the maximum column size but depends on the data type.
OraNullOK	This property indicates if NULLs are permitted for this column.
OraPrecision	This property returns the maximum number of digits in a numeric field.
OraScale	This property returns the number of decimal places in a numeric field.
Name	This property returns the field name.
Size	This property returns the size of the field in characters or bytes (zero for LONG fields).
Truncated	This property indicates whether a LONG or LONG RAW column was only partially retrieved. If True, then you will have to use the GetChunk method.
Type	This property returns a code indicating the expected Visual Basic data type.
Value	This property returns the value of any particular field for the current row.

You will only need the OraFields information if you are writing a generic application that takes different actions depending on the data types it encounters and assuming you do not know which tables you are going to be dealing with beforehand. An example would be a versatile administration-type program similar to the one we developed in Chapter 14, *Data Access Objects*, to create stored procedures.

TABLE 18.13: The Oracle Internal Data Type Codes

Oracle Data Type	Constant	Data Type
CHAR	ORADB_TEXT	String
DATE	ORADB_DATE	Variant
LONG	ORADB_MEMO	String

Continued on next page

TABLE 18.13 CONTINUED: The Oracle Internal Data Type Codes

Oracle Data Type	Constant	Data Type
LONG RAW	ORADB_LONGBINARY	String
NUMBER (1-4,0)	ORADB_INTEGER	Integer
NUMBER (5-9,0)	ORADB_LONG	Long Integer
NUMBER (10-15,0)	ORADB_DOUBLE	Double
NUMBER (16-38,0)	ORADB_TEXT	String
NUMBER (1-15,n)	ORADB_DOUBLE	Double
NUMBER (16-38,n)	ORADB_TEXT	String
RAW	ORADB_LONGBINARY	String
VARCHAR2	ORADB_TEXT	String

Drawbacks to OO4O

Despite the excellent functionality OO4O has—in fact, functionality that is very hard, if not impossible, to achieve with any other data-access method—there are still a few drawbacks.

- Performance in some instances is not the fastest. This is partly because it is an in-process server. Even if you use the techniques in the OO4O Help file for improving performance, OO4O may not be able to keep up with ADO/OLE-DB.

- There is as yet no support for asynchronous operations or events.

- There is no support for the GetRows method. OO4O is mainly designed for updatable dynasets.

- OO4O ties you to Oracle. If you decide to change to another database, the move to RDO or ADO is not trivial.

- OO4O is seldom talked about or written about in database books.

Summary

In this chapter, we covered the final data-access method we will see in this book, Oracle Objects for OLE. We saw its tight integration with the Oracle Server and its support for all the techniques that Oracle supports for input and output of data. This included setting up database connections and creating SELECT SQL queries for retrieving a variety of data. We saw how to use SQL parameters in our queries and PL/SQL parameters in stored procedures. We covered how to execute SQL commands as well as how to retrieve output parameters, cursor variables, and PL/SQL tables from stored procedures. We also saw how to use the stored query OraSQLStmt and, finally, how to detect errors in OO4O.

Epilogue

We have covered a large variety of information in this book. You will find that the more you learn about Oracle, the more useful and interesting your Visual Basic applications will be. In a similar way, the more you learn about Visual Basic data-access techniques, the more of Oracle's capabilities will make themselves available.

With the release of Visual Basic 6 and ADO 2.0 or OO4O, Visual Basic developers now have more capabilities for interfacing with Oracle than ever before. The techniques we have covered will enable you to produce professional applications, rivaling anything available commercially. Despite the move currently underway to supplement Oracle with a Java engine, there can be little doubt that the future for Visual Basic in an Oracle arena is great whether it is for traditional client/server applications or for building the client and middle tiers of multitier applications.

One thing is certain though; the techniques we have covered throughout the book are in a constant state of flux. Some of the techniques will change in their details, and some changes may lead to situations where applications no longer work. You must constantly be undergoing the learning process whether it is through periodicals, technical support databases, or Web sites. The learning process is a life-long one; I wish you enjoyment in that process.

INDEX

Note to the Reader: First-level entries are in **bold**. Page numbers in **bold** indicate the principal discussion of a topic or the definition of a term. Page numbers in *italic* indicate illustrations.

(

D

F

G

H

O

T

SYBEX BOOKS ON THE WEB

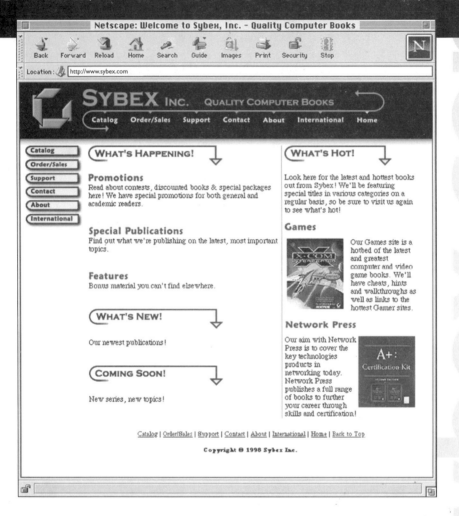

At the dynamic and informative Sybex Web site, you can:

- view our complete online catalog
- preview a book you're interested in
- access special book content
- order books online at special discount prices
- learn about Sybex

www.sybex.com

SYBEX Inc. • 1151 Marina Village Parkway, Alameda, CA 94501 • 510-523-8233